# Contemporary Moral Issues

# Contemporary Moral Issues

## DIVERSITY AND CONSENSUS

*Lawrence M. Hinman*

UNIVERSITY OF SAN DIEGO

*Prentice Hall*
*Upper Saddle River, New Jersey 07458*

*Library of Congress Cataloging-in-Publication Data*

Hinman, Lawrence M.
    Contemporary moral issues: diversity & consensus / Lawrence M.
Hinman.
        p.   cm.
    Includes bibliographical references.
    ISBN 0–13–079435–X
    1. Ethics.   I. Title.
BJ1012.H56   1996                                    95–31450
170—dc20                                             CIP

Acquisitions editor:                              Ted Bolen
Editorial/production supervision and design:      Jenny Moss
Assistant editor:                                 Jennie Katsaros
Buyer:                                            Lynn Pearlman
Editorial assistant:                              Meg McGuane
Cover photo:                                      Digital art/Westlight

Acknowledgments for essay contributions appear on the base
of opening pages, which constitute a continuation of the copyright page.

 © 1996 by Prentice-Hall, Inc.
Simon & Schuster/A Viacom Company
Upper Saddle River, New Jersey 07458

Printed in the United States of America
10  9  8  7  6  5  4  3  2  1

ISBN 0-13-079435-X

Prentice-Hall International (UK) Limited, *London*
Prentice-Hall of Australia Pty. Limited, *Sydney*
Prentice-Hall Canada Inc., *Toronto*
Prentice-Hall Hispanoamericana, S.A., *Mexico*
Prentice-Hall of India Private Limited, *New Delhi*
Prentice-Hall of Japan, Inc., *Tokyo*
Simon & Schuster Asie Pte. Ltd., *Singapore*
Editora Prentice-Hall do Brasil, Ltda., *Rio de Janeiro*

*To Virginia*

# Contents

## 2   Euthanasia                                            101

## 3   Punishment and the Death Penalty                      161

PART TWO: MATTERS OF DIVERSITY AND EQUALITY

## 4    Race and Ethnicity 227

## 5    Gender 275

# 6   Sexual Orientation                                          323

# 7   Poverty and Welfare                                         363

PART THREE: EXPANDING THE CIRCLE

# 8   World Hunger and Poverty                                405

# 9   Living Together with Animals                            451

# 10   Environmental Ethics                                                     501

# Preface

We have only to open the daily newspaper to encounter the issues raised in this book. What restrictions, if any, should be placed on abortion? Should physicians be allowed to hasten the deaths of terminally ill patients? Should the state be allowed to execute certain criminals convicted of heinous crimes? Is affirmative action a violation of equal rights? How should we deal with sexual harassment? Should gays and lesbians be allowed to serve openly in the military? Do people have a right to welfare assistance? Should affluent nations like the United States aid starving countries? Should the government require U.S. fishing boats to take precautions against snagging dolphins, even if other countries do not enforce the same requirements? Should we preserve natural species and habitats even at the expense of jobs in economically disadvantaged areas? These are but some of the questions dealt with in the following readings.

There is no shortage of good anthologies that deal with these issues. In adding yet one more to this list, I have been motivated by several factors. First, few anthologies pay any attention to *personal narratives* in understanding these social issues. Second, many of these anthologies still pay relatively little importance to *issues of diversity*. Finally, most of these anthologies offer comparatively little help to students, especially in the difficult process of *writing papers on moral problems*. Let me say a few words about each of these concerns.

First, the issues discussed in this book—from abortion and euthanasia to questions of famine relief and animal experimentation—are both questions of social policy and issues within individual lives. Indeed, contemporary social ethics exists at the intersection of large-scale policy decisions and personal narratives. Throughout this anthology, I have tried to give voice to the stories of individual lives that are woven—sometimes skillfully, sometimes poorly—into the tapestry of social policy decisions. It is crucial that we understand the way in which these social policies impact individual lives. Thus each chapter contains at least one narrative account that places these larger issues within the context of an individual life. Often truth is to be found in the detail of our personal lives—what philosophers call "thick descriptions"—not just in general principles. It is my hope that these narrative selections will help to provide some of that detail.

Second, issues of diversity play an important role, both in questions of social policy and in the stories of individual lives. Throughout this book, I have tried to provide the opportunity for as many voices of diversity as possible to be heard. In addition to this, one third of this book—Part Two: Matters of Diversity and Equality—is explicitly devoted to a number of specific issues about diversity and equality in regard to race, gender, sexual orientation, and economic status.

Third, I have tried throughout this book to make it "user-friendly" for students. *Critical introductions* to each chapter provide a conceptual map of the moral terrain to be covered, while a short, *general introduction to moral theory* helps to specify some of the common issues that arise in each chapter. Each selection is introduced with *prereading questions* to focus students' attention. *Discussion questions* at the end of each selection are designed to help students develop their own positions on the issues raised, while journal questions—given in italics—explore more personal issues raised by the readings. A *bibliographical essay* at the end of each chapter highlights key works and points the way to valuable resources for students. An *appendix* provides helpful guidelines on critically reading in philosophy and on writing philosophical papers on moral issues. It includes tips on choosing and refining a topic, developing a bibliography, refining arguments, and using counterexamples.

Will the articles in this book change your mind on important moral issues? I don't know, but there is a way for you to find out. At the beginning of this book, I've included an initial self-quiz that surveys your position on a number of issues discussed throughout the book. At the end of each chapter, there is a retest of the relevant questions. Take the initial test before you read any of the individual chapters, and then retake it at the end of each chapter. Check your responses against your initial answers, and see in what ways—if any—you've changed.

This book, like Caesar's Gaul, is divided into three parts. *Part One* centers around issues of life and death, including abortion, *in vitro* fertilization, euthanasia, and the death penalty. Central to this section are the questions of the right to life and the sanctity of human life. *Part Two* deals explicitly with questions of diversity and equality, including issues of race, ethnicity, gender, sexual orientation, and economic status. Here one of the central issues is how we balance the recognition of diversity with the demands for community. *Part Three* turns to a consideration of the boundaries of the moral domain. Morality may begin at home, but how far from home does it extend? Do our moral obligations extend to the poor and starving of other countries? To animals? To the environment? These three questions provide the basis for the final three chapters of this book.

For instructors who are interested in using it, a videotape is available with segments dealing with the topics in each of these chapters. The segments are short (about 12 minutes), and are intended to stimulate discussion of the issues. They are drawn from ABC News sources, primarily *Nightline*.

As this book is going to press, I am developing a World Wide Web site designed to perform several functions. First, continually updated versions of the bibliographical essays in this book will be available on-line, with references to the latest work in each area. Second, hypertext links to numerous World Wide Web sites will provide additional resources for the book. For example, the section on abortion contains links to the Web pages of both pro-choice and pro-life groups, and also contains links to the full texts of major court decisions about abortion. Third, there will be brief descriptions of current news articles and popular books that relate to issues raised in this book. Fourth, an opportunity will be provided for you—both students and instructors—to forward interesting articles, references, etc., for posting on this site. Finally, I hope eventually to provide discussion groups on each of the main topics in this book. The internet address of this site is:

http://pwa.acusd.edu/~hinman

Please come, visit, and contribute.

I wish to thank, first of all, the authors who kindly allowed their work to be reprinted in this book, for it is their contributions that form the heart of this work. Moreover, I would like to thank the reviewers—Joseph M. Yonder, Villa Maria College; Gregory F. Weir, University of South Carolina at Aiken; Edward Kent, Brooklyn College, CUNY; Thomas Auxter, University of Florida at Gainesville; and Orville V. Clark, University of Wisconsin at Green Bay—for their comments and suggestions for making this a better book; any shortcomings are my own. At Prentice Hall, I am especially grateful to Ted Bolen, for his faith in the project and his encouragement, and to Jennie Katsaros and Jenny Moss for their assistance in guiding this project to its completion. At the University of San Diego, many contributed to the success of this project: Pat Drinan, dean of the College of Arts and Sciences, for his support for computer resources that saved me countless hours on this project; the Faculty Research Grants Committee, for its generous reassigned time for this project; Leanna Cummings, our departmental secretary, for invaluable assistance in managing permissions requests; Ed Starkey, our university librarian, for valuable assistance in tracking down references; and many of my colleagues, including Mike Soroka, George Bryjak, Joe Colombo, and Rodney Peffer. Finally, most of all, I would like to thank my wife, Virginia, for her patience as well as support in what proved to be a more arduous and time-consuming project than either of us anticipated.

Finally, I would greatly appreciate comments from readers, both students and professors. Please feel free to write to me either via e-mail (hinman@acusd.edu) or the old-fashioned way to Lawrence M. Hinman, Department of Philosophy, University of San Diego, 5998 Alcalá Park, San Diego, CA 92110-2492. Your comments and suggestions are most welcome.

## ABC News/PH Video Library for *Contemporary Moral Issues: Diversity and Consensus*

Video is the most dynamic of all the supplements you can use to enhance your class. But the quality of the video material and how well it relates to your course can still make all the difference. For these reasons, Prentice Hall and ABC News have decided to work together to bring you the best and most comprehensive video ancillaries available in the college market.

Through its wide variety of award-winning programs—*Nightline, Business World, On Business, This Week with David Brinkley, World News Tonight,* and *The Health Show*—ABC offers a resource for feature and documentary-style videos related to text concepts and applications. The programs have extremely high production quality, present substantial content, and are hosted by well-versed, well-known anchors. Prentice Hall, its authors, and its editors provide the benefit of having selected videos on topics that will work well with this course and text and give the instructor teaching notes on how to use them in the classroom.

"The ABC News/PH Video Library for *Contemporary Moral Issues: Diversity and Consensus*" offers video material for every chapter in the text.

# Introduction

## A Pluralistic Approach to Contemporary Moral Issues

# Moral Disagreement

## The Apparent Prevalence of Moral Disagreement

As we move through the chapters of this book, we will see one area of moral disagreement after another. Abortion, surrogacy, euthanasia, the death penalty, racism, sexism, homosexuality, welfare, world hunger, animal rights, and environmental issues—all are areas characterized by fundamental disagreements that are often intense, sometimes bitter and acrimonious.

This situation is made even more perplexing by the fact that in all of these debates, each side has good arguments in support of its position. In other words, these are not debates in which one side is so obviously wrong that only moral blindness or ill-will could account for its position. Thus we cannot easily dismiss such disagreements by just saying that one side is wrong in some irrational or malevolent way. Ultimately, these are disagreements among intelligent people of good will. And, *it is precisely this fact that makes them so disturbing.* Certainly part of moral disagreement can be attributed to ignorance or ill will, but the troubling part is the moral disagreement among informed and benevolent people.

What kind of sense can we make of such disagreement? Three possible responses deserve particular attention.

## Moral Absolutism

The first, and perhaps most common, response to such disagreements is to claim that there is a single, ultimate answer to the questions being posed. This is the answer of the *moral absolutists,* those who believe there is a single Truth with a capital "T." Usually, absolutists claim to know what that truth is—and it usually corresponds, not surprisingly, to their own position.

Moral absolutists are not confined to a single position. Indeed, absolutism is best understood as much as a way of *holding* certain beliefs as it is an item of such belief. Religious fundamentalists—whether Christian, Muslim, or some other denomination—are usually absolutists. Some absolutists believe in communism, others believe just as absolutely in free-market economics. Some moral philosophers are absolutists, believing that their moral viewpoint is the only legitimate one. But what characterized all absolutists is the conviction that their truth is *the* truth.

Moral absolutists may be right, but there are good reasons to be skeptical about their claims. If they are right, how do they explain the persistence of moral disagreement? Certainly there are disagreements and disputes in other areas (including the natural sciences), but in ethics there seems to be a persistence to these disputes that we usually do not find in other areas. It is hard to explain this from an absolutist standpoint without saying such disagreement is due to ignorance or ill-will. Certainly this is part of the story, but can it account for all moral disagreement? Absolutists are unable to make sense out of the fact that sometimes we have genuine moral disagreements among well-informed and good-intentioned people who are honestly and openly seeking the truth.

## Moral Relativism

The other common response to such disagreement effectively denies that there is a truth in this area, even with a lowercase "t." *Moral relativists* maintain that moral disagreements stem from the fact that what is right for one is not necessarily right for another. Morality is like beauty, they claim, purely relative to the beholder. There is no ultimate standard in terms of which perspectives can be judged. No one is wrong; everyone is right within his or her own sphere.

Notice that these relativists do more than simply acknowledge the existence of moral disagreement. Just to admit that moral disagreement exists is called *descriptive relativism*, and this is a comparatively uncontroversial claim. There is plenty of disagreement in the moral realm, just as there is in most other areas of life. However, *normative relativists* go further. They not only maintain that such disagreement exists; they also say that each is right relative to his or her own culture. Incidentally, it is also worth noting that relativists disagree about precisely what morality is relative *to*. At the one end of the spectrum are those (*cultural moral relativists*) who say that morality is relative to culture; at the other end of the spectrum are those (*moral subjectivists*) who argue that morality is relative to each individual. When we refer to moral relativists here, we will be talking about normative relativists, including both cultural moral relativists and moral subjectivists.

Although moral relativism often appears appealing at first glance, it proves to be singularly unhelpful in the long run. It provides an explanation of moral disagreement, but it fails to provide a convincing account of how moral *agreement* could be forged. In the face of disagreement, what practical advice can relativists offer us? All they can say, it would seem, is that we ought to follow the customs of our society, our culture, our age, or our individual experience. Thus cultural moral relativists tell us, in effect, "When in Rome, do as the Romans do." Moral subjectivists tell us that we should be true, not to our culture, but to our individual selves. But relativists fail to offer us help in how to resolve disputes when they arise. To say that each is right unto itself is of no help, for the issue is what happens when they come together.

While this might have been helpful advice in an age of moral isolationism when each society (or individual) was an island unto itself, it is of little help today. In our contemporary world, the pressing moral question is how we can live together, not how we can live apart. Economies are mutually interdependent; corporations are often multinational; products such as cars are seldom made in a single country. Communications increasingly cut across national borders. Satellite-based telecommunication systems allow international television (MTV is worldwide, and news networks are sure to follow) and international telephone communications. Millions of individuals around the world dial into the Internet, establishing a virtual community. In such a world, relativism fails to provide guidance for resolving disagreements. All it can tell us is that everyone is right in their own world. But the question for the future is how to determine what is right when those worlds overlap.

## Moral Pluralism

Let's return to our problem: in some moral disputes, there seem to be well-informed and good-intentioned people on opposing sides. Absolutism fails to offer a convincing account of how opposing people could be both well-informed and good-intentioned. It says there is only one answer, and those who do not see it are either ignorant or ill-willed. Relativism fails to offer a convincing account of how people can agree. It says no one is wrong, that each culture (or individual) is right unto itself. However, it offers no help about how to resolve these moral disputes.

There is a third possible response here, which I will call *moral pluralism*. Moral pluralists maintain that there are moral truths, but they do not form a body of coherent and consistent truths in the way that one finds in the science or mathematics. Moral truths are real, but partial. Moreover, they are inescapably *plural*. There are many moral truths, not just one—and they may conflict with one another.

Let me borrow an analogy from government. Moral absolutists are analogous to old-fashioned monarchists: there is one leader, and he or she has the absolute truth. Moral relativists are closer to anarchists: each person or group has its own truth. The U.S. government is an interesting example of a tripartite pluralist government. We don't think that the President, the Congress, or the judiciary alone has an exclusive claim to truth. Each has a partial claim, and each provides a check on the other two. We don't—at least not always—view conflict among the three branches as a bad thing. Indeed, such a system of overlapping and at times conflicting responsibilities is a way of hedging our bets. If we put all of our hope in only one of the branches of government, we would be putting ourselves at greater risk. If that one branch is wrong, then everything is wrong. However, if there are three (at least partially conflicting) branches of government, then the effect of one branch's being wrong are far less catastrophic. Moreover, the chance that mistakes will be uncovered earlier is certainly increased when each branch is being scrutinized by the others.

We have an analogous situation in the moral domain. As we shall see, there are conflicting theories about goodness and rightness. Such conflict is a good thing. Each theory contains important truths about the moral life, and none of them contains the whole truth. Each keeps the others honest, as it were, curbing the excesses of any particular moral absolutism. Yet each claims to have the truth, and refuses the relativist's injunction to avoid making judgments about others. Judgment—both making judgments and being judged—is crucial to the moral life, just as it is to the political life. We have differing moral perspectives, but we must often inhabit a common world.

It is precisely this tension between individual viewpoints and living in a common world that lies at the heart of this book. The diversity of viewpoints is not intended to create a written version of those television news shows where people constantly shout at one another. Rather, these selections indicate the range of important and legitimate insights with which we approach the issue in question. The challenge, then, is for us—as individuals, and as a society—to forge a common ground that acknowledges the legitimacy of the conflicting insights but also establishes a minimal area of agreement so that we can live together with our differences. The model this book strives to emulate is not the one-sided monarch who claims to have the absolute truth, nor is it the anarchistic society that contains no basis for consensus. Rather, it is the model of a healthy democracy in which diversity, disagreement, compromise, and consensus are signs of vitality.

## A Pluralistic Approach to Moral Theories

Just as in the political realm there are political parties and movements that delineate the main contours of the political debate, so also in philosophy there are moral theories that provide characteristic ways of understanding and resolving particular moral issues. In the readings throughout this book, we will see a number of examples of these theories in action. Before we examine these theories, it is helpful to look at some of the main characteristics of each of these theories. Just as Republicans and Democrats, liberals and conservatives, and libertarians and socialists all have important, and often conflicting, insights about the political life, so, too, does each of these theories have valuable insights into the moral life. Yet none of them has the whole story. Let's look briefly at each of these approaches.

# Morality As Consequences

What makes an action morally good? For many of us, what counts are *consequences*. The right action is the one that produces good consequences. If I give money to Oxfam to help starving people, and if Oxfam saves the lives of starving people and helps them develop a self-sustaining economy, then I have done something good. It is good because it produced good consequences. For this reason, it is the right thing to do. Those who subscribe to this position are called *consequentialists*. All consequentialists share a common belief that it is consequences that make an action good, but they differ among themselves about precisely which consequences.

## Ethical Egoism

Some consequentialists, called *ethical egoists*, maintain that each of us should look only at the consequences that affect us. In their eyes, each person ought to perform those actions that contribute most to his or her own self-interest. Each person is the best judge of his or her own self-interest, and each person is responsible for maximizing his or her own self-interest. The political expression of ethical egoism occurs most clearly in *libertarianism*, and the best-known advocate of this position was probably Ayn Rand.

Ethical egoism has been criticized on a number of counts, most notably that it simply draws the circle of morality much too closely around the isolated individual. Critics maintain that self-interest is precisely what morality has to overcome, not what it should espouse. Egoism preaches selfishness, but morality should encourage altruism, compassion, love, and a sense of community—all, according to critics, beyond the reach of the egoist.

## Utilitarianism

Once we begin to enlarge the circle of those affected by the consequences of our actions, we move toward a utilitarian position. At its core, *utilitarianism* represents the belief that one ought to do what produces the greatest overall good consequences for *everyone*, not just for oneself. One determines what to do by examining the various courses of action open to us, calculating the consequences associated with each, and then deciding on the one that produces the consequences that provide the greatest overall good for everyone. Utilitarianism is consequentialist and computational. It holds out the promise that moral disputes can be resolved objectively by computing consequences. Part of the attraction of utilitarianism is precisely this claim to objectivity based on a moral calculus.

This is a very demanding moral doctrine for two reasons. First, it asks people to set aside their own individual interests for the good of the whole. Often this can result in great individual sacrifice, if taken seriously. For example, the presence of hunger and starvation in our society (as well as outside of it) places great demands on the utilitarian, for often more good would be accomplished by giving food to the hungry than by eating it oneself. Second, utilitarianism asks us to do whatever produces the *most* good. Far from being a doctrine of the moral minimum, utilitarianism always asks us to do the maximum.

Utilitarians disagree among themselves about what the proper standard is for judging consequences. What are "good" consequences? Are they the ones that produce the most *pleasure*? The most *happiness*? The most truth, beauty, and the like? Or, simply the consequences that satisfy the most people? Each of these standards of utility has its strengths and weaknesses. Jeremy Bentham originally proposed pleasure as the standard of utility. *Pleasure* is comparatively easy to measure, but in many people's eyes it seems to be a rather base standard. Can't we increase pleasure just by putting electrodes in the proper location in a person's brain? Presumably we want something more, and better, than that. John Stuart Mill criticized Bentham's standard of pleasure and argued that happiness should be the standard of utility. *Happiness* seems a more plausible candidate, but the difficulty with happiness is that it is both elusive to define and extremely difficult to measure. This is particularly a problem for utilitarianism, for since its initial appeal rests in part on its claim to objectivity. *Ideals* such as truth and beauty are even more difficult to measure. *Preference satisfaction* is more measurable, but it provides no foundation for distinguishing between morally acceptable preferences and morally objectionable preferences such as racism.

The other principal disagreement that has plagued utilitarianism centers around the question of whether we look at the consequences of each individual act—this is called *act utilitarianism*—or the consequences that would result from everyone following a particular rule—this is called *rule utilitarianism*. The danger of act utilitarianism is that it may justify some particular acts that most of us would want to condemn, particularly those that sacrifice individual life and liberty for the sake of the whole. This classic problem occurs in regard to punishment. We could imagine a situation in which punishing an innocent person—while concealing his innocence, of course—would have consequences that imparted the greatest overall good. If doing so would result in the greatest overall amount of pleasure or happiness, then it would not only be permitted by act utilitarianism, it would be morally required. Similar difficulties arise in regard to an issue such as euthanasia. It is conceivable that overall utility might justify active euthanasia of the elderly and infirm, even involuntary euthanasia, especially of those who leave no one behind to mourn their passing. Yet are there things we cannot do to people, even if utility seems to require it? Many of us would answer such a question affirmatively.

In response to such difficulties, utilitarian theorists pointed out that, while consequences may justify a particular act of punishing the innocent, they could never justify living by a *rule* that said it was permissible to punish the innocent when doing so would produce the greatest utility. Rule utilitarianians agree that we should look only at consequences, but maintain that we should look at the consequences of adopting a particular rule for everyone, not the consequences of each individual action. This type of utilitarianism is less likely to generate the injustices associated with act utilitarianism, but many feel that it turns into rule-worship. Why, critics ask, should we follow the rule in those instances where it does not produce the greatest utility?

### Feminist Consequentialism

During the last twenty years, much interesting and valuable work has been done in the area of feminist ethics. It would be misleading to think of feminist approaches to ethics as falling into a single camp, but certainly some feminist moral philosophers have sketched out consequentialist accounts of the moral life in at least two different ways.

First, some feminists have argued that morality is a matter of consequences, but that consequences are not best understood or evaluated in the traditional computational model offered by utilitarianism. Instead, they focus primarily on the ways in which particular actions have consequences for relationships and feelings. Negative consequences are those that destroy relationships and that hurt others, especially those that hurt others emotionally. Within this tradition, the morally good course of action is that one that preserves the greatest degree of connectedness among all those affected by it. Carol Gilligan has described this moral voice in her book *In a Different Voice*.

Second, other feminists have accepted a roughly utilitarian account of consequences but have paid particular attention to—and often given special weight to—the consequences that affect women. Such consequences, they argue, have often been overlooked by traditional utilitarian calculators, supposedly impartial but often insensitive to harms to women. Unlike the work of Gilligan and others mentioned in the previous paragraph, feminists in this tradition do not question the dominant utilitarian paradigm, but rather question whether it has in fact been applied impartially.

## Conclusion

Despite these disagreements about the precise formulation of utilitarianism, most people would admit that utilitarianism contains important insights into the moral life. Part of the justification for morality, and one of the reasons people accept the burdens of morality, is that it promises to produce a better world than we would have without it. This is undoubtedly part of the picture. But is it the whole picture?

# Morality As Act and Intention

Critics of utilitarianism point out that, for utilitarianism, no actions are good or bad in themselves. All actions in themselves are morally neutral, and, for pure consequentialists, no action is intrinsically evil. Yet this seems to contradict the moral intuition of many people—people who believe that some actions are just morally wrong, even if they have good results. Killing innocent human beings, torturing people, raping them—these are but a few of the actions that many would want to condemn as wrong in themselves, even if in unusual circumstances they may produce good consequences.

How can we tell if some actions are morally good or bad in themselves? Clearly, we must have some standard against which they can be judged. Various standards have been proposed, and most of these again capture important truths about the moral life.

### Conformity to God's Commands

In a number of fundamentalist religious traditions, including some branches of Judaism, Christianity, and Islam, what makes an act right is that it is commanded by God and what makes an act wrong is that it is forbidden by God. In these traditions, certain kinds of acts are wrong just because God forbids them. Usually such prohibitions are contained in sacred texts such as the Bible or the Koran.

There are two principal difficulties with this approach, one external, one internal. The external problem is that, while this may provide a good reason for believers to act in particular ways, it hardly gives a persuasive case to nonbelievers. The internal difficulty is that it is often difficult, even with the best of intentions, to discern what God's commands actually are. Sacred texts, for example, contain numerous injunctions, but it is rare that any religious tradition takes *all* of them seriously. (The Bible tells believers to pick up venomous vipers, but only a handful of Christians engage in this practice.) How do we decide which injunctions to take seriously and which to ignore or interpret metaphorically?

## Natural Law

There is a long tradition, beginning with Aristotle and gaining great popularity in the Middle Ages, that maintains that acts which are "unnatural" are always evil. The underlying premise of this view is that the natural is good, and, therefore, what contradicts it is bad. Often, especially in the Middle Ages, this was part of a larger Christian worldview that saw nature as created by God, who then was the ultimate source of its goodness. Yet it has certainly survived in twentieth-century moral and legal philosophy quite apart from its theological underpinnings. This appeal to natural law occurs at a number of junctures in our readings, but especially in the discussions of reproductive technologies and those of homosexuality. Natural law arguments lead quite easily into considerations of human nature, again with the implicit claim that human nature is good.

Natural law arguments tend to be slippery for two, closely interrelated reasons. First, for natural law arguments to work, one has to provide convincing support for the claim that the natural is (the only) good—or at least for its contrapositive, the claim that the "unnatural" is bad. Second, such arguments presuppose that we can clearly differentiate between the natural and the unnatural. Are floods and earthquakes natural? Is disease natural? Either the natural is not always good, or else we have to adopt a very selective notion of the "natural."

## Proper Intention

A second way in which acts can be said to be good or bad is that they are done for the proper motivation, with the correct intention. Indeed, intentions are often built into our vocabulary for describing actions. The difference between stabbing a person and performing surgery on that person may well reside primarily in the intention of the agent.

*Acting for the sake of duty.*   Again, there is no shortage of candidates for morally acceptable intentions. A sense of duty, universalizability, a respect for other persons, sincerity or authenticity, care and compassion—these are but a few of the acceptable moral motivations. Consider, first of all, the motive of duty. Immanuel Kant argued that what gives an action moral worth is that it is done for the sake of duty. In his eyes, the morally admirable person is the one who, despite inclinations to the contrary, does the right thing solely because it is the right thing to do. The person who contributes to charities out of a sense of duty is morally far superior to the person who does the same thing in order to look good in the eyes of others, despite the fact that the consequences may be the same in both cases.

*Universalizability.*   Yet how do we know what our duty is? Kant wanted to avoid saying duty was simply a matter of "following orders." Instead, he saw duty as emanating from the nature of reason itself. And because reason is universal, duty is also universal. Kant suggested an important test whether our understanding of duty was rational in any particular instance. We always act, he maintained, with a subjective rule or maxim that guides our decision. Is this maxim one that we can will that everyone accept, or is it one that fails this test of universalizability?

Consider cheating. If you cheat on an exam, it's like lying: you are saying something is your work when it is not. Imagine you cheat on all the exams in a course and finish with an average of 98 percent. The professor then gives you a grade of "D." You storm into the professor's office, demanding an explanation. The professor calmly says, "Oh, I lied on the grade sheet." Your natural reply would be: "But you can't lie about my grade!" Kant's point is that, by cheating, you've denied the validity of your own claim. You've implicitly said that it is morally all right for people to lie. But of course you don't believe it's permissible for your professor to lie—only for you yourself to do so. This, Kant says, fails the test of universalizability.

Notice that Kant's argument isn't a consequentialist one. He's not asking what would happen to society if everyone lied. Rather, he's saying that certain maxims are *inconsistent* and thus irrational. You cannot approve of your own lying without approving of everyone else's, and yet the advantage you get depends precisely on other people's honesty. It is the irrationality of making an exception of my own lying in this way that Kant feels violates the moral law. Indeed, we should all examine our own past actions to see where we may have made an exception for ourselves that we know (at least in retrospect) isn't morally justified.

Kant has captured something valuable about the moral life: the insight that what's fair for one is fair for all. Yet Kant's critics were quick to point out that this can hardly be the entire story. Consequences count, and intentions are notoriously slippery. A given act can be described with many different intentions—to cheat on a test, to try to excel, to try to meet your parents' expectations, to be the first in the class—and not all of them necessarily fail the test of universalizability.

*Respect for other persons.*    Kant offered another formulation of his basic moral insight, one that touches a responsive chord in many of us. We should never treat people merely as things, Kant argued. Rather, we should always respect them as autonomous (i.e., self-directing) moral agents. Both capitalism and technology pressure us to treat people merely as things, and many have found Kant's refusal to do this to be of crucial moral importance.

It is easy to find examples at both ends of this spectrum. We use people merely as things when we do not let them make their own decisions and when we harm them for our own benefit without respect for their rights. Consider the now infamous Tuskegee experiment, in which medical researchers tracked the development of syphilis in a group of African-American men for over thirty years, never telling them the precise nature of their malady and never treating them—something that would have been both inexpensive and effective. Instead, the researchers let the disease proceed through its ultimately fatal course in order to observe more closely the details of its progress. These men were used merely as means to the researchers' ends.

Similarly, we have all—I hope—experienced being treated as ends in ourselves. If I am ill, and my physician gives me the details of my medical condition, outlines the available options for treatment (including nontreatment), and is supportive of whatever choice I finally make in this matter, then I feel as though I have been treated with respect. Timothy Quill's selection in the chapter on euthanasia offers a good, real-life example of such respect in the doctor-patient relationship.

The difficulty with this criterion is that there is a large middle ground where it is unclear if acting in a particular way is really using other people merely as things. Indeed, insofar as our economic system is based on the exchange of currency for commodities, we can be assured that this will be a common phenomenon in our society. To what extent is respect for persons attainable in a capitalist and technological society?

*Compassion and caring.* Some philosophers—particularly, but not exclusively, feminist—have urged the moral importance of acting out of motives of care and compassion. Many of these philosophers have argued that caring about other persons is the heart of the moral life, and that a morality of care leads to a refreshingly new picture of morality as centering on relationships, feelings, and connectedness rather than on impartiality, justice, and fairness. In a moral dispute, the justice-oriented person will determine the fair thing to do, and then proceed to follow that course of action, no matter what effect that has on others. The care-oriented individual, on the other hand, will try to find the course of action that best preserves the interests of all involved and does the least amount of damage to the relationships involved.

Many in this tradition have seen the justice orientation as characteristically male and the care orientation as typically female. (Notice that this is not the same as claiming that these orientations are exclusively male or female.) Critics have argued that such correlations are simplistic and misleading. Both orientations may be present to some degree in almost everyone, and particular types of situations may be responsible for bringing one or the other to the fore.

## Respect for Rights

Kant, as we have just seen, told us that we ought to respect other persons. Yet what specific aspects of other persons ought we to respect? One answer, which has played a major political as well as philosophical role during the past two centuries, has been framed in terms of human rights. The Bill of Rights was the first set of amendments to the U.S. Constitution. At approximately the same time, the French were drafting the *Declaration of the Rights of Man and Citizen*. Concern for human rights has continued well into the twentieth century, and the last forty years in the United States have been marked by an intense concern with rights—the civil rights movement for racial equality, the equal rights movement for women, the animal rights movement, the gay rights movement, and the movement for equal rights for Americans with disabilities. Throughout the selections in this book, we will see continual appeals to rights, debates about the extent and even the existence of rights, and attempts to adjudicate conflicts of rights.

Rights provide the final criterion to be considered here for evaluating acts. Those acts that violate basic human rights are morally wrong, this tradition suggests. Torture, imprisoning and executing the innocent, denial of the right to vote, denial of due process—these are all instances of actions that violate human rights. (The fact that an act does not violate basic human rights does not mean that it is morally unobjectionable; there may be other criteria for evaluating it as well as rights.) Human rights, defenders of this tradition maintain, are not subject to nationality, race, religion, class, or any other such limitation. They cannot be set aside for reasons of utility, convenience, or political or financial gain. We possess them simply by virtue of being human beings, and they thus exhibit a universality that provides the foundation for a global human community.

Criticisms of the rights tradition abound. First, how do we determine *which* rights we have? Rights theorists often respond that we have a right to those things—such as life, freedom, and property—which are necessary to human existence itself. Yet many claim that such necessities are contextual, not universal. Moreover, they maintain that there is something logically suspicious about proceeding from the claim that "I need something" to the claim that "I have a right to it." Needs, these critics argue, do not entail rights. Second, critics have asked whether these rights are *negative rights* (i.e., freedoms from certain kinds of interference) or *positive rights* (i.e., entitlements). This is one of the issues at the core of the welfare debate currently raging in the United States. Do the poor have any positive rights to welfare, or do they only have rights not to be discriminated against in various ways? Finally, some critics have argued that the current focus on rights has obscured other, morally relevant aspects of our lives. Rights establish a moral minimum for the ways in which we interact with others, especially strangers we do not care about. But when we are dealing with those we know and care about, more may be demanded of us morally than just respecting their rights.

# Morality As Character

It is rare that a philosophy anthology reaches the best-seller lists, and it is even more unusual when that book is a relatively traditional work about character. William Bennett's *The Book of Virtues* (New York: Simon & Schuster, 1993), however, has done just that. Staying on the best-seller list for week after week, Bennett's book indicates a resurgence of interest in a long-neglected tradition of ethic: Aristotelian virtue theory.

## The Contrast between Act-Oriented Ethics and Character-Oriented Ethics

This Aristotelian approach to ethic, sometimes called *character ethics* or *virtue ethics*, is distinctive. In contrast to the preceding act-oriented approaches, it does not focus on what makes *acts* right or wrong. Rather, it focuses on *people* and their moral character. Instead of asking, "What should I do?" those in this tradition ask, "What kind of person should I strive to be?" This gives a very different focus to the moral life.

An analogy with public life may again be helpful. Consider the American judiciary system. We develop an elaborate set of rules through legislation, and these rules are often articulated in excruciating detail. However, when someone is brought to trial, we do not depend solely on the rules to guarantee justice. Ultimately, we place the fate of accused criminals in the hands of people—a judge and jury. As a country, we bet on both rules and people.

A similar situation exists in ethics. We need good rules—and the preceding sections have described some attempts to articulate those rules—but we also need good people to have the wisdom and good will to interpret and apply those rules. Far from being in conflict with each other, act-oriented and character-oriented approaches to ethics complement one another.

## Human Flourishing

The principal questions that character-oriented approaches to ethics pose are the following: What strengths of character (i.e., virtues) promote human flourishing? And, correlatively, what weaknesses of character (i.e., vices) impede human flourishing? *Virtues* are thus those strengths of character that contribute to human flourishing, while *vices* are those weakness that get in the way of flourishing.

In order to develop an answer to these questions, the first thing that those in this tradition must do is to articulate a clear notion of human flourishing. Here they depend as much on moral psychology as moral philosophy. Aristotle had a vision of human flourishing, but it was one that was clearly limited to his time—one that excluded women and slaves. In contemporary psychology, we have seen much interesting work describing flourishing in psychological terms—Carl Rogers and Abraham Maslow have made but two of the better-known attempts at describing human flourishing in psychological terms. The articulation of a well-founded and convincing vision of human flourishing remains one of the principal challenges of virtue ethics today.

## The Virtue of Courage

We can better understand this approach to ethics if we look at a sample virtue and its corresponding vices. Consider courage. Aristotle analyzes it primarily in military terms, but we now see that it is a virtue necessary to a wide range of human activities—and those who lack courage will rarely flourish. Courage is the strength of character to face and overcome that which we fear. Fears differ from one person to the next, but we all have them. Some may fear physical danger; some may fear intimacy and the psychological vulnerability that comes with it; some may fear commitment; some may fear taking risks to gain what they desire. We all have things we fear, and we must overcome those fears if we are to achieve our goals, to attain what we value in life.

Imagine people who lack the courage to take chances in their careers. They desire a more challenging position, but they are unwilling to give up the old one in order to make the move. Imagine those who fear the vulnerability that comes with genuinely intimate relationships. They long for intimacy, but are unable or unwilling to take the risk necessary to attain it. Those who lack courage will be unable to take the necessary risks, and this is the sense in which cowardice is a vice: it prevents us from flourishing.

Yet Aristotle also suggests that virtues are usually a mean between two extremes. One of the extremes here is clear: cowardice. But what would it mean to have too much courage? It is easy to imagine examples. First, one could be willing to risk too quickly. Rashness is one way of having too much courage. Or one could risk much for too little. To run into a burning building to save a trapped child is courageous; to run into the same building to save an old pair of shoes is foolhardy. Foolhardiness is another way of having too much courage. Of course, the phrase "too much courage" here can be misleading. In the end, too much courage isn't really courage, it's something else.

## Compassion

Aristotle talked a lot about virtues such as proper pride, courage, fortitude, and the like. Compassion was not among them. Yet many today would argue that compassion is a virtue—and this becomes a pivotal issue in a number of our readings in this book. What would an Aristotelian analysis of compassion look like?

First, let's define compassion and bracket it between its two extremes, the vices that correspond to a deficiency or an excess of compassion. *Compassion* itself is a feeling for our fellow moral beings (human beings and perhaps animals). It is literally a "feeling with . . . ," an ability to identify with the feelings of another being, especially feelings of suffering. Moreover, it is usually oriented toward action. The compassionate person is moved to help those who are suffering, and we would doubt the genuineness of the compassion if it never led to action. Those with too little compassion are cold-hearted, indifferent to the suffering of others. Unfortunately, there is no shortage of examples here. Yet what is "too much" compassion? Presumably, it is being overly concerned with the suffering of others. There are several ways in which this could occur. First, we might be so concerned with the suffering of others that we neglect ourselves and those to whom we have direct duties. Second, we might be so concerned with the suffering of others that we neglect the nonsuffering parts of their personalities, turning them into pure victims when they are not. Third, we may be appropriately concerned with the suffering of others, but we may manifest this in inappropriate ways. If compassion for a child crying in pain during a medical procedure leads us to kidnap the child to save it from suffering, we have expressed our compassion in an inappropriate way.

Compassion has an emotional element to it, but it is not just a blind feeling. Rather, it is also a way of perceiving the world—the world looks different through the eyes of the compassionate person than through the eyes of the sociopath. Moreover, it is also a way of thinking about the world, a way of understanding it. Compassion has to make judgments about the nature and causes of suffering, and also about the possible remedies for suffering. Compassion, finally, is also a way of acting, a way of responding to the suffering of the world. Compassion can be both deeply passionate and smart at the same time. As we shall see in our discussion of issues about poverty and starvation, it is not enough to feel compassion. We also have to know how to respond to suffering in effective ways that not only relieve the immediate suffering but also help the sufferers to free themselves from future suffering. Compassion needs to be wise, not just strongly felt.

### Virtue Ethics As the Foundation of Other Approaches to Ethics

We can conclude this section by reflecting once again on the relationship between virtue ethics and action-oriented approaches to ethics. One of the principal problems faced by moral philosophers has been how to understand the continuing disagreement among the various ethical traditions sketched out above. It seems implausible to say that one is right and all the rest are wrong, but it also seems impossible to say that they are all right, for they seem to contradict each other. If we adopt a pluralistic approach, we may say that each contains partial truths about the moral life, but none contains the whole truth. But then the question is: how do we know which position should be given precedence in a particular instance?

There is, I suspect, no *theoretical* answer to this question, no meta-theory that integrates all these differing and at times conflicting theories. However, I think there is a *practical* answer to this question: we ultimately have to put our trust in the wise person to know when to give priority to one type of moral consideration over another. Indeed, it is precisely this that constitutes moral wisdom.

## Analyzing Moral Problems

As we turn to consider the various moral problems discussed in this book, each of these theories will help us to understand aspects of the problem that we might not originally have noticed, to see connections among apparently unconnected factors, and to formulate responses that we might not previously have envisioned. Ultimately, our search is a personal one, a search for wisdom.

But it is also a social approach, one that seeks to discern how to live a good life with other people, how to live well together in community. As we consider the series of moral issues that follows in this book, we will be attempting to fulfill both the individual and the communal goals. We will be seeking to find the course of action that is morally right for us as individuals, and we will be developing our own account of how society as a whole ought to respond to these moral challenges.

# AN INITIAL SELF-QUIZ

## Introduction

Drawing on your current moral beliefs, please answer the following questions as honestly as possible. You may feel that these check boxes do not allow you to state your beliefs accurately enough. Please feel free to add notes, qualifications, etc., in the margins. Also realize that you will be asked to return to your answers to these questions throughout the semester.

### Chapter 1: Reproductive Choices

| Strongly Agree | Agree | Undecided | Disagree | Strongly Disagree | |
|---|---|---|---|---|---|
| 1. ❑ | ❑ | ❑ | ❑ | ❑ | The principal moral consideration about abortion is the question of whether the fetus is a person or not. |
| 2. ❑ | ❑ | ❑ | ❑ | ❑ | The principal moral consideration about abortion is the question of the rights of the pregnant woman. |
| 3. ❑ | ❑ | ❑ | ❑ | ❑ | The only one who should have a voice in making the decision about an abortion is the pregnant woman. |
| 4. ❑ | ❑ | ❑ | ❑ | ❑ | Any procedure that helps infertile couples to have children is good. |
| 5. ❑ | ❑ | ❑ | ❑ | ❑ | Genetic manipulation of embryos should be forbidden. |

### Chapter 2: Euthanasia

| | | | | | |
|---|---|---|---|---|---|
| 6. ❑ | ❑ | ❑ | ❑ | ❑ | Euthanasia is always morally wrong. |
| 7. ❑ | ❑ | ❑ | ❑ | ❑ | Euthanasia should be illegal at least under almost all circumstances. |
| 8. ❑ | ❑ | ❑ | ❑ | ❑ | The principal moral consideration about euthanasia is the question of whether the person chooses it or not. |
| 9. ❑ | ❑ | ❑ | ❑ | ❑ | Sometimes it is more compassionate to terminate someone's life painlessly rather than let them die a natural death in agony. |
| 10. ❑ | ❑ | ❑ | ❑ | ❑ | The only one who should have a voice in making the decision about either passive or active euthanasia is the patient. |

### Chapter 3: Punishment and the Death Penalty

| | | | | | |
|---|---|---|---|---|---|
| 11. ❑ | ❑ | ❑ | ❑ | ❑ | The purpose of punishment is primarily to pay back the offender. |

|  | Strongly Agree | Agree | Undecided | Disagree | Strongly Disagree | |
|---|---|---|---|---|---|---|
| 12. | ❑ | ❑ | ❑ | ❑ | ❑ | The purpose of punishment is primarily to deter the offender and others from committing future crimes. |
| 13. | ❑ | ❑ | ❑ | ❑ | ❑ | Capital punishment is always morally wrong. |
| 14. | ❑ | ❑ | ❑ | ❑ | ❑ | The principal moral consideration about capital punishment is the question of whether it is administered arbitrarily or not. |
| 15. | ❑ | ❑ | ❑ | ❑ | ❑ | The principal moral consideration about capital punishment is that it doesn't really deter criminals. |

### Chapter 4: Race and Ethnicity

|  |  |  |  |  |  | |
|---|---|---|---|---|---|---|
| 16. | ❑ | ❑ | ❑ | ❑ | ❑ | African Americans are still often discriminated against in employment. |
| 17. | ❑ | ❑ | ❑ | ❑ | ❑ | Affirmative action helps African Americans and other minorities. |
| 18. | ❑ | ❑ | ❑ | ❑ | ❑ | Racial separatism is wrong. |
| 19. | ❑ | ❑ | ❑ | ❑ | ❑ | Hate speech should be banned. |
| 20. | ❑ | ❑ | ❑ | ❑ | ❑ | We should encourage the development of racial and ethnic identity. |

### Chapter 5: Gender

|  |  |  |  |  |  | |
|---|---|---|---|---|---|---|
| 21. | ❑ | ❑ | ❑ | ❑ | ❑ | Women's moral voices are different from men's. |
| 22. | ❑ | ❑ | ❑ | ❑ | ❑ | Women are still discriminated against in the workplace. |
| 23. | ❑ | ❑ | ❑ | ❑ | ❑ | Sexual harassment should be illegal. |
| 24. | ❑ | ❑ | ❑ | ❑ | ❑ | Affirmative action helps women. |
| 25. | ❑ | ❑ | ❑ | ❑ | ❑ | Genuine equality for women demands a restructuring of the traditional family. |

### Chapter 6: Sexual Orientation

|  |  |  |  |  |  | |
|---|---|---|---|---|---|---|
| 26. | ❑ | ❑ | ❑ | ❑ | ❑ | Gays and lesbians should be allowed to serve openly in the military. |
| 27. | ❑ | ❑ | ❑ | ❑ | ❑ | Gays and lesbians should not be discriminated against in hiring or housing. |
| 28. | ❑ | ❑ | ❑ | ❑ | ❑ | Homosexuality is unnatural. |
| 29. | ❑ | ❑ | ❑ | ❑ | ❑ | Same-sex marriages should be legal. |
| 30. | ❑ | ❑ | ❑ | ❑ | ❑ | Homosexuality is a matter of personal choice. |

|  | Strongly Agree | Agree | Undecided | Disagree | Strongly Disagree |
|---|---|---|---|---|---|

### Chapter 7: Poverty and Welfare

31. ❑ ❑ ❑ ❑ ❑ People are poor mainly because they do not have the proper ability, training, motivation, or interest in working hard.

32. ❑ ❑ ❑ ❑ ❑ Everyone has a right to a minimum income, whether they work or not.

33. ❑ ❑ ❑ ❑ ❑ Everyone has a right to a minimum income, if they want to work but cannot find a job.

34. ❑ ❑ ❑ ❑ ❑ Society ought to continue welfare support for women with illegitimate children.

35. ❑ ❑ ❑ ❑ ❑ Society ought to provide welfare support to elderly people who are no longer able to work.

### Chapter 8: World Hunger and Poverty

36. ❑ ❑ ❑ ❑ ❑ Only the morally heartless would refuse to help the starving.

37. ❑ ❑ ❑ ❑ ❑ We should help starving nations until we are as poor as they are.

38. ❑ ❑ ❑ ❑ ❑ In the long run, relief aid to starving nations does not help them.

39. ❑ ❑ ❑ ❑ ❑ Overpopulation is the main cause of world hunger and poverty.

40. ❑ ❑ ❑ ❑ ❑ The world is gradually becoming a better place.

### Chapter 9: Living Together with Animals

41. ❑ ❑ ❑ ❑ ❑ There's nothing morally wrong with eating veal.

42. ❑ ❑ ❑ ❑ ❑ It's morally permissible to cause animals pain in order to do medical research that benefits human beings.

43. ❑ ❑ ❑ ❑ ❑ All animals have the same moral standing.

44. ❑ ❑ ❑ ❑ ❑ Zoos are a morally good thing.

45. ❑ ❑ ❑ ❑ ❑ There is nothing morally wrong with hunting.

### Chapter 10: Environmental Ethics

46. ❑ ❑ ❑ ❑ ❑ Nature is just a source of resources for us.

47. ❑ ❑ ❑ ❑ ❑ The government should strictly regulate toxic waste.

48. ❑ ❑ ❑ ❑ ❑ We should make every effort possible to avoid infringing on the natural environment any more than we already have.

49. ❑ ❑ ❑ ❑ ❑ We owe future generations a clean and safe environment.

50. ❑ ❑ ❑ ❑ ❑ We should not impose our environmental concerns on developing nations.

*Part One: Matters of Life and Death*

# Reproductive Choices

# EXPERIENTIAL ACCOUNTS

*Linda Bird Francke is a journalist whose articles have appeared in* The New York Times, Harper's Bazaar, The Washington Post, Esquire, Ms., *and* McCalls. *Her books include* The Ambivalence of Abortion *and* Growing Up Divorced. *She has three children and lives in Sagaponack, New York.*

*The present selection originally appeared anonymously in the Letters to the Editor section of* The New York Times. *The article itself brought forth a number of letters in reply, and Ms. Francke's response to those letters is also included here. Eventually her concern with the issue of abortion led to her book on* The Ambivalence of Abortion, *which presents first-hand accounts of the decision about abortion from women in numerous positions in life.*

~

We were sitting in a bar on Lexington Avenue when I told my husband I was pregnant. It is not a memory I like to dwell on. Instead of the champagne and hope which had heralded the impending births of the first, second and third child, the news of this one was greeted with shocked silence and Scotch. "Jesus," my husband kept saying to himself, stirring the ice cubes around and around. "Oh, Jesus."

Oh, how we tried to rationalize it that night as the starting time for the movie came and went. My husband talked about his plans for a career change in the next year, to stem the staleness that fourteen years with the same investment-banking firm had brought him. A new baby would preclude that option.

The timing wasn't right for me either. Having juggled pregnancies and child care with what freelance jobs I could fit in between feedings, I had just taken on a full-time job. A new baby would put me right back in the nursery just when our youngest child was finally school age. It was time for us, we tried to rationalize. There just wasn't room in our lives now for another baby. We both agreed. And agreed. And agreed.

How very considerate they are at the Women's Services, known formally as the Center for Reproductive and Sexual Health. Yes, indeed, I could have an abortion that very Saturday morning and be out in time to drive to the country that afternoon. Bring a first morning urine specimen, a sanitary belt and napkins, a money order or $125 cash—and a friend.

My friend turned out to be my husband, standing awkwardly and ill at ease as men always do in places that are exclusively for women, as I checked in at nine A.M. Other men hovered around just as anxiously, knowing they had to be there, wishing they weren't. No one spoke to each other.

When I would be cycled out of there four hours later, the same men would be slumped in their same seats, locked downcast in their cells of embarrassment.

The Saturday morning women's group was more dispirited than the men in the waiting room. There were around fifteen of us, a mixture of races, ages and backgrounds. Three didn't speak English at all and a fourth, a pregnant Puerto Rican girl around eighteen, translated for them.

There were six black women and a hodge podge of whites, among them a T-shirted teenager who kept leaving the room to throw up and a puzzled middle-aged woman from Queens with three grown children.

"What form of birth control were you using?" the volunteer asked each one of us. The answer was inevitably "none." She then went on to describe the various forms of birth control available at the clinic, and offered them to each of us.

The youngest Puerto Rican girl was asked through the interpreter which she'd like to use: the loop, diaphragm, or pill. She shook her head "no" three times. "You don't want to come back here again, do you?" the volunteer pressed. The girl's head was so low her chin rested on her breast-bone. "Si," she whispered.

We had been there two hours by that time, filling out endless forms, giving blood and urine, receiving lectures. But unlike any other group of women I've been in, we didn't talk. Our common denominator, the one which usually floods across language and economic barriers into familiarity, today was one of shame. We were losing life that day, not giving it.

The group kept getting cut back to smaller, more workable units, and finally I was put in a small waiting room with just two other women. We changed into paper bathrobes and paper slippers, and we rustled whenever we moved. One of the women in my room was shivering and an aide brought her a blanket.

"What's the matter?" the aide asked her. "I'm scared," the woman said. "How much will it hurt?" The aide smiled. "Oh, nothing worse than a couple of bad cramps," she said. "This afternoon you'll be dancing a jig."

I began to panic. Suddenly the rhetoric, the abortion marches I'd walked in, the telegrams sent to Albany to counteract the Friends of the Fetus, the Zero Population Growth buttons I'd worn, peeled away, and I was all alone with my microscopic baby. There were just the two of us there, and soon, because it was more convenient for me and my husband, there would be one again.

How could it be that I, who am so neurotic about life that I step over bugs rather than on them, who spend hours planting flowers and vegetables in the spring even though we rent out the house and never see them, who make sure the children are vaccinated and inoculated and filled with vitamin C, could so arbitrarily decide that this life shouldn't be?

"It's not a life," my husband had argued, more to convince himself than me. "It's a bunch of cells smaller than my fingernail."

But any woman who has had children knows that certain feeling in her taut, swollen breasts, and the slight but constant ache in her uterus that signals the arrival of a life. Though I would march myself into blisters for a woman's right to exercise the option of motherhood, I discovered there in the waiting room that I was not the modern woman I thought I was.

When my name was called, my body felt so heavy the nurse had to help me into the examining room. I waited for my husband to burst through the door and yell "stop," but of course he didn't. I concentrated on three black spots in the acoustic ceiling until they grew in size to the shape of saucers, while the doctor swabbed my insides with antiseptic.

"You're going to feel a burning sensation now," he said, injecting Novocaine into the neck of the womb. The pain was swift and severe, and I twisted to get away from him. He was hurting my baby, I reasoned, and the black saucers quivered in the air. "Stop," I cried. "Please stop." He shook his head, busy with his equipment. "It's too late to stop now," he said. "It'll just take a few more seconds."

What good sports we women are. And how obedient. Physically the pain passed even before the hum of the machine signaled that the vacuuming of my uterus was completed, my baby sucked up like ashes after a cocktail party. Ten minutes start to finish. And I was back on the arm of the nurse.

There were twelve beds in the recovery room. Each one had a gaily flowered draw sheet and a soft green or blue thermal blanket. It was all very feminine. Lying on these beds for an hour or more were the shocked victims of their sex, their full wombs now stripped clean, their futures less encumbered.

It was very quiet in that room. The only voice was that of the nurse, locating the new women who had just come in so she could monitor their blood pressure, and checking out the recovered women who were free to leave.

Juice was being passed about, and I found myself sipping a Dixie cup of Hawaiian Punch. An older woman with tightly curled bleached hair was just getting up from the next bed, "That was no goddamn snap," she said, resting before putting on her miniskirt and high white boots. Other women came and went, some walking out as dazed as they had entered, others with a bounce that signaled they were going right back to Bloomingdale's.

Finally then, it was time for me to leave. I checked out, making an appointment to return in two weeks for an IUD insertion. My husband was slumped in the waiting room, clutching a single yellow rose wrapped in a wet paper towel and stuffed into a baggie.

We didn't talk the whole way home, but just held hands very tightly. At home there were more yellow roses and a tray in bed for me and the children's curiosity to divert.

It had certainly been a successful operation. I didn't bleed at all for two days just as they had predicted, and then I bled only moderately for another four days. Within a week my breasts had subsided and the tenderness vanished, and my body felt mine again instead of the eggshell it becomes when it's protecting someone else.

My husband and I are back to planning our summer vacation and his career switch.

And it certainly does make more sense not to be having a baby right now—we say that to each other all the time. But I have this ghost now. A very little ghost that only appears when I'm seeing something beautiful, like the full moon on the ocean last weekend. And the baby waves at me. And I wave at the baby. "Of course, we have room," I cry to the ghost. "Of course, we do."

## Journal/Discussion Questions

✍ Write about your reactions to the case described above. What, if anything, touched you the most in Francke's essays? What would be the questions that would run through your mind in this situation? What would you do if you were in this situation?

1. Was there anything about the Francke selection that surprised you? If so, what was it? Explain.

2. Francke says that she does not regret having an abortion. Does that claim seem consistent with the rest of what she says? Explain.

3. Francke says that she is still as strongly "pro-choice" as she ever was. Yet she depicts abortion as a morally profoundly

ambiguous experience? Is this consistent? Explain.

4. Do you think that Francke and her husband make the right decision? What do you mean by "the right decision?" Explain.

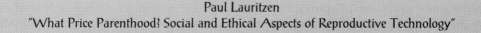

Paul Lauritzen
"What Price Parenthood? Social and Ethical Aspects of Reproductive Technology"

*Paul Lauritzen is the author of* Religious Belief and Emotional Transformation: A Light in the Heart *and* Pursuing Parenthood: Ethical Issues in Assisted Reproduction.

*Drawing on personal experience in infertility therapy as well as recent scholarship in the ethical aspects of reproductive technology, Lauritzen argues that we "must combine careful attention to the experience of pursuing parenthood by technological means with principled reflection on the morality of this pursuit." Lauritzen relates feminist objections to IVF, AID, and surrogacy to his own experience, and concludes that such technologies must be approached with great caution and only—if at all—as a final resort.*

### As You Read, Consider This:

1. What, according to Lauritzen, is the reason for including personal experiences with infertility within a philosophical discussion of the ethical issues raised by reproductive technologies? In what ways does this add or detract from his argument?

2. How, according to Lauritzen, does the very existence of new reproductive technologies become coercive? In what ways do you agree with Lauritzen? Disagree with him?

The ceremony goes as usual.

I lie on my back, fully clothed except for the healthy white cotton underdrawers. What I could see, if I were to open my eyes, would be the large white canopy of Serena Joy's outsized colonial-style four-poster bed, suspended like a sagging cloud above us. . . .

Above me, towards the head of the bed, Serena Joy is arranged, outspread. Her legs are apart, I lie between them, my head on her stomach, her pubic bone on the base of my skull, her thighs on either side of me. She too is fully clothed.

My arms are raised; she holds my hands, each of mine in each of hers. This is supposed to signify that we are one flesh, one being. What it really means is that she is in control, of the process and thus of the product. . . .

My red skirt is hitched up to my waist, though no higher. Below it the Commander is fucking. What he is fucking is the lower part of my body. I do not say making love, because this is not what he's doing. Copulating too would be inaccurate, because it would imply two people and only one is involved. (Margaret Atwood, *The Handmaid's Tale*).

This chilling depiction of the process of reproduction in the fictional Republic of Gilead provides a vision of what many feminists believe will soon be reality if the new reproductive technologies (NRTs) proceed unchecked. Children will be thought of exclusively as products. Women will be valuable merely as breeders. Reproductive prostitution will emerge as women are forced to sell wombs, ovaries, and eggs in reproductive brothels.[1] Men will be more fully in control than ever.

There was a time when I would have dismissed such claims as wildly alarmist. I still believe these worries to be overblown. Yet I have been haunted by this passage from *The Handmaid's Tale* as I have stood, month after month, holding my wife Lisa's hand as she, feet in stirrups, has received my sperm from the catheter that her doctor has maneuvered into her uterus. Indeed, once, when the nurse asked me to stand behind her to hold steady an uncooperative light, I wondered perversely whether I shouldn't, like Serena Joy, play my symbolic pall by moving rhythmically as the nurse emptied the syringe.[2] Having experienced the world of reproductive medicine firsthand, I believe we need to take a closer look at feminist objections to NRTs.

Here, then, I will review objections that some feminists have raised to such technologies as *in vitro* fertilization (IVF), artificial insemination with donor sperm (AID), and surrogate motherhood, and relate these objections to my own experience. I take up feminist objections because, although there is no one "feminist" response to reproductive technology, some of the most forceful objections to this technology have come from writers who are self consciously feminist and understand their opposition to the NRTs to be rooted in their feminism.[3] Moreover, the international feminist organization FINRRAGE (Feminist International Network of Resistance to Reproductive and Genetic Engineering) is committed to opposing the spread of reproductive technology, and it is from this group that we have the most sustained and systematic attack on NRTs in the literature.[4] I relate these objections to my own experience because, in my view, all serious moral reflection must attend to the concrete experience of particular individuals and thus inevitably involves a dialectical movement between general principles and our reactions to particular cases. The need to balance appeals to abstract rules and principles with attention to the affective responses of particular individuals has not always been sufficiently appreciated in moral theory or in medical ethics.[5] Yet such a balance is necessary if we are to understand both how moral decisions are actually made and how to act compassionately when faced with troubling moral situations.

My experience leads me to believe that there are some real dangers in pursuing these technologies, that individuals should resort to them only after much soul searching, and that society should resist efforts to expand their use in ways that would make them available as something other than a reproductive process of last resort. In the case of my wife and me, this soul searching is upon us. It now appears that artificial insemination with my sperm will not be successful. We are thus confronted with the decision of whether to pursue *in vitro* fertilization, artificial insemination with donor sperm, or adoption. This paper is one moment in that process of soul searching.

Like many couples of our generation and background, my wife and I delayed having children until we completed advanced degrees and began our jobs. With careful deliberation, we planned the best time to have children given our two careers, and were diligent in avoiding pregnancy until that time. What we had not planned on was the possibility that pregnancy would not follow quickly once we stopped using birth control. This had not been the experience of our friends whose equally carefully laid plans had all been realized. For them, birth control ended and pregnancy followed shortly thereafter. For us, a year of careful effort, including charting temperatures and cycles, yielded only frustration.

Because we had indeed been careful and deliberate in trying to conceive, we suspected early on that there might be a problem and we thus sought professional help. A post-coital examination by my wife's gynecologist revealed few, and rather immobile sperm. I was referred to a specialist for examination and diagnosed as having two unrelated problems: a varicocele and retrograde ejaculation. A varicocele is a varicose vein in the testicle that is sometimes associated with a reduction in both the numbers and quality of sperm. Retrograde ejaculation is a condition in which a muscle at the neck of the bladder does not contract sufficiently during ejaculation to prevent semen from entering the bladder. As a result, during intercourse semen is ejaculated into the bladder rather than into the vagina. Both conditions are treatable, in many cases. Indeed, the doctor's diagnosis was followed almost immediately by a presentation of possible "therapies," given roughly in the order of the doctor's preferences, all presented as points on the same therapeutic continuum. A varicocele can be repaired surgically. Retrograde ejaculation can sometimes be eliminated through the use of drugs and, failing that, can be circumvented by recovering sperm from urine and using it for artificial insemination. Should both these treatments fail, *in vitro* fertilization might be successful. And, if all else fails, donor insemination is always a possibility.

Since surgery for a valicocele is not always successful and since surgery is more invasive than either of the treatments for retrograde ejaculation, I tried these latter treatments first. Unfortunately, neither drug therapy nor artificial insemination was of any avail. Possibly because of damage done to the sperm as the result of the varicocele, the numbers and quality of sperm recovered from urine for insemination were not such as to make conception likely. After trying artificial insemination (AIH) for six months, we decided to attempt to repair the varicocele. Following this surgery, there is generally a three- to nine-month period in which a patient can expect to see improvement in his sperm count. After nearly seven months, we have seen virtually no improvement. Although we have begun AIH once again, we do not have high hopes for success.

This is the bare chronicle of my infertility experience. A complete record would be too personal, too painful, and too long to present here. But something more should be said. For someone who loves children, who has always planned to have children, infertility is an agonizing experience. In a culture that defines virility so completely in phallocentric terms, infertility can also threaten male identity, for infertility is often confused with impotence. Infertility is damaging in other ways as well. The loss of intimacy as one's sex life is taken over by infertility specialists strains a relationship. More generally, the cycle of hope and then despair that repeats itself month after month in unsuccessful infertility treatment can become unbearable. Nor is the experience of infertility made easier by the unintended thoughtlessness or uncomfortable attempts at humor of others. It is hard to know which is worse: to endure a toast on Father's Day made with great fanfare by someone who knows full well your efforts to become a father or to suffer yet another comment about shooting blanks.

With this as background, I would like to consider four interrelated, but distinct objections that have been raised to NRTs. According to feminist opponents, the new reproductive technologies are inescapably coercive; lead to the dismemberment of motherhood; treat women and children as products; and open the door to widespread genetic engineering.

## The Tyranny of Technology

Although opponents of reproductive technology do not generally distinguish types of coercion, there are typically two sorts of claims made about NRTs. The first is that the very existence (and availability) of these technologies constitutes a sort of coercive *offer*; the second, that the future of these technologies is likely to include coercive *threats* to women's reproductive choices.[6] The first claim is often a response to the standard reasons given for developing these technologies. Advocates of NRTs typically argue that these techniques are developed exclusively to help infertile couples, expanding the range of choices open to them.[7] Moreover, the medical community is portrayed as responding to the needs and interests of infertile patients to find technological means to produce pregnancy if the natural ones fail. IVF programs, for example, are almost always defended on the grounds that however experimental, painful, or dangerous they may be to women, women choose to participate in them. Thus, it is said, IVF increases choice.

Feminists who believe NRTs to be coercive claim that such a choice is illusory, because in a culture that so thoroughly defines a woman's identity in terms of motherhood, the fact that women agree to participate in IVF programs does not mean they are truly free not to participate. According to this view, we must not focus too quickly on the private decisions of individuals.[8] Individual choices are almost always embedded in social contexts, and the context in our culture is such that a childless woman is an unenviable social anomaly. To choose to be childless is still socially disapproved and to be childless in fact is to be stigmatized as selfish and uncaring. In such a situation, to offer the hope of becoming a mother to a childless woman is a coercive offer. Such a woman may well not wish to undergo the trauma of an *in vitro* procedure, but unwillingly does so.

Robyn Rowland has appreciated the significance of this social context for infertile women. "In an ideological context where child bearing is claimed to be necessary for women to fulfill themselves," she writes, "whether this is reinforced by patriarchal structures or by feminist values, discovering that you are infertile is a devastating experience."[9] The response may be a desperate search to find any means of overcoming this infertility, a search that may render the idea of choice in this context largely meaningless.

Moreover, feminists insist, developing these technologies is not about increasing choice. They are not, by and large, available to single women—infertile or not—or to lesbian women. Further, if doctors were truly concerned for the suffering of infertile women, we would expect much greater effort to publicize and to prevent various causes of infertility, including physician-induced sterility, as well as to inform women more fully about the physical and emotional trauma that various types of fertility treatments involve.[10] This neglect became dramatically apparent to me when I discovered Lisa at home weeping quietly but uncontrollably after a "routine" salpingogram for which she was utterly unprepared by her doctor's description of the procedure.[11] I will return to this theme below but I hope the claim of feminist opponents of the NRTs is clear. If doctors were in fact concerned about the well-being of their infertile patients, they would treat them less as objects to be manipulated by technologies and more as persons. The fact that this is often not the case should reveal something about the underlying motivations.[12]

The second claim about the possibility of coercive threats is really a concern about the future. While we may debate whether a desperately infertile woman really is free to choose not to try *in vitro* fertilization, still, no one is forcing her to participate in an IVF program. But what about the future? This question is meant to point to how thoroughly medicine has encroached on the birth process. The use of ultrasound, amniocentesis, genetic testing and counseling, electronic fetal monitoring, and cesarean sections have all increased the medical community's control over the process of birth. Why should the process of conception be any different? If anything, a pattern suggests itself. What was originally introduced as a specialized treatment for a subclass of women quickly expanded to cover a far wider range of cases. What was originally an optional technology may quickly become the norm.[13]

Such interventions can be coercive not only in the sense that, once established as the norm they are difficult to avoid, but in the stricter sense that women may literally be forced to submit to them, as with court-ordered cesarean sections. Will compulsory treatment be true of the new technologies as well? Will the technology that allows for embryo flushing and transfer in surrogate cases be required in the future as part of a process of medical evaluation of the fetus? The concern that the answers to these questions is too likely to be "yes" stands behind some claims that the NRTs are dangerously coercive. The potential for a loss of control over one's reproductive destiny is increased with the development of these technologies. And the coercion that could follow such a loss of control is worrisome.

Have I experienced a loss of control or coercion? The answer is a qualified yes. I certainly have not felt coerced in the second sense. I have not been physically forced to undergo infertility treatment nor has there been any threat, actual or implied, connected with the prospect of avoiding NRTs altogether. Still, I have experienced the existence of these technologies as coercive. And here the notion of a coercive offer is helpful. Although the inability to have children has not threatened my social identity in the same way it might were I a woman, nevertheless, the pressure is real. Having experienced this pressure, and having met others whose desperation to bear a child was almost palpable, I do not doubt that the offer of hope held out by available technologies, however slim and unrealistic in some cases, is indeed a form of coercion.

The problem here might reasonably be called the tyranny of available technologies. This soft form of coercion arises from the very existence of technologies of control. Increased control by the medical profession over the birth process, for example, has not resulted because of a conspiracy to gain control, but rather because, once the technology of control exists, it is nearly impossible not to make use of it. If, as I believe, this pressure to make use of existing technologies is a type of coercion, I have experienced this coercion powerfully during my infertility treatment. If surgery might repair the problem, even if the chances are not great, how can I not have surgery? If surgery and artificial insemination have not worked, but some new technique might, how can I not try the new technique?

The very existence of the technology inevitably changes the experience of infertility in ways that are not salutary. One of the peculiar aspects of infertility is that it is a condition that a couple suffers. Individuals can have retrograde ejaculation or blocked tubes, but only couples can be infertile. As Leon Kass has noted, infertility is as much a relationship as a condition.[14] Yet infertility treatment leads us to view infertility individually, with unfortunate consequences. The reason is that couples will often not be seen together in infertility treatment, and, even when they are, they will receive individual workups and be presented with individual treatment options. Now it might be said that providing individuals with options increases agency rather than diminishes it. Yet with this agency comes a responsibility that may not itself be chosen and that reduces the prospects for genuine choice. For once an individual is presented with a treatment option, not to pursue it is, in effect to choose childlessness and to accept responsibility for it. From a situation in which infertility is a relational problem for which no one is to blame, it becomes an individual problem for which a woman or man who refuses treatment is to blame.[15] Reproductive technology structures the alternatives such that a patient is "free" to pursue every available form of assisted reproduction or to choose to be childless.

This problem is compounded by the fact that infertility specialists simply assume that patients will pursue all available treatments and typically present the variety of treatment options as just different points on the same therapeutic spectrum, distinguished primarily by degree of invasiveness. In our case, taking relatively mild drugs in an effort to make an incontinent muscle more efficient lies at one end of the continuum, at the other end of which lies IVF. Surgery, I suppose, falls somewhere in the middle. At no time in my experience, however, has anyone suggested that treatments differ qualitatively. (The only exception to this was my urologist's opposition to an experimental treatment for malefactor infertility.) It has generally been assumed that if one therapy fails, we will simply move on to the next. And that is the problem. If the technology exists, the expectation is that it will be used. Again, if IVF might work, how can we not try it? The force of these questions covers us like a weight as we consider what to do next.

## The Dismemberment of Motherhood

A second objection raised against the NRTs is that they question the very meaning of motherhood. The reality of oocyte donation, embryo flushing, and embryo transfer produces another possible reality: the creation of a child for whom there are three mothers: the genetic mother, the gestational mother, and the social mother.[16] In such a situation, who is the real mother? In the absence of a compelling answer, the claim of each of these three women to the child will be tenuous. Maternity will be as much in dispute as paternity ever was. And whatever criteria are used to settle this issue, the result for women is that the reproductive experience may become discontinuous in much the way it has traditionally been for men. Just as paternity has been uncertain because the natural, biological relation between the father and child could always be questioned, so too might maternity become a sort of abstract idea rather than a concrete reality. Just as paternity has been a fight rather than a natural relation, so too might maternity become.[17]

The significance of this can be seen if one takes seriously Mary O'Brien's claims that men's reproductive experience of discontinuity, that is, the inevitable uncertainty of genetic continuity, has contributed significantly to men's need to dominate. The problematic nature of paternity, O'Brien suggests, can account for the sense of isolation and separation so common in men, in part because for men the nature of paternity is such that the natural experimental relation of intimacy with another is missing.

Feminists' celebrations of motherhood have also made much of the biological continuity women have traditionally experienced with their children. Caroline Whitbeck and Nancy Hartsock, for example, have both discussed how the biological differences between men and women, especially as they are manifested in reproduction, account for some of the differences in how men and women experience the world.[18] Many women do not experience the sharp separation between self and others so common to male experience, Hartsock and Whitbeck note, a fact both explain by appeal to the way in which female physiology mediates female experience. In the case of women who are mothers, the experience of pregnancy, labor, childbirth, and nursing shape a way of responding to the world and to others. For a mother whose milk lets down at the sound of her child's cry, a sense of deep connection and continuity is established.[19]

On this view, the danger of the new technologies of birth is precisely that they alienate women from procreation and thus rob them of one of the most significant sources of power and identity. It is precisely this realization that leads Connie Ramos, a character in Marge Piercy's *Woman on the Edge of Time*, to react with such horror at the division of motherhood envisioned by Piercy. In a world where gestation takes place in artificial wombs, where men as well as women nurse the young, women have lost something of tremendous value and men have gained something they always wanted: control of reproduction. Connie's response to seeing a breast feeding male poignantly expresses this point:

> She felt angry. Yes, how dare any man share that pleasure. These women thought they had won, but they had abandoned to men the last refuge of women. What was special about being a woman here? They had given it all up, they had let men steal from them the last remnants of ancient power, those sealed in blood and in milk.[20]

One of the gravest concerns raised about the new technologies of birth, then, is that they represent the culmination of a patriarchal imperative: to gain for men what they have always lacked, namely, the power to reproduce. The fear is that this desire is close to realization. Gena Corea has put this point forcefully:

> Now men are far beyond the stage at which they expressed their envy of woman's procreative power through couvade, transvestism, or subincision. They are beyond merely giving spiritual birth in their baptismal-font wombs, beyond giving physical birth with their electronic fetal monitors, their forceps, their knives. Now they have laboratories.[21]

Since this objection essentially focuses on the impact on women of the NRTs, my experience cannot speak directly to this issue. Nevertheless, because part of what is at stake is the importance of the unity of genetic and social parenthood, as well as the unity of genetic and gestational parenthood, this is not a concern exclusively of women; it is a concern I have confronted in reflecting about donor insemination and adoption. One of the most striking aspects of my experience is how powerfully I have felt the pull of biological connection. Does this mean that genetic and social parenthood should never be separated or that parenthood should be defined strictly as a biological relation? I believe the answer to both questions is "no," but my experience leads me to believe also that a unity of genetic, gestational, and social parenthood is an ideal that we ought to strive to maintain.

# The Commodification of Reproduction

The third objection found in some of the feminist literature on NRTs is that they tend to treat human beings as products. Not only can these technologies divide up motherhood, they can divide up persons into parts. Even when they are used to treat infertility, it is often not men or women who are being treated, but testicles, sperm, ovaries, eggs, wombs, etc. While this is true to some extent of all treatment in the specialized world of modern medicine, it is acute in reproductive medicine. Robyn Rowland has described the situation as one in which women especially are treated as "living laboratories" in which body parts and systems are manipulated in dramatic fashion without knowledge about the consequences of such manipulation.[22] Clearly, this has been the case in the development of *in vitro* fertilization, where women have not been adequately informed about the experimental nature of the procedure, possible side effects, or poor success rates.

In addition, the language of reproductive medicine can also be dehumanizing. Eggs are "harvested" as one might bring in a crop. Body parts are personified and thus attributed a sort of individuality and intentionality; cervical mucus is said to be "hostile," the cervix itself is said to be "incompetent," and the list could go on.

Yet as troubling as the language and practice surrounding this technology may be in treating persons like products, it is the application of this technology that treats persons as products that is completely objectionable. This has clearly happened with the development of a commercial surrogate industry and donor sperm banks, and it is the danger that attends the establishment of oocyte donor programs. Indeed, Corea's idea of a reproductive brothel seems inescapable. If there are not yet houses of ill repute where one can go to purchase embryos and women to gestate them, there are brochures available containing pictures and biographical information of women willing to sell their services. Nor can the development of commercial surrogacy arrangements be dismissed as the misguided and unintended application of reproductive techniques, an application of NRTs mistakenly and uncharacteristically driven by the profit motive. Treatment of infertility is big business, and the drive to develop reproductive technology is clearly fueled by financial incentives.[23]

Nothing perhaps illustrates this more clearly than the development of an embryo flushing technique by a team of physicians at Harbor-UCLA Medical Center. In April 1983, this team successfully flushed an embryo from one woman and transferred it to a second woman who carried the fetus to term. The project was funded by Fertility and Genetics Research, a for-profit company begun by two physicians who envisioned the establishment of a chain of embryo transfer clinics where infertile women could purchase embryos to gestate themselves. Indeed, to insure maximum profits for themselves, the Harbor-UCLA team sought to patent the equipment and the technique they developed.[24]

Not only do men and women get treated as products, so do children. The logic here is clear enough. If women are paying for embryos or being paid for eggs, the embryos and the eggs cannot but be understood as products. Because they are products, buyers will place demands on them. We will expect our products to meet certain standards and, if they fail, we will want to be compensated or to return the damaged goods. In a society that sells embryos and eggs for profit, children will inevitably be treated as property to be bought and sold, and just as inevitably it follows that different children will carry different price tags. As Barbara Katz Rothman puts it, "some will be rejects, not salable at any price: too damaged, or the wrong colour, or too old, too long on the shelf."[25]

My own experience leads me to believe that this tendency toward the commodification of reproduction is one of the most worrisome aspects of the NRTs.[26] In part, this tendency is troubling because it manifests itself not simply in commercial surrogacy transactions—transactions that many if not most people find morally problematic—but in applications of these technologies that almost no one questions. For example, few, I believe, would have qualms about the sort of artificial insemination that Lisa and I have undertaken and yet perhaps the most difficult part of AIH for us has been the struggle to maintain a degree of intimacy in the process of reproduction in the midst of a clinical environment designed to achieve results. As Katz Rothman has pointed out, the ideology of technology that fuels this commodification is not reducible to particular technological tools or to particular commercial transactions. Rather it is a way of thinking of ourselves and our world in "mechanical, industrial terms," terms that are incompatible with intimacy.[27] Interestingly, the Roman Catholic Church has rejected AIH precisely because it separates procreation from sexual intercourse and the expression of love manifest in the conjugal act.[28] While I reject the act-oriented natural law reasoning that stands behind this position, there is an insight here that should not be overlooked. Once procreation is separated from sexual intercourse, it is difficult not to treat the process of procreation as the production of an object to which one has a fight as the producer. It is also difficult under these circumstances not to place the end above the means; effectiveness in accomplishing one's goal can easily become the sole criterion by which decisions are made.

This anyway, has been my experience. Although Lisa and I tried for a time to maintain a degree of intimacy during the process of AIH by remaining together during all phases of the procedure as well as after the insemination, we quickly abandoned this as a charade. The system neither encourages nor facilitates intimacy. It is concerned, as it probably should be, with results. And so we have become pragmatists too. We do not much enjoy the process of AIH, to say the least, but we also do not try to make it something it is not. A conception, if it takes place, will not be the result of an act of bodily lovemaking, but a result of technology. We have come to accept this. Yet, such acceptance comes at a price, for our experience of reproduction is discontinuous. A child conceived by this method is lovingly willed into existence, but it is not conceived through a loving, bodily act.

Having accepted the separation of sexual intercourse and procreation, however, it is difficult to resist any sort of technological manipulation of gametes that might result in conception. We have, so to speak, relinquished our gametes to the doctors and once this has been done, how can various technological manipulations be judged other than by criteria of likelihood of success; This is precisely the problem: once one has begun a process that inevitably treats procreation as the production of a product, the methods of production can only be evaluated by the end result.

## Reproductive Technologies and Genetic Engineering

The fourth objection to NRTs is that their general acceptance and use is an inevitable route to widespread use of genetic engineering. It should be no mystery why this might be thought to be the case. Once the embryo, for example, is treated as a product to be bought and sold, there will be great pressure to produce the perfect product. The attraction of genetic engineering under such circumstances should be obvious. Genetic screening and therapy would be a sort of quality control mechanism by which to insure customer satisfaction.[29] Moreover, the greater access to embryos and to eggs provided by IVF and embryo flushing means that genetic manipulation of the eggs or the developing embryo is now more feasible than it once was. Even more importantly, however, this greater access to embryos and eggs, combined with the possibility of freezing and storing those not used to attempt a pregnancy, means that experimentation can go forward at a much faster rate. Scientists have experimented with the injection of genetic material into non-human eggs for some time, and a recent issue of *Cell* reported the introduction of foreign genetic material into mouse sperm.[30] It is not unreasonable to suppose that such manipulations will one day extend to human gametes. Indeed, one experimental technique being developed to treat forms of male infertility in which sperm is unable to penetrate the egg involves isolating a single sperm in order to introduce the sperm directly into the egg.[31] The obvious question is: How will this sperm be selected? The most likely answer will be: by a determination that it is not genetically abnormal.

Thus far, most genetic experimentation, manipulation, and screening has been defended by appeal to the goal of eliminating human suffering. If genetic abnormalities can be detected or even treated, much human suffering might either be avoided or alleviated. Yet, how does one distinguish between attempts to eliminate suffering and attempts at eugenics? The fact that it is so difficult to answer this question is one reason to be concerned about NRTs. Moreover, the equation of genetic abnormality or disability with suffering can be questioned. As Marsha Saxton has pointed out, we cannot simply assume that disabled people "suffer" from their physical conditions any more than any other group or category of individuals "suffer."[32] Indeed, decisions about bearing genetically damaged fetuses are generally made in relative ignorance of what sorts of lives potential offspring might actually have.[33] "Our exposure to disabled children," Saxton writes, "has been so limited by their isolation that most people have only stereotyped views which include telethons, and displays on drugstore counters depicting attractive crippled youngsters soliciting our pity and loose change."[34]

If reproductive technology is developed because every person has a right to bear a child, does it not follow that every person has a right to bear a perfect child? Advocates of NRTs would not admit this, and yet it seems to be the logical conclusion of the commitment to produce a child, no matter the cost. To see the difficulties here, we need only ask how we are to define the perfect child, and whether a commitment to eliminate genetic abnormalities means that women will lose the freedom not to test for or to treat abnormalities.

In my view, the concern here is a real one for, once one has begun to think in terms of producing a product, it becomes exceedingly difficult to distinguish between technological interventions except on the basis of the resulting product. And since the product one desires in this instance is a healthy baby, a technological intervention that helps to achieve this, even one that involves genetic manipulation, is likely to be both initially attractive and ultimately irresistible. My own reaction to the new technique of overcoming male infertility by isolating a single sperm and injecting it into an egg it would otherwise be unable to penetrate is instructive. My initial response was that of tremendous excitement. Here was a treatment that could clearly overcome our problem. The fact that I did not produce great numbers of sperm or that the ones I produced were not likely to be capable of penetrating an egg did not matter. In theory, very few sperm are required and the work of penetration is done for them. The fact that such a technique involves placing an extraordinary amount of control in the hands of the doctor who selects the single sperm from among the many millions that even a man with a low sperm count is likely to produce did not even occur to me. In fact, it was my doctor, who had moral reservations about this technique, who first pointed this out to me. What is perhaps more troubling, however, is that when the issue of control was pointed out to me, I found no immediately compelling reason to object. I had, after all, been routinely providing sperm for a lab to manipulate in an effort to produce a collection that was capable of penetrating my wife's egg. Was selecting a single sperm that could accomplish the goal really so different?

In light of these various objections and my own experience, then, my basic response is one of concern. I do not believe that the predominantly male medical profession is acting in bad faith in developing reproductive technologies, as some critics suggest. Much of the feminist literature on NRTs is cynical and deeply contemptuous of what is seen as a patriarchal and conspiratorial medical establishment. My own experience, however, does not bear this out. Although there is much about my treatment for infertility that I have found frustrating, anxiety-producing, and distasteful, and although I have felt at turns coerced by the existence of the technologies themselves; angry at the loss of intimacy in my relationship with Lisa; and worried by my own near obsession with the goal of achieving a pregnancy, I have never had reason to doubt the sincerity of my doctor's care and concern. That my experience has been so negative despite treating with a doctor who is very much aware of the potentially dehumanizing aspects of infertility treatment is further evidence of how serious the problems with these technologies may be.

This is not to deny that infertility specialists are too concerned with technological fixes; in my view, they are. While there is no conspiracy to gain control of the process of reproduction, there is increased control. And if one theme joins the various objections to the new reproductive technologies, it is that they increase the medical profession's control over the process of reproduction and that such control has deleterious consequences. We have not, by and large, thought through the consequences of this sort of intervention and control. Neither infertile couples nor those who try to alleviate their suffering, nor indeed the community that is generally supportive of the desire to have children has really asked whether that desire should be met at all costs. Is the desire to have children a desire for a basic human good? Can it be met through adoption or only through biological offspring? Are there other, competing social goods that set limits on how far we, as a community, should go to meet this need? These are certainly questions that I had not addressed before my experience of infertility. Even now I am not certain how to answer all of them. I am certain, however, that my desire to have children is strong. I am also equally certain that we need to attend to these questions as a society. For anyone not blinded by self-deception will admit that wanting something does not always make it right.

## Acknowledgments

A number of individuals both encouraged me to go forward with this essay, and provided me with very helpful suggestions for revisions. Thanks to Lisa Cahill, Lisa de Filippis, Howard Eilberg-Schwartz, Tom Kelly, Gilbert Meilaender, Louis Newman, John P. Reeder, Jr., David H. Smith, Claudia Spencer, John Spencer, and Brian Stiltner. I also received very helpful comments from the works-in-progress group at the Center for Bioethics at the Case Western Reserve University School of Medicine and the participants in a NEH-sponsored Humanities and Medicine Institute at Hiram College held in collaboration with the Northeastern Ohio Universities College of Medicine.

## Endnotes

1. See Gena Corea, "The Reproductive Brothel" in *Man-made Woman*, Gena Corea et al., eds. (Bloomington: Indiana University Press, 1987), pp. 38–51.

2. The medical profession has gone to some lengths to insure that artificial insemination is defined as a medical procedure, and thus controlled by doctors. Most of my wife's inseminations have been administered by doctors, even when this has been inconvenient for us. The two exceptions have been when Lisa ovulated on the weekend and then, apparently, insemination did not need to be performed by a doctor.

3. Although for convenience I will refer in this paper to "feminist" objections, I cannot stress enough that there is not one feminist response to reproductive technology, but several. Indeed, feminist responses range from enthusiastic support to moderate and cautious support to radical opposition. See Anne Donchin, "The Future of Mothering: Reproductive Technology and Feminist Theory," *Hypatia* (1986), 121–137.

4. Patricia Spallone and Deborah Lynn Steinberg, eds., *Made to Order* (Oxford: Pergamon Press, 1987).

5. But see Sidney Callahan, "The Role of Emotion in Ethical Decisionmaking," *Hastings Center Report* 18:3 (1988), 9–14.

6. On the difference between coercive offers and coercive threats, see Virginia Held, "Coercion and Coercive Offers," in *Coercion*, J. Roland Pennock and John Chapman, eds. (Chicago: Atherton, 1972), 49–62.

7. I use "couples" here intentionally. The justification for developing reproductive methods is almost always to help infertility within marriage. There is an irony in this: Although physicians tend to treat infertility as a problem for an individual, they insist that that individual be part of a heterosexual marriage. Thus it is not just infertility that is of concern, but infertility in certain types of situations.

8. For a discussion of the difficulty of providing an adequate account of free choice given the assumptions of modern liberalism, see Barbara Katz Rothman, *Recreating Motherhood* (New York: W. W. Norton, 1989), p. 62.

9. Robyn Rowland, "Of Woman Born, But for How Long?" in *Made to Order*, p. 70.

10. See Spallone and Steinberg, eds., *Made to Order*, pp. 6–7.

11. The test involves injecting radiopaque dye into the uterine cavity after which x-rays are taken. The fallopian tubes are outlined wherever the dye has penetrated. Using this procedure, it is sometimes possible to determine whether a woman's tubes are blocked.

12. Here my experience and Lisa's differ dramatically. The infertility specialist I have seen could not be more sensitive or attentive to the human dimension of our difficulties. By contrast, Lisa's experience with the gynecologists involved with insemination has been almost entirely negative, in part because she has not been treated fully as a person by them.

13. Spallone and Steinberg, eds., *Made to Order*, pp. 4–5.

14. Leon Kass, *Toward a More Natural Sex* (New York: The Free Press, 1985), p. 45.

15. I am, in effect, suggesting that more choice is not always better. This is not a popular view in

our culture, but it can be persuasively defended. For such a defense, see Gerald Dworkin, "Is More Choice Better than Less?" *Midwest Studies in Philosophy* 7, Peter A. French, Theodore E. Uehling, Jr., and Howard K. Wettstein, eds. (Minneapolis: University of Minnesota Press, 1982), 47–61.

16. Gena Corea, *The Mother Machine* (New York: Harper and Row, 1985), p. 290.

17. Mary O'Brien, *The Politics of Reproduction* (Boston: Routledge and Kegan Paul, 1981), p. 55.

18. See Nancy Hansock, "The Feminist Standpoint: Developing the Ground for a Specifically Feminist Historical Materialism," in *Discovering Reality*, Sandra Harding and Merrill B. Hintikka, eds. (Dordrecht: D. Reidel, 1983), pp. 283–310; and Caroline Whitbeck, "A Different Reality: Feminist Ontology," in *Beyond Domination*, Carol C. Gould, ed. (Totowa, NJ: Rowman and Allanheld, 1983), pp. 64–88.

19. Emily Martin, *The Woman in the Body* (Boston: Beacon Press, 1987).

20. Marge Piercy, *Woman on the Edge of Time* (New York: Ballantine Books, 1976), p. 134.

21. Corea, *The Mother Machine*, p. 314.

22. Robyn Rowland, "Women As Living Laboratories: The New Reproductive Technologies," in *The Trapped Woman*, Josefina Figueira-McDonough and Rosemary Sani, eds. (Newbury Park, CA: Sage Publications, 1987), pp. 81–112.

23. According to the Office of Technology Assessment, $164 million is paid to close to 11,000 physicians every year for artificial inseminations alone. Add to this the variety of other infertility services provided every year to childless couples and the total cost is at least $1 billion (U.S. Congress, Office of Technology Assessment, *Artificial Insemination Practice in the U.S.: Summary of a 1987 Survey;* Washington: Government Printing Office, 1988).

24. Although there are currently no franchised clinics in the U.S., the ovum transfer procedure using uterine lavage is commonplace. See Leonard Fonnigli, Graziella Fonnigli, and Carlo Roccio, "Donation of Fertilized Uterine Ova to Infertile Women," *Fertility and Sterility* 47:1 (1987), 162–165.

25. Barbara Katz Rothman, "The Products of Conception: The Social Context of Reproductive Choices," *Journal of Medical Ethics* 11 (1985), p. 191.

26. The tendency to treat children as commodities is not solely the product of developing NRTs, of course, but the culmination of a process begun with the old reproductive technology of contraception. Once the inexorable connection between sexual intercourse and procreation was broken, it became possible to choose when to have children. From that point on, it made sense to treat children in some ways as products, the purchase of which, so to speak, could be planned as one planned the purchase of other expensive items.

27. Katz Rothman, *Recreating Motherhood*, p. 49.

28. Sacred Congregation for the Doctrine of the Faith, Instruction on Respect for Human Life in Its Origin and on the Dignity of Procreation, in *Origins* 16 (March 1987), 697–711.

29. Katz Rothman, "The Products of Conception," 188.

30. For a discussion of the transgenic animals that result from the genetic manipulation of eggs,

see V. G. Pursel et al., "Genetic Engineering of Livestock," *Science* 244 (1989), 128–188. Also see M. Lavitrano et al., "Sperm Cells As Vectors for Introducing Foreign DNA into Eggs: Genetic Transformation of Mice," *Cell* 57:5 (1989), 717–724.

31. Actually, there are at least three different techniques being investigated. See Jon W. Gordon et al., "Fertilization of Human Oocytes by Sperm from Infertile Males After Zona Pellucida Drilling," *Fertility and Sterility* 50:1 (1988), 68–73.

32. Marsha Saxton, "Born and Unborn: The Implications of Reproductive Technologies for People with Disabilities," in *Test-tube Women*, Rita Arditti, Renate Duelli Klein, and Shelley Minden, eds. (London: Pandora Press, 1984), pp. 298–313.

33. Anne Finger, "Claiming All of Our Bodies: Reproductive Rights and Disabilities," in *Test-tube Women*, pp. 281–297.

34. See Ruth Hubbard, "'Fetal Rights' and the New Eugenics," *Science for the People* (March/April 1984), 7–9, 27–29.

## Journal/Discussion Questions

✍ *Do you know anyone who has gone through any of the types of fertility programs that Lauritzen describes? In what ways was their experience similar to Lauritzen's? In what ways dissimilar?*

1. Why do feminists think that advances in reproductive technologies actually *reduce* women's choices? Do you agree with this reasoning? Why or why not?

2. Should reproductive technologies be made available to single women? To lesbian women? Why or why not?

3. Lauritzen states that, "A child conceived by this method [AID] is lovingly willed into existence, but it is not conceived through a loving, bodily act." What moral implications follow from this, according to Lauritzen? In what ways do you agree with him? Disagree?

4. Lauritzen asks, "How does one distinguish between attempts to eliminate suffering and attempts at eugenics?" How does he answer this question? In what ways do you agree with him? Disagree?

# AN INTRODUCTION TO THE MORAL ISSUES

## Abortion: The Two Principal Moral Concerns

The ongoing discussion of abortion in American society is often framed as a debate between two sides, usually called *pro-life* and *pro-choice*. The labels themselves are instructive. Whereas one label points our attention toward the fetus, the other emphasizes the pregnant woman. Each position highlights a different aspect of the situation as the principal focus of moral concern. Pro-life supporters emphasize the issue of the rights of the unborn, while pro-choice advocates stress the importance of the rights of the pregnant woman.

Notice that these two moral concerns are not immediately mutually exclusive in the same way that, for example, the pro- and anti-capital-punishment positions are. (They may, of course, be secondarily exclusive insofar as the consequences of one exclude the other.) This results in a certain murkiness in debates about abortion, since the opposing sides are often talking primarily about quite different things, either the moral status of the fetus or the rights of the pregnant woman. Let's examine each of these issues.

## The Moral Status of the Fetus

Initially, much of the debate about abortion centered around the question of the moral status of the fetus—in particular, if and when the fetus is a person. Most participants in the discussion took for granted that if the fetus can be shown to be a person, then abortion is morally wrong. Thus the discussion focused primarily on whether the fetus could be shown to be a person or not. In order to answer this question, it was necessary to specify what we meant by a *person*.

### Criteria of Personhood

In attempting to define personhood, philosophers have looked for the criteria by means of which we determine whether a being is a person or not. This is a search for *sufficient conditions*, that is, conditions which if present would guarantee personhood. The argument moves in the following way. Some criterion is seen as conferring personhood, and personhood is seen as conferring certain rights, including the right to life. Thus the overall structure of the argument looks like this:

*What characteristics does a being have to have in order to be a person?*

> criterion   ⇨   personhood   ⇨   right to life.

We can see the two critical junctures in the argument just by looking at this diagram. The first is in the transition from the criterion to personhood. What justification is there for claiming that this criterion (or group of criteria) justifies the claim that a being is a person? The second transition has sometimes been seen as less problematic, but it may have more difficulties than are initially apparent. The issue in this transition is whether personhood always justifies the right to life.

A number of criteria have been advanced for personhood. Some of these result in conferring personhood quite early in fetal development, sometimes from the moment of conception.

The *conceived-by-humans* criterion is, at least on the surface, the most straightforward: "if you are conceived by human parents, you are human." (Noonan, in Feinberg, p. 9) But this straightforwardness turns out to be misleading. We obviously acknowledge the personhood of anyone *born of human parents*. This is the indisputably true sense of "conceived-by-humans." However, we do not obviously and necessarily acknowledge the personhood of everything "conceived-by-humans" in the strict sense. This either equivocates or begs the question.

The *genetic structure* argument maintains that a human genetic code is a sufficient condition for personhood. All the genetic information for the fully formed human being is present in the fetus at the time of conception; therefore, it has the rights of a person. Nothing more needs to be added, and if nothing interferes with the development of the fetus, it will emerge as a full-fledged human baby.

The *physical resemblance* criterion claims that something that looks human is human. Advocates of this criterion then claim that the fetus is a person because of its physical resemblance to a full-term baby. Movies such as *The Silent Scream* (which graphically depicts the contortions of a fetus during an abortion) depend strongly on such an criterion. This criterion seems rhetorically more powerful than the appeal to DNA (since DNA lacks the same visual and emotive impact), but less rigorous, since resemblance can be more strongly in the eye of the beholder than DNA structures.

The *presence-of-a-soul criterion* is often involved by religious thinkers. The criterion is then used in an argument maintaining that God gives an immortal soul to the fetus at a particular moment, at which time the fetus becomes a person. Although contemporary versions of this argument usually maintain that the implantation of a soul takes place at the time of conception, St. Thomas Aquinas—one of the most influential of modern theologians—claimed that implantation usually occurs at quickening, around the third month. (Aquinas also thought that this event occurred later for females than it did for males.) The principal difficulty with this argument is that it attempts to clarify the opaque by an appeal to the utterly obscure: God's will, at least in matters such as the implantation of a soul, is even more difficult to discern than the personhood of the fetus.

The *viability* criterion sees personhood as inextricably tied to the ability to exist independently of the mother's womb. A fetus is thus seen as a person and having a right to life when it could survive (even with artificial means) outside the body of the mother. This criterion is clearly dependent on developments in medical technology which make it possible to keep increasingly young premature babies alive. If artificial wombs are eventually developed, then viability might be pushed back to a much earlier stage in fetal development.

Finally, the *future-like-ours* criterion maintains that fetuses have a future, just as adult human beings have a future. Just as killing of adults is wrong because it deprives them of everything that comprises their future, so, too, the killing of a fetus deprives it of its future. Don Marquis develops this argument in his selection, "Why Abortion Is Immoral."

Some philosophers have argued that there are other criteria that are *necessary* conditions of personhood, and that fetuses usually lack these characteristics. These are criteria that we usually associate with adult human beings: *reasoning*, a *concept of self*, *use of language*, and so on. (These criteria are often particularly relevant in discussions of the end of life: at what point, if any, does a breathing human being cease to be a person?) There are several dangers with appeals to such criteria. Most notably, such criteria may set the standard of personhood too high and justify not only abortion, but also infanticide, the killing of brain-damaged adults, and involuntary euthanasia.

There are a number of possible responses to this lack of consensus in regard to the conditions of personhood. Two arguments have been advanced that see this lack of consensus as supporting a conservative position on the morality of abortion. The *Let's Play It Safe* argument states that we cannot be absolutely sure when the fetus becomes a person, so let's be careful to err on the safe side. This is often coupled with the *Let's Not Be Arbitrary* argument, which states that, since we do not know precisely the moment at which a fetus assumes personhood, we should assume that it becomes a person at the moment of conception and act accordingly. The moment of conception provides, according to this argument, the only nonarbitrary point of demarcation.

Other philosophers have taken a quite different tack in the face of this disagreement about the conditions of personhood. They have argued that it is impossible to define the concept of a person with the necessary precision. Instead, we should turn to other moral considerations to determine whether and when abortion is morally justified.

## Relevance of Personhood

There was a widespread assumption that if the fetus is a person, then abortion is morally wrong. The first major article to challenge this assumption was Judith Jarvis Thomson's "A Defense of Abortion" (1971), which presented an intriguing example. Imagine that, without your prior knowledge or consent, you are sedated in your sleep and surgically connected to a famous violinist, who must share the use of your kidneys for nine months until he is able to survive on his own. Even granting that the violinist is obviously a full-fledged person, Thomson argues that you are morally justified in disconnecting yourself from the violinist, even if it results in his death. Going back to our diagram of the two main stages of the abortion argument, we can see that Thomson's strategy is to question the transition from "personhood" to "right to life." Even granting that the dependent entity is a full person (whether fetus or violinist), we may still be morally justified in cutting off support and thereby killing that person. Thus, Thomson argues, the morality of abortion does not depend on our answer to the question of whether the fetus is a person or not. A more developed version of Thomson's example is to be found in Jane English's selection, "Abortion and Personhood."

Thomson's article has been criticized on many fronts, but despite these criticisms, the major impact of her piece has been to open the door to the possibility that the answer to the question of abortion does not depend solely on the moral status of the fetus. This opened the door to a more extensive consideration of the other principal moral consideration in this situation, the rights of the pregnant woman.

# The Rights of the Pregnant Woman

The second principal focus of moral concern is on the rights of the pregnant woman. Yet what precisely are these rights? At least four main candidates have been advanced: the right to privacy, the right to ownership and control over one's own body, the right to equal treatment, and the right to self-determination.

## The Right to Privacy

In *Roe* v. *Wade* (1973), the Supreme Court based its support for a woman's right to abortion in part on the claim that the woman has a right to privacy. In constitutional law, the right to privacy seems to have two distinct senses. First, certain behaviors—such as sexual intercourse—are usually thought to be private; the government may not infringe upon these behaviors unless there is some particularly compelling reason (such as preventing the sexual abuse of children) for doing so. Second, some decisions in an individual's life—such as the choice of a mate or a career—are seen as matters of individual autonomy or self-determination; these are private in the sense that the government has no right to tell an individual what to do in such areas. This second sense of privacy will be discussed below in the section on the right to self-determination. In this section, we will confine our attention to the first sense of privacy.

*Does the right to privacy guarantee the right to an abortion?*

This appeal to the right of privacy as the basis for a woman's right to choice has proved to be a peculiar justification for two reasons. First, privacy claims are difficult to justify constitutionally, since in fact there is no explicit mention of a right to privacy in the Constitution or Bill of Rights. Second, the abortion *procedure* is certainly not usually private in the way in which, for example, sexual intercourse is private. It takes place outside of the home (at a clinic or hospital) and involves a second party (a physician and staff). To be sure, the *decision* may be made in private, but what is at issue is the procedure for implementing that decision. Interestingly, this will change significantly if and when the French-developed abortion pill, RU-486, is more widely used. Under new protocols being developed for the drug, the pregnant woman may only have to make a single visit to a physician to obtain the prescription.

## The Right to Ownership of One's Own Body

Some have argued that the right to abortion is based on a woman's right to control her own body, and in some instances this is seen as a property right. This approach also seems wide of the mark. To be sure, no one else owns our bodies, and, in this sense, there seems to be a right to control our own bodies. However, it is doubtful whether the relationship we have with our own bodies is best understood in terms of ownership, nor is the presence of the fetus most perceptively grasped as the intrusion onto private property.

## The Right to Equal Treatment

Some jurists, most notably Ruth Bader Ginsburg, have suggested that a woman's right to abortion may be best justified constitutionally through an appeal to the right to equal protection under the law. Pregnancy results from the combined actions of two people, yet the woman typically bears a disproportionate amount of the responsibility and burden. This line of reasoning certainly seems highly relevant to striking down laws and regulations that discriminate against women because of pregnancy, but it is unclear whether it alone is sufficient to support a right to abortion. In fact, it would seem that there must be some other, more fundamental right that is at stake here.

## The Right to Self-Determination

When we consider the actual conflict that many women experience in making the decision about abortion, it would seem that it centers primarily around the effects that an unwanted pregnancy and child would have on their lives. The most fundamental right at issue for the pregnant woman in this context would seem to be the right to determine the course of her own life. In this context, it is relevant to ask *how much* the pregnancy would interfere with the woman's life. As John Martin Fisher has pointed out, one of the misleading aspects of Thomson's violinist example is that it suggests that pregnancy would virtually eliminate one's choices for nine months. In actuality, the violinist case would be comparable only to the most difficult of pregnancies, those which require months of strict bed rest. Yet in most cases, pregnancy does not involve such an extreme restriction on the woman's everyday life; the restrictions on self-determination are much less.

In what ways do pregnancy and childbirth potentially conflict with self-determination? Consider, first of all, the extremes on the spectrum. On the one hand, imagine a most grave threat to self-determination: a rape that results in an extremely difficult pregnancy that required constant bed rest, childbirth that contained a high risk of the mother's death, and the likelihood that the child would require years of constant medical attention. Conception, pregnancy, delivery, and the child would all severely limit (if not destroy) the mother's choices in life. These carry enormous moral weight. On the other hand, an easy pregnancy and birth of a perfectly healthy baby are potentially much less restrictive to a woman's power of self-determination. Raising a child, of course, is potentially quite restrictive to self-determination, but in those cases where adoption is a reasonable option, raising the child is not necessary.

There is a further perplexity about self-determination. It is reasonable, as Fisher and others have done, to distinguish between what is central to one's self-determination and what is peripheral to it. We intuitively recognize this when we hear, for example, of a pianist whose hands have been crushed. Although such an accident would be terrible for anyone, it is especially terrible for a person whose life is devoted to making music with his or her hands. If the pianist were to become color-blind, this would be much less serious since it would not strike as centrally at the pianist's sense of self. (We would have a quite different assessment of color-blindness in a painter, however.) Yet the perplexity centers around those cases in which people make something central to their sense of identity that we, as outsiders, would consider peripheral at best. For example, the couple who want an abortion because bearing a child would force them to postpone a vacation for two months seems to be giving undue weight to the timing of their vacation. What if, to take an even more extreme case, a woman bank robber decided on an abortion because pregnancy would interfere with robbing banks? Are there any limits to what can legitimately be taken as central to self-determination?

# Other Moral Considerations

## Feminist Concerns about Abortion

For many thinkers, especially feminists, the issue of abortion must be understood within the context of the oppression of women. Indeed, this gives a special importance to the right of self-determination as one which must be defended all the more vigilantly in a context of oppression.

Rape provides the most extreme example of this oppression within the realm of sexuality, but the oppression of women is not confined to this sphere. For some women, rape has become a metaphor for understanding many of the sexual relations between men and women. Whether we choose to use the word "rape" or not, most of us can agree that there are many areas outside of paradigmatic rape cases (forcible intercourse by a stranger) in which sexual intercourse is less than fully consensual. There is a growing recognition that rape often occurs between acquaintances, friends, and even spouses. Moreover, it is increasingly clear that there are many situations in which women are pressured (although the threat of physical force is not present) into sexual intercourse without their full consent. In addition to this, we live in a society in which men value highly the feeling that they are the ones in control of sexuality. Given all of this, feminists argue that it is imperative that women have the right to determine whether to bring a pregnancy to term or not.

## Abortion and Racism

Among some African Americans and other minority groups in the United States, there is a concern that the emphasis on abortion rights has racist overtones. In particular, their concern is that abortion—and forced sterilization—might be used as a means of controlling minority populations. This concern is not limited to the United States; in many countries, members of oppressed minority populations fear that the majority government may be using abortion (and enforced sterilization) as means of reducing the minority population. The history of the relationship between the medical establishment in the United States and African Americans makes such fears understandable. The Tuskegee syphilis experiment, in which African American men were allowed to die from syphilis without treatment until the early seventies in order to further research in this area, typifies the type of cases to which African Americans point in order to make their concerns more understandable to those who have not suffered such discrimination. Similarly, as pressure grows to reduce or eliminate support for Aid to Families with Dependent Children, some see a growing pressure on women, and perhaps especially on minority women, to choose abortion. Ironically, this has resulted in some very conservative, antiabortion Christian groups being on the same side as outspoken opponents of white racism who are at the other end of the political spectrum.

## The Rights of the Father

During the past twenty-five years, there has been an increasing interest in our understanding of fatherhood. This raises important issues in regard to the proper role of the father in making decisions regarding abortion. What rights, if any, does a biological father have when he disagrees with the woman's choice either to have an abortion or not to have an abortion? Are there any circumstances in which the man's choice should take precedence over the woman's preferences? Two types of cases are imaginable. On the one hand, the man may wish to have the fetus brought to term

*What rights, if any, do fathers have in deciding whether their partner should have an abortion?*

but the woman may want to abort it; on the other hand, these roles may be reserved. Under what conditions, if any, do the father's preferences count? Do those conditions have to do with the initial circumstances of conception? With the present state of their relationship? With the assumption of future responsibilities for the child?

Some feminist concerns seem to conflict directly with concerns about the rights of the father in the decision-making process. The issue, of course, is that women's oppression has been primarily at the hands of men—and any attempts at recognizing the rights of the father may seem at the same time to be an act of returning power to the oppressors. Moreover, it seems to ignore the asymmetry between men and women in regard to child-bearing. Although the act of conception requires both a male and female contribution, it is the woman who carries the fetus to term and undergoes childbirth. A man can be a father and never know it, but the same is not true for a woman. A woman bears the direct weight of pregnancy and childbirth is a way that men do not and cannot. The strongest argument against giving the father a decisive voice in this decision is precisely the fact that the woman bears the responsibilities of pregnancy and childbirth so much more directly, strongly, and unavoidably than men.

Given these reservations, two additional points need to be made about the rights of fathers. First, rights entail responsibilities. To the extent that a father has a voice in the decision, he presumably also has correlative responsibilities toward the baby (and indirectly toward the mother). Second, this situation is perhaps not best understood in terms of rights; rather, especially within the context of long-term, committed relationships, the appeal to rights may usually occur only when the situation has disintegrated.

## The Principle of Double Effect

Centuries of Christian theology and philosophy have finely honed what is known as the *Principle of the Double Effect*, which allows us to perform certain actions that would otherwise be immoral. Typically, four conditions have to be met for an action to be morally permissible: (1) the action itself must be either morally good or at least morally neutral; (2) the bad consequences must not be intended; (3) the good consequences cannot be the direct causal result of the bad consequences; and (4) the good consequences must be proportionate to the bad consequences. For example, the principle of the double effect allows a physician to remove a cancerous uterus from a pregnant woman, even if the fetus is thereby killed. Removal of the uterus is in itself morally neutral; it is not done in order to abort the fetus; the elimination of the cancer does not result from the killing of the fetus; and the saving of the woman's life is proportionate to the termination of the pregnancy.

## A Consequentialist Concern

Some philosophers have expressed concern about the possible consequences of widespread abortion if it is used for sex selection. The argument is a simple enough one, even if it is not easy to judge the factual claims on which it is based. If abortion is widely used as a means of choosing to bring primarily male babies to term, it may well create a gender imbalance in society with undesirable long-term consequences. This concern does not center on abortion *per se*, and would be equally applicable to preconception sex-selection methods, if such methods became available.

# Abortion and Compromise: Seeking a Common Ground

Initially, it might seem that there is no room for compromise in matters of abortion. If it is the intentional killing of an innocent human being, then it cannot be countenanced. If it does not involve killing a human being, then it should not be prohibited. It is either wrong or right, and there seems to be little middle ground.

*Is there any common ground that pro-choice and pro-life supporters can accept?*

Yet as we begin to reflect on the issue, we see that there are indeed areas of potential cooperation. Let's briefly consider several such areas here.

## Reducing Unwanted Pregnancies

One of the striking aspects of the abortion issue is its potential avoidability. Abortions occur when there are unwanted pregnancies. To the extent that we can reduce unwanted pregnancies, we can reduce abortions. Certainly there are cases of unwanted pregnancy due to rape or incest, and there are certainly other cases due to the failure of contraceptive devices. Unfortunately, despite our best efforts, none of these types of cases will probably be completely eliminated in the future. Yet they comprise only a small percentage of the cases of unwanted pregnancies; moreover, there is already agreement that these should be further reduced.

The single most common cause of unwanted pregnancies is sexual intercourse without contraception. To the extent that this can be reduced, the number of abortions can be reduced. Conservatives, liberals, and strong feminists can agree on this goal, although they may emphasize quite different ways of achieving it. Conservatives will stress the virtue of chastity and the value of abstinence. Liberals will stress the importance of contraceptives and family planning. Strong feminists will urge social and political changes that will insure that women have at least an equal voice in decisions about sexual intercourse. Some will respond to the conservative call, others to the liberal program, still others to the feminist concerns. Yet the common result may be the reduction of unwanted pregnancies and, with that, the reduction of abortions. In addition to this, an increase in responsibility in the area of sexuality may help to reduce the spread of AIDS and other sexually communicated diseases.

## Ensuring Genuinely Free and Informed Choice

There is widespread agreement among almost all parties that a choice made freely is better than one made under pressure or duress. There are several ways of increasing the likelihood of a genuinely free and informed choice. First, *the earlier the choice, the better*. Many people maintain that the more the fetus is developed, the more morally serious is the abortion decision. Although conservatives would maintain that all abortions are equally wrong, encouraging an early decision would not contradict their beliefs. Second, *women should have the opportunity to make the choice without undue outside pressure*. There are a number of ways in which undue outside pressure can be reduced, most notably through providing genuinely impartial counseling in an atmosphere devoid of coercion (demonstrations, etc.). Third, alternatives to abortion should be available. These include adoption (for those who wish to give their baby up for adoption), aid to dependent children (for those who wish to raise their own babies), daycare (for those who work full-time and raise children), and adequate maternity leave.

## Living Together with Moral Differences

Abortion is a particularly interesting and important moral issue in contemporary America, for it poses most clearly to us as a society the question of how we can live together with deep moral differences. People on all sides of the abortion controversy are intelligent people of good will, genuinely trying to do what they believe is right. The challenge for all of us in such situations is to view one another in this light and to seek to create a community that embraces and respects our differences while at the same time preserving our moral integrity. It is in this spirit that you are urged to approach the articles contained in this section. None provides the final answer to all our questions about the morality of abortion, but each helps to shed light on the moral complexity of the situation and the differing moral insights with which we as a society approach this difficult issue. Even if none of these articles provides the complete answer to the problem of abortion, each does help us to better understand ourselves and others.

# In Vitro Fertilization

Current estimates suggest that one in twelve American couples who want to have a child experience significant medical barriers to fertility. For such couples, once the nature of the medical problem(s) has been diagnosed, there are often initial therapeutic techniques, such as hormone therapy or surgery, that can allow the couple to have children without further medical assistance. However, this is not possible for all. For some couples, it is still impossible to conceive. In those cases, it is necessary to turn to more radical means. If conception cannot take place in the woman, then the next step is to try to bring about conception outside the woman—in a glass laboratory dish, *in vitro*. The man's sperm and the woman's egg are combined in a glass dish (*in vitro* just means "in glass" in Latin) in a way that allows the sperm to fertilize the egg, producing the embryo. This creates a double separation. First, the act of creating a human life is separated from sexual intercourse. Second, and even more importantly, the embryo itself is separate (if only for a short period of time) from the mother. At this point, the embryo is implanted, either in the woman herself or in another woman who will bear the baby.

## The Vocabulary of the New Parenthood

We can begin to see the myriad of possibilities in this arrangement and how our traditional vocabulary fails us. To help describe the various possibilities, we can distinguish among the:

*How many parents can a child have?*

- intentional mother: the woman who wants to have the child;
- intentional father: the man who wants to have the child;
- genetic mother: the woman who supplies the egg for the embryo;
- genetic father: the man who supplies the sperm for the embryo;
- gestational mother: the woman who carries the embryo to term and gives birth to it;
- nurturing mother: the woman who raises and nurtures the child from infancy as her own;
- nurturing father: the man who raises and nurtures the child from infancy as his own.

In the simplest case, both sperm and egg may come from the couple wanting to have the child, and then the embryo may be implanted back in the woman. In this case, we may say that the *intentional parents* are also the *genetic parents*, the *birth parents*, and the *nurturing parents*. However, it is not uncommon for either the sperm or the egg—sometimes, even both—to come from a donor. (The male's sperm count may be too low or too abnormal or unable to penetrate the egg, or the female may be unable to produce eggs that can be fertilized.) In those cases, the genetic mother or father is different from the birth mother and the nurturing parents. The simplest of these cases does not even require *in vitro* fertilization; it can simply be achieved through artificial insemination by a donor (AID). Compared with *in vitro* procedures, AID is comparatively cheap and effective. However, it is only helpful in cases of male infertility. The corresponding procedure for women, which involves donor eggs instead of donor sperm, is much more complicated and expensive and generally requires *in vitro* techniques.

We can easily see the complex possibilities that present themselves. It is possible for a child to have three mothers: a genetic mother (i.e., the one who supplies the egg); a birth mother (i.e., the woman who carries the child and gives birth to it); and a nurturing mother (i.e., the woman who raises the child as her child). (Presumably the intentional mother and the nurturing mother are the same, although in unusual circumstances they could be two different women.) Similarly, a child can have at least two fathers: the genetic father (i.e., the one who supplies the sperm) and the nurturing father (i.e., the one who raises the child as his own).

Who, then, are the *real* parents? Our initial answers often reveal a lot about our most fundamental beliefs about what counts as "real." Some see biology as constituting what is most real, and for them the "real" parents are either the genetic parents or, in some cases, the birth mother. Some see relationships and love as being the most "real," and for them the "real" parents are often the nurturing parents. But there is no simple and unchallenged answer to this question, and little is to be gained by pursuing it too far. Rather, the answer is to be found in making the various senses of "real" more precise and then specifying the ways in which a given person meets, or fails to meet, that more specific sense.

## The Moral Status of the Pre-embryo

We have already discussed many of the arguments about the moral status of the *fetus* in the introduction to this chapter. However, when we are dealing with *in vitro* fertilization, we are dealing with what is sometimes called a "pre-embryo," which arguably has a different moral status than an embryo.

What is a "pre-embryo?" Some have argued that it is simply an embryo at its earliest stage of development, and that the attempt to call it a *pre*-embryo is simply an attempt to make anything relating to it appear morally unobjectionable. Yet giving something a new name does not change its moral status. We will follow common usage and employ the term "pre-embryo," but note that this does not entail any judgment about its moral status.

*Is the pre-embryo a human person?*

At least two points are relevant here to the moral status of the pre-embryo. First, at this early stage, the pre-embryo is microscopic, smaller than the period at the end of this sentence. Usually, it is implanted or frozen when it has reached eight cells. There is nothing visually resembling a human being, although the pre-embryo certainly contains the coded genetic information for a full human being. Second, in contrast to its situation when it is *in utero*, the pre-embryo in a petri dish will not develop into a human being unless someone takes positive steps to implant it. This is very different from the situation of abortion, where someone has to intervene to prevent the pre-embryo from developing. Of course, the positive steps necessary when the pre-embryo is *ex utero* are only necessary because the woman's eggs have been artificially removed and fertilized.

One of the principal moral issues here is that it is standard procedure during *in vitro* fertilization to harvest a number of eggs, to fertilize them outside of the uterus, and then to implant the pre-embryo most likely to thrive. What happens to the remaining pre-embryos? In some instances, they may be frozen in order to be used later by the couple if this attempt is unsuccessful or if they want additional children. Otherwise they are usually destroyed. Some people are opposed to *in vitro* fertilization primarily because it produces pre-embryos that are then discarded.

## Access to *in Vitro* Fertilization

Unusual cases often find their way into the newspaper headlines, and unusual cases involving *in vitro* fertilization are no exception. In 1995 in Italy, a woman in her early sixties gave birth to a healthy baby boy, with the help of donor eggs and her husband's sperm. She decided to try IVF after the death of their seventeen year old son and after they were told that they were too old to adopt. Such a case inevitably raises questions. Should there be age limits on couples seeking IVF? Moreover, should there be any restrictions about motivation? In the Italian case, the woman gave her new baby the same name as her previously deceased son. In another case in 1995, a black woman in Italy with a husband of mixed race obtained *in vitro* fertilization using the eggs of a white woman. One of the reasons she gave was her belief that a light-skinned child would have an easier time in life than a dark-skinned one, given the existence of racism. Again, questions about motivation immediately arise.

What interest, if any, does the state have in regulating such IVF? While we might raise questions about the motives of the women mentioned in the preceding paragraph, we could certainly raise questions about the motives of many parents, and yet that is not sufficient grounds for state intervention. The situation changes significantly if public money is used to finance such procedures; but as long as they are done with private funds, it seems that the state has little basis for questioning the motivation of the couples involved.

## Conflicting Claims: The Embryos of Divorcing Couples

One of the more perplexing issues arising out of the fact that embryos can—at least temporarily—exist outside the mother's womb is that couples, when in the process of divorcing, make competing claims for custody of the embryos. Usually such embryos are frozen, and this allows such battles to be protracted. Several issues are intertwined here.

The first of these issues is the moral status of the pre-embryo, which we have already considered above. If they have the moral status of persons, then they have a right to life. If one member of the couple wants the embryos destroyed, this would not be morally permissible if they have a right to life. If, on the other hand, they do not yet have this moral status, then destroying embryos would be morally permissible.

*Who, if anyone, has the right to frozen embryos when a couple decides to divorce?*

Second, what kind of rights and responsibilities do the genetic parents have toward the embryo *as parents*? Is it a relationship of ownership? Of parenthood? In the case of one divorcing couple, the woman wanted possession of the embryos in order to have them implanted in herself and to bring them to term. The divorcing husband did not want to be the (genetic) father, with its accompanying responsibilities, when he and his wife were getting a divorce. Does the wife have the right to go ahead and have the embryos implanted? Does the husband have the right to have the embryos destroyed, since he no longer wants to be their father? What role should the courts play in settling such disputes?

## Conservative Objections to *in Vitro* Fertilization

Some critics of the current rise in *in vitro* fertilization recognize that it may be effective in achieving its goal, but that it ought not to be used anyway. Several motives come into play in such criticisms.

*Religiously based critiques of assisted reproduction.*   Many religious traditions are profoundly opposed to the development of reproductive technologies. At its deepest level, just as we have seen in our discussion of abortion, this view questions the technological society's presumption that we can control our destiny. Instead, it believes that our fates are ultimately in divine hands, and that intrusive technological procedures are *hubris*.

The second principal concern within religious traditions is that reproductive technologies almost always involve manipulating and destroying embryos. Embryos, many religious thinkers maintain, are persons and thus are not the proper objects of manipulation. Certainly, it is immoral to destroy them. Since *in vitro* fertilization almost inevitably involves such destruction of embryos, many religious thinkers believe it should be condemned.

*Anti-technology critiques of assisted reproduction.*   Not all critics of assisted reproduction are motivated solely by religious concerns. Many are concerned with the way in which technology distorts the reproductive process, as our selection from Paul Lauritzen, "What Price Parenthood?" indicates. Ideally—and almost everyone would admit that the actual case often falls short of the ideal—conception is part of a larger process, one with both human and natural elements. Technological intervention breaks both the natural and the human cycle. Ideally, human intercourse is motivated by love and is open to the possibility that this love will result in children.

# Genetic Manipulation and Parenthood

Two areas of development have recently combined to open possibilities that were previously thought to be only in the realm of science fiction. First, in just the past few years, scientists have developed the ability to *manipulate* the genes of an embryo or fetus. Although such techniques are still in their infancy, as it were, there is little reason to doubt that they will develop further, probably fairly rapidly. Second, in the late 1980s, the U.S. government and others launched the Human Genome Project, which is intended eventually to provide a complete map of the human genome. A vast undertaking, this project is gradually uncovering the genetic markers for numerous diseases as well as for a number of human conditions

*Is it moral to use genetic screening of embryos? To change gene structure?*

that are not diseases. The combination of the technology to manipulate genes and the knowledge of the human genetic code is a powerful and awesome prospect.

## From Abortion to Genetic Manipulation

The moral terrain opened up by advances in genetic manipulation is still largely uncharted. One of the first things we notice is that, with the advent of genetic manipulation, abortion is no longer the only option when tests reveal an unwanted condition in the embryo or fetus. This makes the situation morally much more complex, because it is no longer a question—as it was in the case of abortion—of depriving the fetus of a future through terminating it. Instead, the issue is now one of

*What is the moral difference between abortion and genetic manipulation?*

giving it a *different* future, one that results from conscious human choice rather than genetics.

Some alternative futures are clearly preferable to others, especially when we are dealing with disease. A child facing a future of Tay-Sachs disease or multiple sclerosis or other debilitating and eventually lethal ailments clearly has a bleaker future than a child who does not face that. There seems to be little moral problem here. However, other cases are much more difficult. What do we say about dwarfism? Genetically based deafness? Obesity? Eye color? Skin color? Sex? Sexual orientation? If it is possible do so, do parents have the right to choose whatever characteristics they desire for their child?

Consider the following example. It is already possible to test to determine whether a fetus has the gene for acondroplegia, a form of dwarfism. If the fetus has that gene for both parents—a double dominant—then it can be expected to live only a few days after birth. If it has the gene just from one side, then it will be a dwarf. If it does not have the gene from either side, its height will be normal. It is important to note that dwarfism is not a medical illness and that, although they encounter more problems with back pain and the like, dwarfs are not at medical risk. At present, the only option available to parents is to have the child or to abort it. Should a couple be allowed to abort a fetus because it will be a dwarf? Should a couple, both of whom are dwarfs, be allowed to abort a fetus if it is *not* a dwarf? Should genetic counselors (and genetic testing laboratories) provide prospective parents with such information? Let's imagine, furthermore, that the choice did not involve abortion, but rather genetic manipulation. Should prospective parents be allowed to request genetic manipulation to insure that the child does not die shortly after birth? To insure that the child is not a dwarf? To insure that the child is not of normal height?

## Individual Choices and Social Policy

Once we begin to raise questions about the limits of individual choice in these matters, we also have to distinguish between the moral issues surrounding the individual decision and those that arise if large numbers of people make the same decision. This is not a major issue in regard to acondroplegia, which is a relatively rare condition (it affects one in every 20,000 to 30,000 births) and does not directly impact social policy. Consider two other areas that are more perplexing.

*What limits should be placed on genetic manipulation of embryos?*

First, if it becomes possible genetically to manipulate the sex of an embryo, this could have far-reaching impact on society. If more couples have a preference for a male child than a female, and if an increasing number of couples have only one child, then such selection can seriously upset the balance of males and females in society. We do not know what consequences this may have, but a number of undesirable scenarios—especially undesirable for women—have been sketched out. Many of these involve women, because of their scarcity, being turned into breeding machines in a male-dominated society. If only a handful of parents were to engage in genetic sex selection for their developing embryos, then it may be unnecessary or unwise to legislate such practices. If, however, large numbers of parents do so, and if in doing so they affect the balance of males and females in our society, then there may be harmful effects of the practice as a whole and reasons for intervening.

Second, imagine if it eventually becomes possible to determine sexual orientation. Some researchers feel that they are on the trail of a gene for "gayness." Whether this will actually occur remains an open question, and to many it seems improbable that such a complex thing can be reduced to a single genetic marker. Nonetheless, it is certainly possible. Moreover, it is possible that, if such a genetic marker is found, it may become possible to change it. Several factors might discourage couples for having gay children, if the choice were up to them. First, the vast majority of couples having children are not gay. Second, in our society there is a significant amount of anti-gay sentiment. Some parents may be against having gay children; others may simply feel that a child will have an easier time in our society if he or she is not gay. It is not unimaginable that, given genetic manipulation, the percentage of persons who are gay might decrease.

## Common Ground in a Brave, New World

When we are hiking in a new area, we often are particularly aware of possible dangers. These dangers often serve as landmarks, hazardous and to be avoided. Similarly, as we explore the new moral terrain opened up by recent reproductive technologies, there are several dangers that can serve as initial reference points as we begin to formulate our positions.

### Unforseeable Consequences

Genetic manipulation opens up previously undreamed-of possibilities. It is all too easy, at least for some of us, to focus on the possible benefits of such developments rather than the possible—and, at least in some cases, largely unforseeable—negative effects. It is wise to tread carefully in such uncharted terrain.

### Using Persons As Commodities

Many people, regardless of political and ideological commitments, would agree that one of the principal dangers of contemporary capitalist, technological society is that it turns people into commodities. Persons, Kant once reminded us, are priceless, but mere things can always be bought and sold. We honor this admonition with our firm conviction that people—or even parts of people, their body organs and blood—cannot be bought or sold. The danger we face with the development of reproductive technologies is that this tendency to turn everything into a commodity will only increase. We are moving at least dangerously close—some would say we have already crossed the line—to the buying and selling of sperm, eggs, and even the use of wombs.

# THE ARGUMENTS

## Jane English
## "Abortion and the Concept of a Person"

*Jane English (1947–78) received her doctorate from Harvard University. She wrote several articles in the field of ethics before her untimely death in a mountain climbing accident on the Matterhorn at the age of thirty-one.*

*English challenges a common belief often shared by both advocates and critics of abortion. Both sides often claim that the permissibility of abortion turns on the question of whether the fetus is a person or not. English argues (1) that the notion of personhood is not precise enough to offer a decisive criterion for judging whether the fetus is a person; and (2) that there are a number of cases in which we can reasonably conclude that (a) abortion is permissible even if the fetus is a person, and (b) abortion is not permissible even if the fetus is not a person. The issue of abortion, in other words, does not turn on the issue of the personhood of the fetus.*

### As You Read, Consider This:

1. What reasons does English offer for claiming that the notion of personhood is not precise enough to serve as a foundation for deciding the abortion issue? Do you agree with her reasons?

2. Why, according to English, do we need "an additional premise" to move from the claim that the fetus is a person to the conclusion that abortion is always morally wrong?

The abortion debate rages on. Yet the two most popular positions seem to be clearly mistaken. Conservatives maintain that a human life begins at conception and that therefore abortion must be wrong because it is murder. But not all killings of humans are murders. Most notably, self-defense may justify even the killing of an innocent person.

Liberals, on the other hand, are just as mistaken in their argument that since a fetus does not become a person until birth, a woman may do whatever she pleases in and to her own body. First, you cannot do as you please with your own body if it affects other people adversely.[1] Second, if a fetus is not a person, that does not imply that you can do to it anything you wish. Animals, for example, are not persons, yet to kill or torture them for no reason at all is wrong.

At the center of the storm has been the issue of just when it is between ovulation and adulthood that a person appears on the scene. Conservatives draw the line at conception, liberals at birth. In this paper I first examine our concept of a person and conclude that no single criterion can capture the concept of a person and no sharp line can be drawn. Next I argue that if a fetus is a per-

Jane English, "Abortion and the Concept of a Person." *Canadian Journal of Philosophy* 5, no. 2 (1975). Copyright © 1975, The University of Calgary Press. Reprinted by permission of the University of Calgary Press and the Jane English Memorial Trust Fund.

son, abortion is still justifiable in many cases; and if a fetus is not a person, killing it is still wrong in many cases. To a large extent, these two solutions are in agreement. I conclude that our concept of a person cannot and need not bear the weight that the abortion controversy has thrust upon it.

# I

The several factions in the abortion argument have drawn battle lines around various proposed criteria for determining what is and what is not a person. For example, Mary Anne Warren[2] lists five features (capacities for reasoning, self-awareness, complex communication, etc.) as her criteria for personhood and argues for the permissibility of abortion because a fetus falls outside this concept. Baruch Brody[3] uses brain waves. Michael Tooley[4] picks having-a-concept-of-self as his criterion and concludes that infanticide and abortion are justifiable, while the killing of adult animals is not. On the other side, Paul Ramsey[5] claims a certain gene structure is the defining characteristic. John Noonan[6] prefers conceived-of-humans and presents counterexamples to various other candidate criteria. For instance, he argues against viability as the criterion because the newborn and infirm would then be non-persons, since they cannot live without the aid of others. He rejects any criterion that calls upon the sorts of sentiments a being can evoke in adults on the grounds that this would allow us to exclude other races as non-persons if we could just view them sufficiently unsentimentally.

These approaches are typical: foes of abortion propose sufficient conditions for personhood which fetuses satisfy, while friends of abortion counter with necessary conditions for personhood which fetuses lack. But these both presuppose that the concept of a person can be captured in a straitjacket of necessary and/or sufficient conditions.[7] Rather, "person" is a cluster of features, of which rationality, having a self-concept and being conceived of humans are only part.

What is typical of persons? Within our concept of a person we include, first, certain biological factors: descended from humans, having a certain genetic make-up, having a head, hands, arms, eyes, capable of locomotion, breathing, eating, sleeping. There are psychological factors: sentience, perception, having a concept of self and of one's own interests and desires, the ability to use tools, the ability to use language or symbol systems, the ability to joke, to be angry, to doubt. There are rationality factors: the ability to reason and draw conclusions, the ability to generalize and to learn from past experience, the ability to sacrifice present interests for greater gains in the future. There are social factors: the ability to work in groups and respond to peer pressures, the ability to recognize and consider as valuable the interests of others, seeing oneself as one among "other minds," the ability to sympathize, encourage, love, the ability to evoke from others the responses of sympathy, encouragement, love, the ability to work with others for mutual advantage. Then there are legal factors: being subject to the law and protected by it, having the ability to sue and enter contracts, being counted in the census, having a name and citizenship, the ability to own property, inherit, and so forth.

Now the point is not that this list is incomplete, or that you can find counterinstances to each of its points. People typically exhibit rationality, for instance, but someone who was irrational would not thereby fail to qualify as a person. On the other hand, something could exhibit the majority of these features and still fail to be a person, as an advanced robot might. There is no single core of necessary and sufficient features which we can draw upon with the assurance that they constitute what really makes a person; there are only features that are more or less typical.

This is not to say that no necessary or sufficient conditions can be given. Being alive is a necessary condition for being a person, and being a U.S. Senator is sufficient. But rather than falling inside a sufficient condition or outside a necessary one, a fetus lies in the penumbra region where our concept of a person is not so simple. For this reason I think a conclusive answer to the question whether a fetus is a person is unattainable. Here we might note a family of simple fallacies that proceed by stating a necessary condition for personhood and showing that a fetus has that characteristic. This is a form of the fallacy of affirming the consequent. For example, some have mistakenly reasoned from the premise that a fetus is human (after all, it is a human fetus rather than, say, a canine fetus), to the conclusion that it is a human. Adding an equivocation of "being," we get the fallacious argument that since a fetus is something both living and human, it is a human being.

Nonetheless, it does seem clear that a fetus has very few of the above family of characteristics, whereas a newborn baby exhibits a much larger proportion of them—and a two-year old has even more. Note that one traditional anti-abortion argument has centered on pointing out the many ways in which a fetus resembles a baby. They emphasize its development ("It already has ten fingers . . .") without mentioning its dissimilarities to adults (it still has gills and a tail). They also try to evoke the sort of sympathy on our part that we only feel toward other persons ("Never to laugh . . . or feel the sunshine?"). This all seems to be a relevant way to argue, since its purpose is to persuade us that a fetus satisfies so many of the important features on the list that it ought to be treated as a person. Also note that a fetus near the time of birth satisfies many more of these factors than a fetus in the early months of development. This could provide reason for making distinctions among the different stages of pregnancy, as the U.S. Supreme Court has done.[8]

Historically, the time at which a person has been said to come into existence has varied widely. Muslims date personhood from fourteen days after conception. Some medievals followed Aristotle in placing ensoulment at forty days after conception for a male fetus and eighty days for a female fetus.[9] In European common law since the seventeenth century, abortion was considered the killing of a person only after quickening, the time when a pregnant woman first feels the fetus move on its own. Nor is this variety of opinions surprising. Biologically, a human being develops gradually. We shouldn't expect there to be any specific time or sharp dividing point when a person appears on the scene.

For these reasons I believe our concept of a person is not sharp or decisive enough to bear the weight of a solution to the abortion controversy. To use it to solve that problem is to clarify *obscurum per obscurius*.

## II

Next let us consider what follows if a fetus is a person after all. Judith Jarvis Thomson's landmark article, "A Defense of Abortion,"[10] correctly points out that some additional argumentation is needed at this point in the conservative argument to bridge the gap between the premise that the fetus in an innocent person and the conclusion that killing it is always wrong. To arrive at this conclusion, we would need the additional premise that killing an innocent person is always wrong. But killing an innocent person is sometimes permissible, most notably in self-defense. Some examples may help draw out our intuitions or ordinary judgments about self-defense.

Suppose a mad scientist, for instance, hypnotized innocent people to jump under the bushes and attack innocent passers-by with knives. If you are so attacked, we agree you have a right to kill the attacker in self-defense, if killing him is the only way to protect your life or to save yourself from serious injury. It does not seem to matter here that the attacker is not malicious but himself an innocent pawn, for your killing of him is not done in a spirit of retribution but only in self-defense.

How severe an injury may you inflict in self-defense? In part this depends upon the severity of the injury to be avoided: you may not shoot someone merely to avoid having your clothes torn. This might lead one to the mistaken conclusion that the defense may only equal the threatened injury in severity; that to avoid death you may kill, but to avoid a black eye you may only inflict a black eye or the equivalent. Rather, our laws and customs seem to say that you may create an injury somewhat, but not enormously, greater than the injury to be avoided. To fend off an attack whose outcome would be as serious as rape, a severe beating or the loss of a finger, you may shoot; to avoid having your clothes torn, you may blacken an eye.

Aside from this, the injury you may inflict should only be the minimum necessary to deter or incapacitate the attacker. Even if you know he intends to kill you, you are not justified in shooting him if you could equally well save yourself by the simple expedient of running away. Self-defense is for the purpose of avoiding harms rather than equalizing harms.

Some cases of pregnancy present a parallel situation. Though the fetus is itself innocent, it may pose a threat to the pregnant woman's well-being, life prospects or health, mental or physical. If the pregnancy presents a slight threat to her interests, it seems self-defense cannot justify abortion. But if the threat is on a par with a serious beating or the loss of a finger, she may kill the fetus that poses such a threat, even if it is an innocent person. If a lesser harm to the fetus could have the same defensive effect, killing it would not be justified. It is unfortunate that the only way to free the woman from the pregnancy entails the death of the fetus (except in very late stages of pregnancy). Thus a self-defense model supports Thomson's point that the woman has a right only to be freed from the fetus, not a right to demand its death.[11]

The self-defense model is most helpful when we take the pregnant woman's point of view. In the pre-Thomson literature, abortion is often framed as a question for a third party: do you, a doctor, have a right to choose between the life of the woman and that of the fetus? Some have claimed that if you were a passer-by who witnessed a struggle between the innocent hypnotized attacker and his equally innocent victim, you would have no reason to kill either in defense of the other. They have concluded that the self-defense model implies that a woman may attempt to abort herself, but that a doctor should not assist her. I think the position of the third party is somewhat more complex. We do feel some inclination to intervene on behalf of the victim rather than the attacker, other things equal. But if both parties are innocent, other factors come into consideration. You would rush to the aid of your husband whether he was attacker or attackee. If a hypnotized famous violinist were attacking a skid row bum, we would try to save the individual who is of more value to society. These considerations would tend to support abortion in some cases.

But suppose you are a frail senior citizen who wishes to avoid being knifed by one of these innocent hypnotics, so you have hired a body-guard to accompany you. If you are attacked, it is clear we believe that the bodyguard, acting as your agent, has a right to kill the attacker to save you from a serious beating. Your rights of self-defense are transferred to your agent. I suggest that we should similarly view the doctor as the pregnant woman's agent in carrying out a defense she is physically incapable of accomplishing herself.

Thanks to modern technology, the cases are rare in which a pregnancy poses as clear a threat to a woman's bodily health as an attacker brandishing a switchblade. How does self-defense fare when more subtle, complex and long-range harms are involved?

To consider a somewhat fanciful example, suppose you are a highly trained surgeon when you are kidnapped by the hypnotic attacker. He says he does not intend to harm you but to take you back to the mad scientist who, it turns out, plans to hypnotize you to have a permanent mental block against all your knowledge of medicine. This would automatically destroy your career which would in turn have a serious adverse impact on your family, your personal relationships and your happiness. It seems to me that if the only way you can avoid this outcome is to shoot the innocent attacker, you are justified in so doing. You are defending yourself from a drastic injury to your life prospects. I think it is no exaggeration to claim that unwanted pregnancies (most obviously among teenagers) often have such adverse life-long consequences as the surgeon's loss of livelihood.

Several parallels arise between various views on abortion and the self-defense model. Let's suppose further that these hypnotized attackers only operate at night, so that it is well known that they can be avoided completely by the considerable inconvenience of never leaving your house after dark. One view is that since you could stay home at night, therefore if you go out and are selected by one of these hypnotized people, you have no right to defend yourself. This parallels the view that abstinence is the only acceptable way to avoid pregnancy. Others might hold that you ought to take along some defense such as Mace which will deter the hypnotized person without killing him, but that if this defense fails, you are obliged to submit to the resulting injury, no matter how severe it is. This parallels the view that contraception is all right but abortion is always wrong, even in cases of contraceptive failure.

A third view is that you may kill the hypnotized person only if he will actually kill you, but not if he will only injure you. This is like the position that abortion is permissible only if it is required to save a woman's life. Finally we have the view that it is all right to kill the attacker, even if only to avoid a very slight inconvenience to yourself and even if you knowingly walked down the very street where all these incidents have been taking place without taking along any Mace or protective escort. If we assume that a fetus is a person, this is the analogue of the view that abortion is always justifiable, "on demand."

The self-defense model allows us to see an important difference that exists between abortion and infanticide, even if a fetus is a person from conception. Many have argued that the only way to justify abortion without justifying infanticide would be to find some characteristic of personhood that is acquired at birth. Michael Tooley, for one, claims infanticide is justifiable because the really significant characteristics of a person are acquired some time after birth. But all such approaches look to characteristics of the developing human and ignore the relation between the fetus and the woman. What if, after birth, the presence of an infant or the need to support it posed a grave threat to the woman's sanity or life prospects? She could escape this threat by the simple expedient of running away. So a solution that does not entail the death of the infant is available. Before birth, such solutions are not available because of the biological dependence of the fetus on the woman. Birth is the crucial point not because of any characteristics the fetus gains, but because after birth the woman can defend herself by a means less drastic than killing the infant. Hence self-defense can be used to justify abortion without necessarily thereby justifying infanticide.

# III

On the other hand, supposing a fetus is not after all a person, would abortion always be morally permissible? Some opponents of abortion seem worried that if a fetus is not a full-fledged person, then we are justified in treating it in any way at all. However, this does not follow. Non-persons do get some consideration in our moral code, though of course they do not have the same rights as persons have (and in general they do not have moral responsibilities), and though their interests may be overridden by the interests of persons. Still, we cannot just treat them in any way at all.

Treatment of animals is a case in point. It is wrong to torture dogs for fun or to kill wild birds for no reason at all. It is wrong Period, even though dogs and birds do not have the same rights persons do. However, few people think it is wrong to use dogs as experimental animals, causing them considerable suffering in some cases, provided that the resulting research will probably bring discoveries of great benefit to people. And most of us think it all right to kill birds for food or to protect our crops. People's rights are different from the consideration we give to animals, then, for it is wrong to experiment on people, even if others might later benefit a great deal as a result of their suffering. You might volunteer to be a subject, but this would be supererogatory; you certainly have a right to refuse to be a medical guinea pig.

But how do we decide what you may or may not do to non-persons? This is a difficult problem, one for which I believe no adequate account exists. You do not want to say, for instance, that torturing dogs is all right whenever the sum of its effects on people is good—when it doesn't warp the sensibilities of the torturer so much that he mistreats people. If that were the case, it would be all right to torture dogs if you did it in private, or if the torturer lived on a desert island or died soon afterward, so that his actions had no effect on people. This is an inadequate account, because whatever moral consideration animals get, it has to be indefeasible, too. It will have to be a general proscription of certain actions, not merely a weighing of the impact on people on a case-by-case basis.

Rather, we need to distinguish two levels on which consequences of actions can be taken into account in moral reasoning. The traditional objections to Utilitarianism focus on the fact that it operates solely on the first level, taking all the consequences into account in particular cases only. Thus Utilitarianism is open to "desert island" and "lifeboat" counterexamples because these cases are rigged to make the consequences of actions severely limited.

Rawls's theory could be described as a teleological sort of theory, but with teleology operating on a higher level.[12] In choosing the principles to regulate society from the original position, his hypothetical choosers make their decision on the basis of the total consequences of various systems. Furthermore, they are constrained to choose a general set of rules which people can readily learn and apply. An ethical theory must operate by generating a set of sympathies and attitudes toward others which reinforces the functioning of that set of moral principles. Our prohibition against killing people operates by means of certain moral sentiments including sympathy, compassion and guilt. But if these attitudes are to form a coherent set, they carry us further: we tend to perform supererogatory actions, and we tend to feel similar compassion toward person-like non-persons.

It is crucial that psychological facts play a role here. Our psychological constitution makes it the case that for our ethical theory to work, it must prohibit certain treatment of non-persons which are significantly person-like. If our moral rules allowed people to treat person-like non-persons in ways we do not want people to be treated, this would undermine the system of sympathies and attitudes that makes the ethical system work. For this reason, we would choose in the original position to make mistreatment of some sorts of animals wrong in general (not just wrong in the cases with public impact), even though animals are not themselves parties in the original position. Thus it makes sense that it is those animals whose appearance and behavior are most like those of people that get the most consideration in our moral scheme.

It is because of "coherence of attitudes," I think, that the similarity of a fetus to a baby is very significant. A fetus one week before birth is so much like a newborn baby in our psychological space that we cannot allow any cavalier treatment of the former while expecting full sympathy and nutritive support for the latter. Thus, I think that anti-abortion forces are indeed giving their strongest arguments when they point to the similarities between a fetus and a baby, and when they try to evoke our emotional attachment to and sympathy for the fetus. An early horror story from New York about nurses who were expected to alternate between caring for six-week premature infants and disposing of viable 24-week aborted fetuses is just that—a horror story. These beings are so much alike that no one can be asked to draw a distinction and treat them so very differently.

Remember, however, that in the early weeks after conception a fetus is very much unlike a person. It is hard to develop these feelings for a set of genes which doesn't yet have a head, hands, beating heart, response to touch or the ability to move by itself. Thus it seems to me that the alleged "slippery slope" between conception and birth is not so very slippery. In the early stages of pregnancy, abortion can hardly be compared to murder for psychological reasons, but in the latest stages it is psychologically akin to murder.

Another source of similarity is the bodily continuity between fetus and adult. Bodies play a surprisingly central role in our attitudes toward persons. One has only to think of the philosophical literature on how far physical identity suffices for personal identity or Wittgenstein's remark that the best picture of the human soul is the human body. Even after death when all agree the body is no longer a person, we still observe elaborate customs of respect for the human body; like people who torture dogs, necrophilics are not to be trusted with people.[13] So it is appropriate that we show respect to a fetus as the body continuous with the body of a person. This is a degree of resemblance to persons that animals cannot rival.

Michael Tooley also utilizes a parallel with animals. He claims that it is always permissible to drown newborn kittens and draws conclusions about infanticide.[14] But it is only permissible to drown kittens when their survival would cause some hardship. Perhaps it would be a burden to feed and house six more cats or to find other homes for them. The alternative of letting them starve produces even more suffering than the drowning. Since the kittens get their rights secondhand, so to speak, via the need for coherence in our attitudes, their interests are often overridden by the interests of full-fledged persons. But if their survival would be no inconvenience to people at all, then it is wrong to drown them, contra Tooley.

Tooley's conclusions about abortion are wrong for the same reason. Even if a fetus is not a person, abortion is not always permissible, because of the resemblance of a fetus to a person. I agree with Thomson that it would be wrong for a woman who is seven months pregnant to have an abortion just to avoid having to postpone a trip to Europe. In the early months of pregnancy when the fetus hardly resembles a baby at all, then, abortion is permissible whenever it is in the interests of the pregnant woman or her family. The reasons would only need to outweigh the pain and inconvenience of the abortion itself. In the middle months, when the fetus comes to resemble a person, abortion would be justifiable only when the continuation of the pregnancy or the birth of the child would cause harms—physical, psychological, economic or social—to the woman. In the last months of pregnancy, even on our current assumption that a fetus is not a person, abortion seems to be wrong except to save a woman from significant injury or death.

The Supreme Court has recognized similar gradations in the alleged slippery slope stretching between conception and birth. To this point, the present paper has been a discussion of the moral status of abortion only, not its legal status. In view of the great physical, financial and sometimes psychological costs of abortion, perhaps the legal arrangement most compatible with the proposed moral solution would be the absence of restrictions, that is, so-called abortion "on demand."

So I conclude, first, that application of our concept of a person will not suffice to settle the abortion issue. After all, the biological development of a human being is gradual. Second, whether a fetus is a person or not, abortion is justifiable early in a pregnancy to avoid modest harms and seldom justifiable late in pregnancy except to avoid significant injury or death.

## Endnotes

1. We also have paternalistic laws which keep us from harming our own bodies even when no one else is affected. Ironically, anti-abortion laws were originally designed to protect pregnant women from a dangerous but tempting procedure.

2. Mary Anne Warren, "On the Moral and Legal Status of Abortion," *Monist* 5 (1973), p. 55.

3. Baruch Brody, "Fetal Humanity and the Theory of Essentialism" in Robert Baker and Frederick Elliston (eds.), *Philosophy and Sex* (Buffalo, NY, 1975).

4. Michael Tooley, "Abortion and Infanticide," *Philosophy and Public Affairs* l (1971).

5. Paul Ramsey, "The Morality of Abortion," in James Rachels (ed.), *Moral Problems* (New York, 1971)

6. John Noonan, "Abortion and the Catholic Church: A Summary History," *Natural Law Forum* 12 (1967), 125–131.

7. Wittgenstein has argued against the possibility of so capturing the concept of a game, *Philosophical Investigations* (New York, 1958), §66–71.

8. Not because the fetus is partly a person and so has some of the rights of persons but rather because of the rights of person-like non-persons. This I discuss in part III.

9. Aristotle himself was concerned, however, with the different question of when the soul takes form. For historical data, see Jimmye Kimmey "How the Abortion Laws Happened," *Ms.* I (April 1973), pp. 48 ff. and John Noonan, *loc. cit.*

10. J. J. Thomson, "A Defense of Abortion," *Philosophy and Public Affairs* I (1971).

11. *Ibid.*, p. 52.

12. John Rawls, *A Theory of Justice* (Cambridge, MA, 1971), §§3–4.

13. On the other hand, if they can be trusted with people, then our moral customs are mistaken. It all depends on the facts of psychology.

14. *Op. cit.*, pp. 40, 60–61.

## Journal/Discussion Questions

✍ *In your own experience, do you think of the fetus as a person? In what sense(s)? In what ways did English's remarks shed light on your moral feelings toward the unborn?*

1. English indicates that it is not always morally wrong to kill an innocent person. What support does she give for this claim? Do you agree with her?

2. What does English mean by "coherence of attitudes"? What role does this term play in the development of her argument?

3. Under what circumstances would English hold that abortion is morally wrong? What are her reasons? Do you agree with her? Why or why not?

---

### Stanley Hauerwas
### "Why Abortion Is a Religious Issue"

---

*Stanley Hauerwas is a contemporary theologian who has written extensively in the area of moral theology. His books include* A Community of Character *(from which the present selection is drawn),* Vision and Virtue, *and* Truthfulness and Tragedy.

*Rather than concentrating primarily on the issue of whether the fetus is a person, Hauerwas maintains that for many women the principal factor that affects their choice about abortion is the quality of the relationship between the couple. This suggests that the underlying issue of abortion is actually the issue of parenthood and our faith in our community to provide a world receptive to children—and that is ultimately a religious matter of faith and hope. A society that accepts abortion as a general practice is one that "is afraid of itself and its children."*

### As You Read, Consider This:

1. Hauerwas tries to understand the experiences of women who choose abortions. Mark the places where he discusses them. Do you think his descriptions are accurate? Explain.

2. In the margin, note what you think is Hauerwas's strongest point. Do the same for what you think is his weakest point.

⌒

## Abortion and Ordinary Discourse

. . . I am impressed that in spite of the hundreds of articles published defending or opposed to abortion, the way people decide to have or not to have an abortion rarely seems to involve the issues discussed in those articles. People contemplating abortion do not ask if the fetus has a right to

Stanley Hauerwas, "Why Abortion Is a Religious Issue." From *A Community of Character: Toward a Constructive Christian Social Ethic* by Stanley Hauerwas. Copyright © 1981 by the University of Notre Dame Press. Reprinted by permission of the publisher.

life, or when does life begin, or even if abortion is right or wrong. Rather, the decision seems to turn primarily on the quality of the relationship (or lack of relationship) between the couple.

I have no hard evidence for this contention. The best I can do is to call your attention to Linda Bird Francke's extremely interesting book *The Ambivalence of Abortion*.[1] The primary thrust of Francke's book is to dispel the anti-abortionist claim that abortion has become a matter that women now take lightly and as a matter of routine. The book powerfully demonstrates that abortion is seldom undertaken in a morally insensitive manner; for even the most committed pro-abortionist, abortion in actual practice continues to produce "ambivalence."

The anti-abortionists might well reply that they are less than impressed with such evidence, as "ambivalence" is hardly sufficient to indicate the moral seriousness of abortion. Yet I think such a response fails to do justice to the genuine moral agony of the women and men on whom Francke reports.

More importantly, to read her book from that perspective fails to appreciate the moral argument against abortion to which the book witnesses almost in spite of itself. Few of the women Francke describes claim they are doing a good thing by having an abortion. Rather they say they are acting out of "necessity." Strange as it may seem, they seldom claim to have aborted a fetus—they abort a "child" or a "baby." Thus one of her respondents says,

> If my parents were dead, then I'd have had the baby. But they're here to remind me of guilt and lay on their disapproval. I had my second abortion after I'd been living with a guy for two years. I missed a couple of pills and got knocked up. I must have done it on purpose. I really believe that. I love children, you know. I've been a mother's helper since I was thirteen and spent a whole year as a governess. I was old-fashioned enough with this guy to want to have his baby, but not admitting it to myself. I was really half-assed. He was very sensitive. He sort of wanted to have the baby too, but then he said I better have the abortion. So I did.[2]

The fact that this woman soon felt disgust for her partner and left him aptly illustrates Francke's general observation that the most critical factor in the decision to abort was the relationship with the male partner. Indeed she says that in her research almost every relationship between single people broke up either before or after the abortion. Thus

> if the pregnancy is a result of a one-night stand or a meaningless relationship, the decision is easier. But when it is a result of an ongoing relationship, the emotional issues become myriad. The relationship suddenly reaches a crisis point and can seesaw wildly. Some women are stunned when their partners bolt and run in panic. Others are resentful that their partners support the abortion decision, feeling this represents a lack of commitment. Forced to evaluate the quality of their relationship, other couples split up because the fact of pregnancy and abortion is too weighty for them to handle. Many couples, on the other hand, become closer in facing such an agonizing decision together.[3]

It should not be surprising, of course, that abortion, like any major decision a couple must make, surfaces tensions in a marriage or a relationship that are usually repressed. Yet there seems something peculiar about abortion, as it seems to ask for a vote of confidence in one another and in the relationship like few other decisions. Thus another of Francke's respondents said,

> I think abortion is best for both my husband and me. I'd like to get a little bit of something someday. I had to quit high school in the eleventh grade, and I don't know how to do anything. The problem is deep down I want to keep the baby. I realize it's not the smart thing to do. The abor-

tion will give us more of a chance to get something. But I think about the baby all the time, about my little girl. That's what I had always hoped it would be if I would have had it. If it had been born what would she have looked like? I just guess I feel bad that when my next one comes along that I would have had another one that I loved. I come in tomorrow. I'm going to go through with it. I hope I feel better than I do today. I love the baby. I love my husband. I just think it would be better for him if I had the abortion. I'll get over it. I'm sure there'll be a lot of times when I think about it, but we got so many problems now. So many. I know I can have another baby someday. But it's this one I love now. I just love her so much.[4]

Abortion is often defended as the necessary condition for the freedom of women from male oppression. Yet if we are to believe the testimony of Francke's witnesses, abortion often is the coercive method men use to free themselves from responsibility to women.[5] But even more ironic, for many women, rather than a declaration of independence, abortion is a subtle vote of no-confidence in their ability to determine their destiny: As one man (who generally approved of abortion) put it, "This new breed of women has got it all wrong when they decide not to have children. What these intelligent women owe the world is not just what they do or are—they owe the world a legacy to pass on."[6] And the unwillingness to pass on such a legacy may be a sign of the profoundest self-hate.

I am aware that these passages from Francke's book cannot or should not determine whether abortion is morally acceptable or not. . . . Of course some philosophers or theologians may well argue that all this is beside the point. While Francke's interviews are psychologically or biographically interesting, they have almost nothing to tell us about the morality or immorality of abortion. Indeed, at best all that her book demonstrates is that most people, even those getting abortions, do not understand morally what they are doing. The interviews simply represent philosophically confused positions and attitudes which could be corrected by any moderately good introductory course in philosophy.

Nevertheless, the language used by Francke's respondents is much closer morally to the heart of the matter than the arguments about the status of the fetus made by ethicists. And I think this can be shown philosophically, as arguments concerning our obligation to the fetus often depend on assumptions about the kind of responsibilities we have as parents. . . .

## Religious Convictions and Abortion

Even though I have tried to show that our convictions about the place of children in our lives forge a connection between contraception and abortion, I have not tried to argue for any particular understanding of our willingness to have children or what that might mean for how we form our sexual behavior and our attitudes toward abortion. Now, however, let me consider how certain religious convictions should be central for how Christians understand their obligation to have children and how those convictions form the necessary background for their attitude about abortion.

For most people and for most times, having children was regarded as a "natural" fact. That is, it has been assumed to be an activity that requires little thought or understanding. It is simply something that everyone "wants to do." The question of why we should "want to do" such a thing never comes up. In most cases, it is appropriate that the question never come up, as we are carried along by the sheer vitality of life in a manner that makes the question of "why" seem almost obscene.

But often hidden in the vitality are corrupt and corrupting attitudes toward children and ourselves. Unwillingness to expose our attitudes to critical analysis magnifies the power of our false convictions. There are some things that we prefer not to examine for fear of what we might find or for fear there is nothing to discover. We must face the fact that culturally we are simply not sure what it is we are doing when we have children.[7] We continue to depend on the "habit," but we are no longer sure what does or should inform the "habit" and give it direction. This is not an entirely bad thing: it helps us see, contrary to our first assumption, that having children is not after all a "natural" occurrence. Rather, having children is one of the most morally charged things any community of people does, as nothing else says more about who they are and what they think life is about.

In particular, a community's willingness to encourage children is a sign of its confidence in itself and its people. For children are a community's sign to the future that life, in spite of its hardship and tedium, is worthwhile. Also, children are symbols of our hope—please note that they are not the object of our hope—which sustains us in our day-to-day existence. Life may be hard, but it can be lived. Indeed, it can be lived with zest and interest to the extent that we have the confidence to introduce others to it.

More profoundly, children signal a community's confidence because they are bound to change our society and their existence foretells inevitable challenge. Our stories and traditions are never inherited unchanged. Indeed, the very power and truth of a tradition depends on its adaptation by each new generation. Thus, children represent a community's confidence that its tradition is not without merit and is strong enough to meet the challenge of a new generation.

What then, do these rhetorical flourishes have to do with abortion and, in particular, religious convictions? Put simply, they indicate the background beliefs that make intelligible why abortion is generally a morally objectionable act. When institutionalized and regarded as morally acceptable or at least morally indifferent by society, abortion is an indication that a society is afraid of itself and its children.

## The Christian and Children

The Christian attitude toward children and the family is often identified with our society's ideology about the importance of the family. Thus Christianity is recommended as a "good thing" because it is alleged to keep the family together, and Christians are supposed to be especially loving when it comes to children. Such a view of the relation of Christianity to the family, however, is a lie that fails to do justice to the basic documents of the faith and to our fundamental convictions.

For example, what was remarkable about the early church is not what it said about the family and children, but that it said so little. Most of what it did say about marriage and the family was not exactly complimentary. This negative attitude has often been taken to be a sign that Christians fear or dislike sex, but far more is at stake. What the early church did was establish a community whose understanding of its mission was such that singleness was of equal status with marriage. As a result, the church challenged the natural necessity of marriage, thus making marriage a vocation as serious as singleness.

As a vocation, marriage was understood to have a peculiar service to the community—namely, it served a symbolic function denoting God's loyalty to his people and as such was the appropriate context for reception of new life. And remember, Christians were not called to have children assured that their children were going to be lovely people, nice folk to be with. We forget that the early Christians had deep convictions about the reality and force of sin and they saw no reason why their children were to be exempt from that reality. Nor could they even assume that their children would be Christian, since they knew also that one must be called in order to be a member of the church. Rather, these people were called to marriage and to having children as their obligation. For their children were their pledge to be a community formed by the conviction that, in spite of evidence to the contrary, God rules this world.

Therefore, for Christians, having children or getting married is not a "natural" event but one freighted with the deepest moral and religious significance. Their attitude toward abortion is but an aspect of their conviction that they must be people who are ever ready to welcome children into the world. To be such a people is in a certain sense to "be out of control," for children often have a way of being born when we "are not ready for them." Yet for Christians, to "be in control" to the extent that new life is excluded from their world, is an indication that we are in fact controlled by powers other than the God we know as the mover of the sun and the stars.

## The Non-Christians and Children

It may be objected that the most established so far is that Christian attitudes about abortion involve religious convictions, but that by no means shows that all anti-abortion positions presuppose such assumptions. Of course that is true, but my case is a little stronger than such an objection suggests. For if I am right that the issue of the morality of abortion gains its intelligibility in relation to assumptions about parenting, then the case I have developed at least suggests that both pro- and anti-abortionists may well have attitudes that are functionally equivalent to the Christian. I am not anxious to call such attitudes religious, but I do want to claim that there are matters involved that we Christians think are central to our understanding of the religious life.

Put differently, I am not suggesting that only Christians have good reasons for having children. Rather I have tried to suggest the narrative context that makes the activity of having children intelligible to Christians and why abortion is thus understood in a negative light. I do not know why people who are not Christians have children, nor do I think there is any reason to investigate and make summary judgment about that. What I think I have shown, however, is that their attitudes toward parenting are crucial for determining their understanding of abortion. Or even more strongly, that their attitudes about abortion may be crucial in determining their understanding of what it means to be a parent. Such issues draw on our profoundest assumptions about what makes life worthwhile.

One of Francke's respondents who had had two previous abortions asked what I take to be the crucial question. She says, "I don't think for many women abortion is as blithe an experience as women are led to believe. I know I'm not totally unique, but how many women going into it know what to expect? I have no moral handle on abortion—none at all. I've never been able to work it out. Is there a right and a wrong? I don't know what to tell my own children."[8] For how do we tell our children what we are doing and still make them glad that they are our children?

## Endnotes

1. Linda Bird Francke, *The Ambivalence of Abortion* (New York: Random House, 1978).
2. *Ibid.*, p. 61. Another respondent says, "My feeling at that time was not one of shame, but of sadness. I tried not to think of the fetus as a baby, but I did. I wanted it over as quickly as

possible emotionally. Mostly I wanted the option of divorcing my husband. That was the prime reason for the abortion. He never realized it at that time and still doesn't. We've been married sixteen years, and we've had a difficult time," p. 107.

3. *Ibid.*, p. 47.

4. *Ibid.*, p. 95.

5. *Ibid.*, p. 81.

6. *Ibid.*, p. 133. Or as a Jewish couple responded to their son and daughter-in-law's decision to have an abortion, "It's a special thing, you know, a grandchild. It's continuity. And if you have a strong family, which we do, then it's the first dividend. It's more of a loss of family continuity, too. Jews are being screwed out of existence. Who uses birth control? Who gets all these abortions? We're being physically wiped out," p. 20.

7. For an argument against the whole idea that we "choose" to have children, see my "Having and Learning to Care for Retarded Children," *Truthfulness and Tragedy*, pp. 147–156.

8. Francke, p. 108. One of the often overlooked consequences of abortion is how it implicitly requires us to try to be too "perfect" as parents. For if children are aborted because we are not ready for them, the assumption is that there is a time when we will be "ready" and able to do everything "right." That kind of compulsiveness for perfection can only rob parenting of the joy that comes from the sheer contingencies of our children.

## Journal/Discussion Questions

✍ *Stanley Hauerwas claims that abortion, at least for Christians, is a religious issue. What role does religion play in your views on abortion? Has that role changed over the years in any way?*

✍ *Hauerwas claims that the decision about an abortion often turns on the question of the quality of the relationship between the couple. Have you seen couples who have grappled with this decision? Does Hauerwas's claim seem accurate to you?*

1. In commenting on Linda Bird Francke's book, Stanley Hauerwas notes that women who have an abortion seldom describe what they have done as a *good* thing—rather, they see it as a matter of necessity. First, does this claim seem accurate? Second, if the claim is true, what moral implications follow from it? Does this provide any basis for thinking that these women are right in their claims?

2. Is it (sometimes) morally permissible to do something that is not good but which you feel is necessary? What, exactly, is the basis for saying that something like abortion is necessary? In particular, when we say that something is necessary, this is usually a shorthand way of saying that it is necessary *for something else*. In the case of abortion, the phrase "necessary for . . ." may be completed in a number of different ways: necessary for life, necessary for preserving the relationship, necessary for a career, necessary for a vacation, etc. If abortion is permissible because it is necessary for something else, what are the legitimate things that it may be necessary for?

3. Again drawing on Francke's book, Hauerwas maintains that "abortion often is the coercive method men use to free themselves from responsibility to

women." Do you think this is true? If it is true, how does this affect your view of abortion?

4. Hauerwas argues that our attitudes toward abortion are deeply tied to our attitudes toward bringing children into the world: *"the issue of the morality of abortion gains its intelligibility in relation to assumptions about parenting."* The willingness to bring children into the world is a sign of a community's faith in itself and hope for the future—and that, ultimately, is a religious matter, at least for Christians. Do *you* think that this is a religious matter? What, exactly, makes something a *religious* matter?

5. Consider Hauerwas's claim: *"When institutionalized and regarded as morally acceptable or at least morally indifferent by society, abortion is an indication that a society is afraid of itself and its children."* Do you think that this claim is true? Why or why not?

---

## Don Marquis
## "Why Abortion Is Immmoral"

---

*Don Marquis is a professor of philosophy at the University of Kansas who specializes in medical ethics. He originally became interested in the issue of abortion while teaching medical ethics. He was also motivated by his belief that American involvement in the Vietnam War was profoundly immoral and he wanted to understand why that was so in a philosophically respectable way.*

*In order to demonstrate precisely what is wrong with abortion, Marquis first develops a theory of what is wrong with killing in general. The principal moral objection to killing is that it deprives beings of their futures—their hopes, projects, dreams, etc. If this is what is objectionable about killing, it is easy to see that abortion is morally wrong, for it deprives a living being of its future.*

### As You Read, Consider This:

1. Marquis considers several possible answers to the question of why killing is wrong. Which of these is closest to your own?

2. On what basis does Marquis support his claim that the fetus is an innocent human being?

~

The view that abortion is, with rare exceptions, seriously immoral has received little support in the recent philosophical literature. No doubt most philosophers affiliated with secular institutions of higher education believe that the anti-abortion position is either a symptom of irrational religious dogma or a conclusion generated by seriously confused philosophical argument. The purpose of this essay is to undermine this general belief. This essay sets out an argument that purports to

Don Marquis, "Why Abortion Is Immoral." Reprinted by permission of the author and publisher from *The Journal of Philosophy* LXXXVI, 4 (April 1989). Copyright © 1989 *The Journal of Philosophy*.

show, as well as any argument in ethics can show, that abortion is, except possibly in rare cases, seriously immoral, that it is in the same moral category as killing an innocent adult human being.

The argument is based on a major assumption. Many of the most insightful and careful writers on the ethics of abortion—such as Joel Feinberg, Michael Tooley, Mary Ann Warren, H. Tristram Engelhardt, Jr., L. W. Sumner, John T. Noonan, Jr., and Philip Devine[1]—believe that whether or not abortion is morally permissible stands or falls on whether or not a fetus is the sort of being whose life it is seriously wrong to end. The argument of this essay will assume, but not argue, that they are correct.

Also, this essay will neglect issues of great importance to a complete ethics of abortion. Some anti-abortionists will allow that certain abortions, such as abortion before implantation or abortion when the life of a woman is threatened by a pregnancy or abortion after rape, may be morally permissible. This essay will not explore the casuistry of these hard cases. The purpose of this essay is to develop a general argument for the claim that the overwhelming majority of deliberate abortions are seriously immoral.

# I

A sketch of standard anti-abortion and pro-choice arguments exhibits how those arguments possess certain symmetries that explain why partisans of those positions are so convinced of the correctness of their own positions, why they are not successful in convincing their opponents, and why, to others, this issue seems to be unresolvable. An analysis of the nature of this standoff suggests a strategy for surmounting it.

Consider the way a typical anti-abortionist argues. She will argue or assert that life is present from the moment of conception or that fetuses look like babies or that fetuses possess a characteristic such as a genetic code that is both necessary and sufficient for being human. Anti-abortionists seem to believe that (1) the truth of all of these claims is quite obvious, and (2) establishing any of these claims is sufficient to show that abortion is morally akin to murder.

A standard pro-choice strategy exhibits similarities. The pro-choicer will argue or assert that fetuses are not persons or that fetuses are not rational agents or that fetuses are not social beings. Pro-choicers seem to believe that (1) the truth of any of these claims is quite obvious, and (2) establishing any of these claims is sufficient to show that an abortion is not a wrongful killing.

In fact, both the pro-choice and the anti-abortion claims do seem to be true, although the "it looks like a baby" claim is more difficult to establish the earlier the pregnancy. We seem to have a standoff. How can it be resolved?

As everyone who has taken a bit of logic knows, if any of these arguments concerning abortion is a good argument, it requires not only some claim characterizing fetuses, but also some general moral principle that ties a characteristic of fetuses to having or not having the right to life or to some other moral characteristic that will generate the obligation or the lack of obligation not to end the life of a fetus. Accordingly, the arguments of the anti-abortionist and the pro-choicer need a bit of filling in to be regarded as adequate.

Note what each partisan will say. The anti-abortionist will claim that her position is supported by such generally accepted moral principles as "It is always prima facie seriously wrong to take a human life" or "It is always prima facie seriously wrong to end the life of a baby." Since these are generally accepted moral principles, her position is certainly not obviously wrong. The pro-choicer will claim that her position is supported by such plausible moral principles as "Being a person is what gives an individual intrinsic moral worth" or "It is only seriously prima facie wrong to take the life of a member of the human community." Since these are generally accepted moral principles, the pro-choice position is certainly not obviously wrong. Unfortunately, we have again arrived at a standoff.

Now, how might one deal with this standoff? The standard approach is to try to show how the moral principles of one's opponent lose their plausibility under analysis. It is easy to see how this is possible. On the one hand, the anti-abortionist will defend a moral principle concerning the wrongness of killing which tends to be broad in scope in order that even fetuses at an early stage of pregnancy will fall under it. The problem with broad principles is that they often embrace too much. In this particular instance, the principle "It is always prima facie wrong to take a human life" seems to entail that it is wrong to end the existence of a living human cancer-cell culture, on the grounds that the culture is both living and human. Therefore, it seems that the anti-abortionist's favored principle is too broad.

On the other hand, the pro-choicer wants to find a moral principle concerning the wrongness of killing which tends to be narrow in scope in order that fetuses will *not* fall under it. The problem with narrow principles is that they often do not embrace enough. Hence, the needed principles such as "It is prima facie seriously wrong to kill only persons" or "It is prima facie wrong to kill only rational agents" do not explain why it is wrong to kill infants or young children or the severely retarded or even perhaps the severely mentally ill. Therefore, we seem again to have a standoff. The anti-abortionist charges, not unreasonably, that pro-choice principles concerning killing are too narrow to be acceptable; the pro-choicer charges, not unreasonably, that anti-abortionist principles concerning killing are too broad to be acceptable.

Attempts by both sides to patch up the difficulties in their positions run into further difficulties. The anti-abortionist will try to remove the problem in her position by reformulating her principle concerning killing in terms of human beings. Now we end up with: "It is always prima facie seriously wrong to end the life of a human being." This principle has the advantage of avoiding the problem of the human cancer-cell culture counterexample. But this advantage is purchased at a high price. For although it is clear that a fetus is both human and alive, it is not at all clear that a fetus is a human *being*. There is at least something to be said for the view that something becomes a human being only after a process of development, and that therefore first trimester fetuses and perhaps all fetuses are not yet human beings. Hence, the anti-abortionist, by this move, has merely exchanged one problem for another.[2]

The pro-choicer fares no better. She may attempt to find reasons why killing infants, young children, and the severely retarded is wrong which are independent of her major principle that is supposed to explain the wrongness of taking human life, but which will not also make abortion immoral. This is no easy task. Appeals to social utility will seem satisfactory only to those who resolve not to think of the enormous difficulties with a utilitarian account of the wrongness of killing and the significant social costs of preserving the lives of the unproductive.[3] A pro-choice strategy that extends the definition of "person" to infants or even to young children seems just as arbitrary as an anti-abortion strategy that extends the definition of "human being" to fetuses. Again, we find symmetries in the two positions and we arrive at a standoff.

There are even further problems that reflect symmetries in the two positions. In addition to counterexample problems, or the arbitrary application problems that can be exchanged for them, the standard anti-abortionist principle "It is prima facie seriously wrong to kill a human being," or one of its variants, can be objected to on the grounds of ambiguity. If "human being" is taken to be a *biological* category, then the anti-abortionist is left with the problem of explaining why a merely biological category should make a moral difference. Why, it is asked, is it any more reasonable to base a moral conclusion on the number of chromosomes in one's cells than on the color of one's skin?[4] If "human being," on the other hand, is taken to be a *moral* category, then the claim that a fetus is a human being cannot be taken to be a premise in the anti-abortion argument, for it is precisely what needs to be established. Hence, either the anti-abortionist's main category is a morally irrelevant, merely biological category, or it is of no use to the anti-abortionist in establishing (noncircularly, of course) that abortion is wrong.

Although this problem with the anti-abortionist position is often noticed, it is less often noticed that the pro-choice position suffers from an analogous problem. The principle "Only persons have the right to life" also suffers from an ambiguity. The term "person" is typically defined in terms of psychological characteristics, although there will certainly be disagreement concerning which characteristics are most important. Supposing that this matter can be settled, the pro-choicer is left with the problem of explaining why *psychological* characteristics should make a *moral* difference. If the pro-choicer should attempt to deal with this problem by claiming that an explanation is not necessary, that in fact we do treat such a cluster of psychological properties as having moral significance, the sharp-witted anti-abortionist should have a ready response. We do treat being both living and human as having moral significance. If it is legitimate for the pro-choicer to demand that the anti-abortionist provide an explanation of the connection between the biological character of being a human being and the wrongness of being killed (even though people accept this connection), then it is legitimate for the anti-abortionist to demand that the pro-choicer provide an explanation of the connection between psychological criteria for being a person and the wrongness of being killed (even though that connection is accepted).[5]

Feinberg has attempted to meet this objection (he calls psychological personhood "commonsense personhood"):

> The characteristics that confer commonsense personhood are not arbitrary bases for rights and duties, such as race, sex or species membership; rather they are traits that make sense out of rights and duties and without which those moral attributes would have no point or function. It is because people are conscious; have a sense of their personal identities; have plans, goals, and projects; experience emotions; are liable to pains, anxieties, and frustrations; can reason and bargain, and so on—it is because of these attributes that people have values and interests, desires and expectations of their own, including a stake in their own futures, and a personal well-being of a sort we cannot ascribe to unconscious or nonrational beings. Because of their developed capacities they can assume duties and responsibilities and can have and make claims on one another. Only because of their sense of self, their life plans, their value hierarchies, and their stakes in their own futures can they be ascribed fundamental rights. There is nothing arbitrary about these linkages (*op. cit.*, p. 270).

The plausible aspects of this attempt should not be taken to obscure its implausible features. There is a great deal to be said for the view that being a psychological person under some description is a necessary condition for having duties. One cannot have a duty unless one is capable of behaving morally, and a being's capability of behaving morally will require having a certain psychology. It is far from obvious, however, that having rights entails consciousness or rationality, as Feinberg suggests. We speak of the rights of the severely retarded or the severely mentally ill, yet some of these persons are not rational. We speak of the rights of the temporarily unconscious. The New Jersey Supreme Court based their decision in the Quinlan case on Karen Ann Quinlan's right to privacy, and she was known to be permanently unconscious at that time. Hence, Feinberg's claim that having rights entails being conscious is, on its face, obviously false.

Of course, it might not make sense to attribute rights to a being that would never in its natural history have certain psychological traits. This modest connection between psychological personhood and moral personhood will create a place for Karen Ann Quinlan and the temporarily unconscious. But then it makes a place for fetuses also. Hence, it does not serve Feinberg's pro-choice purposes. Accordingly, it seems that the pro-choicer will have as much difficulty bridging the gap between psychological personhood and personhood in the moral sense as the anti-abortionist has bridging the gap between being a biological human being and being a human being in the moral sense.

Furthermore, the pro-choicer cannot any more escape her problem by making person a purely moral category than the anti-abortionist could escape by the analogous move. For if person is a moral category, then the pro-choicer is left without the resources for establishing (noncircularly, of course) the claim that a fetus is not a person, which is an essential premise in her argument. Again, we have both a symmetry and a standoff between pro-choice and anti-abortion views.

Passions in the abortion debate run high. There are both plausibilities and difficulties with the standard positions. Accordingly, it is hardly surprising that partisans of either side embrace with fervor the moral generalizations that support the conclusions they preanalytically favor, and reject with disdain the moral generalizations of their opponents as being subject to inescapable difficulties. It is easy to believe that the counterexamples to one's own moral principles are merely temporary difficulties that will dissolve in the wake of further philosophical research, and that the counterexamples to the principles of one's opponents are as straightforward as the contradiction between A and O propositions in traditional logic. This might suggest to an impartial observer (if there are any) that the abortion issue is unresolvable.

There is a way out of this apparent dialectical quandary. The moral generalizations of both sides are not quite correct. The generalizations hold for the most part, for the usual cases. This suggests that they are all *accidental* generalizations, that the moral claims made by those on both sides of the dispute do not touch on the *essence* of the matter.

This use of the distinction between essence and accident is not meant to invoke obscure metaphysical categories. Rather, it is intended to reflect the rather atheoretical nature of the abortion discussion. If the generalization a partisan in the abortion dispute adopts were derived from the reason why ending the life of a human being is wrong, then there could not be exceptions to that generalization unless some special case obtains in which there are even more powerful countervailing reasons. Such generalizations would not be merely accidental generalizations; they would point to, or be based upon, the essence of the wrongness of killing, what it is that makes killing wrong. All this suggests that a necessary condition of resolving the abortion controversy is a more theoretical account of the wrongness of killing. After all, if we merely believe, but do not understand, why killing adult human beings such as ourselves is wrong, how could we conceivably show that abortion is either immoral or permissible?

## II

In order to develop such an account, we can start from the following unproblematic assumption concerning our own case: it is wrong to kill us. Why is it wrong? Some answers can be easily eliminated. It might be said that what makes killing us wrong is that a killing brutalizes the one who kills. But the brutalization consists of being inured to the performance of an act that is hideously immoral; hence, the brutalization does not explain the immorality. It might be said that what makes killing us wrong is the great loss others would experience due to our absence. Although such hubris is understandable, such an explanation does not account for the wrongness of killing hermits, or those whose lives are relatively independent and whose friends find it easy to make new friends.

A more obvious answer is better. What primarily makes killing wrong is neither its effect on the murderer nor its effect on the victim's friends and relatives, but its effect on the victim. The loss of one's life is one of the greatest losses one can suffer. The loss of one's life deprives one of all the experiences, activities, projects, and enjoyments that would otherwise have constituted one's future. Therefore, killing someone is wrong, primarily because the killing inflicts (one of) the greatest possible losses on the victim. To describe this as the loss of life can be misleading, however. The change in my biological state does not by itself make killing me wrong. The effect of the loss of my biological life is the loss to me of all those activities, projects, experiences, and enjoyments which would otherwise have constituted my future personal life. These activities, projects, experiences, and enjoyments are either valuable for their own sakes or are means to something else that is valuable for its own sake. Some parts of my future are not valued by me now, but will come to be valued by me as I grow older and as my values and capacities change. When I am killed, I am deprived both of what I now value which would have been part of my future personal life, but also what I would come to value. Therefore, when I die, I am deprived of all of the value of my future. Inflicting this loss on me is ultimately what makes killing me wrong. This being the case, it would seem that what makes killing *any* adult human being prima facie seriously wrong is the loss of his other future.[6]

How should this rudimentary theory of the wrongness of killing be evaluated? It cannot be faulted for deriving an "ought" from an "is," for it does not. The analysis assumes that killing me (or you, reader) is prima facie seriously wrong. The point of the analysis is to establish which natural property ultimately explains the wrongness of the killing, given that it is wrong. A natural property will ultimately explain the wrongness of killing, only if (1) the explanation fits with our intuitions about the matter and (2) there is no other natural property that provides the basis for a better explanation of the wrongness of killing. This analysis rests on the intuition that what makes killing a particular human or animal wrong is what it does to that particular human or animal. What makes killing wrong is some natural effect or other of the killing. Some would deny this. For instance, a divine command theorist in ethics would deny it. Surely this denial is, however, one of those features of divine-command theory which renders it so implausible.

The claim that what makes killing wrong is the loss of the victim's future is directly supported by two considerations. In the first place, this theory explains why we regard killing as one of the worst of crimes. Killing is especially wrong, because it deprives the victim of more than perhaps any other crime. In the second place, people with AIDS or cancer who know they are dying believe, of course, that dying is a very bad thing for them. They believe that the loss of a future to them that they would otherwise have experienced is what makes their premature death a very bad thing for them. A better theory of the wrongness of killing would require a different natural property associated with killing which better fits with the attitudes of the dying. What could it be?

The view that what makes killing wrong is the loss to the victim of the value of the victim's future gains additional support when some of its implications are examined. In the first place, it is incompatible with the view that it is wrong to kill only beings who are biologically human. It is possible that there exists a different species from another planet whose members have a future like ours. Since having a future like that is what makes killing someone wrong, this theory entails that it would be wrong to kill members of such a species. Hence, this theory is opposed to the claim that only life that is biologically human has great moral worth, a claim which many anti-abortionists have seemed to adopt. This opposition, which this theory has in common with personhood theories, seems to be a merit of the theory.

In the second place, the claim that the loss of one's future is the wrong-making feature of one's being killed entails the possibility that the futures of some actual nonhuman mammals on our own planet are sufficiently like ours that it is seriously wrong to kill them also. Whether some animals do have the same right to life as human beings depends on adding to the account of the wrongness of killing some additional account of just what it is about my future or the futures of other adult human beings which makes it wrong to kill us. No such additional account will be offered in this essay. Undoubtedly, the provision of such an account would be a very difficult matter. Undoubtedly, any such account would be quite controversial. Hence, it surely should not reflect badly on this sketch of an elementary theory of the wrongness of killing that it is indeterminate with respect to some very difficult issues regarding animal rights.

In the third place, the claim that the loss of one's future is the wrong-making feature of one's being killed does not entail, as sanctity of human life theories do, that active euthanasia is wrong. Persons who are severely and incurably ill, who face a future of pain and despair, and who wish to die will not have suffered a loss if they are killed. It is, strictly speaking, the value of a human's future which makes killing wrong in this theory. This being so, killing does not necessarily wrong some persons who are sick and dying. Of course, there may be other reasons for a prohibition of active euthanasia, but that is another matter. Sanctity-of-human-life theories seem to hold that active euthanasia is seriously wrong even in an individual case where there seems to be good reason for it independently of public policy considerations. This consequence is most implausible, and it is a plus for the claim that the loss of a future of value is what makes killing wrong that it does not share this consequence.

In the fourth place, the account of the wrongness of killing defended in this essay does straightforwardly entail that it is prima facie seriously wrong to kill children and infants, for we do presume that they have futures of value. Since we do believe that it is wrong to kill defenseless little babies, it is important that a theory of the wrongness of killing easily account for this. Personhood theories of the wrongness of killing, on the other hand, cannot straightforwardly account for the wrongness of killing infants and young children.[7] Hence, such theories must add special ad hoc accounts of the wrongness of killing the young. The plausibility of such ad hoc theories seems to be a function of how desperately one wants such theories to work. The claim that the primary wrong-making feature of a killing is the loss to the victim of the value of its future accounts for the wrongness of killing young children and infants directly; it makes the wrongness of such acts as obvious as we actually think it is. This is a further merit of this theory. Accordingly, it seems that this value of a future-like-ours theory of the wrongness of killing shares strengths of both sanctity-of-life and personhood accounts while avoiding weaknesses of both. In addition, it meshes with a central intuition concerning what makes killing wrong.

The claim that the primary wrong-making feature of a killing is the loss to the victim of the value of its future has obvious consequences for the ethics of abortion. The future of a standard fetus includes a set of experiences, projects, activities, and such which are identical with the futures of adult human beings and are identical with the futures of young children. Since the reason that is sufficient to explain why it is wrong to kill human beings after the time of birth is a reason that also applies to fetuses, it follows that abortion is prima facie seriously morally wrong.

This argument does not rely on the invalid inference that, since it is wrong to kill persons, it is wrong to kill potential persons also. The category that is morally central to this analysis is the category of having a valuable future like ours; it is not the category of personhood. The argument to the conclusion that abortion is prima facie seriously morally wrong proceeded independently of the notion of person or potential person or any equivalent. Someone may wish to start with this analysis in terms of the value of a human future, conclude that abortion is, except perhaps in rare circumstances, seriously morally wrong, infer that fetuses have the right to life, and then call fetuses "persons" as a result of their having the right to life. Clearly, in this case, the category of person is being used to state the *conclusion* of the analysis rather than to generate the *argument* of the analysis.

The structure of this anti-abortion argument can be both illuminated and defended by comparing it to what appears to be the best argument for the wrongness of the wanton infliction of pain on animals. This latter argument is based on the assumption that it is prima facie wrong to inflict pain on me (or you, reader). What is the natural property associated with the infliction of pain which makes such infliction wrong? The obvious answer seems to be that the infliction of pain causes suffering and that suffering is a misfortune. The suffering caused by the infliction of pain is what makes the wanton infliction of pain on me wrong. The wanton infliction of pain on other adult humans causes suffering. The wanton infliction of pain on animals causes suffering. Since causing suffering is what makes the wanton infliction of pain wrong and since the wanton infliction of pain on animals causes suffering, it follows that the wanton infliction of pain on animals is wrong.

This argument for the wrongness of the wanton infliction of pain on animals shares a number of structural features with the argument for the serious prima facie wrongness of abortion. Both arguments start with an obvious assumption concerning what it is wrong to do to me (or you, reader). Both then look for the characteristic or the consequence of the wrong action which makes the action wrong. Both recognize that the wrong-making feature of these immoral actions is a property of actions sometimes directed at individuals other than postnatal human beings. If the structure of the argument for the wrongness of the wanton infliction of pain on animals is sound, then the structure of the argument for the prima facie serious wrongness of abortion is also sound, for the structure of the two arguments is the same. The structure common to both is the key to the explanation of how the wrongness of abortion can be demonstrated without recourse to the category of person. In neither argument is that category crucial.

This defense of an argument for the wrongness of abortion in terms of a structurally similar argument for the wrongness of the wanton infliction of pain on animals succeeds only if the account regarding animals is the correct account. Is it? In the first place, it seems plausible. In the second place, its major competition is Kant's account. Kant believed that we do not have direct duties to animals at all, because they are not persons. Hence, Kant had to explain and justify the wrongness of inflicting pain on animals on the grounds that "he who is hard in his dealings with animals becomes hard also in his dealing with men."[8] The problem with Kant's account is that there seems to be no reason for accepting this latter claim unless Kant's account is rejected. If the alternative to Kant's account is accepted, then it is easy to understand why someone who is indifferent to inflicting pain on animals is also indifferent to inflicting pain on humans, for one is indifferent to what makes inflicting pain wrong in both cases. But, if Kant's account is accepted, there is no intelligible reason why one who is hard in his dealings with animals (or crabgrass or stones) should also be hard in his dealings with men. After all, men are persons: animals are no more persons than crabgrass or stones. Persons are Kant's crucial moral category. Why, in short, should a Kantian accept the basic claim in Kant's argument?

Hence, Kant's argument for the wrongness of inflicting pain on animals rests on a claim that, in a world of Kantian moral agents, is demonstrably false. Therefore, the alternative analysis, being more plausible anyway, should be accepted. Since this alternative analysis has the same structure as the anti-abortion argument being defended here, we have further support for the argument for the immorality of abortion being defended in this essay.

Of course, this value of a future-like-ours argument, if sound, shows only that abortion is prima facie wrong, not that it is wrong in any and all circumstances. Since the loss of the future to a standard fetus, if killed, is, however, at least as great a loss as the loss of the future to a standard adult human being who is killed, abortion, like ordinary killing, could be justified only by the most compelling reasons. The loss of one's life is almost the greatest misfortune that can happen to one. Presumably abortion could be justified in some circumstances, only if the loss consequent on failing to abort would be at least as great. Accordingly, morally permissible abortions will be rare indeed unless, perhaps, they occur so early in pregnancy that a fetus is not yet definitely an individual. Hence, this argument should be taken as showing that abortion is presumptively very seriously wrong, where the presumption is very strong—as strong as the presumption that killing another adult human being is wrong.

### III

How complete an account of the wrongness of killing does the value of a future-like-ours account have to be in order that the wrongness of abortion is a consequence? This account does not have to be an account of the necessary conditions for the wrongness of killing. Some persons in nursing homes may lack valuable human futures, yet it may be wrong to kill them for other reasons. Furthermore, this account does not obviously have to be the sole reason killing is wrong where the victim did have a valuable future. This analysis claims only that, for any killing where the victim did have a valuable future like ours, having that future by itself is sufficient to create the strong presumption that the killing is seriously wrong.

One way to overturn the value of a future-like-ours argument would be to find some account of the wrongness of killing which is at least as intelligible and which has different implications for the ethics of abortion. Two rival accounts possess at least some degree of plausibility. One account is based on the obvious fact that people value the experience of living and wish for that valuable experience to continue. Therefore, it might be said, what makes killing wrong is the discontinuation of that experience for the victim. Let us call this the *discontinuation account*.[9] Another rival account is based upon the obvious fact that people strongly desire to continue to live. This suggests that what makes killing us so wrong is that it interferes with the fulfillment of a strong and fundamental desire, the fulfillment of which is necessary for the fulfillment of any other desires we might have. Let us call this the *desire account*.[10]

Consider first the desire account as a rival account of the ethics of killing which would provide the basis for rejecting the anti-abortion position. Such an account will have to be stronger than the value of a future-like-ours account of the wrongness of abortion if it is to do the job expected of it. To entail the wrongness of abortion, the value of a future-like-ours account has only to provide a sufficient, but not a necessary, condition for the wrongness of killing. The desire account, on the other hand, must provide us also with a necessary condition for the wrongness of killing in order to generate a pro-choice conclusion on abortion. The reason for this is that presumably the argument from the desire account moves from the claim that what makes killing wrong is interference with a very strong desire to the claim that abortion is not wrong because the fetus lacks a strong desire to live. Obviously, this inference fails if someone's having the desire to live is not a necessary condition of its being wrong to kill that individual.

One problem with the desire account is that we do regard it as seriously wrong to kill persons who have little desire to live or who have no desire to live or, indeed, have a desire not to live. We believe it is seriously wrong to kill the unconscious, the sleeping, those who are tired of life, and those who are suicidal. The value-of-a-human-future account renders standard morality intelligible in these cases; these cases appear to be incompatible with the desire account.

The desire account is subject to a deeper difficulty. We desire life, because we value the goods of this life. The goodness of life is not secondary to our desire for it. If this were not so, the pain of one's own premature death could be done away with merely by an appropriate alteration in the configuration of one's desires. This is absurd. Hence, it would seem that it is the loss of the goods of one's future, not the interference with the fulfillment of a strong desire to live, which accounts ultimately for the wrongness of killing.

It is worth noting that, if the desire account is modified so that it does not provide a necessary, but only a sufficient, condition for the wrongness of killing, the desire account is compatible with the value of a future-like-ours account. The combined accounts will yield an anti-abortion ethic. This suggests that one can retain what is intuitively plausible about the desire account without a challenge to the basic argument of this paper.

It is also worth noting that, if future desires have moral force in a modified desire account of the wrongness of killing, one can find support for an anti-abortion ethic even in the absence of a value of a future-like-ours account. If one decides that a morally relevant property, the possession of which is sufficient to make it wrong to kill some individual, is the desire at some future time to live—one might decide to justify one's refusal to kill suicidal teenagers on these grounds, for example—then, since typical fetuses will have the desire in the future to live, it is wrong to kill typical fetuses. Accordingly, it does not seem that a desire account of the wrongness of killing can provide a justification of a pro-choice ethic of abortion which is nearly as adequate as the value of a human-future justification of an anti-abortion ethic.

The discontinuation account looks more promising as an account of the wrongness of killing. It seems just as intelligible as the value of a future-like-ours account, but it does not justify an anti-abortion position. Obviously, if it is the continuation of one's activities, experiences, and projects, the loss of which makes killing wrong, then it is not wrong to kill fetuses for that reason, for fetuses do not have experiences, activities, and projects to be continued or discontinued. Accordingly, the discontinuation account does not have the anti-abortion consequences that the value of a future-like-ours account has. Yet, it seems as intelligible as the value of a future-like-ours account, for when we think of what would be wrong with our being killed, it does seem as if it is the discontinuation of what makes our lives worthwhile which makes killing us wrong.

Is the discontinuation account just as good an account as the value of a future-like-ours account? The discontinuation account will not be adequate at all, if it does not refer to the *value* of the experience that may be discontinued. One does not want the discontinuation account to make it wrong to kill a patient who begs for death and who is in severe pain that cannot be relieved short of killing. (I leave open the question of whether it is wrong for other reasons.) Accordingly, the discontinuation account must be more than a bare discontinuation account. It must make some reference to the positive value of the patient's experiences. But, by the same token, the value of a future-like-ours account cannot be a bare future account either. Just having a future surely does not itself rule out killing the above patient. This account must make some reference to the value of the patient's future experiences and projects also. Hence, both accounts involve the value of experiences, projects, and activities. So far we still have symmetry between the accounts.

The symmetry fades, however, when we focus on the time period of the value of the experiences, etc., which has moral consequences. Although both accounts leave open the possibility that the patient in our example may be killed, this possibility is left open only in virtue of the utterly bleak future for the patient. It makes no difference whether the patient's immediate past contains intolerable pain, or consists in being in a coma (which we can imagine is a situation of indifference), or consists in a life of value. If the patient's future is a future of value, we want our account to make it wrong to kill the patient. If the patient's future is intolerable, whatever his or her immediate past, we want our account to allow killing the patient. Obviously, then, it is the value of that patient's future which is doing the work in rendering the morality of killing the patient intelligible.

This being the case, it seems clear that whether one has immediate past experiences or not does no work in the explanation of what makes killing wrong. The addition the discontinuation account makes to the value of a human future account is otiose. Its addition to the value-of-a-future account plays no role at all in rendering intelligible the wrongness of killing. Therefore, it can be discarded with the discontinuation account of which it is a part.

## IV

The analysis of the previous section suggests that alternative general accounts of the wrongness of killing are either inadequate or unsuccessful in getting around the anti-abortion consequences of the value of a future-like-ours argument. A different strategy for avoiding these anti-abortion consequences involves limiting the scope of the value of a future argument. More precisely, the strategy involves arguing that fetuses lack a property that is essential for the value-of-a-future argument (or for any anti-abortion argument) to apply to them.

One move of this sort is based upon the claim that a necessary condition of one's future being valuable is that one values it. Value implies a valuer. Given this one might argue that, since fetuses cannot value their futures, their futures are not valuable to them. Hence, it does not seriously wrong them deliberately to end their lives.

This move fails, however, because of some ambiguities. Let us assume that something cannot be of value unless it is valued by someone. This does not entail that my life is of no value unless it is valued by me. I may think, in a period of despair, that my future is of no worth whatsoever, but I may be wrong because others rightly see value—even great value—in it. Furthermore, my future can be valuable to me even if I do not value it. This is the case when a young person attempts suicide, but is rescued and goes on to significant human achievements. Such young people's futures are ultimately valuable to them, even though such futures do not seem to be valuable to them at the moment of attempted suicide. A fetus's future can be valuable to it in the same way. Accordingly, this attempt to limit the anti-abortion argument fails.

Another similar attempt to reject the anti-abortion position is based on Tooley's claim that an entity cannot possess the right to life unless it has the capacity to desire its continued existence. It follows that, since fetuses lack the conceptual capacity to desire to continue to live, they lack the right to life. Accordingly, Tooley concludes that abortion cannot be seriously prima facie wrong (*op. cit.*, pp. 46–7).

What could be the evidence for Tooley's basic claim? Tooley once argued that individuals have a prima facie right to what they desire and that the lack of the capacity to desire something undercuts the basis of one's right to it (*op. cit.*, pp. 44–5). This argument plainly will not succeed in the context of the analysis of this essay, however, since the point here is to establish the fetus's right to life on other grounds. Tooley's argument assumes that the right to life cannot be established in general on some basis other than the desire for life. This position was considered and rejected in the preceding section of this paper.

One might attempt to defend Tooley's basic claim on the grounds that, because a fetus cannot apprehend continued life as a benefit, its continued life cannot be a benefit or cannot be something it has a right to or cannot be something that is in its interest. This might be defended in terms of the general proposition that, if an individual is literally incapable of caring about or taking an interest in some X, then one does not have a right to X or X is not a benefit or X is not something that is in one's interest.[11]

Each member of this family of claims seems to be open to objections. As John C. Stevens[12] has pointed out, one may have a right to be treated with a certain medical procedure (because of a health insurance policy one has purchased), even though one cannot conceive of the nature of the procedure. And, as Tooley himself has pointed out, persons who have been indoctrinated, or drugged, or rendered temporarily unconscious may be literally incapable of caring about or taking an interest in something that is in their interest or is something to which they have a right, or is something that benefits them. Hence, the Tooley claim that would restrict the scope of the value of a future-like-ours argument is undermined by counterexamples.[13]

Finally, Paul Bassen[14] has argued that, even though the prospects of an embryo might seem to be a basis for the wrongness of abortion, an embryo cannot be a victim and therefore cannot be wronged. An embryo cannot be a victim, he says, because it lacks sentience. His central argument for this seems to be that, even though plants and the permanently unconscious are alive, they clearly cannot be victims. What is the explanation of this? Bassen claims that the explanation is that their lives consist of mere metabolism and mere metabolism is not enough to ground victimizability. Mentation is required.

The problem with this attempt to establish the absence of victimizability is that both plants and the permanently unconscious clearly lack what Bassen calls "prospects" or what I have called "a future life like ours." Hence, it is surely open to one to argue that the real reason we believe plants and the permanently unconscious cannot be victims is that killing them cannot deprive them of a future life like ours; the real reason is not their absence of present mentation.

Bassen recognizes that his view is subject to this difficulty, and he recognizes that the case of children seems to support this difficulty, for "much of what we do for children is based on prospects." He argues, however, that, in the case of children and in other such cases "potentiality comes into play only where victimizability has been secured on other grounds" (ibid., p. 333).

Bassen's defense of his view is patently question-begging, since what is adequate to secure victimizability is exactly what is at issue. His examples do not support his own view against the thesis of this essay. Of course, embryos can be victims: when their lives are deliberately terminated, they are deprived of their futures of value, their prospects. This makes them victims, for it directly wrongs them.

The seeming plausibility of Bassen's view stems from the fact that paradigmatic cases of imagining someone as a victim involve empathy, and empathy requires mentation of the victim. The victims of flood, famine, rape, or child abuse are all persons with whom we can empathize. That empathy seems to be part of seeing them as victims.[15]

In spite of the strength of these examples, the attractive intuition that a situation in which there is victimization requires the possibility of empathy is subject to counterexamples. Consider a case that Bassen himself offers: "Posthumous obliteration of an author's work constitutes a misfortune for him only if he had wished his work to endure" (*op cit.*, p. 318). The conditions Bassen wishes to impose upon the possibility of being victimized here seem far too strong. Perhaps this author, due to his unrealistic standards of excellence and his low self-esteem, regarded his work as unworthy of survival, even though it possessed genuine literary merit. Destruction of such work would surely victimize its author. In such a case, empathy with the victim concerning the loss is clearly impossible.

Of course, Bassen does not make the possibility of empathy a necessary condition of victimizability; he requires only mentation. Hence, on Bassen's actual view, this author, as I have described him, can be a victim. The problem is that the basic intuition that renders Bassen's view plausible is missing in the author's case. In order to attempt to avoid counterexamples, Bassen has made his thesis too weak to be supported by the intuitions that suggested it.

Even so, the mentation requirement on victimizability is still subject to counterexamples. Suppose a severe accident renders me totally unconscious for a month, after which I recover. Surely killing me while I am unconscious victimizes me, even though I am incapable of mentation during that time. It follows that Bassen's thesis fails. Apparently, attempts to restrict the value of a future-like-ours argument so that fetuses do not fall within its scope do not succeed.

# V

In this essay, it has been argued that the correct ethic of the wrongness of killing can be extended to fetal life and used to show that there is a strong presumption that any abortion is morally impermissible. If the ethic of killing adopted here entails, however, that contraception is also seriously immoral, then there would appear to be a difficulty with the analysis of this essay.

But this analysis does not entail that contraception is wrong. Of course, contraception prevents the actualization of a possible future of value. Hence, it follows from the claim that futures of value should be maximized that contraception is prima facie immoral. This obligation to maximize does not exist, however; furthermore, nothing in the ethics of killing in this paper entails that it does. The ethics of killing in this essay would entail that contraception is wrong only if something were denied a human future of value by contraception. Nothing at all is denied such a future by contraception, however.

Candidates for a subject of harm by contraception fall into four categories: (1) some sperm or other, (2) some ovum or other, (3) a sperm and an ovum separately, and (4) a sperm and an ovum together. Assigning the harm to some sperm is utterly arbitrary, for no reason can be given for making a sperm the subject of harm rather than an ovum. Assigning the harm to some ovum is utterly arbitrary, for no reason can be given for making an ovum the subject of harm rather than a sperm. One might attempt to avoid these problems by insisting that contraception deprives both the sperm and the ovum separately of a valuable future like ours. On this alternative, too many futures are lost. Contraception was supposed to be wrong, because it deprived us of one future of value, not two. One might attempt to avoid this problem by holding that contraception deprives the combination of sperm and ovum of a valuable future like ours. But here the definite article misleads. At the time of contraception, there are hundreds of millions of sperm, one (released) ovum and millions of possible combinations of all of these. There is no actual combination at all. Is the subject of the loss to be a merely possible combination? Which one? This alternative does not yield an actual subject of harm either. Accordingly, the immorality of contraception is not entailed by the loss of a future-like-ours argument simply because there is no nonarbitrarily identifiable subject of the loss in the case of contraception.

# VI

The purpose of this essay has been to set out an argument for the serious presumptive wrongness of abortion subject to the assumption that the moral permissibility of abortion stands or falls on the moral status of the fetus. Since a fetus possesses a property, the possession of which in adult human beings is sufficient to make killing an adult human being wrong, abortion is wrong. This way of dealing with the problem of abortion seems superior to other approaches to the ethics of abortion, because it rests on an ethics of killing which is close to self-evident, because the crucial morally relevant property clearly applies to fetuses, and because the argument avoids the usual equivocations on "human life," "human being," or "person." The argument rests neither on religious claims nor on Papal dogma. It is not subject to the objection of "speciesism." Its soundness is compatible with the moral permissibility of euthanasia and contraception. It deals with our intuitions concerning young children.

Finally, this analysis can be viewed as resolving a standard problem—indeed, *the* standard problem—concerning the ethics of abortion. Clearly, it is wrong to kill adult human beings. Clearly, it is not wrong to end the life of some arbitrarily chosen single human cell. Fetuses seem to be like arbitrarily chosen human cells in some respects and like adult humans in other respects. The problem of the ethics of abortion is the problem of determining the fetal property that settles this moral controversy. The thesis of this essay is that the problem of the ethics of abortion, so understood, is solvable.

## Endnotes

1.  Feinberg, "Abortion," in *Matters of Life and Death: New Introductory Essays in Moral Philosophy*, Tom Regan, ed. (New York: Random House, 1986), pp. 256–293; Tooley, "Abor-

tion and Infanticide," *Philosophy and Public Affairs* 11, 1 (1972), 37–65, Tooley, *Abortion and Infanticide* (New York: Oxford, 1984); Warren, "On the Moral and Legal Status of Abortion," *The Monist* LVIX, 1 (1973), 4361; Engelhardt, "The Ontology of Abortion," *Ethics* LXXXIV, 3 (1974), 217–234; Sumner, *Abortion and Moral Theory* (Princeton: University Press, 1981); Noonan "An Almost Absolute Value in History," in *The Morality of Abortion: Legal and Historical Perspectives*, Noonan, ed. (Cambridge: Harvard, 1970); and Devine, *The Ethics of Homicide* (Ithaca: Cornell, 1978).

2. For interesting discussions of this issue, see Warren Quinn, "Abortion: Identity and Loss," *Philosophy and Public Affairs* XIII, 1 (1984), 24–54; and Lawrence C. Becker, "Human Being: The Boundaries of the Concept," *Philosophy and Public Affairs* IV, 4 (1975), 334–359.

3. For example, see my "Ethics and The Elderly: Some Problems," in Stuart Spicker, Kathleen Woodward, and David van Tassel, eds., *Aging and the Elderly: Humanistic Perspectives in Gerontology* (Atlantic Highlands, NJ: Humanities, 1978), pp. 341–355.

4. See Warren, *op. cit.*, and Tooley "Abortion and Infanticide."

5. This seems to be the fatal flaw in Warren's treatment of this issue.

6. I have been most influenced on this matter by Jonathan Glover, *Causing Death and Saving Lives* (New York: Penguin, 1977), ch. 3; and Robert Young, "What Is So Wrong with Killing People?" *Philosophy* LIV, 210 (1979), 515–528.

7. Feinberg, Tooley, Warren, and Engelhardt have all dealt with this problem.

8. "Duties to Animals and Spirits," in *Lectures on Ethics,* Louis Infeld, trans. (New York: Harper, 1963), p. 239.

9. I am indebted to Jack Bricke for raising this objection.

10. Presumably a preference utilitarian would press such an objection. Tooley once suggested that his account has such a theoretical underpinning. See his "Abortion and Infanticide," pp. 44–5.

11. Donald VanDeVeer seems to think this is self-evident. See his "Whither Baby Doe?" in *Matters of Life and Death*, p. 233.

12. "Must the Bearer of a Right Have the Concept of That to Which He Has a Right?" *Ethics* XCV, 1 (1984), 68–74.

13. See Tooley again in "Abortion and Infanticide," pp. 47–49.

14. "Present Sakes and Future Prospects: The Status of Early Abortion," *Philosophy and Public Affairs* XI, 4 (1982), 322–326.

15. Note carefully the reasons he gives on the bottom of p. 316.

## Journal/Discussion Questions

✍ *Take some time to reflect on what makes killing wrong for you. Why do you think it is wrong? Is it because you believe people have a right to life? If so, what is the basis for that right? Is it because of the suffering that the person being killed experiences? What if the killing were sudden and painless? Would that make it less objectionable?*

1. Marquis maintains that what's wrong with killing someone is that the person who is killed suffers the loss of his or her life, and "the loss of one's life deprives one of all the experiences, activities, projects, and enjoyments that would otherwise have constituted one's future." Do you agree that this is what makes killing wrong?

2. At the beginning of his article, Marquis dismisses two proposed candidates for explaining the wrongness of killing—the effects on the perpetrator and the effects on the victim's family and friends—in favor of his own analysis. Why do you think that Marquis considers and rejects these two particular claims? Can there be more than one thing that is wrong with killing people, or must wrongness always be reduced to a single factor?

3. Imagine that you are the First Officer of the U.S.S. Enterprise and head of a landing party being beamed down to a planet that you don't have any previous knowledge of. How would you decide which beings on the planet ought not to be killed? Marquis suggests that it would be morally wrong to kill any being that has a future like ours. Is this the criterion that you would use?

4. Marquis argues that "personhood theories of the wrongness of killing . . . cannot straightforwardly account for the wrongness of killing infants and young children." Recall the discussion of personhood theories presented in Jane English's article. Do you think that Marquis's criticism of such theories is justified? Why?

5. The future-like-ours argument, Marquis maintains, does not entail the claim that contraception is morally wrong. Do you think that Marquis is justified in this claim? Does it depend on the kind of contraception? At what point does an entity have a future-like-ours? At the moment of conception? Implantation? Or later?

6. Do you think that abortion involves killing an innocent human being? If it does, is it murder?

---

## George W. Harris
### "Fathers and Fetuses"

*George Harris, as associate professor of philosophy at the College of William and Mary, specializes in ethics and social and political philosophy.*

*In this article, Harris directs his attention toward a largely neglected topic in the discussion of abortion: the moral standing of the father's wishes in the decision about abortion. Centering his argument on the concept of respect for autonomy, he attempts to specify the conditions under which a woman's decision to have an abortion would be a wrongful harm to the father and thus be morally impermissible.*

George W. Harris, "Fathers and Fetuses," *Ethics* 96 (1986). Copyright © 1986, The University of Chicago Press. Reprinted by permission of the publisher and the author.

## As You Read, Consider This:

1. Under what circumstances, if any, does Harris think it would be morally wrong for a woman to have an abortion if the father of the fetus did not want her to do so?

2. What role do considerations about respecting autonomy play in Harris's argument?

⁓

Conspicuously absent from most discussions of the abortion issue are considerations of third-party interests, especially those of the father. A survey of the literature reveals an implicit assumption by most writers that the issue is to be viewed as a two-party conflict—the rights of the fetus versus the rights of the mother—and that an adequate analysis of the balance of these rights is sufficient to determine the conditions under which abortion is morally permissible. I shall argue, however, that in some cases it would be morally impermissible for a woman to have an abortion because it would be a wrongful harm to the father and a violation of his autonomy. Moreover, I shall argue for this on principles that I believe require a strong stand on women's rights.

# I

The issue I wish to discuss then is whether or not it would ever be morally wrong for a woman to have an abortion on the grounds that it would be a wrong done to the father. I leave aside the issue of the rights of the fetus since I do not consider here whether abortion under the circumstances raised might be wrong on other grounds.

Consider then the following cases which are arranged to elucidate the moral considerations involved in the analysis. The extreme cases 1 and 5 are included not so much for their intrinsic importance but because of the light they shed on the analysis of cases 2, 3, and 4. Now, to the cases.

*Case 1.* Karen, a healthy twenty-five-year-old woman, becomes pregnant as the result of being raped by a man with severe psychological problems. After therapy and significant improvement in his mental health, the man recognizes what he has done and is willing to accept liability for the harms he has caused and even punishment should the victim deem it necessary. His only plea is that Karen carry the fetus to term and then give it to him if she does not care to raise the child herself. Unable, however, to disassociate the fetus from the trauma of the rape, Karen decides to abort.

*Case 2.* Jane and Jack, two attractive, healthy individuals, meet at a party given by mutual friends. During the weeks and months that follow, a casual but pleasant sexual relationship develops between them. As a result, Jane becomes pregnant. But after learning of the pregnancy, Jack reveals that he is a moderately serious Catholic and from a combined sense of guilt, responsibility, and parental instinct proposes that they be married. Jane, on the other hand, being neither Catholic nor desirous of a husband, decides to abort. Respecting her religious differences and her right to marry whomever she pleases, Jack offers to pay all of Jane's medical expenses, to take complete responsibility for the child after it is born, and to pay her a large sum of money to carry the fetus to term. Jane nonetheless decides to proceed with the abortion.

*Case 3.*    Susan and Charles, both in perfect health, are in the fifth year of their marriage. Aside from his love for Susan, the prospect of raising a family is the most important thing in Charles's life—more important than career, possessions, sports, or any of the other things thought to be of the utmost importance to men. Susan, on the other hand, is secretly ambivalent about having children due to her indecisiveness between having a career and having a family. But because of her love for Charles and the fear of causing him what she believes might be unnecessary anxiety, she allows him to believe that her reluctance is only with when rather than with whether to have children. And despite reasonable efforts at birth control, Susan becomes pregnant just at a point at which her career takes a significant turn for the better. In the situation, it is a career rather than children that she wants, and she decides to have an abortion. Distraught, Charles tries to dissuade her by offering to forgo his own career and to take on the role traditionally reserved for mothers. But to no avail.

*Case 4.*    Michelle and Steve, like Susan and Charles, are also in the fifth year of their marriage. And Steve, like Charles, is equally and similarly desirous of a family. Michelle, however, knows all along that she does not want children but avoids discussing the issue with Steve, allowing him to think that the beginning of their family is just a matter of time. She believes that eventually she can disabuse him of the values of family life in favor of a simple life together. But due to the unpleasantness of broaching the subject, Michelle procrastinates and accidentally becomes pregnant. And despite Steve's expectations, his pleas, and his offer to take on the major responsibilities of raising the child, Michelle decides to abort.

*Case 5.*    Anne is a man hater. Resentment brought on in part by traditional male chauvinistic attitudes toward women has led her to stereotype all men as little more than barbarians. Mark is a reasonably decent man, who, like Charles and Steve, desires very much to be a parent. After meeting Mark, Anne devises a plan to vicariously vent her rage through Mark on the entire male sex. Carefully playing the role of a conventionally attractive woman with traditional life plans, she sets out to seduce Mark. Soon he falls in love with her and, thinking that he has met the ideal mate, proposes marriage. She accepts and after the wedding convinces Mark that if they are to have a happy married life and a healthy environment in which to raise children he must give up his lucrative realty business and the house he inherited from his parents. Valuing his life with Anne and the prospects of a family more than his career, he sells the business at a considerable loss and takes a less lucrative job. He also sells his home and buys another, again at a considerable financial loss. Finally, Anne becomes pregnant. Initially, she plays the adorable expectant mother, intentionally heightening Mark's expectations. But later she has an abortion. Relishing Mark's horror, she further reveals her scheme and explains that his pain and loss are merely the just deserts of any man for the things that men have done to women.

In all these cases, the issue is this: if we assume that all the men could be acceptable parents and that the pregnancies are physically normal, would any of the abortions by the women in these cases constitute a moral wrong done to any of the men? In the following sections, I shall argue that only in the third, fourth, and fifth cases is a wrongful harm done to the father and that only in the fourth and fifth cases would it be morally impermissible for the woman to proceed with the abortion. By a "wrongful harm," I shall mean a harm that could reasonably have been avoided. I shall argue that in the cases where abortion is claimed to be morally impermissible it is so on the grounds that it violates the father's autonomy; that is, it invades the man's morally legitimate interest in self-determination. The Kantian notion of treating persons as ends—as autonomous agents in pursuit of morally legitimate interests—underlies my argument. Its role will become clearer as the argument proceeds.

## II

Much of the analysis presented here turns on the issue of when it is morally significant to say that the fetus is the father's as well as the mother's. One of the things that a woman can do without violating her interest in the autonomous control of her own body is to have a baby. I do not mean that she can do this alone but that, with the cooperation of a man, she can become pregnant as a matter of unencumbered choice. And though things are a bit more difficult for a man, one of the things he can do with his body, in cooperation with a woman, is to bring new life into the world. The interest in autonomy and the interest in procreation are therefore quite compatible and are common to both women and men. The significance of this, I believe, is that when a man and a woman autonomously decide to become parents together, a harm done to the fetus by a third party without the consent of both parents is a prima facie wrong done both to the man and to the woman because it is an interference with his autonomy as well as with hers. Moreover, a harm done to the fetus is a harm done to the man as well as to the woman because the fetus is both the object and the result of his pursuing a morally legitimate interest, that is, the interest in procreation. To harm the fetus, then, is to invade the morally legitimate interest in procreation of both the father and the mother and thereby to interfere with the man's as well as the woman's autonomy. Further exploration of these observations, I believe, is crucial to the analysis of the cases already presented.

In the first case, Karen's abortion, whatever its moral standing relative to the fetus, is not a wrong done to the man who raped her. This is true despite the fact that the man was not in control of his behavior and therefore was not responsible for his actions. The biological connection between the fetus and the father in this case is not sufficient to establish that the fetus is a morally legitimate object of interest for the man. The reason is obvious. Although procreation is a morally legitimate interest that men can have, the pursuit of this interest is restricted by the requirement that men respect the autonomy of women in this regard. And since the fetus was forced upon Karen by the man, she is not required to view the fetus as a legitimate object of interest for him. The fetus then is his only in a biological sense. Any harm done to the fetus is therefore neither a violation of his autonomy nor a harm done to him by Karen. It is important to note, however, that she could decide to keep it without violating her own or anyone else's autonomy. And this makes the fetus hers in a way that it is not the man's.

Similarly, in the second case, the fetus is Jane's in a way that it is not Jack's. The reasons, however, are slightly different than in the first case. Although Jane and Jack here each autonomously decide to pursue their interests in sex, neither has decided to pursue an interest in procreation. The fact that Jack has neglected to reveal his beliefs about abortion vitiates any claim he has that a harm done to the fetus is a violation of his autonomous pursuit of procreation. Rather, he has left it to Jane to assume that his only interest is in the pleasure of sex with her, and it is only this interest that she has a moral obligation to honor in terms of his autonomy. Had she promised him love and a family in order to have sex with him, she would have violated his autonomy both in regard to his interest in sex with love and his interest in procreation. Neither of these has occurred here. But though Jane is free from considerations of Jack's autonomy in deciding whether to abort or to keep the fetus, she could decide to keep it without violating her own sense of autonomy. It is this fact that makes the fetus hers in a way that it is not Jack's.

Yet by parity of reasoning, Jack is equally free from any responsibility to Jane in terms of the fetus should she decide to keep it. For, like Jane he has not given his consent to the use of his body for the pursuit of her interest in procreation. He could, however, autonomously decide to take on the responsibility for the fetus. But she could not lay claim to a violation of her autonomy if he did not so choose. Had he promised her love and a family in order to have sex with her, he would have violated her autonomy in regard to her interest in sex with love and her interest in procreation. But since he has done neither of these, she has no valid claim that the fetus is a moral liability for him.[1] Thus the pursuit of casual sex can be quite compatible with the principle of autonomy; it is nonetheless morally perilous for both men and women.

In the third case, Charles is the victim of a wrongful harm and his autonomy has been violated. Due to the fact that both men and women have a morally legitimate interest in procreation, couples have an obligation to each other to be forthright and informative about their desires and reservations about family planning. Such forthrightness is necessary if each is to pursue morally legitimate interests without violating the autonomy of the other. Susan, in this case, has clearly been negligent in this responsibility to Charles. She has allowed him to believe that his sex life with her is more than casual and includes more than an expression of his love for her; it is, in part, a legitimate pursuit of his interest in procreation.

Moreover, he has not violated her autonomy as the rapist did with Karen in the first case. Consequently, the fetus is a morally legitimate object of interest for him, and to harm it is to harm Charles—a harm that could reasonably have been avoided by Susan had she told him about her reservations and informed him that should a pregnancy occur she might very well decide in favor of abortion. And it is no excuse that she had not led Charles to believe that she would carry through with any pregnancy, for she has led him to believe that she would carry through with some pregnancy and has now made a decision that thwarts any such expectation. As a result of Susan's negligence, then, the abortion causes a wrongful harm to Charles and is a violation of his autonomy because the fetus is his as well as hers.

But does it follow from this that the abortion is morally impermissible for Susan? The abortion would be morally impermissible if and only if she has a moral obligation to carry the fetus to term. And the issue we are considering here is whether she has such an obligation to Charles. By withholding important information relevant to her own interest in procreation, she has violated his autonomy in regard to two of his legitimate interests—his interest in procreation and his interest in respecting her autonomy in regard to procreation. Therefore, since the fetus is the result of his pursuing a morally legitimate interest in a morally legitimate way with due respect for her autonomy, the fetus is his as well as hers and she has a prima facie obligation to him not to harm it. What considerations then could possibly absolve her of her obligation to Charles?

The answer cannot be found in ranking the interest in a career over an interest in procreation; I cannot see that a career is a more legitimate means of self-determination than procreation or vice versa. Rather, I believe that the answer can be found in Susan's general interest in the control of her own body when compared with the nature of her negligence. To undertake a pregnancy is a serious investment of a woman's bodily and psychological resources—an undertaking that is not similarly possible for a man. The fetus then is a threat to the mother's autonomy in a way that it is not to the father's. And though Susan is responsible for being forthright about such matters, it is certainly understandable for a woman, as it is for a man, to be undecided about how to rank an interest in a career versus an interest in a possible family. Moreover, it is understandable, though far from mature or laudable, for a person to find it difficult to talk with his or her spouse about such matters when the spouse has strong desires for a family. To say that Susan has an obligation to carry his fetus to term in this case and to sacrifice the control of her own body is, it seems to me, to overestimate the fault of her negligence by not allowing for understandable weaknesses in regard to the responsibilities of autonomy. But we must be careful not to underestimate it. She has caused Charles a serious harm, and she has violated his autonomy. For that, she is guilty.

The fourth case is much like the third except the violation of Steve's autonomy and the consequent wrongful harm are done with deceit rather than negligence. The burden to overcome the prima facie obligation not to harm the fetus is therefore stronger for Michelle than it was for Susan because Michelle could have been expected more reasonably to have avoided the harm. Again it is understandable, though neither mature nor laudable, for a person who is deeply in love with someone with significantly different life plans, perhaps as a result of self-deception, to think that the other person can be brought around to seeing things the other way. But it is not excusable. Surely, given the importance the interest in procreation plays in the lives of some people, a normal adult can be expected on the grounds of the other person's autonomy to be honest in such situations. If so, then in the absence of countervening moral considerations it would be a wrong to Steve for Michelle to have the abortion.

The fifth case involves malicious deceit with the intent to cause harm. Only a crazed ideologue could think that the harm caused Mark is not wrongful. And only someone who thinks that men have no legitimate moral interest in procreation could think that Anne's plan does not involve a violation of his autonomy. The fetus is clearly a morally legitimate object of interest for him and therefore his as well as hers. To harm the fetus then is a prima facie harm done to Mark. And given the extent of his sacrifices, the intensity of his expectations, and the depravity of Anne's intentions, it is difficult to see how the general interest in the autonomous control of one's own body could ever be morally significant enough to allow a woman like Anne to culminate the harm she has planned by having the abortion unless the fetus seriously threatened her most fundamental welfare. To think that the general interest in the autonomous control of one's body allows a woman this kind of freedom is to sanctify female autonomy and to trivialize male autonomy—the mirror image of the chauvinism Anne claims to despise. Assuming then that Anne is physically healthy and the pregnancy is not a threat to her fundamental welfare, for her to abort is morally wrong. She has an obligation to Mark to carry through with the pregnancy. . . .

## IV

Someone might argue, however, that the wrongs in these cases can be accounted for on moral grounds that are independent of special considerations of the father or the fetus. The negligence of Susan, the deceit of Michelle, the malice of Anne, all—it might be argued—are wrongs independent of abortion, and there is nothing special about abortion amid these wrongs.

Certainly negligence, deceit, and malice are wrongs independent of abortion, but it does not follow from this that there is nothing special about the wrongs here. Susan, Michelle, and Anne would, respectively, be guilty of negligence, deceit, and malice even had Charles, Steve, and Mark turned out unknowingly to be sterile. But the fact that the men were not sterile and the fact that the women did become pregnant make possible an additional wrong that is special to the abortion issue and that involves fathers and fetuses. The nonmalicious deceit of Michelle illustrates this well. Had Steve been unknowingly sterile, Michelle would have wronged him by lying to him, but she would not have wrongfully harmed him. In fact, the particular harm Anne planned to inflict upon Mark would have been impossible had he been sterile. And had he been knowingly sterile, Anne could not have violated his autonomy by invading an interest that was impossible for him to pursue. Nonetheless, she would have wronged him in other ways. The fact that these other wrongs can affect a man's legitimate interest in procreation gives them special significance here.

It might also be objected that one disquieting implication of the argument is that abortion would be said to constitute a "wrongful harm" to anyone and anything that has a "morally legitimate interest" in it. So, for example, in an underpopulated country like Norway or Australia, society might have a morally legitimate interest in childbearing, and every woman opting for an abortion might be said to do a "wrongful harm to society." Or grandparents might have a "morally legitimate" interest in grandchildren being born; and a woman aborting would be said to have done a "wrongful harm" to the would-be grandparents.[2]

Certainly these results are unacceptable, but I do not believe that they are consistent with the concept of autonomy I have in mind here. We might distinguish between interests that are prima facie morally legitimate and those that are morally legitimate simpliciter or legitimate after all moral considerations are in. An interest that is prima facie morally legitimate is one that in itself is a morally permissible interest to have. The interest in sex and the interest in procreation are two such interests, as are the interest in grandparents having grandchildren and the interest of a country in having a larger population. But one way in which prima facie morally legitimate interests can fail to be morally legitimate simpliciter is for a person who has these interests to pursue them in ways that are morally illegitimate.

Assume that the rapist has an interest in sex (which is doubtful, at least that it is his primary interest.) This interest fails to be morally legitimate simpliciter when the pursuit of it invades the morally legitimate interest his victim has in her choice of sexual partners. And it is the primacy of the importance of individual choice and its moral legitimacy that is at the heart of the concept of autonomy employed here. Thus a prima facie morally legitimate interest can fail to be morally legitimate simpliciter if it is pursued in a way that does not respect the autonomy of others to pursue their morally legitimate interests. So like the rapist who has an interest in sex, there is nothing wrong with what the country wants in wanting a larger population or in what potential grandparents want in wanting grandchildren. These interests become morally illegitimate, however, when the autonomy of the women involved is violated by the rapist, the country, or the grandparents in the pursuit of their interests. And it is the importance of autonomy to my argument that prevents the disquieting implication.

A final objection might be that too much of the argument turns on the extremity and implausibility of case 5. There is an ambiguity, however, in the charge of "implausibility." On the one hand, it might mean that the case is far-fetched in that cases like it are not at all likely to occur. Or on the other hand, it might mean that the analysis of the case is either unconvincing or that it sheds no light on the other cases.

The first construal of the charge renders it irrelevant. We hope that there are and will be no such cases. But this is beside the point. If the analysis of the case can be defended against the charge of implausibility of the second kind, the case serves to shed light on moral issues in other contexts. This is what Judith Jarvis Thomson's violinist example and Jane English's mad scientist example are designed to do.[3] And no one thinks that these examples are implausible on the grounds that they are unlikely to occur. Those who think of these examples as implausible think so on the grounds that they are misleading or otherwise uninformative in terms of analysis.[4] The objection then turns on the second construal of the charge.

That the analysis is unconvincing might be argued either by claiming that Anne has not wronged Mark or that the wrong is independent of the abortion issue. Since I do not believe that anyone would upon reflection seriously claim the former and since I have already addressed the latter claim, the second charge must turn on the claim that the case fails to illuminate the issues in other contexts. But I believe that it does illuminate the issues of other cases. Most important, it establishes that a serious wrong that a woman can do to a man is to harm him by killing his fetus, and it shows how this might involve other wrongs that are done with intentional malice. Once these two points are established, the issue naturally arises as to whether the wrong of harming a man by killing his fetus might be done in other ways involving other wrongs that are not accompanied by malicious intent. I have argued that abortion constitutes a wrongful harm in cases involving neglect and nonmalicious deceit. Viewed from this perspective, cases 3 and 4 are illuminated by case 5. And viewed from this perspective, we can see that there are other ways—ways that are more likely to occur—in which we can wrong others by failing to take their autonomy and their interests seriously than just in cases where we intentionally and maliciously set out to do so. The latter cases are easy to recognize; the former are not always. Being alive to this is important, and that is why cases 3 and 4 and perhaps other more subtle ones are most important in the analysis.

I have spoken about the rights of autonomy. It is time now to say something about its responsibilities. On any plausible view of the importance of autonomy, anyone who claims to have a right that others respect his or her autonomy must recognize the obligation to take seriously the autonomy of others. Men and women in their relations with each other as members of the opposite sex have not always done this. Let me briefly mention two ways in which men and women have failed in this responsibility.

The first has to do with equality. If the interest in procreation and the interest in, say, a career are equally legitimate, then a man cannot consistently require a woman with whom he is involved to take seriously his interest in a family if he does not take seriously her interest in a career. It is notoriously true that many men are chauvinistic in this regard. But by the same taken, a woman cannot consistently require a man with whom she is involved to take seriously her interest in a career if she does not take seriously his interest in a family. This does not mean that she must have children with him, but it does mean that in working out her relationship with him she must grant that men have as legitimate an interest in being parents as do women. I am not sure that many women—nor for that matter that many men—are emotionally prepared to admit this. Although we are making some progress in thinking that women have an equal right to a career as men and that men have equal obligations in child rearing as women, we are still hesitant to think that a man could be an equal to a woman in parenthood.

The second way in which men and women have failed to take each other's autonomy seriously involves forthrightness. Men, it is said with some justification, are unwilling to talk about their feelings. This often puts an unfair burden on the woman with whom a man is involved to understand what his interests are, and without adequate information regarding his interests, the woman is poorly positioned to respect his autonomy in regard to those interests. Thus one aspect of the responsibility to be forthright involves letting the other person know what your interests are so that your autonomy can be respected. This was Jack's failure in case 2.

Another aspect of the responsibility to be forthright has to do with allowing the other person to make an informed choice. Certainly, it is an interference with another person's autonomy to purposefully provide them with or knowingly allow them to believe erroneous information relevant to their choices. This is what Susan, Michelle, and Anne have done in the cases considered. Such motivation to be less than forthright is not always selfish, but it is almost always a failure to take autonomy seriously.

## V

To summarize: In order for a man to lay claim to the fetus being his in a sense that the mother is obligated to respect, the fetus must be the result of his pursuing the legitimate interest in procreation in a morally legitimate way. In cases 1 and 2, the men—in different ways—have not satisfied the requirement of acting in a way that is consistent with the responsibilities of autonomy. It would therefore not be a wrong done to these men for Karen and Jane to have their abortions. However, when a man has satisfied the requirements of autonomy in regard to the interest in procreation both in regard to himself and to his sexual partner, the woman has a prima facie obligation to him not to harm the fetus. And unless there is some countervening moral consideration to override this prima facie obligation, the abortion of the fetus is morally impermissible. I have argued that the latter is true in cases 4 and 5.

### Endnotes

1. These observations do not contradict the practice of the courts in holding liable for support men who have simply become uninterested in their wives and children. What is being maintained is that the fact that a man is the biological father of a child is not sufficient either to give him rights to the child or to put him under an obligation to it or to the mother.

2. I owe this objection to Robert Goodin. The grandparents case was also mentioned to me by James F. Hill.

3. See Judith Jarvis Thomson, "A Defense of Abortion," *Philosophy and Public Affairs* I (1971), 47–66; and Jane English, "Abortion and the Concept of a Person," *Canadian Journal of Philosophy* 5 (1975), 233–243. [Reprinted above.]

4. I find these examples quite helpful, especially English's.

# Journal/Discussion Questions

*✍ Have you ever known men who were involved with the decision about whether a woman who had gotten pregnant by them should have an abortion? What did you learn from observing the situation?*

1. In ruling out the legitimacy of the father's interest in the Case 1, Harris advances an interesting principle: "Although procreation is a morally legitimate interest that men can have, the pursuit of this interest is restricted by the requirement that men respect the autonomy of women in this regard." Thus, where the interest in procreation was pursued through rape, there was no respect for the autonomy of women and consequently the man has no morally legitimate interest in the pregnancy. Do you agree with Harris's claim about this? What other circumstances, besides rape, reveal a lack of respect for the autonomy of women in this regard?

2. In discussing Case 2, Harris suggests that Jack is "free from any responsibility to Jane in terms of the fetus should she decide to keep it" because "he has not given his consent to the use of his body for the pursuit of her interest in procreation." This suggests that responsibility is solely dependent on consent, which in turn suggests a view of the moral world as constituted primarily of freely-chosen contracts. Does this seem like an accurate view of the moral life? Can you think of any circum-

stances in which people have responsibilities thrust upon them without their consent? Give an example. Does this have any implications for Harris's position?

3. In his discussion of Case 3, Harris does not see Susan's choice as turning (morally) on the question of whether career or procreation should be given a higher rank; rather, he sees it primarily as a question of the woman's general interest in the control of her own body and what it would take to override that interest. When, if ever, should other factors be allowed to override a woman's general interest in the control of her own body in regard to reproductive decisions?

4. Harris argues that in Cases 4 and 5, the woman's decision to have an abortion is morally impermissible because it violates the father's "morally legitimate interest in self-determination," that is, his autonomy. Do you agree with his reasoning here? What about the autonomy of the mother?

5. Autonomy, Harris suggests, implies responsibility. If we want others to respect our autonomy, we ought to respect theirs, and this involves respecting their morally legitimate interests. Both men and women, Harris maintains, have a (morally) equally legitimate interest in being parents. Do you agree with this claim? Why or why not?

Richard A. McCormick
"Should We Clone Humans? Wholeness, Individuality, Reverence"

*Richard A. McCormick, S. J., is a Catholic moral theologian and philosopher who specializes in biomedical ethics. His earlier work includes* How Brave A New World.

*In contrast to those who maintain that decisions about human cloning and genetic manipulation are personal matters of individual autonomy, McCormick argues that they are profoundly social issues. He proposes three fundamental values—wholeness, individuality, and reverence—to serve as guides in decision-making in this area.*

## As You Read, Consider This:

1. McCormick claims that the assumption that "anything that helps overcome infertility is morally appropriate" is "frighteningly myopic." What does he mean by this? Do you agree?

2. What, according to McCormick, is the moral status of the pre-embryo?

The cloning of human embryos by Dr. Jerry L. Hall at George Washington University Medical Center last month has set off an interesting ethical debate. Should it be done? For what purposes? With what controls? It is not surprising—though I find it appalling—that some commentators see the entire issue in terms of individual autonomy. Embryos belong to their producers, they argue, and it is not society's business to interfere with the exercise of people's privacy (see comments in *The New York Times*, October 26, 1993).

One's approach to cloning will vary according to the range of issues one wants to consider. For example, some people will focus solely on the role of cloning in aiding infertile couples—and they will likely conclude that there is nothing wrong with it. The scarcely hidden assumption is that anything that helps overcome infertility is morally appropriate. That is, I believe, frighteningly myopic.

Human cloning is an extremely social matter, not a question of mere personal privacy. I see three dimensions to the moral question: the wholeness of life, the individuality of life, and respect for life.

*Wholeness.*   Our society has gone a long way down the road of positive eugenics, the preferential breeding of superior genotypes. People offhandedly refer to "the right to a healthy child." Implied in such loose talk is the right to discard the imperfect. What is meant, of course, is that couples have a claim to reasonably available means to ensure that their children are born healthy. We have pre-implementation diagnosis for genetic defects. We have recently seen several cases of "wrongful life" where the child herself or himself is the plaintiff. As a member of the ethics committee of the American Fertility Society, I regularly receive brochures from sperm banks stating the donors' race, education, hobbies, height, weight and eye color. We are rapidly becoming a pick-and-choose society with regard to our prospective children. More than a few couples withhold acceptance of their fetuses pending further testing. This practice of eugenics raises a host of problems: What qualities are to be maximized? What defects are intolerable? Who decides? But the critical flaw in "preferential breeding" is the perversion of our attitudes: we begin to value the person in terms of the particular trait he or she was programmed to have. In short, we reduce the whole to a part. People who do that are in a moral wilderness.

*Individuality.* Uniqueness and diversity (sexual, racial, ethnic, cultural) are treasured aspects of the human condition, as was sharply noted by a study group of the National Council of Churches in 1984 (*Genetic Engineering: Social and Ethical Consequences*). Viewed theologically, human beings, in their enchanting, irreplaceable uniqueness and with all their differences, are made in the image of God. Eugenics schemes that would bypass, downplay or flatten human diversities and uniqueness should be viewed with a beady eye. In the age of the Genome Project it is increasingly possible to collapse the human person into genetic data. Such reductionism could shatter our wonder at human individuality and diversity at the very time that, in other spheres of life, we are emphasizing it.

*Life.* Everyone admits that the pre-embryo (preimplanted embryo) is human life. It is living, not dead. It is human, not canine. One need not attribute personhood to such early life to claim that it demands respect and protection.

Two considerations must be carefully weighed as we try to discern our obligations toward pre-embryonic life. The first consideration is for the potential of the pre-embryo. Under favorable circumstances, the fertilized ovum will move through developmental individuality and then progressively through functional, behavioral, psychic and social individuality. In viewing the first stage, one cannot afford to blot out subsequent stages. It retains its potential for personhood and thus deserves profound respect. This is a weighty matter for the believer who sees the human person as a member of Gods family and the temple of the Spirit. Interference with such a potential future cannot be a light undertaking.

The second consideration concerns our own human condition. I would gather these concerns under the notion of "uncertainty." There is uncertainty about the extent to which enthusiasm for human research can be controlled. That is, if we concluded that pre-embryos need not be treated in all circumstances as persons, would we little by little extend this to embryos? Would we gradually trivialize the reasons justifying pre-embryo manipulation? These are not abstract worries; they have become live questions.

Furthermore, there is uncertainty about the effect of pre-embryo manipulation on personal and societal attitudes toward nascent human life in general. Will there be further erosion of our respect? I say "further" because of the widespread acceptance and practice of abortion. There is grave uncertainty about our ability to say no and backtrack when we detect abuses, especially if they have produced valuable scientific and therapeutic data or significant treatment. Medical technology ("progress") has a way of establishing irreversible dynamics.

Because the pre-embryo does have intrinsic potential and because of the many uncertainties noted above, I would argue that the pre-embryo should be treated as a person. These obligations, may be prima facie—to use W. D. Ross's phrase—and subject to qualifications. But when we are dealing with human life, the matter is too important to be left to local or regional criteria and controls. We need uniform national controls. Without them, our corporate reverence for life, already so deeply compromised, will be further eroded.

In sum, human cloning is not just another technological step to be judged in terms of its effects on those cloned. What frightens me above all is what human cloning would do to all of us—to our sense of the wholeness, individuality and sanctity of human life. These are intertwined theological concerns of the first magnitude.

## Journal/Discussion Questions

✍ *McCormick expresses his concerns as "theological." Do you think these concerns are limited only to those who share his religious beliefs? Discuss.*

1. "Preferential breeding," as McCormick calls it, undermines the value of wholeness. Explain his reasoning for this claim. In what ways do you agree with him? Disagree? Should wholeness be an important value?

2. To what extent do advances in cloning threaten diversity? Do you think that diversity is an important value in this context? Explain.

3. McCormick maintains that the pre-embryo should be treated as a person. What support does he offer for this claim? Do you agree or disagree? Why?

# QUESTIONS FOR DISCUSSION AND REVIEW

## Where Do You Stand Now?

**Instructions:**

You have already answered the following questions in your moral problems self-quiz at the beginning of this book. Now that you have studied the material in this section, take a moment to answer the same questions again.

|  | *Strongly Agree* | *Agree* | *Undecided* | *Disagree* | *Strongly Disagree* | *Chapter 1: Reproductive Choices* |
|---|---|---|---|---|---|---|
| 1. | ❏ | ❏ | ❏ | ❏ | ❏ | The principal moral consideration about abortion is the question of whether the fetus is a person or not. |
| 2. | ❏ | ❏ | ❏ | ❏ | ❏ | The principal moral consideration about abortion is the question of the rights of the pregnant woman. |
| 3. | ❏ | ❏ | ❏ | ❏ | ❏ | The only one who should have a voice in making the decision about an abortion is the pregnant woman. |
| 4. | ❏ | ❏ | ❏ | ❏ | ❏ | Any procedure that helps infertile couples to have children is good. |
| 5. | ❏ | ❏ | ❏ | ❏ | ❏ | Genetic manipulation of embryos should be forbidden. |

Now compare your answers to the present self-quiz with the answers to the initial self-quiz. How, if at all, have your answers changed? How have the *reasons* for your answers changed?

## Journal/Discussion Questions

✍ You have now read, thought, and discussed a number of aspects of the morality of the abortion decision. How have your views changed and developed? What idea had the greatest impact on your thinking about abortion?

✍ Imagine that a close friend at another college just called you to tell you that she was pregnant and that she didn't know what to do. Although she is not asking you to tell her what to do, she does ask you to tell her what you *believe about* abortion. Write her a letter in which you tell her what your own beliefs are. Talk, among other things, about what sorts of factors should be taken into consideration.

✍ In "Why Abortion Is a Religious Issue," Stanley Hauerwas claims that most people make the decision about abortion for reasons that have relatively little to do with the types of arguments that philoso-

*phers usually advance. Looking back
over your readings on this issue, do you
think that Hauerwas was correct? If so,
what follows from his claim?*

✍ *If you were going to have a baby, to what
extent would you want to select its characteristics in advance? Which characteristics, if any, would you not want to consciously select? Physical characteristics?
Physical and mental capabilities? Personality traits? Sex? Sexual orientation?*

1. What, in the readings in this chapter, was
   the most thought-provoking idea you encountered? In what ways did it prompt
   you to reconsider some of your previous
   beliefs?

2. Has your overall position on the morality
   of abortion changed? If so, in what
   way(s)? If your position has not changed,

have your reasons developed in any way?
If so, in what way(s)? Has your understanding changed of the reasons supporting other positions that are different from
your own? If so, in what way(s)?

3. In light of the readings in this chapter,
   what new issues about reproductive technologies were most interesting to you?
   Which ones do you think will be most
   difficult for us as a society to resolve?

4. Should there be any limits on couples
   who wish to use artificial means in order
   to have children? Should there be any
   limits on individuals who wish to do so?

5. Should society regulate the practice of
   surrogacy? In what ways? How should it
   deal with surrogate mothers who change
   their minds?

# FOR FURTHER READING:
## A BIBLIOGRAPHICAL GUIDE
## TO REPRODUCTIVE CHOICES

## Journals

There are a number of excellent journals in ethics that contain articles on virtually all of the topics treated in this book. These include *Ethics*, the oldest and arguably the finest of the ethics journals; *Philosophy and Public Affairs*, which—as its name implies—places special emphasis on questions of public rather than private morality; *Journal of Social Philosophy*, which often contains articles on the cutting edge of social controversies; *Social Philosophy and Policy*, which is devoted to a particular topic each issue (such as Liberalism and the Economic Order; Altruism; Property Rights; and Crime, Culpability, and Remedy); and *Public Affairs Quarterly*, which contains a number of articles on the ethical dimensions of public policy issues. In addition to these, see the *Hastings Center Reports*, *BioEthics*, *Kennedy Institute of Ethics*, *Journal of Medicine and Philosophy* and *Law, Medicine & Health Care* for discussion of issues relating specifically to biomedical ethics. For current developments, see my World Wide Web site mentioned in the Preface.

## Review Articles and Reports

For a comprehensive bibliographical guide to *abortion*, see Diane E. Fitzpatrick, *A History of Abortion in the United States: A Working Bibliography of Journal Articles* (Monticello, IL: Vance Bibliographies, 1991). For excellent surveys of the philosophical issues, see Mary Anne Warren, "Abortion," in *A Companion to Ethics*, edited by Peter Singer (Oxford: Blackwell, 1991), pp. 303–314, and Nancy (Ann) Davis, "Abortion," *Encyclopedia of Ethics*, ed. Lawrence C. Becker and Charlotte B. Becker (New York: Garland, 1992), vol. I, pp. 2–6. For demographic data, see Paul Sachdev, *International Handbook on Abortion* (New York: Greenwood Press, 1988). There are a number of helpful bibliographies available on issues relating to *reproductive technologies*; see Mary Carrington Coutts, "Human Gene Therapy," *Scope Note 24.* (Washington, D.C.: Georgetown University, 1994); and Walters, LeRoy, and Kahn, Tamar Joy, eds., *Bibliography of Bioethics*, vols. 1–19 (Washington, D.C.: Kennedy Institute of Ethics, Georgetown University). For a review of some of the moral issues raised by new reproductive technologies, see Helen Bequaert Holmes, "Reproductive Technologies," *Encyclopedia of Ethics*, ed. Lawrence C. Becker and Charlotte B. Becker (New York: Garland 1992), vol. II, pp. 1083–1089.

There have been a number of national commissions, both here and in England, that have prepared reports and policy recommendations on these issues. See, among others, The President's Commission for the Study of Ethical Problems in Medicine and Biomedical and Behavior Research, *Splicing Life: The Social and Ethical Issues of Genetic Engineering with Human Beings* (Washington, D.C.: GPO, 1982); Mary Warnock, *A Question of Life: The Warnock Report on Human Fertilization and Embryology* (Oxford: Basil Blackwell, 1985); Jonathan Glover et al., *Fertility and the Family: The Glover Report on Reproductive Technologies to the European Commission* (London: Fourth Estate, 1989); American Fertility Society, Ethics Committee, *Ethical*

*Considerations of the New Reproductive Technologies*, in *Fertility and Sterility*, vol. 46, no. 3, supplement 1 (1986) and *Fertility and Sterility*, vol. 53, no. 6, supplement 2 (1990). For a religious response to the Warnock report by the Regius Professor of Moral and Pastoral Theory in the University of Oxford, see Oliver O'Donovan, *Begotten or Made?* (Oxford: Clarendon Press, 1984). For a survey of results of such reports, see LeRoy Walters, "Ethical Aspects of the New Reproductive Technologies," *Annals of the New York Academy of Sciences*, no. 541 (1988), 646–664.

## Anthologies and Books

There are a number of excellent *anthologies* of selections dealing solely with the issue of abortion. *The Problem of Abortion*, 2nd ed., edited by Joel Feinberg (Belmont, CA: Wadsworth, 1984) contains a number of important pieces covering a wide range of positions, as does *The Ethics of Abortion: Pro-Life vs. Pro-Choice*, rev. ed., ed. Robert M. Baird and Stuart E. Rosenbaum (Buffalo: Prometheus Books, 1993). Lewis M. Schwartz's *Arguing about Abortion* (Belmont, CA: Wadsworth, 1993) not only contains a number of important essays, but also (a) provides a well-done introduction to reconstructing and evaluating argumentative discourse and (b) offers an outline and analysis of six of the essays contained in the anthology. *Abortion: Moral and Legal Perspectives*, ed. Jay L. Garfield and Patricia Hennessey (Amherst: University of Massachusetts Press, 1984) contains several new essays as well as reprints of some previously published pieces. See also Marshall Cohen, Thomas Nagel, and Thomas Scanlon, eds., *Rights and Wrongs of Abortion* (Princeton: Princeton University Press, 1974) and John T. Noonan, Jr., ed., *The Morality of Abortion: Legal and Historical Perspectives* (Cambridge: Harvard University Press, 1970). The anthology *Abortion: Understanding Differences*, ed. Sidney Callahan and Daniel Callahan (Plenum Press, 1984) contains a number of perceptive essays. For an excellent selection of both philosophical and popular articles, see *Abortion: Opposing Viewpoints*, ed. Charles P. Cozic and Stacey L. Tripp (San Diego: Greenhaven Press, 1991).

There are a number of excellent anthologies available in the area of reproductive technologies. Among the general anthologies on issues in bioethics, see the excellent *Contemporary Issues in Bioethics*, ed. Tom L. Beauchamp and LeRoy Walters, 4th ed. (Belmont: Wadsworth, 1994); for an excellent selection of both philosophical and non-philosophical authors, see *Genetic Engineering: Opposing Viewpoints* (San Diego: Greenhaven Press, 1994) and Carol Levine, ed., *Taking Sides: Clashing View on Controversial Bioethical Issues* (Guilford, CN: Dushkin, 1995).

One of the principal areas of concern in regard to genetic screening is *sex selection*. See Mary Anne Warren, *Gendercide: The Implications of Sex Selection* (Totowa, NJ: Rowman and Allanheld, 1985); and her "IVF and Women's Interests: An Analysis of Feminist Concerns," *Bioethics* 2, no. 1 (1988), pp. 37–57; for a review on recent feminist work in this and related areas, see Anne Donchin, "The Growing Feminist Debate Over the New Reproductive Technologies," *Hypatia*, vol. 4, no. 3 (1989), pp. 136–149 (also see several other related articles in this volume); and Helen Bequaert Holmes, "Sex Preselection: Eugenics for Everyone?" *Biomedical Ethics Reviews—1985*, ed. J. Humber and R. Almeders (Clifton, NJ: Humana Press, 1985). Also see Michelle Stanworth, *Reproductive Technologies: Gender, Motherhood, and Medicine* (Minneapolis: University of Minnesota Press, 1987).

For some excellent resources in regard to questions of *genetic engineering*, see *Ethical Issues in the New Reproductive Technologies*, ed. Richard Hull (Belmont: Wadsworth, 1990);

Kenneth D. Alpern, *The Ethics of Reproductive Technology* (New York: Oxford University Press, 1992); Sherill Cohen and Nadine Taub, eds., *Reproductive Laws for the 1990s* (Clifton, NJ: Humana Press, 1989); Ruth F. Chadwick, ed., *Ethics, Reproduction, and Genetic Control* (London: Croom Helm, 1987); Elaine Baruch, et al., *Test Tube Women: What Future for Motherhood?* (London: Pandora, 1984) contains essays mostly against new reproductive technologies; Clifford Grobstein's *From Chance to Purpose: An Appraisal of External Human Fertilization* (Reading, MA: Addison-Wesley, 1981) and his later *Science and the Unborn: Choosing Human Futures* (New York: Basic Books, 1988); Joseph Fletcher's *The Ethics of Genetic Control: Ending Reproductive Roulette* (Buffalo, NY: Prometheus Books, 1988) strongly presents the case in favor of genetic manipulation, while Gena Corea's *The Mother Machine: Reproductive Technologies from Artificial Insemination to Artificial Wombs* (New York: Harper and Row, 1985) gives a strong presentation of arguments against such manipulation.

Among the many excellent books on abortion, see L. W. Sumner, *Abortion and Moral Theory* (Princeton: Princeton University Press, 1981) for a carefully reasoned moderate view on the permissibility of abortion. Rosiland Hursthouse's *Beginning Lives* (Oxford: Basil Blackwell, 1987) includes a perceptive account of the issue of abortion. John T. Noonan, Jr., who represents a conservative Catholic view, has several books on this issue, including *A Private Choice: Abortion in America in the Seventies* (New York: The Free Press, 1979); Germain G. Grisez's *Abortion: The Myths, the Realities, and the Arguments* (New York: Corpus Books, 1970) also argues for a strongly conservative view. Baruch Brody's *Abortion and the Sanctity of Human Life: A Philosophical View* (Cambridge, MA: The M.I.T. Press, 1975) defends a fairly conservative view, arguing that the fetus becomes a person when brain activity begins. Michael Tooley's *Abortion and Infanticide* (Oxford: Clarendon Press, 1983) presents some controversial arguments in support of abortion and situates the issue within the larger context of infanticide and the killing of nonhuman animals. Bonnie Steinbock's *Life Before Birth: The Moral and Legal Status of Embryos and Fetuses* (New York: Oxford, 1992) concentrates primarily on the issue of the status of embryos and fetuses, while F. M. Kamm's *Creation and Abortion* (New York: Oxford, 1992) develops a broader theory of creating new people responsibility, and explores the issue of abortion within this context. Also see Stephen D. Schwarz, *The Moral Question of Abortion* (Chicago: Loyola University Press, 1990).

## Key Essays

Among philosophers, there are several key essays that have set the stage for the philosophical discussion of abortion. The most reprinted essay in contemporary philosophy is probably Judith Jarvis Thomson's "A Defense of Abortion," which originally appeared in the inaugural issue of *Philosophy and Public Affairs* 1, no. 1 (Fall 1971), 47–66 and is reprinted in her *Rights, Restitution, & Risk: Essays in Moral Theory* (Cambridge; Harvard University Press, 1986)—which also contains her "Rights and Deaths," a reply to several critics of her initial essay—and in both the Feinberg and the Schwartz anthologies cited above. Thomson's article has elicited a number of replies; one of the more recent and insightful of these is John Martin Fisher, "Abortion and Self-Determination," *Journal of Social Philosophy*, XXII, no. 2 (Fall 1991), 5–13. John T. Noonan, Jr.'s "An Almost Absolute Value in History," is also widely reprinted (including in Noonan's *The Morality of Abortion*, cited above) and is a strong, classic statement of the conservative view. Joel

Feinberg's "Abortion," in *Matters of Life and Death*, ed. Tom Regan (New York: Random House, 1980), pp. 183–217, is a careful and nuanced discussion of the question of the moral status of the fetus. Roger Werthheimer's "Understanding the Abortion Argument," *Philosophy and Public Affairs* 1, no. 1 (Fall 1971), 67–95, presents strong arguments for a fairly conservative view. Mary Anne Warren's "On the Moral and Legal Status of Abortion," *The Monist* 57 (1973) argues for a strongly liberal position, maintaining that the fetus is not a person.

On the issue of *genetic engineering*, see the issue of *The Hastings Center Report* 24, no. 2 (March, 1994), with articles by Joseph Palca, "A Word to the Wise: On the Approval of *in vitro* Fertilization Research"; John A. Robertson, "The Question of Human Cloning"; and Richard A. McCormick, "Blastomere Separation: Some Concerns: Embryo Splitting As a Treatment to *in Vitro* Fertilization." For a good collection of essays on the status of the fetus, see *Biomedical Ethics Reviews: Bioethics and the Fetus: Medical, Moral, and Legal Issues*, ed. James M. Humber and Robert Almeder (Clifton, NJ: Humana Press, 1991) and Peter Singer et al., eds., *Embryo Experimentation* (New York: Cambridge University Press, 1990). For a critique of the philosophical viability of the notion of the "*pre-embryo*," see A. A. Howsepian, "Who or What Are We?" *Review of Metaphysics* 45, no. 3, 483–502, which replied to Richard McCormick's "Who or What is the Preembryo?" in the *Kennedy Institute of Ethics Journal* 1 (1991), 1–15; Alan Holland, "A Fortnight of My Life Is Missing: A Discussion of the Status of the Human 'Pre-Embryo,'" *Applied Philosophy*, ed. Brenda Almond and Donald Hill (London: Routledge and Kegan Paul, 1991), pp. 299–311.

For background on the *principle of double effect*, see Joseph T. Mangan, "An Historical Analysis of the Principle of Double Effect," *Theological Studies*, 10 (1949), 41–61. G. E. M. Anscombe's "Modern Moral Philosophy," *Philosophy*, 33 (1958), 26–42, raises important questions about the distinction between intended consequences and forseen consequences. Phillipa Foot expresses doubts about the moral significance of this distinction in her article, "Abortion and the Doctrine of Double Effect," in her *Virtues and Vices and Other Essays* (Berkeley: University of California Press, 1978), pp. 19–32. For a short survey of the philosophical issues surrounding this principle, see William David Solomon, "Double Effect," *Encyclopedia of Ethics*, ed. Lawrence C. Becker and Charlotte B. Becker (New York: Garland , 1992), vol. I, pp. 268–269.

## Narratives

On *women's experiences with the abortion decision*, see Carol Gilligan, *In a Different Voice* (Cambridge: Harvard University Press, 1982), which contains in-depth interviews with young women who have faced the abortion decision. Linda Bird Francke's *The Ambivalence of Abortion* (New York: Random House, 1978) is an excellent source of interviews with women of all ages who have had abortions. Martha Bolton's "Responsible Women and Abortion Decisions," in *Having Children: Philosophical and Legal Reflections* (New York: Oxford University Press, 1979), pp. 40–51, places the decision within the context of the narratives of individual women's lives. For collections of narratives about abortion, see *The Choices We Made: Twenty-five Women and Men Speak Out About Abortion*, ed. Angela Bonavoglia (New York: Random House, 1991). For a fascinating portrait of individuals involved on all sides of the abortion controversy, see Faye D. Ginsburg, *Contested Lives: The Abortion Debate in an American Community* (Berkeley: University of California Press, 1989). Also see Denise Winn, *Experiences of Abortion* (London: Macdonald, 1988) and Ellen Messer and Kathryn E. May, *Back Rooms: Voices from the Abortion Era* (New

York: Simon & Schuster, 1988) and *The Voices of Women: Abortion, in Their Own Words* (Washington, D.C.: National Abortion Rights Action League, 1989).

## Abortion and the Law

On *Roe* v. *Wade*, see especially David J. Garrow, *Liberty and Sexuality: The Right to Privacy and the Making of* Roe *v.* Wade (New York: Macmillan, 1994). For a broader history, see Mary Ann Glendon, *Abortion and Divorce in Western Law* (Cambridge: Harvard University Press, 1987).

## On Finding a Common Ground

Several recent contributions to the search for common ground in the abortion discussion are Laurence H. Tribe, *Abortion: The Clash of Absolutes* (New York: Norton, 1992); Roger Rosenblatt, *Life Itself* (New York: Vintage Books, 1992); Ronald Dworkin, *Life's Dominion: An Argument about Abortion, Euthanasia, and Individual Freedom* (New York: Knopf, 1993); and Elizabeth Mensch and Alan Freeman, *The Politics of Virtue. Is Abortion Debatable?* (Durham: Duke University Press, 1993). For an excellent review of Tribe's book, see Nancy (Ann) Davis, "The Abortion Debate: The Search for Common Ground," *Ethics* 103, no. 3 (April 1993), 516–539 and 103, no. 4 (July 1993), 731–778. For a discussion of abortion within the general context of a theory of compromise, see Martin Benjamin, *Splitting the Difference: Compromise and Integrity in Ethics and Politics* (Lawrence, KS: University of Kansas Press, 1990), esp. pp. 151–171.

# 2

# Euthanasia

**Videotape:**

|            |                                    |
|------------|------------------------------------|
| *Topic:*   | The Right to Die—Dr. Kevorkian     |
| *Source:*  | *Nightline* (December 13, 1993)    |
| *Anchor:*  | Cokie Roberts                      |

# EXPERIENTIAL ACCOUNTS

Anonymous
"It's Over, Debbie"

*The author of this essay remains anonymous; at the time this was written, he or she was a gynecology resident. After the publication of this essay in* JAMA, The Journal of the American Medical Association, *unsuccessful attempts were made to indict the resident for murder.*

*This article describes an actual instance of euthanasia by a physician who at that time was a resident in gynecology. The case of Debbie, as it has come to be known, is discussed in several selections later in this chapter.*

The call came in the middle of the night. As a gynecology resident rotating through a large, private hospital, I had come to detest telephone calls, because invariably I would be up for several hours and would not feel good the next day. However, duty called, so I answered the phone. A nurse informed me that a patient was having difficulty getting rest, could I please see her. She was on 3 North. That was the gynecologic-oncology unit, not my usual duty station. As I trudged along, bumping sleepily against walls and corners and not believing I was up again, I tried to imagine what I might find at the end of my walk. Maybe an elderly woman with an anxiety reaction, or perhaps something particularly horrible.

I grabbed the chart from the nurses station on my way to the patient's room, and the nurse gave me some hurried details: a twenty-year-old girl named Debbie was dying of ovarian cancer. She was having unrelenting vomiting apparently as the result of an alcohol drip administered for sedation. Hmmm, I thought. Very sad. As I approached the room I could hear loud, labored breathing. I entered and saw an emaciated, dark-haired woman who appeared much older than twenty. She was receiving nasal oxygen, had an IV, and was sitting in bed suffering from what was obviously severe air hunger. The chart noted her weight at eighty pounds. A second woman, also dark-haired but of middle age, stood at her right, holding her hand. Both looked up as I entered. The room seemed filled with the patient's desperate effort to survive. Her eyes were hollow, and she had suprasternal and intercostal retractions with her rapid inspirations. She had not eaten or slept in two days. She had not responded to chemotherapy and was being given supportive care only. It was a gallows scene, a cruel mockery of her youth and unfulfilled potential. Her only words to me were, "Let's get this over with."

I retreated with my thoughts to the nurses station. The patient was tired and needed rest. I could not give her health, but I could give her rest. I asked the nurse to draw 20 mg. of morphine sulfate into a syringe. Enough, I thought, to do the job. I took the syringe into the room and told the two women I was going to give Debbie something that would let her rest and to say good-bye. Debbie looked at the syringe, then laid her head on the pillow with her eyes open, watching what was left of the world. I injected the morphine intravenously and watched to see if my calculations would be correct. Within seconds her breathing slowed to a normal rate, her eyes closed, and her features softened as she seemed restful at last. The older woman stroked the hair of the now-sleeping patient. I waited for the inevitable next effect of depressing the respiratory drive. With clocklike certainty, within four minutes the breathing rate slowed even more, then became irregular, then ceased. The dark-haired woman stood erect and seemed relieved.

It's over, Debbie.

## Journal/Discussion Questions

✍ *As you develop your own position on the morality and legality of euthanasia, in what ways does this article help you to develop your own thinking?*

1. If you had been the resident in this situation, what would you have done? Why?

2. One of the major issues in euthanasia is the question of informed consent. Do you think the resident had informed consent? What more, if anything, should have been done to insure informed consent?

3. If you were the district attorney for the city in which this took place, would you seek to charge the resident with a crime? Why or why not?

---

Timothy E. Quill, M.D.
"Death and Dignity:
A Case of Individualized Decision Making"

*Timothy Quill, M.D., specializes in internal medicine, has had experience as a hospice director, and is an associate professor of medicine and psychiatry at the University of Rochester School of Medicine and Dentistry. His book,* Death and Dignity: Making Choices and Taking Charge, *argues in favor of physician-assisted euthanasia.*

*In sharp contrast to the previous selection, this piece depicts a strong and long relationship between a physician and his patient. As the patient, Diane, confronts her terminal cancer, she decides that she does not want extraordinary medical care. Her doctor, Timothy Quill, must then face crucial issues about how willing he is to help to alleviate Diane's suffering and support her choice to die.*

⌒

Diane was feeling tired and had a rash. A common scenario, though there was something subliminally worrisome that prompted me to check her blood count. Her hematocrit was 22, and the white-cell count was 4.3 with some metamyelocytes and unusual white cells. I wanted it to be viral, try-

Timothy Quill, "Death and Dignity," *New England Journal of Medicine* 324 (1991), 691–694. Copyright © 1991, Massachusetts Medical Society. All rights reserved. Reprinted by permission of *The New England Journal of Medicine*.

ing to deny what was staring me in the face. Perhaps in a repeated count it would disappear. I called Diane and told her it might be more serious than I had initially thought—that the test needed to be repeated and that if she felt worse, we might have to move quickly. When she pressed for the possibilities, I reluctantly opened the door to leukemia. Hearing the word seemed to make it exist. "Oh, shit!" she said. "Don't tell me that." Oh, shit! I thought, I wish I didn't have to.

Diane was no ordinary person (although no one I have ever come to know has been really ordinary). She was raised in an alcoholic family and had felt alone for much of her life. She had vaginal cancer as a young woman. Through much of her adult life, she had struggled with depression and her own alcoholism. I had come to know, respect, and admire her over the previous eight years as she confronted these problems and gradually overcame them. She was an incredibly clear, at times brutally honest, thinker and communicator. As she took control of her life, she developed a strong sense of independence and confidence. In the previous 3½ years, her hard work had paid off. She was completely abstinent from alcohol, she had established much deeper connections with her husband, college-age son, and several friends, and her business and her artistic work were blossoming. She felt she was really living fully for the first time.

Not surprisingly, the repeated blood count was abnormal, and detailed examination of the peripheral-blood smear showed myelocytes. I advised her to come into the hospital, explaining that we needed to do a bone marrow biopsy and make some decisions relatively rapidly. She came to the hospital knowing what we would find. She was terrified, angry, and sad. Although we knew the odds, we both clung to the thread of possibility that it might be something else.

The bone marrow confirmed the worst: acute myelomonocytic leukemia. In the face of this tragedy, we looked for signs of hope. This is an area of medicine in which technological intervention has been successful, with cures 25 percent of the time—long-term cures. As I probed the costs of these cures, I heard about induction chemotherapy (three weeks in the hospital, prolonged neutropenia, probable infectious complications, and hair loss; 75 percent of patients respond, 25 percent do not). For the survivors, this is followed by consolidation chemotherapy (with similar side effects; another 25 percent die, for a net survival of 50 percent). Those still alive, to have a reasonable chance of long-term survival, then need bone marrow transplantation (hospitalization for two months and whole-body irradiation, with complete killing of the bone marrow, infectious complications, and the possibility for graft-versus-host disease—with a survival of approximately 50 percent, or 25 percent of the original group). Though hematologists may argue over the exact percentages, they don't argue about the outcome of no treatment—certain death in days, weeks, or at most a few months.

Believing that delay was dangerous, our oncologist broke the news to Diane and began making plans to insert a Hickman catheter and begin induction chemotherapy that afternoon. When I saw her shortly thereafter, she was enraged at his presumption that she would want treatment, and devastated by the finality of the diagnosis. All she wanted to do was go home and be with her family. She had no further questions about treatment and in fact had decided that she wanted none. Together we lamented her tragedy and the unfairness of life. Before she left, I felt the need to be sure that she and her husband understood that there was some risk in delay, that the problem was not going to go away, and that we needed to keep considering the options over the next several days. We agreed to meet in two days.

She returned in two days with her husband and son. They had talked extensively about the problem and the options. She remained very clear about her wish not to undergo chemotherapy and to live whatever time she had left outside the hospital. As we explored her thinking further, it became clear that she was convinced she would die during the period of treatment and would suffer unspeakably in the process (from hospitalization, from lack of control over her body, from the side effects of chemotherapy, and from pain and anguish). Although I could offer support and my best effort to minimize her suffering if she chose treatment, there was no way I could say any of this would not occur. In fact, the last four patients with acute leukemia at our hospital had died very painful deaths in the hospital during various stages of treatment (a fact I did not share with her). Her family wished she would choose treatment but sadly accepted her decision. She articulated very clearly that it was she who would be experiencing all the side effects of treatment and that odds of 25 percent were not good enough for her to undergo so toxic a course of therapy, given her expectations of chemotherapy and hospitalization and the absence of a closely matched bone marrow donor. I had her repeat her understanding of the treatment, the odds, and what to expect if there were no treatment. I clarified a few misunderstandings, but she had a remarkable grasp of the options and implications.

I have been a longtime advocate of active, informed patient choice of treatment or nontreatment, and of a patient's right to die with as much control and dignity as possible. Yet there was something about her giving up a 25 percent chance of long-term survival in favor of almost certain death that disturbed me. I had seen Diane fight and use her considerable inner resources to overcome alcoholism and depression, and I half expected her to change her mind over the next week. Since the window of time in which effective treatment can be initiated is rather narrow, we met several times that week. We obtained a second hematology consultation and talked at length about the meaning and implications of treatment and nontreatment. She talked to a psychologist she had seen in the past. I gradually understood the decision from her perspective and became convinced that it was the right decision for her. We arranged for home hospice care (although at that time Diane felt reasonably well, was active, and looked healthy), left the door open for her to change her mind, and tried to anticipate how to keep her comfortable in the time she had left.

Just as I was adjusting to her decision, she opened up another area that would stretch me profoundly. It was extraordinarily important to Diane to maintain control of herself and her own dignity during the time remaining to her. When this was no longer possible, she clearly wanted to die. As a former director of a hospice program, I know how to use pain medicines to keep patients comfortable and lessen suffering. I explained the philosophy of comfort care, which I strongly believe in. Although Diane understood and appreciated this, she had known of people lingering in what was called relative comfort, and she wanted no part of it. When the time came, she wanted to take her life in the least painful way possible. Knowing of her desire for independence and her decision to stay in control, I thought this request made perfect sense. I acknowledged and explored this wish but also thought that it was out of the realm of currently accepted medical practice and that it was more than I could offer or promise. In our discussion, it became clear that preoccupation with her fear of a lingering death would interfere with Diane's getting the most out of the time she had left until she found a safe way to ensure her death. I feared the effects of a violent death on her family, the consequences of an ineffective suicide that would leave her lingering in precisely the state she dreaded so much, and the possibility that a family member would be forced to assist her, with all the legal and personal repercussions that would follow. She discussed this at length with her family. They believed that they should respect her choice. With this in mind, I told Diane that information was available from the Hemlock Society that might be helpful to her.

A week later she phoned me with a request for barbiturates for sleep. Since I knew that this was an essential ingredient in a Hemlock Society suicide, I asked her to come to the office to talk things over. She was more than willing to protect me by participating in a superficial conversation about her insomnia, but it was important to me to know how she planned to use the drugs and to be sure that she was not in despair or overwhelmed in a way that might color her judgment. In our discussion, it was apparent that she was having trouble sleeping, but it was also evident that the security of having enough barbiturates available to commit suicide when and if the time came would leave her secure enough to live fully and concentrate on the present. It was clear that she was not despondent and that in fact she was making deep, personal connections with her family and close friends. I made sure that she knew how to use the barbiturates for sleep, and also that she knew the amount needed to commit suicide. We agreed to meet regularly, and she promised to meet with me before taking her life, to ensure that all other avenues had been exhausted. I wrote the prescription with an uneasy feeling about the boundaries I was exploring— spiritual, legal, professional, and personal. Yet I also felt strongly that I was setting her free to get the most out of the time she had left, and to maintain dignity and control on her own terms until her death.

The next several months were very intense and important for Diane. Her son stayed home from college, and they were able to be with one another and say much that had not been said earlier. Her husband did his work at home so that he and Diane could spend more time together. She spent time with her closest friends. I had her come into the hospital for a conference with our residents, at which she illustrated in a most profound and personal way the importance of informed decision making, the right to refuse treatment, and the extraordinarily personal effects of illness and interaction with the medical system. There were emotional and physical hardships as well. She had periods of intense sadness and anger. Several times she became very weak, but she received transfusions as an outpatient and responded with marked improvement of symptoms. She had two serious infections that responded surprisingly well to empirical courses of oral antibiotics. After three tumultuous months, there were two weeks of relative calm and well-being, and fantasies of a miracle began to surface.

Unfortunately, we had no miracle. Bone pain, weakness, fatigue, and fevers began to dominate her life. Although the hospice workers, family members, and I tried our best to minimize the suffering and promote comfort, it was clear that the end was approaching. Diane's immediate future held what she feared the most—increasing discomfort, dependence, and hard choices between pain and sedation. She called up her closest friends and asked them to come over to say good-bye, telling them that she would be leaving soon. As we had agreed, she let me know as well. When we met, it was clear that she knew what she was doing, that she was sad and frightened to be leaving, but that she would be even more terrified to stay and suffer. In our tearful good-bye, she promised a reunion in the future at her favorite spot on the edge of Lake Geneva, with dragons swimming in the sunset.

Two days later her husband called to say that Diane had died. She had said her final good-byes to her husband and son that morning, and asked them to leave her alone for an hour. After an hour, which must have seemed an eternity, they found her on the couch, lying very still and covered by her favorite shawl. There was no sign of struggle. She seemed to be at peace. They called me for advice about how to proceed. When I arrived, her husband and son were quiet. We talked about what a remarkable person she had been. They seemed to have no doubts about the course she had chosen or about their cooperation, although the unfairness of her illness and the finality of her death were overwhelming to us all.

I called the medical examiner to inform him that a hospice patient had died. When asked about the cause of death, I said, "acute leukemia." He said that was fine and that we should call a funeral director. Although acute leukemia was the truth, it was not the whole story. Yet any mention of suicide would have given rise to a police investigation and probably brought the arrival of an ambulance crew for resuscitation. Diane would have become a "coroner's case," and the decision to perform an autopsy would have been made at the discretion of the medical examiner. The family or I could have been subject to criminal prosecution, and I to professional review, for our roles in support of Diane's choices. Although I truly believe that the family and I gave her the best care possible, allowing her to define her limits and directions as much as possible, I am not sure the law, society, or the medical profession would agree. So I said "acute leukemia" to protect all of us, to protect Diane from an invasion into her past and her body, and to continue to shield society from the knowledge of the degree of suffering that people often undergo in the process of dying. Suffering can be lessened to some extent, but in no way eliminated or made benign, by the careful intervention of a competent, caring physician, given current social constraints.

Diane taught me about the range of help I can provide if I know people well and if I allow them to say what they really want. She taught me about life, death, and honesty and about taking charge and facing tragedy squarely when it strikes. She taught me that I can take small risks for people that I really know and care about. Although I did not assist in her suicide directly, I helped indirectly to make it possible, successful, and relatively painless. Although I know we have measures to help control pain and lessen suffering, to think that people do not suffer in the process of dying is an illusion. Prolonged dying can occasionally be peaceful, but more often the role of the physician and family is limited to lessening but not eliminating severe suffering.

I wonder how many families and physicians secretly help patients over the edge into death in the face of such severe suffering. I wonder how many severely ill or dying patients secretly take their lives, dying alone in despair. I wonder whether the image of Diane's final aloneness will persist in the minds of her family, or if they will remember more the intense, meaningful months they had together before she died. I wonder whether Diane struggled in that last hour, and whether the Hemlock Society's way of death by suicide is the most benign. I wonder why Diane, who gave so much to so many of us, had to be alone for the last hour of her life. I wonder whether I will see Diane again, on the shore of Lake Geneva at sunset, with dragons swimming on the horizon.

## Journal/Discussion Questions

✍ *Have you ever known anyone in a situation similar to Diane's? How did they deal with it? How would you have dealt with it?*

1. Do you think that Dr. Quill made the right decision in this case? Why or why not? How would you have responded to Diane's decision?

2. Do you think physicians should ever be allowed to assist patients in ending their own lives? What guidelines, if any, would you propose for physicians who face this choice?

# AN INTRODUCTION TO THE MORAL ISSUES

## Introduction

As we consider the details of the issue of euthanasia, it is helpful to begin by realizing the pervasiveness of the issue. Increasingly, people die in a medical context—often a hospital—that is unfamiliar to them and populated primarily by strangers. Currently, 85 percent of Americans die in some kind of health-care facility (this includes not only hospitals, but nursing homes, hospices, etc.); of this group, 70 percent (which is equivalent to almost 60 percent of the population as a whole) choose to withhold some kind of life-sustaining treatment.[1] It is highly likely that each of us will eventually face that same decision about ourselves; it is even more likely that we will indirectly be involved in that decision as family members and loved ones face death.

Dying in a hospital is particularly difficult, for there is nothing within medicine itself—which is tenaciously committed to winning every possible battle with death, even though there is no hope of ever winning the war—that helps physicians to let go, to allow an individual to die peacefully. There are certainly many physicians who show great wisdom in dealing with this issue (the selection from Dr. Quill reprinted below is a good example of this), but their wisdom flows primarily from their character as persons rather than from their medical knowledge. Medical knowledge alone does not tell us when to let go, and medical practice—perhaps quite rightly—is often committed to fighting on and on, no matter what the odds. Yet this means that each of us as patients must face this question squarely.

## What Are We Striving for?

Before we begin to consider some of the intricate conceptual issues posed by euthanasia, it is important to ask ourselves what our goal is in this area. In our discussion of abortion, almost everyone would agree that our ultimate goal was to have a society in which there were no unwanted pregnancies; at that point, abortion would disappear as a moral issue. Obviously, in the case of euthanasia, things are much different. Clearly, we are not striving for a society in which there are no unwanted deaths. That would not only be impossible, but also—as least from a population point of view—undesirable. We cannot do away with death or avoid it.

Given this basic fact, our goal in this area presumably centers around *how* we die, not whether we die. The word "euthanasia" comes from the Greek, *eu*, which means "good" or "well," and the Greek word for death, *thanatos*. In its broadest sense, euthanasia is about dying well. How do we do this?

The first, and most obvious, point is that dying well is intimately linked to living well. It is highly unlikely that we will die well if we have not been able to live well. Those who die surrounded by loved ones and at peace with themselves are those who have lived lives filled with love and who have come to peace with their lives; their lives are, in a certain fundamental sense, complete and not marred by unresolved fundamental regrets. It is very different, I think, for those who have not found love or peace in their lives; their deaths are often characterized by loneliness and a sense of incompleteness, a grasping for what could have been. Much of what needs to be said about euthanasia is not about death, but about life. A good life is the best preparation for a good death. Unfortunately, even a good life is no guarantee of a good death; chance can always intervene to make one's death untimely, unbearably painful, or uncharacteristically lonely.

There is a second, and much narrower, sense of euthanasia: a (relatively) painless death free from the pain and the intrusion of medical attempts to sustain life. Most of the philosophical discussion has centered around this second sense of euthanasia, but some of the difficulties that arise in this second and narrower sense of euthanasia can be reduced if it is placed within the context of this wider sense of euthanasia. All too often, we try through medical means to help an individual to die well, when in actuality all that is within reach medically is to help the person to die painlessly and quickly. A quick and painless death is not the same thing as a good death, but sometimes it is the best we can do.

## Some Initial Distinctions

Recent discussions of euthanasia have been dominated by several important distinctions—and by disagreement over exactly how the distinctions are to be drawn and what significance they should have. The three most important of these are the distinction between active and passive euthanasia, voluntary and involuntary euthanasia, and assisted and unassisted euthanasia. Let's consider each of these in turn.

### Active versus Passive Euthanasia

The distinction between active and passive euthanasia seems, on the surface, easy enough. *Active euthanasia* occurs in those instances in which someone takes active means, such as a lethal injection, to bring about someone's death; *passive euthanasia* occurs in those instances in which someone simply refuses to intervene in order to prevent someone's death. In a hospital setting, a DNR (do not resuscitate) order is one of the most common means of passive euthanasia.

*Conceptual clarity.* This distinction has been attacked in at least two ways. First, some have attacked the *conceptual clarity* of the distinction, arguing that the line between active and passive is much more blurred than one might initially think. One reason this distinction becomes conceptually slippery, especially in regard to the notion of passive euthanasia, is that it is embedded in a background set of assumptions about what constitutes normal care and what the normal duties of care givers are. In typical hospital settings, there is a distinction between ordinary and extraordinary care. At one end of the spectrum, giving someone food and water is clearly ordinary care; at the other end of the spectrum, giving someone an emergency heart and lung transplant to save that person's life is

*How do we draw the line between killing and letting die?*

clearly extraordinary care. Refusing to give food and water seems to be different than refusing to perform a transplant. Both are passive, but one involves falling below the expectations of normal care while the other does not. Typically, DNRs would fall somewhere in the middle ground on this scale. The source of this bit of conceptual slipperiness comes from that we need to distinguish between two levels of passive euthanasia: (a) refusing to provide extraordinary care, and (b) refusing to provide any life-sustaining care at all. Just as in daily life we would distinguish between the person who refuses to jump into a turbulent sea to save a drowning child and the person who refuses to reach into a bathtub to save a baby drowning there, so, too, in medical contexts, we must distinguish between refusing to take extraordinary means to prevent death and refusing to provide normal care (such as nutrition and hydration) to sustain life.

There is at least a second reason why this distinction is conceptually slippery, especially in regard to the notion of active euthanasia. As we have already seen in our discussion of abortion, philosophers distinguish between the intended consequences of an action and the unintended (but foreseeable) consequences of an action. This distinction is crucial to the principle of the double effect, which under certain specifiable conditions morally permits an individual to perform an action that would otherwise not be allowed. Many Catholic ethicians, for example, would argue that a physician might be morally permitted to perform a surgical procedure such as a hysterectomy to remove a cancerous uterus even if this results in the death of a fetus, as long as the intention was not to kill the fetus, the cause was serious, and there was no other means to that end. Similarly, physicians might give certain terminal patients pain-killers in large dosages, realizing that such dosages might cause death but having no other way of alleviating the patient's extreme pain.

*Moral significance.*    In addition to attacking the conceptual clarity of the active/passive distinction, some ethicists have attacked the *moral significance* of this distinction. The standard view is that active euthanasia is morally much more questionable than passive euthanasia, since it involves actively choosing to bring about the death of a human being. Critics of the moral significance of this distinction have argued that active euthanasia is often more compassionate than passive euthanasia and morally preferable to it. The typical type of case they adduce is one in which (a) there is no doubt that the patient will die soon, (b) the option of passive euthanasia causes significantly more pain for the patient (and often the family as well) than active euthanasia and does nothing to enhance the remaining life of the patient, and (c) passive measures will not bring about the death of the patient. Certain types of cancers are not only extremely painful but also very resistant to pain-killing medications in dosages that still permit patients to be aware of themselves and those around them. It is not uncommon for situations to occur in which patients will undoubtedly die (within several days, if not hours) and in which their remaining time will be filled either with extreme pain or unconsciousness resulting from pain medication. Removal of life-support may not bring about the death of such patients if their heart and respiratory systems have not been seriously compromised. In such situations, passive euthanasia seems to be *crueler* than active euthanasia and therefore morally less preferable.

## Voluntary, Nonvoluntary, and Involuntary Euthanasia

The second crucial distinction in discussion of euthanasia is among voluntary, nonvoluntary, and involuntary euthanasia. Voluntary euthanasia occurs when the individual chooses to die; nonvoluntary euthanasia occurs when the individual's death is brought about (either actively or passively) without the individual's choosing to die; involuntary euthanasia occurs when the individual's death is brought about against the individual's wishes. Several points need to be made about this distinction.

*The Distinction between nonvoluntary and involuntary.*   Involuntary euthanasia covers those cases in which an individual does not want to be euthanized; nonvoluntary euthanasia refers to those in which the individual cannot make an expressed choice at all. The former class of cases is clearly troubling: the individual wishes to live and someone else intentionally terminates that individual's life. Most would say that this is simply murder. The latter class of cases is more common and morally more ambiguous. How do we treat those individuals, usually terminally ill and unable to choose (due to coma or some other medical condition), who may be in great pain and who have never clearly expressed their wishes about euthanasia in the past? Similarly, infants are unable to express their wishes about this (or any other) matter. If euthanasia is employed in such cases, it is involuntary, but not in the same sense as it is involuntary when the patient has expressed a clear wish not to be euthanized. Thus we get the following type of division.

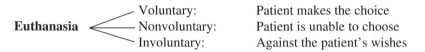

|  |  |  |
|---|---|---|
| | Voluntary: | Patient makes the choice |
| **Euthanasia** | Nonvoluntary: | Patient is unable to choose |
| | Involuntary: | Against the patient's wishes |

The morally most troubling of these cases will be those of involuntary euthanasia where the patient is unable to choose.

## Assisted versus Unassisted Euthanasia

The final important distinction in the discussion of euthanasia centers about the fact that many instances of euthanasia occur when an individual is no longer physically able to carry out the act. Assistance becomes necessary, either to perform the action at all or at least to die in a relatively painless and nonviolent way. Several important points need to be noted about this distinction. This chart helps us to see the ways in which these basic distinctions relate to one another, the types of acts they designate, and their current legal status in the United States.

### Euthanasia: Some Fundamental Distinctions

|  | Passive | Active: Not Assisted | Active: Assisted |
|---|---|---|---|
| Voluntary | Currently legal; often contained in living wills | Equivalent to suicide for the patient | Equivalent to suicide for the patient; Possibly equivalent to murder for the assistant |
| Nonvoluntary: Patient Not Able to Choose | Sometimes legal, but only with court permission | Not possible | Equivalent to either suicide or being murdered for the patient; Legally equivalent to murder for the assistant |
| Involuntary: Against Patient's Wishes | Not Legal | Not possible | Equivalent to being murdered for the patient; Equivalent to murder for assistant |

Equipped with these distinctions, let's now turn to a consideration of the fundamental moral issues raised by euthanasia, looking first at the justifications that have been offered for and against euthanasia and then considering the three most typical types of cases: defective newborns, adults with profoundly diminished lives, and those in the final and painful phase of a terminal illness.

## Euthanasia As the Compassionate Response to Suffering

One of the principal moral motives that moves us toward euthanasia is compassion: we see needless suffering, whether in ourselves or others, we want to alleviate or end it, and euthanasia is the only means of doing so. The paradigmatic situation here is that of a patient who is near death, who is in great pain that is not responsive to medication, and who has made an informed choice to die. At that juncture, those who care about the patient simply want the patient's suffering to end—there seems to be no point in further suffering, for there is no hope of recovery—and euthanasia becomes the way of ending it.

It is important to understand the *intention* contained in this kind of response. The direct intention is not to kill the patient; neither is it is utilitarian intention concerning the reduction of the overall amount of suffering; nor is it an egoistic intention that simply seeks to be rid of an annoying relative. Rather, the direct intention is simply to stop the patient's pointless suffering. In passive euthanasia, the means is the withholding or withdrawal of life-sustaining treatment; in active euthanasia, the means for ending that suffering is some action—such as a lethal injection—that brings about the death of the patient. There are certainly situations in which passive euthanasia would not quickly end the suffering; patients may continue to live, sometimes for days, in great agony once life-support has been removed. In such cases, active euthanasia offers the only avenue for ending the pain. It is precisely this type of response that has come to be known as "mercy killing." If any situation justifies active euthanasia, this would seem to be it.

*Is euthanasia a proper way to express one's compassion for the suffering of the dying?*

Some cases of compassionate euthanasia can be viewed as an instance of the principle of double effect, but only when the intention was still to relieve pain. If a physician was administering increasingly large doses of pain medication which eventually and foreseeably resulted in the patient's death, this could be covered under the principle of the double effect as long as the intention throughout was to relieve the patient's pain. It's not clear, however, whether this is really euthanasia; it seems better described as a last-ditch, high-risk attempt to alleviate the patient's suffering.

There is a sense in which the motivation and justification of compassionate euthanasia may appear to be utilitarian, or at least consequentialist, in character: the concern is with eliminating pointless suffering. It asks what good comes from the suffering and what bad comes from the termination of the suffering. But there are two ways in which the motivation for this response is not utilitarian in the standard sense. First, it is concerned principally, perhaps even exclusively, with the welfare of the patient, not with the *overall* welfare. Second, it is not a *calculated* response in the way in which classical utilitarianism is; rather, it is a response from the heart, a compassionate response that seeks to eliminate the pointless suffering of someone we care about. It arises, not out of calculation, but out of care.

The adjective "pointless" is crucial here for two reasons. First, it indicates that euthanasia is not a proper response to *all* suffering, only to that suffering which serves no purpose. Generally, suffering that results in the patient's getting better (or at least improving to some minimally accept-able level) is not seen as pointless. Second, it helps explain part of the disagreement in our own so-ciety about the morality of euthanasia. Our views on euthanasia will depend in part on our back-ground assumptions about the nature and purpose of suffering. Once again, we see that there are at least two distinct traditions here. On the one hand, many in our society hold that suffering always has a purpose—usually a purpose that God can discern, even if we mere mortals cannot. It may build character, purify an individual, provide an example to others, provide retribution, or serve some part in a larger plan beyond our grasp. On this view, even the suffering in the final stage of a terminal illness serves some purpose, although we may not be able to say what it is. On the other hand, many others in our society believe that suffering is simply an unqualified evil that should be eradicated whenever possible. Suffering, on this view, is always pointless in itself, even if it is sometimes unavoidable for the sake of some other goal such as recovering from an illness. These two views on suffering will be discussed in more detail in the next section.

This compassionate response may not be limited just to cases of extreme pain in terminally ill patients; it may extend, at least in respect to passive euthanasia, to cases of extreme physical debility or to cases of Alzheimer's where the individual's personal identity has long ago been lost. The prin-cipal criterion here would seem to be the individual's wish no longer to be alive under such condi-tions—whether that wish is currently expressed or had been expressed clearly at an earlier point in life. Again, the focus here is on what the person wants and what is in the person's best interest.

## The Sanctity of Life and the Right to Die

There are very few villains in the debate over euthanasia, but there are disagreements about the in-terpretation and relative place of certain fundamental values and rights. One of the most prominent areas of conflict centers around the relationship between the sanctity of life and the right to die.

### The Sanctity of Life

Human life, many of us believe, is sacred. In its original form, this belief is a religious one; the sanctity of life is an indication that life is a gift from God and therefore cannot be ended by human hand without violating God's law or rejecting God's love. Moreover, in its original form—one sees this most clearly in Buddhism, but also in other religious traditions—this belief encom-passes *all* life, not just human life. In this form, it is not only a tradition that encompasses pacifism and opposes capital punishment, abortion, and euthanasia, but also one that respects the lives of an-imals and the living environment as a whole. Life is a sacred gift from God, and it is not the proper role of human beings to take it away from anyone. Respect for life, in the words of one Catholic bishop, is a "seamless garment" which covers the entire fabric of living creation. No distinction is drawn about the quality of life. All life is to be respected, loved, and cared for. It is this tradition that leads to the compassion of the Buddha and of Mother Theresa.

Followers of this tradition do not support either active or passive euthanasia in the senses discussed here. However, they certainly are committed to the broader sense of "dying well" dis-cussed above, and spiritual discipline is often part of that commitment. So, too, is ministering to the sick and dying. Their alternative to active or passive euthanasia in the Western sense is not ne-glect, but compassion and love and ministering to the sick, the infirm, and the dying.

## The Right to Die

Those who argue that human beings have a right to die usually differ from those who stress the sanctity of life on two principal points. First, and more importantly, they do not see life as a gift from God that cannot be disposed of at will; instead, they often see life ontologically as an accident and almost always morally as the possession of an individual. The dominant metaphor here is of life as property rather than gift. In this tradition, each person is seen as *owning* his or her own life, and owners are allowed to do whatever they want with their property. Second, respect for life in this tradition entails allowing the proper owner—that is, the individual—to decide for himself or herself whether to continue living. Notice that this tradition does not deny respect for life; rather, it has a different view of the source of life and of who holds proper dominion over life.

*Do we have a right to die?*

Those in this tradition respond quite differently to illnesses that profoundly reduce the quality of an individual's life or produce great and needless pain. Their focus is on reducing suffering, maintaining a minimal threshold of quality for the individual's life, and encouraging individuals to make their own decisions about the termination of their own life. The focus is thus on the quality of life and individual autonomy. The types of cases that those in this tradition point to are usually cases in which individuals want to die in order to end their suffering but are kept alive against their own wishes because a family member, the court, or in some cases the administrators of health care facilities—ever fearful of suits and federal investigations—are unwilling to let them die.

Yet there is also an irony in this tradition, for its emphasis on technology and control helps to create the very problem that it then seeks to solve through euthanasia. Just as it prolongs life through technology, it then must figure out how to end life technologically. Active euthanasia for the chronically ill and slowly dying rarely arises as an issue in nontechnological societies because, prior to the introduction of modern, high-tech medicine, people either died or got better.

## The Conflict of Traditions

It is important to understand the nature of this disagreement—and it is especially important to avoid certain easy ways of misunderstanding it. This is not a conflict between those who respect life and those who do not, nor is it a conflict between those who are indifferent to suffering and those who seek to eliminate it. Rather, it is a conflict between two types traditions, both of which respect life and both of which encourage compassion and the reduction of suffering. The differences between them center around how they understand life and what they accept as legitimate ways of reducing suffering.

How do we respond to such a conflict? Certainly one common response is to look for a winner, marshaling arguments in support of one tradition and against the other. My own inclination, however, is quite different. I think that we are better off as a society precisely because both of these traditions are present and vital. Each keeps the other in check, as it were. The sanctity-of-life tradition continually reminds us of our own frailty, of the fact that we are not masters of the universe; it checks our inclination toward *hubris*. The right-to-die tradition, on the other hand, stresses the importance of reducing suffering in the world and increasing individual autonomy. I think our moral world would be impoverished if we had only one of these traditions. Let's see how this works out in practice.

## The Value of Life and the Cost of Caring

In the *Groundwork of a Metaphysics of Morals*, Immanuel Kant drew a crucial moral distinction between rational beings and mere things.[2] Everything, Kant maintains, has either a *price* or a *dignity*. Mere things always have a price, that is, an equivalent value of some kind (usually a monetary one); they can be exchanged one for the other. Rational beings, however, have dignity, for the value of a human being is such that it is beyond all calculations of price; they cannot be exchanged, one for the other. In drawing this distinction, Kant articulated a moral insight that remains powerful today: the belief that human life is priceless and that we therefore ought not to put a price tag on it. Human life is to be preserved at all costs, for the value of human life is beyond that of any costs. Indeed, this may well be one of the motivations in critical care situations when the full arsenal of medicine's skill and technology is brought to bear on a frail, old, dying person in order to prolong his or her life for a few days, weeks, or even months. We cannot put a price tag on human life, the Kantian inside us says. There is something morally odious about thinking that a human life can be traded for something else.

*Can we put a price tag on human life?*

Many of us find that Kant's insight strikes a resonant chord in our moral lives, but that there is another, potentially dissonant note in all of this. Costs *do* matter, as utilitarians make clear, although there is much disagreement about the kinds of costs and how much they matter. We can see this on both the personal level and on the level of social policy. On the personal level, individuals and families struggle with this issue. Imagine a family, such as the one given in the case study at the beginning of this chapter, with a member who requires costly and continual medical care that goes well beyond insurance; family resources—emotional as well as financial—may be drained in the attempt to continue care. Here costs are not simply monetary, but also emotional and spiritual. Financial costs are not limited simply to restrictions on the family vacation, but may extend into areas such as education that directly affect the welfare of the children in the family. Similarly, emotional and spiritual costs to the family may be quite high, although these costs may be more evenly distributed over the range of options.

On the social policy level, we recognize that an amazingly large percentage of our health care dollars are spent on persons during the final weeks of their lives, and ethicists such as Daniel Callahan have maintained that we ought not to spend our money and resources in this way. Although firmly opposing active euthanasia, Callahan maintains that we should respect the natural life span and we should not use intrusive means—such as respirators and feeding tubes—to keep the elderly alive. Here we have some degree of passive involuntary euthanasia, at least for those who lack the private financial resources to pay for continued extraordinary care. This raises the specter of involuntary passive euthanasia for all but the rich. Of course, this is only an inequity if we believe that a longer life under such conditions is better than a shorter one.

## Slippery Slopes

Even among those who are not opposed to euthanasia in principle, there are serious reservations about the possibility that legalizing euthanasia could lead to abuses. Once the door is opened even a little, the danger is that more will be permitted—either through further legalization or because of objectionable but common abuses which, while not permitted by the new proposal, could not be effectively curbed—than we would originally wanted. History makes us cautious. Euthanasia of the physically and mentally handicapped was part of Hitler's plan, and by some estimates as many as 200,000 handicapped people were killed as part of the Nazi eugenics program. Not surprisingly, many are watching the Netherlands very carefully now, for active euthanasia has been tolerated there for a number of years and legalized in 1994.

## Undervalued Groups

The slippery slope argument has an added dimension when placed within a social context of discrimination. In a society in which the lives of certain classes of people are typically undervalued, legalized euthanasia could become a further instrument of discrimination. The classes discriminated against may vary from society to society, and the classes may be based on race, ethnicity, gender, social orientation, religious beliefs, social class, age, or some other characteristic. However the classes are determined, the point remains the same: legalized euthanasia would be more likely to encourage the early deaths of members of those classes that are discriminated against in society. For this argument to work, it must either presuppose that euthanasia is bad in itself or

*Would the legalization of euthanasia open the door to further abuses?*

else that it would encourage certain morally unjustified kinds of euthanasia such as involuntary euthanasia. The latter line of argument seems to be plausible, namely, that the legalization of voluntary euthanasia would result in undue pressure on certain segments of society to "choose" euthanasia when they did not really want to do so.

There is certainly no shortage of undervalued groups in the United States. Some groups are racially constituted: some Native Americans and some African Americans feel that their people have been treated in ways that have genocidal overtones. For them, it is extremely important that they have especially strong guarantees that they will not be the objects of euthanasia disproportionately. Similar issues exist for the poor and the homeless, but they are often less able to advance their own interests in public forums. Finally, and perhaps most pervasively, the elderly in the United States (and elsewhere as well) form a group that is highly undervalued. Several factors contribute to this. First, our society tends to value youth rather than age, aggressive problem-solving intelligence and new ideas rather than the wisdom of long experience. Second, our society tends to value work, and the elderly are often retired and no longer able to be productive. Third, our society tends to be highly mobile, and as a result elderly parents often live in a different location from their children; extended, loving families are hard to find. Fourth, as the percentage of the entire population that is over sixty-five grows, this will put increasing pressure on our social welfare resources; the possibility of increasing resentment toward the aged by younger generations in our society is certainly great.

## Moral Pluralism

Any satisfactory proposal for liberalizing the euthanasia laws must contain adequate provisions to prevent it from sliding down the slope to unacceptable practices. It is here that a pluralistic approach has much to recommend itself, for by encouraging both traditions it provides a check on each. Just as pro-choice forces will try to minimize cases in which people are kept alive and suffering against their will, so, too, pro-life forces will try to ensure that euthanasia is used only in cases where everyone wants it. It is precisely the tension between traditions that helps to reduce the likelihood that one will slide down the slope.

### Endnotes

1. Miles S. Gomez C., *Protocols for Elective Use of Life-Sustaining Treatment* (New York: Springer-Verlag, 1988). Cited in Margaret Battin, "Euthanasia: The Way We Do It, the Way They Do It," *Journal of Pain and Symptom Management* 6, no. 5, 298–305.
2. Immanuel Kant, *The Moral Law: Kant's Groundwork of the Metaphysic of Morals,* trans. and anal. H. J. Paton (London: Hutchinson University Library, 1969), pp. 96–97.

## Journal Questions

✍ *Under what conditions, if any, would you want others to withhold medical treatment from you? To withhold fluids and nutrition? To actively terminate your life?*

✍ *Write your own living will, including in it all instructions and requests you think are relevant.*

# THE ARGUMENTS

**Kenneth L. Vaux**
"The Theologic Ethics of Euthanasia"

*Kenneth L. Vaux is professor of theological ethics at Ganett-Evangelical Theological Seminary at Northwestern University. His books include* Will to Live, Will to Die: Ethics and the Search for a Good Death; Birth Ethics: Religious and Cultural Values in the Genesis of Life; Death Ethics: Religious and Cultural Values in Prolonging and Ending Life; *and* Ethics and the Gulf War: Religion, Rhetoric, and Righteousness.

*Situating the issue of euthanasia within the context of Christian religious belief, Vaux argues against acting with the intention of bringing about death; he accepts, however, that it is morally acceptable "to administer potentially lethal analgesia in the relief of pain."*

## As You Read, Consider This:

1. How, according to Vaux, should the physician have responded to "Debbie"? In what ways do you agree and disagree with Vaux's analysis of this case?

2. What values does Vaux claim are at the heart of his "transcendant ethic"? To what extent are these values dependent on his particular religious beliefs?

As Easter approached, the contrast of the two pronouncements kept going through my mind:

> I injected the morphine intravenously . . . within seconds her breathing slowed to a normal rate. Her eyes closed and her features softened. She seemed restful at last. The older woman stroked the hair of the now-sleeping patient. I waited for the inevitable next effect of depressing the respiratory drive . . . the breathing slowed . . . became irregular, then ceased. It's over, Debbie.[1]

> The strife is o'er, the battle done, the victory o'er death is won. The song of triumph has begun. Hallelujah![2]

Debbie's was one of those epochal cases that seem to engage our whole society in an issue that troubles everyone to the very core of his being. Current practices in Holland and political initiatives in the United States suggest an urgency to debate on euthanasia with implications spanning personal, professional, and legal concerns. How shall we personally meet a good death? How shall physicians act in the face of terminal illness and imminent death? What policy, if any, shall our society promulgate?

# A Transcendant Ethic

The questions of deliberate death and euthanasia present issues that move our reflection beyond the customary modes of ethical analysis. We are no longer faced with the gruesome stipulates of an "ecological ethic" of weeding out the old and the weak. Here also we move beyond the philosophic ethic that speaks of a "right to die," a professional ethic that affirms a "duty to preserve life," and the legal ethic that proscribes acts of medical murder, even if the victim is a pleading patient and the perpetrator a compassionate physician. At times such as this, what is called for is an ethic transcending both reason and convention, an ethic rooted in patient plight and the ultimate ground of being. For here we touch the mysteries of life and death, and face the human impulses of risk, guilt, and sacrifice. In these moments, and "borderline situations," other parameters of ethics do not fit.

Yet the radical and "different" ethic required is also traditional, in that its elements are imbedded in particular cultures. The dominant moral ethos in America is Christian, commingled with Judaism and secular humanism. Our religio-moral ethos is anchored in beliefs of radical ethical freedom, the sacred origin and destiny of the human soul, persistent sin, and the drama of suffering, death, and transfiguration as a decisional paradigm for difficult choices. It is grounded in belief in the sacredness of the human being in vitality and in frailty, and in the ultimacy of grace and forgiveness. These convictions should profoundly influence our perspectives on euthanasia.

When a situation or moral decision is viewed theologically in this manner, three new ethical perspectives are disclosed. First, when God is acknowledged as the giver, sustainer, and receiver of life, we see and evaluate that life with awe and wonder; responses of quick dispatch or highly principled withdrawal are no longer possible. We also view death as transparent and nonfinal. Though death is feared because life is celebrated, this fear is transformed by belief in the reality of life hereafter. Finally, we are prompted to give "intensive" care and companionship to the dying.

What implications does this system of theological ethics hold for the issue of euthanasia?

# Types of Euthanasia

Let us begin with the most easily justifiable class of cases, passive euthanasia, in which death occurs in the course of treating a terminally ill person by forgoing potentially life-prolonging measures. It is not considered obligatory to initiate CPR, antimicrobial therapy, mechanical ventilation, or artificial nutrition and hydration when it is futile or only marginally helpful. Patients are not obliged to accept surgery, organ transplantation, or mechanical organs when hearts or kidneys fail. We are learning when to partake in technology's feast and when to decline—what Ivan Illich calls a "technofast." As free, responsible, and immortal creatures, we will often find passive euthanasia acceptable.

A second class of actions can be designated "double effect euthanasia." Theologically and morally it is acceptable for a patient to choose palliative treatments that may result in death and for a physician to administer potentially lethal analgesia in the relief of pain. And many ethicists argue that the administrator of a lethal dosage is not culpable if his primary intent is to relieve suffering, though the ensuing death may be foreseeable, so long as the patient and family consent.

We might understand Debbie's case best from this perspective. Debbie suffered from ovarian cancer; she was given morphine to relieve her suffering, but it also happened to hasten her death.

This type of double-edged intention and bivalent action is certainly the most difficult to assess morally. The unfortunate side-effect was grievous, but not unethical. In the narrative, the doctor's stated intent seemed to be to provide relief and restfully aware that the merciful analgesia might end the patient's life. We can also infer that the slated intent to kill was not serious, but rather a melodramatic or anguished afterthought. Morphine is not normally a drug used for suicide or homicide. Often it does not depress respiratory function and since pain increases respiration the relief given by morphine usually diminishes a respiratory crisis. Moreover, twenty milligrams of morphine for a terminal cancer patient in intense pain is, in the words of one expert on oncologic analgesia, "a piddly dose." In cancer clinics today patients are given 140, 400, even in exceptional cases 700 mg per hour of morphine. The resident could not possibly know in advance that this dosage would cause certain death. I would infer from both the choice and dosage of medication that this was a case of double effect euthanasia, even if the expressed premeditation and volition were ambiguous. This doctor entertained, I believe, both the hope of rest and relief and the probability of death.

Our moral heritage condones mercy in the face of suffering, courage in the face of uncertainty, and forgiveness in the face of tragic extremes; my colleagues in the Roman Catholic tradition, for example, counsel that compassion dictates that one offer relief to someone in Debbie's situation. It would be unconscionable to condemn a patient to greater anguish because of guilt-ridden hesitancy to risk death. Our moral tradition demands that we act courageously, even though our actions might result in double effect euthanasia.

## Exceptional Case Euthanasia

A third and controversial type of action, active euthanasia, must be proscribed in principle, but the tradition of medicine, religious tradition, and contemporary precedent may permit it in exceptional cases. This permission has always existed alongside the dominant ethic of prolonging and sustaining life. Paul Carrick, a scholar of ancient medical ethics, contends that the physician "possessed what might be described as a discretionary professional right to assist in abortion or voluntary euthanasia."[3]

The position of "exceptional case" euthanasia is grounded in classical clinical wisdom. In this tradition the physician was discouraged from invading the atrium of death therapeutically or technologically. Attempts to cure were now to yield to attempts to comfort. In the Hippocratic treatise *The Art*, the *techne iatrihe* is defined as follows:

> In general terms, it is (1) to do away with the sufferings of the sick, (2) to lessen the violence of their diseases, and (3) to refuse to treat those who are overmastered by their diseases, realizing that in such cases medicine is powerless.[4]

This reflects the fundamental religious and ethical genius of classical ethics: In the atrium of death, one's life is given over to the transcending spirit who gave it. The god known by the Pythagorean mystics at the vortex of temporal perfection, at the junction of the finite and the infinite, was the lord of death. In both a natural and a transcendent perspective it is a graceful virtue to accept death.

In Hebraic and Christian medicine, art becomes ministry and service. In Judaism the *gosos*, or imminently dying one, is treated with reverence and respect. Christianity, which historically extolled and endorsed the moral and spiritual excellence of the sect of Hippocrates, exhibited the same awe and reverence for the dying individual. However, Greek contempt for the material body was transformed into esteem and stewardship, and the centrality of the crucified one in faith created a new positive meaning to excruciating suffering.

It is remarkable that, with these prolongevist impulses, the tradition contended that death could be greeted boldly and triumphantly, and that no one should impede another in his appointed hour. In the Christian perspective the recognition of impending death initiated the *ars moriendi*. The art of dying now included the individual's preparations for and orchestration of the dying process, and signaled the withdrawal to only modest medical activity. In the English *Prayerbook* one prays to be delivered from a swift and unexpected death, where one is denied the grace of such preparation and orchestration.

Beginning in the middle decades of this century we transformed death into an act of human deliberation and technological manipulation. How has this come about? First of all, modern diseases have displaced earlier diseases; newer chronic conditions have replaced acute illness. By significantly checking infections with vaccines and antibiotics we have opened the door of morbidity, which like the door of mortality seems to be a constant in human history. Now it has been opened to chronic diseases like Alzheimer's, osteoporosis, arthritis, and cancer.

Today a vivid set of cases involving patients who are not dying but are suffering from the final stages of Lou Gehrig's disease, cystic fibrosis, cerebral palsy, or other irreversible and fatal afflictions have been set before us in newspapers, courts, and television dramas. Some of these patients eventually ask their physicians to disconnect life-supports and ease them into death with barbiturates and muscle relaxants.[5] In my view such cases are compelling and justify active euthanasia.

The most moving evidence I have witnessed for this direction in my twenty-five years as a consultant in medical ethics is the testimony of ethical and humane physicians who out of love would give a lethal dose to their wife, parent, or other loved one if his or her dying was marked by suffering and agony. I find it strange and hypocritical that the imperative of compassion would allow an action with loved ones but not with patients. This may say that we have lost empathy, sympathy, and the covenant of care with those who have entrusted their lives to us because they believe we embody those very qualities.

## Physician Participation

The life-and-death nature of a scenario like Debbie's is in a sense a contrivance of our own making. Chemotherapy radically altered her entire physiology and biochemistry. Her pain thresholds and equilibrium were modified by the disease and by analgesia, and her nutritional state maintained completely by artificial means. She is dying in a hospital. The entire situation is one of technological and institutional contrivance. Now, in the words of the Czech playwright Capek, we must become accountable for "what we have wrought." It would be a moral cop-out to act boldly and put a Swann-Ganz catheter in her neck and a mechanical respirator tube down her throat to save her life, and then plead incompetence and reluctant conscience to remove them when it becomes clear she cannot recover.

In Debbie's case more faithful care would have been slow and deliberate, across several hours. The physician should have drained the effusion in her chest, titrated morphine every two minutes until her pain was relieved, and then made considerate decisions with her about the need for resuscitation and other expected events. All this should have been done with the fully informed consent of the primary physician, health team, chaplain, ethics committee, and loved ones. This more customary protocol should have been followed not to draw out her suffering—an absolute ethical prohibition—but rather to attend her need in the most humane and sensitive manner possible.

If this line of argument is valid, it follows that the physician should superintend and participate in his patient's dying. The patient and physician should come to "will one will" together in receiving death. This new engagement with the patient, involving informing, consenting, and to use Paul Ramsey's felicitous phrase, "co-adventuring," is incurred by the changes in the patient's readiness for death, brought about by the preceding series of interventions.

Death is different in our time. Some will succumb to sudden coronary death, others to stroke or myocardial infarction. Some will contract pneumonia and die swiftly. Others will commit suicide. Yet a large number of people will move toward chronic patterns of demise. Patients with cancer, arthritis, Alzheimer's, AIDS, emphysema, and other afflictions will now have the occasion to deliberate and decide the time and manner of their own deaths. This opportunity will give patients, physicians, and pastors new possibilities for courage, responsibility, and sympathetic cooperation.

We must, at this point, acknowledge and respond to a formidable conviction that presents a different conclusion. As he confronted his own terminal illness and impending death, Paul Ramsey wrote an essay entitled, "Should Physicians Hasten the Death Angel When She Pauses in Her Flight?" in which he argued that the medical-ethical and biblical traditions, the normative centers of our moral system, absolutely condemn "the intention to cause death."[6] In his inimitable way he criticized both the active euthanasic modes of "strychnine, gun, and morphine" and the passive modes of withdrawing nutrition and hydration. For Ramsey the will is decisive; paraphrasing papal teaching, he concluded that "any act or omission that by design and in reality brings on death is wrong morally."

While I wholeheartedly agree with the general tenor of Ramsey's view, I suggest that he has not fully understood how we have already "designed" the death-defying and death-prolonging situation. We have created the conditions for suspension of mortality so that it becomes morally incumbent upon us willfully to offer at some point a fissure of release in our own barricade. Having barred the door to Death, are we not then obliged at some point to open it?

Resisting death is indeed noble; we must do it. But we must finally yield. As Teilhard said:

> We must struggle against death with all our force, for it is our fundamental duty as living creatures. But when by virtue of a state of things, death takes us, we must experience that paroxysm of faith in life that causes us to abandon ourselves to death as to a falling into a greater life.[7]

We must beware of allowing a case like Debbie's to create a general medical precedent. But neither should our fearful antipathy toward what happened to her make us inhumanely force individuals to outlive themselves. Just as physicians must not be accomplices to the modern euthanasic ritual we euphemistically call cost cutting, they must never open themselves to the currently widespread criticism that they cruelly prolong patients' dying. Our irresistible technology, joined to an insatiable need to help and an incoherent fear of death, could do this to us. Alternatively a new courage, grace, and reciprocity may mark our future, if we choose.

## Endnotes

1. Full discussion of the Debbie case can be found in the *Journal of the American Medical Association* 259, no. 2 (1988), 292; 259, no. 14 (1988), 2094–2098, 2139–2143; 260, no. 6 (1988), 787–789.

2. Easter hymn.

3. Paul Carrick, *Medical Ethics in Antiquity* (Boston: D. Reidel, 1985), p. 158.

4. Hippocrates, *The Art,* II, p. 193.

5. Andrew H. Malcolm, "To Suffer a Prolonged Illness or Elect to Die," *The New York Times,* 16 December 1984, pp. 1, 18.

6. To appear in *Covenants of Life: Contemporary Medical Ethics in Light of the Thought of Paul Ramsey—Essays and Response*, ed. Kenneth Vaux (Urbana, IL: University of Illinois Press) (forthcoming).

7. Pierre Teilhard de Chardin, *On Suffering* (New York: Harper & Row, 1979), p. 58.

## Journal/Discussion Questions

✍ *Vaux's article raises questions of the relationship between religious beliefs and ethics. How, if at all, do your religious beliefs and values affect your standing on euthanasia?*

1. When, according to Vaux, is active euthanasia morally permissible? What justification does he offer for this position? Do you agree? Why or why not?

2. Vaux discusses the *principle of the double effect.* What is this principle? In what ways do you agree and disagree with Vaux's application of this principle to the issue of euthanasia?

## James Rachels
## "Active and Passive Euthanasia"

*James Rachels is one of the most prominent of contemporary moral philosophers, especially in the area of applied ethics. His books include* Created from Animals: The Moral Implications of Darwinism, The Elements of Moral Philosophy, *and* The End of Life: The Morality of Euthanasia.

*This article, originally published in a medical journal and directed toward physicians, was the first major challenge to the moral significance of the distinction between active and passive euthanasia.*

James Rachels, "Active and Passive Euthanasia," *New England Journal of Medicine* 292 (1975), 78–80. Reprinted by permission of *The New England Journal of Medicine*.

## As You Read, Consider This:

1. Why, according to Rachels, is active euthanasia morally preferable to passive euthanasia in some cases?
2. What, according to Rachels, is the difference between killing and letting die?

⌒

The distinction between active and passive euthanasia is thought to be crucial for medical ethics. The idea is that it is permissible, at least in some cases, to withhold treatment and allow a patient to die, but it is never permissible to take any direct action designed to kill the patient. This doctrine seems to be accepted by most doctors, and it is endorsed in a statement adopted by the House of Delegates of the American Medical Association on December 4, 1973:

> The intentional termination of the life of one human being by another—mercy killing—is contrary to that for which the medical profession stands and is contrary to the policy of the American Medical Association.
> The cessation of the employment of extraordinary means to prolong the life of the body when there is irrefutable evidence that biological death is imminent is the decision of the patient and/or his immediate family. The advice and judgment of the physician should be freely available to the patient and/or his immediate family.

However, a strong case can be made against this doctrine. In what follows I will set out some of the relevant arguments, and urge doctors to reconsider their views on this matter.

To begin with a familiar type of situation, a patient who is dying of incurable cancer of the throat is in terrible pain, which can no longer be satisfactorily alleviated. He is certain to die within a few days, even if present treatment is continued, but he does not want to go on living for those days since the pain is unbearable. So he asks the doctor for an end to it, and his family joins in the request.

Suppose the doctor agrees to withhold treatment, as the conventional doctrine says he may. The justification for his doing so is that the patient is in terrible agony, and since he is going to die anyway, it would be wrong to prolong his suffering needlessly. But now notice this. If one simply withholds the treatment, it may take the patient longer to die, and so he may suffer more than he would if more direct action were taken and a lethal injection given. This fact provides strong reason for thinking that, once the initial decision not to prolong his agony has been made, active euthanasia is actually preferable to passive euthanasia, rather than the reverse. To say otherwise is to endorse the option that leads to more suffering rather than less, and is contrary to the humanitarian impulse that prompts the decision not to prolong his life in the first place.

Part of my point is that the process of being "allowed to die" can be relatively slow and painful, whereas being given a lethal injection is relatively quick and painless. Let me give a different sort of example. In the United States about one in 600 babies is born with Down's syndrome. Most of these babies are otherwise healthy—that is, with only the usual pediatric care, they will proceed to an otherwise normal infancy. Some, however, are born with congenital defects such as intestinal obstructions that require operations if they are to live. Sometimes, the parents and the doctor will decide not to operate, and let the infant die. Anthony Shaw describes what happens then:

. . . When surgery is denied [the doctor] must try to keep the infant from suffering while natural forces sap the baby's life away. As a surgeon whose natural inclination is to use the scalpel to fight off death, standing by and watching a salvageable baby die is the most emotionally exhausting experience I know. It is easy at a conference, in a theoretical discussion, to decide that such infants should be allowed to die. It is altogether different to stand by in the nursery and watch as dehydration and infection wither a tiny being over hours and days. This is a terrible ordeal for me and the hospital staff—much more so than for the parents who never set foot in the nursery.[1]

I can understand why some people are opposed to all euthanasia, and insist that such infants must be allowed to live. I think I can also understand why other people favor destroying these babies quickly and painlessly. But why should anyone favor letting "dehydration and infection wither a tiny being over hours and days"? The doctrine that says that a baby may be allowed to dehydrate and wither, but may not be given an injection that would end its life without suffering, seems so patently cruel as to require no further refutation. The strong language is not intended to offend, but only to put the point in the clearest possible way.

My second argument is that the conventional doctrine leads to decisions concerning life and death made on irrelevant grounds.

Consider again the case of the infants with Down's syndrome who need operations for congenital defects unrelated to the syndrome to live. Sometimes, there is no operation, and the baby dies, but when there is no such defect, the baby lives on. Now, an operation such as that to remove an intestinal obstruction is not prohibitively difficult. The reason why such operations are not performed in these cases is, clearly, that the child has Down's syndrome and the parents and doctor judge that because of that fact it is better for the child to die.

But notice that this situation is absurd, no matter what view one takes of the lives and potentials of such babies. If the life of such an infant is worth preserving, what does it matter if it needs a simple operation? Or, if one thinks it better that such a baby should not live on, what difference does it make that it happens to have an unobstructed intestinal tract? In either case, the matter of life and death is being decided on irrelevant grounds. It is the Down's syndrome, and not the intestines, that is the issue. The matter should be decided, if at all, on that basis, and not be allowed to depend on the essentially irrelevant question of whether the intestinal tract is blocked.

What makes this situation possible, of course, is the idea that when there is an intestinal blockage, one can "let the baby die," but when there is no such defect there is nothing that can be done, for one must not "kill" it. The fact that this idea leads to such results as deciding life or death on irrelevant grounds is another good reason why the doctrine should be rejected.

One reason why so many people think that there is an important moral difference between active and passive euthanasia is that they think killing someone is morally worse than letting someone die. But is it? Is killing, in itself, worse than letting die? To investigate this issue, two cases may be considered that are exactly alike except that one involves killing whereas the other involves letting someone die. Then, it can be asked whether this difference makes any difference to the moral assessments. It is important that the cases be exactly alike, except for this one difference, since otherwise one cannot be confident that it is this difference and not some other that accounts for any variation in the assessments of the two cases. So, let us consider this pair of cases:

In the first, Smith stands to gain a large inheritance if anything should happen to his six-year-old cousin. One evening while the child is taking his bath, Smith sneaks into the bathroom and drowns the child, and then arranges things so that it will look like an accident.

In the second, Jones also stands to gain if anything should happen to his six-year-old cousin. Like Smith, Jones sneaks in planning to drown the child in his bath. However, just as he enters the bathroom Jones sees the child slip and hit his head, and fall face down in the water. Jones is delighted; he stands by, ready to push the child's head back under if it is necessary, but it is not necessary. With only a little thrashing about, the child drowns all by himself, "accidentally," as Jones watches and does nothing.

Now Smith killed the child, whereas Jones "merely" let the child die. That is the only difference between them. Did either man behave better, from a moral point of view? If the difference between killing and letting die were in itself a morally important matter, one should say that Jones's behavior was less reprehensible than Smith's. But does one really want to say that? I think not. In the first place, both men acted from the same motive, personal gain, and both had exactly the same end in view when they acted. It may be inferred from Smith's conduct that he is a bad man, although that judgment may be withdrawn or modified if certain further facts are learned about him—for example, that he is mentally deranged. But would not the very same thing be inferred about Jones from his conduct? And would not the same further considerations also be relevant to any modification of this judgment? Moreover, suppose Jones pleaded, in his own defense, "After all, I didn't do anything except just stand there and watch the child drown. I didn't kill him; I only let him die." Again, if letting die were in itself less bad than killing, this defense should have at least some weight. But it does not. Such a "defense" can only be regarded as a grotesque perversion of moral reasoning. Morally speaking, it is no defense at all.

Now, it may be pointed out, quite properly, that the cases of euthanasia with which doctors are concerned are not like this at all. They do not involve personal gain or the destruction of normal, healthy children. Doctors are concerned only with cases in which the patient's life is of no further use to him, or in which the patient's life has become or will soon become a terrible burden. However, the point is the same in these cases: The bare difference between killing and letting die does not, in itself, make a moral difference. If a doctor lets a patient die, for humane reasons, he is in the same moral position as if he had given the patient a lethal injection for humane reasons. If his decision was wrong—if, for example, the patient's illness was in fact curable—the decision would be equally regrettable no matter which method was used to carry it out. And if the doctor's decision was the right one, the method used is not in itself important.

The AMA policy statement isolates the crucial issue very well; the crucial issue is "the intentional termination of the life of one human being by another." But after identifying this issue, and forbidding "mercy killing," the statement goes on to deny that the cessation of treatment is the intentional termination of a life. This is where the mistake comes in, for what is the cessation of treatment, in these circumstances, if it is not "the intentional termination of the life of one human being by another." Of course it is exactly that, and if it were not, there would be no point to it.

Many people will find this judgment hard to accept. One reason, I think, is that it is very easy to conflate the question of whether killing is, in itself, worse than letting die, with the very different question of whether most actual cases of killing are more reprehensible than most actual cases of letting die. Most actual cases of killing are clearly terrible (think, for example, of all the murders reported in the newspapers), and one hears of such cases every day. On the other hand, one hardly ever hears of a case of letting die, except for the actions of doctors who are motivated by humanitarian reasons. So one learns to think of killing in a much worse light than of letting die. But this does not mean that there is something about killing that makes it in itself worse than letting die, for it is not the bare difference between killing and letting die that makes the difference in these cases. Rather, the other factors—the murderer's motive of personal gain, for example, contrasted with the doctor's humanitarian motivation—account for different reactions to the different cases.

I have argued that killing is not in itself any worse than letting die; if my contention is right, it follows that active euthanasia is not any worse than passive euthanasia. What arguments can be given on the other side? The most common, I believe, is the following:

"The important difference between active and passive euthanasia is that, in passive euthanasia, the doctor does not do anything to bring about the patient's death. The doctor does nothing, and the patient dies of whatever ills already afflict him. In active euthanasia, however, the doctor does something to bring about the patient's death: he kills him. The doctor who gives the patient with cancer a lethal injection has himself caused his patient's death; whereas if he merely ceases treatment, the cancer is the cause of the death."

A number of points need to be made here. The first is that it is not exactly correct to say that in passive euthanasia the doctor does nothing, for he does do one thing that is very important: he lets the patient die. "Letting someone die" is certainly different, in some respects, from other types of action—mainly in that it is a kind of action that one may perform by way of not performing certain other actions. For example, one may let a patient die by way of not giving medication, just as one may insult someone by way of not shaking his hand. But for any purpose of moral assessment, it is a type of action nonetheless. The decision to let a patient die is subject to moral appraisal in the same way that a decision to kill him would be subject to moral appraisal: it may be assessed as wise or unwise, compassionate or sadistic, right or wrong. If a doctor deliberately let a patient die who was suffering from a routinely curable illness, the doctor would certainly be to blame for what he had done, just as he would be to blame if he had needlessly killed the patient. Charges against him would then be appropriate. If so, it would be no defense at all for him to insist that he didn't "do anything." He would have done something very serious indeed, for he let his patient die.

Fixing the cause of death may be very important from a legal point of view, for it may determine whether criminal charges are brought against the doctor. But I do not think that this notion can be used to show a moral difference between active and passive euthanasia. The reason why it is considered bad to be the cause of someone's death is that death is regarded as a great evil—and so it is. However, if it has been decided that euthanasia—even passive euthanasia—is desirable in a given case, it has also been decided that in this instance death is no greater an evil than the patient's continued existence. And if this is true, the usual reason for not wanting to be the cause of someone's death simply does not apply.

Finally, doctors may think that all of this is only of academic interest—the sort of thing that philosophers may worry about but that has no practical bearing on their own work. After all, doctors must be concerned about the legal consequences of what they do, and active euthanasia is clearly forbidden by the law. But even so, doctors should also be concerned with the fact that the law is forcing upon them a moral doctrine that may well be indefensible, and has a considerable effect on their practices. Of course, most doctors are not now in the position of being coerced in this matter, for they do not regard themselves as merely going along with what the law requires. Rather, in statements such as the AMA policy statement that I have quoted, they are endorsing this doctrine as a central point of medical ethics. In that statement, active euthanasia is condemned not merely as illegal but as "contrary to that for which the medical profession stands," whereas passive euthanasia is approved. However, the preceding considerations suggest that there is really no moral difference between the two, considered in themselves (there may be important moral differences in some cases in their consequences, but, as I pointed out, these differences may make active euthanasia, and not passive euthanasia, the morally preferable option). So, whereas doctors may have to discriminate between active and passive euthanasia to satisfy the law, they should not do any more than that. In particular, they should not give the distinction any added authority and weight by writing it into official statements of medical ethics.

## Endnote

1. Anthony Shaw, "Doctor, Do We Have a Choice?" *The New York Times Magazine,* January 30, 1972), p. 54.

## Journal/Discussion Questions

✍ *Rachels maintains that active euthanasia is sometimes justified on the basis of a desire to alleviate suffering, and that it is more humane than passive euthanasia. What limits are there on compassionate action? Can compassion ever be a legitimate reason for ending someone's life?*

1. Rachels offers two principal arguments against the distinction between active and passive euthanasia. What are these arguments?

2. What objections to his position does Rachels consider? Are you convinced by his replies to those objections? Can you think of any objections that Rachels does not consider? What are they?

3. Rachels claims that "killing is not in itself any worse than letting die." What support does he offer for this claim? Do you agree? Why or why not?

---

## Richard Doerflinger
### "Assisted Suicide: Pro-Choice or Anti-Life?"

---

*Richard Doerflinger is associate director of the Office for Pro-Life Activities of the National Conference of Catholic Bishops, Washington, D.C.*

*In this article, Doerflinger argues that respect for life is incompatible with assisting in active euthanasia. He argues, furthermore, that liberalization of the euthanasia laws is dangerous, because it could combine with other factors at work in society to threaten the value of individual lives.*

## As You Read, Consider This:

1. On what basis does Doerflinger claim that arguments in favor of assisted suicide presuppose a viewpoint on the value of life?

2. What, according to Doerflinger, are the two kinds of slippery slope arguments? Why is this dinstinction crucial for understanding the euthanasia issue?

~

The intrinsic wrongness of directly killing the innocent, even with the victim's consent, is all but axiomatic in the Jewish and Christian worldviews that have shaped the laws and mores of Western civilization and the self-concept of its medical practitioners. This norm grew out of the conviction that human life is sacred because it is created in the image and likeness of God, and called to fulfillment in love of God and neighbor.

With the pervasive secularization of Western culture, norms against euthanasia and suicide have to a great extent been cut loose from their religious roots to fend for themselves. Because these norms seem abstract and unconvincing to many, debate tends to dwell not on the wrongness of the act as such but on what may follow from its acceptance. Such arguments are often described as claims about a "slippery slope," and debate shifts to the validity of slippery slope arguments in general.

Since it is sometimes argued that acceptance of assisted suicide is an outgrowth of respect for personal autonomy, and not lack of respect for the inherent worth of human life, I will outline how autonomy-based arguments in favor of assisting suicide do entail a statement about the value of life. I will also distinguish two kinds of slippery slope argument often confused with each other, and argue that those who favor social and legal acceptance of assisted suicide have not adequately responded to the slippery slope claims of their opponents.

## Assisted Suicide versus Respect for Life

Some advocates of socially sanctioned assisted suicide admit (and a few boast) that their proposal is incompatible with the conviction that human life is of intrinsic worth. Attorney Robert Risley has said that he and his allies in the Hemlock Society are "so bold" as to seek to "overturn the sanctity of life principle" in American society. A life of suffering, "racked with pain," is "not the kind of life we cherish."[1]

Others eschew Risley's approach, perhaps recognizing that it creates a slippery slope toward practices almost universally condemned. If society is to help terminally ill patients to commit suicide because it agrees that death is objectively preferable to a life of hardship, it will be difficult to draw the line at the seriously ill or even at circumstances where the victim requests death.

Some advocates of assisted suicide therefore take a different course, arguing that it is precisely respect for the dignity of the human person that demands respect for individual freedom as the noblest feature of that person. On this rationale a decision as to when and how to die deserves the respect and even the assistance of others because it is the ultimate exercise of self-determination—"ultimate" both in the sense that it is the last decision one will ever make and in the sense that through it one takes control of one's entire self. What makes such decisions worthy of respect is not the fact that death is chosen over life but that it is the individual's own free decision about his or her future.

Thus Derek Humphry, director of the Hemlock Society, describes his organization as "prochoice" on this issue. Such groups favor establishment of a constitutional "right to die" modeled on the right to abortion delineated by the U.S. Supreme Court in 1973. This would be a right to choose whether or not to end one's own life, free of outside government interference. In theory, recognition of such a right would betray no bias toward choosing death.

## Life versus Freedom

This autonomy-based approach is more appealing than the straightforward claim that some lives are not worth living, especially to Americans accustomed to valuing individual liberty above virtually all else. But the argument departs from American traditions on liberty in one fundamental respect.

When the Declaration of Independence proclaimed the inalienable human rights to be "life, liberty, and the pursuit of happiness," this ordering reflected a long-standing judgment about their relative priorities. Life, a human being's very earthly existence, is the most fundamental right because it is the necessary condition for all other worldly goods including freedom; freedom in turn makes it possible to pursue (without guaranteeing that one will attain) happiness. Safeguards against the deliberate destruction of life are thus seen as necessary to protect freedom and all other human goods. This line of thought is not explicitly religious but is endorsed by some modern religious groups:

> The first right of the human person is his life. He has other goods and some are more precious, but this one is fundamental—the condition of all the others. Hence it must be protected above all others.[2]

On this view suicide is not the ultimate exercise of freedom but its ultimate self-contradiction: A free act that by destroying life, destroys all the individual's future earthly freedom. If life is more basic than freedom, society best serves freedom by discouraging rather than assisting self-destruction. Sometimes one must limit particular choices to safeguard freedom itself, as when American society chose over a century ago to prevent people from selling themselves into slavery even of their own volition.

It may be argued in objection that the person who ends his life has not truly suffered loss of freedom, because unlike the slave he need not continue to exist under the constraints of a loss of freedom. But the slave does have some freedom, including the freedom to seek various means of liberation or at least the freedom to choose what attitude to take regarding his plight. To claim that a slave is worse off than a corpse is to value a situation of limited freedom less than one of no freedom whatsoever, which seems inconsistent with the premise of the "pro-choice" position. Such a claim also seems tantamount to saying that some lives (such as those with less than absolute freedom) are objectively not worth living, a position that "pro-choice" advocates claim not to hold.

It may further be argued in objection that assistance in suicide is only being offered to those who can no longer meaningfully exercise other freedoms due to increased suffering and reduced capabilities and lifespan. To be sure, the suffering of terminally ill patients who can no longer pursue the simplest everyday tasks should call for sympathy and support from everyone in contact with them. But even these hardships do not constitute total loss of freedom of choice. If they did, one could hardly claim that the patient is in a position to make the ultimate free choice about suicide. A dying person capable of making a choice of that kind is also capable of making less monumental free choices about coping with his or her condition. This person generally faces a bewildering array of choices regarding the assessment of his or her past life and the resolution of relationships with family and friends. He or she must finally choose at this time what stance to take regarding the eternal questions about God, personal responsibility, and the prospects of a destiny after death.

In short, those who seek to maximize free choice may with consistency reject the idea of assisted suicide, instead facilitating all choices *except* that one which cuts short all choices.

In fact proponents of assisted suicide do not consistently place freedom of choice as their highest priority. They often defend the moderate nature of their project by stating, with Derek Humphry, that "we do not encourage suicide for any reason except to relieve unremitting suffering." It seems their highest priority is the "pursuit of happiness" (or avoidance of suffering) and not "liberty" as such. Liberty or freedom of choice loses its value if one's choices cannot relieve suffering and lead to happiness; life is of instrumental value insofar as it makes possible choices that can bring happiness.

In this value system, choice as such does not warrant unqualified respect. In difficult circumstances, as when care of a suffering and dying patient is a great burden on family and society, the individual who chooses life despite suffering will not easily be seen as rational, thus will not easily receive understanding and assistance for this choice.

In short, an unqualified "pro-choice" defense of assisted suicide lacks coherence because corpses have no choices. A particular choice, that of death, is given priority over all the other choices it makes impossible, so the value of choice as such is not central to the argument.

A restriction of this rationale to cases of terminal illness also lacks logical force. For if ending a brief life of suffering can be good, it would seem that ending a long life of suffering may be better. Surely the approach of the California "Humane and Dignified Death Act"—where consensual killing of a patient expected to die in six months is presumably good medical practice, but killing the same patient a month or two earlier is still punishable as homicide—is completely arbitrary.

## Slippery Slopes, Loose Cannons

Many arguments against sanctioning assisted suicide concern a different kind of "slippery slope": Contingent factors in the contemporary situation may make it virtually inevitable in practice, if not compelling at the level of abstract theory, that removal of the taboo against assisted suicide will lead to destructive expansions of the right to kill the innocent. Such factors may not be part of euthanasia advocates' own agenda; but if they exist and are beyond the control of these advocates, they must be taken into account in judging the moral and social wisdom of opening what may be a Pandora's box of social evils.

To distinguish this sociological argument from our dissection of the conceptual *logic* of the rationale for assisted suicide, we might call it a "loose cannon" argument. The basic claim is that socially accepted killing of innocent persons will interact with other social factors to threaten lives that advocates of assisted suicide would agree should be protected. These factors at present include the following:

## The Psychological Vulnerability of Elderly and Dying Patients

Theorists may present voluntary and involuntary euthanasia as polar opposites; in practice there are many steps on the road from dispassionate, autonomous choice to subtle coercion. Elderly and disabled patients are often invited by our achievement-oriented society to see themselves as useless burdens on younger, more vital generations. In this climate, simply offering the option of "self-deliverance" shifts a burden of proof, so that helpless patients must ask themselves why they are not availing themselves of it. Society's offer of death communicates the message to certain patients that they *may* continue to live if they wish but the rest of us have no strong interest in their survival. Indeed, once the choice of a quick and painless death is officially accepted as rational, resistance to this choice may be seen as eccentric or even selfish.[3]

## The Crisis in Health Care Costs

The growing incentives for physicians, hospitals, families, and insurance companies to control the cost of health care will bring additional pressures to bear on patients. Curt Garbesi, the Hemlock Society's legal consultant, argues that autonomy-based groups like Hemlock must "control the public debate" so assisted suicide will not be seized upon by public officials as a cost-cutting device. But simply basing one's own defense of assisted suicide on individual autonomy does not solve the problem. For in the economic sphere also, offering the option of suicide would subtly shift burdens of proof.

Adequate health care is now seen by at least some policymakers as a human right, as something a society owes to all its members. Acceptance of assisted suicide as an option for those requiring expensive care would not only offer health care providers an incentive to make that option seem attractive—it would also demote all other options to the status of strictly private choices by the individual. As such they may lose their moral and legal claim to public support—in much the same way that the U.S. Supreme Court, having protected abortion under a constitutional "right of privacy," has quite logically denied any government obligation to provide public funds for this strictly private choice. As life-extending care of the terminally ill is increasingly seen as strictly elective, society may become less willing to appropriate funds for such care, and economic pressures to choose death will grow accordingly.

## Legal Doctrines on "Substituted Judgment"

American courts recognizing a fundamental right to refuse life-sustaining treatment have concluded that it is unjust to deny this right to the mentally incompetent. In such cases the right is exercised on the patient's behalf by others, who seek either to interpret what the patient's own wishes might have been or to serve his or her best interests. Once assisted suicide is established as a fundamental right, courts will almost certainly find that it is unjust not to extend this right to those unable to express their wishes. Hemlock's political arm, Americans Against Human Suffering, has underscored continuity between "passive" and "active" euthanasia by offering the Humane and Dignified Death Act as an amendment to California's "living will" law, and by including a provision for appointment of a proxy to choose the time and manner of the patient's death. By such extensions our legal system would accommodate nonvoluntary, if not involuntary, active euthanasia.

## Expanded Definitions of Terminal Illness

The Hemlock Society wishes to offer assisted suicide only to those suffering from terminal illnesses. But some Hemlock officials have in mind a rather broad definition of "terminal illness." Derek Humphry says "two and a half million people alone are dying of Alzheimer's disease."[4] At Hemlock's 1986 convention, Dutch physician Pieter Admiraal boasted that he had recently broadened the meaning of terminal illness in his country by giving a lethal injection to a young quadriplegic woman—a Dutch court found that he acted within judicial guidelines allowing euthanasia for the terminally ill, because paralyzed patients have difficulty swallowing and could die from aspirating their food at any time.

The medical and legal meaning of terminal illness has already been expanded in the United States by professional societies, legislatures, and courts in the context of so-called passive euthanasia. A Uniform Rights of the Terminally Ill Act proposed by the National Conference of Commissioners on Uniform State Laws in 1986 defines a terminal illness as one that would cause the patient's death in a relatively short time if life-preserving treatment is not provided—prompting critics to ask if all diabetics, for example, are "terminal" by definition. Some courts already see comatose and vegetative states as "terminal" because they involve an inability to swallow that will lead to death unless artificial feeding is instituted. In the Hilda Peter case, the New Jersey Supreme Court declared that the traditional state interest in "preserving life" referred only to "cognitive and sapient life" and not to mere "biological" existence, implying that unconscious patients are terminal, or perhaps as good as dead, so far as state interests are concerned. Is there any reason to think that American law would suddenly resurrect the older, narrower meaning of "terminal illness" in the context of active euthanasia?

## Prejudice against Citizens with Disabilities

If definitions of terminal illness expand to encompass states of severe physical or mental disability, another social reality will increase the pressure on patients to choose death: long-standing prejudice, sometimes bordering on revulsion, against people with disabilities. While it is seldom baldly claimed that disabled people have "lives not worth living," able-bodied people often say they could not live in a severely disabled state or would prefer death. In granting Elizabeth Bouvia a right to refuse a feeding tube that preserved her life, the California Appeals Court bluntly stated that her physical handicaps led her to "consider her existence meaningless" and that "she cannot be faulted for so concluding." According to disability rights expert Paul Longmore, in a society with such attitudes toward the disabled, "talk of their 'rational' or 'voluntary' suicide is simply Orwellian newspeak."[5]

## Character of the Medical Profession

Advocates of assisted suicide realize that most physicians will resist giving lethal injections because they are trained, in Garbesi's words, to be "enemies of death." The California Medical Association firmly opposed the Humane and Dignified Death Act, seeing it as an attack on the ethical foundation of the medical profession.

Yet California appeals judge Lynn Compton was surely correct in his concurring opinion in the *Bouvia* case, when he said that a sufficient number of willing physicians can be found once legal sanctions against assisted suicide are dropped. Judge Compton said this had clearly been the case with abortion, despite the fact that the Hippocratic Oath condemns abortion as strongly as it condemns euthanasia. Opinion polls of physicians bear out the judgment that a significant number would perform lethal injections if they were legal.

Some might think this division or ambivalence about assisted suicide in the medical profession will restrain broad expansions of the practice. But if anything, Judge Compton's analogy to our experience with abortion suggests the opposite. Most physicians still have qualms about abortion, and those who perform abortions on a full-time basis are not readily accepted by their colleagues as paragons of the healing art. Consequently, they tend to form their own professional societies, bolstering each other's positive self-image and developing euphemisms to blunt the moral edge of their work.

Once physicians abandon the traditional medical self-image, which rejects direct killing of patients in all circumstances, their new substitute self-image may require ever more aggressive efforts to make this killing more widely practiced and favorably received. To allow killing by physicians in certain circumstances may create a new lobby of physicians in favor of expanding medical killing.

## The Human Will to Power

The most deeply buried yet most powerful driving force toward widespread medical killing is a fact of human nature: Human beings are tempted to enjoy exercising power over others; ending another person's life is the ultimate exercise of that power. Once the taboo against killing has been set aside, it becomes progressively easier to channel one's aggressive instincts into the destruction of life in other contexts. Or as James Burtchaell has said: "There is a sort of virginity about murder; once one has violated it, it is awkward to refuse other invitations by saying, 'But that would be murder!'"[6]

Some will say assisted suicide for the terminally ill is morally distinguishable from murder and does not logically require termination of life in other circumstances. But my point is that the skill and the instinct to kill are more easily turned to other lethal tasks once they have an opportunity to exercise themselves. Thus Robert Jay Lifton has perceived differences between the German "mercy killings" of the 1930s and the later campaign to annihilate the Jews of Europe, yet still says that "at the heart of the Nazi enterprise . . . is the destruction of the boundary between healing and killing."[7] No other boundary separating these two situations was as fundamental as this one, and thus none was effective once it was crossed. As a matter of historical fact, personnel who had conducted the "mercy killing" program were quickly and readily recruited to operate the killing chambers of the death camps.[8] While the contemporary United States fortunately lacks the anti-Semitic and totalitarian attitudes that made the Holocaust possible, it has its own trends and pressures that may combine with acceptance of medical killing to produce a distinctively American catastrophe in the name of individual freedom.

These "loose cannon" arguments are not conclusive. All such arguments by their nature rest upon a reading and extrapolation of certain contingent factors in society. But their combined force provides a serious case against taking the irreversible step of sanctioning assisted suicide for any class of persons, so long as those who advocate this step fail to demonstrate why these predictions are wrong. If the strict philosophical case on behalf of "rational suicide" lacks coherence, the pragmatic claim that its acceptance would be a social benefit lacks grounding in history or common sense.

### Endnotes

1. Presentation at the Hemlock Society's Third National Voluntary Euthanasia Conference, "A Humane and Dignified Death," Washington, D.C., September 2–27, 1986. All quotations from Hemlock Society officials are from the proceedings of this conference unless otherwise noted.

2. Vatican Congregation for the Doctrine of the Faith, *Declaration on Procured Abortion* (1974), para. 11.

3. I am indebted for this line of argument to Dr. Eric Chevlen.

4. Denis Herbstein, "Campaigning for the Right to Die," *International Herald Tribune,* 11 September 1986.

5. Paul K. Longmore, "Elizabeth Bouvia, Assisted Suicide, and Social Prejudice," *Issues in Law Medicine* 3, no. 2 (1987), 168.

6. James T. Burtchaell, *Rachel Weeping and Other Essays on Abortion* (Kansas City: Andrews & McMeel, 1982), p. 188.

7. Robert Jay Lifton, *The Nazi Doctors: Medical Killing and the Psychology of Genocide* (New York: Basic Books, 1986), p. 14.

8. Yitzhak Rad, *Belzec, Sobibor, Treblinka* (Bloomington, IN: Indiana University Press, 1987), pp. 11, 16–17.

## Journal/Discussion Questions

✍ *Doerflinger's analysis takes place within the larger context of a Christian worldview. Do you share this worldview? Do you agree with Doerflinger's conclusions about euthanasia?*

1. According to Doerflinger, the prohibition against killing the innocent is grounded in the Judeo-Christian conviction that life is sacred. Do you think that the religious belief that human life is sacred necessarily leads to the conclusion that voluntary euthanasia is always morally wrong? Do other religious traditions permit euthanasia? Discuss.

2. Both Doerflinger and Vaux ("The Theologic Ethics of Euthanasia") claim to present Christian positions. How are their positions different? Are they both Christian? Discuss.

3. Doerflinger argues that proponents of eu-

thanasia claim that liberty is their highest value, but this claim is misleading. Why, according to Doerflinger, is it misleading?

4. In the "loose cannon" argument, Doerflinger maintains that legalizing euthanasia will interact with seven other factors in our society in ways that are ultimately harmful. What are these other factors? How plausible do you think each of these seven arguments is? Which of the seven factors do you think is the greatest threat?

5. Doerflinger sees euthanasia as related to "the human will to power." What does he mean by this? Are you convinced by his analysis? Discuss.

---

## Gregory S. Kavka
## "Banning Euthanasia"

*Gregory Kavka is the author of* Hobbesian Moral and Political Theory *and* Moral Paradoxes of Nuclear Deterrence *as well as numerous articles in moral and political philosophy. He died of cancer in 1994 at the age of forty-six.*

*In the following article, Kavka maintains that it is wrong to prevent people from rescuing others in great suffering, and that banning voluntary euthanasia does precisely this, for it prevents some people (usually physicians) from rescuing someone else (usually a patient) from great suffering.*

### As You Read, Consider This:

1. What is the basic moral principle that Kavka's argument rests on?
2. On what basis does Kavka prevent his argument from justifying (assisted) suicide in general?

⁓

Recently, the Dutch Parliament has made active voluntary euthanasia "quasi-legal" in the Netherlands by voting to formally protect from prosecution physicians who carry it out under strict and clearly defined guidelines.[1] Yet, with the failure of Proposition 161 in the November 1992 election in California, active voluntary euthanasia remains illegal in all fifty states of the United States. Indeed, the legislature of the state of Michigan has recently passed a law specifically designed to prevent retired Pathologist Jack Kevorkian (or any of his followers) from euthanizing patients by assisting them in committing suicide.[2]

In this paper, I will present a simple, but novel, moral argument for legalizing active voluntary euthanasia. In brief, I argue that banning active voluntary euthanasia, by forbidding it either in law or in professional codes of medical practice, is very morally wrong because it prevents some people from rescuing others from great suffering. Spelled out more fully, my argument rests on some general, but highly plausible, factual claims combined with a simple and attractive moral

---

Gregory Kavka, "Banning Euthanasia." Prevously unpublished. Reprinted by permission of the author.

principle. Below, I set out the argument by presenting its factual and moral elements in turn, explaining its conclusion, and defending it from some important objections.

# The Argument

## Factual Premises

The factual premises of my argument concern, respectively, those who may wish to be euthanized and those (especially some physicians) who might be willing to euthanize them. First, it is evident that there are some people who are in such great suffering due to irreversible and adverse medical circumstances that they wish to have their lives ended very soon, even though they are aware that—in their own case—this can be done only by active euthanasia (e.g., a fatal injection). This is merely to say that there are some patients who would want active euthanasia if it were available to them.[3] Second, banning active voluntary euthanasia—by law or codes of medical ethics—deters some people (in particular, some physicians) from actively euthanizing some people who want to have their lives ended in this manner.[4] In other words, if medical codes and laws were liberalized to allow active voluntary euthanasia, there would be more physicians who would make this option available to more patients. Putting these two simple assertions together yields the main conclusion of the factual component of my argument: *Banning active voluntary euthanasia prevents some people (physicians) from rescuing some others (patients) from great suffering in a manner in which these others wish to be rescued.*

## The Moral Principle

*The case of the evil Colonel.* Turning to the moral component of my argument, let us begin our inquiry by imagining a non-medical situation in which a person's only release from great suffering is death. An evil Colonel is the unrestrained ruler of his military district in some backward country, and he is greatly angered at some unfortunate Private (e.g., for not showing the Colonel sufficient respect). He begins to slowly and agonizingly torture the Private to death over a period of weeks, making no bones of his aim of inflicting maximum suffering ending in death. After only a few hours of torture, the Private (even during intervals between the torture sessions) begs repeatedly to be killed immediately by any means rather than have the torture go on. The only one—besides the heartless Colonel—in a position to save him from weeks of torture (without sharing his fate) is the Water Boy who periodically brings water for the Private to drink. In the kitchen, he slips a fatal dose of poison in the cup of water he is about to take to the prisoner. (The poison will kill the prisoner in a short time, but is not likely to be discovered—the Colonel is not the type to ask for an autopsy when a prisoner drops dead during torture.) The Cook in the kitchen sees what the Water Boy is doing and stops him by threatening to tell the Colonel if the Water Boy delivers the poison to the Private.

It is clear that in this situation the Cook has acted wrongly, very wrongly. He has eliminated the Private's only real hope of rescue from weeks of agonizing torture. His conduct is not, of course, as wrongful as that of the Colonel, but that is hardly to say anything in its favor. It is also worth noting that what the Cook does is *much worse* than merely allowing torture to go forward without intervening. Suppose, for example, that the Water Boy had declined to poison the water even though he was certain he could do so without risk of detection. Whether, in that case, he acts wrongly in failing to rescue to the Private is, perhaps, a difficult question to answer. But the Cook does not merely fail to rescue, he prevents a rescue-in-progress from taking place. That this is much worse is evident when we consider the parallel case of aiding the world's starving poor. Philosophers have extensively debated the issue of whether citizens in wealthy nations are failing to live up to their obligations if they do not provide aid to the world's starving poor.[5] But it is not debatable that it would be very wrong to prevent others who are willing to provide such aid from doing so. No one, for example, would regard a law preventing U.S. citizens or charities from providing aid to the world's starving poor as anything but iniquitous. Clearly, however bad it is to fail to rescue someone in dire need, it is worse to actively intervene to prevent someone else from rescuing them.

These considerations flowing from our hypothetical torture case suggest the following moral principle: *It is very wrong to prevent someone from rescuing someone else from great suffering (in a manner in which the latter person wishes to be rescued).* It is this principle which explains what the Cook has done wrong. He has prevented one person, the Water Boy, from rescuing another, the Private, from great suffering, the Colonel's torture, in a manner in which the Private—in his constant pleading for an early death—wishes to be rescued.

Combining this simple moral principle with the earlier factual claim that banning active voluntary euthanasia prevents some people from rescuing others from great suffering in a manner in which the latter wish to be rescued immediately yields the conclusion that *banning active voluntary euthanasia is very wrong.*[6] And it is wrong for one of the same reasons that torture is wrong: it involves acting in such a way as to insure that people experience great suffering that they would not experience, save for the actor's intervention.[7] (The Private's continued great suffering, past the point at which the Water Boy would have poisoned him absent the Cook's threat, is the result of the interventions of both the Colonel and the Cook.) Of course, if banning active voluntary euthanasia is very wrong, as this argument indicates, legislators and physicians' organizations should act forthwith to remove their blanket bans on it.

Note, however, that the argument allows for the legitimacy of strict restrictions on the practice of active euthanasia, to insure both the voluntariness of the patient's choice and the presence of great suffering brought on by a medical condition. The Dutch rules, for example, state that "the request for euthanasia must come from a patient who is doing so voluntarily, who is mentally competent, has a hopeless disease without prospect for improvement, and is undergoing unbearable physical or mental suffering."[8] Such restrictions conflict with neither the spirit nor the letter of my argument. It is only in those cases in which considerations concerning the patient's well being (i.e., ending of great suffering from a hopeless medical condition) and her autonomous choices concur in recommending early death as the best course of action, that my argument implies we may not prevent physicians from pursuing this course. It is an argument for legalizing active voluntary euthanasia, *not* for allowing suicide (or assisted suicide) *in general.*

Notice, however, that my argument does *not* require that the patient be in terminal condition. Why not? Because if it is wrong to prevent a terminal patient being relieved of a short period of great suffering, it is at least as wrong to prevent non-terminal patients being relieved of longer periods of great suffering. Intuitively, we tend to recoil from this conclusion. If, for example, you survey a large class of undergraduates, you typically find a large majority in favor of euthanasia for the terminally ill who are suffering, and a large majority against euthanasia for patients suffering from horrible chronic conditions that are not terminal.[9] You can bring out the tension between these two beliefs by simply asking them, "Which is worse, suffering for a short time or suffering for a long time?"[10] The same point can be made by considering a variation of our earlier torture case in which the Colonel plans to extend the Private's torture over months and years. The Cook's interference with the Water Boy's rescue-by-poisoning plan would be even more reprehensible in this case than in the case described earlier. For it would doom the Private to a much longer period of extreme misery.

## Objections and Replies

*First objection.*   Having set out my main argument, and having clarified the sorts of restrictions on active voluntary euthanasia it supports, I proceed to defend the argument by answering six objections to it. The first objection says that it is permissible—even obligatory—to stop someone from being rescued from great suffering if they will die as the result of the "rescue." Thus, for example, if someone is suffering greatly from a painful but life-saving medical procedure, and an onlooker attempts to interrupt the proceedings to stop the patient's pain, it would be correct for you to subdue the onlooker so that the procedure may continue.

This objection establishes that some rescues to prevent great suffering may be permissibly prevented on the grounds that the rescue would result in the sufferer's death. But it fails to establish that such prevention is permissible whenever the rescue would kill the sufferer. For consider our earlier example of the Private being tortured by the Colonel. The Water Boy's rescue-by-poisoning would kill the Private, yet we judge the Cook's interference with this rescue to be wrong in full knowledge of this fact, because the rescue is in the Private's interest and has his consent. And clearly the physician who provides a fatal injection to a patient suffering horribly from an irreversible medical condition is acting in a situation parallel to that of the Water Boy, rather than that of the onlooker who attempts to disrupt a painful life-saving procedure.

This reply may not satisfy the objector. For he may believe in absolute deontological prohibitions against certain kinds of actions, including deliberately (or intentionally) killing the innocent. Even if there are such absolute prohibitions, it does not follow immediately that they should be enshrined in, or enforced by, law. For example, while deceitful betrayal of a close friend, or blasphemy against the true deity, are kinds of acts that may always be wrong, it might be unwise and harmful to legally punish such acts. Still, the prohibition on deliberately killing the innocent might be regarded as so central to social life that it must be enshrined in law.

But is there any such absolute prohibition? Supposing so has wildly counterintuitive implications concerning a class of cases I call Extra Death cases. In such cases, deliberately killing an innocent person is the only way to prevent that person and other innocent persons from being killed. In such cases, if we refrain from killing, innocent people will die that we could have saved, and no innocent people will be saved. A common case of this sort arises fairly frequently if—at least for the sake of argument—we regard the human fetus as a person. When an abortion can save the mother's life, but both mother and fetus will die if one is not performed, we have an Extra Death case. The fetus perishes whatever is done, but aborting saves the mother. Yet the absolute prohibition view says—quite implausibly—that we must not abort, that we must sacrifice the mother's life, even though the fetus cannot benefit.[11]

Would it help to modify the absolute prohibition view to allow killing the innocent when other lives are saved and the victim consents? It does make the view more plausible, but only at the cost of undermining the objection to my argument. Suppose, for example, that the modified doctrine allows physicians to kill a terminal patient, with her consent, to allow her still healthy kidneys to be transplanted to save the lives of two of her children who each need one of her kidneys to live. If this is so, it would seem arbitrary to deny the permissibility of the same action to save her children the sufferings involved in a lifetime of kidney-dialysis. But if she may be killed, with her consent, to prevent the great suffering of others, it would be outrageous to suppose that she could not be killed, with her consent, to prevent her own great suffering. Thus, the objection based on an absolute prohibition on deliberately killing the innocent leads to a painful dilemma for its supporters: either they accept the highly implausible implications of their view in Extra Death cases, or they allow for reasonable modifications in their absolutism and end up unable to condemn voluntary euthanasia. We may leave them impaled on the horns of this dilemma and move on.

*Second objection.*    A second objection notes that my argument implicitly (and wrongly) assumes that early death may benefit a person in great suffering. Despite rejection of this assumption by some writers on euthanasia,[12] I feel safe in relying on it. Can we deny that the dead victims of torture would have been better off if they had died earlier in the horrible process? Can we deny that some of those who endure the "natural tortures" imposed by painful and debilitating illnesses without hope of recovery would benefit from an early death? If we do deny this, if we hold that early death harms all patients, then we must oppose passive as well as active euthanasia, a position that few would be willing to accept.

*Third objection.*    Another implicit assumption of my argument—that death is the only alternative to great suffering—leads to a third objection. In my torture cases, I have stipulated that the Private may be rescued from torture only by death. Otherwise, if—for example—the cavalry is on the way to capture the Colonel, the Water Boy is wrong to poison the Private and the Cook is right to stop him. But, continues the objection, in the real world, the cavalry is on the way for suffering patients, in the form of better medical treatment for pain. Thus, active euthanasia is no longer justified, because it is no longer needed.[13]

To the extent that improved pain management techniques make life bearable and worth continuing for the afflicted, the urgency of legalizing active voluntary euthanasia is reduced. But no one is supposing that now, or in the near future, all the afflicted will be successfully treated by these techniques. Pain-killers do not address all of the sufferings of the afflicted: the disabilities, the mental anguish, the loss of the enjoyments of normal life, the loss of independence, and so on.[14] And even if all significant physical pain could be eliminated short of death *in principle* (an unrealistic prospect in any case), real suffering patients actually being relieved of their physical pains by an overburdened and imperfect medical system is too much to expect. For those whose sufferings remain untreatable, or untreated, death may remain the only way *in fact* in their own case to relieve their suffering. If and when pain management techniques overcome the need for voluntary euthanasia, patients will stop requesting it. In the meantime, it is wrong to deprive those who do request it of their only practical succor from great suffering by preventing willing physicians from euthanizing them under appropriate safeguards.

*Fourth objection.*    Perhaps the most likely objection to my argument that it is wrong to ban active voluntary euthanasia is the claim that regardless of the beneficial effects such acts of euthanasia may have for particular patients, legalizing euthanasia would have bad effects on society as a whole. Various possible negative effects are often cited in this context, including negative effects on the morale of medical personnel, and reduction of incentives to manage pain. But the most common, and significant objection of this form is a slippery slope argument: if we legalize active voluntary euthanasia, this will eventually lead to the legalization of other, more objectionable, forms of euthanasia, to the great detriment of society.

Now to succeed, slippery slope arguments must establish two things: first, that following policy A is likely to lead to later policy or effect B, and that B is socially harmful or morally odious. In other words, we should not adopt A, because we will then slide down the slippery slope *and end up at an undesirable place.* But there are two different possible long-range effects of legalizing active voluntary euthanasia—the legalization of active *non-voluntary* euthanasia (e.g., of the permanently comatose and others who cannot express their will) and the legalization of active *involuntary* euthanasia (e.g., of those who do not want to die but are pressured into saying that they do, or are killed against their wishes to economize on medical costs). Legalization of active non-voluntary euthanasia might well follow from the legalization of active voluntary euthanasia, but it is unclear that this is undesirable if there are appropriate restrictions and safeguards. Active involuntary euthanasia, on the other hand, is clearly undesirable—tantamount to murder, we might say without much exaggeration. But it seems highly unlikely, in a civilized society, that its legalization would result from legalizing active voluntary euthanasia. So legalizing active voluntary euthanasia has one purported "slippery slope" effect that is bad (i.e., legalized active involuntary euthanasia), and one that is likely (i.e., legalized non-voluntary euthanasia), but none that is both bad and likely. Hence, the slippery slope argument against active voluntary euthanasia apparently fails.[15]

The objection to legalization of active voluntary euthanasia based on bad social consequences—whether or not it is formulated as a slippery slope argument—fails for a more general reason. Preventing patients who wish to be euthanized from being rescued from their great sufferings, in order to benefit society, would unfairly sacrifice their vital individual interests to the end of collective benefit. Most philosophers find strict utilitarian moral theory unacceptable for precisely this reason—it allows, indeed requires, the well-being of individuals to be sacrificed to promote group good.[16] This is especially outrageous when the individual losses are large, concrete, certain, and fall on some of society's least fortunate members (e.g., those in the most hopeless and painful medical conditions), while the group gains are indirect, diffuse, and speculative. And this is precisely the situation as regards the banning of active voluntary euthanasia.

*Fifth objection.*    But perhaps the worry of opponents of legalizing euthanasia is not about social harm, but the harm to individuals who might be euthanized against their wills. And even if a slide down the slippery slope to *legalized* involuntary euthanasia is unlikely, it is more plausible to claim that once any form of euthanasia is legalized, safeguards will inevitably be abused so that many patients end up being killed against their wills. Indeed, critics of legalized euthanasia have contended that the Dutch experience validates this claim, with statistics indicating that about 140 patients a year in the Netherlands are actively euthanized without being consulted, even though they were competent to be consulted and to give or withhold consent.[17] The implication is that some of these people would not have consented, and hence were killed against their wills.

Others have interpreted the Dutch data differently. They point out that these "unconsulted competent" patients were all in a hopeless terminal condition, a significant fraction of them had previously expressed a desire for early life-termination, that families were consulted in nearly all cases, and that life expectancy was less than a day for more than half these patients, and less than a week for eighty-seven per cent of them.[18] Thus, one knowledgeable observer writes, "There is no evidence of any patient being put to death *against* his or her implied wish."[19] It has also been observed that there are characteristics of the American legal system that would make involuntary euthanasia less likely here than in Holland if voluntary euthanasia were legalized,[20] and that there are a number of institutional safeguards that can be instituted to prevent involuntary euthanasia from occurring in a significant number of cases.[21] In light of this, it seems that to oppose legalizing euthanasia in the United States one must either (1) take a quite pessimistic view of our legal and medical systems' capacities to enact, heed and enforce such safeguards, or (2) must consider it more important to save a few imminently terminal patients from unwanted earlier deaths than to save very many times that number of patients from great, unwanted, and unnecessary suffering. In my view, we should not be so cynical about our institutions, or so convinced of the great value of life irrespective of its quality for the person whose life it is, as to endorse either of these attitudes.

*Sixth objection.*    A final objection to my argument is that—contrary to my conclusion—laws prohibiting active voluntary euthanasia are morally permissible because as individuals have no right to be euthanized, society has no obligation to allow euthanasia. The astute deontological ethicist F. M. Kamm presents a version of this argument in the following passage:

> Yet even if it is permissible to perform voluntary active euthanasia, we are not obligated to do so, and so even the person who requests it does not have a right to active euthanasia. And even though many people are willing to kill someone for his own good, many others are not. . . . Although many people who wish to be actively euthanized may not get their wish if we do not permit active euthanasia, they also will not have their rights violated, nor will we fail in our duties to them if there is a law prohibiting active euthanasia.[22]

Now I would agree that individuals have no *unconditional* right to be actively euthanized—that is, a right to be actively euthanized even if no one volunteers to perform this service for them. And this is so for the very reason that Kamm suggests: some people object to performing active euthanasia, and no one who so objects should be obligated to do so. But it does not follow that individuals lack the *conditional* right to be actively euthanized, the right to be actively euthanized (under appropriate circumstances) provided there are volunteers who are willing to supply this service. This can readily be seen by considering the right to marry. This is clearly not a right to be married regardless of whether anyone wants to marry you, but a conditional right to marry if a volunteer can be found. The fact that some people (indeed most) would not wish to marry you in no way implies that you lack this conditional right. But this conditional right to marry would be violated, or negated, by a law banning marriage, as the conditional right to be actively euthanized by a willing volunteer is violated by laws banning active euthanasia. Thus, Kamm's argument that we may permissibly ban active euthanasia turns out to be a *non sequitur*, apparently brought on by failure to note in this context the important moral difference between failing to rescue someone from suffering and preventing a willing third-party from carrying out such a rescue. Even lacking an unconditional right to be rescued, we may possess a right that third parties not interfere with (or prevent) our rescue by a willing party.

Of course, even the conditional right to be actively euthanized has been challenged. Leon Kass writes,

> Even if we . . . merely allow those to practice it [active voluntary euthanasia] who are freely willing, our society would be drastically altered. For unless the state accepts the job of euthanizer, which God forbid that it should, it would thus surrender its monopoly on the legal use of lethal force, a monopoly it holds and needs if it is to protect innocent life, its first responsibility.[23]

How are we to understand this argument? If the state's "first responsibility" of protecting innocent life is understood to include protecting a suffering patient from active euthanasia at his own request, Kass' argument begs the question by assuming what is to be proved: that the state should prevent voluntary active euthanasia. But if protecting innocent life does not include this sort of protection, an argument is needed why the state's surrendering authority over this particular use of lethal force (e.g., to physicians) would undermine its effective exercise of its right to use force to protect innocent life in other contexts. Are we to suppose that legalizing active voluntary euthanasia will undermine the efforts of the police and courts to deter and punish crime, or of the armed forces to defend the state in just wars? If so, Kass owes us an argument to that effect.

In closing, I should note that the success of my argument does not strictly depend on asserting possession of an individual right to be actively euthanized, even the conditional right to be actively euthanized at your request if conditions are appropriate and there is a willing volunteer. Rather, my argument establishes that it is morally wrong for the state (and medical groups) to prevent physicians from rescuing patients from great suffering at the patients' request by blanket bans on active euthanasia. My argument does not assert that this is wrong because of some right the patient has, but rather because it is wrong to make a person undergo great, unwanted, and unnecessary suffering if we can prevent that suffering by merely standing aside and letting a willing volunteer rescue that person from it.

## Acknowledgments

An earlier version of this paper was presented to the Moral and Political Philosophy Society of Orange County (MAPPS) and to the Liberty Society of Irvine. I am grateful to members of those groups, and to Jefferson McMahan, for helpful comments. Ronald B. Miller and Kurt Norlin provided useful references.

## Endnotes

1. "Dutch Parliament Approves Law Permitting Euthanasia," *The New York Times*, International Edition, February 10, 1993, Section A, p. 5.
2. "Dr. Kevorkian's Death Wish," *Newsweek*, March 8, 1993, pp. 46–48. In this paper, I treat assisted suicide of those facing a life not worth living because of their medical condition as a special case of voluntary euthanasia.

3. It would be hard for opponents of legalizing active voluntary euthanasia to reject this premise. If it were false, legalization would not have a significant practical effect for want of any volunteers.

4. Again, opponents of active voluntary euthanasia would have to acknowledge the truth of this premise or admit that laws banning active voluntary euthanasia have only a symbolic function.

5. William Aiken and Hugh LaFollette, eds., *World Hunger and Moral Obligation* (Englewood Cliffs, NJ: Prentice Hall, 1977).

6. Since a legal ban prevents rescue from great suffering in *many* cases, it is presumably much worse than preventing rescue from suffering in a single instance, other things being equal.

7. There is another possible difference between preventing rescue from human torture and preventing rescue from the "natural torture" endured by some patients. Torture, unlike a patient's suffering, may be thought of as a bad with two components—the natural evil of the patient's horrible experience, and the moral evil of its deliberate infliction by the torturer. It might therefore be thought that, other things being equal, it is more important to prevent torture inflicted by people than torture inflicted by nature. If so, it would perhaps be worse to prevent the prevention of torture in a particular instance (e.g., stop the Water Boy from poisoning the Private) than to prevent the prevention of natural suffering in a particular instance (e.g., by restraining a Dr. Kevorkian from assisting a patient in committing suicide). Whether this argument works, however, depends on whether you think the moral evil created by the Colonel is diminished if the Private drops dead of poison before the Colonel is finished with him. I am inclined to doubt that it is.

    Jefferson McMahan has suggested to me the following additional argument (which he attributes to Thomas Scanlon) that it is not more important to stop harms caused by evil people than by natural events. If it were, then we should choose to rescue nineteen people from suffering (or death) caused by evil people rather than save twenty others from equal suffering (or death) caused by natural disaster. But, faced with such a choice, and all other things being equal, it seems clear we should save the greater number.

8. "Dutch Parliament Approves Law Permitting Euthanasia," *op. cit.*

9. I owe this point to Virginia Warren.

10. Favoring euthanasia only in terminal cases could make sense if accompanied by certain empirical background assumptions, e.g., suffering is much worse in the terminal stages of illness, non-terminal patients may be saved by new miracle cures.

11. For an example of an otherwise well-argued deontological view that founders on its failure to recognize and address the Extra Death problem, see Charles Fried, *Right and Wrong* (Cambridge, MA: Harvard University Press, 1978). The various attempts of supporters of the Doctrine of Double Effect to get around this problem face an unsolved dilemma: if they allow sufficient "redescription" in this sort of case so that the fetus' death turns out unintended (hence permissible), similar redescriptions will vitiate the bite of the Doctrine so that it cannot proscribe what its supporters want it to proscribe, e.g., civilian bombing in warfare.

12. Leon R. Kass ("Is There a Right to Die?" *Hastings Center Report,* 23 [January–February, 1993], 42) writes: "[W]e cannot serve the patient's good by deliberately eliminating the patient."

13. An argument of this form is suggested in Alexander Morgan Capron, "At Law—Even in Defeat, Proposition 161 Sounds a Warning," *Hastings Center Report* 23 (January–February, 1993), 32–34.

14. While 46 percent of patients in the Netherlands requesting euthanasia gave "pain" as a reason for their request, an equal percentage mentioned "unworthy dying," and a greater number (57 percent) mentioned "loss of dignity." See Paul J. Van Der Maas et al., "Euthanasia and Other Medical Decisions Concerning the End of Life," *The Lancet* 338 (Sept. 14, 1991), 669–674, at 672.

15. For a more detailed reply to the Slippery Slope argument, along somewhat similar lines, see Dan Brock, "Voluntary Active Euthanasia," *Hastings Center Report* 22 (1992), 10–22.

16. See, for example, John Rawls, *A Theory of Justice* (Cambridge, MA: Harvard University Press, 1971), pp. 22–27.

17. Richard Fenigsen, "The Report of the Dutch Governmental Committee on Euthanasia," *Issues in Law and Medicine* 7 (1991), 339–344, at 342.

18. Chris Ciesielski-Carlucci, "The Termination of Life without Request in the Netherlands," *VES News* (May 1993), London, forthcoming.

19. Margaret P. Battin, "Seven (More) Caveats Concerning the Discussion of Euthanasia in the Netherlands," *American Philosophical Association Newsletter on Philosophy and Medicine* 92 (1993), 76–80, at 78.

20. Gary Seay, review of Carlos Gomez, *Regulating Death: Euthanasia and the Case of the Netherlands, American Philosophical Association Newsletter on Medicine and Philosophy* 92 (1993), 89–92, at 91.

21. Margaret Battin, "Voluntary Euthanasia and the Risks of Abuse: Can We Learn Anything from the Netherlands," *Law, Medicine, and Health Care* 20 (1992), 133–143.

22. F. M. Kamm, *Creation and Abortion: A Study in Moral and Legal Philosophy* (New York: Oxford University Press, 1992), p. 35.

23. "Is There a Right to Die?" p. 42.

## Journal/Discussion Questions

✍ *Kavka's objection to banning euthanasia centers, in part, on the claim that it is wrong to prevent someone from rescuing someone else from great suffering. The focus, in other words, is on rescuing someone from suffering. Presuming you were qualified to do so (e.g., that you were a physician), how would you respond to a request from someone in great and terminal pain to save that person from further suffering through euthanasia? What would the moral issues be for you?*

1. According to Kavka, people do not have to be in terminal condition in order to justifiably request euthanasia. Why not? Do you agree?

2. Some opponents of euthanasia maintain that human life is sacred and that we therefore must never intentionally kill any human being. How does Kavka reply to supporters of this position? Do you agree or disagree with his reply? Explain.

3. How does Kavka deal with the "slippery slope" objection to legalizing euthanasia? Are you convinced by his reply?

## Daniel Callahan
## "Pursuing a Peaceful Death"

*A co-founder of* The Hastings Center, *Daniel Callahan has been a major voice in biomedical ethics for the last thirty years. His books include* Abortion: Law, Choice, and Morality; Abortion: Understanding Differences, *edited with Sidney Callahan;* Setting Limits: Medical Goals in an Aging Society; *and* The Troubled Dream of Life: Living with Mortality. *He has a particular interest in the relationship of ethics and culture, and of the way in which problems require not only careful rational analysis, but also a feel for culture, for one's own understanding of the world, and for the way we are individually and socially shaped by the technologies and artifacts of our society.*

*Recognizing that modern medicine has made dying much more difficult than before, Callahan considers some of the ways in which this may deform the process of dying. He then sketches out what a "good death" would involve, and argues that medicine should see one of its tasks as helping people to die well.*

### As You Read, Consider This:

1. How does Callahan define a "peaceful death"? What things would you add or subtract from his list of characteristics?
2. What does Callahan mean by "medical futility"? What role does this notion play in his argument?

⌒

On the face of it, one might be forgiven for thinking that death at the hands of modern technological medicine should be a far more benign, sensitive event than it was in earlier times. Do we not have a much greater biological knowledge, thus enabling more precise prognoses of death? Do we not have more powerful analgesics, thereby enhancing the capacity to control pain?

Do we not possess more sophisticated machines, capable of better managing organs gone awry? Do we not have greater psychological knowledge, suitable to relieve the anxieties and suffering of an anticipated death? Do we not, adding all that up, have at hand exactly what we need to enhance the possibility of a peaceful death?

The answer in each case is yes and no. Yes, we do have much more knowledge than we did prior to modern medicine. But no, that knowledge has not made death a more peaceful event, either in reality or in anticipation. The enhanced biological knowledge and technological skill have served to make our dying all the more problematic: harder to predict, more difficult to manage, the source of more moral dilemmas and nasty choices, and spiritually more productive of anguish, ambivalence, and uncertainty. In part this is because, with the advent of modern medicine, the earlier superstructure of meaning and ritual was dismantled, thus setting death adrift in a world of uncertain value and import. But also in part it is because modern medicine brought with it a stance toward death that is ambivalent about its necessity and inevitability.

In response to that ambivalence, without knowing it, without using quite that language, we have come to feel only now the loss of what the late French historian Philippe Aries called a "tame" death.[1] By that he meant a death that was tolerable and familiar, affirmative of the bonds of community and social solidarity, expected with certainty and accepted without crippling fear. That kind of human ending, common to most people throughout history until recently, Aries contrasted with the "wild" death of technological medicine. The latter death—which began to occur in the nineteenth century—is marked by undue fear and uncertainty, by the presence of medical powers not quite within our mastery, by a course of decline that may leave us isolated and degraded. It is wild because it is alien from and outside of the cycle of life, because modern technologies make its course highly uncertain, and because it seems removed from a full, fitting presence in the life of the community.

The technologies of that death, ever more clever in their ability to sustain failing organs, provide a set of tools that endlessly sustain our ambivalence and allow it to be played out in tortuous detail. Precisely because they have opened up new possibilities in the ancient struggle with our mortality, those technologies have made our understanding of that mortality all the more difficult. To confound us more, they have misled us into thinking we have a greater dominance over our mortality than was earlier the case.

What can be done to gain a better way of thinking about medical technology and our human mortality? How can that technology be made to serve a peaceful death, not to be its enemy? What can be done to bring about a change? I want to try to make plausible a different way of thinking about the use of technology and then suggest some ways of implementing it. The change I propose can be put very simply, however strange and odd it may sound. We should begin backward. Death should be seen as the necessary and inevitable end point of medical care.

## Death As the End Point of Medical Care

In considering its appropriate goals, medicine should, so to speak, simultaneously work backward as well as forward. Medicine now characteristically works forward only, looking to promote the good of life, both to lengthen life and improve its quality. Death is reluctantly admitted into the realm of medicine as the limit to achieving those ends, but that limit is itself uncertain at its boundary, not readily located. Thus also is the termination of treatment judged to be a lesser moral evil, because the quality of life cannot be sustained at the level at which, ideally, medicine would like to sustain it.

What if, however we began our thinking with death? What if we asked how medicine should conduct itself to promote both a good life and a peaceful death? What if medicine once and for all accepted death as a limit that cannot be overcome and used that limit as an indispensable focal point in thinking about illness and disease? The reality of death as a part of our biological life would be seen, not as a discordant note in the search for health and well-being, but as a foreseeable endpoint of its enterprise, and its pacification as a proper goal of medicine from the outset. What if the aim of scientific medicine was not an endless struggle against death, with the fight against disease as the token of that struggle, but helping humans best live a mortal, not immortal, life?

These questions are almost naive. But I see no evidence that they are deeply and persistently asked in modern medicine. If they were, then death would have to be taken seriously, allowed an honored role in the ideals of medicine, not treated as only a necessary evil and a temporary scientific failure. The acceptance, management, and understanding of death would become as fully a part of the mainline enterprise of medicine as the pursuit of health. It would not be necessary even to conceive of a hospice movement, a separate system of caring for the dying; that would be taken for granted as central to the enterprise of medicine itself, not a specially constructed sideshow, out of sight of the main tent.

If the ordinary goal of medicine is the preservation or restoration of health, death should be the understood and expected ultimate outcome of that effort, implicitly and inherently there from the start. The only question is when and how, not whether. Medicine's pursuit of health should be leavened by its need when health fails, as it must, to prepare the way for as peaceful a death as possible. If death is part of the human life cycle, then care for the dying body must be integral to the ends of medicine.

Death is, to sharpen the point, that to which medical care should be oriented from the outset in the case of all serious, potentially life-threatening illnesses, or of a serious decline of mental and physical capacities as a result of age or disease. Of each serious illness—especially with the elderly—a question should be asked and a possibility entertained: could it be that this illness is the one that either will be fatal or, since some disease must be fatal, should soon be allowed to be fatal? If so, then a different strategy toward it should come immediately into play, an effort to work toward a peaceful death rather than fight for a cure.

What am I saying that is different from the present stance of medicine? At present medicine takes as its task only the pursuit of health, or the preservation of a decent quality of life, with death as the accidental result of illnesses and diseases thought to be avoidable and contingent, even though in fact still fatal. Death is what happens when medicine fails, and is thus outside its proper scientific scope. That is why, I surmise, a great medical classic, *Cecil Textbook of Medicine*, a primary guide for physicians, refers in only twenty-five of its twenty-three hundred pages to death (and only in five to pain).[2] For a book filled with accounts of lethal diseases and ways to treat them, there is a strikingly scant discussion—three pages only of treatment for those in the terminal phase of disease. It tells what to do to hold off death, but not what is to be done when that is not possible. That omission is a stark example of the way death is kept beyond the borders of medicine, an unwelcome, unwanted, unexpected, and ultimately accidental intruder. What if, by contrast, every section of that book dealing with potentially fatal diseases had a part dealing with the care of those dying from the disease? The care of the dying cancer patient is not identical with the care of a person dying from congestive heart disease or kidney failure. But this could never be guessed from reading standard treatment textbooks.

An incorporation of that approach in textbooks and clinical training would make clear, in the most direct way, that this disease may be, sometimes voluntarily and sometimes not, the cause of death—death, which must come to all and is thus no accident. Then the physician's task would become that of accepting a particular illness as the likely cause of death, opening the way for a peaceful death by choosing that combination of treatment and palliation of the accepted condition most likely to make it possible. The objective here would be exactly the opposite of technological brinkmanship, which goes as far as possible with aggressive treatment, stopping only when it is useless to go further. In the task of allowing a peaceful death, brinkmanship would be repudiated from the outset. Active treatment to cure disease and stop death from coming would stop well short of its technical possibilities, at that point when a peaceful death could be most assured and best managed. The worry that a patient might die sooner than technologically necessary would be actively balanced by anxiety that a patient might die later than was compatible with a peaceful death.

# Deforming Our Dying

A peaceful death can be understood both positively and negatively. I will begin with the latter, specifying some ways in which our dying can be deformed. If we can better discern some of the ways that happens, the ideal of a peaceful death can be given greater substance. Our dying can be deformed in three ways: by deforming the process of dying, by deforming the dying self, and by deforming the community of the living.

## Deforming the Process of Dying

The process of dying is deformed when it is subject to the violence of technological attenuation, drawn out and unduly extended by medical interventions, directly or indirectly. Technological brinkmanship is the most common way of creating the deformity—that is, pushing aggressive treatment as far as it can go in the hope that it can be stopped at just the might moment if it turns out to be futile. That brinkmanship and the gamble it represents can both save life and ruin dying; that is the dilemma it poses. The most obvious kind of technological violence comes when a particular course of treatment—some forms of chemotherapy for cancer, or cardiopulmonary resuscitation for a dying person—itself directly imposes the violence.

Less noticed, but bound to become increasingly important, is the violence done when the cure of one disease sets the stage for the advent of another, perhaps even more cruel than the death one has just averted. Consider, for instance, the person cured of cancer at seventy-five who is set up for the enhanced risk, by virtue of age alone, of the onset of a fatal case of Alzheimer's disease at eighty, or for an excessively long period of severe frailty. We increase the likelihood of spending our declining years helpless, demented, and incontinent if medicine saves our lives long enough to help us avert all of the lethal diseases that stand in the way of that (not so splendid) final outcome.

We may of course gain some extra good years before that happens, and for some it will not happen at all. I only want to underscore the gamble implicit here, a kind of technological Russian roulette with one's last years of life. We must reckon whether it is a good or bad gamble, and how much we are prepared to accept a deformed dying as a result. Increasing frailty and bodily decline are themselves part of the aging process, the wasting away that ordinarily precedes death in old age. There is no inherent evil in the dependency that withering can bring. My complaint is instead directed against a kind of medicine that drives us toward technological brinkmanship and thus needlessly exacerbates and attenuates the withering in destructive ways, genuinely deforming the process of dying. The process of dying is deformed when, through overconfidence in our power to manage technology and to manage our own ambivalence toward death, we fail to take account of what an overzealous medicine can do.

The process of dying is also deformed when there is an extended period of a loss of consciousness well before we are actually dead. It is deformed when there is an exceedingly and unduly long period of debility and frailty before death. It is deformed when there is a lengthy period of pain and suffering prior to death. Note the words I have used: "extended," "exceedingly," "unduly," and "lengthy." By these I mean to say that death may well and unavoidably be preceded by some pain and suffering, some loss of consciousness, some debility and frailty, but that we human beings have generated our own miseries when we allow technology to create a situation that produces exceedingly long periods of those evils. I offer no precise definition of "exceedingly." Frailty and debility can be tolerated for longer periods of time than straight pain and suffering, and a few days even of unconsciousness might be tolerable.

It is when those evils go on and on that a problem, a desperate one, arises. Left unattended, the biological process of dying would not ordinarily lead to such deformities, even if it will happen in some minority of cases. That is something we can know from the dying of other biological organisms, especially higher animals, and from the historical record of human death itself before our modern era, where an extended period of dying was the exception rather than the rule. Our contemporary deformities of dying, it is then fair to say, ordinarily arise only as the result of human medical intervention.

## Deforming the Dying Self

The most obvious way the dying self can be deformed is by allowing the fear of death, or the fear of what dying may do to our ideal self, itself to corrupt the self. Obsessions with a loss of control, or with a diminishment of the idealized optimal self, or with the prospect of pain, are other ways this can happen. That is to turn our dying into an occasion of unrelenting self-pity and self-castigation: I can never be again what I once was, I do not want to be what I now am, and I do not want to be what I will become as my death draws even closer.

Some delicacy is in order in trying to make this point. It is understandable that we should not want to lose all control or to become less of a self than we once were, or that we should fear pain. Anxiety, even terror, is to be expected as we approach our death, both because of the physical threats of dying and because of the challenge to our sense of self-worth and self-coherence. It is the preoccupation with those evils that introduces the potential deformity, the feeling that we cannot be worthy human beings if they are our fate, and an inability to think of anything but our losses, our failures, our diminution.

## Deforming the Community of the Living

Just as we can harm the self, our sense of self-worth, in responding to the threat of death, so too can we do harm to others. If the horror of death—or, more likely, of illness, decline, and dying together—yields social policies designed to relieve that suffering at all costs, then the community of the living is put at risk. A society that takes the relief of the ordinary burdens of life (of which death is surely one) as a goal to be pursued with singular dedication must ultimately fail, putting its members in harm's way even as it does so.

This can happen when the pursuit of health and the avoidance of death become an excessively high priority, gained at the cost of ignoring other social evils. It can happen when the medical community comes to believe it must, as the price of relieving suffering, be prepared to kill or assist in suicide, thus distorting its oldest and most central traditions. It can happen when, as a community ideal, a life that includes any suffering is rejected as intolerable. It can happen when a life thought "not worth living" (the Nazi expression) is one marked by suffering, a less than ideal self, and a failure to make adequate contributions to society.

The possibility of a peaceful death will, then, require as a minimal condition that death not be deformed, either individually or socially. But more will be required to enhance its possibility.

## Defining a Peaceful Death

It is not difficult, just listening to the way people talk about the kind of death they would like, to gain a decent sense of what they would count as a peaceful death. I could try to do that, but I would prefer to put it in my own voice, recognizing that there may be individual variations:

- I want to find some meaning in my death or, if not a full meaning, a way of reconciling myself to it. Some kind of sense must be made of my mortality.
- I hope to be treated with respect and sympathy, and to find in my dying a physical and spiritual dignity.
- I would like my death to matter to others, to be seen in some larger sense as an evil, a rupturing of human community, even if they understand that my particular death might be preferable to an excessive and prolonged suffering, and even if they understand death to be part of the biological nature of the human species.
- If I do not necessarily want to die in the public way that marked the era of a tame death, with strangers coming in off the streets, I do not want to be abandoned, psychologically ejected from the community, because of my impending death. I want people to be with me, at hand if not in the same room.
- I do not want to be an undue burden on others in my dying, though I accept the possibility that I may be some burden. I do not want the end of my life to be the financial or emotional ruination of another life.
- I want to live in a society that does not dread death—at least an ordinary death from disease at a relatively advanced age—and that provides support in its rituals and public practices for comforting the dying and, after death, their friends and families.
- I want to be conscious very near the time of my death, and with my mental and emotional capacities intact. I would be pleased to die in my sleep, but I do not want a prolonged coma prior to my death.
- I hope that my death will be quick, not drawn out.
- I recoil at the prospect of a death marked by pain and suffering, though I would hope to bear it well if that is unavoidable.

There is a difference between this desired peaceful death and Philippe Aries's tame death. Technological advances make it possible to manage better those conditions that could not, in the past, be made amenable to a tame death, especially the degenerative diseases of aging. We can, that is, have both the advantages of the older tame death and, with the help of technology, many improvements in contemporary death.

The most evident characteristic of a peaceful death as I have outlined it is the way it blends personal, medical, and social strands. Whatever meaning we find in our dying and death must come from within ourselves, though we may and probably will of course draw upon religious and other traditions for important help. We could also reasonably look to the larger society for public practices, rituals, and attitudes that can provide a more comforting context for the acceptance of death. A modified return to special symbols of mourning, such as black armbands for men and dark clothes for women, as well as the enhancement of groups organized for grieving spouses, or religious services, would be examples of the possibilities here. As for the relief of pain, there we can look to medical practice, and even expect from that practice some help with suffering, a more subtle condition stemming in part from an interior perception of the significance of dying and from the kind of external support we are given in the face of our anxieties.

Could a peaceful death be assured every patient? No. Medicine cannot now and probably never will be able to avert all pain and suffering or ensure a tranquil course of illness. No society could wholly overcome the fear of death or the rending of community that is death. No one can be confident that fear, anguish, or a sense of pointlessness and futility will not be one's lot, even if one has lived the kind of life most conducive to reducing that possibility. Since no one can give us, as our own, a meaning to our dying and death, we must find that for ourselves; some of us will never find it.

Since there can be no guarantee that a peaceful death will be ours, some store of courage must be available. If I am correct in my surmise that the obsessively feared loss of control of our dying is itself part of the problem—a fear that we will not be either ourselves or in command of ourselves—then one way to resist the force of this fear is to be willing to accept some loss of control. The price of obsession is undue fear. Relief can be sought in a willingness to live with, and die with, less than perfection here. Yet if we can understand that there is a middle way, then the possibility of a peaceful death can be greatly enhanced. It is at least as likely that we could create the possibility of a peaceful death for a majority of people by changing our medical attitudes and expectations as by the more violent course of euthanasia and assisted suicide, and with far less loss of other values in the process.

## Medical Futility

The general orientation and resource allocation priorities of the health care system can make a considerable difference, albeit indirectly for the most part, in the care of the dying. Of more direct and immediate impact will be the aggregate effect of what clinicians at the bedside come to consider futile or marginally useful treatment. As a concept, futility has both medical and moral dimensions.[3] Its medical feature is that of a probability that a particular treatment for a particular person will not be efficacious, that is, it will not return the patient to good health or sustain the patient in any medically viable way. The moral feature is a judgment that some forms of medical treatment, with either a low or no probability of success, should be morally judged to be useless. Taken together, then, a judgment of medical futility is medical insofar as it relies on judgments of probability of medical outcome, and moral in that it relies upon judgments about whether the pursuit of low-probability outcomes is morally required.

There is already considerable pressure from physicians to be allowed to make judgments of medical futility on their own, without having to ask patients or their families. Their goal is not to avoid a doctor-patient interaction, but to be spared the pressure of unrealistic patient demands. It is one thing, they say, to be asked by patients or their families to stop treatment; that is acceptable. It is still another to be asked to provide treatment of a kind physicians think futile or useless; that they take to be unacceptable, a threat to their professional integrity.

Their instinct is correct and reasonable. Physicians ought not to be required to perform procedures or provide treatment that they believe will do no good. Yet it would be arbitrary to allow physicians unilaterally to make those judgments, given the fights of patients to be informed of their situation. It would be better if the standards here were established collectively, by joint bodies of lay people and physicians.

This might best be done in individual hospitals, where joint medical-lay panels could help establish an institutional policy sensitive to local needs and values. It should not, I believe, be done with individual patients on a case-by-case basis. Judgments of futility could then be made, and treatment denied, but on the basis of consensual norms and publicly visible policies.[4] The development of such policies would, of course, have a potentially significant impact on the options available to patients. Some general societal standards would come to replace unlimited patient choice.

What would be the pertinence of such a development for the termination of treatment? It would be valuable if in coming years some consensus were achieved about futile treatment. Futility needs, however, to be understood in two senses: futile because no benefit whatever can be achieved from treatment, and futile because, given resource limitations, the treatment is economically unjustifiable. Thus we must have a general social agreement on the right of physicians to withhold medical treatment from persons in the persistent vegetative state, and an agreement on the forms of medical treatment that would be considered futile for those faced with imminent death from an acute or chronic illness or from the slow death of dementia.

A standard of futility compatible with the goal of avoiding an unnecessarily painful or extended death would be most valuable. The test of futility could be twofold: first, an inability to arrest more than momentarily (by a few days or weeks) a downward, deteriorating course; and second, the probability, should that kind of effort be made, that a peaceful death would become increasingly unlikely. At that point, curative medical treatment has indeed become futile and ought to be stopped. The standard is thus one that looks to the possibility of sustaining life in some decent fashion, but also and simultaneously to the choices necessary for enhancing the possibility of a peaceful death.

The most difficult but impending problem of futility judgments is whether to embody them in public policy. As matters now stand, it is customary for both federal and private health care plans to provide reimbursement for the care of those in a persistent vegetative state; families and medical staffs that want medical treatment to be continued for these patients can be reimbursed for its cost. Should financial support continue in the future? I believe that, in principle, it should not. Ideally speaking, it makes no sense in light of budget restraints or humane public policy to use medical technology to sustain for an extended period the life of someone who will almost certainly never return to consciousness.

The temptation here is to adopt an either-or approach. If we consider the patient alive, then we think we should provide the patient with all those forms of health care that we would provide any other live person; or if we simply consider the patient as dead, even if not legally so, we think we should stop all care. The problem, however, is that we as a society remain uncertain about the status of patients who manage to combine, in a bewildering way, elements of both life and death. An appropriate compromise, I believe, would be to provide minimal nursing care but not the extended artificial nutrition and hydration that many institutions now routinely provide—probably because of public disagreement about the moral status of someone in that condition.

My guess is that increasingly few people will for long believe that this form of "life" merits being called human. It is a moribund life sustained by technological artifact in the face of a biological condition crying out to come to an end, as in nature it ordinarily would. Yet as long as disagreement persists, it would be unwise to stop treatment precipitately or high-handedly. That could seem to bespeak an indifference to the important convictions of some people, convictions not without some merit. But every effort should slowly be made to change those convictions so that a social consensus could build to form the basis of new policy that would refuse reimbursement for patients in that condition. A softer, perhaps more tolerable alternative would be to assign a low priority to such treatment, to help assure it would not capture resources that could be better spent on more needy patients with a chance of real recovery or amelioration of their condition.

A peaceful death should have both an individual and a public face. For the individual it can bring life to a fitting close, marked by connection to the self through reason and self-consciousness, and by connection to others through dying within the circle of human companionship and caring. But death should also have a peaceful public face. The control and management of death, understood as an unavoidable part of life, should not consume an undue share of resources, as if keeping death at bay represented society's most important goal. People should have a chance to live a healthy life, avoid premature death, and then die without that technological brinkmanship that knows no boundaries in the war against mortality.

I would define a peaceful death in a public context as a death that, on the one hand, rejected a disproportionate share of resources which, through a kind of economic violence, threatened other societal goods such as education and housing; and, on the other hand, rejected euthanasia and assisted suicide as still other forms of violence, though medical and social rather than economic.

What about family burdens as a form of quasi-domestic violence? It is not improper for people to worry about being a burden on their families or to wish they could spare them undue emotional and financial hardship. We can readily recognize the possibility of taking down with us, in a parallel destruction, those family members whose devotion—economic or emotional or both—is pressed too far. It is hard to see how a death that impoverishes a family, or destroys the later years of an elderly spouse, or wrecks the family life of a dutiful child caring for an elderly parent, can be called entirely peaceful.

At the same time, however, it is right and proper that we bear one another's illness and dying. We should not only be willing to care for others; no less important, we should allow them to care for us if there is no moral or humane way to avoid that burden. We do not need a medical system and a set of moral values that will impose upon families the drain of extended illness and death, especially when that has been brought about not by natural forces but by an excessive application of life-sustaining technologies. We should be willing to bear what nature and human mortality bring to us. But there is no reason why we should have to bear artificially extended deaths. A patient should reject them for the sake of the family's welfare after he or she is gone. And when a patient is incompetent and death on the way, family members should not be forced, through guilt or a confusion about killing and allowing to die, to believe that a termination of treatment is wrongful killing. It is not killing at all.

## Endnotes

1. Philippe Aries, *The Hour of Our Death*, trans. Helen Weaver (New York: Knopf, 1981), pp. 5–28; see also Philippe Aries, *Western Attitudes Toward Death*, trans. Patricia M. Ranum (Baltimore: The Johns Hopkins University Press, 1974).

2. James R. Wyngaarden, Lloyd H. Smith, and J. Claude Bennett, eds., *Cecil Textbook of Medicine,* 19th ed. (Philadelphia: W. B. Saunders, 1992).

3. See Lawrence J. Schneiderman, Nancy S. Jecker, and Albert R. Jonsen, "Medical Futility: Its Meaning and Ethical Implications," *Annals of Internal Medicine* 112, no. 12 (1990), 949–954; John D. Lantos et al., "The Illusion of Futility, in Medical Practice," *American Journal of Medicine* 87 (July 1980), 81–84; Tom Tomlinson and Howard Brody, "Futility and the Ethics of Resuscitation," *JAMA* 264, no. 10 (1990), 1276–1280; Stuart J. Youngner, "Who Defines Futility?" *JAMA* 260, no. 14 (1988), 2094–2095.

4. See Daniel Callahan, "Medical Futility, Medical Necessity: The Problem-Without-A-Name," *Hastings Center Report* 21, no. 4 (1991), 30–35.

## Journal/Discussion Questions

✍ *What kind of death do you want to have? What do you think will be the greatest barriers to dying in the way you want?*

1. To what extent, according to Callahan, has modern medicine changed the ways in which we die? In what ways has dying been deformed? Why has this given rise to a *moral* problem?

2. How would Callahan's suggestions change the way in which physicians today typically treat dying patients? Discuss.

# QUESTIONS FOR DISCUSSION AND REVIEW

## Where Do You Stand Now?

### Instructions

You have already answered the following questions in your moral problems self-quiz at the beginning of this book. Now that you have studied the material in this section, take a moment to answer the same questions again.

| | Strongly Agree | Agree | Undecided | Disagree | Strongly Disagree | Chapter 2: Euthanasia |
|---|---|---|---|---|---|---|
| 6. | ❑ | ❑ | ❑ | ❑ | ❑ | Euthanasia is always morally wrong. |
| 7. | ❑ | ❑ | ❑ | ❑ | ❑ | Euthanasia should be illegal at least under almost all circumstances. |
| 8. | ❑ | ❑ | ❑ | ❑ | ❑ | The principal moral consideration about euthanasia is the question of whether the person freely chooses to die or not. |
| 9. | ❑ | ❑ | ❑ | ❑ | ❑ | Actively killing someone is always morally worse than just letting them die. |
| 10. | ❑ | ❑ | ❑ | ❑ | ❑ | We should never allow terminally ill newborns to die. |

Compare your answers to the present self-quiz with the answers to the initial self-quiz. How, if at all, have your answers changed? How have the *reasons* for your answers changed?

## Journal/Discussion Questions

✍ *Under what conditions, if any, would you want others to withhold medical treatment from you? To withhold fluids and nutrition? To actively terminate your life?*

✍ *Write your own living will, including in it all instructions and requests you think are relevant.*

1. You have now read, thought, and discussed a number of aspects of the morality of the euthanasia decision. How have your views *changed* and developed? Has your understanding changed of the reasons supporting other positions that are different from your own? What issue(s) remain unresolved for you at this point?

2. What, in the readings in this section, was the most thought-provoking idea you encountered? In what ways did it prompt you to reconsider some of your previous beliefs?

3. In light of the preceding readings, what do you think is the single most compelling reason for legalizing euthanasia? What do you think is the single most compelling reason for *not* doing so? If euthanasia were to be legalized, what do you think would be the most important safeguard that should accompany it?

# FOR FURTHER READING:
## A BIBLIOGRAPHICAL GUIDE
## TO EUTHANASIA

### Journals

In addition to the standard journals in ethics mentioned in Chapter 1, see *The Hastings Center Reports*, *The Journal of Medicine and Philosophy*, *Bioethics*, and *The Kennedy Institute of Ethics Journal*.

### Anthologies

There are several very helpful *anthologies* that deal with euthanasia. *Beneficent Euthanasia,* ed. by Marvin Kohl (Buffalo: Prometheus Books, 1975) contains a very good range of pieces; *Ethical Issues Relating to Life and Death*, ed. John Ladd (New York: Oxford University Press, 1979); *Euthanasia: The Moral Issues*, ed. Robert M. Baird and Stuart E. Rosenbaum (Buffalo: Prometheus Books, 1989) contains a nice balance of philosophical and popular pieces; *Euthanasia: Opposing Viewpoints*, ed. Carol Wekesser (San Diego: Greenhaven Press, 1995) also contains a good balance of philosophical and popular pieces, all in relatively short segments. Also see, *Voluntary Euthanasia*, ed. A. B. Downing and Barbara Smoker (London: Peter Owen, 1986), which includes a number of important essays, including an exchange between Yale Kamisar and Glanville Williams; and *The Dilemmas of Euthanasia*, ed. J. A. Behnke and Sissela Bok (New York, 1975); and *Suicide and Euthanasia*, ed. Baruch Brody (Dordrecht: Kluwer). On the distinction between killing and letting die, see *Killing and Letting Die*, ed. Bonnie Steinbock and Alastair Norcross, 2nd ed. (New York: Fordham University Press, 1994), which contains virtually all the major essays on this topic; it also contains an excellent bibliography.

### Review Articles

For an excellent survey of the philosophical issues (and a very helpful annotated bibliography), see Marvin Kohl, "Euthanasia," *Encyclopedia of Ethics*, ed. Lawrence C. Becker and Charlotte B. Becker (New York: Garland, 1992), pp. 335–339.

### Journal Articles

The *distinction between active and passive euthanasia* was seriously questioned in our selection from James Rachels, "Active and Passive Euthanasia," *New England Journal of Medicine* 292, no. 2 (January 9, 1975), 78–80. Rachels's position has been criticized by a number of philosophers, including Tom L. Beauchamp, "A Reply to Rachels on Active and Passive Euthanasia," in *Social Ethics,* ed. Thomas A. Mappes and Jane S. Zembaty (New York: McGraw-Hill, 1977), pp. 67–76; Thomas D. Sullivan, "Active and Passive Euthanasia: An Impertinent Distinction?", in *Social Ethics,* 4th ed., ed. Thomas A. Mappes and Jane S. Zembaty (New York: McGraw-Hill, 1992), pp. 115–121; Rachels's reply to Sullivan is variously reprinted, including in Mappes and

Zembaty's *Social Ethics*, 4th ed., pp. 121–131. Also see Bonnie Steinbock, "The Intentional Termination of Life," *Ethics in Science and Medicine* 6, no. 1 (1979), 59–64.

Among the important philosophical essays, see Philippa Foot, "Euthanasia," reprinted in her *Virtues and Vices* (Berkeley: University of California Press, 1978), pp. 33–61; Judith Jarvis Thomson's "Killing, Letting Die, and the Trolley Problem," and "The Trolley Problem," reprinted in her *Rights, Restitution, and Risk,* ed. William Parent (Cambridge: Harvard University Press, 1986), pp. 78–93, 94–116; in "Euthanasia: A Christian View," *Philosophic Exchange* 2, no. 2 (1975), pp. 43–52, R. M. Hare develops a version of the Golden Rule argument against euthanasia.

## Books

Among the *philosophical books devoted primarily to euthanasia and decisions at the end of life*, see especially James Rachels, *The End of Life: The Morality of Euthanasia* (New York: Oxford University Press, 1986); Fred Feldman, *Confrontations with the Reaper: A Philosophical Study of the Nature and Value of Death* (New York: Oxford University Press, 1992); Jay F. Rosenberg, *Thinking Clearly about Death* (Englewood Cliffs, NJ: Prentice Hall, 1983); Marvin Kohl, *The Morality of Killing: Sanctity of Life, Abortion, and Euthanasia* (New York: Humanities Press, 1974); Kenneth L. Vaux, *Death Ethics: Religious and Cultural Values in Prolonging and Ending Life* (Philadelphia: Trinity Press International, 1992); Daniel Callahan, *Setting Limits: Medical Goals in an Aging Society* (New York: Simon and Schuster, 1987); and Margaret Battin, *The Least Worst Death: Essays in Bioethics on the End of Life* (New York: Oxford, 1994).

Among the more *popular literature* on euthanasia, see Derek Humphrey's *Final Exit: The Practicalities of Self-Deliverance and Assisted Suicide for the Dying* (Eugene, OR: Hemlock Society, 1991). Perhaps the most (in)famous public figure in this area is Jack Kevorkian; see *Prescription—Medicide: The Goodness of Planned Death* (Buffalo, NY: Prometheus Books, 1991). For a much more moderate voice, see C. Everett Koop, *The Right to Live, the Right to Die* (Wheaton, IL: Tyndale House Publishers, 1976). In *Death and Dignity: Making Choices and Taking Charge* (New York: W. W. Norton, 1993), Timothy E. Quill, M.D., argues, at least in part on the basis of his experience as a hospice director, in favor of physician-assisted euthanasia; for an interesting contrast, see *Euthanasia Is Not the Answer: A Hospice Physician's View,* by David Cundiff (Totowa, NJ: Humana Press, 1992).

On the *Nazi euthanasia program,* see most recently Michael Burleigh's *Death and Deliverance* (Cambridge: Cambridge University Press, 1994) as well as Robert Jay Lifton's *The Nazi Doctors* (New York: Basic Books, 1986).

## Suicide

There are a number of excellent *anthologies* of selections dealing solely with the issue of suicide. These include: *On Suicide,* Introduction by Robert Coles, ed. John Miller (San Francisco: Chronicle Books, 1992); and *Essays in Self-Destruction,* edited by Edwin S. Shneidman (New York: J. Aronson, 1967). For a more strictly philosophical approach, see the anthologies *Suicide, the Philosophical Issues,* ed. M. Pabst Battin and David J. Mayo (New York: St. Martin's Press, 1980) and *Suicide: Right or Wrong?* ed. John Donnelly (Buffalo: Prometheus Press, 1990) for excellent selections of philosophical works on suicide.

A. Alvarez's *The Savage God: A Study of Suicide* (New York, Random House, 1972) is a classic study. On the effects of *depression*, see especially William Styron, *Darkness Visible* (New York: Random House, 1990).

Among contemporary *philosophical approaches to suicide*, see the interesting contrast between the Kantian approach of Thomas E. Hill, Jr., "Self-Regarding Suicide: A Modified Kantian View," *Autonomy and Self-Respect* (Cambridge: Cambridge University Press, 1991), pp. 85–103 and the utilitarian perspective of Richard Brandt, "The Morality and Rationality of Suicide," in his *Morality, Utilitarianism, and Rights* (Cambridge: Cambridge University Press, 1992), pp. 315–335. For an excellent longer study, see Margaret Pabst Battin, *Ethical Issues in Suicide* (Englewood Cliffs, NJ: Prentice Hall, 1982).

# Punishment and the Death Penalty

**Videotape:**

       *Topic:*   The Death Penalty—Crime and Punishment

       *Source:*  *Nightline* (January 16, 1995)

       *Anchor:*  Ted Koppel

# EXPERIENTIAL ACCOUNTS

Helen Prejean, C.S.J.
"Crime Victims on the Anvil of Pain"

*Sister Helen Prejean, C.S.J., is a native of Louisiana, a member of the Sisters of St. Joseph of Medaille, and a spiritual counselor both to inmates on death row and to the families of their victims. Her book,* Dead Man Walking: An Eyewitness Account of the Death Penalty in the United States, *quickly became one of the most influential works questioning the morality of the death penalty.*

*In the following newspaper article from 1988, Helen Prejean tries to do justice both to her firm conviction that the death penalty is wrong and her compassion for those who have lost a family member to a violent crime. She describes, briefly but graphically, the pain of both and the effects of their pain on her.*

## As You Read, Consider This:

1. Do you think that Sister Prejean perceives the death row inmates clearly? The families of the victims?
2. What moves you about Sister Prejean's account of her ministry to death row inmates and to the families of their victims?

I stand outside the door and take a deep breath. It's my first meeting with the New Orleans Chapter of Parents of Murdered Children, a support group for people whose children have met violent deaths.

Vernon Harvey, my nemesis of sorts, waits for me on the other side of the door. His step-daughter, Faith, was murdered by Robert Lee Willie. I was Robert's spiritual adviser. Both of us witnessed Robert's execution in the electric chair.

Prior to the execution, both of us had appeared at the Pardon Board hearing—he, urging Robert's death; I, pleading for his life. He was furious at me.

"You should be helping victims' families," he had told me.

Finally, at his urging I was coming to this meeting.

People ask me how I got involved in all this. Good question. I ask it of God sometimes when I pray.

For 20 years I did what most other Catholic nuns were doing—teaching the young, conducting religious education programs in a suburban church parish. But in 1981 I moved into a steamy public housing project in New Orleans and for the first time in my life tasted the struggle of those who live on the "underside of history."

One day a friend in prison ministry asked me to become a pen pal to someone on death row. "Sure," I said, having no idea what lay in store for me. I wrote to Elmo Patrick Sonnier, then I became his spiritual adviser, then I watched him die in the electric chair. I became a strong advocate for death row inmates and their families.

I am with Elmo Patrick Sonnier in the death house. The guards are in his cell, shaving his head, his left ankle. . . .

He returns to the metal door where I sit on the other side. His body sags in the chair. He looks naked, stripped. He smokes cigarettes and drinks black coffee.

I've known him for two years. As a child he alternated between divorced parents and he was out on his own by the time he was 16. He had done his share of settling life's challenges with his fists, but never anything like Nov. 5, 1977, when he and his brother killed a teen-age couple. The fathers of the victims will be there to witness his execution.

He's talking non-stop . . . snatches from the past . . . how good it felt to go hunting when the weather was cool . . . driving 18 wheelers . . . "thank you for your love . . . please take care of my Mama . . ."

We pray together. "God, just give me the strength to make that last walk." He starts to shiver. A guard puts a denim jacket over his shoulders.

It's midnight. "Time to go, Sonnier," the warden says.

We walk to the electric chair, my hand on his shoulder as I read from the Bible. We stop. I look up and see the chair. The guards are leading me away. "Pray for me, Pat." He turns around. "I will, Sister Helen, I will."

His last words . . . he looks at the parents of the murdered teen-agers. "Forgive me for what me and my brother did."

He sits in the chair. The guards move quickly, strapping his arms, his legs. He finds my face among the witnesses. "I love you," he says.

I turn the doorknob and enter the room where the Parents of Murdered Children are meeting. Vernon comes over to greet me. His eyes say, "You're coming around—at last."

The meeting begins. The motto of the group is "Give sorrow words."

- "Laura was stabbed by my son's best friend one week before her 12th birthday. Her skiing outfit is still hanging in the closet . . . five years now. I just can't give it away."

- "When my child was killed, it took over a week to find her body. The police treated us like we were the criminals. They brushed us off whenever we phoned."

- "I got to witness the son of a b—— fry who killed our daughter. The chair is too quick. I hope he's burning in hell."

- "I'm beginning to let my anger go. I put John's picture on the Christmas tree. My Christmas angel, I call him."

- "Friends avoid us. If you try to bring up your child's death, they change the subject."

I leave the meeting stunned by the pain I have been allowed to touch. On the anvil of that pain I forge a new commitment to expend my energies for victims' families as well as death row inmates. Now I work on a task force to see that victims' families get state-allotted funds for counseling, unemployment compensation, funeral expenses. Only a handful of sheriff's offices in Louisiana bother to appoint the personnel to administer these funds. Related, I think, to a mind-set prevalent in our criminal justice system: big on recrimination; short on healing.

As I see it, the death penalty is just another killing (and a highly selective one at that; two-thirds of all executions happen in four southern states). Obviously executions don't do anything for the criminal, and, from what I've seen, they don't do much for victims' families either.

Our need to protect ourselves from killers is real. When I walk to my car at night I glance often over my shoulder. I know now that really bad things can happen to really good people. But surely in 1988 we who purport to be the most civilized of societies can find a way to incapacitate dangerous criminals without imitating their tragic, violent behavior.

## Journal/Discussion Questions

✍ *Sister Prejean's reactions to both the death row inmates and to the families of their victims are probably different from our own—certainly the combination is most unusual, for she seems able to appreciate the humanity of both without idealizing either. Do you think that her perceptions are correct? If they are different from your own and you think they are correct, what makes it difficult for you fully to perceive the humanity of these murderers? Of their victims?*

1. How does Sister Prejean reconcile her commitment to the death row inmates and to the families of their victims? Does this have more moral force than if she were just committed to one or the other alone? Why?

2. Why is Sister Prejean opposed to the death penalty? What does she suggest as an alternative?

# AN INTRODUCTION TO THE MORAL ISSUES

## Introduction

In the mid-1990s, we have seen increasing calls to "get tough" in regard to punishment, in particular punishment for crimes of violence and punishment for repeat offenders. Eager to capitalize on public fear, politicians have proposed increasingly stringent penalties for particular crimes of violence and for those who have been convicted of crimes in the past. Yet all of this remains troubling, for it is not clear that things are getting any better. We punish more and more in America, but it doesn't seem that our society is safer or that criminals are really deterred by the threat of punishment. Indeed, the United States currently has more individuals in prison today that any other industrialized country, and there seems to be little end in sight.

## Justifications of Punishment

Punishment needs justification. The very idea of punishment is that we impose something unpleasant—perhaps even painful or horrible, such as hanging or electrocution—on people against their will. On what basis do we claim the right to do something that odious? It is to this question that justifications of punishment are directed.

Justifications of punishment generally fall into one of two types: *backward-looking* justifications, which essentially see punishment as retribution for a past offense, and *forward-looking* accounts, which see the justification of punishment in some future state of affairs (such as reduction of crime or even rehabilitation of the criminal) that it may bring about. Of the forward-looking accounts, the most common is a deterrence model, which sees the justification of punishment to be located primarily in the ways in which it deters future crime. Rehabilitative models, which see punishment as being more properly replaced by rehabilitation, are also forward-looking, but there is some dispute about whether they genuinely involve punishment. So, too, are models of punishment that see that justification of punishment as being in the type of society that it produces.

In addition to distinguishing between backward-looking and forward-looking accounts of the justification of punishment, we can also distinguish between accounts of punishment in general as an institution (i.e., why are we justified in punishing *at all*?), accounts of the justification of particular punishments (i.e., why is this particular punishment justified for this particular *type* of offense), and justifications of specific instances of punishment (i.e., why is this *particular* individual given this *particular* sentence?). As we shall see, the justification of punishment in general need not be the same as the justification of particular punishments. In this context, we will not be concerned with any specific instances of punishment.

### Retributivism: An Eye for an Eye

Retributivist accounts of punishment see it essentially as a kind of paying-back, a retribution for past offenses. A person has been wronged, and the state is jus-

*Is punishment just a matter of "an eye for an eye"?*

tified in inflicting on the wrongdoer the same degree of pain or suffering that the wrongdoer inflicted on the victim. With this comes some rough principle of proportionality, which came to be
associated with the Old Testament maxim of "an eye for an eye, a tooth for a tooth," the *lex talionis*. As we shall see, there are difficulties in interpreting this maxim too literally, but the power of
the metaphor is obvious once one acknowledges that it is a metaphor and not a literal guide to behavior. Punishment, retributivists claim, must fit the crime.

*Retributivism as revenge.*   The crudest account of retributivist justifications of punishment sees
them simply as a more or less disguised version of revenge. Friedrich Nietzsche, for example,
maintained that revenge was at the heart of the modern notion of punishment. Some have criticized
and rejected retributivist accounts of punishment because of this link between retributivism and revenge. Retributivism, they claim, is simply our primitive desire to hit back dressed up in moral
clothing.

   Defenders of retributivism can respond with two types of replies. On the one hand, they can
admit the link between retributivism and revenge but deny that this is grounds for rejecting retributivism. Revenge, they can argue, is a fundamental moral impulse of human beings that places a
check on external aggression. Without the desire for revenge, we would be willing accomplices in
our own victimization. Revenge, in other things, is not such a bad thing after all, and is certainly
not sufficient grounds for rejecting retributivism.

   On the other hand, retributivists can argue that retribution is not about revenge, or at least not
in any exclusive sense or in any morally shallow sense. Retribution, they argue, is about something
more: about balancing the scales of justice, about safeguarding the rights of victims, and about
changing perpetrators. Let's look briefly at each of these claims.

*The scales of justice.*   Several different reasons have been advanced in support of this general
claim of retributivism. First, underlying some retributivist thought is a metaphor of *moral balance*
which is closely associated with the notion of justice. Punishment resets the moral scales, as it
were, of society after they have been upset through an offense. Think, for example, of the punishment of Nazis who ran the death camps. Such punishment was often seen as balancing the scales of
justice, and many felt it was morally odious for such actions to go unpunished.

*The rights of victims.*   Some retributivists have taken a somewhat different tact: *victims*, they
argue, have a right to see that the perpetrators suffer their just desserts. Clearly it would be anarchy
if victims were to take this task upon themselves, so punishment becomes the proper domain of the
state. Indeed, the very idea of having rights in a particular state is that the state guarantees those
rights, by preventing others from violating them when possible and punishing violators.

*The effect on perpetrators.*   Finally, some retributivists focus on the effect that punishment should
have on those who perpetrate offenses. First, punishment should bring about some kind of insight.
The Kantian account of this insight is that, by willing the crime (e.g., a theft), the perpetrator wills
that the maxim behind it (that one person is entitled to appropriate another person's property without permission) be a universal law; thus the perpetrator is in effect willing that others are equally
entitled to take the perpetrator's property. What's fair for one is fair for all. Others have argued that
perpetrators should experience the pain, suffering, etc. that they have inflicted on their victims. In-

deed, there is something profoundly moral about this which has nothing to do with revenge *per se*. Many, including Josiah Royce, have argued that the essence of the moral point of view is the realization that the suffering of others is of equal value to one's own suffering. Think, for example, of punishments of drunk drivers that require them to ride with paramedics to the scenes of auto accidents, to visit victims of other drunk drivers in hospitals and rehabilitation facilities, to talk to families who have lost loved ones in accidents caused by drunk drivers. From a moral point of view, such punishments are best understood as programs that help perpetrators understand the real and potential pain and suffering that their offenses can cause.

Second, punishment should "wipe the slate clean." Again, this is part of the balance metaphor insofar as once the scales are back in correct balance, there is nothing left to over to be an object of resentment. Yet this is also a corollary of the intended effect of punishment on perpetrators: if they realize how wrong their deeds were, then they have made a kind of moral progress which entitles them for full reinstatement in the moral community. Many thinkers, not just retributivists, have argued that perpetrators give up their membership in the moral community through their crimes, and it is in part the insights gained through their own punishment—as well as the suffering endured—that entitle them to reinstatement in the moral community.

*Criticisms of retributivism.* When strict retributivists are asked to justify the institution of punishment, they are at something of a disadvantage. In order to justify something like the institution of punishment, we have to point to something else—and that something else is usually consequentialist and forward-looking in character. Retributivists often seem stuck with simply saying, "Well, it's just *right* that criminals should be punished." If they go further and maintain that it's right because . . . , then what follows the "because" is usually a forward-looking consequentialist concern. It may be that it's right because without punishment society would run amok, or it may be right because it teaches people important lessons about society, but in any case the "because" clause usually turns out to be a forward-looking one.

Second, critics of strict retributivism argue that the *lex talionis*, the law of "an eye for an eye, a tooth for a tooth," is much less simple that it would appear. If someone is convicted of torture, do we then torture that person as a punishment? If someone is convicted of rape, are they to be raped in return? What do we do with someone who has hijacked a bus? Plagiarized a term paper? Desecrated an historical monument? Robbed a bank? The *lex talionis*, in other words, appears to offer literal guidance on punishment, but on closer inspection it can only be interpreted as metaphorical.

Finally, some critics of strict retributivism maintain that it can lead to individual punishments in particular cases that are cruel or that do not serve the ends of justice. Think, for example, of those who committed serious but undetected crimes in their youth and then led exemplary lives, only to have their crime uncovered in old age. Strict retributivists would seem to be committed to punishment that is equally severe, whether the crime is discovered minutes after its commission or decades later. It may be possible to temper this with some degree of mercy, but mercy has no necessary place in the retributivist's world.

## Deterrence

One of the principal forward-looking justifications of punishment is its deterrent effect. There are two aspects to such deterrence. The first, and more immediate, is the deterrent effect on the perpetrators who are convicted: punishment deters them from committing such crimes again.

The second level of deterrence is more general: punishment of perpetrators deters others, those who have not committed such crimes but may be inclined to do so, from committing them. Common to both is the simple claim that punishment deters crime, and it is upon this that its justification rests.

There is much to be said for forward-looking justifications of the institution of punishment as a whole. Indeed, we do not have to stop with deterrence of further crimes in our forward-looking justifications, for we can then point out why such deterrence would be valuable to society: the greater sense of public safety, the elimination of societal resources destroyed through crime, etc. Overall, the forward-looking claim is a clearly utilitarian one: societies that have the institution of punishment are better than those that do not. Overall, punishment makes society a better place in which to live.

*Normative and empirical considerations.*   Notice that deterrence-based justifications of punishment contain both normative and empirical premises. In order to justify punishment on the basis of its deterrent effect, we really need two types of premises. First, we need an *empirical claim* that punishment does in fact deter. Second, we need a *normative claim* that deterrence (or a society with deterrence) is *good.* Thus our argument looks like this:

> *Empirical Premise:*     Punishment reduces crime.
>
> *Normative Premise:*     Reducing crime is good.
>
> *Conclusion:*     Punishment is good.

Obviously, neither of these premises is controversial, at least in its most general form. Although there is a lot of controversy about the deterrent effects of particular punishments, it seems uncontroversially true that overall punishment reduces crime. Similarly, it is uncontroversially true that reducing crime is good. However, when we look more closely, problems begin to emerge.

*Paths to deterrence.*   The potential difficulties with this argument begin to emerge when we look more closely at the premises. The empirical premise about the deterrent effect of punishment is generally true, but as it stands it only refers to punishment in general, not particular punishments. Moreover, it leaves open the possibility that something else may also reduce crime, perhaps even more effectively. Some candidates for other general societal factors that reduce crime may include a strong moral education, strong family support, the reduction of physical and sexual abuse in childhood, reduction of dependency on drugs and alcohol, and the reduction of poverty and discrimination; some, more specifically crime-related factors, include increased funding for community policing, more intensive parole programs, and more research on factors that reduce the occurrence of crime. Clearly, we do not want to say that *only* punishment reduces crime. The question then becomes whether punishment is the best means or—presuming that we do not want to consider these as mutually exclusive alternatives—what the proper mixture should be between punishment and other means of reducing crime.

*Punishment and prevention.*   These considerations have a particular relevance when we are thinking of punishment in general as an institution and the distribution of resources in society. There is an interesting analogy here between crime and lung cancer. Punishment is one of the ways that society seeks to reduce crime, but it is often a last-ditch effort. Just as surgery, radiation, and chemotherapy may be effective therapies against lung cancer, so too imprisonment (and perhaps even the death penalty) may be effective responses to crime, but there is a sense in which they all come too late. They arrive on the scene after the event has happened and the damage has been done. Preventive approaches are far more effective, but much less visible—and thus it may be much harder to obtain funding for them. It makes good sense to spend more of our resources on reducing the causes of cancer—such as smoking and environmental factors—than on developing increasingly effective surgical and therapeutic techniques for curing existing cases of cancer. Similarly, when we consider how we want to distribute our total resources as a society in regard to crime, it makes good sense to concentrate on changing the conditions that give rise to criminal behavior rather than focusing primarily on punishing that behavior once it has occurred. Increasingly severe punishments do not provide the most effective long-term answer to the question of crime. The answer is not to punish crime more severely and more often after it happens, but to support those changes that will reduce the occurrence of crime in the first place.

*Conflicting goods.*    Although the normative premise looks uncontroversial, it too needs at least additional precision. Reducing crime is clearly good, but it is not the *only* good that we strive for, and we must insure that in seeking to reduce crime we do not impinge upon other, perhaps even more important rights and goods. Reducing crime is good, but so too is respecting individual rights, and these two goods often come into conflict. We could easily reduce the level of crime by more extensive surveillance of citizens, by restrictive curfews, by permitting police searches and seizures at will, by outlawing the possession of any weapons, and the like. However, we don't do these things because they conflict with individual rights to liberty, and the preservation of those rights is a good that we strive to realize. We can accept the premise that reducing crime is good, but we must not overlook the fact that it is not the only good.

*Disproportionate punishments.*    One of the greatest potential dangers of deterrence-based models of punishment is that they seem to open the door to justifying punishment, or a severity of punishment, disproportionate to the offense. Recall, for example, the case of Michael Fay, who was sentenced to caning (and also to prison and to fines) for various acts of vandalism in Singapore. Many Americans were outraged at the severity of the sentence, but officials in Singapore pointed out that the penalty was their standard penalty, that everyone knows what the penalties are (including Mr. Fay), and that their society has an amazingly low incident of crime as a result. In other words, they said, this punishment deters, so what's wrong with it? Indeed, many Americans agreed, perhaps indicating their discontent with the American criminal justice system rather than their allegiance to Singapore's.

The philosophical issue here is an important one. If the *only* justification for punishment is deterrence, then it would seem to follow that the more a punishment deters, the more justified it is. Let's furthermore presume that punishments that are inevitable, swift, and public are more likely to deter than punishments that are not. A department store that is bothered by shoplifting, for example, may want to have surveillance equipment, roving undercover police, and roving magistrates to arrest shoplifters, try them on the spot, and then impose a swift, certain, severe, and public punishment such as cutting off a hand for first offenders, cutting off the other hand for second offenders.

This would, one suspects, reduce the amount of shoplifting—indeed, it would probably reduce even the *appearance* of shoplifting—but our immediate reply to such a proposal would presumably be twofold. First, we would say that such punishment violates the shoplifter's rights. But doesn't all punishment do so? Indeed, the whole idea of punishment is to do something to offenders that they don't like—otherwise it wouldn't be punishment. Second, we would say that such punishment is disproportionate to the offense. But proportionality is really a retributivist concept. For the strict deterrence theorist, proportionality just isn't an issue.

*Punishing the innocent.*   In the most extreme cases, deterrence seems to justify punishing the innocent if doing so would result in a significant deterrent effect. The acceptability of this practice seems to follow from a pure deterrence theory. If the sole justification of punishment is deterrence, and if in a particular case punishing an innocent person—who the public thought was guilty—would have a significant deterrent effect, then punishing an innocent person in that context would be justified. Imagine, for example, that a distinguished diplomat from a foreign country with nuclear capabilities is killed in mysterious circumstances. The United States authorities do not know who killed the diplomat, but they realize that an international incident—perhaps culminating in a nuclear attack—could occur if someone is not arrested immediately. Determined to avoid such a thing, officials arrange the arrest of an innocent man—who in fact is only months from death by cancer—whose generalized guilt is so great that he can be enticed into confessing to the crime. He is then executed, and the crisis is avoided.

In discussing these kinds of cases, which he calls *telishment*, John Rawls points out that they can only be justified from a utilitarian perspective if we consider them as individual cases. However, if we asked whether we could justify a rule permitting telishment from a utilitarian standpoint, we clearly could not do so. Rule utilitarian justifications are not subject to the same potential abuses as act utilitarian ones are.

## Rehabilitation

Typically, retributivist models of punishment see moral agents as autonomous agents who have chosen to do something wrong. Deterrence models are largely indifferent to questions about the autonomy of offenders; they are only concerned with preventing crime in the future. Rehabilitation models typically begin with a different model of the moral agent, one that sees offenders

*Should punishment seek to rehabilitate?*

as having in some sense diminished moral capacity—often due to societal factors—and thus more in need of rehabilitation than punishment.

Although most Americans are not enthusiastic about rehabilitative models of punishment, they are distressed because their prisons often seem to do more harm than good: inexperienced criminals emerge hardened and more inclined than ever toward a life of crime. Prisons seem to be a training school for criminals, an intensive internship program in criminal values and techniques. Although they deter the criminals from committing (at least most of) their usual crimes while in prison, those criminals often return to the streets tougher, meaner, and more skilled in crime than when they entered prison.

One of the difficulties of rehabilitation as a goal of punishment is that it makes punishment more open-ended, which in some cases can result in a longer period of loss of freedom for the offender. Furthermore, some kinds of rehabilitation treat offenders as though they were not fully responsible moral and legal agents. Such programs are also very expensive to administer, and they seem to offer criminals positive opportunities not always available to the general citizen. Finally, it is far from clear that such programs work often enough to justify their expense.

## Reconciliation and Healing

Unfortunately, there has been no shortage in recent years (or at virtually any other time in human history, for that matter) of horrible, systematic violations of human rights by governments and their representatives. Think of the Nazi persecution of Jews and others, of the human rights violations in Latin America, of the horrors of apartheid in South Africa. When societies begin to come to terms with such offenses, they face a difficult challenge, for they must both punish and heal. Sometimes these seem like incompatible goals. Punishment seems divisive, while reconciliation seems to demand that offenders be allow to go free without punishment.

Consider South Africa. After many decades of brutal torture and murder on the part of the South African government against the indigenous population (and their sympathizers), the white South African government relinquished power, allowing a majority government by blacks and persons of mixed raced. As a society, South Africa faced a crucial question. Should it attempt to punish all those guilty of torture and murder over the years, or should it set aside such considerations of justice in order to avoid the divisiveness of such trials and their accompanying punishments? Nelson Mandela, the first black president of South Africa, set the tone for the new government by inviting his jailer of thirty years to attend his inauguration. In doing so, Mr. Mandela sent a clear message that he would pursue a path of reconciliation rather than retribution. This is an extremely morally demanding path, for it is important to note that it is most morally demanding on those who have suffered the most. Those who have suffered, the victims and their families, have a morally understandable desire for retribution. Yet it is often precisely the divisiveness generated by such trials that threatens the often fragile social fabric of a new regime. The danger of ignoring retribution is twofold. First, those who have suffered will feel that they have not been avenged properly. Second, it can be interpreted as sending a message that possible future acts of political oppression will be unpunished as well. Some countries, most notably in Latin America, have tried to find a middle ground here by holding investigative hearings intended to establish an accurate public record of abuses—thereby recognizing the suffering of victims—but have not pursued punishment for the offenders in the interests of national reconciliation.

A corresponding issue exists on the individual level. Those who have been wronged have to face the issue of how to put the crime "behind them." Punishment alone rarely brings healing, but for many it is the precondition for healing. The families of murder victims, for example, often await the execution of the murderer as a necessary step in their healing process. For others, the road to healing is through mercy and forgiveness. In their eyes, punishment may be justified, but it may nonetheless not be the best course of action.

## Mixed Justifications

Some philosophers, most notably John Rawls, have argued that retributivist and consequentialist accounts of punishment can be combined, and that each has distinctive strengths in particular areas and that the combination avoids the weaknesses each typically have. The general strategy in such approaches has been to distinguish between the justification of punishment as an institution in general and the justification of particular punishments. They then consider the liabilities associated with each of the two major approaches to punishment, the retributivist and the deterrence-based theories. Typically, retributivist justifications of the *institution* of punishment are weak and open to the charge that punishment is simply revenge dressed up in legal clothing. Similarly, deterrence-based (and consequentialist in general) justifications of particular punishments run the risks of disproportionate punishment and punishment of the innocent when such punishment is the best deterrent. On the other hand, each of these positions is seen as having a unique strength. Retributivism contains a doctrine of proportionality that seems appropriate in determining the nature and severity of particular punishments. Similarly, consequentialist theories are certainly correct in saying that the overall justification for punishing at all is that it has good effects for society as a whole, especially in terms of deterrence. Thus, in order to avoid the difficulties associated with each position and retain the benefits of each, mixed justifications typically argue that the institution of punishment in terms of its benefit to society as a whole, while the severity of particular punishments is justified on the basis of a retributivist's principle of proportionality.

Although there is much to recommend such mixed theories, the principal drawback seems to be precisely their mixed character. Just as physics is continually searching for a Grand Unified Theory that explains everything in terms of a few simple principles that apply everywhere, so, too, philosophers want a theory that illuminates the continuity of our moral experience. Mixed theories fail to do that, and their failure raises the suspicion that we are employing theories in an ad hoc manner—that is, applying them when they yield the results we want, and ignoring them when they do not. However, the whole idea of a theory is that it is *not* ad hoc, that it applies uniformly. We still seem to lack a grand unified theory of punishment.

## The Limits of Punishment

In light of these considerations, we can formulate at least some of the general restrictions that ought to be imposed on punishment in general. Some of these are general considerations following from the nature of law, others derive specifically from our preceding discussion.

*Public notice of offenses.*   First, and most uncontroversially, we clearly are not entitled to punish people if we do not tell them in advance that something is an offense. Laws must be publicly proclaimed, and that it is fundamental principle of all law, not just criminal law.

*Authority to punish.*   Second, punishment can only be administered by those who are legally entitled to do so. Part of being a member of a state is that we cede to the state certain powers, including the power to punish. On the retributivist view, when the state punishes someone who has committed a crime against me, it does so in my name.

*Guilt.*   Third, we should punish *only* the guilty. Whatever utilitarian justification might be given for intentionally punishing the innocent, telishment is not permissible.

*Reasonable doubt.* Fourth, we should punish only when we have a reasonable degree of certitude that they are guilty. The greater the potential severity of the punishment, the greater the level of certitude.

*Equitable administration.* Fifth, we should punish *all* the guilty in the same way—or at least punishment must also be administered equitably, that is, certain groups ought not to be treated differently on irrelevant grounds. This is a basic requirement of justice. In the United States, this is particularly an issue in regard to race, and especially in regard to the death penalty and African Americans, which will be discussed below.

*Proportionality.* Sixth, the punishment must be proportional to the offense. To hang pickpockets, for example, is to punish disproportionately.

*"Cruel and unusual."* Seventh, some punishments, even if they are proportional to the offense, are too cruel ever to be used. Some people have committed truly heinous crimes—the torture, mutilation, and killing of infants and young children is the most obvious example—and they *deserve* the same suffering in return. However, for us to *administer* this suffering would be to debase ourselves. Such punishments are too cruel, too inhumane for us to administer without damaging ourselves.

*Punishment and social conditions that give rise to crimes.* Like cancer and other diseases, crime is best dealt with through preventive measures before it occurs. When confronted by an increase in crime, we must respond not only with short-term answers (such as imprisonment), but also with long-term answers that address the root conditions that give rise to crime.

## Punishment and Imagination

There are, as we have seen, many possible purposes of punishment, but certainly one of the legitimate purposes is to bring the perpetrator back into the moral community. Crime is a rupture in the moral fabric of society, and punishment attests to the nature and seriousness of that rupture. What often seems missing in punishment is a realization on the part of perpetrators of the consequences of their deeds. We often want to say, as a society (and especially on behalf of the victims) to perpetrators: "Look, *this* is what you did—this is the horror, and the pain, and the suffering, and perhaps even the death, that you have caused." Only when they realize the depth of the harm that they have caused will they change, and only when they have changed in this way are they worthy of being readmitted back into the moral community.

Punishment may be a means of helping criminals to realize what they have done. Certainly this motivation is compatible with the *lex talionis*—an eye for an eye—insofar as, by imposing on perpetrators the same harm they have imposed on their victims, perpetrators may come to understand what they have done to someone else. It may also be compatible with deterrence-based accounts of punishment insofar as realizing the harm one has inflicted may serve to deter a person from committing the same crime again.

One of the principal difficulties that faces us in structuring punishment is that we often lack imagination. We are unable to devise new ways of helping criminals to see the true consequences of their crimes for others. There is no necessary correlation between sitting in prison for years and realizations of this kind. However, programs of punishment that bring offenders face-to-face with the consequences of their misdeeds offer some hope of effecting the type of change of heart that heralds genuine rehabilitation.

# Capital Punishment

If punishment in general is problematic, capital punishment is especially so. The United States is one of the few major industrialized countries in the world to practice capital punishment, and one of an even smaller group that permits the death penalty for crimes committed by minors.

## A Life for a Life

Advocates of the death penalty often invoke the *lex talionis*, the law of "an eye for an eye, a tooth for a tooth," as their justification for the death penalty. If we take that law literally, then it becomes "a death for a death." It is, however, more helpful to take this law metaphorically as one of proportionality: our harshest punishment for our worst crimes. This is in fact the way in which it has been interpreted in the United States, where the death penalty is reserved for aggravated murder and a handful of other, similarly egregious crimes.

Yet the legitimacy of this metaphorical interpretation raises interesting questions. Why don't we take the *lex talionis* literally? Why shouldn't a torturer be tortured as punishment? Why shouldn't a rapist endure the agony of being raped as punishment? Why shouldn't someone who has raped, tortured, and killed a person be punished in the same way? As we reflect on these questions, we discover that capital punishment isn't the worst possible punishment—there are other punishments, such as torture and rape and mutilation, which are worse *in some way*. When we try to specify the exact way in which they are worse, we get an interesting answer. They aren't worse in the sense that they are more final, that they destroy more possibilities. Clearly the death penalty is the worst in this respect, since it eliminates any further possibilities for the person being executed. Rather, it is worse in the sense that it is *crueler*. If we ranked punishments along a continuum according to their *level of cruelty*, we might get something like this:

*When are we justified in killing someone as punishment?*

### Punishments: Scale of Cruelty

Monetary Fines  ⇨  Day Service ⇨  Imprisonment ⇨ Execution  ⇨  Rape and Torture

This is a different scale than we might get if we ranked punishments according to the *extent to which they destroyed a person's future possibilities*. Then we might get something like this:

### Punishments: Scale of Destruction of Life Possibilities

Monetary Fines  ⇨  Day Service ⇨  Imprisonment ⇨ Rape and Torture  ⇨ Execution

The metaphorical interpretation of the *lex talionis* comes into play when the literal interpretation results in a punishment that is too far to the right on the cruelty scale. Clearly, everyone admits that some punishments are too cruel. The issue then becomes one of drawing the line: at what point do we say that the literal interpretation of the *lex talionis* results in a punishment that is too cruel? The claim of opponents of the death penalty is that the line should be drawn before execution; advocates of the death penalty draw the line after execution.

We now can see that there is a sense in which the death penalty is the worst possible punishment (it completely destroys all future life possibilities) and a sense in which it isn't the worst (other punishments may be crueler). While literal interpretations of the *lex talionis* would seem to justify crueler punishments such as torture for convicted torturers, we are barred from such punishments because of their cruelty; yet the death penalty seems acceptable for the most heinous of crimes because it is the worst possible punishment in another sense.

## The Sanctity of Life

Opponents of the death penalty are often motivated by a moral concern for the sanctity of life. We can distinguish three versions of this concern. First, the *strong version*, such as we find among Quakers and Buddhists, maintains an absolute prohibition on the taking of *any* human life. It is thus opposed to the death penalty because it involves intentionally killing a human being, just as it would be opposed to war and even killing in self-defense. Second, the *moderate version*, which we find in many religious traditions, is opposed to any taking of *innocent* human life. This version would also be opposed to practices such as active euthanasia as well as the death penalty. It would be opposed to the death penalty insofar as its administration inevitably involves inadvertently executing innocent people occasionally. Finally, the *weak version* of this view maintains that any practice involving the intentional killing of other human beings must have an extremely strong justification—and that the justification of the death penalty instead of life imprisonment simply isn't strong enough to warrant its use.

For those who support the strong or moderate versions of the sanctity of life, the potential deterrent effect of capital punishment is not really an issue. In their eyes, even if capital punishment deters more effectively than alternative punishments, it still is not justified, for it involves the intentional taking of a human life.

## Hope and the Possibility of Change

Opponents of the death penalty are often motivated by another, less articulated concern. For many of them, the death penalty is a sign of giving up, a sign that we have concluded—at least in this particular instance—that there is nothing salvageable about this criminal, that there is nothing that redeems that person's life and justifies his (and it is almost always "his," not "her") continued existence. Sometimes this is part of a larger religious worldview that sees hope for all human beings, no matter what their situation; sometimes it is part of a purely humanistic worldview that sees human beings as fundamentally good at the core and only brutalized and deformed through external influences.

For those who share this belief, in whatever form, the death penalty is an act of breaking faith with ourselves, with our humanity, an act of despair from people who no longer know what else to do.

### The Effect of the Death Penalty: Deterrence or Brutalization?

What effect does the death penalty have? Two competing and incompatible claims have been advanced in answer to this question. On the one hand, some have argued that it has a deterrence effect, that is, that it reduces the number of potential future crimes for which it is a punishment. On the other hand, others have argued that it results in what has been called the *brutalization effect*; that is, that the number of capital crimes actually *increases* as a result of executions.

*The empirical findings.*    There are two distinct issues here: an empirical one and a normative one. The *empirical question* is in the domain of social scientists, and their answer is by no means univocal. This is hardly surprising, given the complexity of the issue. One not only has to show that the death penalty deters, but that it deters more effectively than alternative punishments such as life imprisonment. Moreover, even if the death penalty as presently administered doesn't deter more effectively than the alternatives, there is still the question of whether it might be a more effective deterrent if it were administered differently (more often, more quickly, etc.).

The empirical findings on the effects of capital punishment have been mixed. They range between two extremes. On the one hand, some researchers have argued that the death penalty was responsible for saving seven or eight lives (of innocent potential victims) per year in the United States while it was being used.[1] On the other hand, others have claimed that the number of capital offenses goes up immediately following an execution.[2] One of the more interesting studies has compared *contiguous states*, such as North and South Dakota, where one has the death penalty and the other does not, but which in many other respects are similar. If the death penalty were an effective deterrent, one would expect that the rate of capital crimes would decline in the state with the death penalty, but this has not been the case.

*The argument from common sense.*    Some theorists have argued that we need not be bothered by these contradictory findings; all we need to do is to reflect for a moment, and common sense will give us the answer to our question about the deterrent effects of capital punishment. When prisoners are given a choice between life in prison and the death penalty, they inevitably choose life in prison. We don't find "lifers" trying to get their sentence changed to death; on the other hand, we find there are plenty of prisoners on death row who are trying to get their sentences changed to life in prison. Common sense and a moment's reflection tell us that virtually everyone considers execution to be worse than life in prison. And if everyone considers it to be worse, then they will be more deterred by it than by a life sentence.

The common sense argument, at least in its initial version, falls short of the mark in at least two respects. First, granting the premises of the argument, we still have an additional question: do potential criminals, when contemplating a capital offense, think that they will receive the death penalty rather than life in prison? For deterrence to work, it must be effective *before* the crime is committed, and the argument from common sense does not assure us that it is. Second, the argument ignores any other factors as influencing the situation. (This is a problem with hypothetical examples in general: often we only discover in them the factors that we wanted to be there in the first place; real life cases are messier, more surprising, and consequently more instructive.) For example, it ignores the possibility that potential criminals might feel that since the state kills (through executions), it's okay for them to kill.

*The moral issue.*   The *moral issue* on which deterrence turns is distinct from the empirical question: if it turns out that capital punishment deters significantly more effectively than alternative punishments, then ought we to employ it? After all, the death penalty is the intentional killing of another human being—in the eyes of some, murder by the state. It is certainly consistent to say that capital punishment deters and still be opposed to it

*If the death penalty deters, is it thereby justified?*

because it violates the sanctity of human life (as we have already seen), because of the high probability that some innocent people will be executed, or because it is administered in our society in an unavoidably arbitrary manner.

*Deterrence and publicity.*   If capital punishment is justified in terms of its deterrent effect, then it would seem to follow that it should be administered in such a way as to maximize its potential as a deterrent. If we are executing criminals in order to deter other (potential) criminals from committing the same crime, then shouldn't we execute them in such a way as to have the greatest possible impact on anyone else who might commit such a crime? Two possible changes might increase the deterrent effect.

First, as mentioned above, punishments that are administered quickly and surely are, all other things being equal, more likely to be effective deterrents than punishments that are administered long after the fact and sporadically. In capital punishment cases, every effort should be made to hasten the judicial process and the execution if the point of such punishment is deterrence.

Second, the more vivid the realization of the consequences, the more effectively they influence behavior. In the case of capital punishment, this would seem to justify public, televised executions, presuming that they increase the deterrent effect of capital punishment. Indeed, if deterrence is the justification for such punishment, then it seems to be wasting an individual's execution if the government does not maximize its potential deterrent effects. Of course, this would have to be done in a way that properly shelters children, and so on, and at the same time is most likely to reach those most likely to commit capital crimes.

## The Irrevocability of Capital Punishment

One of the common objections to capital punishment is that it is irrevocable: once an innocent person is executed, there is no way to bring that person back to life again. Yet when we reflect on this argument, we see that it is not stated very precisely, for *all* punishment (except, perhaps, monetary fines, which can be returned with interest) is in a very real sense irrevocable. Twenty years in prison cannot be given back to someone who was falsely convicted. The real issue is that there is no way of even attempting to compensate for the injustice when someone has been executed, since the person is no longer alive to receive the compensation.

## The Demand for Certitude

The high stakes in capital punishment create an additional demand in terms of the level of certitude required to carry out the punishment. Precisely because there is no way to undo a mistake in capital punishment, we must be more certain than would otherwise be required that we are in fact executing the guilty party.

In evaluating this argument, we can again look at two distinct issues. The first is an empirical one. How often do mistakes get made? One recent estimate claimed that in the United States since 1900, fifty-seven innocent persons—or, more precisely, persons whose innocence can be *proved* in retrospect—have been executed.[3] The further claim is that, if this number can be shown to have been innocent, how many more were innocent that we did not know about? This is a difficult empirical matter, but it seems reasonable to conclude that at least some times, innocent persons are executed, even if we are not certain how many. This situation is exacerbated by the increase in executions in recent years and by the Supreme Court decisions that exclude the uncovering of new evidence of innocence as a basis for reconsideration of a case.

The second issue raised by this argument is a normative one. If capital punishment results in the taking of innocent life, at what point do we say that this invalidates its use? Those who oppose the taking of any innocent life at all would say that capital punishment ought to be abandoned if it results in the taking of even one innocent life. Utilitarians, in contrast, would be concerned about the numbers. They would ask how many innocent lives are apt to be lost as opposed to alternative punishments (such as life in prison without parole)? However, the calculations here become tricky, because presumably the utilitarian has to calculate the total number of innocent lives saved, not just innocent lives on death row. At that juncture, deterrence becomes relevant, since effective deterrence also saves innocent lives—the lives of potential victims. Imagine if utilitarians were faced with a choice between two alternatives.

*Alternative # 1:* No capital punishment; life imprisonment instead
        saves 8 innocent lives of prisoners per decade
        saves no innocent lives of potential victims over Alternative #2

*Alternative # 2:* Capital punishment
        cost 8 innocent lives of prisoners per decade
        saves 20 innocent lives of potential victims per decade

*If* the numbers worked out this way (and these numbers are purely hypothetical), and if everything else is equal (and it never is in real life), then the utilitarian would have to be in favor of capital punishment, even though it costs the lives of some innocent persons, because it costs fewer innocent lives *overall.*

Interestingly, there is little that retributivists have to contribute to this discussion. Their concern is exclusively with justified punishment, and there is nothing internal to retributivism itself that provides us with moral guidance about mistakes. Obviously, no moral system *espouses* mistakes.

## Racial Bias

There is little doubt that the death penalty in the United States is administered in a way that exhibits racial bias, although that does not mean that the individuals who reach these judgments are intentionally racist. The bias is most evident when dealing with African Americans, and two aspects of it are especially noteworthy. First, if the murderer is an African American male, he is somewhat more likely than his Caucasian counterpart to receive the death penalty. Second, and much more significantly, if the *victim* is Caucasian, the murderer is much more likely to receive the death penalty than if he is Caucasian. The race of the victim is the most significant racial factor, and African Americans who kill Caucasians are the most likely to receive the death penalty.

*The subtlety of racial bias.*   Several factors need to be noted about the influence of race on sentences of death, and the first of these is an appreciation of the various levels on which such bias can be influential. Long before a jury begins to deliberate on a case, numerous decisions are made that contribute to the final decision. The extent of public and political pressure for a public verdict in a case (as opposed to plea bargaining), the zeal (or lack thereof) with which law enforcement investigators pursue their inquiries, and the extent to which the prosecution is willing to look for and identify special circumstances (which justify asking for the death penalty) are but a few of the factors that influence whether juries are even presented with a case in which the death penalty is permitted and requested.

*The empirical evidence.*   What empirical evidence is available for the claim that the death penalty is administered in a racially biased way? The consensus[4] seems to be that the *race of the victim* is a very significant factor in a prosecutor's decision to seek the death penalty: prosecutors are four times more likely to seek the death penalty in cases in which African Americans kill Caucasians than in cases in which African Americans kill African Americans. Nor is this the only significant factor. Obviously, it makes a major difference which state the murder was committed in, since only some states permit capital punishment; furthermore, 50 percent of all executions occur in two states (Florida and Texas). Furthermore, prosecutors in rural counties are more likely to seek the death penalty than their counterparts in large urban areas. Both the race of the victim and where the murder is committed are important factors in prosecutors' decisions to seek the death penalty.

*The reply of death penalty supporters.*   Advocates of the use of the death penalty, such as Ernest van den Haag, have an interesting reply to such claims of bias. They are willing to admit, at least on occasion, that there is some arbitrariness in the administration of the death penalty, but they have a reply that is at least initially plausible. Imagine a dozen cars speeding on the freeway, and a police officer pulls one over and gives its driver a ticket. We can hardly claim that the driver does not deserve the ticket because there were others who were also speeding who got away? Clearly the fact that some of the guilty are not punished does not mean that we should refrain from punishing those that we have caught. Similarly, though there may be some perpetrators of capital offenses who are not convicted of them, that does not mean we are not entitled to execute those who are properly convicted. The fact that the death penalty is administered somewhat arbitrarily does not mean that it should not be used at all. If anything, it only means that we should try to execute more people, all offenders who deserve it.

*Are the criteria for capital crimes clear and well-justified?*   Opponents of the death penalty say that such analogies are misleading in at least three respects. First, the criteria for speeding are clear and well-defined, and the means for determining whether someone is violating the speed limit are relatively well-established. The criteria for capital offenses are much more vague and much harder to apply consistently. Although legislatures have attempted to specify the aggravating circumstances that transform a simple murder into a capital offense, many—including most recently

Justice Harry A. Blackmun—have concluded that, despite extensive guidelines, the United States has simply failed to reduce the arbitrariness with which the death penalty is applied.

*Are people who do not deserve the death penalty executed?*   Second, the speeding analogy suggests that the police arrest only those who are actually speeding. However, in regard to the death penalty, there is reasonable evidence—as mentioned above—that some innocent persons are executed.

*Is the death penalty sought for morally suspect reasons?*   Finally, the speeding example suggests that it was a matter of pure chance that some drivers were arrested while others got away. However, we would be more suspicious if the police arrested only speeding drivers with, say, red hair or Chicago Bulls bumper stickers. In the case of the death penalty, it appears that it is administered in a systematically uneven way that treats those who kill whites more harshly than those who kill blacks. Such a pattern of discrimination becomes a part of a much larger societal pattern of discrimination that ought to be opposed in its various manifestations. Thus when it is said that the death penalty is administered in an arbitrary manner, that does not mean it is applied randomly—there is a pattern to its application.

*Two senses of justice.*   Telling though these replies may seem, many still feel that the execution of criminals who have perpetrated particularly heinous crimes is right. Isn't it, after all, simply a matter of *justice* that those who have committed especially gruesome murders be executed, no matter what might happen to other offenders?

There is a sense in which this is true, and an examination of that sense reveal two distinct meanings of justice. First, there is what Joel Feinberg has called noncomparative justice, which is simply a matter of dessert, of what one deserves. But there is also a second, comparative sense of justice, which involves treating everyone (in a given class) the same. It is in this sense that the administration of the death penalty is unjust: there are insufficient morally relevant reasons why it is applied in some cases and not in others.

## Diversity and Consensus

As always in this book, each of us has to come to a considered, reflective judgment that weighs complex and competing claims. Indeed, that's the very nature of the problems selected for this book—the easy problems have been omitted, since we need little help in resolving them. We can, however, draw some conclusions which may provide part of the common ground we need here to reach a societal consensus on the issue of the death penalty.

First, many people on both sides of this debate agree that the *empirical evidence about the deterrent effect of capital punishment is inconclusive.* There is no incontrovertible evidence that the death penalty is a more effective deterrent than life imprisonment, but neither is there clear evidence that it is not. Moreover, this remains such an empirically tricky question to settle that there is little likelihood that there will be an indisputable empirical answer to the question of the death penalty's deterrent effect.

Second, most people agree that human life is sacred or at least extremely valuable (for those who do not frame the issue in religious terms), but this shared belief leads to opposite conclusions. For some, it leads to a prohibition against capital punishment because it involves the intentional taking of human life. For others, it leads to support of the death penalty as either the proper penalty for violating the sanctity of life or as the deterrent most likely to preserve the sanctity of innocent life.

Third, almost everyone would agree that a society in which capital crimes do not occur is better than one in which they occur and are punished. Our long-range focus needs to be on reducing the number of crimes that could be classified as capital, and the most effective long-term use of our resources is toward that end. It is an empirical question what will most effectively promote that goal—some suggestions include more community-based policing, more rehabilitation in and out of prison, more programs that reduce drug and alcohol use (which are often associated with crime), more programs that strengthen family and community values, and more research into which programs are most effective in reducing crime—and it is a question well worth pursuing.

Finally, I would hope—and this is a personal hope rather than a statement of societal consensus—that many will agree that capital punishment, no matter how deserved it is on the basis of the crime (and surely there are crimes which justify it), is unworthy of us. It diminishes us, the ones in whose name it is administered. And it is, finally, an act of despair, a declaration that the person to be executed is beyond hope, beyond redemption. This may in fact be a realistic assessment of that individual, but there is moral merit in living in the area between realism and hope.

## Endnotes

1. See Isaac Ehrlich, "The Deterrent Effect of Capital Punishment: A Question of Life or Death," *American Economic Review* 65 (June 1975), 397–417; also see the discussion of this issue below in Jeffrey Reiman's "Justice, Civilization, and the Death Penalty," and the bibliography in his footnote 35.

2. W. Bowers and G. Pierce in "Deterrence or Brutalization: What is the Effect of Executions?" *Crime & Delinquency* 26 (1980), 453–484.

3. See especially, the study by Hugo A. Bedeau and M. L. Radelet, "Miscarriages of Justice in Potentially Capital Cases," *Stanford Law Review* 40 (1987), 21–179.

4. See, for example, Raymond Paternoster, "Race of the Victim and Location of Crime: The Decision to Seek the Death Penalty in South Carolina," *Journal of Criminal Law and Criminology* 74 (1983), 754–785 and S. R. Gross, "Race and Death: The Judicial Evaluation of Discrimination in Capital Sentencing" *U.C. Davis Law Review* 18 (1985), 1275–1325 and Gross's *Death and Discrimination: Racial Disparities in Capital Sentencing* (Boston: Northeastern University Press, 1989); see also W. Bowers and G. Pierce, "Arbitrariness and Discrimination under Post-*Furman* Capital Statutes," *Crime & Delinquency* 26 (1980), 563–635.

# THE ARGUMENTS

Richard Dagger
"Playing Fair with Punishment"*

*Richard Dagger, a professor of political science at Arizona State University, is the author of articles on rights, obligations, citizenship, and other topics in legal and political philosophy. He is also the co-author (with Terence Ball) of* Political Ideologies and the Democratic Ideal *and his book,* Civil Virtues: Rights, Citizenship, and Republican Liberalism, *is forthcoming.*

*This article, which appeared in the journal* Ethics *in 1993, is an attempt to restore the principle of fair play as the principal justification of punishment. Seeing society as a cooperative venture secured by coercion, Dagger argues that the institution of punishment is necessary if we are to maintain social order. Those who reap the benefits of the social order must also pay its price, namely, fair social cooperation. Criminals are people who act unfairly to others by taking advantage of the legal order, and punishment of individual criminals is justified in order to reinstate the principle of fairness. Dagger considers six objections to this conception of punishment as grounded in fair play, and argues that none of them undermines his fundamental conception of punishment as being grounded in fair play.*

## As You Read, Consider This:

1. How does Dagger use his discussion of each of the six objections to build and further refine his notion of punishment as grounded in fair play?
2. Why, according to Dagger, is it insufficient for criminals simply to make restitution to those they have wronged? Do you agree? What conclusion does Dagger draw from this?

In his influential essay "Are There Any Natural Rights?" H. L. A. Hart appealed to a "mutuality of restrictions" to account for the obligation to obey the law. As Hart put it, "when a number of persons conduct any joint enterprise according to rules and thus restrict their liberty, those who have submitted to these restrictions when required have a right to a similar submission from those who have benefited by their submission."[1] As developed by John Rawls and others, Hart's "mutuality of restrictions" acquired a new name—the principle of fairness (or fair play)—and soon played a leading part in discussions not only of legal obligation, but of legal punishment as well.[2] For if

*Although he is an apostate in these matters, I am indebted to Jeffrie Murphy for a number of stimulating conversations on topics relating to obligation, fair play, and punishment. I am also grateful for the thoughtful comments of Alan Ryan, an anonymous reviewer, and two anonymous *Ethics* associate editors.

considerations of fairness or reciprocity account for the obligation to obey the law, as the principle's proponents argued, then they should presumably justify the punishment of those who fail to fulfill this obligation.

Now, nearly forty years after the publication of Hart's essay, the principle of fair play figures prominently in a lively debate on the question of whether there is or can be a general obligation to obey the law, with advocates and critics of the principle vigorously arguing their cases.[3] Punishment remains the center of an equally lively debate, but in this case the principle of fairness seems no longer to play a significant role. Indeed, critics have raised so many serious objections that they seem to have overwhelmed those who once regarded the principle of fair play as the best justification of punishment. These objections, however, are not as damaging as they appear. Or so I shall argue in this article, which attempts to restore the principle of fair play to a central place in discussions of the justification of punishment.

Before I examine the objections to the principle, it is first necessary to explain briefly how fair play provides a justification of punishment. This, in turn, requires a few words about what counts as a justification of punishment. Here I follow Stanley Benn's observation that any attempt to justify punishment must supply a justification at two different levels, for both the institution of punishment and its application in particular instances must be justified.[4] This distinction is important, as Benn noted, because what serves as a satisfactory justification at one level may be entirely unsatisfactory at the other. If we want to provide a justification for legal punishment, then, we must answer two distinct questions: (1) What justifies punishment as a social practice? and (2) What justifies punishing particular persons? The principle of fair play is an especially attractive theory of punishment, I shall argue, because it offers plausible and compelling answers to both these questions. I shall also suggest that there is a third question—How should we punish those who commit crimes?—that fair play cannot answer without help from other sources.

# I

As it applies to punishment, the principle of fair play begins with a conception of society as a cooperative endeavor secured by coercion. To think of society in this way is to recognize that the individuals who compose a society enjoy a number of benefits available only because of the cooperation of their fellows. The social order enables us to work together for common purposes and to pursue in peace our private interests. But we can do these things only when others, through their cooperation, help to maintain this order. This has two important implications. The first is that rules or conventions of some sort become necessary, for we need to know what the required acts of cooperation are. The second is that those who enjoy the benefits of society owe their own cooperation to the other members of society. Because the cooperation of others makes these benefits available to me, fairness demands that I help provide these benefits for them by cooperating in turn. When other things are equal, then, I owe it to the others to obey the rules; if I fail to do so, I take unfair advantage of them.

There are, however, two complications. One is that we are sometimes required to do things for the sake of cooperation that we find unpleasant or burdensome—paying taxes, driving within the speed limit, respecting the persons or property of others, and so on. In all but the smallest and most closely knit societies, moreover, it is often possible to receive the benefits without bearing the burdens of cooperation. This is due to the second complicating feature of the social order—that it provides public goods. One of these, perhaps the most important, is the rule of law. Like other public goods, the rule of law provides benefits for those who do not cooperate as well as for those who do. Under these circumstances the rational course of action for each individual is to withhold cooperation—to be a free rider—whenever cooperation is unpleasant.

This is where punishment enters the picture. Even if people want to cooperate by obeying the rules of the social order, they will find it unwise to do so when there is widespread disobedience. In some circumstances, where the sense of community is especially strong, the threat of coercion may not be necessary to ensure cooperation. But these circumstances are not likely to obtain in the legal systems of modern states. With the aid of the institution of punishment, however, we can provide a guarantee that "those who would voluntarily obey shall not be sacrificed to those who would not."[5]

This is to say that punishment as a practice is justified because it is necessary to the maintenance of the social order. As long as the social order is itself just, or reasonably so, and as long as we cannot trust everyone to obey its rules, we may use punishment to secure its survival. To justify the institution of punishment is not to justify its applications to particular cases, however. Hence Benn's second question must be asked: Whom may we punish?

The answer again follows from the conception of society as a cooperative venture secured by coercion. In this case, though, the relationship between the individuals who compose the society is more important than its security. This is because these individuals are under an obligation to one another to obey the laws of their society. According to the principle of fair play, anyone who takes part in a cooperative practice and accepts the benefits it provides is obligated to bear his or her share of the burdens of the practice. In the case of the legal order this means that everyone who profits from others' obedience to the law is under an obligation to reciprocate by obeying the law in turn. As Jeffrie Murphy once put it, "in order to enjoy the benefits that a legal system makes possible, each man must be prepared to make an important sacrifice—namely, the sacrifice of obeying the law even when he does not desire to do so. Each man calls on others to do this, and it is only just or fair that he bear a comparable burden when his turn comes."[6]

The problem is that people do not always act justly or fairly, especially when they can be free riders or gain in some other way from their unfair actions. As we have seen, one of the purposes of punishment is to discourage us from taking unfair advantage of those who, through their obedience to the law, enable us to enjoy the benefits of the social order. For some, the mere threat of punishment will not be a sufficient deterrent; and in these cases punishment itself is justified.

Punishment is justified, ceteris paribus, because the persons who disobey the law fail to meet their obligations to the other members of society. In this sense every crime is a crime of unfairness, whatever else it may be. Criminals act unfairly when they take advantage of the opportunities the legal order affords them without contributing to the preservation of that order. In doing so, they upset the balance between benefits and burdens at the heart of the notion of justice. Justice requires that this balance be restored, and this can only be achieved through punishment or pardon. As Herbert Morris has argued, "A person who violates the rules has something others have—the benefits of the system—but by renouncing what others have assumed, the burdens of self-restraint, he has acquired an unfair advantage. Matters are not even until this advantage is in some way erased. . . . [H]e owes something to others, for he has something that does not rightfully belong to him. Justice—that is, punishing such individuals—restores the equilibrium of benefits and burdens by taking from the individual what he owes, that is, exacting the debt."[7]

This, according to the advocates of fair play, is how we must justify punishing particular individuals. But we must be careful to note what this implies. If we hold that punishment is a means to the end of restoring equilibrium between benefits and burdens, then we must also hold that punishment is warranted only when this equilibrium has been disturbed. We are presuming, in other words, that benefits and burdens were in balance before the person we intend to punish upset matters by breaking the law. And this means that punishment is justified only when there is a just balance of benefits and burdens to begin with—when the social order is just, or reasonably so.[8]

When the social order does come reasonably close to balancing the costs and rewards of cooperation, however, punishment is justified as an institution and society is justified in punishing those who break the law. At both the levels Benn distinguished, then, the principle of fair play provides a justification for punishment.

## II

Nevertheless, the attempt to ground punishment in fair play has been the subject of serious criticism by a number of philosophers. Society may well have a right to punish those who break its laws, they say, but this right cannot follow from the principle of fair play. The philosophers who make this complaint typically acknowledge that fair play or reciprocity is an attractive and plausible foundation for punishment. Yet they proceed to argue that closer inspection reveals serious flaws in this foundation. Exactly what those flaws are is the subject of some disagreement—indeed, they sometimes criticize one another's criticisms—but among them the critics have uncovered six principal reasons for rejecting fair play.[9] None of the six provides a conclusive objection to the fair play account of punishment, however, as I shall now try to show. Indeed, these criticisms often rest on a misunderstanding of the nature of the benefits and burdens involved in fair play.

### First Objection: Neither Prohibit nor Punish

The first complaint is that the principle of fair play can justify neither prohibiting nor punishing those who break the law. This is because the principle, as Morris elaborates it, requires that a just balance be maintained between the benefits and burdens of social cooperation. Lawbreakers upset this balance by taking benefits that do not belong to them and by shirking burdens that do. To restore the proper balance, society must remove the extra benefit from the offender while reimposing the burdens of social cooperation—that is, obeying the law. But this need not mean that the offender must be punished. As Herbert Fingarette insists, restoring the balance and punishing the offender are quite different from one another.

> On [Morris's] view, provided the books are ultimately balanced, I would seem to have two equally legitimate options—paying my debts earlier in cash, or paying later in punishment. But surely that's not the intent of the law prohibiting stealing. The intent is precisely to deny us a legitimate alternative to paying the storekeeper for what we take. And even if I restore the balance by returning the stolen goods, and by paying back any incidental losses incurred by the storekeeper, it still remains intelligible and important—not only in principle but in the practice of the law—to ask whether I should also be punished. So Morris's kind of view . . . fails to account for law as prohibition, and . . . to make intelligible the question of punishment as something over and above the equitable distribution of burdens and benefits.[10]

This criticism rests on a misconception of the relationship between reciprocity and punishment. There is, to be sure, a distinction between restoring the balance and punishing offenders. If a payroll clerk mistakenly pays an employee more than he or she is supposed to, the clerk may have to retrieve the money from the employee, or take it out of the employee's next pay check, in order to balance the books. This need not involve punishment, either of the clerk or the other employee. But balancing the books in this case does not require a balance of benefits and burdens, which makes it very different from the kind of case Morris has in mind. The clerk and the other employee do not stand in the same relation to one another as the law-abiding citizen (the storekeeper in Fingarette's example) and the lawbreaker (the thief). To restore the balance between the second set is to preserve or restore the balance between the benefits and burdens of cooperation under the rule of law. Indeed, when the thief steals from the storekeeper, he upsets the balance not only with regard to her, but to all law-abiding citizens.

The benefit that the thief gains, in other words, is not simply whatever he steals from the storekeeper. This can be repaid, as Fingarette says, without punishment. Instead, the benefit is to be understood as the double advantage of not obeying the law when it suits one's purposes while also enjoying the advantages of the rule of law provided by the law-abiding citizens. This benefit cannot be repaid simply by forcing the thief not to break the law again—that would leave the "books" unbalanced. So, to restore the balance, the lawbreaker must be punished. The whole point of the principle, then, is to secure a cooperative practice such as the rule of law by prohibiting actions that will undermine the practice and by punishing those who nevertheless do them. The first criticism simply fails to see this.[11]

## Second Objection: Sufficient, but Not Necessary

The second criticism holds that acting unfairly may be a sufficient warrant for legal punishment, but it cannot be necessary. There are many people who deserve to be punished, on this view, not because they have acted unfairly, but because they have done something far worse. Put in terms of the distinction between acts that are *mala prohibita* [prohibited evils] and those that are *mala in se* [evil in themselves], the point of this criticism is that some misdeeds should be punished because they take unfair advantage of others, thus falling into the first category, while other and more serious crimes deserve punishment because they are intrinsically wrong. Rape, murder, and other forms of assault are wrong, and they ought to be proscribed; but we cannot explain their wrongness in terms of a violation of fair play or a lack of reciprocity. As R. A. Duff says, "Such talk of the criminal's unfair advantage implies that obedience to the law is a burden for us all: but is this true of such *mala in se*? Surely many of us do not find it a *burden* to obey the laws against murder and rape, or need to *restrain* ourselves from such crimes: how then does the murderer or rapist gain an unfair advantage over the rest of us, by evading a burden of self-restraint which we accept?"[12] The problem with fair play, then, is that it justifies punishment in some cases, but not in all—and not in the cases in which punishment seems most obviously deserved.

There is something to this charge. Rape and murder and other acts of violence are wrong for reasons that have nothing to do with fairness. But this is not to say that considerations of reciprocity play no part in our condemnation and punishment of those who are guilty of such crimes. All crimes, I have said, are in some sense crimes of unfairness. They may be *more than* crimes of unfairness, as rape, robbery, and murder surely are, but they must be *at least* crimes of this sort.

This is true whenever the rule of law is in effect. Murders and rapes and other vicious acts may take place when it is not, of course, but then the character of the offense is different. In such circumstances the offense may be taken to be a private matter involving only the offender and the victim; or it may be regarded as an offense against family honor, or perhaps against the gods or the proper order of things. But it cannot be an offense against the public, or society, unless there is some sense that the members of society are bound together under the rule of law that it is wrong, ceteris paribus, to violate. Nor can the offender suffer legal punishment unless the rule of law obtains. He may suffer revenge, or the punishment of the gods, but not punishment under the law.

The contrast between these two attitudes toward offenses and offenders is one of the themes of Aeschylus's *Oresteia*. So, too, is the advantage of living under the rule of law. In place of the blood feuds and ceaseless quarrels of the lawless life, the rule of law at least promises us the chance to live under rules made and enforced by impartial authorities. To achieve the security and freedom thus promised, we must be willing to forgo the private "punishment" of those who have, we believe, injured us. When we do this, we recognize that an injury to one person is not only an injury to her and her kin, but an offense against the law itself—and therefore a wrong done to all those who make the rule of law possible.

It is in this sense, that all crimes (under the rule of law) are crimes of unfairness. The robber, the rapist, and the murderer do terrible things to the specific victims of their crimes, and the charge of unfairness does not capture this. But what gives society, rather than the victim or his or her kin, the right to punish is the criminals' violation of fairness and reciprocity. The criminals want the security and freedom afforded by the rule of law, but they are not willing to grant this same security and freedom to their victims. They enjoy the benefits of cooperation without bearing a full share of its burdens. When they commit their crimes, therefore, they wrong all the law-abiding members of society. For this crime of unfairness they may properly be punished, as well as for the additional wrong they have done to their particular victims. All crimes (under the rule of law) are crimes of unfairness, in short, even if some are much more than that.

## Third Objection: What Benefit? What Burden?

In rejecting the foregoing criticisms I have relied in part on the claim that the critics misunderstand the nature of the benefits and burdens involved in a cooperative practice governed by fair play. But what exactly are these benefits and burdens? Is there really a balance to be struck between them? Can we really justify the practice and infliction of punishment by appeal to such notions? Not according to the third criticism, which holds that the principle of fair play offers no coherent and plausible account of benefits and burdens.

The problem stems, again, from the difficulty of seeing how some crimes are to be analyzed in terms of an unfair distribution of benefits and burdens. To return to Duff's example, it is easy enough to see how the would-be rapist or murderer will find compliance with the laws against rape or murder burdensome; but those who are never tempted to commit one of these crimes will not feel the restrictions of these laws at all. Insofar as rape is defined as unlawful carnal knowledge of a female by a male, moreover, it seems that a man cannot benefit from its proscription, at least not in the same way a woman can. For that matter, the man who wants to commit rape, or the person who wants to be cruel to animals, may derive no benefit at all from laws against these acts.[13] There are, it seems, laws that provide no benefit to some people and laws that impose no burden on some people. That being so, it must be impossible to balance benefits and burdens in these cases. Does this mean that these laws should be eliminated? No, because these laws are among those most of us consider most important. It means, instead, that the principle of fair play cannot provide the ground for a justification of criminal punishment.

This criticism is effective only if we take the benefits and burdens in question to be the benefits provided and burdens imposed by obedience to particular laws. But this is not what the principle of fair play requires. The benefits and burdens in question are those that follow from obedience to the laws of a cooperative practice—in this case, the rule of law in a reasonably just society.[14] When these circumstances obtain, everyone engaged in the practice is free to act, to enjoy his or her rights, with a security that would otherwise be impossible. This is a benefit everyone shares. But everyone also shares the burden of self-restraint. The freedom one gains as a result of the cooperation of others, in other words, must be balanced by a restriction on one's freedom, on one's right to act, in order to make freedom under law possible. Everyone thus receives the same benefit—freedom under law—and bears the same burden—obedience to the law. Rights and obligations are in balance, furthermore, for every person in the practice has a right to the cooperation of the others and an obligation to cooperate in turn.

This balance is upset when someone breaks the law. In some cases the lawbreaker may have good, even public-spirited reasons for disobedience. In most cases, however, the lawbreaker seeks a double benefit for himself. He seeks to enjoy the benefits of freedom under law, that is, while enjoying freedom from the burden of obedience as well. If he succeeds, the lawbreaker achieves an excess of freedom over the law-abiding members of society.[15] He enjoys the benefit of cooperation, then, without bearing its burden. It is in this sense that the balance of benefits and burdens is upset.

The offender achieves this, furthermore, by doing what he cannot want everyone else to do. This is the Kantian aspect of reciprocity that Murphy has emphasized.[16] The lawbreaker is typically someone who wants the advantages of the rule of law, but who is unwilling to make the sacrifice of self-restraint. By taking advantage of the obedience of others to enjoy benefits for himself, he treats the law-abiding citizens as means to his own ends.

### Fourth Objection: How to Punish?

The fourth criticism is that fair play cannot provide a satisfactory basis for punishment because it cannot tell us how, or to what extent, we are to punish offenders. If all crimes are (at least) crimes of unfairness, then does it follow that all criminals are to suffer the same punishment? If so, we shall have no way to account for the different degrees of seriousness we attach to different crimes.

One possible escape from this difficulty is to look for some sense of proportionality in the principle of fair play. Beginning with the notion that the principle requires us to restore the balance of benefits and burdens under the rule of law, one might say that those who commit the most serious offenses throw the distribution of benefits and burdens further out of balance than those who commit petty crimes. To restore the balance, then, the murderer must be punished more severely than the robber, who must be punished more severely than the thief, and so on.

The trouble with this defense of fair play, as Richard Burgh argues, is that it requires us to look not only to the gravity of the crime in question, but to the benefits and burdens involved. If the benefit the criminal receives is relief from the burden of self-restraint, with the extra freedom this brings, we must then find some way of understanding what the force of the burden of obeying the law is. "Now," Burgh says, "one way of understanding this burden is to see it in terms of the strength of the inclination to commit the crime. The stronger the inclination, the greater the burden one undertakes in obeying the law. Hence, if the strength of the inclination to commit one crime is stronger than another, a greater advantage will be derived from committing that crime. If the basis of desert is the removing of the advantage, then the person who commits the crime will be deserving of more punishment."[17] The consequences of such a policy, Burgh continues, are surely unacceptable. The crimes we ordinarily consider the most serious are the ones that most people are least inclined to commit, while the ones most people are most inclined to commit are usually regarded as the least serious. But this will change if we base punishment on the strength of the inclination to break the law. As Burgh puts it, "Insofar as we think of the burden of self-restraint in terms of the strength of inclination to violate the law, it probably follows that a greater burden is renounced with regard to tax fraud than with respect to murder." Accepting the principle of fair play thus seems to entail the surrender of "the rather central intuition that punishment must be proportional to the gravity of the crime. In fact, if this analysis yields the result that the tax evader deserves a greater punishment than the murderer, then I think most would be inclined to reject the analysis."[18]

As Burgh says, "one way of understanding" the burden of obedience is in terms of the strength of the inclination to commit a particular crime. This is not the only way to understand this burden, however, nor is it the right way. Here, as with my response to the second criticism, the key is to distinguish between the burden of obeying a particular law and the burden of obeying the law in general. Reciprocity does not mean that everyone must benefit from and feel the burden of each and every law. On the contrary it is the system of laws—law as a cooperative practice—from which each must benefit, and to which each must contribute by bearing the burden of cooperation. Cooperation will not always be burdensome; if it were, the practice would probably collapse. But there are times for almost all of us when we would like to have the best of both worlds—that is, the freedom we enjoy under the rule of law plus freedom from the burden of obeying laws. Because the rule of law is a public good, it is sometimes possible to do this—up to the point, at least, where disobedience is widespread enough to threaten the breakdown of law. Punishment is the device we use to prevent this from happening.

This way of understanding the burden of obedience saves fair play from Burgh's criticism. Still, it does not address the more general point, namely, Does fair play tell us how, or to what extent various offenders are to be punished? The answer is that it does not. Fair play tells us that those who take unfair advantage of the cooperating members of a cooperative practice should be punished—allowing, of course, for the possibility of overriding considerations. But it does not tell us how they should be punished. Nor should it.

The principle of fair play enables us to see how certain actions constitute offenses against society because those who engage in these actions take advantage of the law-abiding citizens who make the rule of law possible. From this point of view, as I have said, all crimes are crimes of unfairness. From this point of view, furthermore, that is all that they are. The murderer and the tax cheater are on a par in this respect. Both are guilty of taking unfair advantage of those who obey the law, and both should be punished accordingly. Exactly how they should be punished is something fair play cannot tell us. That will depend upon the circumstances of the society in question, and perhaps even on the circumstances of the individuals in question, since what counts as an efficacious punishment at one place and time may not count at another. But the murderer and tax cheater should be punished to the same extent for their crimes of unfairness.

This is not to say that the murderer and the tax cheater should receive the same punishment *tout court*. For the murderer has committed two crimes, in a sense, but the tax cheater only one. The murderer has simultaneously committed a crime of unfairness (a *malum prohibitum*) and a crime against her particular victim (a *malum in se*). For these two offenses, as it were, she must suffer two punishments. The first serves to discharge her debt to society by restoring the balance of benefits and burdens under the rule of law. The second punishment must be justified and established on other grounds.[19]

It is true, then, that the principle of fair play does not tell us everything we need to know about punishment. But this does not mean that it is unsatisfactory as a grounding principle. On the contrary, it simply means that reciprocity must be supplemented by other considerations—for example, deterrence, reform, moral education, restitution—when it is time to decide how exactly to punish wrongdoers. But it is important to notice that none of these other considerations provides a satisfactory account of society's right to punish. For that we must rely on the principle of fair play.

### Fifth Objection: Restitution or Compensation, Not Punishment

A different kind of objection tries to sever the connection between fair play and punishment. In this case the complaint is that fair play or reciprocity may provide a sound foundation for a system of criminal justice, but such a system will not include punishment. If the point of criminal justice is to maintain the balance of benefits and burdens on the part of those who live under the rule of law, the argument goes, then it is by no means clear that punishment is necessary to secure or restore this balance. "For it remains to be seen," as Richard Wasserstrom argues, "how it is that punishing the wrongdoer constitutes a taking of the wrongfully appropriated benefit away from him or her. . . . [C]ompensation or restitution to the victim by the wrongdoer, not his or her punishment, appears to be the natural and direct way to restore the balance in respect to wrongful appropriation of something that belonged to the victim."[20] All crimes may be (at least) crimes of unfairness, in other words, and society may have a right to respond to these crimes, but there is no reason to believe that punishment is the proper response.

Although I do not want to insist that punishment should be the sole response to crime, I do want to resist the conclusion that it is not a proper response. There are two primary reasons for taking this position.

First, there is no entirely suitable substitute for punishment. Restitution and compensation to victims both have their place, as I have argued elsewhere, but they work best when they are regarded as forms of or supplements to punishment.[21] Pure (as opposed to punitive) restitution promises to restore the balance of benefits and burdens between the criminal and his or her direct victims, or the victims' beneficiaries; it offers little, however, to the indirect or secondary victims who must endure the anxiety, frustration, and insurance costs that accompany crime.[22] Nor can pure restitution deal adequately with those offenses, such as tax evasion or violation of antipollution statutes, in which there are no specific victims to be identified for purposes of restitution. Requiring some form of community service may be the appropriate response to crimes of this sort, but community service is usually taken to be a form of punitive restitution.

As for compensation to the victims of crime, another set of problems arises. Compensation may help to restore the victims to their previous condition in some sense, but it falls far short of restoring the balance of benefits and burdens under the rule of law. For if compensation is made from public funds, then it is principally the law-abiding who are responsible for compensating the victims for their losses and suffering. This simply imposes an additional burden on those who are already bearing the indirect costs of crime, thereby throwing the benefits and burdens of the rule of law farther out of balance.[23] Another tactic might be to pay a reward of some sort to people who obey the law. This might serve to secure the benefits of the rule of law without resorting to punishment. In this case, however, everyone would be taxed to provide these rewards to people who either would obey the laws anyhow or who obey only to gain the reward. But in this case those who would willingly obey the law would find themselves paying what amounts to extortion to those who would otherwise break it—and that hardly counts as restoring the balance.

These problems lead me to believe that there are no entirely suitable substitutes for punishment. Punishment provides something that these other approaches necessarily lack—which brings me to my second reason for believing that is a proper response to criminal wrongdoing. Punishment rests on the notion that certain actions are wrong, either as *mala in se* or *mala prohibita*. That is why we must draw a distinction, to return to Fingarette's argument, between restoring the balance and punishing offenders. We may restore the balance, as I suggested earlier, without implying that anyone is guilty of criminal intent or misconduct. If a payroll clerk mistakenly pays an employee too much, then steps should be taken to correct the mistake and prevent its happening again. If the clerk and the other employee are working together to steal from their employer, however, simply restoring the balance in the sense of regaining the money is not a sufficient response. These criminals have wronged both their employer and, I have argued, the law-abiding people who make it possible for them to enjoy the benefits of the rule of law. Steps must be taken to make the offenders and others aware of the wrong they have done. These actions are necessary to restore the benefits and burdens under the rule of law. Making restitution to the employer is not enough to restore the balance between the offenders and the law-abiding members of society. To do that, some form of punishment—some form that affirms the belief that it is wrong to take advantage of those whose cooperation makes the rule of law possible—seems necessary.

Punishing offenders is a way of restoring the balance in these cases because it responds to a disruption of the equality that everyone is supposed to enjoy in the eyes of the law. Insofar as people are members of a society governed by the rule of law, that is, they all should have the same rights and obligations. All should be equal and alike as subjects of the law, no matter how different and unequal they are in other respects. The criminal, however, sets himself apart. By taking advantage of the cooperation of others to advance his own interests, he says in effect that others are less important than he. He wants them to bear the burdens of cooperation while he receives only benefits. In Kantian language, he treats others as mere means to his ends; he fails to show respect for their dignity as persons. Such an attitude threatens the rule of law. It must be condemned in order to maintain equality in the eyes of the law. The balance to be restored, then, is the balance between people *qua* equal subjects of the law. Punishing those who upset this equality is the closest we can come to restoring the balance in this sense.

## Sixth Objection: Does the Law Play Fair?

This leads us to the final objection. In this case the complaint is that the notion of fair play simply fails to capture important features of law and punishment. The belief that we should obey the law because we owe obedience to the cooperating members of society may make sense in some circumstances, according to the objection, but not in all. Laws that prohibit certain forms of sexual relations seem to have nothing to do with fairness, for instance. Should two consenting adults who find themselves behind closed doors really refrain from engaging in proscribed sexual activity on the grounds that disobeying the law would be taking unfair advantage of others? Do considerations of fairness even play a part in this and similar cases? If they do not, as it appears, then fairness cannot provide the foundation for the rule of law and the practice of punishment.[24]

This in a way is the other side of the second objection, which holds that fair play cannot account for rape, robbery, murder, and other acts that are *mala in se.* In this case the complaint is that fairness or reciprocity requires people to obey, on utterly inappropriate grounds, laws that probably ought not to be laws in the first place. This is a forceful objection. Yet we may admit its force without abandoning the principle of fair play. In fact, it is possible to respond to this objection in a way that strengthen the case for fair play. This response involves three steps.

First, we should notice once again that all crimes must be, on the fair play theory, crimes of unfairness. But this does not mean, as we have seen, that actions are or should be criminal only if they are ordinarily understood to be unfair. Some actions should be outlawed because they are unfair, others because they are wrong in some other way. The principle of fair play, however, is concerned with the overall balance of benefits and burdens in society, especially the benefits and burdens involved in the rule of law. If we live in a society that may be reasonably regarded as a cooperative venture under the rule of law, then fairness requires us to obey the law, even if the particular law in question seems to have nothing to do with fairness.

The second step in the response is to recall that this general obligation to obey the law is defeasible. It holds only when one's society is reasonably just, and even then it may be overridden by more pressing moral considerations. No society will be perfectly just, so it is always possible that an unjust law will be on the books of a reasonably just society. That may be the case now with laws prohibiting certain kinds of sexual conduct, for instance. If so, a person may well conclude that he or she may, or even should, disobey the laws in question. Or there may be other laws that are not in themselves unjust, but seem to require pointless obedience—such as stopping at a red light in the early morning hours when it is clear that there is no one else on the road. Here again there is an obligation to obey, but it is a relatively weak obligation, and it may therefore be overridden more easily than, say, the obligation to pay one's taxes.[25]

But how are we to distinguish just laws from unjust, or weak obligations from strong? The answer, at least in part, is to look to considerations of fairness and reciprocity. This forms the third step in the response to the final objection. Those laws that have the strongest force are those that are most essential to the maintenance of a cooperative venture under the rule of law. Laws that place unfair burdens on some or give unfair benefits to others serve to undermine cooperation and the rule of law, so they cannot be just. In the case of private, consensual sexual conduct, for example, laws proscribing certain activities seem to place an unfair burden on some people—namely, the burden of repressing their sexual inclinations and activities while others are legally free to pursue theirs. Other things being equal, such laws are neither just nor in harmony with the principle of fair play. Until they are abolished, those who are affected by these laws have reason to believe that their obligation to obey them is of little force.

# III

It seems, in sum, that the principle of fair play does a better job of accounting for crime and punishment than its critics suspect. Indeed, if the arguments I have presented are correct, the principle's ability to meet the six objections considered in this article strongly suggests that it provides the basis for the practice of punishment. The principle does not tell us everything we need to know about punishment—it does not tell us exactly how to punish every offender, as I have noted, or what the fitting punishment is for every crime—but it does provide the foundation from which we can go on to address these matters.

The principle of fair play, then, provides plausible answers to Benn's two questions about the justification of punishment—What justifies punishment as a practice? What justifies punishing particular individuals?—and it provides a partial answer to a third. If this is not reason enough to recognize fair play as the true or the best philosophical account of punishment, it is surely reason to restore it to a central place in the debate over punishment's justification.

## Endnotes

1. H. L. A. Hart, "Are There Any Natural Rights?" in *Human Rights*, ed. A. I. Melden (Belmont, CA: Wadsworth, 1970), p. 70. Hart's essay originally appeared in *Philosophical Review* 64 (1955), 175–191. For an earlier, but less influential, statement of this view, see C. D. Broad, "On the Function of False Hypotheses in Ethics," *International Journal of Ethics* 26 (1915–1916), 377–397.

2. John Rawls, "Legal Obligation and the Duty of Fair Play," in *Law and Philosophy*, ed. Sidney Hook (New York: New York University Press, 1964).

3. Important criticisms of the fair play theory of legal obligation include M. B. E. Smith, "Is There a Prima Facie Obligation to Obey the Law?" *Yale Law Journal* 82 (1973), 950–976; Robert Nozick, *Anarchy, State, and Utopia* (New York: Basic, 1974), pp. 90–95; and A. John Simmons, *Moral Principles and Political Obligations* (Princeton, NJ: Princeton University Press, 1979), chap. 5. For defenses, see, inter alia: Richard Arneson, "The Principle of Fairness and Free-Rider Problems," *Ethics* 92 (1982), 616–633; Richard Dagger, "Rights, Boundaries, and the Bonds of Community: A Qualified Defense of Moral Parochialism," *American Political Science Review* 79 (1985), 436–447, esp. pp. 443–446; and George Klosko, *The Principle of Fairness and Political Obligation* (Lanham, MD: Rowman & Littlefield, 1992).

4. Stanley Benn, "An Approach to the Problems of Punishment," *Philosophy* 33 (1958), 325–341.

5. H. L. A. Hart, *The Concept of Law* (Oxford: Clarendon Press, 1961), p. 193.

6. Jeffrie Murphy, "Three Mistakes about Retributivism," *Analysis* 31 (1971), 166–169; see also his *Retribution, Justice, and Therapy* (Dordrecht: D. Reidel 1979), p. 77. For Murphy's

more recent doubts about the adequacy of this principle, see his "Retributivism, Moral Education, and the Liberal State," *Criminal Justice Ethics* 4 (1985), 3–11, esp. 6–7, and his review of George Sher's *Desert* in *Philosophical Review* 99 (April 1990), 280–283.

7. Herbert Morris, "Persons and Punishment," *Monist* 52 (1968), 475–501, esp. p. 478.

8. On the connection between punishment and social justice, see Jeffrie Murphy "Marxism and Retribution," *Philosophy and Public Affairs* 2 (1973), 217–243; also see Murphy, *Retribution, Justice, and Therapy,* pp. 93–115.

9. For a criticism of criticisms, see Richard Burgh, "Do the Guilty Deserve Punishment?" *Journal of Philosophy* 79 (1982), 193–213.

10. Herbert Fingarette, "Punishment and Suffering," *Proceedings and Addresses of the American Philosophical Association* 50 (1977), 499–525, 502; emphasis in original.

11. See Burgh, "Do the Guilty Deserve Punishment?" p. 203, n. 18, for a related criticism of Fingarette's argument.

12. R. A. Duff, *Trials and Punishments* (Cambridge: Cambridge University Press 1986), p. 213; emphasis in original. See also Richard Wasserstrom, *Philosophy and Social Issues* (Notre Dame, IN: University of Notre Dame Press, 1980), pp. 143–146.

13. As Burgh says in "Do the Guilty Deserve Punishment?" p. 205.

14. Burgh, ibid., recognizes this, but argues that this "retreat to a second-order set of benefits, viz., those received from obedience to law in general" must fail because it entails "that all offenders are, regardless of the offense they committed, deserving of the same punishment" (p. 206). I respond to this . . . , under "Fourth Objection."

15. Here I follow George Sher, *Desert* (Princeton, NJ: Princeton University Press, 1987), pp. 78–80.

16. See esp. Jeffrie G. Murphy, "Kant's Theory of Criminal Punishment," in Murphy, *Retribution, Justice, and Therapy,* pp. 82–92.

17. Burgh, "Do the Guilty Deserve Punishment?" p. 209.

18. Ibid., pp. 209–210. For a related criticism, see David Dolinko, "Some Thoughts about Retributivism," *Ethics* 101 (1991), 537–559, esp. pp. 546–549.

19. This should help to alleviate at least part of Murphy's concern about the phrase debt to society. "The idiom of owing and paying a debt is misleading," he says, "in that it tends to obscure the fact that (i) criminal 'debts' differ from ordinary debts in that we have an antecedent moral obligation not to incur them and (ii) undergoing punishment for (say) murder, unlike paying the final installment on a loan, can hardly be said to make things all right again, to make the world morally as it was before" (*Retribution, Justice, and Therapy,* p. 78). On my analysis, the criminal's punishment for the crime of unfairness repays the debt to society. This does not "make the world morally as it was before"—perhaps nothing can do that—but that is asking for more than a debt to society can entail.

20. Wasserstrom, *Philosophy and Social Issues,* p. 145; emphasis in original.

21. I make a case for restitution as an especially valuable form of punishment in "Restitution, Punishment, and Debts to Society," in *Victims, Offenders, and Alternative Sanctions,* ed. J. Hudson and B. Galaway (Lexington, MA: Lexington Books, 1980), pp. 11–18, and in "Restitution: Pure or Punitive?" *Criminal Justice Ethics* 10 (1991), 29–39.

22. In addition to the articles cited in the previous note, see Franklin Miller, "Restitution and Punishment: A Reply to Barnett," *Ethics* 88 (1978), 358–360; and Margaret Holmgren, "Punishment as Restitution: The Rights of the Community," *Criminal Justice Ethics* 2 (1983), 36–49, for this and other criticisms of pure restitution.

23. For a scheme in which all crime victims are to receive compensation from those criminals who are apprehended and convicted, see Mane Hajdin, "Criminals as Gamblers: A Modified Theory of Pure Restitution," *Dialogue* 26 (1987), 77–86. I criticize Hajdin's proposal in "Restitution: Pure or Punitive?" esp. pp. 33–35.

24. Jeffrie Murphy raises this objection in his review of Sher's *Desert*.

25. In this and the succeeding paragraph I draw on George Klosko, "The Moral Force of Political Obligations," *American Political Science Review* 84 (1990), 1235–1250.

## Journal/Discussion Questions

✍ *Have you ever been the victim of a crime? If so, reflect on that experience and ask whether Dagger's analysis sheds helpful light on your experience as a victim. Does it illuminate why you felt what the criminal did was* wrong?

1. According to Dagger, "all crimes (under the rule of law) are crimes of unfairness." In what sense do you think that this is true? In what sense do you think that it misses something essential about the nature of some crimes?

2. In what sense, according to Dagger, do lawbreakers seek a double benefit for themelves? Does this seem true about all cases of law-breaking?

3. In what way does the idea that certain acts are evil in themselves (*mala in se*) a challenge to Dagger's account of punishment? Do you think he successfully responded to this challenge?

---

### Jeffrey H. Reiman
### "Justice, Civilization, and the Death Penalty"

---

*Jeffrey Reiman is professor of philosophy and justice at the American University in Washington, D.C. He is the author of several books, including* The Rich Get Richer and the Poor Get Prison *and* Justice and Modern Moral Philosophy.

*This article stakes out an interesting position. In contrast to most abolitionists, Reiman admits that the death penalty is a just punishment for murder. However, he still argues against the death penalty in states such as ours, maintaining that abolition of the death penalty is part of the process of becoming more civilized.*

Jeffrey H. Reiman, "Justice, Civilization, and the Death Penalty: Answering van den Haag," *Philosophy and Public Affairs* 14 (Spring 1985). Copyright © 1985, Princeton University Press. Reprinted by permission of the publisher and the author.

## As You Read, Consider This:

1. What, according to Reiman, is the heart of the retributivist position? How does it differ from sheer revenge?

2. What, according to Reiman, makes the death penalty so horrible? Should horribleness be part of some punishments? Why or why not?

⌒

On the issue of capital punishment, there is as clear a clash of moral intuitions as we are likely to see. Some (now a majority of Americans) feel deeply that justice requires payment in kind and thus that murderers should die; and others (once, but no longer, nearly a majority of Americans) feel deeply that the state ought not be in the business of putting people to death. Arguments for either side that do not do justice to the intuitions of the other are unlikely to persuade anyone not already convinced. And, since, as I shall suggest, there is truth on both sides, such arguments are easily refutable, leaving us with nothing but conflicting intuitions and no guidance from reason in distinguishing the better from the worse. In this context, I shall try to make an argument for the abolition of the death penalty that does justice to the intuitions on both sides. I shall sketch out a conception of retributive justice that accounts for the justice of executing murderers, and then I shall argue that *though the death penalty is a just punishment for murder*, abolition of the death penalty is part of the civilizing mission of modern states. Before getting to this, let us briefly consider the challenges confronting those who would argue against the death penalty. In my view, these challenges have been most forcefully put by Ernest van den Haag.

## I. The Challenge to the Abolitionist

The recent book, *The Death Penalty: A Debate*, in which van den Haag argues for the death penalty and John P. Conrad argues against, proves how difficult it is to mount a telling argument against capital punishment.[1] Conrad contends, for example, that "To kill the offender [who has committed murder in the first degree] is to respond to his wrong by doing the same wrong to him" (p. 60). But this popular argument is easily refuted. Since we regard killing in self-defense or in war as morally permissible, it cannot be that we regard killing per se as wrong. It follows that the wrong in murder cannot be that it is killing per se, but that it is (among other things) the killing of an innocent person. Consequently, if the state kills a murderer, though it does the same physical act that he did, it does not do the wrong that he did, since the state is not killing an innocent person (see p. 62). Moreover, unless this distinction is allowed, all punishments are wrong, since everything that the state does as punishment is an act which is physically the same as an act normally thought wrong. For example, if you lock an innocent person in a cage, that is kidnapping. If the state responds by locking you in prison, it can hardly be said to be responding to your wrong by doing you a wrong in return. Indeed, it will be said that it is precisely because what you did was wrong that locking you up, which would otherwise be wrong, is right.

Conrad also makes the familiar appeal to the possibility of executing an innocent person and the impossibility of correcting this tragic mistake. "An act by the state of such monstrous proportions as the execution of a man who is not guilty of the crime for which he was convicted should be avoided at all costs. . . . The abolition of capital punishment is the certain means of preventing the worst injustice" (p. 60). This argument, while not so easily disposed of as the previous one, is, like all claims about what "should be avoided at all costs," neither very persuasive. There is invariably some cost that is prohibitive such that if, for example, capital punishment were necessary to save the lives of potential murder victims, there must be a point at which the number of saved victims would be large enough to justify the risk of executing an innocent—particularly where trial and appellate proceedings are designed to reduce this risk to a minimum by giving the accused every benefit of the doubt. Since we tolerate the death of innocents, in mines or on highways, as a cost of progress, and, in wars, as an inevitable accompaniment to aerial bombardment and the like, it cannot convincingly be contended that, kept to a minimum, the risk of executing an innocent is still so great an evil as to outweigh all other considerations (see pp. 230–231).

Nor will it do to suggest, as Conrad does, that execution implies that offenders are incapable of change and thus presumes the offenders' "total identification with evil," a presumption reserved only to God or, in any case, beyond the province of (mere) men (p. 27; also, pp. 42–43). This is not convincing since no punishment, whether on retributive or deterrent grounds, need imply belief in the total evilness of the punishee—all that need be believed (for retribution) is that what the offender has done is as evil as the punishment is awful, or (for deterrence) that what he has done is awful enough to warrant whatever punishment will discourage others from doing it. "Execution," writes van den Haag, "merely presumes an identification [with evil] sufficient to disregard what good qualities the convict has (he may be nice to animals and love his mother). . . . No total identification with evil—whatever that means—is required; only a sufficiently wicked crime" (p. 35).

Thus far I have tried to indicate how difficult it is to make an argument for the abolition of the death penalty against which the death penalty advocate cannot successfully defend himself. But van den Haag's argument is not merely defensive—he poses a positive challenge to anyone who would take up the abolitionist cause. For van den Haag, in order to argue convincingly for abolition, one must prove either that "no [criminal] act, however horrible, justifies [that is, deserves] the death penalty," or that, if capital punishment were found to deter murder more effectively than life imprisonment, we should still "prefer to preserve the life of a convicted murderer rather than the lives of innocent victims, even if it were certain that these victims would be spared if the murderer were executed" (p. 275).

If van den Haag is right and the abolitionist cause depends on proving either or both of these assertions, then it is a lost cause, since I believe they cannot be proven for reasons of the following sort: If people ever deserve anything for their acts, then it seems that what they deserve is something commensurate in cost or in benefit to what they have done. However horrible executions are, there are surely some acts to which they are commensurate in cost. If, as Camus says, the condemned man dies two deaths, one on the scaffold and one anticipating it, then isn't execution justified for one who has murdered two people? if not two, then ten?[2] As for the second assertion, since we take as justified the killing of innocent people (say, homicidal maniacs) in self-defense (that is, when necessary to preserve the lives of their innocent victims), then it seems that we must take as justified the killing of guilty people if it is necessary to preserve the lives of innocent victims. Indeed, though punishment is not the same as self-defense, it is, when practiced to deter crimes, arguably a form of social defense—and parity of reason would seem to dictate that if killing is justified when necessary for self-defense, then it is justified when necessary for social defense.

It might be thought that injuring or killing others in self-defense is justifiable in that it aims to stop the threatening individual himself, but that punishing people (even guilty people) to deter others is a violation of the Kantian prohibition against using people merely as means to the well-being of others. It seems to me that this objection is premised on the belief that what deters potential criminals are the individual acts of punishment. In that case, each person punished is truly being used for the benefit of others. If, however, what deters potential criminals is the existence of a functioning punishment system, then everyone is benefited by that system, including those who end up being punished by it, since they too have received the benefit of enhanced security due to the deterring of some potential criminals. Even criminals benefit from what deters other criminals from preying on them. Then, each act of punishment is done as a necessary condition of the existence of a system that benefits all; and no one is used or sacrificed merely for the benefit of others.

If I am correct in believing that the assertions that van den Haag challenges the abolitionist to prove cannot be proven, then the case for the abolition of the death penalty must be made while accepting that some crimes deserve capital punishment, and that evidence that capital punishment was a substantially better deterrent to murder than life imprisonment would justify imposing it. This is what I shall attempt to do. Indeed, I shall begin the case for the abolition of the death penalty by defending the justice of the death penalty as a punishment for murder.

## II. Just Deserts and Just Punishments

In my view, the death penalty is a just punishment for murder because the *lex talionis*, an eye for an eye, and so on, is just, although, as I shall suggest at the end of this section, it can only be rightly applied when its implied preconditions are satisfied. The *lex talionis* is a version of retributivism. Retributivism—as the word itself suggests—is the doctrine that the offender should be paid back with suffering he deserves because of the evil he has done, and the *lex talionis* asserts that injury equivalent to that he imposed is what the offender deserves. But the *lex talionis* is not the only version of retributivism. Another, which I shall call "proportional retributivism," holds that what retribution requires is not equality of injury between crimes and punishments, but "fit" or proportionality, such that the worst crime is punished with the society's worst penalty, and so on, though the society's worst punishment need not duplicate the injury of the worst crime. Later, I shall try to show how a form of proportional retributivism is compatible with acknowledging the justice of the *lex talionis*. Indeed, since I shall defend the justice of the *lex talionis*, I take such compatibility as a necessary condition of the validity of any form of retributivism.

There is nothing self-evident about the justice of the *lex talionis* nor, for that matter, of retributivism. The standard problem confronting those who would justify retributivism is that of overcoming the suspicion that it does no more than sanctify the victim's desire to hurt the offender back. Since serving that desire amounts to hurting the offender simply for the satisfaction that the victim derives from seeing the offender suffer, and since deriving satisfaction from the suffering of others seems primitive, the policy of imposing suffering on the offender for no other purpose than giving satisfaction to his victim seems primitive as well. Consequently, defending retributivism requires showing that the suffering imposed on the wrongdoer has some worthy point beyond the satisfaction of victims. In what follows, I shall try to identify a proposition—which I call the *retributivist principle*—that I take to be the nerve of retributivism. I think this principle accounts for the justice of the *lex talionis* and indicates the point of the suffering demanded by retributivism. Not to do too much of the work of the death penalty advocate, I shall make no extended argument for this principle beyond suggesting the considerations that make it plausible. I shall identify these considerations by drawing, with considerable license, on Hegel and Kant.

I think that we can see the justice of the *lex talionis* by focusing on the striking affinity between it and the *golden rule*. The *golden rule* mandates "Do unto others as you would have others do unto you," while the *lex talionis* counsels "Do unto others as they have done unto you." It would not be too far-fetched to say that the *lex talionis* is the law enforcement arm of the golden rule, at least in the sense that if people were actually treated as they treated others, then everyone would necessarily follow the golden rule because then people could only willingly act toward others as they were willing to have others act toward them. This is not to suggest that the *lex talionis* follows from the golden rule, but rather that the two share a common moral inspiration: the equality of persons. Treating others as you would have them treat you means treating others as equal to you, because adopting the golden rule as one's guiding principle implies that one counts the suffering of others to be as great a calamity as one's own suffering, that one counts one's right to impose suffering on others as no greater than their right to impose suffering on one, and so on. This leads to the *lex talionis* by two approaches that start from different points and converge.

I call the first approach "Hegelian" because Hegel held (roughly) that crime upsets the equality between persons and retributive punishment restores that equality by "annulling" the crime.[3] As we have seen, acting according to the golden rule implies treating others as your equals. Conversely, violating the golden rule implies the reverse: Doing to another what you would not have that other do to you violates the equality of persons by asserting a right toward the other that the other does not possess toward you. Doing back to you what you did "annuls" your violation by reasserting that the other has the same right toward you that you assert toward him. Punishment according to the *lex talionis* cannot heal the injury that the other has suffered at your hands, rather it rectifies the indignity he has suffered, by restoring him to equality with you.

"Equality of persons" here does not mean equality of concern for their happiness, as it might for a utilitarian. On such a (roughly) utilitarian understanding of equality, imposing suffering on the wrongdoer equivalent to the suffering he has imposed would have little point. Rather, equality of concern for people's happiness would lead us to impose as little suffering on the wrongdoer as was compatible with maintaining the happiness of others. This is enough to show that retributivism (at least in this "Hegelian" form) reflects a conception of morality quite different from that envisioned by utilitarianism. Instead of seeing morality as administering doses of happiness to individual recipients, the retributivist envisions morality as maintaining the relations appropriate to equally sovereign individuals. A crime, rather than representing a unit of suffering added to the already considerable suffering in the world, is an assault on the sovereignty of an individual that temporarily places one person (the criminal) in a position of illegitimate sovereignty over another (the victim). The victim (or his representative, the state) then has the right to rectify this loss of standing relative to the criminal by meting out a punishment that reduces the criminal's sovereignty in the degree to which he vaunted it above his victim's. It might be thought that this is a duty, not just a right, but that is surely too much. The victim has the right to forgive the violator without punishment, which suggests that it is by virtue of having the right to punish the violator (rather than the duty), that the victim's equality with the violator is restored.

I call the second approach "Kantian" since Kant held (roughly) that, since reason (like justice) is no respecter of the sheer difference between individuals, when a rational being decides to act in a certain way toward his fellows, he implicitly authorizes similar action by his fellows toward him.[4] A version of the golden rule, then, is a requirement of reason: acting rationally, one always acts as he would have others act toward him. Consequently, to act toward a person as he has acted toward others is to treat him as a rational being, that is, as if his act were the product of a rational decision. From this, it may be concluded that we have a duty to do to offenders what they have done, since this amounts to according them the respect due rational beings.[5] Here too, however, the assertion of a duty to punish seems excessive, since, if this duty arises because doing to people what they have done to others is necessary to accord them the respect due rational beings, then we would have a duty to do to all rational persons *everything*—good, bad, or indifferent—that they do to others. The point rather is that, by his acts, a rational being *authorizes* others to do the same to him, he doesn't compel them to. Here too, then, the argument leads to a right, rather than a duty, to exact the *lex talionis*. And this is supported by the fact that we can conclude from Kant's argument that a rational being cannot validly complain of being treated in the way he has treated others, and where there is no valid complaint, there is no injustice, and where there is no injustice, others have acted within their rights.[6] It should be clear that the Kantian argument also rests on the equality of persons, because a rational agent only implicitly authorizes having done to him action similar to what he has done to another, if he and the other are similar in the relevant ways.

The "Hegelian" and "Kantian" approaches arrive at the same destination from opposite sides. The "Hegelian" approach starts from the victim's equality with the criminal, and infers from it the victim's right to do to the criminal what the criminal has done to the victim. The "Kantian" approach starts from the criminal's rationality, and infers from it the criminal's authorization of the victim's right to do to the criminal what the criminal has done to the victim. Taken together, these approaches support the following proposition: The equality and rationality of persons implies that an offender deserves and his victim has the right to impose suffering on the offender equal to that which he imposed on the victim. This is the proposition I call the *retributivist principle*, and I shall assume henceforth that it is true. This principle provides that the *lex talionis* is the criminal's just desert and the victim's (or as his representative, the state's) right. Moreover, the principle also indicates the point of retributive punishment, namely, it affirms the equality and rationality of persons, victims and offenders alike. And the point of this affirmation is, like any moral affirmation, to make a statement, to the criminal, to impress upon him his equality with his victim (which earns him a like fate) and his rationality (by which his actions are held to authorize his fate), and to the society, so that recognition of the equality and rationality of persons becomes a visible part of our shared moral environment that none can ignore in justifying their actions to one another.

When I say that with respect to the criminal, the point of retributive punishment is to impress upon him his equality with his victim, I mean to be understood quite literally. If the sentence is just and the criminal rational, then the punishment should normally *force* upon him recognition of his equality with his victim, recognition of their shared vulnerability to suffering and their shared desire to avoid it, as well as recognition of the fact that he counts for no more than his victim in the eyes of their fellows. For this reason, the retributivist requires that the offender be sane, not only at the moment of his crime, but also at the moment of his punishment—while this latter requirement would seem largely pointless (if not downright malevolent) to a utilitarian. Incidentally, it is, I believe, the desire that the offender be forced by suffering punishment to recognize his equality with his victim, rather than the desire for that suffering itself, that constitutes what is rational in the desire for revenge.

The retributivist principle represents a conception of moral desert whose complete elaboration would take us far beyond the scope of the present essay. In its defense, however, it is worth noting that our common notion of moral desert seems to include (at least) two elements: (1) a conception of individual responsibility for actions that is "contagious," that is, one which confers moral justification on the punishing (or rewarding) reactions of others; and (2) a measure of the relevant worth of actions that determines the legitimate magnitude of justified reactions. Broadly speaking, the "Kantian" notion of authorization implicit in rational action supplies the first element, and the "Hegelian" notion of upsetting and restoring equality of standing supplies the second. It seems, then, reasonable to take the equality and rationality of persons as implying moral desert in the way asserted in the retributivist principle. I shall assume henceforth that the retributivist principle is true.

The truth of the retributivist principle establishes the justice of the *lex talionis*, but, since it establishes this as a right of the victim rather than a duty, it does not settle the question of whether or to what extent the victim or the state should exercise this right and exact the *lex talionis*. This is a separate moral question because strict adherence to the *lex talionis* amounts to allowing criminals, even the most barbaric of them, to dictate our punishing behavior. It seems certain that there are at least some crimes, such as rape or torture, that we ought not try to match. And this is not merely a matter of imposing an alternative punishment that produces; an equivalent amount of suffering, as, say, some number of years in prison that might "add up" to the harm caused by a rapist or a torturer. Even if no amount of time in prison would add up to the harm caused by a torturer, it still seems that we ought not torture him even if this were the only way of making him suffer as much as he has made his victim suffer. Or, consider someone who has committed several murders in cold blood. On the *lex talionis*, it would seem that such a criminal might justly be brought to within an inch of death and then revived (or to within a moment of execution and then reprieved) as many times as he has killed (minus one), and then finally executed. But surely this is a degree of cruelty that would be monstrous.

Since the retributivist principle establishes the *lex talionis* as the victim's right, it might seem that the question of how far this right should be exercised is "up to the victim." And indeed, this would be the case in the state of nature. But once, for all the good reasons familiar to readers of John Locke, the state comes into existence, public punishment replaces private, and the victim's right to punish reposes in the state. With this, the decision as to how far to exercise this right goes to the state as well. To be sure, since (at least with respect to retributive punishment) the victim's right is the source of the state's right to punish, the state must exercise its right in ways that are faithful to the victim's right. Later, when I try to spell out the upper and lower limits of just punishment, these may be taken as indicating the range within which the state can punish and remain faithful to the victim's right.

I suspect that it will be widely agreed that the state ought not administer punishments of the sort described above even if required by the letter of the *lex talionis*, and thus, even granting the justice of *lex talionis*, there are occasions on which it is morally appropriate to diverge from its requirements. We must, of course, distinguish such morally based divergence from that which is based on practicality. Like any moral principle, the *lex talionis* is subject to "ought implies can." It will usually be impossible to do to an offender exactly what he has done—for example, his offense will normally have had an element of surprise that is not possible for a judicially imposed punishment, but this fact can hardly free him from having to bear the suffering he has imposed on another. Thus, for reasons of practicality, the *lex talionis* must necessarily be qualified to call for doing to the offender *as nearly as possible* what he has done to his victim. When, however, we refrain from raping rapists or torturing torturers, we do so for reasons of morality, not of practicality. And, given the justice of the *lex talionis*, these moral reasons cannot amount to claiming that it would be *unjust* to rape rapists or torture torturers. Rather the claim must be that, even though it would be just to rape rapists and torture torturers, other moral considerations weigh against doing so.

On the other hand, when, for moral reasons, we refrain from exacting the *lex talionis*, and impose a less harsh alternative punishment, it may be said that we are not doing full justice to the criminal, but it cannot automatically be the case that we are doing an *injustice* to his victim. Otherwise we would have to say it was unjust to imprison our torturer rather than torturing him or to simply execute our multiple murderer rather than multiply "executing" him. Surely it is counterintuitive (and irrational to boot) to set the demands of justice so high that a society would have to choose between being barbaric or being unjust. This would effectively price justice out of the moral market.

The implication of this is that there is a range of just punishments that includes some that are just though they exact less than the full measure of the *lex talionis*. What are the top and bottom ends of this range? I think that both are indicated by the retributivist principle. The principle identifies the *lex talionis* as the offender's desert and since, on retributive grounds, punishment beyond what one deserves is unjust for the same reasons that make punishment of the innocent unjust, the *lex talionis* is the upper limit of the range of just punishments. On the other hand, if the retributivist principle is true, then denying that the offender deserves suffering equal to that which he imposed amounts to denying the equality and rationality of persons. From this it follows that we fall below the bottom end of the range of just punishments when we act in ways that are incompatible with the *lex talionis* at the top end. That is, we fall below the bottom end and commit an injustice to the victim when we treat the offender in a way that is no longer compatible with sincerely believing that he deserves to have done to him what he has done to his victim. Thus, the upper limit of the range of just punishments is the point after which more punishment is unjust to the offender, and the lower limit is the point after which less punishment is unjust to the victim. In this way, the range of just punishments remains faithful to the victim's right which is their source.

This way of understanding just punishment enables us to formulate proportional retributivism so that it is compatible with acknowledging the justice of the *lex talionis*: If we take the *lex talionis* as spelling out the offender's just deserts, and if other moral considerations require us to refrain from matching the injury caused by the offender while still allowing us to punish justly, then surely we impose just punishment if we impose the closest morally acceptable approximation to the *lex talionis*. Proportional retributivism, then, in requiring that the worst crime be punished by the society's worst punishment and so on, could be understood as translating the offender's just desert into its nearest equivalent in the society's table of morally acceptable punishments. Then the two versions of retributivism (*lex talionis* and proportional) are related in that the first states what just punishment would be if nothing but the offender's just desert mattered, and the second locates just punishment at the meeting point of the offender's just deserts and the society's moral scruples. And since this second version only modifies the requirements of the *lex talionis* in light of other moral considerations, it is compatible with believing that the *lex talionis* spells out the offender's just deserts, much in the way that modifying the obligations of promisers in light of other moral considerations is compatible with believing in the binding nature of promises.

Proportional retributivism so formulated preserves the point of retributivism and remains faithful to the victim's right which is its source. Since it punishes with the closest morally acceptable approximation to the *lex talionis,* it effectively says to the offender, you deserve the equivalent of what you did to your victim and you are getting less only to the degree that *our* moral scruples limit us from duplicating what you have done. Such punishment, then, affirms the equality of persons by respecting as far as is morally permissible the victim's right to impose suffering on the offender equal to what he received, and it affirms the rationality of the offender by treating him as authorizing others to do to him what he has done though they take him up on it only *as far as is morally permissible.* Needless to say, the alternative punishments must in some convincing way be comparable in gravity to the crimes which they punish, or else they will trivialize the harms those crimes caused and be no longer compatible with sincerely believing that the offender deserves to have done to him what he has done to his victim and no longer capable of impressing upon the criminal his equality with the victim. If we punish rapists with a small fine or a brief prison term, we do an injustice to their victims, because this trivializes the suffering rapists have caused and thus is incompatible with believing that they deserve to have done to them something comparable to what they have done to their victims. If, on the other hand, instead of raping rapists we impose on them some grave penalty, say a substantial term of imprisonment, then we do no injustice even though we refrain from exacting the *lex talionis.*

To sum up, I take the *lex talionis* to be the top end of the range of just punishments. When, because we are simply unable to duplicate the criminal's offense, we modify the *lex talionis* to call for imposing on the offender as nearly as possible what he has done, we are still at this top end, applying the *lex talionis* subject to "ought implies can." When we do less than this, we still act justly as long as we punish in a way that is compatible with sincerely believing that the offender deserves the full measure of the *lex talionis*, but receives less for reasons that do not underline this belief. If this is true, then it is not unjust to spare murderers as long as they can be punished in some other suitably grave way. I leave open the question of what such an alternative punishment might be, except to say that it need not be limited to such penalties as are currently imposed. For example, though rarely carried out in practice, a life sentence with no chance of parole might be a civilized equivalent of the death penalty—after all, people sentenced to life imprisonment have traditionally been regarded as "civilly dead."

It might be objected that no punishment short of death will serve the point of retributivism with respect to murderers because no punishment short of death is commensurate with the crime of murder since, while some number of years of imprisonment may add up to the amount of harm done by rapists or assaulters or torturers, no number of years will add up to the harm done to the victim of murder. But justified divergence from the *lex talionis* is not limited only to changing the form of punishment while maintaining equivalent severity. Otherwise, we would have to torture torturers rather than imprison them if they tortured more than could be made up for by years in prison (or by the years available to them to spend in prison, which might be few for elderly torturers), and we would have to subject multiple murderers to multiple "executions." If justice allows us to refrain from these penalties, then justice allows punishments that are not equal in suffering to their crimes. It seems to me that if the objector grants this much, then he must show that a punishment less than death is not merely incommensurate to the harm caused by murder, but so far out of proportion to that harm that it trivializes it and thus effectively denies the equality and rationality of persons. Now, I am vulnerable to the claim that a sentence of life in prison that allows parole after eight or ten years does indeed trivialize the harm of (premeditated, cold-blooded) murder. But I cannot see how a sentence that would require a murderer to spend his full natural life in prison, or even the lion's share of his adult life (say, the thirty years between age twenty and age fifty), can be regarded as anything less than extremely severe and thus no trivialization of the harm he has caused.

I take it then that the justice of the *lex talionis* implies that it is just to execute murderers, but not that it is unjust to spare them as long as they are systematically punished in some other suitably grave way. Before developing the implications of this claim, a word about the implied preconditions of applying the *lex talionis* is in order.

Since this principle calls for imposing on offenders the harms they are responsible for imposing on others, the implied preconditions of applying it to any particular harm include the requirement that the harm be one that the offender is fully responsible for, where responsibility is both psychological, the capacity to tell the difference between right and wrong and control one's actions, and social. If people are subjected to remediable unjust social circumstances beyond their control, and if harmful actions are a predictable response to those conditions, then those who benefit from the unjust conditions and refuse to remedy them share responsibility for the harmful acts—and thus neither their doing nor their cost can be assigned fully to the offenders alone. For example, if a slave kills an innocent person while making his escape, at least part of the blame for the killing must fall on those who have enslaved him. And this is because slavery is unjust, not merely because the desire to escape from slavery is understandable. The desire to escape from prison is understandable as well, but if the imprisonment were a just sentence, then we would hold the prisoner, and not his keepers, responsible if he killed someone while escaping.

Since I believe that the vast majority of murders in America are a predictable response to the frustrations and disabilities of impoverished social circumstances,[7] and since I believe that that impoverishment is a remediable injustice from which others in America benefit, I believe that we have no right to exact the full cost of murders from our murderers until we have done everything possible to rectify the conditions that produce their crimes. But these are the "Reagan years," and not many—who are not already susceptible—will be persuaded by this sort of argument. This does not, in my view, shake its validity; but I want to make an argument whose appeal is not limited to those who think that crime is the result of social injustice. I shall proceed then, granting not only the justice of the death penalty, but also, at least temporarily, the assumption that our murderers are wholly deserving of dying for their crimes. If I can show that it would still be wrong to execute murderers, I believe I shall have made the strongest case for abolishing the death penalty.

## III. Civilization, Pain, and Justice

As I have already suggested, from the fact that something is justly deserved, it does not automatically follow that it should be done, since there may be other moral reasons for not doing it such that, all told, the weight of moral reasons swings the balance against proceeding. The same argument that I have given for the justice of the death penalty for murderers proves the justice of beating assaulters, raping rapists, and torturing torturers. Nonetheless, I believe, and suspect that most would agree, that it would not be right for us to beat assaulters, rape rapists, or torture torturers, *even though it were their just deserts*—and even if this were the only way to make them suffer as much as they had made their victims suffer. Calling for the abolition of the death penalty, though it be just, then, amounts to urging that as a society we place execution in the same category of sanction as beating, raping, and torturing, and treat it as something it would also not be right for us to do to offenders, *even if it were their just deserts.*

To argue for placing execution in this category, I must show what would be gained therefrom; and to show that, I shall indicate what we gain from placing torture in this category and argue that a similar gain is to be had from doing the same with execution. I select torture because I think the reasons for placing it in this category are, due to the extremity of torture, most easily seen—but what I say here applies with appropriate modification to other severe physical punishments, such as beating and raping. First, and most evidently, placing torture in this category broadcasts the message that we as a society judge torturing so horrible a thing to do to a person that we refuse to do it even when it is deserved. Note that such a judgment does not commit us to an absolute prohibition on torturing. No matter how horrible we judge something to be, we may still be justified in doing it if it is necessary to prevent something even worse. Leaving this aside for the moment, what is gained by broadcasting the public judgment that torture is too horrible to inflict even if deserved?

I think the answer to this lies in what we understand as civilization. In *The Genealogy of Morals*, Nietzsche says that in early times "pain did not hurt as much as it does today."[8] The truth in this puzzling remark is that progress in civilization is characterized by a lower tolerance for one's own pain and that suffered by others. And this is appropriate, since, via growth in knowledge, civilization brings increased power to prevent or reduce pain and, via growth in the ability to communicate and interact with more and more people, civilization extends the circle of people with whom we empathize. If civilization is characterized by lower tolerance for our own pain and that of others, then publicly refusing to do horrible things to our fellows both signals the level of our civilization *and, by our example, continues the work of civilizing.* And this gesture is all the more powerful if we refuse to do horrible things to those who deserve them. I contend then that the more things we are able to include in this category, the more civilized we are and the more civilizing. Thus we gain from including torture in this category, and if execution is especially horrible, we gain still more by including it.

Needless to say, the content, direction, and even the worth of civilization are hotly contested issues, and I shall not be able to win those contests in this brief space. At a minimum, however, I shall assume that civilization involves the taming of the natural environment and of the human animals in it, and that the overall trend in human history is toward increasing this taming, though the trend is by no means unbroken or without reverses. On these grounds, we can say that growth in civilization generally marks human history, that a reduction in the horrible things we tolerate doing to our fellows (even when they deserve them) is part of this growth, and that once the work of civilization is taken on consciously, it includes carrying forward and expanding this reduction.

This claim broadly corresponds to what Emile Durkheim identified, nearly a century ago, as "two laws which seem . . . to prevail in the evolution of the apparatus of punishment." The first, the law of quantitative change, Durkheim formulates as:

> *The intensity of punishment is the greater the more closely societies approximate to a less developed type—and the more the central power assumes an absolute character.*

And the second, which Durkheim refers to as the law of qualitative change,

> *Deprivations of liberty, and of liberty alone, varying in time according to the seriousness of the crime, tend to become more and more the normal means of social control.*[9]

Several things should be noted about these laws. First of all, they are not two separate laws. As Durkheim understands them, the second exemplifies the trend toward moderation of punishment referred to in the first. Second, the first law really refers to two distinct trends, which usually coincide but do not always. That is, moderation of punishment accompanies both the movement from less to more advanced types of society and the movement from more to less absolute rule. Normally these go hand in hand, but where they do not, the effect of one trend may offset the effect of the other. Thus, a primitive society without absolute rule may have milder punishments than an equally primitive but more absolutist society. This complication need not trouble us, since the claim I am making refers to the first trend, namely, that punishments tend to become milder as societies become more advanced; and that this is a trend in history is not refuted by the fact that it is accompanied by other trends and even occasionally offset by them. Moreover, I shall lose this article with a suggestion about the relation between the intensity of punishment and the justice of society, which might broadly be thought of as corresponding to the second trend in Durkheim's first law. Finally, and most important for our purposes, is the fact that Durkheim's claim that punishment becomes less intense as societies become more advanced is a generalization that he supports with an impressive array of evidence from historical societies from pre-Christian times to the time in which he wrote—and this in turn supports my claim that the reduction in the horrible things we do to our fellows is in fact part of the advance of civilization.

Against this it might be argued that many things grow in history, some good, some bad, and some mixed, and thus the fact that there is some historical trend is not a sufficient reason to continue it. Thus, for example, history also brings growth in population, but we are not for that reason called upon to continue the work of civilization by continually increasing our population. What this suggests is that in order to identify something as part of the work of civilizing, we must show not only that it generally grows in history, but that its growth is, on some independent grounds, clearly an advance for the human species—that is, either an unmitigated gain or at least consistently a net gain. And this implies that even trends which we might generally regard as advances may in some cases bring losses with them, such that when they did it would not be appropriate for us to lend our efforts to continuing them. Of such trends we can say that they are advances in civilization except when their gains are outweighed by the losses they bring—and that we are only called upon to further these trends when their gains are *not* outweighed in this way. It is clear in this light that increasing population is a mixed blessing at best, bringing both gains and losses. Consequently, it is not always an advance in civilization that we should further, though at times it may be.

What can be said of reducing the horrible things that we do to our fellows even when deserved? First of all, given our vulnerability to pain, it seems clearly a gain. Is it however an unmitigated gain? That is, would such a reduction ever amount to a loss? It seems to me that there are two conditions under which it would be a loss, namely, if the reduction made our lives more dangerous, or if not doing what is justly deserved were a loss in itself. Let us leave aside the former, since, as I have already suggested and as I will soon indicate in greater detail, I accept that if some horrible punishment is necessary to deter equally or more horrible acts, then we may have to impose the punishment. Thus my claim is that reduction in the horrible things we do to our fellows is an advance in civilization *as long as our lives are not thereby made more dangerous*, and that it is only then that we are called upon to extend that reduction as part of the work of civilization. Assuming then, for the moment, that we suffer no increased danger by refraining from doing horrible things to our fellows when they justly deserve them, does such refraining to do what is justly deserved amount to a loss?

It seems to me that the answer to this must be that refraining to do what is justly deserved is only a loss where it amounts to doing an injustice. But such refraining to do what is just is not doing what is unjust, unless what we do instead falls below the bottom end of the range of just punishments. Otherwise, it would be unjust to refrain from torturing torturers, raping rapists, or beating assaulters. In short, I take it that if there is no injustice in refraining from torturing torturers, then there is no injustice in refraining to do horrible things to our fellows generally, when they deserve them, as long as what we do instead is compatible with believing that they do deserve them. And thus that if such refraining does not make our lives more dangerous, then it is no loss, and given our vulnerability to pain, it is a gain. Consequently, reduction in the horrible things we do to our fellows, when not necessary to our protection, is an advance in civilization that we are called upon to continue once we consciously take upon ourselves the work of civilization.

To complete the argument, however, I must show that execution is horrible enough to warrant its inclusion alongside torture. Against this it will be said that execution is not especially horrible since it only hastens a fate that is inevitable for us. I think that this view overlooks important differences in the manner in which people reach their inevitable ends. I contend that execution is especially horrible, and it is so in a way similar to (though not identical with) the way in which torture is especially horrible. I believe we view torture as especially awful because of two of its features, which also characterize execution: intense pain and the spectacle of one human being completely subject to the power of another. This latter is separate from the issue of pain since it is something that offends us about unpainful things, such as slavery (even voluntarily entered) and prostitution (even voluntarily chosen as an occupation). Execution shares this separate feature, since killing a bound and defenseless human being enacts the total subjugation of that person to his fellows. I think, incidentally, that this accounts for the general uneasiness with which execution by lethal injection has been greeted. Rather than humanizing the event, it seems only to have purchased a possible reduction in physical pain at the price of increasing the spectacle of subjugation—with no net gain in the attractiveness of the death penalty. Indeed, its net effect may have been the reverse.

In addition to the spectacle of subjugation, execution, even by physically painless means, is also characterized by a special and intense psychological pain that distinguishes it from the loss of life that awaits us all. Interesting in this regard is the fact that although we are not terribly squeamish about the loss of life itself, allowing it in war, self-defense, as a necessary cost of progress, and so on, we are, as the extraordinary hesitance of our courts testifies, quite reluctant to execute. I think this is because execution involves the most psychologically painful features of deaths. We normally regard death from human causes as worse than death from natural causes, since a humanly caused shortening of life lacks the consolation of unavoidability. And we normally regard death whose coming is foreseen by its victim as worse than sudden death, because a foreseen death adds to the loss of life the terrible consciousness of that impending loss. As a humanly caused death whose advent is foreseen by its victim, an execution combines the worst of both.

Thus far, by analogy with torture, I have argued that execution should be avoided because of how horrible it is to the one executed. But there are reasons of another sort that follow from the analogy with torture. Torture is to be avoided not only because of what it says about what we are willing to do to our fellows, but also because of what it says about us who are willing to do it. To torture someone is an awful spectacle not only because of the intensity of pain imposed, but because of what is required to be able to impose such pain on one's fellows. The tortured body cringes, using its full exertion to escape the pain imposed upon it—it literally begs for relief with its muscles as it does with its cries. To torture someone is to demonstrate a capacity to resist this begging, and that in turn demonstrates a kind of hard-heartedness that a society ought not parade.

And this is true not only of torture, but of all severe corporal punishment. Indeed, I think this constitutes part of the answer to the puzzling question of why we refrain from punishments like whipping, even when the alternative (some months in jail versus some lashes) seems more costly to the offender. Imprisonment is painful to be sure, but it is a reflective pain, one that comes with comparing what is to what might have been, and that can be temporarily ignored by thinking about other things. But physical pain has an urgency that holds body and mind in a fierce grip. Of physical pain, as Orwell's Winston Smith recognized, "you could only wish one thing: that it should stop."[10] Refraining from torture in particular and corporal punishment in general, we both refuse to put a fellow human being in this grip and refuse to show our ability to resist this wish. The death penalty is the last corporal punishment used officially in the modern world. And it is corporal not only because administered via the body, but because the pain of foreseen, humanly administered death strikes us with the urgency that characterizes intense physical pain, causing grown men to cry, faint, and lose control of their bodily functions. There is something to be gained by refusing to endorse the hardness of heart necessary to impose such a fate.

By placing execution alongside torture in the category of things we will not do to our fellow human beings even when they deserve them, we broadcast the message that totally subjugating a person to the power of others *and* confronting him with the advent of his own humanly administered demise is too horrible to be done by civilized human beings to their fellows even when they have earned it. Too horrible to do, and too horrible to be capable of doing. And I contend that broadcasting this message loud and clear would in the long run contribute to the general detestation of murder and be, to the extent to which it worked itself into the hearts and minds of the populace, a deterrent. In short, refusing to execute murderers though they desire it both reflects and continues the taming of the human species that we call civilization. Thus, I take it that the abolition of the death penalty, though it is a just punishment for murder, is part of the civilizing mission of modern states.

## IV. Civilization, Safety, and Deterrence

Earlier I said that judging a practice too horrible to do even to those who deserve it does not exclude the possibility that it could be justified if necessary to avoid even worse consequences. Thus, were the death penalty clearly proven a better deterrent to the murder of innocent people than life in prison, we might have to admit that we had not yet reached a level of civilization at which we could protect ourselves without imposing this horrible fate on murderers, and thus we might have to grant the necessity of instituting the death penalty. But this is far from proven. The available research by no means clearly indicates that the death penalty reduces the incidence of homicide more than life imprisonment does. Even the econometric studies of Isaac Ehrlich, which purport to show that each execution saves seven or eight potential murder victims, have not changed this fact, as is testified to by the controversy and objections from equally respected statisticians that Ehrlich's work has provoked.[11]

Conceding that it has not been proven that the death penalty deters more murders than life imprisonment, van den Haag has argued that neither has it been proven that the death penalty does not deter more murders,[12] and thus we must follow common sense which teaches that the higher the cost of something, the fewer people will choose it, and therefore at least some potential murderers who would not be deterred by life imprisonment will be deterred by the death penalty. Van den Haag writes:

> . . . our experience shows that the greater the threatened penalty, the more it deters.
> . . . Life in prison is still life, however unpleasant. In contrast, the death penalty does not just threaten to make life unpleasant—it threatens to take life altogether. This difference is perceived by those affected. We find that when they have the choice between life in prison and execution, 99% of all prisoners under sentence of death prefer life in prison. . . .
> From this unquestioned fact a reasonable conclusion can be drawn in favor of the superior deterrent effect of the death penalty. Those who have the choice in practice . . . fear death more than they fear life in prison. . . . If they do, it follows that the threat of the death penalty, all other things equal, is likely to deter more than the threat of life in prison. One is most deterred by what one fears most. From which it follows that whatever statistics fail, or do not fail, to show, the death penalty is likely to be more deterrent than any other. [Pp. 68–69][13]

Those of us who recognize how common-sensical it was, and still is, to believe that the sun moves around the earth, will be less willing than Professor van den Haag to follow common sense here, especially when it comes to doing something awful to our fellows. Moreover, there are good reasons for doubting common sense on this matter. Here are four:

*1.* From the fact that one penalty is more feared than another, it does not follow that the more feared penalty will deter more than the less feared, unless we know that the less feared penalty is not fearful enough to deter everyone who can be deterred—and this is just what we don't know with regard to the death penalty. Though I fear the death penalty more than life in prison, I can't think of any act that the death penalty would deter me from that an equal likelihood of spending my life in prison wouldn't deter me from as well. Since it seems to me that whoever would be deterred by a given likelihood of death would be deterred by an *equal* likelihood of life behind bars, I suspect that the common-sense argument only seems plausible because we evaluate it unconsciously assuming that potential criminals will face larger likelihoods of death sentences than of life sentences. If the likelihoods were equal, it seems to me that where life imprisonment was improbable enough to make it too distant a possibility to worry much about, a similar low probability of death would have the same effect. After all, we are undeterred by small likelihoods of death every time we walk the streets. And if life imprisonment were sufficiently probable to pose a real deterrent threat, it would pose as much of a deterrent threat as death. And this is just what most of the research we have on the comparative deterrent impact of execution versus life imprisonment suggests.

*2.*   In light of the fact that roughly 500 to 700 suspected felons are killed by the police in the line of duty every year, and the fact that the number of privately owned guns in America is substantially larger than the number of households in America, it must be granted that anyone contemplating committing a crime *already* faces a substantial risk of ending up dead as a result. It's hard to see why anyone *who is not already deterred by this* would be deterred by the addition of the more distant risk of death after apprehension, conviction, and appeal. Indeed, this suggests that people consider risks in a much cruder way than van den Haag's appeal to common sense suggests—which should be evident to anyone who contemplates how few people use seatbelts (14% of drivers, on some estimates), when it is widely known that wearing them can spell the difference between life (outside prison) and death.

*3.*   Van den Haag has maintained that deterrence doesn't work only by means of cost-benefit calculations made by potential criminals. It works also by the lesson about the wrongfulness of murder that is slowly learned in a society that subjects murderers to the ultimate punishment (p. 63). But if I am correct in claiming that the refusal to execute even those who deserve it has a civilizing effect, then the refusal to execute also teaches a lesson about the wrongfulness of murder. My claim here is admittedly speculative, but no more so than van den Haag's to the contrary. And my view has the added virtue of accounting for the failure of research to show an increased deterrent effect from executions *without having to deny the plausibility of van den Haag's common-sense argument that at least some additional potential murderers will be deterred by the prospect of the death penalty.* If there is a deterrent effect from not executing, then it is understandable that while executions will deter some murderers, this effect will be balanced out by the weakening of the deterrent effect of not executing, such that no net reduction in murders will result. And this, by the way, also disposes of van den Haag's argument that, in the absence of knowledge one way or the other on the deterrent effect of executions, we should execute murderers rather than risk the lives of innocent people whose murders might have been deterred if we had. If there is a deterrent effect of not executing, it follows that we risk innocent lives either way. And if this is so, it seems that the only reasonable course of action is to refrain from imposing what we know is a horrible fate.

*4.*   Those who still think that van den Haag's common-sense argument for executing murderers is valid will find that the argument proves more than they bargained for. Van den Haag maintains that, in the absence of conclusive evidence on the relative deterrent impact of the death penalty versus life imprisonment, we must follow common sense and assume that if one punishment is more fearful than another, it will deter some potential criminals not deterred by the less fearful punishment. Since people sentenced to death will almost universally try to get their sentences changed to life in prison, it follows that death is more fearful than life imprisonment, and thus that it will deter some additional murderers. Consequently, we should institute the death penalty to save the lives these additional murderers would have taken. But, since people sentenced to be tortured to death would surely try to get their sentences changed to simple execution, the same argument proves that death-by-torture will deter still more potential murderers. Consequently, we should institute death-by-torture to save the lives these additional murderers would have taken. Anyone who accepts van den Haag's argument is then confronted with a dilemma: Until we have conclusive evidence that capital punishment is a greater deterrent to murder than life imprisonment, he must grant either that we should not follow common sense and not impose the death penalty; or we should follow common sense and torture murderers to death. In short, either we must abolish the electric chair or reinstitute the rack. Surely, this is the *reductio ad absurdum* of van den Haag's common-sense argument.

## Conclusion: History, Force, and Justice

I believe that, taken together, these arguments prove that we should abolish the death penalty though it is a just punishment for murder. Let me close with an argument of a different sort. When you see the lash fall upon the backs of Roman slaves, or the hideous tortures meted out in the period of the absolute monarchs, you see more than mere cruelty at work. Surely you suspect that there is something about the injustice of imperial slavery and royal tyranny that requires the use of extreme force to keep these institutions in place. That is, for reasons undoubtedly related to those that support the second part of Durkheim's first law of penal evolution, we take the amount of force a society uses against its own people as an inverse measure of its justness. And though no more than a rough measure, it is a revealing one nonetheless, because when a society is limited in the degree of force it can use against its subjects, it is likely to have to be a juster society since it will have to gain its subjects' cooperation by offering them fairer terms than it would have to, if it could use more force. From this we cannot simply conclude that reducing the force used by our society will automatically make our society more just—but I think we can conclude that it will have this tendency, since it will require us to find means other than force for encouraging compliance with our institutions, and this is likely to require us to make those institutions as fair to all as possible. Thus I hope that America will pose itself the challenge of winning its citizens' cooperation by justice rather than force, and that when future historians look back on the twentieth century, they will find us with countries like France and England and Sweden that have abolished the death penalty, rather than with those like South Africa and the Soviet Union and Iran that have retained it—with all that this suggests about the countries involved.

### Acknowledgment

This paper is an expanded version of my opening statement in a debate with Ernest van den Haag on the death penalty at an Amnesty International conference on capital punishment, held at John Jay College in New York City, on October 17, 1983. I am grateful to the Editors of *Philosophy and Public Affairs* for very thought-provoking comments, to Hugo Bedau and Robert Johnson for many helpful suggestions, and to Ernest van den Haag for his encouragement.

### Endnotes

1. Ernest van den Haag and John P. Conrad, *The Death Penalty: A Debate* (New York: Plenum Press, 1983). Unless otherwise indicated, page references in the text and notes are to this book.

2. "As a general rule, a man is undone by *waiting* for capital punishment well before he dies. Two deaths are inflicted on him, the first being worse than the second, whereas he killed but once" (Albert Camus, "Reflections on the Guillotine," in *Resistance, Rebellion and Death* [New York: Knopf, 1969], p. 205). Based on interviews with the condemned men on Al-

abama's death row, Robert Johnson presents convincing empirical support for Camus' observation, in *Condemned to Die: Life Under Sentence of Death* (New York: Elsevier, 1981).

3. Hegel writes that "The sole positive existence which the injury [i.e., the crime] possesses is that it is the particular will of the criminal [i.e., it is the criminal's intention that distinguishes criminal injury from, say, injury due to an accident]. Hence to injure (or penalize) this particular will as a will determinately existent is to annul the crime, which otherwise would have been held valid, and to restore the right." (G. W. F. Hegel, *The Philosophy of Right*, trans. T. M. Knox [Oxford Clarendon Press, 1962; originally published in German in 1821], p. 69; see also p. 331n). I take this to mean that the right is a certain equality of sovereignty between the wills of individuals, crime disrupts that equality by placing one will above others, and punishment restores the equality by annulling the illegitimate ascendance. On these grounds, as I shall suggest below, the desire for revenge (strictly limited to the desire "to even the score") is more respectable than philosophers have generally allowed. And so Hegel writes that "The annulling of crime in this sphere where right is immediate [i.e., the condition prior to conscious morality] is principally revenge, which is just in its content in so far as it is retributive" (ibid., p. 73).

4. Kant writes that "any undeserved evil that you inflict on someone else among the people is one that you do to yourself. If you vilify him, you vilify yourself; if you steal from him, you steal from yourself; if you kill him, you kill yourself." Since Kant holds that "If what happens to someone is also willed by him, it cannot be a punishment," he takes pains to distance himself from the view that the offender wills his punishment. "The chief error contained in this sophistry," Kant writes, "consists in the confusion of the criminal's [that is, the murderer's] own judgment (which one must necessarily attribute to his reason) that he must forfeit his life with a resolution of the will to take his own life" (Immanuel Kant, *The Metaphysical Elements of Justice, Part I of The Metaphysics of Morals*, trans. J. Ladd [Indianapolis: Bobbs-Merrill, 1965; originally published in 1797], pp. 101, 105–106). I have tried to capture this notion of attributing a judgment to the offender rather than a resolution of his will with the term "authorizes."

5. "Even if a civil society were to dissolve itself by common agreement of all its members . . . , the last murderer remaining in prison must first be executed, so that everyone will duly receive what his actions are worth" (Kant, ibid., p. 102).

6. Kant, *Metaphysical Elements of Justice*, p. 104; see also p. 133.

7. "In the case of homicide, the empirical evidence indicates that poverty and poor economic conditions are systematically related to higher levels of homicide" (Richard M. McGahey, "Dr. Ehrlich's Magic Bullet: Economic Theory, Econometrics, and the Death Penalty," *Crime & Delinquency* 26, no. 4 [October 1980], 502). Some of that evidence can be found in Peter Passell, "The Deterrent Effect of the Death Penalty: A Statistical Test," *Stanford Law Review* (November 1975), 61–80.

8. Friedrich Nietzsche, *The Birth of Tragedy and The Genealogy of Morals* (New York: Doubleday, 1956), pp. 199–200.

9. Emile Durkheim, "Two Laws of Penal Evolution," *Economy and Society* 2 (1973), 285 and 294; italics in the original. This essay was originally published in French in *Année Sociologique* 4 (1899–1900).

10. George Orwell, *1984* (New York: New American Library, 1983; originally published in 1949), p. 197.

11. Isaac Ehrlich, "The Deterrent Effect of Capital Punishment: A Question of Life or Death," *American Economic Review* 65 (June 1975), 397–417. For reactions to Ehrlich's work, see Alfred Blumstein, Jacqueline Cohen, and Daniel Nagin, eds., *Deterrence and Incapacitation: Estimating the Effects of Criminal Sanctions on Crime Rates* (Washington, DC: National Academy of Sciences, 1978), esp. pp. 59–63 and 336–360; Brian E. Forst, "The Deterrent Effect on Capital Punishment: A Cross-State Analysis," *Minnesota Law Review* 61 (May 1977), 743–767. Deryck Beyleveld, "Ehrlich's Analysis of Deterrence," *British Journal of Criminology* 22 (April 1982),101–123, and Isaac Ehrlich, "On Positive Methodology, Ethics and Polemics in Deterrence Research," *British Journal of Criminology* 22 (April 1982),124–139. Much of the criticism of Ehrlich's work focuses on the fact that he found a deterrence impact of executions in the period from 1933–1969, which includes the period of 1963–1969, a time when hardly any executions were carried out and crime rates rose for reasons that are arguably independent of the existence or nonexistence of capital punishment. When the 1963–1969 period is excluded, no significant deterrent effect shows. Prior to Ehrlich's work, research on the comparative deterrent impact of the death penalty versus life imprisonment indicated no increase in the incidence of homicide in states that abolished the death penalty and no greater incidence of homicide in states without the death penalty compared to similar states with the death penalty. See Thorsten Sellin, *The Death Penalty* (Philadelphia: American Law Institute, 1959).

12. Van den Haag writes: "Other studies published since Ehrlich's contend that his results are due to the techniques and periods he selected, and that different techniques and periods yield different results. Despite a great deal of research on all sides. one cannot say that the statistical evidence is conclusive. Nobody has claimed to have disproved that the death penalty may deter more than life imprisonment. But one cannot claim, either, that it has been proved statistically in a conclusive manner that the death penalty does deter more than alternative penalties. This lack of proof does not amount to disproof" (p. 65).

13. An alternative formulation of this "common-sense argument" is put forth and defended by Michael Davis in "Death, Deterrence, and the Method of Common Sense," *Social Theory and Practice* 7, no. 2 (Summer 1981), 145–177.

## Journal/Discussion Questions

✍ *Have you ever known someone who experienced the murder of a close family member? How did this affect their feelings about capital punishment? How does this relate to Reiman's Kantian and Hegelian analyses of retributivism?*

1. Reiman's position is an unusual one in that it accepts the justice of the death penalty but still argues for its abolition. In what ways does it differ from your own? Did reading his article prompt you to reconsider any elements of your own position?

2. What, according to Reiman, is the difference between the *lex talionis* and proportional retributivism? Why is this distinction important to his argument?

3. What is the *retributivist principle*? What are its Kantian and Hegelian foundations? How is it related to the Golden Rule?

4. Why, according to Reiman, should we refrain from raping rapists and torturing torturers? Why should we refrain from executing murderers?

5. Reiman considers the "common-sense argument" that capital punishment deters. What objections does he raise to it? Are those objections convincing?

---

## Walter Berns
## "The Morality of Anger"

*Walter Berns is a resident scholar at the American Enterprise Institute.*

*In this selection, which is drawn from his* For Capital Punishment: Crime and the Morality of the Death Penalty, *Berns argues in favor of the moral force of anger and its place in punishment.*

### As You Read, Consider This:

1. Compare and contrast your reactions to Simon Wiesenthal and Berns's reactions. Do they indicate any differences in your respective positions on the death penalty and the general purpose of punishment?

2. In what ways, according to Berns, is anger connected to punishment and to justice?

~

Until recently, my business did not require me to think about the punishment of criminals in general or the legitimacy and efficacy of capital punishment in particular. In a vague way, I was aware of the disagreement among professionals concerning the purpose of punishment—whether it was intended to deter others, to rehabilitate the criminal, or to pay him back—but like most laymen I had no particular reason to decide which purpose was right or to what extent they may all have been right. I did know that retribution was held in ill repute among criminologists and jurists—to them, retribution was a fancy name for revenge, and revenge was barbaric—and, of course, I knew that capital punishment had the support only of policemen, prison guards, and some local politicians, the sort of people Arthur Koestler calls "hanghards" (Philadelphia's Mayor Rizzo comes to mind). The intellectual community denounced it as both unnecessary and immoral. It was the phenomenon of Simon Wiesenthal that allowed me to understand why the intellectuals were wrong and why the police, the politicians, and the majority of the voters were right: We punish criminals principally in order to pay them back, and we execute the worst of them out of moral necessity. Anyone who respects Wiesenthal's mission will be driven to the same conclusion.

Of course, not everyone will respect that mission. It will strike the busy man—I mean the sort of man who sees things only in the light cast by a concern for his own interests—as somewhat bizarre. Why should anyone devote his life—more than thirty years of it!—exclusively to the task of hunting down the Nazi war criminals who survived World War II and escaped punishment? Wiesenthal says his conscience forces him "to bring the guilty ones to trial." But why punish them? What do we hope to accomplish now by punishing SS Obersturmbannführer Adolf Eichmann or SS Obersturmbannführer Franz Stangl or someday—who knows?—Reichsleiter Martin Bormann? We surely don't expect to rehabilitate them, and it would be foolish to think that by punishing them we might thereby deter others. The answer, I think, is clear: We want to punish them in order to *pay them back*. We think they must be made to pay for their crimes with their lives and we think that we, the survivors of the world they violated, may legitimately exact that payment because we, too, are their victims. By punishing them, we demonstrate that there are laws that bind men across generations as well as across (and within) nations, that we are not simply isolated individuals, each pursuing his selfish interests and connected with others by a mere contract to live and let live. To state it simply, Wiesenthal allows us to see that it is right, morally right, to be angry with criminals and to express that anger publicly, officially, and in an appropriate manner, which may require the worst of them to be executed.

Modern civil-libertarian opponents of capital punishment do not understand this. They say that to execute a criminal is to deny his human dignity; they also say that the death penalty is not useful, that nothing useful is accomplished by executing anyone. Being utilitarians, they are essentially selfish men, distrustful of passion, who do not understand the connection between anger and justice, and between anger and human dignity.

Anger is expressed or manifested on those occasions when someone has acted in a manner that is thought to be unjust, and one of its origins is the opinion that men are responsible, and should be held responsible for what they do. Thus, as Aristotle teaches us, anger is accompanied not only by the pain caused by the one who is the object of anger, but by the pleasure arising from the expectation of inflicting revenge on someone who is thought to deserve it. We can become angry with an inanimate object (the door we run into and then kick in return) only by foolishly attributing responsibility to it, and we cannot do that for long, which is why we do not think of returning later to revenge ourselves on the door. For the same reason, we cannot be more than momentarily angry with any one creature other than man; only a fool and worse would dream of taking revenge on a dog. And, finally, we tend to pity rather than to be angry with men who—because they are insane, for example—are not responsible for their acts. Anger, then, is a very human passion not only because only a human being can be angry, but also because anger acknowledges the humanity of its objects: it holds them accountable for what they do. And in holding particular men responsible, it pays them the respect that is due them as men. Anger recognizes that only men have the capacity to be moral beings and, in so doing, acknowledges the dignity of human beings. Anger is somehow connected with justice, and it is this that modern penology has not understood; it tends, on the whole, to regard anger as a selfish indulgence.

Anger can, of course, be that; and if someone does not become angry with an insult or an injury suffered unjustly, we tend to think he does not think much of himself. But it need not be selfish, not in the sense of being provoked only by an injury suffered by oneself. There were many angry men in America when President Kennedy was killed; one of them—Jack Ruby—took it upon himself to exact the punishment that, if indeed deserved, ought to have been exacted by the law. There were perhaps even angrier men when Martin Luther King, Jr., was killed, for King, more than anyone else at the time, embodied a people's quest for justice; the anger—more, the "black rage"—expressed on that occasion was simply a manifestation of the great change that had occurred among black men in America, a change wrought in large part by King and his associates in the civil rights movement: the servility and fear of the past had been replaced by pride and anger, and the treatment that had formerly been accepted as a matter of course or as if it were deserved was now seen for what it was, unjust and unacceptable. King preached love, but the movement he led depended on anger as well as love, and that anger was not despicable, being neither selfish nor unjustified. On the contrary, it was a reflection of what was called solidarity and may more accurately be called a profound caring for others, black for other blacks, white for blacks, and, in the world King was trying to build, American for other Americans. If men are not saddened when someone else suffers, or angry when someone else suffers unjustly, the implication is that they do not care for anyone other than themselves or that they lack some quality that befits a man. When we criticize them for this, we acknowledge that they ought to care for others. If men are not angry when a neighbor suffers at the hands of a criminal, the implication is that their moral faculties have been corrupted, that they are not good citizens.

Criminals are properly the objects of anger, and the perpetrators of terrible crimes—for example, Lee Harvey Oswald and James Earl Ray—are properly the objects of great anger. They have done more than inflict an injury on an isolated individual; they have violated the foundations of trust and friendship, the necessary elements of a moral community, the only community worth living in. A moral community, unlike a hive of bees or a hill of ants, is one whose members are expected freely to obey the laws and, unlike those in a tyranny, are trusted to obey the laws. The criminal has violated that trust, and in so doing has injured not merely his immediate victim but the community as such. He has called into question the very possibility of that community by suggesting that men cannot be trusted to respect freely the property, the person, and the dignity of those with whom they are associated. If, then, men are not angry when someone else is robbed, raped, or murdered, the implication is that no moral community exists, because those men do not care for anyone other than themselves. Anger is an expression of that caring, and society needs men who care for one another, who share their pleasures and their pains, and do so for the sake of the others. It is the passion that can cause us to act for reasons having nothing to do with selfish or mean calculation; indeed, when educated it can become a generous passion, the passion that protects the community or country by demanding punishment for its enemies. It is the stuff from which heroes are made.

A moral community is not possible without anger and the moral indignation that accompanies it. Thus the most powerful attack on capital punishment was written by a man, Albert Camus, who denied the legitimacy of anger and moral indignation by denying the very possibility of a moral community in our time. The anger expressed in our world, he said, is nothing but hypocrisy. His novel *L'Étranger* (variously translated as *The Stranger* or *The Outsider*) is a brilliant portrayal of what Camus insisted is our world, a world deprived of God, as he put it. It is a world we would not choose to live in and one that Camus, the hero of the French Resistance, disdained. Nevertheless, the novel is a modern masterpiece, and Meursault, its antihero (for a world without anger can have no heroes), is a murderer.

He is a murderer whose crime is excused, even as his lack of hypocrisy is praised, because the universe, we are told, is "benignly indifferent" to how we live or what we do. Of course, the law is not indifferent; the law punished Meursault and it threatens to punish us if we do as he did.

But Camus the novelist teaches us that the law is simply a collection of arbitrary conceits. The people around Meursault apparently were not indifferent; they expressed dismay at his lack of attachment to his mother and disapprobation of his crime. But Camus the novelist teaches us that other people are hypocrites. They pretend not to know what Camus the opponent of capital punishment tells: namely, that "our civilization has lost the only values that, in a certain way, can justify that penalty . . . [the existence of] a truth or a principle that is superior to man." There is no basis for friendship and no moral law; therefore, no one, not even a murderer, can violate the terms of friendship or break that law; and there is no basis for the anger that we express when someone breaks that law. The only thing we share as men, the only thing that connects us one to another, is a "solidarity against death," and a judgment of capital punishment "upsets" that solidarity. The purpose of human life is to stay alive.

Like Meursault, Macbeth was a murderer, and like *L'Étranger*, Shakespeare's *Macbeth* is the story of a murder; but there the similarity ends. As Lincoln said, "Nothing equals *Macbeth*." He was comparing it with the other Shakespearean plays he knew, the plays he had "gone over perhaps as frequently as any unprofessional reader . . . *Lear, Richard Third, Henry Eighth, Hamlet*"; but I think he meant to say more than that none of these equals *Macbeth*. I think he meant that no other literary work equals it. "It is wonderful," he said. *Macbeth* is wonderful because, to say nothing more here, it teaches us the awesomeness of the commandment "Thou shalt not kill."

What can a dramatic poet tell us about murder? More, probably, than anyone else, if he is a poet worthy of consideration, and yet nothing that does not inhere in the act itself. In *Macbeth*, Shakespeare shows us murders committed in a political world by a man so driven by ambition to rule that world that he becomes a tyrant. He shows us also the consequences, which were terrible, worse even than Macbeth feared. The cosmos rebelled, turned into chaos by his deeds. He shows a world that was not "benignly indifferent" to what we call crimes and especially to murder, a world constituted by laws divine as well as human, and Macbeth violated the most awful of those laws. Because the world was so constituted, Macbeth suffered the torments of the great and the damned, torments far beyond the "practice" of any physician. He had known glory and had deserved the respect and affection of king, countrymen, army, friends, and wife; and he lost it all. At the end he was reduced to saying that life "is a tale told by an idiot, full of sound and fury, signifying nothing"; yet, in spite of the horrors provoked in us by his acts, he excites no anger in us. We pity him; even so, we understand the anger of his countrymen and the dramatic necessity of his death. *Macbeth* is a play about ambition, murder, tyranny; about horror, anger, vengeance, and perhaps more than any other of Shakespeare's plays, justice. Because of justice, Macbeth has to die, not by his own hand—he will not "play the Roman fool, and die on [his] sword"—but at the hand of the avenging Macduff. The dramatic necessity of his death would appear to rest on its *moral* necessity. Is that right? Does this play conform to our sense of what a murder means? Lincoln thought it was "wonderful."

Surely Shakespeare's is a truer account of murder than the one provided by Camus, and by truer I mean truer to our moral sense of what a murder is and what the consequences that attend it must be. Shakespeare shows us vengeful men because there is something in the souls of men— then and now—that requires such crimes to be revenged. Can we imagine a world that does not take its revenge on the man who kills Macduff's wife and children? (Can we imagine the play in which Macbeth does not die?) Can we imagine a people that does not hate murderers? (Can we imagine a world where Meursault is an outsider only because he does not *pretend* to be outraged by murder?) Shakespeare's poetry could not have been written out of the moral sense that the death penalty's opponents insist we ought to have. Indeed, the issue of capital punishment can be said to turn on whether Shakespeare's or Camus' is the more telling account of murder.

There is a sense in which punishment may be likened to dramatic poetry. Dramatic poetry depicts men's actions because men are revealed in, or make themselves known through, their actions; and the essence of a human action according to Aristotle, consists in its being virtuous or vicious. Only a ruler or a contender for rule can act with the freedom and on a scale that allows the virtuousness or viciousness of human deeds to be fully displayed. Macbeth was such a man, and in his fall, brought about by his own acts, and in the consequent suffering he endured, is revealed the meaning of morality. In *Macbeth* the majesty of the moral law is demonstrated to us; as I said it teaches us the awesomeness of the commandment Thou shalt not kill. In a similar fashion, the punishments imposed by the legal order remind us of the reign of the moral order; not only do they remind us of it, but by enforcing its prescriptions, they enhance the dignity of the legal order in the eyes of moral men, in the eyes of those decent citizens who cry out "for gods who will avenge injustice." That is especially important in a self-governing community, a community that gives laws to itself.

If the laws were understood to be divinely inspired or, in the extreme case, divinely given, they would enjoy all the dignity that the opinions of men can grant and all the dignity they require to ensure their being obeyed by most of the men living under them. Like Duncan in the opinion of Macduff, the laws would be "the Lord's anointed," and would be obeyed even as Macduff obeyed the laws of the Scottish kingdom. Only a Macbeth would challenge them, and only a Meursault would ignore them. But the laws of the United States are not of this description; in fact, among the proposed amendments that became the Bill of Rights was one declaring not that all power comes from God, but rather "that all power is originally vested in, and consequently derives from the people"; and this proposal was dropped only because it was thought to be redundant: the Constitution's preamble said essentially the same thing, and what we know as the Tenth Amendment reiterated it. So Madison proposed to make the Constitution venerable in the minds of the people, and Lincoln, in an early speech, went so far as to say that a "political religion" should be made of it. They did not doubt that the Constitution and the laws made pursuant to it would be supported by "enlightened reason," but fearing that enlightened reason would be in short supply, they sought to augment it. The laws of the United States would be obeyed by some men because they could hear and understand "the voice of enlightened reason," and by other men because they would regard the laws with that "veneration which time bestows on everything."

Supreme Court justices have occasionally complained of our habit of making "constitutionality synonymous with wisdom." But the extent to which the Constitution is venerated and its authority accepted depends on the compatibility of its rules with our moral sensibilities; despite its venerable character, the Constitution is not the only source of these moral sensibilities. There was even a period, before slavery was abolished by the Thirteenth Amendment, when the Constitution was regarded by some very moral men as an abomination: Garrison called it "a covenant with death and an agreement with Hell," and there were honorable men holding important political offices and judicial appointments who refused to enforce the Fugitive Slave Law even though its constitutionality had been affirmed. In time this opinion spread far beyond the ranks of the original abolitionists until those who held it composed a constitutional majority of the people, and slavery was abolished.

But Lincoln knew that more than amendments were required to make the Constitution once more worthy of the veneration of moral men. That is why, in the Gettysburg Address, he made the principle of the Constitution an inheritance from "our fathers." That it should be so esteemed is especially important in a self-governing nation that gives laws to itself, because it is only a short step from the principle that the laws are merely a product of one's own will to the opinion that the only consideration that informs the law is self-interest; and this opinion is only one remove from lawlessness. A nation of simple self-interested men will soon enough perish from the earth.

It was not an accident that Lincoln spoke as he did at Gettysburg or that he chose as the occasion for his words the dedication of a cemetery built on a portion of the most significant battlefield of the Civil War. Two and a half years earlier, in his First Inaugural Address, he had said that Americans, north and south, were not and must not be enemies, but friends. Passion had strained but must not be allowed to break the bonds of affection that tied them one to another. He closed by saying this: "The mystic chords of memory, stretching from every battlefield, and patriot grave, to every living heart and hearthstone, all over this broad land, will yet swell the chorus of the Union, when again touched, as surely they will be, by the better angels of our nature." The chords of memory that would swell the chorus of the Union could be touched, even by a man of Lincoln's stature, only on the most solemn occasions, and in the life of a nation no occasion is more solemn than the burial of the patriots who have died defending it on the field of battle. War is surely an evil, but as Hegel said, it is not an "absolute evil." It exacts the supreme sacrifice, but precisely because of that it can call forth such sublime rhetoric as Lincoln's. His words at Gettysburg serve to remind Americans in particular of what Hegel said people in general needed to know, and could be made to know by means of war and the sacrifices demanded of them in wars: namely, that their country is something more than a "civil society" the purpose of which is simply the protection of individual and selfish interests.

Capital punishment, like Shakespeare's dramatic and Lincoln's political poetry (and it is surely that, and was understood by him to be that), serves to remind us of the majesty of the moral order that is embodied in our law, and of the terrible consequences of its breach. The law must not be understood to be merely a statute that we enact or repeal at our will, and obey or disobey at our convenience—especially not the criminal law. Wherever law is regarded as merely statutory, men will soon enough disobey it, and will learn how to do so without any inconvenience to themselves. The criminal law must possess a dignity far beyond that possessed by mere statutory enactment or utilitarian and self-interested calculations. The most powerful means we have to give it that dignity is to authorize it to impose the ultimate penalty. The criminal law must be made awful, by which I mean inspiring or commanding "profound respect or reverential fear." It must remind us of the moral order by which alone we can live as *human* beings, and in America, now that the Supreme Court has outlawed banishment, the only punishment that can do this is capital punishment.

The founder of modern criminology, the eighteenth-century Italian Cesare Beccaria, opposed both banishment and capital punishment because he understood that both were inconsistent with the principle of self-interest, and self-interest was the basis of the political order he favored. If a man's first or only duty is to himself, of course he will prefer his money to his country he will also prefer his money to his brother. In fact, he will prefer his brother's money to his brother, and a people of this description, or a country that understands itself in this Beccarian manner, can put the mark of Cain on no one. For the same reason, such a country can have no legitimate reason to execute its criminals, or, indeed, to punish them in any manner. What would be accomplished by punishment in such a place? Punishment arises out of the demand for justice, and justice is demanded by angry, morally indignant men; its purpose is to satisfy that moral indignation and thereby promote the law-abidingness that, it is assumed, accompanies it. But the principle of self-interest denies the moral basis of that indignation

Not only will a country based solely on self-interest have no legitimate reason to punish; it may have no need to punish. It may be able to solve what we call the crime problem by substituting a law of contracts for a law of crimes. According to Beccaria's social contract, men agree to yield their natural freedom to the "sovereign" in exchange for his promise to keep the peace. As it becomes more difficult for the sovereign to fulfill his part of the contract, there is a demand that he be made to pay for his nonperformance. From this comes compensation or insurance schemes embodied in statutes whereby the sovereign (or state), being unable to keep the peace by punishing criminals, agrees to compensate its contractual partners for injuries suffered at the hands of criminals, injuries the police are unable to prevent. The insurance policy takes the place of law enforcement and the *posse comitatus*, and John Wayne and Gary Cooper give way to Mutual of Omaha. There is no anger in this kind of law, and none (or no reason for any) in the society. The principle can be carried further still. If we ignore the victim (and nothing we do can restore his life anyway), there would appear to be no reason why—the worth of a man being his price, as Beccaria's teacher, Thomas Hobbes, put it—coverage should not be extended to the losses incurred in a murder. If we ignore the victim's sensibilities (and what are they but absurd vanities?), there would appear to be no reason why—the worth of a woman being *her* price—coverage should not be extended to the losses incurred in a rape. Other examples will no doubt suggest themselves.

This might appear to be an almost perfect solution to what we persist in calling the crime problem, achieved without risking the terrible things sometimes done by an angry people. A people that is not angry with criminals will not be able to deter crime, but a people fully covered by insurance has no need to deter crime: they will be insured against all the losses they can, in principle, suffer. What is now called crime can be expected to increase in volume, of course, and this will cause an increase in the premiums paid, directly or in the form of taxes. But it will no longer be necessary to apprehend, try, and punish criminals, which now costs Americans more than $1.5 billion a month (and is increasing at an annual rate of about 15 percent), and one can buy a lot of insurance for $1.5 billion. There is this difficulty, as Rousseau put it: To exclude anger from the human community is to concentrate all the passions in a "self-interest of the meanest sort, and such a place would not be fit for human habitation.

When, in 1976, the Supreme Court declared death to be a constitutional penalty, it decided that the United States was not that sort of country; most of us, I think, can appreciate that judgment. We want to live among people who do not value their possessions more than their citizenship, who do not think exclusively or even primarily of their own rights, people whom we can depend on even as they exercise their rights, and whom we can trust, which is to say, people who, even in the absence of a policeman, will not assault our bodies or steal our possessions, and might even come to our assistance when we need it, and who stand ready, when the occasion demands it, to risk their lives in defense of their country. If we are of the opinion that the United States may rightly ask of its citizens this awful sacrifice, then we are also of the opinion that it may rightly impose the most awful penalty, if it may rightly honor its heroes, it may rightly execute the worst of its criminals. By doing so, it will remind its citizens that it is a country worthy of heroes.

# Journal/Discussion Questions

✍ *Consider your reaction to the bombing of the federal building in Oklahoma City. To what extent does Berns's analysis shed light on your feelings? What shortcomings does his analysis have in light of your own experience?*

1. Berns sees the function of punishment to be, in part, one of "paying back." What, precisely, are we paying the criminal back for? How does this relate to Dagger's analysis?

2. Why, according to Berns, is it important to stay in touch with our anger about criminals and their crimes? Do you agree? What are the dangers of this position?

# QUESTIONS FOR DISCUSSION AND REVIEW

## Where Do You Stand Now?

**Instructions**

You have already answered the following questions in your moral problems self-quiz at the beginning of this book. Now that you have studied the material in this section, take a moment to answer the same questions again.

| | Strongly Agree | Agree | Undecided | Disagree | Strongly Disagree | *Chapter 3: Punishment and the Death Penalty* |
|---|---|---|---|---|---|---|
| 11. | ❏ | ❏ | ❏ | ❏ | ❏ | The purpose of punishment is primarily to pay back the offender. |
| 12. | ❏ | ❏ | ❏ | ❏ | ❏ | The purpose of punishment is primarily to deter the offender and others from committing future crimes. |
| 13. | ❏ | ❏ | ❏ | ❏ | ❏ | Capital punishment is always morally wrong. |
| 14. | ❏ | ❏ | ❏ | ❏ | ❏ | The principal moral consideration about capital punishment is the question of whether it is administered arbitrarily or not. |
| 15. | ❏ | ❏ | ❏ | ❏ | ❏ | The principal moral consideration about capital punishment is that it doesn't really deter criminals. |

Compare your answers to the present self-quiz with the answers to the initial self-quiz. How, if at all, have your answers changed? How have the *reasons* for your answers changed?

## Journal/Discussion Questions

✍ *Imagine that you are on a jury. You have just found a young adult guilty of a particularly heinous rape/torture/murder of a small child. The defendant appears to be unrepentant. Now you are being asked to consider sentencing. The prosecution is asking for the death penalty, while the defense is requesting a sentence of life imprisonment. How would you vote? What factors would you consider? What*

*would be the major stumbling block to changing your mind and voting the other way? Given your answers to these questions, how does your position fit in with the positions and issues discussed in this chapter?*

1. You have now read, thought, and discussed a number of aspects of punishment in general and the use of the death penalty in particular. How have your

views *changed* and developed? Has your understanding changed of the *reasons* supporting other positions that are different from your own? If so, in what way(s)? What idea had the greatest impact on your thinking about punishment? About the death penalty? Why?

2. Imagine that a close family member was murdered. How, if at all, would this affect your views on punishment? On capital punishment? Presuming that the murderer were caught, what would you like punishment to accomplish?

3. Imagine that you are a new member of the Senate, and that you have just been given an assignment to the Senate committee that is responsible for recommendations about criminal punishment on the state and local levels as well as nationally. Your committee is asked to determine (a) what aspects of our current punishment practices are in need of revision and (b) what changes you would recommend for the future. At the first meeting of the committee, the committee chair asks each member to state their initial general views on these two issues. What would your response be?

# FOR FURTHER READING:
# A BIBLIOGRAPHICAL GUIDE
# TO PUNISHMENT AND THE DEATH PENALTY

## Punishment

There are a number of excellent *anthologies on punishment*, many of which contain articles on the death penalty in particular. See *Punishment and the Death Penalty: The Current Debate*, ed. Robert M. Baird and Stuart E. Rosenbaum (Buffalo, New York: Prometheus Books, 1995); *Punishment: A Philosophy and Public Affairs Reader*, ed. A. John Simmons, Marshall Cohen, Joshua Cohen, and Charles R. Beitz (Princeton: Princeton University Press, 1995); *Philosophy of Punishment*, ed. Robert M. Baird and Stuart E. Rosenbaum (Buffalo, NY: Prometheus Books, 1988); *Punishment: Selected Readings*, ed. Joel Feinberg and Hyman Gross (Encino, CA: Dickenson, 1975); *Philosophical Perspectives on Punishment*, ed. Gertrude Ezorsky (Albany: State University of New York Press, 1972); *The Philosophy of Punishment: A Collection of Papers*, ed. H. B. Acton (New York: St. Martin's Press, 1969); *Theories of Punishment*, ed. Stanley E. Grupp (Bloomington: Indiana University Press, 1971). In contrast to such comparatively modern problems as abortion and *in vitro* fertilization, punishment has been a theme for philosophers for centuries.

The anthology by Ezorsky contains an excellent selection of *classical sources* as well as contemporary authors. See also Plato's *Laws*, Jeremy Bentham's *An Introduction to the Principles of Morals and Legislation* (Oxford: Blackwell, 1967), especially chap. 13, sec. 2; Immanuel Kant, *The Metaphysical Elements of Justice, Part I of The Metaphysics of Morals*, trans. John Ladd (Indianapolis: Bobbs-Merrill, 1965); and G. W. F. Hegel, *The Philosophy of Right*, trans. T. M. Knox (Oxford Clarendon Press, 1962).

Among the influential *contemporary articles and books*, see especially Jeffrie G. Murphy's "Marxism and Retribution," *Philosophy and Public Affairs* 2, no. 3 (Spring 1973), 217–243, in which he argues in favor of a retributivist view of punishment that is compatible with the Marxist tradition; also see his *Retribution, Justice and Therapy* (Dordrecht: Reidel, 1979). Edmund L. Pincoffs, *The Rationale of Legal Punishment* (New York: Humanities Press, 1966) is an eloquent defense of a retributivist view of punishment. Also see Ernest van den Haag, *Punishing Criminals* (New York: Basic Books, 1975). John Cottingham, "Punishment," *The Encyclopedia of Ethics*, ed. Lawrence C. Becker and Charlotte B. Becker (New York: Garland, 1992), vol. II, pp. 1053–1055 and Stanley I. Benn, "Punishment," *The Encyclopedia of Philosophy*, vol. 7, ed. Paul Edwards (New York: Macmillan, 1967), pp. 29–36 both offer excellent surveys of the major issues about punishment. Among the noteworthy articles, see Andrew von Hirsch, "Doing Justice: The Principle of Commensurate Deserts," and Hyman Gross, "Proportional Punishment and Justifiable Sentences," in *Sentencing*, eds. H. Gross and A. von Hirsch (New York: Oxford University Press, 1981), pp. 243–256 and 272–283, respectively, offer perspicuous discussions of retributivism and punishment. Also see Michael Davis, "How to Make the Punishment Fit the Crime," *Ethics* 93 (July 1983), 744 ff. and Herbert Morris, "Persons and Punishment," *The Monist* 52, no. 4 (October 1968), 475–50l, which argues that criminals have a natural, inalienable and absolute right to be punished that derives from their fundamental right to be treated as a person. For a detailed and nuanced discussion of the issue of retributivism in punishment, see Marvin Henberg, *Retribution: Evil for Evil in Ethics, Law, and Literature* (Philadelphia: Temple University Press, 1990).

## Capital Punishment

Among the many *books and anthologies on the death penalty*, see the selections and exchanges in Hugo Adam Bedau, *The Death Penalty in America,* 3rd ed. (New York: Oxford University Press, 1982); Ernest van den Haag and John P. Conrad, *The Death Penalty: A Debate* (New York: Plenum Press, 1983). Also see Walter Berns, *For Capital Punishment: Crime and the Morality of the Death Penalty* (New York: Basic Books, 1979); Charles Black, *Capital Punishment: The Inevitability of Caprice and Mistake,* 2nd ed. (New York: W. W. Norton, 1976); Robert Johnson, *Condemned to Die: Life Under Sentence of Death* (New York: Elsevier, 1981); Jeffrey H. Reiman, *The Rich Get Richer and the Poor Get Prison: Ideology, Class, and Criminal Justice,* 2nd ed. (New York: Wiley, 1984); Stephen Nathanson, *An Eye for an Eye: The Morality of Punishing by Death* (Totowa: Rowman & Littlefield, 1987); and *The Death Penalty: Opposing Viewpoints*, ed. Carol Wekesser (San Diego: Greenhaven Press, 1991) contains a good balance of short pieces.

Among the many helpful *articles* on capital punishment, see Hugo Adam Bedau's excellent overview, analysis, and bibliography in "Capital Punishment," *The Encyclopedia of Ethics,* ed. Lawrence C. Becker and Charlotte B. Becker (New York: Garland, 1992), vol. I, pp. 122–125; Stanley I. Benn, "Punishment," *The Encyclopedia of Philosophy* 7, ed. Paul Edwards (New York: Macmillan, 1967), p. 32 ff.; and Richard Wasserstrom, "Capital Punishment as Punishment: Some Theoretical Issues and Objections," *Midwest Studies in Philosophy,* vol. 7, pp. 473–502, who raises a number of objections to capital punishment, not because it is capital, but because it is punishment. On the *inhumanity of the death penalty*, Michael Davis has recently argued in "The Death Penalty, Civilization, and Inhumaneness," *Social Theory and Practice* 16, no. 2 (Summer 1990), pp. 245–259, that the "argument from inhumaneness" advanced by Reiman and Bedau lacks an adequate account of inhumaneness. Jeffrey Reiman replied to Davis in "The Death Penalty, Deterrence, and Horribleness: Reply to Michael Davis," *Social Theory and Practice* 16, no. 2 (Summer 1990), pp. 261–272. See also Thomas A. Long, "Capital Punishment—'Cruel And Unusual'?" *Ethics* 83 (April 1973), pp. 214–223 and the reply by Robert S. Gerstein, "Capital Punishment— 'Cruel And Unusual': A Retributivist Response," *Ethics* 85 (October 1974), pp. 75–79. On the *irrevocability of capital punishment*, see Michael Davis, "Is the Death Penalty Irrevocable?" *Social Theory and Practice* 10 (Summer 1984), 143–156, argues that there is no morally significant sense in which the death penalty is more irrevocable than life imprisonment; the death penalty is only distinctive in regard to the more modest claim about what we can do to correct error in application. On the *arbitrariness of the death penalty*, see especially Christopher Meyers, "Racial Bias, the Death Penalty, and Desert," *Philosophical Forum* (Winter 1990–91), 139–148, which supports *McCleskey* v. *Kemp* (1987), in which the Supreme Court ruled that racial bias was not sufficient ground for overturning a death sentence, as long as punishment is seen as retribution and as long as defendants do not receive more punishment than they deserve; Brian Calvert, in "Retribution, Arbitrariness and the Death Penalty," *Journal of Social Philosophy* 23, no. 3 (Winter 1992), 140–165, which argues that the administration of the death penalty is arbitrary because there is not a sufficiently clear distinction in kind between murders that deserve execution and murders that deserve life imprisonment. On the *deterrent effect of the death penalty*, see Ernest Van Den Haag, "Deterrence and the Death Penalty: A Rejoinder," *Ethics* 81 (October 1970), 74–75; Hugo Adam Bedau, "A Concluding Note," *Ethics* 81, (October 1970), 76; Michael Davis, "Death, Deterrence, and the Method of Common Sense," *Social Theory and Practice* 7, (Summer 1981), 145–178, uses what he calls the "method of common sense" to show that the death penalty is the most effective humane deterrent available to us. Steven Goldberg, "On Capital Punishment," *Ethics* 85 (October 1974), 67–74, argues in favor of capital punishment for its deterrent effect on potential criminals and George Schedler, "Capital Punishment and Its Deterrent Effect," *Social Theory and Practice* 4 (Fall 1976), 47–56 refutes the "innocent people" argument. David A. Conway, "Capital Punishment and Deterrence: Some Considerations in Dialogue Form," *Philosophy and Public Affairs* 3, no. 4 (Summer 1974), 433 ff.

# Race and Ethnicity

**Videotape:**

|  |  |
|---|---|
| *Topic:* | Race Relations in America |
| *Source:* | *This Week with David Brinkley* (May 20, 1990) |
| *Anchors:* | David Brinkley; Dena Reynolds |

# EXPERIENTIAL ACCOUNTS

Naomi Zack
"An Autobiographical View of Mixed Race and Deracination"

*Naomi Zack, as assistant professor of philosophy at the State University of New York at Albany, has written extensively on race and related issues. This essay formed the basis of the first chapter of her* Mixed-Race and Anti-Race: A Critique of American Racial Inheritance and Identity.

*In this autobiographical essay, Ms. Zack discusses the issue of mixed race, the disjunctive character of American racial categories, and her own refusal to accept such categories.*

## The Subject

American racial categories are exclusively disjunctive: Thou shalt have a race, and, thy race must be black or white, but not both! As a result of this imperative disjunction, the person of mixed black and white race may pose a problem for others. The mixed-race person may also encounter contradictory identities in her view of herself. These contradictory identities do not admit of any easeful resolution.

In racial matters self-emancipation may be a last recourse. But self-emancipation can lead the person of mixed race to conclusions which are jarring in their ahistoricality, and unacceptable to people whose racial identities are not self-contradictory. I will call the awareness of the problem of mixed race, by a person of mixed race, the problematization of mixed race. And I will call the solution to the problematization of mixed race, deracination. Deracination is a problem for people with black or white racial identities. An awareness of the problem of deracination by a deracinated person could be called the problematization of deracination. These distinctions between problems and problematizations are merely a preliminary way of demarcating racial existence, which includes experience, values and ideology, from racial theory. Problematization is on the side of theory.

## The First Person

I am going to begin by describing some facts about myself which it has taken me many years to be able to describe evenly. It has taken me a long time to be able to even describe these facts, publicly, because of warps in my psychology, warps which I do not consider it irresponsible to insist are the effects of warps in external social reality.

Naomi Zack, "An Autobiographical View of Mixed Race and Deracination," *American Philosophical Association Newsletters* 91, no. 1 (Spring 1992). Copyright © 1992, American Philosophical Association. Reprinted by permission of the publisher and the author.

My mother was a Jew whose parents came to this country from Lithuania, in 1903. My father was an African American whose father was born a slave and whose mother claimed Sioux (Native American) descent. My parents were never married to each other and only my mother raised me. My mother was ashamed of her relationship with my father and she encouraged me to deny my black ancestry. She was not an observant Jew and neither am I. But she saw the world through (what I take to be) Jewish eyes and felt the world with (what I take to be) Jewish fears, and I have never been able to avoid (what I take to be) the same apperceptions. In other words, I believe I "identify" with my mother.

My mother knew herself to be a Jew, totally. Many Jews believe that if one's mother is a Jew, then one is a Jew oneself and it does not matter what one's father is. In American society, Jews are classified as white racially. For these reasons, I have usually been designated as white on official documents, especially those which do not have a category of undesignated "other." I do not like to explicitly say that I am white because that is a lie—in American society, if one has a black parent, then one is black. I am black.

There are known to be blacks in the USA who have become Jews by religious conversion, but there is no widely recognized category of hereditary Jews who are racially black. Until recently, the American Jews I have known, have, with varying degrees of (slight) skepticism, accepted me as a Jew, with the understanding that my father was not a Jew—they have not been specially concerned with how he was not a Jew.[1] But my husbands and the close friends of my adult life have been white gentiles, for the most part. After I have told them that my father was black, a veil has often dropped over any understanding they had about how one inherits a Jewish identity. They have often made the judgment that I have been passing (for white), and that I cannot be a Jew because my father was black.[2] This judgment has been echoed by some blacks I have known. In a way that I intuitively understand, the judgment by blacks that I have been passing (for white) has sometimes been accompanied by resentment and implied moral condemnation.

I am a Jew and therefore I am white. I am black and therefore I am not white. This contradiction is very difficult to think about without momentum from self-emancipation. Self-emancipation is a movement of values.

## Self-Emancipation and Valuation

What am I? The racial and ethnic answers to this question can have a direct bearing on how I feel and whether my life, in general, is bearable to me. This question, What am I? as a question about racial and ethnic identity, divides into three categories: what I think I am; what others think I am; what I want others to think I am. The answers have value-neutral, value-positive and value-negative, first-, second- and third-person aspects. The goal of self-emancipation is to unite a value-positive answer to the question, What do I think I am? with a value-positive answer to the question, What do others think I am? This movement from a value-positive, first-person description of myself, to a value-positive second- or third-person description of me, is contained in how I want others to value me. Thus, first I aim to feel good about myself and then I aim to get others to have good feelings toward me; although at stake is something more stringent than feelings, more than a matter of being liked, something which at the least involves respect. Self-emancipation is thereby a social activity which begins with positive self-valuation. Oppression is also a social activity, although it need not begin in value-negative, third-person judgments; oppression may begin with self-interest, for example.

Self-emancipation is difficult to get started because the self which needs to be positively revalued in order to overcome oppression has already been identified by negative valuations from others. Every step up in value will be resisted by those who not only devalue me but consider it their right to do so. Solitary acts of self-revaluation may at the outset be indistinguishable from delusions of grandeur and other alienated and isolated anti-social expressions of inner life, which have little to do with freedom. Positive self-valuation about race and ethnicity requires that negative valuations which express racism and ethnocentricity be somehow overcome. There are few forms of negative valuation in the USA which are more oppressive than racial designations. American racial designations are based on a kinship schema of black and white racial inheritance. A person of mixed race must begin with this schema in order to answer the question, What am I?

## The Kinship Schema of Black and White Racial Inheritance

There is a strong asymmetry between black and white racial inheritance. If a person has a black parent, a black grand-parent or a black great "$n$" grand-parents (where $n$ is indeterminate, in principle), then that person is considered black. But if a person has a white parent, or three white grand-parents, or $X$ white great "$n$" grand-parent (where $X$ is any odd number and $n$ is still indeterminate, in principle), then that person is not thereby considered white. This is a kinship schema and it means that whiteness is nothing more than the absence of any black forebears, and blackness is nothing more than the presence of one black forebear. Apart from this cultural schema, there is no natural black or white racial substratum or essence which anyone can identify in physiological terms. Nevertheless, the kinship schema of racial inheritance is so widely accepted that it is assumed to have a physiological basis. It is assumed that if one refers to a person's race according to this schema, then one is referring to some objective and universal-to-that-race characteristic of the person.

As a social entity, the black race in America is perceived to have an ethnic cohesion based on family affiliation; the recognition of black people by white people and other black people; the general negative value of being black; and the shared cultural practices, preferences, aspirations and experiences of black people. This entire social situation contributes to black ethnicity or black identity.[3] Given the false identification of race with a physiological substratum, an analogy could be drawn between race and ethnicity, and sex and gender. But the analogy breaks down insofar as there is now less tolerance of critiques of ethnicity than critiques of gender.

In contrast to black ethnic identity, white ethnic identity in the USA is usually based on differences in the national origins of the forebears of white people. Thus, while black ethnic identity is believed to be racial, white ethnic identity refers to foreign nationality.[4] Two exceptions to this rule come to mind, however: White supremacists appear to base their ethnicity solely on the absence of non-white forebears in their heredity. And some white ethnic groups, such as Jews, and perhaps Roman Catholics, seem to base their ethnic identity primarily on their religion.

The above sketch of the schema of black and white racial inheritance and the description of racial ethnicity in the USA is not new and neither does it contradict the common sense racial and ethnic categorizations which most American people make.[5] If one adds the negative valuation of blacks in comparison to whites, to the strong asymmetry in the schema of black and white racial inheritance, it is impossible to escape the conclusion that the schema is both racist in favor of whites and unjust. The schema is racist in favor of whites because it automatically excludes some people, who have white ancestors, from membership in the white race, while others with white ancestry are not thereby excluded. This exclusionary force of the schema reinforces social beliefs about the superiority of whites in comparison to blacks. The schema is unjust because it denies individuals with black forebears the right to claim anything of positive racial value on the basis of having white forebears. Thus, the schema discriminates against people with black forebears, with respect to their having white forebears, solely because they have black forebears.

## The Problematization of Multi-Race

I mean to distinguish between the problem of mixed race and the problematization of mixed race. The problem of mixed race is a problem for white people, mainly, because historically sexual relations between white people and black people were socially taboo—they were also illegal for long periods of American history. The existence of an individual of mixed race was, and still is, proof that these taboos had been violated, and it was proof which many proponents of the prohibitions valued negatively in social and moral spheres. The problematization of mixed race is formulated by a person of mixed race when she thinks about the schema of racial inheritance and the prevailing attitudes about race and ethnicity. Except in cases of extreme despair, the person of mixed race does not have a problem with mixed race because she does not have a problem with the bare fact of her own existence.

The first part of the problematization of mixed race is in the designation of the term "mixed race" for someone who has both black and white forebears. Strictly speaking, the designation should never be made and fails to make sense. According to the accepted schema of racial inheritance, everyone with at least one black forebear is black and everyone with all white forebears is white. Therefore everyone is either black or white. There are no people of mixed race.

Black people are likely to perceive the person who is culturally or ethnically white, but racially black, as an inauthentic black person, someone who is disloyal to other black people or who evades or denies racial discrimination by attempting to pass (for white). From a black ethnic perspective it is not plausible that someone who is designated as of mixed race in white contexts, might have spent so much of her life in white contexts that she does not have a black ethnic identity. The (authentic) racial and ethnic black person will hold the person of mixed race responsible for not having had the courage (and good faith) to acquire a black ethnic identity as soon as she became aware of the injustice of racism and racial discrimination against black people. There is a moral injunction here that one ought not to benefit from a loophole in what one knows to be an unjust situation. The black person, who functions as a white person in white contexts, under the honorarium of a mixed race designation, has an obligation, supererogatory though it may be, to insist that her skills be recognized by white people as the skills of a black person. If this person of mixed race does not do that, then it can only be because she agrees with the negative valuation of black people by white people. This, then, is how I understand the implied moral argument.

I think that the argument is persuasive up to a point. The argument is only persuasive as long as one accepts the strongly asymmetrical kinship schema of racial designation. The argument ceases to be persuasive when one's racial existence does not support this schema. If one spent one's formative years with white people and failed to realign one's ethnic identity in adolescence, when it may still have been possible, then the moral argument may not so much be a spur to action as the cause of bad conscience. My bad conscience is not assuaged by claims of Jewish ethnic identity because the difficulty of the Jewish experience is not immediate in contemporary American society. While I do not think that it can be conclusively argued that in a conflict between two allegiances, morality is always on the side of the claim which represents the greater present suffering, if present action is called for, one is obligated to respond to the present situation. Any bad conscience can be a spur to an intellectual and moral position which has merits in spite of it origins. The bad conscience which has grown out of my problematization of mixed race, has at times led me to a position of deracination. But regardless of my conscience, the position of deracination has strong merits.

## Deracination

This is the position of deracination: The schema of racial inheritance in the USA is racist and unjust. As a rational woman with both black and white forebears, I do not accept this schema. I refuse to be pressured into denying the existence of black forebears to please whites, and I refuse to be pressured into denying my white ethnicity and my white forebears, to please blacks. There is no biological foundation of the concept of race. The concept of race is an oppressive cultural invention and convention, and I refuse to have anything to do with it. I refuse to be reasonable in order to placate either blacks or whites who retain non-empirical and irrational categorizations. Therefore, I have no racial affiliation and will accept no racial designations. If more people joined me in refusing to play the unfair game of race, fewer injustices based on the concept of race would be perpetrated.

The literal meaning of the term 'deracination' is "to be plucked up by the roots." What is it in me that is supposed to have roots? What is the "soil" in which these "roots" have a natural and not-to-be-disturbed location? Affiliations with others in the present, mental reconstructions of the past and plans for the future based on my "roots," and their "soil," especially plans which I would have to impose on my children, are all active, deliberate doings, which require choices and expenditures of energy in the present and future. There is no automatic "claim" exerted by "roots." I am not a fish out of water, a cat up a tree, or any kind of plant. If I cannot follow the imperative disjunction, Thou shalt have a race, and, thy race shall be black or white!, then perhaps I can construct a racial identity of mixed race. Failing that construction, perhaps there are some shreds of benign universalism with which I can cover my deracinated self, or maybe there is still some humanistic soil in which an aracial self can be "implanted."

Even if I had a black ethnic identity from childhood or had developed one as an adult, any attempt to synthesize black and white ethnic identities would be doomed to fail as soon as I confronted the racial antagonisms and tensions in wider social reality. Any attempt to base my identity on membership in both black and white races could only take place on a level not subject to racial tensions and antagonisms. The level on which I could be both black and white would be culturally isolated.[6] If racial identity is based on wider group membership, then a black and white racial identity would be but another form of deracination, and perhaps a needlessly complicated one.

The new use of the term "of color" may represent an effort to by-pass some of the contradictions and bitterness in racial categorization. Anyone who is not white is a person of color. But to say that I am a person of color is merely to say what I am not racially, i.e., not white. This categorization glides over my diverse ethnic experiences and cannot even begin to describe the ways in which I am not white. Using the term 'of color' in effect deracinates non-whites within the category of non-white. It is but another instance of the tendency of whites to assign race itself to non-whites, perhaps analogously to the way in which men assign sex itself to members of the female gender. What is needed is a term which will deracinate people who are white, as well as non-white, some racial analogue to the designation "no religious affiliation."

The position of deracination could lead to conflicts at the intersection of racial identity and family membership. If a person is deracinated because she has both black and white forebears, her relatives may not have the same racial heredity, or if they do, they may not share her position of deracination. But the insistence on racial uniformity within a family is no more or less worthy of fulfillment than other forms of family uniformity, such as political or religious sameness, for example. If people who are biologically related have divisive differences, then those differences ought to be addressed on their own merits (as they often are during times of rapid social change).

## The Problematization of Deracination

Again, I want to distinguish between the problem and the problematization. Deracination is a problem for people who belong to races and wish to categorize everyone else in racial terms as well. The problematization of deracination, as I have proposed it, has to do with the viewpoint of a deracinated person.

In ordinary, walking-around reality, the deracinated person will not have solved anything. People will still insist on categorizing her racially and her explicit refusal to participate in their (racializing) attempts will only add to their scorn and dislike of her. In her own mind she will be relieved from many contentious dialogues and ambivalent impulses. But as soon as she puts her position into plain language, she will have a problem with others.

Intellectually, deracination is not in harmony with the spirit of the times. For the past two or three decades, there has been an intensification of ethnicity and in expressions of pride in the culture of forebears, among different groups in America. This has its correlative in the critiques by feminists and other marginal spokespersons of the perceived white, upper class, heterosexist, male tradition in philosophy. Continental philosophy, since Martin Heidegger, as well as deconstructionist literary theory, has been increasingly preoccupied with the limitations imposed on thought by different European languages, and with the question of whether translation is even possible. In philosophy of science, the idea that competing theories may be incommensurable has unsettled much contemporary discussion. Politically, nationalism has probably never been as insistent a theme in any other period of world peace as it has in recent years. These generalities about diversities, as well as practical considerations, make it unlikely that a case for universalism of any kind can be formulated in a convincing manner at this time. But this is not to say that the case cannot be formulated at all a philosophic analysis of American concepts of race might leave no rational alternative.

With deracination, one may come full circle to an old ideal of universalism within the refuge of abstract thought. This is a treacherous place because the universalism may once more conceal a bias in favor of certain groups. In this new universalism the bias would be in favor of raceless races—it would be a bias of anti-race. But unlike racism, which is an asymmetrical privileging of race, anti-race would be a theoretical move that blocks the privileging of race by undermining racial designations. Furthermore, the risk of this anti-race bias may be outweighed by the gains of self-emancipation. In self-emancipation, it may be necessary to deracinate oneself in order to understand the problems and problematizations of race and ethnicity, and to address them evenly. It may also be necessary to remove everything concerning race from oneself, in order to feel good about being the self who is obliged to ask and answer the question, What am I?

## Endnotes

1. American concepts of race and ethnic identity are not stable over time. In recent years, I have noticed that some American Jews have become more insistent on their racial whiteness. Furthermore, it is by no means a foregone conclusion that a majority of Jews accept someone who does not have two Jewish parents, as a Jew. For a discussion of contemporary themes about white Americans who have only one Jewish parent, see Charlotte Anker, "We Are the Children You Warned Our Parents About," *Moment* 16, no. 1 (February 1991), 34–40.

2. The matrilinear nature of the inheritance of Jewish identity may at times have some bearing on the different perceptions of black inheritance by Jews and Gentiles.

3. It is important to remember that these generalizations only hold true in American society. In European society there is a longer history of the identification of race with ethnicity, especially by anti-Semites. The French anti-Semite, for example, bases both his own racial identity and his ethnic pride on the fact that his forebears originated in the same place where he lives. See Jean-Paul Sartre's analysis in *Anti-Semite and Jew* (New York: Schocken Books, 1948), esp. pp. 7–30.

4. Again, the situation is different in European history, where Jews were designated as a race with complicated references to their lack of homeland.

5. Cf. Anthony Appiah, "'But Would That Still Be Me?': Notes on Gender, 'Race,' Ethnicity as Sources of Identity," *The Journal of Philosophy* LXXVII, no. 10, (October 1990), 493–499.

6. There have always been isolated individuals and small groups without voices of authority who have refused to be pressured into identities of black or white racial designations. See for example, *Interrace*, a magazine which features interracial heterosexual relationships and persons of mixed-race in the entertainment industry.

## Journal/Discussion Questions

✍ In what ways have you experienced, either directly or indirectly, the issues of mixed race that Zack raises?

1. What does Zack mean by "the problematization of mixed race," by "the problem of mixed race," by "deracination," and by "the problematization of deracination"?

2. According to Zack, the question "What am I?" divides into three subquestions. What are these three questions? How does this relate to her discussion of self-emancipation?

3. Zack says that, "The schema of racial inheritance in the USA is racist and unjust." What support does she offer for this claim? What conclusions does she draw from it?

## Studs Turkel
## "Race: How Blacks and Whites Think and Feel about the American Obsession"

*Studs Turkel, a longtime Chicagoan and host for the past thirty-five years of a talk show on WFMT radio in Chicago, is the author of several oral histories, including* Working *and* The Good War. *This interview is drawn from his book,* Race: How Blacks and Whites Think and Feel about the American Obsession.

*This selection, entitled "Clarence Page: 'It's a Boy!'" is a 1990 interview by Studs Turkel with Clarence Page, a columnist of the Chicago* Tribune *and member of its editorial board. Mr. Page won the Pulitzer Prize for Commentary. He frequently appears as a television commentator. Except for a four-year absence, when he worked for the Chicago CBS station, he has been with the newspaper twenty years. He was the second black reporter ever hired by the* Tribune *as a full-time employee.*

～

When I broke in here as a police reporter, I learned a new phrase, "cheap it out." News out of black neighborhoods were viewed as cheap news. [Laughs.] If I got a tip on a double homicide, they'd say, "Oh, South Side. Cheap it out." Some old-timers still use the phrase. It was demeaning to me to see how this double standard worked.

If I was going to survive and make it as a reporter, I had to understand how news judgment was made. I got to be an assistant city editor. But it was so demoralizing to be a lonely voice around a big table of fellows who were largely suburban white male. Trying to sell them on the idea of a South Side homicide being as important as a North Side homicide was as incomprehensible as my speaking Martian. Eventually I decided I didn't want to be management anymore. I'd fight my battles elsewhere.

You could say there's a triple standard in black, white, and Hispanic news; rich, poor, and middle-class. One of my white colleagues said, "News is what happens near the news editor's house." That's why it's so important to have a multicultural newsroom.

The double standard is still there. A fire death in the inner city is not worth a fire death in the outer city. [Laughs.] Isn't that an interesting phrase, "inner city"? So is the word "underclass." When I say underclass to a black person, he tends to think of a specific pathological group with a specific set of problems. When I use the word with a white person, chances are better than even that he'll think black. Whites tend to generalize about blacks. We do the same thing, in a lot of ways. I may be doing it at this moment. All of us learn racial generalizations early on and it sticks with us. It frustrates me as a journalist.

I am optimistic. It comes from being around long enough to have seen things worse than they are. Twenty years ago, I was the only black person here. We have quite a few now—not enough, but a lot more than we used to.

I was in high school when the Voting Rights Act was passed. Segregation didn't bend with its passage. When we got a black mayor elected in Chicago, I saw a low-intensity race war break out. The young blacks find white people not nearly as enlightened as they expected. They find out how lonely it is to walk into a predominantly white newsroom. You're dealing with the same questions as a new arrival in town, as well as with some extra ones.

I learned that if it's dark out and I see a white friend, don't approach him too quickly. Don't startle him because the first thing he's going to see is a black man. I have startled people without meaning to. If I'm walking with a group of black males down the street, I'm aware that a white guy passing by might be scared. I imagine those black kids in Central Park were well aware of just how intimidating their presence was. To a large degree, they acted out what was expected of them.

If you expect a kid to be a thug, he's going to be one, nine times out of ten. If you have low expectations, he'll meet them. Today, our society has low expectations of young black males.

When I wake up in the morning and see my pregnant wife beside me, I know from ultra-sound we'll probably have a boy. A young black male. How different I think as the father of a young black male than if I were a white father of a white male. There's a certain level of expectations society has of my kid different from the other one. If he's a teen-aged boy walking down the street wearing Adidas basketball shoes, jeans, and a troop jacket, he's regarded differently from a white teen-ager in Adidas basketball shoes, jeans, and a troop jacket. They wear the same outfit, yet are looked upon so differently.

I think of moving to the suburbs because of the schools. But I think: "Where will I be welcome? Where will I be possibly burned out?" In 1990, I think about that. If I were to move into a predominantly white suburb, the first thing that crosses their mind is not the Pulitzer Prize, it's "a black family in our neighborhood." Even among the most liberal white families, the question is: is it bad for my property values?

What else do I think of when I wake up in the morning? Getting to work. I hope the weather's nice, because if it's bad, a taxi will pass me by and pick up a white person halfway down the block. It happens to me all the time. I'm dressed in a suit, tie, carry a briefcase. Just like the white guy who got the cab. I'm a member of the Tribune editorial board, right? I dress the role, right? Just getting to work, I think about that.

I'm conscious of how I'm dressed because I want this cabdriver to see that I'm not a welfare recipient. The average white guy may go out there in dirty blue jeans and expect the taxi to stop just like that. And it will. It will stop for him more quickly than for me, three-piece suit and everything.

When I'm on the El, I see people reacting certain ways. I've got prejudices, too, because I've dealt with pickpockets and purse-snatchers. I have formed a profile in my mind of such a potential thief: a young black male. I don't want to project that image to others, but I'm thinking it.

Black people are more afraid of crime than whites. They've got reason to be. We are victims of it more often. I've experienced a mugging, I've had a gun pointed at me, and a knife, and I've given over my wallet. I've had to deal with high-crime neighborhoods a lot. My family has experienced crime.

If you are Bernard Goetz with a gun in your pocket, I don't want you to feel intimidated. He shot four individuals, two of whom were going through the motions of intimidating him. Another was sitting on the bench, not even close to him, the one Goetz shot and paralyzed. He fell on the floor and played dead. Goetz looked at him and said, "You're not hurt so bad, here's another." So he pierced his spine and paralyzed the kid for life. This kid didn't even have a record. Because he was black and with the group, Goetz generalized. He shot them all.

The kid was from a middle-class home. He was eleven when his father died. His mother, now a single mom, low-income, moves back to the Bronx from which they had escaped. His life changed overnight. What would happen to my wife and child if I died? What happens to people who are a paycheck away from poverty? This is something white folks don't think about when they see this new class of black folks getting into the mainstream. They don't think how many of us are only a paycheck away from poverty.

I don't worry about it as much as I used to. I'm finally starting to get comfortable with the fact that I'm not going to fall back out of the middle class. It took me years. Often, I wished I had the cavalier attitude of some of my white peers who grew up middle-class.

When my wife told me she was half white, I asked her what she considered herself. She said, "I was raised by my mother to think I was mixed and I still think of myself that way. But society says I'm black, so I go along with it."

Black people are already a rainbow coalition, because even if you're black and Asian, you're black.

I'm always wondering what other people think of me. Even now. What they think of why I am where I am. Am I where I am because I'm black? It used to be: Would I be further advanced if I were white? Nowadays, people wonder: Am I being advanced because I'm black?

Now that I won the Pulitzer Prize, I wonder if people wonder if I won it because I'm non-white. [Laughs. ] My predecessors, who deserved it, who toiled in the vineyards longer than I—did the judges feel obliged to give it to me? I have aspired to a new level of insecurity.

In my younger, single days, I'd go to these Rush Street bars just to spite them. I'd better explain. There are bars on the street that still have a reputation of giving young black people a hard time. We've learned to be sensitive about going where we're welcome and where we're not.

It didn't matter if I was a professional, they'd always give me the once-over and say, "You can't come in wearing jeans." I looked past the door and saw most of the guys in jeans. "You haven't got enough IDs." I always had a bunch of them with me.

Things have improved a lot. Kids who are fresh off the campus are a lot more comfortable with whites than my generation was. But the discomfort level is still there. You don't see any more of a black-white mix than you did twenty years ago.

Know what the problem is? We black folks didn't live up to the expectations of the white folks who helped us out during the civil-rights movement. They didn't live up to our expectations either, because we were expecting more of white folks than this.

We didn't live up to the expectations Jews had of us. They expected blacks, once Jim Crow was beaten, to aspire toward success the way Jews did: education. Blacks decided to aspire the way the Irish did: City Hall. Politics.

Black-Jewish tensions have been considerably overblown by the media. The coverage of Louis Farrakhan says it all. Among the great many black people, he's rated as useful and entertaining. An educated clown. People will fill Madison Square Garden and watch him for his entertainment value. How many have joined his movement? Very few. He can say anything and the media will rush out there.

When I worked for Channel 2, they chartered a plane and flew me and a crew to Indianapolis to cover a routine Farrakhan speech. We had to put it on the air that night. It was his usual stuff, nothing extraordinary. I know why they sent me down there. They were hoping he'd say something outrageous. This is their thing.

Naturally, Farrakhan welcomes all this attention. What respect he has from black people comes to anybody who stands up to white folks and tells it like it is. My wife was thrilled when I took her to see him. She heard so much about him as entertaining. Did she become a follower? No. There is a side of us as black people that resents the way we are ignored as individuals, the way mainstream America insults us. In a way, Farrakhan is feeding off that sentiment.

I wake up in the morning, watch the news, and hear of a heinous crime. "I hope he's not black" is the first thought that crosses my mind. Before I even see the picture on TV. A lot of black folks are the same way. When I was a kid, my uncle used to say, "Please, Lord, don't let it be black."

A white backlash is the last thing that worries us now. We've always had a backlash, but never called it that. Why should we worry about it now? The truth is we don't fear white people anymore. We don't have the kind of fear our fathers and grandfathers had.

Our lives are still controlled by white people, and that's still on our minds. Malcolm X once put the question: Why do the media never refer to all-white neighborhoods as segregated? An all-black neighborhood is always referred to as segregated. Why? Because they know who's doing the segregating. Black people didn't segregate themselves. An all-white neighborhood is never referred to as a ghetto, yet the youngsters who grow up there are socially deprived of the benefits that come from a pluralistic society. Many grow up socially disabled.

So when I wake up in the morning and see my pregnant wife and the odds are overwhelming it's going to be a boy, a young black male. . . . [Trails off.]*

## Journal/Discussion Questions

✍ *Reflect on your own reactions to this interview. To what extent does your own race and ethnicity shape those reactions?*

1. Truth is often found, not just in general theories, but in the details of everyday life. What aspects of this interview surprised you? What details revealed truths not generally acknowledged?

2. Do you agree with Mr. Page about the extent of racism in our own society today? Discuss.

*It was a boy.

# AN INTRODUCTION TO THE MORAL ISSUES

The issues of race and ethnic identity have always been central to American society, yet at the same time our American identity as a "melting pot" has in part been forged on the basis of denying this as the principal basis of our identity.

Recall our threefold structure for analyzing these issues: the problem, the ideal, and the means for going from one to the other. We will begin by considering the facts of racism, turn to a consideration of the various ideals, and then discuss which means offer the most hope of moving us from an actual situation toward the ideal. But first, a few words about a basic distinction.

## Race and Ethnicity

Although distinct concepts, race and ethnicity are obviously related to one another. Generally, anthropologists see *race* as a physical characteristic. They recognize the existence of three or four major racial groups: Caucasoid, Negroid, Mongoloid and sometimes Australoid. (The United States Census Bureau, on the other hand, recognizes four races, adding Native American—which anthropologists consider part of Mongoloid—to the first three.) *Ethnicity*, on the other hand, refers primarily to social and cultural forms of identification and self-identification. There are many more ethnic identities than racial ones. The English, French, Italians, Germans, and Poles all share a common race, but they consider themselves ethnically different.

*What is the difference between race and ethnicity?*

Several points should be noted about these concepts. First, race inevitably has a socially constituted meaning, and it this point the distinction between race and ethnicity is somewhat less clear-cut. Whatever race is, it isn't *just* a physical characteristic. Second, although we have a clear term to denote discrimination based on race (namely, racism), we lack a corresponding term to indicate discrimination based on ethnicity. However, ethnically based discrimination (witness the atavistic conflicts of eastern Europe) is often of the same structure as racism and sometimes masquerades as racially based when it is actually ethnically grounded. Third, it is worth noting that, at least in the United States, we tend to think of racial categories as mutually exclusive. In forms asking about race, we are usually asked to "check one of the following: white, black, Asian, or American Indian." However, some of us are either remotely (i.e., back at least two generations) or recently (i.e., our parents or grandparents) of mixed race. Forms that allow individuals to acknowledge the plurality of their racial and ethnic identities would not only be more accurate, but also less polarizing for society as a whole.

## The Facts of Racism

Racism has been a pervasive and disturbing fact of American society. The very founding of the United States is inextricably bound up with the racism that characterized our treatment of Native Americans and, soon thereafter, with the racism that helped to make slavery possible. The legacy, and in some cases the continuing reality, of that racism is still with us today. Most Americans in

239

their forties and older grew up in a world in which racial discrimination was still legally sanctioned. African Americans (and others as well) were *legally* denied access to schools, jobs, neighborhoods, churches, clubs, and the voting booth well into the middle 1960s. Although such discrimination continues to some extent today, it is no longer done under the sanction of law.

The word *racism* is both descriptive and evaluative. As a *descriptive* term, it refers to certain attitudes and actions that (a) single out certain people on the basis of their racial—or, in some cases, ethnic—heritage and (b) disadvantage them in some way on this basis. (The second element, disadvantaging someone on the basis of race, has to be present or else simple categorization—such as one finds in a census—would be racist.) College admissions policies that excluded African Americans on the basis of their race would be a clear example of racism. Yet *racism* also has an *evaluative* element: it conveys a negative value judgment that racism is morally objectionable, evil. The evaluative element may refer primarily to the *intention* behind the practice or to the *consequences* of such a practice.

This distinction between intention and consequences also provides part of the foundation for a distinction between *overt racism* and *institutional racism*. Gertrude Ezorsky, for example, sees overt racist action as grounded in "the agent's racial bias against the victim or in a willingness to oblige the racial prejudice of others".[1] In the case of institutional racism, no negative value judgment is made about the agents' intentions. Their actions might not be intended to harm a particular racial group at all, although this may be an unintended consequence. The negative value judgment is reserved primarily for the *consequences* of such actions and policies.

It is important, both morally and politically, to distinguish between government-sanctioned racism and racism that occurs without such official endorsement. When our government enacts racist laws—such as separate schooling, housing, and so on—then it acts in our name as citizens, and it seems reasonable to argue that we as citizens are under an obligation to those who have been wronged. On the other hand, when an individual restaurant owner illegally discriminates against a potential patron on the basis of race, it does not seem that we as citizens are under the same kind of obligation to those who have been wronged because the restaurant owner was not acting in our names. Virtually all ethnic minorities have been subject to unfair treatment at one time or another in American history, but only a few—most notably, Native Americans, African Americans, and Japanese Americans—have been the object of governmentally sanctioned discrimination. The government would seem to have a special obligation in those cases in which groups have been wronged, not just by individuals, but by the government itself. Furthermore, we as citizens may be obligated to compensate wronged groups because such discrimination was done in our name.

## Compensatory Programs

How do we respond morally to the fact of racism in our society and the role that it has played in our history? One response has been to suggest that we owe *compensation* to those who have been wrong. Compensatory programs, which seek to indemnify previously wronged individuals or groups, are essentially backward-looking; they seek to determine who has been wronged in the past and to make up for it in the present and future. Here the issue of governmental sanction assumes special importance. Insofar as racist discrimination was legally required in the past, it was done in our name as citizens. Consequently, we as citizens have a debt to compensate such discrimination. We do not have the same debt in the case of illegal discriminatory acts by individuals. In those cases, racist individuals may owe a debt of compensation to those they have discriminated against; but since they did not discriminate in our name, we are not under the same compensatory debt merely as citizens.

Presumably compensatory programs are limited in scope to a repayment of the debt incurred by the wrong. There is a strong case, for example, that the United States as a whole owes a compensatory debt to many Native American tribes for the various ways in which those tribes have been mistreated by the U.S. government. Moreover, the death of those who have been wronged does not nullify the compensatory debt. It makes both moral and legal sense to compensate the descendants of those who have been wronged or the group as a whole, even if those who were originally wronged are not dead.

Similarly, compensatory programs do not necessarily demand that the current recipients be in a negative condition. Consider, for example, the Japanese who were wrongfully incarcerated during World War II. It is certainly possible that we might conclude that they should be compensated for the wrong imposed upon them by our government, even if they have subsequently achieved economic success. This is little different, some would argue, from repaying a debt: the obligation to repay is not diminished by the fact that the person to whom the debt is owed has just won the lottery.

It is important to realize the morally symbolic value of such programs, which is often as important as any monetary value. When we commit ourselves as a country to compensate those who have been wronged by us as a country—the case of the indemnification of Japanese Americans interned in detention camps is an example of this—we are acknowledging our guilt as a country and stating our willingness to rectify the harm that we have caused. There is, as it were, a totaling of the public moral ledger that is often important in the process of moral reconciliation. When those who have been harmed feel that the perpetrators (a) genuinely recognize that they have done wrong, and (b) are genuinely trying to make up for the actual harm they caused, then it becomes much easier for the victims to put the wrong behind them and heal the moral rift between them and the perpetrators.

Such compensatory programs are different, at least in their moral logic, from future-oriented programs—whether equal rights approaches or affirmative action programs—that seek to create some future goal of equality. Similarly, because compensatory programs are essentially backward-looking, differing ideals of the place of race and ethnicity in society are irrelevant to them. In future-oriented programs, on the other hand, the ideals we are striving to realize are of paramount importance. Let us now turn to a consideration of such future-oriented programs, beginning first with a consideration of the ideals that they may be striving to implement.

## Ideals of the Place of Race in Society

What, precisely, is our ideal in regard to the place of race and ethnicity in our society? Several possible models suggest themselves, ranging from strongly separatist models to highly assimilationist ones. The ideal to which we are committed will have important implications for the means we choose for eradicating racism. Let's briefly consider each type of ideal.

## Separatist Models

Despite claims about being a "melting pot," the United States has a long history of racial—and, often, ethnic—separatism. Sometimes separatism is imposed from outside the group, sometimes it comes from within. Racial separatism was often imposed in laws against Native Americans, African Americans, and (during World War II) Japanese and Japanese Americans. The intent of such legislation was both to keep the races separate and to maintain the supremacy of the white race in particular.

Separatism has often been a comparatively attractive option for comparatively small groups whose culture would easily be obliterated by the larger culture of the society if it were not protected in some way. Some native American tribes (members of the Acoma Pueblo, for example) have chosen to maintain a largely separate life, sheltered from the intrusions of outsiders, as a way of preserving their own identity. Separatist groups may be constituted along strictly ethnic lines—the major eastern cities of the United States often contained numerous ethnic neighborhoods in which residents could easily go about their day-to-day affairs without having to know English—and sometimes on the

*Why do some groups find separatism an attractive option in the United States?*

basis of religious commitments. The Amish and the Mennonites, for example, have long been committed to a largely separatist view of their place in American society as a whole, and many major religions exhibit a separatist current in monasteries, cloistered convents, and the like. Similarly, some utopian communities have preferred a separatist model of their place in society. Typically, most of these groups ask little from the larger world around them except to be left alone.

Clearly, there is no moral justification for *imposing* separatism on others, and such attempts are almost always conjoined with either overt or covert beliefs in the racial supremacy of those in control. Self-imposed separatism is a morally more ambiguous matter, and key to its evaluation are the questions of what the proponents of separatism propose to preserve and why they want to preserve it. Moreover, we must recognize that separatism is usually a matter of degree. Only a few are at the far extreme of not wanting to share anything—language, products, transportation—with the surrounding society.

The strongest argument in support of self-imposed racial or ethnic separatism is what we can call *the identity argument.* It maintains that a firm sense of one's race and ethnicity is a necessary component of one's identity as a person, and that this sense of racial and ethnic identity can be preserved only through separatism. These issues are often discussed under the heading of "the politics of identity" or "the politics of recognition," and this has been a principal concern for many racial and ethnic groups that fear their identities will be lost through immersion in the larger society.

Critics of such separatist models maintain that, while some degree of separatism may be workable, strongly separatist models threaten to undermine the sense in which we have a national identity at all. Moreover, some argue that some separatists are inconsistent: they both want to be left alone by the larger society and at the same time be provided with the benefits of that larger society.

## Assimilationist Models

The "melting pot" metaphor of American society suggests a model of American society that is primarily assimilationist. Differences are largely obliterated, melted down, and the result is a homogeneous nation of citizens. Indeed, this seems to have occurred with most immigrant groups from western and eastern Europe. Many whose ethnic background is European identify themselves primarily as American and only secondarily—and sometimes not at all—in terms of their ethnic European background. Traditional liberalism in the United States has been strongly committed to an assimilationist model, at least within the political realm.

The tension between separatist and assmilationist models comes out in various areas of daily life and public policy. For example, one of the principal issues in publicly funded education is whether it should seek to encourage such assimilation or whether it should seek to encourage the preservation and development of racial and ethnic identity.

## Pluralistic Models

Somewhere between these two extremes is a middle ground that both respects diversity and at the same time tries to establish the minimal conditions necessary to a common life—a shared political life even if not a shared community. The principal thrust of a pluralistic model is to suggest, first, that there are certain minimal conditions necessary to the establishment of a common life; second, that specific groups may maintain a partially separate identity without negating that common life; and, third, that the identity of any given individual is constituted through both participation in the common life and through identification with any number of specific groups.

*What model of race and ethnicity do pluralists support?*

Pluralists do not even need to posit that different groups in society exhibit some fundamental agreement with one another. Consider an analogous issue: pacifism. I am not a pacifist. I do not believe that all killing of human beings is wrong, but I am glad that I live in a society in which some people are pacifists. Their presence reminds me of a truth, albeit a partial truth, that human life is of inestimable importance and ought not to be destroyed if that can be avoided. On the other hand, I am glad that I do not live in a society in which everyone was a pacifist. Not only would I feel morally lonely in such a world, but I would fear that it would lack the resilience to defend itself in the face of aggressive evil if faced with such a challenge. The tension between pacifists and nonpacifists is a good thing for our society as a whole and for each of us as individuals, and our lives would be diminished if we did not have one of these two opposing groups. Nor are these opposing groups without common ground. They both respect life—or, at least, most of both groups do most of the time. No one advocates indiscriminate killing, and those who defend killing at all usually do so through an appeal to some core values, including the value of innocent life (which can be preserved through self-defense or whose loss can be avenged through capital punishment).

So, too, with racial and ethnic pluralism. Our world is richer for the diversity of our traditions, and there is no need to make everyone be like us. Indeed, I can feel that our world is a better place precisely because there are people who are *not* like me. The diversity of racial and ethnic traditions is a source of richness for the society as a whole, providing a wealth of possibilities far beyond the scope of any single ethnic tradition. That wealth of possibilities becomes especially important whenever we need help, whenever we run out of possibilities dealing with a specific issue, for we can then turn to the wisdom of other ethnic traditions to discover new and potentially better ways of dealing with that issue.

Finally, we should note that pluralism is multidimensional in the following sense. Pluralists would typically not only favor a diversity of ethnic traditions, but would also maintain that we as individuals are members of a wide range of communities, many of which may have little or nothing to do with race and ethnicity. There are many lines of affiliation in which ethnicity plays no role: computer hackers, smokers, people who hate to fly. Pluralists typically see a plurality of identities within the individual, not just within society as a whole.

## Multiculturalism, Separatism, and Pluralism

*Descriptive multiculturalism.*   In the last decade, multiculturalism has become a buzz word whose meaning is far from clear. All too often, it becomes a political rallying cry for both its opponents and proponents. At its most innocuous, *multicultural* is simply a descriptive term referring to societies that contain more than one cultural tradition within themselves. Using this definition of *multicultural*, many societies are multicultural. Yet

*What is multiculturalism?*

there is a second, more normative meaning of *multicultural* that sets forth an *ideal* of how societies should treat the various cultural traditions in their midst.

*Separatist multiculturalism.*   There is no single, normative sense of the ideal of multiculturalism, but for the purposes of analysis we can distinguish two currents that run through contemporary discussions of multiculturalism. One ideal of multiculturalism is separatist in character. It sees racial or ethnic identity as the principal—or at least omnipresent—component of personal identity, and it emphasizes racial and ethnic affiliations. *Who you are* is constituted, first and foremost, by your race and ethnicity; consequently, you are first and foremost *the same as* those who have the same race or ethnicity and *different from* anyone who does not share that race or ethnicity. Identity is constituted by race and ethnicity, and races and ethnicities are mutually exclusive. If you're one race and ethnicity, you're not the other. This seems, at least to me, to emphasize the ways in which races and ethnicities are different, to accentuate what sets them apart and to deemphasize what they have in common.

*Pluralistic multiculturalism.*   There is a second sense of multiculturalism which is more closely affiliated with pluralism. This strain of multiculturalism sees racial and ethnic diversity as good, but (a) does not see racial and ethnic identities as necessarily exclusive and (b) sees individual identity as only partially constituted by racial or ethnic affiliations. Let's consider each of these two points.

First, in this pluralistic model of multiculturalism, an individual may have several racial or ethnic affiliations and affirming one need not be done at the expense of affirming the others. One may, for example, be African American and Jewish, and affirming one identity does not entail denying the other identity.

Second, in the pluralistic model of multiculturalism, one's principal identity may not have much to do with one's race or ethnicity. One's principal identity may be religious—one may be a Baha'i or a Pentecostal or a Buddhist, and one's sense of self may be primarily constituted along that axis. Or, one's primary identity may be constituted through parenting, job, avocation, or any number of other factors. Identity, in other words, is a more widely varied and richly textured thing than separatist multiculturalism would suggest.

Pluralistic multiculturalism, in other words, is not committed either to belief that racial and ethnic identities are mutually exclusive or to the belief the personal identities are necessarily primarily constituted along racial or ethnic lines.

Pluralistic multiculturalism also allows us to recognize that race and ethnicity may not even be the principal issues in some disputes. For example, the moral issue about separatist groups in the United States may not actually be primarily along the separatist/assimilationist axis, but rather along a quite different axis that sometimes overlaps with the issue of separatist: the group's attitude toward outside groups. To the extent that group identity is tied up with hatred or oppression of other groups, then we are morally justified in objecting to that particular aspect of the group's identity. Although such hatred and oppression are perhaps more characteristic of separatist groups simply because it would be inconsistent to advocate assimilation of groups one hates or oppresses, there is nothing intrinsic to separatism that entails hatred or oppression of other groups. Lawrence A. Blum's article, "Philosophy and the Values of a Multicultural Community," provides an insightful discussion of the minimal values we should encourage in multicultural communities.

# The Means to Our Ideals

Let's imagine, simply for the sake of discussion, that we have general agreement about our actual situation and about the ideal condition toward which we are striving. The question that then presents itself is how we are to move from one to the other. In general, we can distinguish several kinds of approaches. First, *equal rights approaches* seek to insure that previously discriminated against groups are henceforth treated in a scrupulously fair manner. Such approaches seek to eliminate discrimination in the future, but are often unable to significantly reduce the cumulative and continuing effects of past patterns of discrimination. Second, *affirmative action approaches* attempt to provide some kind of special support, consideration, or advantage to groups that have previously been discriminated against. These have the advantage of seeking to undue the residual effects of past discrimination, but they run the risk of being viewed as further discrimination. Finally, *special protection approaches* provide selected groups with stronger-than-usual protection of the law in specific areas relating to their identity as a group. Regulations banning hate speech, for example, give extra protection of law to certain groups. Such approaches stand midway between equal rights approaches and affirmative action approaches, providing more than extra protection but less than affirmative action in protection of certain groups.

## Equal Rights Approaches

Since the *Brown* v. *Board of Education* decision in 1954, the United States has increasingly committed itself to equal rights for all citizens, regardless of race. The Civil Rights Act of 1964 extended and deepened this commitment, and there are few today who would argue publicly that some citizens ought to be denied their civil rights on the basis of race or discriminated against because of race. Such a commitment was implicit in our Constitution and is increasingly central to our identity as a nation.

It is important to note, however, that there is often a huge gulf between commitment to the general principle of equal rights and commitment to the specific means of insuring such equality. This is particularly the case where there are existing, often deeply ingrained patterns of discrimination. To what extent does the government take an active role in (a) discouraging such attitudes of discrimination and (b) punishing acts of discrimination? Consider, for example, the issue of discrimination in housing. Is the cause of equal rights in this area adequately served by simply passing a law forbidding such discrimination? Should special enforcement agencies be established?

## Affirmative Action Programs

*Four senses of affirmative action.*   Affirmative action is a notoriously slippery term, and it is important to define precisely what we mean when we use it. There are several possible senses of the term. If we consider it just within the context of hiring potential employees, we can distinguish four senses, two of which are weak, the other two of which are strong.

*What are the various meanings of the term "affirmative action"?*

- *Weak senses of affirmative action:*
  1. Encouraging the largest possible number of minority applications in the applicant pool, and then choosing the best candidates regardless of gender, race, and so on.
  2. When the two best candidates are equally qualified and one is a minority candidate, choosing the minority candidate.
- *Strong senses of affirmative action:*
  3. From a group of candidates, all of whom are qualified, choosing the minority candidate over better-qualified nonminority ones.
  4. Choosing an unqualified minority candidate over a qualified nonminority one.

The third and fourth alternatives involve choosing a minority candidate over a better-qualified nonminority one. Almost no one *advocates* the fourth alternative, although critics sometimes claim that support for the third alternative in theory leads, in practice, to the fourth alternative. Many are willing to support the third alternative. Proponents of affirmative action often argue that the first two types of affirmative action, although commendable, are often insufficient to break the cycle of past discrimination and that a more active program—that is, the third type of program—is necessary if affirmative action is to achieve its goal.

Forward-looking defenses of strong affirmative action programs usually contain three crucial elements. First, they need some criterion for determining when racist discrimination exists in a particular area. Second, they need to show that affirmative action programs are the best means of achieving the desired equality. Finally, they need to deal with the objection that merit, not race, should determine who gets jobs and admissions to educational institutions. Let's look at each of these three elements.

*Equality, equal representation, and quotas.*   The general goal of affirmative action programs is a discrimination-free society. The question immediately arises as to how we determine when we have reached a discrimination-free society, when we have achieved genuine equality of opportunity. One commonly proposed indicator that we have reached this goal is the proportional representation of racial groups in various types of jobs. If there is proportional representation of whites, blacks, Asians, and Native Americans among physicians, for example, this is taken as evidence that we have genuine equality of opportunity and that there is no racism at work here. Conversely, lack of proportional representation is taken as *prima facie* evidence of racism, and it is this course of reasoning that leads so easily to quotas. Critics of this argument maintain that lack of proportional representation might be due to numerous other factors besides racism. Inequality of outcome, they argue, does not necessarily entail inequality of opportunity.

*The best means to achieving equality.*    Secondly, defenders of affirmative action must show that such programs are the only—or at least the best, the most efficient, or the speediest—way of reaching the goal of equality in society. If, they argue, we are committed to a society in which all professions are equally accessible to all groups, and if one of the conditions of accessibility is that a significant number of one's own group *already* be represented in that profession, then some type of active intervention would seem to be necessary in order to change the composition of that profession. Strong affirmative action is seen as the only way of breaking the circle of disadvantage. Presumably, once proportional representation is achieved, then the need for such programs will diminish.

Such forward-looking justifications of strong affirmative action assume, however, that affirmative action programs will have the intended consequences—and only those consequences. This is an empirical claim and open to much dispute. Part of the dispute over affirmative action during the last decade has been an empirical one. What are the *actual* consequences of affirmative action programs? Critics of such programs point out that affirmative action programs have had unintended and undesirable consequences that undermine their effectiveness. They have stigmatized minorities in professions shaped by such programs, undermining the accomplishments of those minority persons who have succeeded without the help of affirmative action programs. Moreover, advocates of such programs have underestimated the degree of resentment such programs have created among nonminorities, especially white males. Finally, some have maintained that such programs foster a culture of dependency and victimhood that is ultimately not beneficial to anyone.

*The critique of meritocracy.*    Since the most common objection to affirmative action programs of the third type is that the job should go to the most qualified candidates, the defense of type three programs is often supplemented with an attack on both the theory and the practice of meritocracy. The *theory* of meritocracy (i.e., jobs should always go to the most qualified) is attacked in two ways. First, one may argue that merit is only one among many possibly relevant criteria that can be used when giving people jobs or admitting people to schools. After all, don't many colleges and universities have strong affirmative action programs for recruiting student athletes in money-making sports such as college football? Second, one can enlarge the notion of merit and qualification to include other factors (such as race, ethnicity, or gender) not usually included. For example, if one wants to increase the number of role models of physicians for African Americans, then race might become a relevant qualification for medical school. The *practice* of meritocracy is also often attacked, and here the argument is that institutions do not in fact live up to their own professed standards of meritocratic neutrality. Colleges and universities may, for example, give special consideration to the children of their alums; employers may give jobs to relatives; superficially neutral requirements such as letters of recommendation may actually be part of an insiders' network, often an "old boys' network." The significance of these various attacks is to undermine the claim that a position either should or even usually does go to the most qualified candidate.

*Extended senses of affirmative action.*    Affirmative action programs are not limited to employment and admissions requirements. School busing programs that are designed to achieve racial balance in city schools are a species of affirmative action program, and we can draw a parallel distinction in this area between equal rights approaches and affirmative action programs. Equal rights approaches would prohibit any school district from rejecting any otherwise qualified applicant on the basis of race or ethnicity. The limitation of such approaches, however, is that schools then continue to perpetuate the racial divisions of historically segregated neighborhoods, neighborhoods that may still be economically segregated in ways that reflect earlier patterns of racial segregation. Busing then becomes a way of acting affirmatively to establish racial balance in schools that otherwise would not be so balanced.

In awarding government contracts, the government often provides financial incentives to firms that either are minority-owned or who subcontract a certain percentage of their work to minority-owned businesses. This, too, is an extended form of affirmative action, one which the Supreme Court has now ruled must be subject to strict scrutiny.

In American society today, affirmative action programs are the focus of tremendous controversy. As the readings in this section show, this is not simply a division between those in favor of racial equality and those opposed to it. It is a far more complex problem, with both black and white advocates of racial equality on both sides of the question and with charges of racism being leveled against both proponents and opponents of strong affirmative action.

## Special Protection Programs

In recent years, some attempts have been made to provide special protection to particular groups on the basis of race. Such programs do not qualify as affirmative action programs, but they clearly go beyond simple equal rights guarantees. Consider two examples: interracial adoptions and hate speech laws.

*Interracial adoption.*    As the number of interracial adoptions began to increase in the 1960s, the National Association of Black Social Workers urged in 1972 that "Black children should be placed only with black families whether for foster care or for adoption, because black children in white homes are cut off from the healthy development of themselves as black people." Many local child welfare agencies soon developed guidelines that forbid interracial adoptions, even when this resulted in many children not being adopted. The principal rationale was that children need to be in the same-race family in order to develop a sense of their racial identity and that the government is committed to fostering the development of that sense of identity. Some African Americans go further, arguing that such adoptions are a form of racial genocide and that the government must provide special protection to them as a result.

*Hate speech.*    Another area in which attempts at special protection have been made is hate speech. Advocates of such protection maintain that racist speech is often deeply damaging to minorities and that the government ought to provide special protection to them against such speech. This special protection has been criticized on three grounds. First, it severely limits the right of free speech, which has a very strong constitutional foundation in the United States. In the eyes of the critics of such restrictions, it is not clear that the possible benefits outweigh the accompanying loss of freedom. Second, such restrictions are usually framed in such a way as to protect minorities in particular from such speech, but in the interests of equality shouldn't such protection be extended to all races and ethnicities? Yet in the past when it has existed, hate speech laws have typically been used to oppress racial minorities rather than protect them. Finally, there is a disturbingly large element of vagueness in such legislation. Precisely what counts as "hate speech" and what doesn't?

## Common Ground

As a nation, we have clearly committed ourselves to a society in which racism is not to be tolerated. We certainly sometimes fail to live up to this commitment, some of us may not share the commitment, and some may even view some of the remedies (such as affirmative action) as further instances of the problem (i.e., racism), but virtually no one advocates a society in which basic human rights are distributed differentially according to race.

Some in our society, even if they don't advocate unequal civil rights, do advocate hatred of other racial and ethnic groups. Few, however, truly believe that other groups should hate *them*. Their racially based hatred, in other words, is not something that they are willing to universalize. Nor is it something that we have to condone.

The elimination, or at least reduction, of inequalities caused by racial and ethnic discrimination is a complex matter, and here we find, even among people of good will who are committed to eradicating the legacy of racism in our society, there is deep disagreement about how this can best be accomplished. Certain programs, most notably strong affirmative action programs, have elicited great controversy and resentment. If there is a common ground here, it is probably to be found in searching for other means that promote the same goal with fewer liabilities.

### Endnote

1. Gertrude Ezorsky, *Racism & Justice* (Ithaca: Cornell University Press, 1991), p. 9.

# THE ARGUMENTS

Charles Murray
"Affirmative Racism: How Preferential Treatment Works against Blacks"

*Charles Murray is a well-known conservative thinker and a fellow at the Manhattan Institute for Policy Research. He is the author of numerous articles and books, including most recently (as co-author)* The Bell Curve *and* Losing Ground: American Social Policy 1950–1980.

*Murray argues that "there is no such thing as good racial discrimination" and that preferential treatment is racial discrimination that ultimately works against blacks as well as against whites and that it ought to be abolished.*

## As You Read, Consider This:

1. Some of Murray's assertions are supported by reference to empirical studies, other are not. Assess the reliability of his claims about what both blacks and whites really think and feel.

2. In the course of his essay, Murray traces the career of three hypothetical individuals: John, William, and Carol. Do you think these examples are typical? Discuss.

⌒

A few years ago, I got into an argument with a lawyer friend who is a partner in a New York firm. I was being the conservative, arguing that preferential treatment of blacks was immoral; he was being the liberal, urging that it was the only way to bring blacks to full equality. In the middle of all this he abruptly said, "But you know, let's face it. We must have hired at least ten blacks in the last few years, and none of them has really worked out." He then returned to his case for still stronger affirmative action, while I wondered what it had been like for those ten blacks. And if he could make a remark like that so casually, what remarks would he be able to make some years down the road, if by that time it had been fifty blacks who hadn't "really worked out"?

My friend's comment was an outcropping of a new racism that is emerging to take its place alongside the old. It grows out of preferential treatment for blacks, and it is not just the much-publicized reactions, for example, of the white policemen or firemen who are passed over for promotion because of an affirmative action court order. The new racism that is potentially most damaging is located among the white elites—educated, affluent, and occupying the positions in education, business, and government from which this country is run. It currently focuses on blacks; whether it will eventually extend to include Hispanics and other minorities remains to be seen.

The new racists do not think blacks are inferior. They are typically longtime supporters of civil rights. But they exhibit the classic behavioral symptom of racism: they treat blacks differently from whites, because of their race. The results can be as concretely bad and unjust as any that the

Charles Murray, "Affirmative Racism," *The New Republic* 191 (December 31, 1984). Copyright © 1984, The New Republic. Reprinted by permission of the publisher.

old racism produces. Sometimes the effect is that blacks are refused an education they otherwise could have gotten. Sometimes blacks are shunted into dead-end jobs. Always, blacks are denied the right to compete as equals.

The new racists also exhibit another characteristic of racism: they think about blacks differently from the way they think about whites. Their global view of blacks and civil rights is impeccable. Blacks must be enabled to achieve full equality. They are still unequal, through no fault of their own (it is the fault of racism, it is the fault of inadequate opportunity, it is the legacy of history). But the new racists' local view is that the blacks they run across professionally are not, on the average, up to the white standard. Among the new racists, lawyers have gotten used to the idea that the brief a black colleague turns in will be a little less well-rehearsed and argued than the one they would have done. Businessmen expect that a black colleague will not read a balance sheet as subtly as they do. Teachers expect black students to wind up toward the bottom of the class.

The new racists also tend to think of blacks as a commodity. The office must have a sufficient supply of blacks, who must be treated with special delicacy. The personnel problems this creates are more difficult than most because whites barely admit to themselves what's going on.

What follows is a foray into very poorly mapped territory. I will present a few numbers that explain much about how the process gets started. But the ways that the numbers get translated into behavior are even more important. The cases I present are composites constructed from my own observations and taken from firsthand accounts. All are based on real events and real people, stripped of their particularities. But the individual cases are not intended as evidence, because I cannot tell you how often they happen. They have not been the kind of thing that social scientists or journalists have wanted to count. I am writing this because so many people, both white and black, to whom I tell such stories know immediately what I am talking about. It is apparent that a problem exists. How significant is it? What follows is as much an attempt to elicit evidence as to present it.

As in so many of the crusades of the 1960s, the nation began with a good idea. It was called "affirmative action," initiated by Lyndon Johnson through Executive Order 11246 in September 1965. It was an attractive label and a natural corrective to past racism: actively seek out black candidates for jobs, college, or promotions, without treating them differently in the actual decision to hire, admit, or promote. The term originally evoked both the letter and the spirit of the order. Then, gradually, affirmative action came to mean something quite different. In 1970 a federal court established the legitimacy of quotas as a means of implementing Johnson's executive order. In 1971 the Supreme Court ruled that an employer could not use minimum credentials as a prerequisite for hiring if the credential acted as a "built-in headwind" for minority groups—even when there was no discriminatory intent and even when the hiring procedures were "fair in form." In 1972 the Equal Employment Opportunity Commission acquired broad, independent enforcement powers.

Thus by the early 1970s it had become generally recognized that a good-faith effort to recruit qualified blacks was not enough—especially if one's school depended on federal grants or one's business depended on federal contracts. Even for businesses and schools not directly dependent on the government, the simplest way to withstand an accusation of violating Title VII of the Civil Rights Act of 1964 was to make sure not that they had not just interviewed enough minority candidates, but that they had actually hired or admitted enough of them. Employers and admissions committees arrived at a rule of thumb: if the blacks who are available happen to be the best candidates, fine; if not, the best available black candidates will be given some sort of edge in the selection process. Sometimes the edge will be small; sometimes it will be predetermined that a black candidate is essential, and the edge will be very large.

Perhaps the first crucial place where the edge applies is in admission to college. Consider the cases of the following three students: John, William, and Carol, 17 years old and applying to college, are all equal on paper. Each has a score of 520 in the mathematics section of the Scholastic Aptitude Test, which puts them in the top third—at the 67th percentile—of all students who took the test. (Figures are based on 1983 data.)

John is white. A score of 520 gets him into the state university. Against the advice of his high school counselor, he applies to a prestigious school, Ivy U., where his application is rejected in the first cut—its average white applicant has math scores in the high 600s.

William is black, from a middle-class family who sent him to good schools. His score of 520 puts him at the 95th percentile of all blacks who took the test. William's high school counselor points out that he could probably get into Ivy U. William applies and is admitted—Ivy U. uses separate standards for admission of whites and blacks, and William is among the top blacks who applied.

Carol is black, educated at an inner-city school, and her score of 520 represents an extraordinary achievement in the face of terrible schooling. An alumnus of Ivy U. who regularly looks for promising inner-city candidates finds her, recruits her, and sends her off with a full scholarship to Ivy U.

When American universities embarked on policies of preferential admissions by race, they had the Carols in mind. They had good reason to be optimistic that preferential treatment would work—for many years, the best universities had been weighting the test scores of applicants from small-town public schools when they were compared against those of applicants from the top private schools, and had been giving special breaks to students from distant states to ensure geographic distribution. The differences in preparation tended to even out after the first year or so. Blacks were being brought into a long-standing and successful tradition of preferential treatment. In the case of blacks, however, preferential treatment ran up against a large black-white gap in academic performance combined with ambitious goals for proportional representation. This gap has been the hardest for whites to confront. But though it is not necessary or even plausible to believe that such differences are innate, it is necessary to recognize openly that the differences exist. By pretending they don't, we begin the process whereby both the real differences and the racial factor are exaggerated.

The black-white gap that applies most directly to this discussion is the one that separates blacks and whites who go to college. In 1983, for example, the mean Scholastic Aptitude Test score for all blacks who took the examination was more than 100 points below the white score on both the verbal and the math sections. Statistically, it is an extremely wide gap. To convert the gap into more concrete terms, think of it this way: in 1983, the same Scholastic Aptitude Test math score that put a black at the 50th percentile of all blacks who took the test put him at the 16th percentile of all whites who took the test.

These results clearly mean we ought to be making an all-out effort to improve elementary and secondary education for blacks. But that doesn't help much now, when an academic discrepancy of this magnitude is fed into a preferential admissions process. As universities scramble to make sure they are admitting enough blacks, the results feed the new racism. Here's how it works:

In 1983, only 66 black students nationwide scored above 700 in the verbal section of the Scholastic Aptitude Test, and only 205 scored above 700 in the mathematics section. This handful of students cannot begin to meet the demand for blacks with such scores. For example, Harvard, Yale, and Princeton have in recent years been bringing an aggregate of about 270 blacks into each entering class. If the black students entering these schools had the same distribution of scores as that of the freshman class as a whole, then every black student in the nation with a verbal score in the 700s, and roughly 70 percent of the ones with a math score in the 700s, would be in their freshman classes.

The main problem is not that a few schools monopolize the very top black applicants, but that these same schools have much larger implicit quotas than they can fill with those applicants. They fill out the rest with the next students in line—students who would not have gotten into these schools if they were not black, who otherwise would have been showing up in the classrooms of the nation's less glamorous colleges and universities. But the size of the black pool does not expand appreciably at the next levels. The number of blacks scoring in the 600s on the math section in 1983, for example, was 1,531. Meanwhile, 31,704 nonblack students in 1983 scored in the 700s on the math section and 121,640 scored in the 600s. The prestige schools cannot begin to absorb these numbers of other highly qualified freshmen, and they are perforce spread widely throughout the system.

At schools that draw most broadly from the student population, such as the large state universities, the effects of this skimming produce a situation that confirms the old racists in everything they want most to believe. There are plenty of outstanding students in such student bodies (at the University of Colorado, for example, 6 percent of the freshmen in 1981 had math scores in the 700s and 28 percent had scores in the 600s), but the skimming process combined with the very small raw numbers means that almost none of them [is] black. What students and instructors see in their day-to-day experience in the classroom is a disproportionate number of blacks who are below the white average, relatively few blacks who are at the white average, and virtually none who are in the first rank. The image that the white student carries away is that blacks are less able than whites.

I am not exalting the SAT as an infallible measure of academic ability, or pointing to test scores to try to convince anyone that blacks are performing below the level of whites. I am simply using them to explain what instructors and students already notice, and talk about, among themselves.

They do not talk openly about such matters. One characteristic of the new racism is that whites deny in public but acknowledge in private that there are significant differences in black and white academic performance. Another is that they dismiss the importance of tests when black scores are at issue, blaming cultural bias and saying that test scores are not good predictors of college performance. At the same time, they watch anxiously over their own children's test scores.

The differences in academic performance do not disappear by the end of college. Far from narrowing, the gap separating black and white academic achievement appears to get larger. Various studies, most recently at Harvard, have found that during the 1970s blacks did worse in college (as measured by grade point average) than their test scores would have predicted. Moreover, the black-white gap in the Graduate Record Examination is larger than the gap in the Scholastic Aptitude Test. The gap between black and white freshmen is a bit less than one standard deviation (the technical measure for comparing scores). Black and white seniors who take the Graduate Record Examination reveal a gap of about one and a quarter standard deviations.

Why should the gap grow wider? Perhaps it is an illusion—for example, perhaps a dispro-portionate number of the best black students never take the examination. But there are also reasons for suspecting that in fact blacks get a worse education in college than whites do. Here are a few of the hypotheses that deserve full exploration.

Take the situation of William—a slightly above-average student who, because he is black, gets into a highly competitive school. William studies very hard during the first year. He nonethe-less gets mediocre grades. He has a choice. He can continue to study hard and continue to get mediocre grades, and be seen by his classmates as a black who cannot do very well. Or he can ex-plicitly refuse to engage in the academic game. He decides to opt out, and his performance gets worse as time goes on. He emerges from college with a poor education and is further behind the whites than he was as a freshman.

If large numbers of other black students at the institution are in the same situation as William, the result can be group pressure not to compete academically. (At Harvard, it is said, the current term among black students for a black who studies like a white is "incognegro.") The re-sponse is not hard to understand. If one subpopulation of students is conspicuously behind another population and is visibly identifiable, then the population that is behind must come up with a good excuse for doing poorly. "Not wanting to do better" is as good as any.

But there is another crucial reason why blacks might not close the gap with whites during college: they are not taught as well as whites are. Racist teachers impeding the progress of stu-dents? Perhaps, but most college faculty members I know tend to bend over backward to be "fair" to black students—and that may be the problem. I suggest that inferior instruction is more likely to be a manifestation of the new racism than the old.

Consider the case of Carol, with outstanding abilities but deprived of decent prior schooling: she struggles the first year, but she gets by. Her academic skills still show the after-effects of her inferior preparation. Her instructors diplomatically point out the more flagrant mistakes, but they ignore minor lapses, and never push her in the aggressive way they push white students who have her intellectual capacity. Some of them are being patronizing (she is doing quite well, considering). Others are being prudent: teachers who criticize black students can find themselves being called racists in the classroom, in the campus newspaper, or in complaints to the administration.

The same process continues in graduate school. Indeed, because there are even fewer blacks in graduate schools than in undergraduate schools, the pressures to get black students through to the degree, no matter what, can be still greater. But apart from differences in preparation and abil-ity that have accumulated by the end of schooling, the process whereby we foster the appearance of black inferiority continues. Let's assume that William did not give up during college. He goes to business school, where he gets his masters degree. He signs up for interviews with the corporate recruiters. There are 100 persons in his class, and William is ranked near the middle. But of the 5 blacks in his class, he ranks first (remember that he was at the 95th percentile of blacks taking the Scholastic Aptitude Test). He is hired on his first interview by his first-choice company, which also attracted the very best of the white students. He is hired alongside 5 of the top-ranking white members of the class.

William's situation as one of 5 blacks in a class of 100 illustrates the proportions that prevail in business schools, and business schools are by no means one of the more extreme examples. The pool of black candidates for any given profession is a small fraction of the white pool. This works out to a 20-to-1 edge in business; it is even greater in most of the other professions. The result, when many hiring institutions are competing, is that a major gap between the abilities of new black and white employees in any given workplace is highly likely. Everyone needs to hire a few blacks, and the edge that "being black" confers in the hiring decision warps the sequence of hiring in such a way that a scarce resource (the blacks with a given set of qualifications) is exhausted at an artificially high rate, producing a widening gap in comparison with the remaining whites from which an employer can choose.

The more aggressively affirmative action is enforced, the greater the imbalance. In general, the first companies to hire can pursue strategies that minimize or even eliminate the difference in ability between the new black and white employees. IBM and Park Avenue law firms can do very well, just as Harvard does quite well in attracting the top black students. But the more effectively they pursue these strategies, the more quickly they strip the population of the best black candidates.

To this point I have been discussing problems that are more or less driven by realities we have very little hope of manipulating in the short term except by discarding the laws regarding preferential treatment. People do differ in acquired abilities. Currently, acquired abilities in the white and black populations are distributed differently. Schools and firms do form a rough hierarchy when they draw from these distributions. The results follow ineluctably. The dangers they represent are not a matter of statistical probabilities, but of day-to-day human reactions we see around us.

The damage caused by these mechanistic forces should be much less in the world of work than in the schools, however. Schools deal in a relatively narrow domain of skills, and "talent" tends to be assigned specific meanings and specific measures. Workplaces deal in highly complex sets of skills, and "talent" consists of all sorts of combinations of qualities. A successful career depends in large part upon finding jobs that elicit and develop one's strengths.

At this point the young black professional must sidestep a new series of traps laid by whites who need to be ostentatiously nonracist. Let's say that William goes to work for the XYZ Corporation, where he is assigned with another management trainee (white) to a department where much of the time is spent preparing proposals for government contracts. The white trainee is assigned a variety of scut work—proofreading drafts, calculating the costs of minor items in the bid, making photocopies, taking notes at conferences. William gets more dignified work. He is assigned portions of the draft to write (which are later rewritten by more experienced staff), sits in on planning sessions, and even goes to Washington as a highly visible part of the team to present the bid. As time goes on, the white trainee learns a great deal about how the company operates, and is seen as a go-getting young member of the team. William is perceived to be a bright enough fellow, but not much of a detail man and not really much of a self-starter.

Even if a black is hired under terms that put him on a par with his white peers, the subtler forms of differential treatment work against him. Particularly for any corporation that does business with the government, the new employee has a specific, immediate value purely because he is black. There are a variety of requirements to be met and rituals to be observed for which a black face is helpful. These have very little to do with the long-term career interests of the new employee; on the contrary, they often lead to a dead end as head of the minority-relations section of the personnel department.

Added to this is another problem that has nothing to do with the government. When the old racism was at fault (as it often still is), the newly hired black employee was excluded from the socialization process because the whites did not want him to become part of the group. When the new racism is at fault, it is because many whites are embarrassed to treat black employees as badly as they are willing to treat whites. Hence another reason that whites get on-the-job training that blacks do not: much of the early training of an employee is intertwined with menial assignments and mild hazing. Blacks who are put through these routines often see themselves as racially abused (and when a black is involved, old-racist responses may well have crept in). But even if the black is not unhappy about the process, the whites are afraid that he is, and so protect him from it. There are many variations, all having the same effect: the black is denied an apprenticeship that the white has no way of escaping. Without serving the apprenticeship, there is no way of becoming part of the team.

Carol suffers a slightly different fate. She and a white woman are hired as reporters by a major newspaper. They both work hard, but after a few months there is no denying it: neither one of them can write. The white woman is let go. Carol is kept on, because the paper cannot afford to have any fewer blacks than it already has. She is kept busy with reportorial work, even though they have to work around the writing problem. She is told not to worry—there's lots more to being a journalist than writing.

It is the mascot syndrome. A white performing at a comparable level would be fired. The black is kept on, perhaps to avoid complications with the Equal Employment Opportunity Commission (it can be very expensive to fire a black), perhaps out of a more diffuse wish not to appear discriminatory. Everybody pretends that nothing is wrong—but the black's career is at a dead end. The irony, of course, is that the white who gets fired and has to try something else has been forced into accepting a chance of making a success in some other line of work whereas the black is seduced into not taking the same chance.

Sometimes differential treatment takes an even more pernicious form: the conspiracy to promote a problem out of existence. As part of keeping Carol busy, the newspaper gives her some administrative responsibilities. They do not amount to much. But she has an impressive title on a prominent newspaper and she is black—a potent combination. She gets an offer from a lesser paper in another part of the country to take a senior editorial post. Her current employer is happy to be rid of an awkward situation and sends along glowing references. She gets a job that she is unequipped to handle—only this time, she is in a highly visible position, and within a few weeks the deficiencies that were covered up at the old job have become the subject of jokes at the office. Most of the jokes are openly racist.

It is important to pause and remember who Carol is: an extremely bright young woman, not (in other circumstances) a likely object of condescension. But being bright is no protection. Whites can usually count on the market to help us recognize egregious career mistakes and to prevent us from being promoted too far from a career line that fits our strengths, and too far above our level of readiness. One of the most prevalent characteristics of white differential treatment of blacks has been to exempt blacks from these market considerations, substituting for them a market premium attached to race.

The most obvious consequence of preferential treatment is that every black professional, no matter how able, is tainted. Every black who is hired by a white-run organization that hires blacks preferentially has to put up with the knowledge that many of his co-workers believe he was hired because of his race; and he has to put up with the suspicion in his own mind that they might be right.

Whites are curiously reluctant to consider this a real problem—it is an abstraction, I am told, much less important than the problem that blacks face in getting a job in the first place. But black professionals talk about it, and they tell stories of mental breakdowns; of people who had to leave the job altogether; of long-term professional paralysis. What white would want to be put in such a situation? Of course it would be a constant humiliation to be resented by some of your co-workers and condescended to by others. Of course it would affect your perceptions of yourself and your self-confidence. No system that produces such side effects—as preferential treatment must do— can be defended unless it is producing some extremely important benefits.

And that brings us to the decisive question. If the alternative were no job at all, as it was for so many blacks for so long, the resentment and condescension are part of the price of getting blacks into the positions they deserve. But is that the alternative today? If the institutions of this country were left to their own devices now, to what extent would they refuse to admit, hire, and promote people because they were black? To what extent are American institutions kept from being racist by the government's intervention?

It is another one of those questions that are seldom investigated aggressively, and I have no evidence. Let me suggest a hypothesis that bears looking into: that the signal event in the struggle for black equality during the last thirty years, the one with real impact, was not the Civil Rights Act of 1964 or Executive Order 11246 or any other government act. It was the civil rights movement itself. It raised to a pitch of acute and lasting discomfort the racial consciousness of the generations of white Americans who are now running the country. I will not argue that the old racism is dead at any level of society. I will argue, however, that in the typical corporation or in the typical admissions office, there is an abiding desire to be not-racist. This need not be construed as brotherly love. Guilt will do as well. But the civil rights movement did its job. I suggest that the laws and the court decisions and the continuing intellectual respectability behind preferential treatment are not holding many doors open to qualified blacks that would otherwise be closed.

Suppose for a moment that I am right. Suppose that, for practical purposes, racism would not get in the way of blacks if preferential treatment were abandoned. How, in my most optimistic view, would the world look different?

There would be fewer blacks at Harvard and Yale; but they would all be fully competitive with the whites who were there. White students at the state university would encounter a cross-section of blacks who span the full range of ability, including the top levels, just as whites do. College remedial courses would no longer be disproportionately black. Whites rejected by the school they wanted would quit assuming they were kept out because a less-qualified black was admitted in their place. Blacks in big corporations would no longer be shunted off to personnel-relations positions, but would be left on the main-line tracks toward becoming comptrollers and sales managers and chief executive officers. Whites would quit assuming that black colleagues had been hired because they were black. Blacks would quit worrying that they had been hired because they were black.

Would blacks still lag behind? As a population, yes, for a time, and the nation should be mounting a far more effective program to improve elementary and secondary education for blacks than it has mounted in the last few decades. But in years past virtually every ethnic group in America has at one time or another lagged behind as a population, and has eventually caught up. In the process of catching up, the ones who breached the barriers were evidence of the success of that group. Now blacks who breach the barriers tend to be seen as evidence of the inferiority of that group.

And that is the evil of preferential treatment. It perpetuates an impression of inferiority. The system segments whites and blacks who come in contact with each other so as to maximize the likelihood that whites have the advantage in experience and ability. The system then encourages both whites and blacks to behave in ways that create self-fulfilling prophecies even when no real differences exist.

It is here that the new racism links up with the old. The old racism has always openly held that blacks are permanently less competent than whites. The new racism tacitly accepts that, in the course of overcoming the legacy of the old racism, blacks are temporarily less competent than whites. It is an extremely fine distinction. As time goes on, fine distinctions tend to be lost. Preferential treatment is providing persuasive evidence for the old racists, and we can already hear it sotto voce: "We gave you your chance, we let you educate them and push them into jobs they couldn't have gotten on their own and coddle them every way you could. And see: they still aren't as good as whites, and you are beginning to admit it yourselves." Sooner or later this message is going to be heard by a white elite that needs to excuse its failure to achieve black equality.

The only happy aspect of the new racism is that the corrective—to get rid of the policies encouraging preferential treatment—is so natural. Deliberate preferential treatment by race has sat as uneasily with America's equal-opportunity ideal during the post-1965 period as it did during the days of legalized segregation. We had to construct tortuous rationalizations when we permitted blacks to be kept on the back of the bus—and the rationalizations to justify sending blacks to the head of the line have been just as tortuous. Both kinds of rationalization say that sometimes it is all right to treat people of different races in different ways. For years, we have instinctively sensed this was wrong in principle but intellectualized our support for it as an expedient. I submit that our instincts were right. There is no such thing as good racial discrimination.

## Journal/Discussion Questions

1. What does Murray mean by "the new racism"? What are the characteristics of this new racism? Is this really racism? Do you think it exists and is as prevalent as he implies? On what basis?

2. Murray hypothesizes that black university students may not be getting as good an education as their nonblack counterparts. Explain his support for this claim and evaluate it.

3. Murray claims that "Every black who is hired by a white-run organization that hires blacks preferentially has to put up with the knowledge that many of his co-workers believe he was hired because of his race; and he has to put up with the suspicion in his own mind that they might be right." Do you agree? Discuss.

4. Do you agree with Murray's claim that "the laws and the court decisions and the continuing intellectual respectability behind preferential treatment are not holding many doors open to qualified blacks that would otherwise be closed." Why or why not?

## Derek Bok
## "The Case for Racial Preferences"

*Derek Bok, one of the most noted educators of our day, was president of Harvard University.*

*Replying to Charles Murray's article, Bok maintains that Murray's claims are based on subjective reaction rather than objective data. There are strong empirical reasons, Bok claims, to believe that preferential policies in admissions have worked.*

## As You Read, Consider This:

1. Do you think that Bok gives an accurate and fair depiction of Murray's position? Does Murray offer empirical data that Bok ignores?
2. What, in Bok's eyes, is the strongest argument in favor of affirmative action programs?

For 15 years, colleges and universities have sought to increase educational opportunities for minority students by admitting blacks (as well as Hispanics and Native Americans) with SAT scores lower than those of white applicants. In the December 31 issue of *The New Republic*, Charles Murray criticizes this policy and accuses higher education of helping to foster a new racism. In his view, preferential admissions practices, and affirmative action programs by employers, only demoralize blacks by forcing them to compete beyond their abilities while fostering stereotypes among whites that blacks really are inferior.

Murray offers a simple solution to this problem. Treat all applicants equally in admissions (and hiring), and allow them to make their way without any discrimination or preference on grounds of race. The immediate consequence, he admits, will be a severe drop in the number of black students, especially at more selective colleges and universities. Eventually, however, blacks will participate fully and successfully in American life just as other initially disadvantaged ethnic groups have done.

Murray's arguments are not new. Even so, they may gain a wider following at a time when the nation seems to be reassessing many of its priorities and practices. University administrators need to take the criticisms seriously rather than ignore them in the hope that they will disappear.

Murray mentions only the disappointments and failures of preferential admissions without recognizing its many successes. Since his conclusions are subjective and not based on data, it is also hard to know what to make of his assertions about the effects of preferential admissions on white and black attitudes. For what it's worth, his impressions do not accord with the anonymous survey results at the one institution I know. In a Harvard poll of 1,200 undergraduates conducted in 1978, many students said they suspected that "others" might question the ability of blacks. But less than five percent of black undergraduates felt they had moderate to severe doubts about their own academic ability, and over 75 percent reported no doubts whatsoever. Almost 60 percent of white undergraduates believed that they had no such doubts about blacks, and barely 10 percent indicated moderate or severe doubts.

Historical evidence also cuts against Murray's proposals. In 1965 most colleges and universities outside the South were following the policy that Murray advocates now; they neither discriminated against black applicants nor gave them any preference. And what were the results? A full century after the Civil War, only two percent of the nation's doctors and under two percent of the lawyers were black. Although *Brown* v. *Board of Education* had been decided more than a decade earlier, the proportions of black students preparing for the major professions were still abysmally low. Only slightly more than one percent of the nation's law students were black, and a mere handful of blacks attended the predominantly white graduate schools of medicine and business. Little or no progress had been made in raising these proportions over the preceding generation.

Murray professes a desire to help blacks by warding off a new racism hardly less vicious than the old. If so, he should explain in detail just how his policies would work and why they would fare any better now than they did prior to 1965. It is surely not enough merely to draw an analogy to the experience of other ethnic groups with backgrounds and problems that differ markedly from the legacy of slavery and discrimination that black people have had to overcome. Years of experience with this model yielded little or no progress for blacks and engendered prejudices and resentments just as severe as any that have accompanied affirmative action.

Murray may respond that 1985 is not 1965, and that blacks would now apply and be admitted to universities in much larger numbers than they were 20 years ago. If this is his argument, he should recognize that the very policies he deplores played a major role in encouraging more blacks to seek a college and professional education after 1965. Since he is ultimately concerned with the feelings, attitudes, and stereotypes that result from current admissions practices, he should also explain how universities could suddenly (by his own figures) reduce black enrollments to 1.5 percent or less in scores of selective colleges and professional schools without a devastating effect on the morale and aspirations of blacks—not to mention a strengthening of racial stereotypes on the part of many whites.

I do not mean to overlook the resentments that can arise on the part of whites who feel unjustly excluded from the school of their choice. These disappointments are real, although I wonder why there are not similar resentments against other groups of favored applicants, such as athletes and alumni offspring. I also do not condone everything that has been done in the name of preferential admissions. Some schools have undoubtedly reached too far by admitting blacks with all but insurmountable academic handicaps. Some black students have failed to apply themselves sufficiently, and others have been too quick to reject efforts to help them academically as racist and insulting. Many universities have not been persistent or imaginative enough in developing special ways of assisting blacks and others needing help to overcome deficiencies in their academic backgrounds.

Notwithstanding these defects, most universities have had clear reasons for seeking to admit black students in significant numbers—better reasons, I believe, than those Murray advances to oppose preferential admissions. In the first place, admissions officers do not feel that high scores on SATs and other standardized tests confer a moral entitlement to admission, since such tests are only modestly correlated with subsequent academic success and give no reliable indication of achievement in later life. Instead, they believe that it is educationally enriching for blacks and whites, and important for the country as a whole, for students of all races to live and study together. Academic officials also feel that blacks will have unusual opportunities to contribute to our society in the coming generation and that higher education can play a useful role by helping them to make the most of these possibilities. Finally, educators believe that the growing numbers of black doctors, lawyers, businessmen, and other professionals will serve as examples to encourage more black youths to set higher educational and career goals for themselves.

In adopting these policies, universities have taken the long view. Academic achievement and persistence depend in some significant part on the parents' education, income, and occupation. A promising long-term strategy for helping overcome the racial handicaps of the past is to do what we can to increase the number of blacks with an education, income, and occupational background that will not only serve their own interests, but also help to instill higher educational aspirations and achievement in their children. The hoped-for results may not be fully realized for several decades, and there will be plenty of disappointments along the way. But no one should ever have supposed that we could solve in a single generation problems that were the bitter fruit of so many years of oppression and discrimination.

In the end, the vital question is not whether preferential admission is a success after 15 years, but whether it has made more progress toward overcoming the legacy of discrimination than other strategies that universities might have pursued. On that crucial point, Murray is not convincing. The policies he advances did not work in the past, and he offers no arguments and advances no data to suggest why they would work today. Instead, he gives us his pessimistic impressions of the current situation and compares them unfavorably with his hope of what might occur in some distant, unspecified future if we but followed his prescription. In the face of such arguments, universities should stick by their conviction that a judicious concern for race in admitting students will eventually help to lift the arbitrary burdens that have hampered blacks in striving to achieve their goals in our society.

## Journal/Discussion Questions

✍ *One of the arguments Bok advances is the role model argument: "the growing numbers of black doctors, lawyers, businessmen, and other professionals will serve as examples to encourage more black youths to set higher educational and career goals for themselves." What place have role models (or the lack of them) had in your own development? Discuss.*

1. Bok suggests that "admissions officers do not feel that high scores on SATs and other standardized tests confer a moral entitlement to admission, since such tests are only modestly correlated with subsequent academic success and give no reli-

able indication of achievement in later life." Do you agree with Bok's claims here? Discuss.

2. Bok recognizes "the resentments that can arise on the part of whites who feel unjustly excluded from the school of their choice. These disappointments are real, although I wonder why there are not similar resentments against other groups of favored applicants, such as athletes and alumni offspring." How do you answer his question?

| Lawrence A. Blum |
| "Philosophy and the Values of a Multicultural Community" |

*Lawrence Blum is a professor of philosophy at the University of Massachusetts, Boston. He is the author of numerous articles and books in ethics, including* Friendship, Altruism and Morality *and* Moral Perception and Particularity, *a collection of his recent essays.*

*What values are desirable in a multiracial, multicultural campus? In this essay, Blum explores three values he considers crucial in such a community: opposition to racism, multiculturalism, and a sense of community, connection, or common humanity.*

## As You Read, Consider This:

1. How does Blum define "racism" and "racist"? Is there anything controversial about his definitions?

2. How is multiculturalism different from mere opposition to racism? What, exactly, is the relationship between multiculturalism and ethnocentrism?

⌐∾

Many philosophers are wary about recent calls for greater cultural diversity in university curricula, especially demands that non-Western traditions and modes of thought be given significant recognition. Philosophy departments are often among the last to institute such changes and to join interdisciplinary efforts at implementing this diversity. But I will argue that attention to multiculturalism should be seen as a boon to philosophy.

Philosophy can come into the educational debate over cultural diversity in two places. One concerns philosophy as a specific intellectual discipline among others, and the way diversity is to be explained, justified, and incorporated within its courses. The other is philosophy as contributing to the overall exploration of the issues of multiculturalism as they apply not only to course content but to the classroom and the university as multiracial and multicultural communities of learning. Important as the first is, we should not confine ourselves to a narrow disciplinary focus but should see philosophy as having its role to play in creating what the recent Carnegie Foundation Report "Campus Life: In Search of Community" expressed as a community which is, among other things, just, caring, open, and civil.[1] Taking this role seriously can also show how philosophy can expand to include issues of race, culture, and ethnicity into many courses in ethics, social, and political philosophy, and perhaps other areas of philosophy as well. I would like to begin such an exploration of philosophy and multicultural community today.

I will discuss three distinct values desirable in a multiracial, multicultural campus. They are: (1) opposition to racism, (2) multiculturalism, (3) sense of community, connection, or common humanity. These values are seldom clearly distinguished, and are often entirely run together, defeating clear thought about the real goals and possibilities of multicultural communities.[2] Failure to

Lawrence A. Blum, "Philosophy and the Values of a Multicultural Community," *Teaching Philosophy* 14, no. 2 (June 1991). Copyright © Teaching Philosophy. Reprinted by permssion of the publisher.

make these distinctions blinds us both to possible tensions among these distinct values and to the raising of the question of how best to realize them all so as to minimize that tension.

## 1. Opposition to Racism

The notion of "racism" is highly charged emotionally, and the term is used in contemporary parlance in a number of ways. There has been a well-documented increase in what are unquestionably racist incidents on campus, but also frequent yet more controversial *charges* of racism for any number of remarks and behavior. I want to suggest that the core meaning of "racism" is connected with the *domination or victimization* of some groups by others, and with the notion of the subordinate groups as inferior or less worthy than the dominant group. I will call an act or reaction "racist" if it expresses a notion of a member of a different racial group as being inferior.[3]

On this view the following phenomena, often called "racist" by many students, are not (necessarily, or usually) racist: (1) Departure from pure meritocratic justice: Affirmative action programs which prefer a minority student with lower test scores to a Caucasian student with higher ones. (2) Minority exclusiveness: Black students sitting together in the college dining room, thereby making it uncomfortable for whites to join them. (3) Stereotyping: A white student's unthinkingly assuming that a Latino student is from a lower socio-economic background than his own.

None of these actions express beliefs of superiority toward other groups; this is why they should not (I suggest) be called "racist." This does not mean that these actions and policies cannot be criticized as violating some other moral value appropriate to multi-racial communities, especially college communities. My point is precisely that there are several values relevant to a multiracial community—values which are distinct from one another.

While all racism is bad, on the definition of racism as dominance-attitude, not all manifestations of racism are *equally* bad. To oversimplify a complex issue here, racist attitudes which lend support to an existing structure of racism in which the possessor of the racist attitude is a member of a dominant group are worse than racist attitudes of a member of a subordinate group toward a member of a dominant group, for the latter do not support an existing structure of domination. For example, beliefs and doctrines of Caucasian inferiority to people of color are genuinely racist and worthy of condemnation. Yet these manifestations of racism toward whites are not *as* bad, dangerous, or condemnable as doctrines of white superiority to people of color (or attitudes expressing those doctrines), since the latter, and not the former, play a role in supporting actual structures of domination. The source of the value asymmetry here is that racism supporting existing subordination invokes and reinforces the social weight of this structure of dominance, bringing it down against its victim, and thus (other things being equal) more deeply shames and harms its victim than does subordinate-to-dominant racism, which does not carry that social and historical resonance. (The different force of the formally similar expressions "honkie" and "nigger" illustrates this point.) [4]

This asymmetry helps clarify the frequent mutual incomprehension between white and non-white students concerning racism. Many black students tend to think of racism solely as a phenomenon of whites against blacks or other non-whites. White students by contrast tend to equate—and condemn equally—all attitudes of racial insult, exclusion, or differentiation, by any racial group toward any other.

Aside from the point made earlier that some of what these white students call "racism" is not actually racism (according to my account), each group holds part of the truth. The non-white students see that the core and most socially dangerous phenomenon of racism is the actual, historical domination or victimization of one group by another, and attitudes of superiority (whether conscious or not) which directly support that domination. Many white students fail entirely to see this, not acknowledging—or not acknowledging the significance of—continuing subordinate status (in the United States) of people of color.

The white students, on the other hand, are correct to see clearly that *all* manifestations of racial contempt and superiority are worthy of condemnation, precisely because they are the *sorts* of attitudes which do underpin racial subordination. The non-white students' attitude has the effect of entirely letting non-whites off the hook for objectionable attitudes of superiority or contempt toward other groups.[5]

To state briefly what is involved in learning to oppose racism, and in embodying that value in an educational community: There is a philosophical component involved in understanding why racism is wrong, involving among other things learning how racism damages its victims; but learning the psychological, sociological, economic, and historical dynamics of racism and of resistance to it are essential as well. Public condemnation of racism on the campus is also essential.

# 2. Multiculturalism

Like "racism," this is a term of great currency and imprecise usage. I will use it to encompass the following two components: (a) understanding and valuing one's own cultural heritage, and (b) having respect for and interest in the cultural heritage of members of groups other than one's own. Note that condition (b) takes multiculturalism beyond what is often referred to as "cultural pluralism"—a situation in which different groups are each turned inward into their own group, valuing and learning about their own cultural heritage but being indifferent to that of others. While the idea of cultural pluralism perhaps contains the notion of tolerance for and recognition of the right of others to pursue their own cultural exploration and learning, "multiculturalism" as I am understanding it goes beyond this to encompass a positive interest in and respect for other cultures.

Often the initial association with "cultural diversity" or "multiculturalism"—for example when implying a policy to diversify the curriculum—is as (1) giving non-Caucasian students an understanding of and validation of their own cultural heritages (and thereby also broadening the sense of inclusion in the university's intellectual enterprise), and (2) expanding Caucasian students' intellectual horizons and reducing their ethnocentrism. Yet these two albeit crucial goals do not comprise the whole of what I mean by "multiculturalism." For in addition, my definition implies that members of *every* group (whites and non-whites alike) be involved in overcoming their own ethnocentrism, one possible curricular implication being that every student ought to study, say, two cultures other than her own.

Bypassing for this short presentation further difficulties regarding the definition of multiculturalism (e.g., what constitutes a "culture," which cultures should count for curricular and noncurricular attention, how respect for different cultures is consistent with criticism of them), I want to focus on how what I have called *multiculturalism* is a distinct value from what I have called *opposition to racism*, yet how both are essential in a multiracial community. First, each involves looking at the same group through distinct lenses. From the viewpoint of anti-racism, groups are divided into dominant and subordinate. From an anti-racist perspective, to study for example Native Americans or African Americans involves looking at the way these groups have been oppressed undermined, damaged, and the like by white America, at the beliefs and policies which have supported this mistreatment, and at the subordinate group's resistance to this subordination. It is to study subordinate groups primarily in their role as victims and resisters.

By contrast, to learn about cultural groups from a multicultural perspective involves studying the group's customs, rituals, language, systems of thought and religion, forms of cultural expression, accomplishments and contributions to the wider societies of which they are a part, and the like. The contrast resides not so much in distinct aspects of the groups in question focused on by the multicultural *versus* the anti-racist perspective; for subordinate groups' forms of cultural expressions are often so intimately bound up with their oppressed status and history that no simple delineation is possible. (Consider, for example, Afro-American music, Jewish humor.) The point is that both anti-racism and multiculturalism bring an analytical perspective on the study of cultural groups that the other lacks.

"Multiculturalism" is the preferred rubric of many educators.[6] But multiculturalism without anti-racism projects a world (or society) of cultural groups, each with its own way of life, forms of cultural expression, accomplishments and the like, all existing on something like an equal level. While this sense of equality—to teach and learn informed respect for every culture—may be appropriately (if only roughly) seen as an appropriate aspiration taken purely by itself, it obscures the fact that in our world and our society some of these cultures have been subordinated, undermined, and mistreated by other ones. It is as if one could just affirm that each group is equal, without taking into account the fact that in the world they are not treated as equal; it is this lack of equality that the anti-racist perspective keeps before us.

At the same time, the anti-racist perspective is also by itself incomplete. First, seeing a culture in terms of its victimization—or even its victimization and its resistance to that victimization—is an only partial perspective on that culture, omitting (or omitting important dimensions of) cultural expression and accomplishment. Second, the value perspective of anti-racism is itself only partial. To see that racism is wrong—and to firmly believe that it is wrong—is not the same as, and does not even require, actually having a positive appreciation for the culture of the subordinate group. In fact it is possible to be genuinely anti-racist while knowing little about the cultures of different groups that have been discriminated against. For example, many European, Christian, rescuers of Jews during the Nazi occupation expressed a fully anti-racist outlook in attempting their noble and dangerous rescue efforts; but few had genuine respect for Jews as a distinct cultural/religious group.[7]

While I have been arguing for the distinctness of anti-racism and multiculturalism as goals and values, they are also, or can be, mutually supportive. Learning to value a different culture can certainly help to bring home to a student the wrongness of that culture's mistreatment (even if the student were already in agreement on the abstract point that racism is wrong). It can awaken students for whom opposition to racism does not run very deep to the humanity of others—in its particular manifestation in the culture being studied. Both anti-racism and multiculturalism involve taking those outside one's own group seriously. Though they do so in different ways, both have the power to combat egoism and ethnocentrism.

## 3. Sense of Community, Connection, or Common Humanity

In addition to exemplifying the values of opposition to racism and multiculturalism, one also wants the college community to constitute and to foster a crossracial sense of connection or community. At first glance, this might not seem a distinct value. For isn't opposition to racism grounded in a sense of common humanity? Isn't racism wrong because it violates that common humanity? And doesn't the mutual respect involved in multiculturalism also express a sense of community?

But a sense of (cross-racial) community is, I want to argue, a distinct value. For a genuinely anti-racist individual does not necessarily have a sense of connection to those of another race, even while she or he regards those others as equals. For this sense of community can be negated not only by regarding others as *inferior* but simply by experiencing them as "other," as apart from, distant from, oneself, as persons one does not feel comfortable with because they are not members of one's own group.

It seems clear that many college students do not feel a genuine or full sense of cross-racial community, even though these same students are not racist in the sense defined here; they do not regard the other groups as inferior. Yet to be a genuine *community*, and not just a collection of people seeing each others as equals, a learning community must embody more than anti-racism.

There are ways of teaching and learning about racism which may fail to create, or even to hinder, a cross-racial sense of community. These ways reinforce a "we/they" consciousness in both the white and the non-white students; for example, never mentioning whites who stood against racism but projecting simply a (not really incorrect, but only partial) image of racism as "white oppressing black." It is undoubtedly true that learning about racism and why it is wrong has the inherent potentiality to undermine or strain this sense of connection. And classes on this subject might find ways within the pedagogical structure of the class to meliorate that effect—for example by having cross-racial groups work on class projects. Ultimately, however, such classes are necessary to help reconstruct or create a sense of community at a more informed level. Without a firm anti-racist component, any sense of cross-racial community will fail to involve true equals.

A sense of (cross-racial) connection is distinct from multiculturalism as well, even though multiculturalism teaches respect for others. The more minimal condition of valuing one's own culture and tradition goes nowhere toward creating a sense of cross-racial community, and its inward-turning can serve to undermine that connection (though at the same time for some minority students this aspect of multiculturalism might be a necessary condition for their being able to experience a sense of connection with white students—from a base of cultural self-respect.)

Even including the second condition of multiculturalism (respect for other cultures) does not guarantee a sense of community. For there are ways of presenting other cultures which can simultaneously promote a sense of respect yet of distance from members of that culture—for example placing too much emphasis on the self-enclosed, self-coherent, and differentness of each culture. Such a presentation would be *intellectually* deficient in not recognizing the multiplicity within each culture, its changes over time, its influences from other cultures, and (in most cases) values or elements it shares with other cultures. But my point here is that this intellectual error also has the unfortunate moral effect of helping to create or perpetuate among students a sense of distance between members of different cultures.

Recognizing these potentially divisive or distancing effects of both anti-racism and multiculturalism has been one source of opposition to both of them. "Why don't we just emphasize commonalities among our students, and reinforce them through a curriculum emphasizing a common Western and national tradition," say some (for example, occasionally in the "Point of View" column of the *Chronicle of Higher Education*). But ignoring both racism and genuinely culturally distinct sources of identity will not make these go away. Moreover, as I have tried to argue, both anti-racism and multiculturalism represent distinct and worthy goals, which an educational community must uphold and institutionalize. Any sense of community in the absence of a recognition of these values will in any case be a false and deceptive one.

What is necessary, I suggest, is to take seriously the three distinct goals, to recognize that it may not always be possible to realize all simultaneously, but to search for ways—in the curriculum, the classroom, and the organization of life on campus—to minimize the conflict among them, and to teach those values in ways that do mutually enhance one another to the greatest extent possible.

What I have presented here is a mere sketch of a nest of complex philosophical and value issues concerning multi-racial college classrooms and communities. Philosophy should not cede the discussion of these issues to social scientists, historians, and literature teachers, as we have tended to do. There is clarificatory and constructive work to be done here to which philosophy brings a necessary perspective. That work needs to be done in various courses in moral, social, and political philosophy, as well as in contributions to campus-wide debate.

## Endnotes

1. Carnegie Foundation For the Advancement of Teaching, *Campus Life: In Search of Community* (1990).

2. For example, the excellent Carnegie study mentioned above takes up racial/cultural issues primarily in its "A Just Community" chapter, misleadingly implying a conceptual unity to the distinct issues of access and retention, ignorance of groups and traditions other than one's own, outright discrimination, and minority in-group exclusiveness.

3. To simplify, I will continue to use the language of "dominant/subordinate," though this by-passes not insignificant differences among the terms "subordination," "victimization," "exploitation," "oppression," being "dominated," being "discriminated against," being "mistreated," being an "object of injustice"—all of which terms are used in this context.

4. This too-brief account of moral asymmetries in manifestations of racism is spelled out in my (unpublished) talk in the "Ethics and Society" Lecture Series, Stanford University, April 1990.

5. Note that the forgoing analysis does not concern racism of one subordinate or vulnerable group toward another—e.g., Koreans toward blacks, or blacks toward Jews. This complex matter is discussed in the manuscript mentioned in the previous footnote.

6. Cf. the excellent article defending multicultural education, but in distinction from and even denial of the anti-racist perspective by Diane Ravitch, "Diversity and Democracy: Multicultural Education in America," *American Educator* (Spring 1990).

7. On this see the L. Blum "Altruism and the Moral Value of Rescue: Resisting Persecution, Racism, and Genocide," in L. Baron, L. Blum, D. Krebs, P. Oliner, S. Oliner and Z. Smolenska, *Embracing the Other: Philosophical, Psychological, and Historical Perspectives on Altruism* (New York: NYU Press, 1992).

# Journal/Discussion Questions

✍ *As a college student, you are involved in a community that is probably multiracial and multicultural. What are the most important values for people on your campus? How does this relate to Blum's values?*

1. Blum says that "not all manifestations of racism are *equally* bad." What makes some manifestations of racism worse than others?

2. What does Blum mean by *multiculturalism*? What is the difference between *multiculturalism* and *opposition to racism*?

Why does each perspective need to be complemented by the other?

3. Some critics of multiculturalism ask, "Why don't we just emphasize commonalities among our students, and reinforce them through a curriculum emphasizing a common Western and national tradition?" How does Blum reply to this question? In what ways do you agree with his reply? Disagree?

4. What other values, if any, do you think are essential to a multicultural community?

# QUESTIONS FOR DISCUSSION AND REVIEW

## Where Do You Stand Now?

### Instructions

You have already answered the following questions in your moral problems self-quiz at the beginning of this book. Now that you have studied the material in this section, take a moment to answer the same questions again.

| | | | | | |
|---|---|---|---|---|---|
| *Strongly Agree* | *Agree* | *Undecided* | *Disagree* | *Strongly Disagree* | |

### *Chapter 4: Race and Ethnicity*

16. ❏ ❏ ❏ ❏ ❏   African Americans are still often discriminated against in employment.

17. ❏ ❏ ❏ ❏ ❏   Affirmative action helps African Americans and other minorities.

18. ❏ ❏ ❏ ❏ ❏   Racial separatism is wrong.

19. ❏ ❏ ❏ ❏ ❏   Hate speech should be banned.

20. ❏ ❏ ❏ ❏ ❏   We should encourage the development of racial and ethnic identity.

Compare your answers to the present self-quiz with the answers to the initial self-quiz. How, if at all, have your answers changed? How have the *reasons* for your answers changed?

## Journal/Discussion Questions

✍ *In light of the readings in this chapter, would you change the way in which you understand any of your personal experiences in regard to issues of race or ethnicity?*

1. Do you think that racially based injustices still occur in our society? If so, how do you think these can best be rectified and eliminated in the future?

2. What is your vision of a future ideal society in the United States in regard to the issues of race and ethnicity? How does that ideal relate to some of the ideals we have seen in this chapter? How do you think we can best move toward your ideal? What are the greatest possible objections to your ideal?

# FOR FURTHER READING:
# A BIBLIOGRAPHICAL GUIDE
# TO RACE AND ETHNICITY

## Review Article

Bernard R. Boxill's "Racism and Related Issues," *Encyclopedia of Ethics*, ed. Lawrence and Charlotte Becker (New York: Garland, 1992), vol. II, pp. 1056–1059, provides an excellent overview of work on race and related issues.

## Racism

There is an extensive and often powerful *literature dealing with the prevalence of racism in our society.* Derrick Bell's *Faces at the Bottom of the Well: The Permanence of Racism* (New York: Basic Books, 1992) provides a penetrating look at the pervasiveness of racism in the United States today. Patricia J. Williams's *The Alchemy of Race and Rights* (Cambridge, MA: Harvard University Press, 1991) is part autobiography, part feminist legal philosophy, and part cultural critique. Cornel West's *Race Matters* (Boston: Beacon Press, 1993) and his *Prophetic Thought in Postmodern Times* (Monroe, ME: Common Courage Press, 1993) are both well-argued analyses by one of the foremost contemporary African American thinkers. Shelby Steele's *The Content of Our Character: A New Vision of Race in America* (New York: HarperCollins, 1990) offers a much more conservative interpretation of these phenomena. Stephen L. Carter's *Reflections of an Affirmative Action Baby* (New York: Basic Books, 1991) stresses the ambiguity of affirmative action for African Americans. *Lure and Loathing: Essays on Race, Identity, and the Ambivalence of Assimilation*, ed. Gerald Early (New York: Penguin Press, 1993) contains a number of insightful autobiographical essays on the ambivalence toward assimilation experienced by many contemporary African Americans. Naomi Zack's *Race and Mixed Race* (Philadelphia: Temple University Press, 1993) offers a perceptive analysis of many of the issues surrounding mixed race in our society.

Several excellent *anthologies* contain shorter selections on these issues. See, especially, *Racism in America: Opposing Viewpoints*, ed. William Dudley (San Diego, CA: Greenhaven Press, 1991), which contains an excellent selection of largely popular pro-and-con pieces on a number of topics related to racism; *Taking Sides: Race and Ethnicity*, ed. Richard C. Monk (Guilford, CN: Dushkin, 1994), which treats a wide range of issues relating to ethnicity as well as race; *Race, Class, and Gender in the United States*, 3rd ed., ed. Paula S. Rothenberg (New York: St. Martin's Press, 1995), which is a gold mine of eloquent selections; *Bigotry, Prejudice, and Hatred: Definitions, Causes, and Solutions*, ed. Robert M. Baird and Stuart E. Rosenbaum (Buffalo: Prometheus Books, 1993), which contains an number of excellent philosophical selections; and *Anatomy of Racism*, ed. David Theo Goldberg (Minneapolis: University of Minnesota Press, 1990), which contains pieces by Appiah, Outlaw, Fanon, Barthes, Kristeva, Said, Goldberg, and Gates. The transcript of a two-day conference on "Race and Racism" is printed in *Salmagundi*, nos. 104–105 (Fall 1994–Winter 1995), 3–155; this consists of a roundtable discussion including

Orlando Patterson, Christopher Lasch, Dinesh D'Souza, Anthony Appiah, Jean Elshtain, David Rieff, Michelle Moody-Adams, Norman Birnbaum, and Gerald Early. See also *Women of Color in U.S. Society*, ed. Maxine Baca Zinn and Bonnie Thornton Dill (Philadelphia: Temple University Press, 1994), a collection of sixteen essays, largely from social scientific standpoints.

Among the specifically *philosophical approaches to racism* and related issues, see the issue of *Philosophia* [vol. 8, no. 2–3 (November 1978)] that contains several articles on racism, including Marcus George Singer, "Some Thoughts on Race and Racism," 153–183; Kurt Baier, "Merit and Race," 121–151; and Peter Singer, "Is Racial Discrimination Arbitrary?" 185–203; see also the double issue of *Philosophical Forum* [vol. 9, nos. 2–3 (1977–78)], entitled "Philosophy and the Black Experience" and the triple issue, "African-American Perspectives and Philosophical Traditions" [vol. XXIV, nos. 1–3 (Fall–Spring, 1992–1993)]. See Kwama Anthony Appiah, "Illusions of Race," *In My Father's House: Africa in the Philosophy of Culture* (New York: Oxford University Press, 1992), pp. 28–46, for a discussion of the slipperiness of the concept of race.

On the relationship between *racism and sexism*, see Richard A. Wasserstrom, "On Racism and Sexism," in *Today's Moral Problems*, 3rd ed., ed. Richard A. Wasserstrom (New York: Macmillan, 1985), pp. 1–28; and Laurence Thomas, "Sexism and Racism: Some Conceptual Differences," *Ethics* 90 (January 1980), 239–247.

Claims of racially based differences in *intelligence* have been frequent over the ages. In recent times, see Arthur Jenson, "How Much Can We Boost I.Q. and Scholastic Achievement?" *Harvard Educational Review* 39, no. 1 (1969), 1–123; William Schockley, "Dysgenecs, Geniticity, and Raciology," *Phi Delta Kappan* (January 1972), 297–307; and, most recently, Charles Murray and Richard Herrnstein, *The Bell Curve* (New York: Free Press, 1994). Equally common have been strong critiques of such connections, including Steven Jay Gould, *Ever Since Darwin* (New York: W. W. Norton, 1977) and Ashley Montagu, *Man's Most Dangerous Myth: The Fallacy of Race,* 4th ed. (Cleveland: World, 1964).

## Multiculturalism

Some of the initial articles on multiculturalism are to be found in *Debating P.C.*, ed. Paul Berman (New York: Laurel, 1992) and *Culture Wars: Opposing Viewpoints*, ed. Fred Whitehead (San Diego: Greenhaven Press, 1994). For perceptive comments on these issues, see Henry Louis Gates, Jr., *Loose Cannons: Notes on the Culture Wars* (New York: Oxford University Press, 1993). Among the critics of multiculturalism are, Arthur M. Schlesinger, Jr., *The Disuniting of America* (New York: W. W. Norton, 1992), William J. Bennett, *The De-Valuing of America* (New York: Summit Books, 1992), Dinesh D'Souza, *Illiberal Education: The Politics of Race and Sex on Campus* (New York: Vintage, 1992), and Robert Hughes, *Culture of Complaint* (New York: Oxford University Press, 1993).

For an excellent discussion of the philosophical and political dimensions of multiculturalism, see Amy Gutmann, "The Challenge of Multiculturalism in Political Ethics," *Philosophy and Public Affairs* 22, no. 3 (1993), 171–206 and the essays in *Defending Diversity: Contemporary Philosophical Perspectives on Pluralism and Multiculturalism*, ed. Lawrence Foster and Patricia Herzog (Amherst, MA: University of Massachusetts Press, 1994). For a philosophically sophisticated account of the question of identity within this context, see Charles Taylor, *Multiculturalism and "The Politics of Recognition,"* with commentary by Amy Gutman, Steven C. Rockefeller, Michael

Walzer, and Susan Wolf (Princeton: Princeton University Press, 1992). On the issue of identity, see also the papers by Anthony Appiah and others at the APA Symposium on Gender, Race, and Ethnicity, *Journal of Philosophy* 87, no. 10 (October 1990), 493–499. See also the articles on multiculturalism and philosophy that appeared in *Teaching Philosophy* 14, no. 2 (June 1991).

The issue of *banning hate speech* has received a lot of attention in the past decade. Some of the most influential essays are gathered together in Mari J. Matsuda, et al., *Words That Wound: Critical Race Theory, Assaultive Speech, and the First Amendment* (Boulder, CO: Westview Press, 1993) and Henry Louis Gates, Jr., et al., *Speaking of Race, Speaking of Sex, Hate Speech, Civil Rights, and Civil Liberties*, with an introduction by Ira Glesser (New York: New York University Press, 1994); see also Gates's "Let Them Talk: Why Civil Liberties Pose No Threat to Civil Rights," *The New Republic* 209, no. 12–13 (September 20, 1993), 37 ff.; Andrew Altman, "Liberalism and Campus Hate Speech: A Philosophical Examination," *Ethics* 103, no. 2 (January 1993), 302–317. See also Catharine A. MacKinnon, *Only Words* (Cambridge: Harvard University Press, 1993).

## Affirmative Action

There are a number of excellent *anthologies* dealing with the issue of affirmative action. These include *Social Justice and Preferential Treatment*, ed. William T. Blackstone and Robert Heslep (Athens: University of Georgia Press, 1976), *Equality and Preferential Treatment*, ed. Marshall Cohen, Thomas Nagel, and Thomas Scanlon (Princeton: Princeton University Press, 1977); *Affirmative Action and the University: A Philosophical Inquiry*, ed. Steven M. Cahn (Philadelphia: Temple University Press, 1993); *Reverse Discrimination*, ed. Barry R. Gross (Buffalo: Prometheus Books, 1977); *Equal Opportunity*, ed. Norman E. Bowie (Boulder, CO: Westview Press, 1988); *Discrimination, Affirmative Action, and Equal Opportunity: An Economic and Social Perspective*, ed. by W. E. Block and M. A. Walker (Vancouver, BC: Fraser Institute, 1981), which includes contributions by Gary Becker, Thomas Sowell, and Kurt Vonnegut, Jr.; *Racial Preference and Racial Justice: The New Affirmative Action Controversy*, ed. Russell Nieli (Washington, DC: Ethics and Public Policy Center, 1991); and, most recently, *Debating Affirmative Action: Race, Gender, Ethnicity, and the Politics of Inclusion*, ed. and with an introduction by Nicolaus Mills (New York: Delta, 1994).

Among *books* arguing one side of this issue, see especially Bernard R. Boxill, *Blacks and Social Justice* (Totowa, NJ: Rowman & Allanheld, 1984); Gertrude Ezorsky, *Racism and Justice: The Case for Affirmative Action* (Ithaca: Cornell University Press, 1991); Robert K. Fullinwider, *The Reverse Discrimination Controversy: A Moral and Legal Analysis* (Totowa, NJ: Rowman & Littlefield, 1980); Nathan Glazer, *Affirmative Discrimination: Ethnic Inequality and Public Policy* (New York: Basic Books, 1975); Nicholas Capaldi, *Out of Order: Affirmative Action and the Crisis of Doctrinaire Liberalism* (Buffalo, NY: Prometheus Books, 1985); Frederick R. Lynch, *Invisible Victims: White Males and the Crisis of Affirmative Action* (New York: Greenwood Press, 1989); Alan H. Goldman, *Justice and Reverse Discrimination* (Princeton, NJ: Princeton University Press, 1979); Barry R. Gross, *Discrimination in Reverse: Is Turnabout Fair Play?* (New York: New York University Press, 1978); Michael Rosenfeld, *Affirmative Action and Justice: A Philosophical and Constitutional Inquiry* (New Haven: Yale University Press, 1991); and Iris Marion

Young, *Justice and the Politics of Difference* (Princeton: Princeton University Press, 1990), especially the chapter on "Affirmative Action and the Myth of Merit," pp. 192–225.

Among the many important *philosophical articles* on this set of topics, see W. Blackstone, "Reverse Discrimination and Compensatory Justice," *Social Theory and Practice* 3 (1975), 258–271; Bernard R. Boxill's "The Morality of Reparations," *Social Theory and Practice* 2 (1972), 113–124 and "The Morality of Preferential Hiring," *Philosophy and Public Affairs* 7 (1978), 246–268; H. McGary, Jr., "Justice and Reparations," *Philosophical Forum* 9 (1977–1978), 250–263; Thomas Nagel, "Equal Treatment and Compensatory Discrimination," *Philosophy and Public Affairs* 2 (1973), 348–363; and Thomas E. Hill, Jr., "The Message of Affirmative Action," *Social Philosophy and Policy* 8 (Spring 1991), 108–129.

# 5

# Gender

**Videotape:**

     *Topic:*   Sexual Harassment in the Workplace
    *Source:*  *Nightline* (October 9, 1991)
   *Anchors:*  Ted Koppel; Jeff Greenfield

# EXPERIENTIAL ACCOUNTS

### Elizabeth L'Hommedieu and Frances Conley, M.D.
### "Walking Out on the Boys"

*One of the first board-certified female neurosurgeons in the United States, Frances Conley was a tenured professor of surgery at Stanford Medical School. She submitted her resignation because of the cumulative effects of sexism. She later withdrew her resignation after disciplinary action was taken against one of her male colleagues. Elizabeth L'Hommedieu conducted the interview for* Time.

*In this interview, Dr. Conley discusses some of the instances of "gender insensitivity" that led her to submit her resignation to Stanford Medical School and some of the ways in which such sexism might be mitigated.*

**Q.** After 16 years as a professor at Stanford, you resigned abruptly, charging what you called "gender insensitivity" on the part of male colleagues. Most people interpreted that to mean sexual harassment. Were you sexually harassed?

**A.** I am not talking about sexual harassment. I think harassment is too volatile a term. Sexism is one way of describing it. It is a pervasive attitude problem. The examples I can give will seem trivial, but they are real, and they do affect a person who has a professional life. If I am in an operating room, I have to be in control of the team that is working with me. That control is established because people respect who I am and what I can do. If a man walks into the operating room and says, "How's it going, honey?" what happens to my control? It disappears because every woman who is working in that room with me has also been called "honey" by this same guy, and it means all of a sudden I don't have the status of a surgeon in control of the case being done. I have suddenly become a fellow "honey."

**Q.** Surely there is more to it than being called "honey." Are there any other examples?

**A.** When I was younger I would be repeatedly asked to bed by fellow doctors. This would always happen in front of an audience. It was always done for effect. Another common example is that if I have a disagreement with my male counterparts, I generally tend to get the label of being "difficult" because I am suffering from PMS syndrome or because I am "on the rag." That is a gender-identification problem. You can't say that to a male counterpart who disagrees with you. These men tend to use the female image and those things that are perceived by society as making women inferior, i.e., the fact that we are different biologically, and they make that the focus of their dealing with me. I define that as sexism. It is not sexual harassment. I have had male doctors run their hands up my leg, never in an operating room, but in meetings. It is always done for an audience. Two months ago, I stood up to leave a meeting of all men and me, and as I stood up one of them said to me, "Gee, I can see the shape of your breasts, even through your white coat." I am sorry, but to me that is not right.

**Q.** Why wouldn't men do this to you simply because you are an attractive woman?

**A.** I have analyzed it, and I believe it's because they cannot see me as a peer. They have to establish a relationship that makes me inferior to them. The one they can immediately grab onto is a sexual relationship where the man is supposed to be dominant and the woman subservient.

**Q.** You've said twice now that these sexist remarks are made in front of an audience. Why would that be?

**A.** They have to show their peers that they do not accept this woman as an equal.

**Q.** You have been a surgeon for 25 years. Why did you tolerate this kind of treatment for so long?

**A.** In order for a female to get taken into the club, which is necessary in order to get cases and to get trained, you have to become a member. I decided that I would go along because I wanted to get to where I wanted to be. I really wanted to be a neurosurgeon. I thought I could be a good neurosurgeon. Had I made an issue of some of the things that were happening during the time that I was a resident, I wouldn't have gotten to where I am.

**Q.** How pervasive do you think this kind of treatment of female doctors is?

**A.** The vast majority of men that I have worked with—and there have been a lot of them—are wonderful, warm, supportive human beings who make me feel good about me when I am with them. It is just a few bad apples, but those bad apples can make you feel pretty small.

**Q.** Are all the "bad apples" concentrated in the Stanford neurosurgery department?

**A.** No, they are not. I would say they are much more concentrated in the surgery department across all specialties rather than in, say, pediatric medicine or anesthesia.

**Q.** What do you think you have accomplished by resigning?

**A.** First, I will be able to rebuild myself and regain my self-dignity. When I resigned, I had not intended to make a statement. As it turned out, I did, because I wrote a letter to a local newspaper, and that does make a statement. Many media people said, "You are so naive." I really had not anticipated the reaction to the editorial I wrote. I have been amazed. It is like an abscess that has been festering for years. It's been getting bigger and bigger. What I did was throw a scalpel at it and opened it. Now there is pus running all over the floor. What I have done, I hope, is help others open up a dialogue about this. If we can get men and women to start talking to one another about what gender insensitivity means, then we will have accomplished a great deal.

**Q.** The day after you resigned, you attended a student-faculty senate meeting at which one student described a teacher's using a sex doll to "spice up" a lecture, and another student said her breasts had been fondled. This must have struck a chord with you.

**A.** I think the thing that hit me the most was realizing that these were medical students complaining, and they are having these kinds of problems in their learning place, where they are supposed to be free to learn and to train to become professionals. This is a pervasive, global problem for women who are trying to get into professional careers. I think the reason it is coming out is because of the critical numbers. Since close to 50% of Stanford's medical classes can be women, when you do something in a class that is sexist in nature, you're offending not four people but 40.

**Q.** Stanford President Donald Kennedy has just brought disciplinary charges of sexual harassment and professional misconduct against a male cardiology professor. The charges are based on complaints that two female medical students filed with the university several months prior to your resignation. Do you think your resignation played a part in the university's decision to take action?

**A.** No. I do not believe that my situation influenced this decision. I know nothing about this case. I have enough faith in the people who run the university to feel that they are doing what is right regardless of whether or not I have made a flap. I do not think that Kennedy or any other people would have taken my resignation into account.

**Q.** You have said that the structure of medicine was set up for men by men. How do you think medicine would differ were it to be set up by women?

**A.** It would be far less dictatorial. It would be management by committee—by teamwork. Uniformly, my operating room is a team, and I believe this to be true of most women's O.R.s. The people who work with me are respected, professional, and do a job. We are all doing a job to reach a common goal, and that is to take good care of that patient. I think the nurses feel as if they have tremendous self-worth when they are in my O.R. There are lots of pleases and lots of thank yous. My operating room is a happy environment.

**Q.** Where does Stanford President Donald Kennedy stand on all this?

**A.** I have spoken with Kennedy, and I think he is very supportive. I am not sure he was aware that the gender-relationship problems were quite as significant as they are, and I think he has been most surprised by that. I know he has been getting an earful, because I have been getting copies of many letters that have been sent to him.

**Q.** You have said that with so many more females in medical schools across the country, their environments must change. What steps would you suggest?

**A.** One is to raise the level of consciousness about this type of behavior so that the consciousness is ongoing. The second is to be sure that the appointments that are made to executive positions are made with a great deal of care as to what that person's feelings are and how they relate not only to women but also to minorities, nurses and secretaries. It has to be an environment where people are respected for being people—where every person has self-worth and dignity. There would also be value in having more women in higher administrative positions in medical schools, where the decisions are being made.

**Q.** What has been your husband's reaction to your resignation?

**A.** He has been very supportive of it, primarily because he has been very aware of my unhappiness. He, too, has been flabbergasted by the supportive response and feels that it should have come out a long time ago.

**Q.** How has he handled all your private complaints over the years?

**A.** He has always let me be a very independent person, and that has been terribly important for me so that I could develop as a professional the way I wanted to. I think at times he has been distressed by my complaints. He will occasionally make sniping comments at people who he thinks have been demeaning to me, but he hasn't wanted to jeopardize that which I have done. He has been very careful not to be actively entered into the situation, but he has always been phenomenally supportive of me.

## Journal/Discussion Questions

✍ *If you had been in Dr. Conley's place, how would you have dealt with this problem?*

1. How does Conley distinguish between "gender insensitivity" and "sexual harassment"?

2. If you were the dean of Stanford Medical School, how would you have dealt with this issue in your school?

# AN INTRODUCTION
# TO THE MORAL ISSUES

As we turn to a consideration of the issue of gender, we discover that a wide range of moral issues presents itself. Some have to do with equality and the various ways in which women have been denied equality in our society: sex discrimination, sexist language, sexual harassment, rape, pornography, hate speech, and reproductive rights. Others have to do with issues of diversity: not only diverse ideals of the place of gender in society but also the issue of whether women have a distinctive moral voice. In this introduction, we shall survey these issues, seeking to illuminate what is at stake in each of these areas and highlighting some of the questions each of us must answer in regard to this issue. Then we shall turn to a discussion of competing models of the place of gender in society and conclude with a discussion of the means of remedying some of the problems discussed here. First, however, let's take a quick look at the ways in which the issue of gender is similar to, and different from, ethnicity.

## Gender and Ethnicity

The issue of gender raises a number of issues of diversity and equality that echo those encountered in our discussion of race and ethnicity, but there are also a number of important differences. Principal among these is that there is no natural attraction among the races in the same way that there is between the sexes and that there is nothing comparable to procreation, childbirth, and child rearing that binds the races together in the way that males and females are brought together for these purposes. Nor is separatism as viable an option as it is for races and ethnicities. There have never been purely male or female countries in the way in which we have countries that are composed predominantly of one racial group or another, nor did we ever have male and female neighborhoods in cities in the way in which we have had ethnic neighborhoods. Finally, there is another important difference between racially-based discrimination and gender-based discrimination: there are more indirect ways in which men suffer from discrimination against women who are in their family (wife, daughters, and other relatives) than there are ways in which one race suffers from discrimination against other races.

*In what ways do issues of gender differ from those of ethnicity?*

Yet the types of discrimination that women and racial minorities have suffered show striking similarities, and the remedies proposed to rectify these injustices also overlap in important ways. Although non–African American women were not enslaved in the way that both African Americans males and females were, women not only lacked the vote until the twentieth century, but also lacked legal standing in other respects as well. Often unable to own property when married or to testify in court on their own behalf, women lacked many of the protections of the law accorded to white males. Even after achieving political equality through the vote, women often lacked legal protections when discriminated against and are still battling for economic equality.

# Defining the Problems: Issues of Sexism

Sexism is a notoriously difficult term to define precisely, but its overall elements are clear. It refers to both *attitudes* and *behavior.* Sexist attitudes are attitudes that hold that individuals, solely because of their gender, are "less than" their male or female counterparts. For example, although both are equally competent, Jane is seen by her employer as less competent than her co-worker John; the employer is exhibiting a sexist attitude. If the employer then goes ahead and, on the basis of this distorted perception, promotes John but does not promote Jane, then the employer is behaving in a sexist manner. Sexist *attitudes* refer to our perceptions and feelings; sexist *behavior* to our actions.

## Overt and Institutional Sexism

Just as we did with racism, we can distinguish between overt and institutional sexism. *Overt sexism* is the intentional discrimination against a person because of that person's gender. For example, if a person is denied a job because that person is a male or female, that is an act of overt sexism. In contrast to this, *institutional sexism* occurs when a person is (perhaps unintentionally) discriminated against because of factors that pertain to that person's gender. For example, in some college sports such as basketball and football, women may be underrepresented if teams were open to both male and female applicants; if athletic scholarship money was given only to those who made the team, the indirect result would be that far fewer women would receive athletic scholarships than men. Although there may be no intent to discriminate in athletic scholarships against women, the net result might be precisely such institutional sexism.

## Sexist Language

One of the more contentious areas of discussion in regard to sexism is language. There are two distinct aspects to this issue: (1) the gendered structure of our language and (2) its specific vocabulary. In regard to linguistic structure, many have pointed out that English, like many other languages, is gendered; we often are forced by our language to identify a person as either male or female, even when we don't know the person's gender. Since the masculine gender is the default gender in cases where we don't know, we usually supply the masculine pronouns and adjectives. It is very awkward to say, "The pioneer rode on his or her wagon." Instead, we usually say, "The pioneer rode on his wagon," thereby giving the false impression that the only pioneers are men. Advocates of a gender-neutral language have tried, with only partial success, to encourage us to use language in gender-neutral ways. This demands that we pay attention to our use of language, but that is usually something good. With some degree of care, it is usually possible to reformulate our language in gender-neutral ways. I have often used plural constructions in this book precisely for this reason.

Sexist vocabulary abounds in our language. Sometimes it is rooted in differential perceptions: a man is seen as "assertive," a woman behaving in exactly the same way is perceived as "aggressive." Sometimes the specific words tell us a lot. Obscene, transitive verbs describing sexual intercourse (e.g., "screw") are usually used in such a way as to place women as the direct object and are usually synonymous in English with "to harm or to hurt." This suggests a view of sexual intercourse that few of us would commend. Sexist language is often used to exert power. In the interview with Dr. Frances Conley, we see some of the ways in which her male colleagues used sexist language to intimidate and establish their own superior position of power.

Although it is easy to parody some attempts to eliminate sexist language, the point underlying such attempts is both clear and commendable. When we respect and care about someone, we speak both to them and about them in ways that manifest that respect and concern. In the final analysis, we try to avoid sexist language because we care about persons and respect them, and such language is incompatible with such caring and respect. If, on the other hand, we do not care for and respect others, our sexist language only solidifies and exacerbates that lack of caring and respect. The language is not the root problem, but the symptom of something deeper that has gone wrong. But just as it is valuable in medicine to reduce symptoms of disease, so too there is a value in reducing sexist language, even though such reductions are far from a cure for the underlying ailment.

## Sex Discrimination

Discrimination based on gender has certainly diminished over the years, but it still remains an important issue in American society. Although the Equal Rights Amendment was never ratified by the required number of states, there are a number of legal guarantees available to individuals, especially women, who are the objects of sex discrimination. Moreover, numerous affirmative action programs have helped to increase the representation of women in places where they had previously been discriminated against.

*Overt job discrimination.*   Overt discrimination, by which a woman is denied a job or promotion solely because she is a woman or is paid less than her male counterpart in the same job, has decreased significantly in recent years. In the 1960s, women made 59 cents for every dollar earned by men. In 1990, this figure was 72 cents, and, for younger women during that year, it was 80 cents. How much of this remaining discrepancy is due to discrimination and how much is due to other factors (women, on average, work fewer hours per week than their male counterparts, many have fewer years of work experience than men of the same age, some leave the job force earlier when the family no longer needs the second income, etc.) is unclear, but it is clear that the relative position of women to men in the marketplace—although still subordinate—is definitely improving. Those who are discriminated against in these ways have legal recourse, even without the ERA, and there is an increasingly wide consensus in American society that we ought not to discriminate against people on the basis of gender. Although we may fail to live up to our ideals in this area, clearly, equal pay for equal work has become one of our accepted ideals.

*Comparable worth.*   One of the more subtle ways in which sex discrimination occurs is when predominantly female occupations are paid less than comparable occupations whose employees are predominantly male. Examples come easily enough to mind: plumbers and truck drivers versus cleaning staff and secretaries. Although intuitively this seems true (at least to me), there are two significant problems in translating this intuition into something more concrete and effective. First, the notion of "comparable," although intuitively plausible, is very difficult to make precise. Second, many (especially market conservatives) are very wary of intervening in the market to regulate wages.

*Legal protection: theory and implementation.*    Finally, it is important to note that it is often insufficient simply to pass legislation prohibiting something like sex discrimination unless there is a monitoring and enforcement structure to implement the legislation. Often, the impact of the legislation can be undermined if there is insufficient funding for its implementation.

## Sexual Harrassment

Harassment in general consists of using undue and unwelcome *means*—usually short of outright violence—to pressure someone to some *end*, usually to do something that the harrassee does not want to do. Thus there are two crucial components of harassment: the means and the end. Workers might try to force a fellow worker to quit by pouring coffee in his locker, letting the air out of his car's tires, calling him on the phone repeatedly in the middle of the night. Such actions would be the means of harassment, while the end would be forcing the other worker to quit.

Sexual harassment is usually sexual in two senses: (1) the *end* is usually to pressure someone (usually a woman) to have sexual intercourse with the harasser; and (2) the *means* to this end are usually things such as repeated sexual innuendoes, unwanted fondling, showing pictures, and so on. Sometimes, however, the means may be comparatively unrelated to sex; they may be threats about losing one's job, a promotion, a raise, or something else that the harasser controls. Sometimes, too, the end may not even really be sexual: it may simply be about power. In the interview with Dr. Frances Conley, she speculates that her male harassers were primarily concerned with establishing their own dominance.

Several points need to be made about sexual harassment. First, most of us would agree that the less harassment in society, the better. This applies to all types of harassment, not just sexual harassment. Second, we are particularly wary of harassment of those who are most vulnerable to the intimidation of harassment: individuals of little power (usually women, often financially vulnerable) who have something (sex) that the harasser wants. Third, it is sometimes difficult to make judgments about incidents of harassment, especially when dealing with a single incident in isolation and without witnesses. However, in practice, harassment is often repeated and often done in front of other people. Fourth, sometimes appropriate expressions of sexual interest may cross the line into sexual harassment, either due to the insensitivity of the harasser or to the oversensitivity of the harassee.

Given these general points about harassment, the central question facing us as a society in this regard is the extent to which we want actively to discourage sexual harassment, to provide special protection to those who may be victimized by it, and to punish those who harass. Sexual harassment can be discouraged through educational programs (beginning in schools, continuing on the job), the media, and the like. This is by no means limited to government initiatives; individuals can decide to provide appropriate models for dealing with harassment in their personal and public lives,

> *What can we do to reduce sexual harassment in our society?*

in their business dealings, and so on. Potential victims can be afforded special protection through tough antiharassment laws and through vigorous prosecution of those laws. Yet again, this is not simply a matter of legislation. Individuals can speak out against harassment when they witness it, even though it does not directly affect them. Companies can have strong internal policies against it, and it can be a serious factor in personnel decisions. Finally, we can pass strong legislation at various levels of government that discourage and punish sexual harassment.

## Rape

One of the ways in which women's experience of the world differs from that of men is that it includes the possibility of rape as a much more omnipresent and real threat. Indeed, except for the unusual circumstances of homosexual rape in prisons, men are virtually free from this threat in their everyday lives. Women, however, encounter it lurking in the corners of their everyday world: a deserted parking lot late at night, a seldom-used staircase in an office building, getting one's keys out in order to open the front door of one's apartment.

No one defends rape, so that is hardly a moral issue. However, many things may contribute indirectly toward taking rape less seriously than we should—pornography, media depictions of violence against women, and so on—and certainly one of the moral issues is the extent to which these should be regulated in order to reduce the climate of violence toward women. Moreover, there are issues of conflicting rights in rape trials—the victim's right to protection versus the defendant's right to a strong defense—that bear directly on how women can bring charges of rape against an individual without having the trial itself become another ordeal of violation. Finally, there are important issues of definition. Date rape, for example, raises important issues about the definition of consent. Some feminists go further and see rape as a metaphor—indeed, almost a literal description—for typical interactions between men and women, but there is a danger in such claims. If many things that do not involve forced sexual intercourse are seen as rape, then the danger is that standard instances of rape will be taken less seriously.

For women to be as safe from rape as men, special measures seem appropriate in at least three areas. First, we should do whatever we can, consistent with the rights of free speech, to reduce the climate of violence against women. The focus here need not be on government restrictions, although those may have their place. A refusal to patronize things that advocate such violence (particular movies, rap music groups, authors, etc.) does not deny the right of free speech, it simply asserts the right to be opposed to the content of some free speech as morally wrong. Similarly, a personal willingness to stand up and speak out individually when one encounters such violence is crucial. Second, our criminal justice system must insure that accusers are not treated like criminals and that trials do not repeat the victim's violation. Much has been done in this area with teams specially trained to handle rape cases, but much remains to be done. If my house is burglarized, the principal issue is not whether I locked the front door securely enough; similarly, in rape cases the principal issue should not be the consent of the victim. Finally, if the purpose of punishment is (at least in part) deterrence, then every effort needs to be made to punish offenders in ways that minimize the chance of recurrence.

## Pornography

Supporters of increased respect for women find the issue of pornography particularly troubling. On the one hand, it is clear that most pornography that depicts women does so in ways that debase women and that often make them the objects of violence. Such depictions, many believe, contribute to an atmosphere of disrespect toward women and implicitly sanction violence toward women. On the other hand, most supporters of women's rights consider the right to free speech to be fundamental to our society, and, as a result, they are very wary of legislation that restricts freedom of speech. Indeed, they realize that there is no shortage of persons who are willing to censor feminist ideas and that encouraging restrictions in the case of pornography may well open the door to censorship of their own views. Furthermore, they realize that proposals to ban pornography often ally them politically with conservatives whom they oppose in many other respects.

Some feminists, most notably Catharine MacKinnon, have argued that sometimes words are like deeds and that the case for banning pornography rests in part on its status as an offensive action. Yet many have argued that it is dangerous to blur the distinction between words and deeds in the ways that MacKinnon suggests. To do so extends the concept of an offensive action too far, and the net result is that everything gets trivialized. If uttering a sexist epithet is viewed as an act of rape, then violent rape by a stranger would seem to be in the same category as sexist slurs. Both are objectionable, but they are so different in degree that it seems misleading to lump them into a single category.

## Reproductive Rights

One of the more controversial areas in regard to the status of women in society is the issue of reproductive rights. This encompasses a range of issues, including contraception and abortion and the responsibility of fathers.

*Pregnancy control.*    Advocates of women's rights maintain that one of the most important of women's rights is the right to choose whether and when to bear children. This right, they argue, can never be implemented unless women and girls of childbearing age have adequate access to reliable information about birth control and adequate access to the technology of birth control and, finally, the opportunity to use the means of birth control that they choose. This involves organizations and sometimes schools providing information, often at an early age when the risk of pregnancy is high, to all, but especially to females. It also involves providing contraceptive means (birth control pills, etc.), if requested. Finally, it involves discouraging any sexual relationships in which girls and women are not allowed to use the birth control means of their choice.

Opponents of such proposals often see them as conflicting with parental authority and as encouraging sexual behavior that they—that is, the opponents—would like to discourage. This is particularly an issue for parents with teen-age daughters, where issues of parental rights often conflict with adolescent rights. There is much greater agreement that adult women ought to be able to exert the level of control over pregnancy that they feel is appropriate.

*Abortion.*    Some feminists see abortion solely as an issue of women's rights, and they maintain that no woman ought to be forced to bear a child against her will. Whether the pregnancy resulted involuntarily, accidentally, or even by choice, strong advocates of women's reproductive rights maintain that a woman should be free to choose to terminate the pregnancy if she wishes. We have discussed this issue at length in Chapter 1.

## Women's Moral Voice

During the 1970s, while doing work on the psychology of moral development that originally had nothing to do with gender issues, Carol Gilligan gradually came to realize that the dominant psychological framework for understanding moral development (developed by Lawrence Kohlberg)[1] failed to illuminate women's psychological development in a satisfactory way. Indeed, trying to categorize females' responses to moral dilemmas within Kohlberg's framework, which was originally developed solely with male subjects in mind, was like trying to fit round pegs into square holes. Gilligan became increasingly interested in articulating the distinctive characteristics of females' moral experiences, and a series of her essays appeared in

*Do women speak in a different moral voice than men? If so, is it equal, better, or worse than that of men?*

1982 in the volume *In a Different Voice* (Harvard University Press). The book quickly struck a resonant chord with many scholars in a wide range of disciplines, and soon there was an extensive discussion of women's "voices" not only in morality, but in literature, religion, the natural sciences, the social sciences, and the arts.

Gilligan argues that whereas men typically think of moral issues in terms of rights, justice, fairness, and duty, women are much more likely to think of these same issues in terms of connectedness, caring, compromise, and interpersonal responsibility. Although the exact relationship between these two voices in Gilligan's view (are they separate but equal, complementary, antithetical, or is one superior to the other?) is unclear, her work has provoked a tremendous amount of research and speculation on gender differences, especially within the moral realm.

While many find Gilligan's work refreshing and liberating, others are disturbed by the ways in which her characterization of women's moral voices seems to echo a traditional stereotype of women as concerned more with feelings than rules, more concrete than abstract, more sympathetic than just. There are, in fact, two issues here. First, there are *empirical* questions about the accuracy of Gilligan's findings. These are the domain of moral psychologists. Second, there are *normative* questions about the validity of each of these voices, and those questions fall primarily in the realm of moral philosophy. To what extent, in other words, are each of these voices *right*? Patricia Ward Scaltsas' "Do Feminist Ethics Counter Feminist Aims?" provides a careful and insightful evaluation of these and many other issues related to Gilligan's work.

## Models of the Place of Gender in Society

Just as we saw that there was disagreement about the role of race in society, so, too, we find that there is a significant degree of disagreement about precisely what the role of gender ought to be in society. The fundamental question that we face here is how we envision a future ideal society in regard to gender. Would it be one in which men and women occupy relatively traditional roles such as were common a generation ago? Is it one in which all references to gender have been banished, a unisex society? Is it one in which we still have some traditional roles but individuals—whether male or female—are free to choose whatever roles they want? Let's turn to a closer consideration of each of these three models of the place of gender in society.

## The Traditional Model

Advocates of the traditional model of gender roles see the place of women as primarily in the home and the place of men as primarily in the workplace. Even within the home, the husband is seen as head of the family and the wife is viewed as subservient to him. For a man, his home is his castle; for his wife, the home is all too often something to be cleaned and a place of unpaid work. In the workplace, traditionalists usually—either explicitly in earlier times, or now implicitly—advocate a gender-based division of labor in which women occupy only low-paying (maids), menial (cleaning women), subservient (secretaries), and child-related (elementary school teachers) jobs that typically receive less pay than their male counterparts.

Critics of the traditional model argue that it places women in an inferior position in the home and in the workplace as well. Women's work in the home is unpaid, and their labor in the workplace is underpaid. Moreover, women's options are most severely limited in this model, and they are especially limited from jobs that bring wealth and power. Moreover, in an age when men are freer to divorce their wives in midlife and marry younger women after their family is grown, and in an age when all too many fathers ignore child support, women are especially vulnerable to financial abandonment in middle age. In a society that is reluctant to hire middle-aged people, especially those without a strong employment history, such women face great challenges when they try to return to the work force. Some critics of this model also add that the model is also injurious to men, forcing them into an emotionally-constricting gender-based stereotype that denies them the joys of close relationships and places the burdens of financial support squarely on their shoulders.

Defenders of the traditional model center around the necessity of this model for a strong family life and the importance of strong family life for society as a whole. Although talk about family values is often vague and misleading, there is clearly a sound point here: the most effective juncture for dealing with many widespread social problems is before they begin, and the best time to do this is when children are young and in the home. We shall return to a discussion of this topic below when we consider gender roles and the family.

## The Androgynous Model

At the other extreme from the traditional model, some have advocated a model of society in which gender would be as irrelevant as, for example, eye color presently is. Just as eye color makes no difference in job selection, salary, voting, child care, or anything else remotely similar, so, too—according to the androgynous model—gender should make no differences in these things either. Defenders of androgyny differ about how extensive the domain of the androgynous ought to be. The most extreme position, *strong androgyny*, maintains that sex- and gender-based distinctions ought to be eliminated whenever possible in all areas of life. *Weak androgyny* maintains that gender-based discrimination ought to be eliminated in the public realm (i.e., the workplace and the political realm), but in the private realm of personal relationships it may be unobjectionable.

Among the objections raised to androgyny, three stand out. First, many argue that strong androgyny is impossible. There are simply too many differences between men and women for it to be possible to fit all into the same inevitably constricting mold. Indeed, recent research—which is quickly echoed in pop psychology and therapy—seems to suggest that there are many such differences, including in areas such as communication styles. Trying to cram everyone into a single model would undo the progress we have made in understanding and appreciating our differences.

The merit of this claim will be discussed below in the section of the nature-nurture controversy. Second, many claim that, even if strong androgyny were possible, it is hardly desirable. Just as we seek to encourage diversity and difference in society as a whole, so too, such critics argue, we should try to encourage diversity and difference in the domain of gender. Finally, some have argued that strong androgyny is part of a larger view that sees men primarily as oppressors and women primarily as victims. This larger view, which Christina Hoff Sommers in *Who Stole Feminism?*[2] labels *gender feminism*, sees maleness as oppressive and envisions an androgynous society as banishing such oppressiveness.

Some defenders of strong androgyny reply to such criticisms by defending a weaker version of their position, which simply seeks to abolish sex-based stereotyping and prohibit, at least within the realm of work and politics, discrimination based on gender. At the juncture, androgyny comes increasingly close to the next model, which emphasizes the importance of freedom of choice for all persons.

## The Maximal Choice Model

Finally, many have argued in favor of a model that seeks to eliminate any gender-based restrictions on individual choice. In contrast to advocates of strict androgyny, supporters of the maximal choice model do not seek a unisex society. They are willing to accept that men and women may typically develop different personality traits and that there might even be typical differences in behavior. However, they stress the centrality of establishing a society that promotes *freedom of choice*, so that individuals can make whatever choices they want in both public and private life irrespective of their gender. Gender-based discrimination in the workplace and in the political realm would be abolished, and equally qualified men and women would have equal accessibility to any job, profession, or office they desire. Similarly, within the family, men and women would be equally free to occupy any combination of roles traditionally associated with either men or women.

Criticisms of this model come from both sides. Traditionalists maintain that this model leads to great confusion in roles for everyone, and that social coherence is reduced as a result. Strong androgynists claim that, unless freedom of choice is reinforced with a strong restructuring of gender-based societal roles and expectations, the "freedom" is illusory: people will be subtly shifted into roles that correspond to the majority's expectations. Only a more radical form of androgyny will establish the social order necessary to insure genuine freedom of choice.

## The Nature-Nurture Controversy

Obviously, the choice of models in this realm will depend in part on the extent to which a choice is possible. Some have argued that choice is limited by human nature, and that nature fixes (at least to some extent) our gender roles. Others have claimed that these roles are established primarily (perhaps even exclusively) through nurture and are thus open to change. Advocates of change support the nurture side of this controversy, while advocates of the status quo (or, in some cases, an idealized version of it) support the nature side of the debate.

Although this controversy obviously cannot be settled here, it is important to distinguish three questions when evaluating arguments in this area. First, to what extent do differences between the sexes actually exist? This is an empirical question best answered through careful research, especially in the natural and social sciences. Second, if differences do exist, what is their basis? Are they genetically-based, "hard-wired" differences that remain unaffected by environmental changes or are they part of our "software" that can be reprogrammed through changes in child rearing, education, and the like? This is also an empirical question, but a more difficult one since it is asking about the *causes* of certain empirical conditions, not simply whether the empirical conditions exist. Third, whether there are differences or not, we must ask whether there *ought* to be differences and, if so, what those differences ought to be.

### Gender Roles and the Family

The place of gender in the family is one of the most difficult and controversial areas in which to seek common ground. As we indicated above in the discussion of the traditional model of gender roles, women pay a high price in their lives for their commitment to family—often a higher price than their male counterparts. As women have sought more equal access to the rewards of the workplace and more equal distribution of the responsibilities of home and family life, many men and women have been forced to rethink the ideal of the family and the way in which responsibilities have been apportioned by gender.

*If we genuinely treat men and women equally, what happens to the family?*

As Susan Moller Okin shows in the selection from her *Justice, Gender, and the Family,* we would have to reorganize the family significantly if we were to make the family a just institution. In particular, responsibilities for the home and for children would have to be distributed evenly, and this entails a significant restructuring of roles. Such restructuring need not conflict with important social values, but it certainly involves a significant reordering of priorities and responsibilities for men.

## How Should We Try to Realize Our Ideal Society?

We have seen that, once we are concerned about gender equality, we must face a wide range of issues. Some of these are relatively specific: gender discrimination in employment, sexual harassment, and pornography. Some are more global in character: whether there are distinctive moral voices for men and women, what kind of gender roles we want to endorse in society.

As we develop a position on each of these issues, we must also ask how we can best move toward realizing that position. We have seen that, in regard to specific issues, some mixture of legislation and individual and group initiative seems to offer the best hope of a more just society. Just as we did in regard to issues of race and ethnicity, we can distinguish among (1) *strict equality legislation*, which seeks to insure that women are not treated any differently than men; (2) *special protection legislation*, which seeks to provide special protections to people (usually women) in especially vulnerable situations such as rape or sexual harassment; and (3) *affirmative action legislation*, which seeks to remedy inequalities through various types of affirmative action programs that are basically like those developed for race.

Yet it is important to see these specific issues within the larger context of our ideal for the place of gender in society, for it is our ultimate vision of the role of gender in society that guides our decisions on particular issues. What kind of a relationship do we envision between men and women in the future?

## Endnotes

1. Lawrence Kohlberg, *The Philosophy of Moral Development* (San Francisco: Harper & Row, 1981).
2. Christina Hoff Sommers, *Who Stole Feminism?* (New York: Simon and Schuster, 1994).

# THE ARGUMENTS

Susan M. Dodds, Lucy Frost, Robert Pargetter, and Elizabeth W. Prior
"Sexual Harassment"

*Susan Dodds is a lecturer in philosophy at the University of Wollongong; Lucy Frost is a reader in English at La Trobe University; Robert Pargetter is deputy vice-chancellor of Monash University; and Elizabeth Prior Honson is a senior lecturer in geography and environmental science at Monash University.*

*If we are to develop and enforce laws and policies that discourage sexual harassment, we must be able to define it clearly in a way that allows us to recognize it when it occurs. Dodds et al. argue, through a careful analysis of a series of examples, that it is impossible to define sexual harassment through reference to sex discrimination (Part 1), to negative consequences for the harassee (Part 2), to the misuse of power (Part 3), or to the mental states of the people involved (Part 4). If it is to be a useful concept, sexual harassment must be defined behaviorally, and Part 5 offers just such an account of sexual harassment as "behavior which is typically associated with a mental state representing an attitude which seeks sexual ends without any concern for the person from whom those ends are sought, and which typically produces an unwanted and unpleasant response in the person who is the object of the behavior."*

## As You Read, Consider This:

1. Evaluate the way Dodd et al. use examples. Are there any instances where you disagree with their analysis of the examples? Where you would offer counter-examples?

2. Are there any characteristics of sexual harassment that Dodd et al. reject as necessary but which you think are necessary characteristics of sexual harassment?

～

Mary has a problem. Her boss, Bill, gives her a bad time. He is constantly making sexual innuendoes and seems always to be blocking her way and brushing against her. He leers at her, and on occasion has made it explicitly clear that it would be in her own best interests to go to bed with him. She is the one woman in the office now singled out for this sort of treatment, although she hears that virtually all other attractive women who have in the past worked for Bill have had similar experiences. On no occasion has Mary encouraged Bill. His attentions have all been unwanted. She has found them threatening, unpleasant and objectionable. When on some occasions she has made these reactions too explicit, she has been subjected to unambiguously detrimental treatment. Bill has no genuinely personal feelings for Mary, is neither truly affectionate nor loving: his motivation is purely sexual.

Susan M. Dodds, et al., "Sexual Harassment," *Social Theory and Practice* 14, no. 2 (Summer 1988). Copyright © 1988 Social Theory and Practice. Reprinted by permission of the publisher and the authors.

Surely this is a paradigmatic case of sexual harassment. Bill discriminates against Mary, and it seems that he would also discriminate against any other attractive woman who worked for him. He misuses his power as an employer when he threatens Mary with sex she does not want. His actions are clearly against her interests. He victimizes her at present and will probably force her to leave the office, whatever the consequences to her future employment.

Not all cases of sexual harassment are so clear. Indeed, each salient characteristic of the paradigmatic case may be missing and yet sexual harassment still occurs. Even if all the features are missing, it could still be a case of sexual harassment.

We aim to explicate the notion of sexual harassment. We note that our aim is not to provide an analysis of the ordinary language concept of sexual harassment. Rather we aim to provide a theoretical rationale for a more behavioral stipulative definition of sexual harassment. For it is an account of this kind which proves to be clearly superior for policy purposes. It provides the basis for a clear, just and enforceable policy, suitable for the workplace and for society at large. Of course ordinary language intuitions provide important touchstones. What else could we use to broadly determine the relevant kind of behavior? But this does not mean that all ordinary language considerations are to be treated as sacrosanct. Sexual harassment is a concept with roots in ordinary language, but we seek to develop the concept as one suitable for more theoretical purposes, particularly those associated with the purposes of adequate policy development.

In brief we aim to provide an account which satisfies three desiderata. The account should:

a. show the connection between harassment in general and sexual harassment
b. distinguish between sexual harassment and legitimate sexual interaction
c. be useful for policy purposes.

## 1. Sexual Harassment and Sexual Discrimination

It seems plausible that minimally harassment involves discrimination, and more particularly, sexual harassment involves sexism. Sexual discrimination was clearly part of the harassment in the case of Mary and Bill.

The pull towards viewing sexual harassment as tied to sexual discrimination is strengthened by consideration of the status of most harassers and most harassees. In general harassers are men in a position of power over female harassees. The roles of these men and women are reinforced by historical and cultural features of systematic sexual discrimination against women. Generally men have control of greater wealth and power in our society, while women are economically dependent on men. Men are viewed as having the (positive) quality of aggression in sexual and social relations, while women are viewed as (appropriately) passive. These entrenched attitudes reflect an even deeper view of women as fundamentally unequal, that is in some sense, less fully persons than men. Sexual harassment, then, seems to be just one more ugly manifestation of the sexism and sexual inequality which is rampant in public life.

MacKinnon sees this connection as sufficient to justify treating cases of sexual harassment as cases of sexual discrimination.[1] Sexual discrimination, for MacKinnon, can be understood through two approaches. The first is the "difference approach," under which a "differentiation is based on sex when it can be shown that a person of the opposite sex in the same position is not treated the same." The other is the "inequality approach," which "requires no comparability of situation, only that a rule or practice disproportionately burden one sex because of sex."[2] Thus, even when no comparison can be made between the situation of male and female employees (for example, if the typing pool is composed entirely of women, then the treatment a woman in the pool receives cannot be compared with the treatment of a man in the same situation), if a rule or practice disproportionately burdens women, because they are women, that rule or practice is sexually discriminatory. For MacKinnon all cases of sexual harassment will be cases of sexual discrimination on one or other of these approaches.

Closer consideration reveals, however, that while discrimination may be present in cases of harassment, it need not be. More specifically while sexual discrimination may be (and often is) present in cases of sexual harassment, it is not a necessary feature of sexual harassment.

The fact that in most cases women are (statistically, though not necessarily) the objects of sexual harassment is an important feature of the issue of sexual harassment, and it means that in many cases where women are harassed, the harassment will involve sexual discrimination. However, sexual harassment need not entail sexual discrimination.

Consider the case of Mary A and Bill A, a case very similar to that of Mary and Bill. The only relevant difference is that Bill A is bisexual and is sexually attracted to virtually everyone regardless of sex, appearance, age or attitude. Perhaps all that matters is that he feels that he has power over them (which is the case no matter who occupies the position now occupied by Mary A). Mary A or anyone who filled her place would be subjected to sexual harassment.

The point of this variant case is that there appears to be no discrimination, even though there clearly is harassment. Even if it is argued that there is discrimination against the class of those over whom Bill A has power, we can still describe a case where no one is safe. Bill A could sexually harass anyone. This particular case clearly defeats both of MacKinnon's conceptual approaches to sexual discrimination; it is neither the case that Bill A treats a man in Mary A's position differently from the way in which he treats Mary A, nor is it the case that (in Bill A's office) the burden of Bill A's advances is placed disproportionately on one sex, because of that person's sex (for the purpose of sex, perhaps, but not on account of chromosomes).[3]

A different point, but one worth making here, is that there is a difference between sexual harassment and sexist harassment. A female academic whose male colleagues continually ridicule her ideas and opinions may be the object of sexist harassment, and this sexist harassment will necessarily involve sexual discrimination. But she is not, on this basis, the object of sexual harassment.

## 2. Negative Consequences and Interests

Perhaps sexual harassment always involves action by the harasser which is against the interests of the harassee, or has overall negative consequences for the harassee.

However, consider Mary B who is sexually harassed by Bill B. Mary B gives in, but as luck would have it, things turn out extremely well; Mary B is promoted by Bill B to another department. The long term consequences are excellent, so clearly it has been in Mary B's best interests to be the object of Bill B's attentions. One could also imagine a case where Mary B rejects Bill B with the (perhaps unintentional) effect that the overall consequences for Mary B are very good.

Crosthwaite and Swanton argue for a modification of this view. They urge that, in addition to being an action of a sexual nature, an act of sexual harassment is an action where there is no adequate consideration of the interests of the harassee. They in fact suggest that this is both a necessary and sufficient condition for sexual harassment.[4]

We think it is not sufficient. Consenting to sex with an AIDS carrier is not in an antibody-negative individual's best interests. If the carrier has not informed the other party, the antibody-positive individual has not given adequate consideration to those interests. But this case need not be one of sexual harassment.

Nor is this condition necessary for sexual harassment. Of course Bill B may believe that it is in Mary B's interests to come across. (A sexual harasser can be deceitful or just intensely egotistical.) Bill B may believe that it would conform with Mary B's conception of her interests. And, as we noted earlier, it may even be objectively in her own best interests. Yet still we think this would not prevent the action of Bill B against Mary B—which is in other ways similar to Bill's actions against Mary—being a case of sexual harassment.

In general, harassment need not be against the interests of the harassee. You can be harassed to stop smoking, and harassed to give up drugs. In these cases the consequences may well be good, and the interests of the harassee adequately considered and served, yet it is still harassment. This general feature seems equally applicable to sexual harassment.

## 3. Misuse of Power

Bill has power over Mary and it is the misuse of this power which plays an important role in making his treatment of Mary particularly immoral. For, on almost any normative theory, to misuse power is immoral. But is this misuse of power what makes this action one of sexual harassment?

If it is, then it must not be restricted to the formal power of the kind which Bill has over Mary—the power to dismiss her, demote her, withhold benefits from her, and so on. We also usually think of this sort of formal power in cases of police harassment. But consider the harassment of women at an abortion clinic by Right-To-Lifers. They cannot prevent the women having abortions and indeed lack any formal power over them. Nonetheless, they do possess important powers—to dissuade the faint-hearted (or even the over-sensitive), and to increase the unpleasantness of the experience of women attending the clinic.

Now consider the case of Mary C. Bill C and Mary C are co-workers in the office, and Bill C lacks formal power over Mary C. He sexually harasses her—with sexual innuendoes, touches, leers, jokes, suggestions, and unwanted invitations. To many women Bill C's actions would be unpleasant. But Mary C is a veteran—this has happened to her so many times before that she no longer responds. It is not that she desires or wants the treatment, but it no longer produces the unpleasant mental attitudes it used to produce—it just rolls off her. She gives the negative responses automatically, and goes on as though nothing had happened.

It would still seem to us that Mary C has been sexually harassed. But what power has Bill C misused against Mary C? He has not used even some informal power which has caused her some significantly unpleasant experience.

Crosthwaite and Swanton also argue against the necessary connection between misuse of power and sexual harassment. They note that one case where there is a lack of power and yet harassment takes place (like the Mary C and Bill C case), is the case where there is a use of pornographic pictures and sexist language by work colleagues. They also note that there are cases in which a sexually motivated misuse of power leads to events advantaging the woman in the long run. Misuse of power cannot in itself therefore constitute sexual harassment.[5]

# 4. Attitudes, Intentions and Experiences

In our discussions so far, it seems that we have not taken into account, to any significant extent, how Mary and Bill feel about things. It may be argued that what defines or characterizes sexual harassment is the mental state of the harasser, or harassee, or both.

Bill wanted to have sex with Mary. He perceived her as a sex object. He failed to have regard for her as a person. He failed to have regard for how she might feel about things. And his actions gave him egotistical pleasure. These attitudes, intentions and experiences may help constitute Bill's action as a case of sexual harassment.

Mary also had very specific kinds of mental states. She found Bill's actions unpleasant, and unwanted. She wished Bill would not act in that way towards her, and she disliked him for it. She was angry that someone would treat her that way, and she resented being forced to cope with the situation. So again we have attributed attitudes and mental experiences to Mary in describing this case as one of sexual harassment.

We do not want to have to label as sexual harassment all sexual actions or approaches between people in formally structured relationships. Cases of sexual harassment and nonharassing sexual interaction may appear very similar (at least over short time intervals). It seems that in the two kinds of cases only the mental features differ. That is, we refer to attitudes, intentions or experiences in explaining the difference between the two cases. But attention to this feature of sexual harassment is not enough in itself to identify sexual harassment.

We will now consider one of the more salient features of the mental attitudes of Bill and Mary, and show that sexual harassment is not dependent on these or similar features. Then we shall describe a case where the mental experiences are very different, but where sexual harassment does, in fact, still occur.

Consider the claim that Bill uses (or tries to use) Mary as a sex object. The notion of sex object is somewhat vague and ill-defined, but we accept that it is to view her as merely an entity for sexual activity or satisfaction, with no interest in her attributes as a person and without any intention of developing any personal relationship with her.

This will not do as a sufficient condition for sexual harassment. We normally do not think of a client sexually harassing a prostitute. And surely there can be a relationship between people where each sees the other merely as a sex object without there being harassment. Nor is viewing her merely as a sex object a necessary condition.[6] For surely Bill could love Mary deeply, and yet by pursuing her against her wishes, still harass her.

Now consider the claim that what is essential is that Mary not want the attentions of Bill. This is not a sufficient condition—often the most acceptable of sexual approaches are not wanted. Also a woman may not want certain attentions, and even feel sexually harassed, in situations which we would not want to accept as ones of sexual harassment.

Imagine that Mary D is an abnormally sensitive person. She feels harassed when D comments that the color she is wearing suits her very well, or even that it is a cold day. D is not in the habit of making such comments nor is he in the habit of harassing anyone. He is just making conversation and noting something (seemingly innocuous) that has caught his attention. Mary D feels harassed even though she is not being harassed.

Perhaps this condition is a necessary one. But this too seems implausible. Remember Mary C, the veteran. She is now so immune to Bill C that she has no reaction at all to approaches. He does not cause unpleasantness for her for she does not care what he does. Yet nonetheless Bill C is harassing Mary C.

Mary E and Bill E interact in a way which shows that sexual harassment is not simply a matter of actual attitudes, intentions or experiences. Bill E is infatuated with Mary E and wants to have sex with her. In addition to this, he genuinely loves her and generally takes an interest in her as a person. But he is hopeless on technique. He simply copies the brash actions of those around him and emulates to perfection the actions of the sexual harasser. Most women who were the object of his infatuation (for instance, someone like our original Mary) would feel harassed and have all the usual emotions and opinions concerning the harasser. But Mary E is different. Outwardly, to all who observe the public interactions between them, she seems the typical harassee—doing her best to politely put off Bill E, seeming not to want his attentions, looking as though she is far from enjoying it. That is how Bill E sees it too, but he thinks that that is the way women are.

Inwardly Mary E's mental state is quite different. Mary E is indifferent about Bill E personally, and is a veteran like Mary C in that she is not distressed by his actions. But she decides to take advantage of the situation and make use of Bill E's attentions. By manipulating the harassing pressures and invitations, she believes she can obtain certain benefits that she wants and can gain certain advantages over others. The attention from Bill E is thus not unwanted, nor is the experience for her unpleasant. In this case neither the harasser nor the harassee have mental states in any way typical of harassers and harassees, yet it is a case of sexual harassment.

Such a case, as hypothetical and unlikely as it is, demonstrates that the actual mental states of the people involved cannot be what is definitive of sexual harassment. They are not even necessary for sexual harassment.

## 5. A Behavioral Account of Sexual Harassment

The case of Mary E and Bill E persuades us that we require a behavioral account of sexual harassment. For a harasser to sexually harass a harassee is for the harasser to behave in a certain way towards the harassee. The causes of that behavior are not important, and what that behavior in turn causes is not important. The behavior itself constitutes the harassment.

But how then are we to specify the behavior that is to count as sexual harassment? We shall borrow a technique from the functionalist theory of the mind.

Functionalists usually identify mental states in terms of the functional roles they play. However, some functionalist theories allow a variation on this. If we talk instead of the kind of mental state which *typically* fills a functional role or the functional role *typically* associated with a mental state, we maintain the functionalist flavor, but allow unusual combinations of kinds of inner states and kinds of functional roles to be accommodated. We shall follow a similar technique when describing the kinds of behavior associated with sexual harassment.

Consider the behavior which is typically associated with a mental state representing an attitude which seeks sexual ends without any concern for the person from whom those ends are sought, and which typically produces an unwanted and unpleasant response in the person who is the object of the behavior. Such behavior we suggest is what constitutes sexual harassment. Instances of the behavior are instances of sexual harassment even if the mental states of the harasser or harassee (or both) are different from those typically associated with such behavior. The behavior constitutes a necessary and sufficient condition for sexual harassment.

According to this view, the earlier suggestion that attitudes, intentions and experience are essential to an adequate characterization of sexual harassment is correct. It is correct to the extent that we need to look at the mental states typical of the harasser, rather than those present in each actual harasser, and at those typical of the harassee. The empirical claim is that connecting these typical mental states is a kind of behavior—behavior not incredibly different from instance to instance, but with a certain sameness to it. Thus it is a behavior of a definite characteristic *type*. This type of behavior is sexual harassment.

This proffered account may at first appear surprising. But let us look at some of its features to alleviate the surprise, and at the same time increase the plausibility of the account.

Most importantly, the account satisfies our three desiderata: to show the connection between harassment in general and sexual harassment, to distinguish between sexual harassment and legitimate sexual interaction, and to assist in guiding policy on sexual harassment.

The relationship between harassment and sexual harassment is to be accounted for in terms of a behavioral similarity. This at first may seem to be a sweeping suggestion, since *prima facie*, there need be no descriptive similarity between sexual harassment, harassment by police, harassment of homosexuals, harassment of Jews, and so on. But the behavioral elements on which each kind of harassment supervenes will have enough in common to explain our linking them all as harassment, while at the same time being sufficiently different to allow for their differentiation into various kinds of harassment. The most plausible similarity, as we shall argue later, will be in the presence of certain behavioral dispositions, though the bases for these dispositions may differ.

Our approach allows for an adequate distinction between sexual harassment and legitimate sexual approaches and interactions. The approach requires that this be a behavioral difference. There is something intrinsically different about the two kinds of activity. Given that the typical causal origin of each of the kinds of behavior is different and so too is the typical reaction it in turn produces, it is to be expected that there would be a difference in the behavior itself. It is important to note that the constitutive behavior will be within a particular context, in particular circumstances. (The importance of this is well illustrated in cases such as a student and her lecturer at a university.[7]) Further it will include both overt and covert behavior (subtle differences count). In many cases it will also be behavior over a time interval, not just behavior at a time.

From the policy guiding perspective the account is very attractive. It is far easier to stipulate a workable, practical, defensible, and legally viable policy on harassment if it is totally definable in behavioral terms. Definition in terms of mental experiences, intentions and attitudes spells nothing but trouble for a viable social policy on sexual harassment.

The analysis we have offered entails that if there were no such characteristic kind of behavior there would be no sexual harassment. This seems to be right. In this case no legislation to ground a social policy would be possible. We would instead condemn individual actions on other moral grounds—causing pain and distress, acting against someone's best interests, misusing power, and so on.

In addition to satisfying these three desiderata, our account has numerous other positive features. First our account is culturally relative. It is highly likely that the kind of behavior constitutive of sexual harassment will vary from culture to culture, society to society. That is, it will be a culture-relative kind of behavior that determines sexual harassment. In any culture our reference to the typical mental states of the harasser and harassee will identify a kind of behavior that is constitutive of sexual harassment in that culture. This kind of behavior matches well with the empirical observations. There is so much variation in human behavior across cultures that behavior which may be sexual harassment in one need not be in another. The same is true of other kinds of human behavior. In the middle east, belching indicates appreciation of a meal. In western society, it is considered bad manners. The practice of haggling over the price of a purchase is acceptable (indeed expected) in some societies, and unacceptable in others. But in almost any culture, some kind of behavior may reasonably be judged to be sexual harassment.

Second, while we have cast our examples in terms of a male harasser and female harassee, there is nothing in the account which necessitates any gender restriction on sexual harassment. All that is required is that the behavior is sexual in nature and has other behavioral features which make it an instance of sexual harassment. The participants could be of either sex in either role, or of the same sex.

We acknowledge that we use the notion of an action being sexual in nature without attempting any explication of that notion. Such an explication is a separate task, but we believe that for our purposes there is no problem in taking it as primitive.

Third, the account allows for the possibility of sexual harassment without the presence of the mental states typical of the harasser or the harassee. There is an important connection between these typical mental states and sexual harassment, but it does not restrict instances of sexual harassment to instances where we have these typical mental states.

Further as the account focuses on behavior, rather than mental states, it explains why we feel so skeptical about someone who behaves as Bill behaves, yet pleads innocence and claims he had no bad intentions. The intentions are not essential for the harassment, and such a person has an obligation to monitor the responses of the other person so that he has an accurate picture of what is going on. Moreover, he has an obligation to be aware of the character of his own behavior. He also has an obligation to give due consideration to the strength and the weight of the beliefs upon which he is operating before he makes a decision to act in a manner that may have unpleasant consequences for others. Strength of belief concerns the degree of confidence it is rational to have in the belief, given the evidence available. Weight of belief concerns the quality of the evidential basis of the belief, and the reasonableness of acting on the evidence available.[8] If a person is acting in a way which has a risk of bad consequences for others, that person has an obligation to be aware of the risks and to refrain from acting unless he has gained evidence of sufficient strength and weight to be confident that the bad consequences will not arise. In the case of someone who wishes to engage in legitimate sexual interaction and to avoid sexual harassment, he must display a disposition to be alive to the risks and to seek appropriate evidence from the other person's behavior, as to whether that person welcomes his attentions. He must also display a disposition to refrain from acting if such evidence is lacking.

In the case of Mary E and Bill E, Bill E relies on the harassing behavior of other men as a guide to his actions regarding Mary E. Mary E has displayed standard forms of avoidance behavior (although she has ulterior motives). Bill E does not pay sufficient heed to the strength and weight of the beliefs which guide his actions, and it is just fortunate that Mary E is not harmed by what he does. Given Bill E's total disregard of Mary E's interests and reactions, it seems that his behavior could have caused, just as easily, significant distress to any other Mary who might have filled that role. A policy intended to identify sexual harassment should not rely on such luck, although the actual mental states (where they are as atypical as Mary E's) may mitigate blameworthiness. Bill E's harassing behavior should be checked and evaluated, regardless of any of Mary's actual mental states.[9]

Consider an example taken from an actual case[10] which highlights this obligation. Suppose Tom is married to Jane. He invites Dick (an old friend who has never met Jane) home to have sex with Jane. He tells Dick that Jane will protest, but that this is just part of the game (a game she very much enjoys). Dick forces Jane, who all the time protests violently, to have sex with him. Jane later claims to have been raped. Dick has acted culpably because he has acted without giving due consideration to the weight of the belief which guided his action, that is, to how rational it was to act on the belief given such a minimal evidential base. The only evidence he had that Jane did consent was Tom's say-so, and the consequences of acting on the belief were very serious. All of Jane's actions indicated that she did not consent.

In the case of Bill E and Mary E, Bill has an obligation to consider the strength and weight of the beliefs which guide his action before he acts. He is not justified in claiming that he is innocent, when he has been provided with signals that indicate that Mary does not welcome his attentions.

We acknowledge that it will be difficult in many situations to obtain sufficient evidence that a proposed act will not be one of sexual harassment. This will be true especially in cases where the potential harassee may believe that any outward indication of her displeasure would have bad consequences for her. The awareness of this difficulty is probably what has led others to promote the policy of a total ban on sexual relationships at the office or work place. While we acknowledge the problem, we feel that such a policy is both unrealistic and overrestrictive.

Fourth, the account allows an interesting stance on the connection between sexual harassment and morality. For consequentialist theories of morality, it is possible (though unlikely) that an act of sexual harassment may be, objectively, morally right. This would be the case if the long term good consequences outweighed the bad effects (including those on the harassee at the time of the harassment). For other moral theories it is not clear that this is a possibility, except where there are sufficiently strong overriding considerations present, such as to make the sexual harassment morally permissible. From the agent's point of view, it would seem that the probable consequences of sexual harassment (given the typical attitude of the typical harasser and the typical effects on the typical harassee) will be bad. Hence it is very likely, on any moral theory, that the agent evaluation for a harasser will be negative. The possible exceptions are where the harasser's actual mental state is not typical of a harasser, or the harassee's is not typical of a harassee.

Further, on this account many of the salient features of the case of Mary and Bill—such as misuse of power, discrimination, unfair distribution of favors, and so on—are not essential features of sexual harassment. They are usually immoral in their own right, and their immorality is not explained by their being part of harassment. But the behavior characteristic of sexual harassment will be constituted by features which we commonly find in particular instances of sexual harassment. For sexual harassment must supervene on the behavioral features which constitute its instances, but there is a range of such behavior, no one element of which need be present on any particular occasion. Similarly the morality of an instance of sexual harassment (at least for the consequentialist) will supervene on the morality of those same features of behavior.

## 6. Objections to the Behavioral Account

It may be objected that we have made no significant progress. We acknowledged at the beginning of the paper that many different kinds of behavior were instances of sexual harassment, even though there seemed to be no specific kind of behavior commonly present in all these instances.

Our reply is to concede the point that there is no first order property commonly possessed by all the behaviors. However, other important similarities do exist.

The property of being an instance of sexual harassment is a second order property of a particular complex piece of behavior. It is a property of the relevant specific behavioral features, and these features may be from a list of disjunctive alternatives (which may be altered as norms of behavior change). Also, the behavior of a typical harassee will possess the property of being an instance of avoidance behavior. Avoidance behavior is a disposition. Hence, even if two lots of behavior are descriptively similar they may differ in their dispositional properties. Finally the behavior of the typical harasser will possess the property of being sexually motivated, which again is dispositional in nature.

A second objection goes as follows: couldn't we have the very same piece of behavior and yet have no sexual harassment? To take the kind of example well tried as an objection to behaviorism, what would we say about the case of two actors, acting out a sexual harassment sequence?

There are a variety of replies we may make here. We could "bite the bullet" and admit the case to be one of sexual harassment. On the model proposed, we may do this while still maintaining that the behavior in this case is not morally wrong. Or, instead, we could insist that certain kinds of behavior only become harassment when they are carried on over a sufficiently lengthy time interval, the circumstances surrounding the behavior also being relevant. The case of the actors would not count as an instance of harassment because the behavior has not been recurrent over a sufficiently long period of time, especially as the behavior before and after the acting period are significantly different. Also the circumstances surrounding an acting exercise would be typically different from those of an instance of sexual harassment.

Still another response to the acting example is to argue that if the actual mental states of "harasser" and "harassee" are sufficiently different from those of the prototypical harasser and harassee, there can be no sexual harassment as there will be behavioral differences. This is not a logical necessity, but a physical one given the causal relations which hold between the mental states and the behavior. We should also keep in mind that many of the features of sexual harassment are dispositional. Thus, even if such features of sexual harassment are not manifested in particular circumstances, they would in other circumstances, and it is in these other circumstances that the observable behavior would be significantly different if it is the manifestation of harassment from that which would be associated with non-harassment.[11]

A third objection to our behavioral account focuses on our use of the mental state *typical* of harassers and harassees. We have noted that it is possible that some instances of harassment will involve a harasser or harassee with mental states significantly different from those of the typical harasser or harassee. So it is possible that the harassee is not even offended or made to feel uncomfortable, and it is possible that the harasser did not have intentions involving misuse of power against, and disregard for the interests of, the harassee. It is even possible that one or both of the harasser and harassee could know about the atypical mental states of the other. Why, at least in this last case, insist that the behavior is sufficient for sexual harassment?

From our concern to provide an account of sexual harassment adequate for policy purposes, we would be inclined to resist this kind of objection, given the clear advantage in policy matters of a behavioral account. But there is more to say in reply to this objection. Policy is directed at the action of agents, and in all cases except where at least one of the agents involved has justified beliefs about the atypical actual mental states of the agents involved, it is clearly appropriate to stipulate behavior associated with the states of mind typical of harassers and harassees as sexual harassment. For agents ought to be guided by what it is reasonable to predict, and rational prediction as to the mental states of those involved in some kind of behavior will be determined by the mental states typically associated with that behavior. So only in cases where we have reliable and justified knowledge of atypical mental states does the objection have any substance at all.

But even in these cases it seems the behavior should not be regarded as innocuous. Instances of behavior all form parts of behavioral patterns. People are disposed to behave similarly in similar circumstances. Hence we ought not to overlook instances of behavior which would typically be instances of sexual harassment. Agents ought not be involved in such patterns of behavior. It is for similar reasons that while we allow for cultural relativity in the behavior constitutive of sexual harassment, this relativity should not be taken to legitimate patterns of behavior which do constitute sexual harassment but which are taken as the standard mode of behavior by a culture.[12]

There are three final notes about our account of sexual harassment. Provided that the kind of behavior so specified is characteristically different from behavior having other typical causes and effects, the desired distinction between sexual harassment and other kinds of sexual activity is assured.

The required connection between sexual harassment and other forms of harassment seems assured by a kind of behavioral similarity. Other forms of harassment are not sexual and vary in many ways from the pattern of behavior characteristic of sexual harassment. But there will be corresponding accounts for each kind of harassment in terms of typical causes and typical effects. The connection between all the different kinds of harassment may well be revealed by looking at these typical causes and typical effects. But despite the noted differences, the contention is that there will be an empirically verifiable behavioral similarity, and this will justify the claim that they are all forms of harassment. It may be that the relevant features of the behavior characteristic of the various forms of harassment are dispositional.

We have made two claims about behavior constitutive of sexual harassment, and we should now see how they relate. The behavior is identified in terms of its typical causes and typical effects, that is, in terms of the typical mental states of harassers and harassees. But harassment is recognized by reference to features of the behavior itself, and any legislation to ground social policy will also refer to such features. The philosophical claim is that there will be a range of such behavior features some combination of which will be present in each case of sexual harassment. The empirical job is to tell us more about the nature of such behavior and help determine the practical social policy and legislation.[13]

# Endnotes

1. Catherine MacKinnon, *Sexual Harassment of Working Women* (London: Yale University Press, 1979), chap. 6.

2. MacKinnon, p. 225.

3. Given that sexual harassment is possible between men, by a woman harassing a man, among co-workers, and so on, MacKinnon's view of sexual harassment as nothing but one form of sexual discrimination is even less persuasive. It is also interesting that the problems which MacKinnon recognizes in trying to characterize "offence" of sexual harassment (p. 162 ff.), indicate a need for a behavioral analysis of sexual harassment, like the one we offer.

4. Jan Crosthwaite and Christine Swanton, "On the Nature of Sexual Harassment," *Women and Philosophy: Australasian Journal of Philosophy,* supplement to 64 (1986), 91–106; esp. 100–101.

5. Crosthwaite and Swanton, 99.

6. If it is, it needs to be connected to a general view that women are sex objects, for pornographic pin-ups and sexist jokes and language may harass a woman without anyone viewing *that* woman as a sex object. (See Nathalie Hadjifotiou, *Women and Harassment at Work* (London: Pluto Press, 1983), p. 14.) Note that we have urged that sexual harassment should be a special case of harassment. But what is the general form of the sex object account? It seems implausible that for each form of harassment there is something corresponding to the notion of sex object.

7. See, for example, Billie Wright Dzeich and Linda Weiner, *The Lecherous Professor: Sexual Harassment on Campus* (Boston: Beacon Press, 1984).

8. For a discussion of this concept of weight see Barbara Davidson and Robert Pargetter, "Weight," *Philosophical Studies* 49 (1986), 219–230.

9. Some might say that this behavioristic account of sexual harassment is similar to having strict liability for murder, that is to say, that mental states do need to be taken into account when judging and penalizing someone's actions. What we are arguing for is a way of *identifying* sexual harassment, not how (or even if) it should be *penalized.* The appropriate response to a case of sexual harassment may very well take mental states into account, along with the harm caused, or likely to be caused, and so forth. One advantage of our account is that it demands that potential harassers become aware of their behavior and to be alert to the responses of those around them. The response of Bill E (that he thought women liked to be treated that way) ought not be considered adequate especially in public life where a person's livelihood could hang in the balance.

10. This example is based on the British case, *D.P.P.* v. *Morgan* (1975), 2 All E.R. 347 (House of Lords): Morgan (1975), 1 All E.R. 8 (Court of Appeal); see also Frank Jackson, "A Probabilistic Approach to Moral Responsibility," in Ruth Barcan Marcus, et al. (eds.), *Logic, Methodology and Philosophy of Science Vll* (North Holland, 1986), pp. 351–366.

11. For a useful account of dispositional properties, their manifestations, and their categorical bases, see Elizabeth Prior, Robert Pargetter and Frank Jackson, "Three Theses about Dispositions," *American Philosophical Quarterly* 19 (1982), 251–258.

The case of pressing solicitation by a prostitute towards a reluctant john can be viewed in the same manner as that of the actors. It is quite likely that there would be sufficient difference in the mental states of the pressing prostitute and the typical harasser to yield behavioral differences (for instance the prostitute is more interested in making money than having sex, so her behavior will reflect this insofar as, say, she would not keep on pressing if the john proved to have no money). The pressing behavior of the prostitute may be seen as a nuisance by the reluctant john, but it is not sexual harassment.

12. What will be culturally relative are types of behavior incidental to their being viewed as constituting sexual harassment in a particular culture. Acceptable standards concerning modes of address, physical proximity, touching, and so forth will vary among cultures, so the behavior patterns which will constitute sexual harassment will also vary. Of course, we must be careful not to confuse socially accepted behavior with behavior which is not sexually harassing, especially in cultures where men have much greater power to determine what is to count as socially acceptable behavior. However, so long as there are typical mental states of harassers and harassees, the behavior which constitutes sexual harassment will be identifiable in each culture.

13. We acknowledge useful comments from Robert Young and various readers for *Social Theory and Practice*.

## Journal/Discussion Questions

✍ *Have you ever been the object of sexual harassment? Discuss the ways in which your experience relates to the issues raised in this article.*

1. What, according to Dodds et al., is the difference between sexual harassment and sexist harassment? Can one occur without the other? Can both occur together? What does it mean to harass?

2. How do you draw the line between sexual harassment and morally permissible instances of sexual advances that prove to be unwelcome? How do Dodds et al. answer this question?

3. How, if at all, should sexual harassment be regulated? How, and by whom, should the regulations be enforced?

---

### Susan Moller Okin
### "Justice, Gender, and the Family"

*Susan Moller Okin, a professor of political science at Stanford University, is the author of* Women in Western Political Thought *(Princeton, 1979).*

*This selection is the concluding chapter of Professor Okin's* Justice, Gender, and the Family, *in which she addresses the question of how we can make the family a more just institution that reduces the vulnerability of women and children and at the same time respects individual freedom of choice. Okin adopts a Rawlsian approach, asking what policies we would agree to about marriage, family, and related responsibilities if we did not know in advance whether we would find ourselves in the position of men or women. From this standpoint (which Rawls calls the original position), we can envision a society in which gender plays a much smaller role.*

## As You Read, Consider This:
1. What is Okin's view of "a just society" in regard to gender? How does this differ from your own view?
2. How would everyday family life as you have known it change in light of Okin's suggestions?

The family is the linchpin of gender, reproducing it from one generation to the next. As we have seen earlier in *Justice, Gender, and the Family*, family life as typically practiced in our society is not just, either to women or to children. Moreover, it is not conducive to the rearing of citizens with a strong sense of justice. In spite of all the rhetoric about equality between the sexes, the traditional or quasi-traditional division of family labor still prevails. Women are made vulnerable by constructing their lives around the expectation that they will be primary parents; they become more vulnerable within marriages in which they fulfill this expectation, whether or not they also work for wages; and they are most vulnerable in the event of separation or divorce, when they usually take over responsibility for children without adequate support from their ex-husbands. Since approximately half of all marriages end in divorce, about half of our children are likely to experience its dislocations, often made far more traumatic by the socioeconomic consequences of both gender-structured marriage and divorce settlements that fail to take account of it. I have suggested that, for very important reasons the family *needs* to be a just institution, and have shown that contemporary theories of justice neglect women and ignore gender. How can we address this injustice?

This is a complex question. It is particularly so because we place great value on our freedom to live different kinds of lives, there is no current consensus on many aspects of gender, and we have good reason to suspect that many of our beliefs about sexual difference and appropriate sex roles are heavily influenced by the very fact that we grew up in a gender-structured society. All of us have been affected, in our very psychological structures, by the fact of gender in our personal pasts, just as our society has been deeply affected by its strong influence in our collective past. Because of the lack of shared meanings about gender, it constitutes a particularly hard case for those who care deeply about both personal freedom and social justice. The way we divide the labor and responsibilities in our personal lives seems to be one of those things that people should be free to work out for themselves, but because of its vast repercussions it belongs clearly within the scope of things that must be governed by principles of justice. Which is to say, in the language of political and moral theory, that it belongs both to the sphere of "the good" and to that of "the right."

I shall argue here that any just and fair solution to the urgent problem of women's and children's vulnerability must encourage and facilitate the equal sharing by men and women of paid and unpaid work, of productive and reproductive labor. We must work toward a future in which all will be likely to choose this mode of life. A just future would be one without gender. In its social structures and practices, one's sex would have no more relevance than one's eye color or the length of one's toes. No assumptions would be made about "male" and "female" roles; childbearing would be so conceptually separated from child rearing and other family responsibilities that it would be a cause for surprise, and no little concern, if men and women were not equally responsible for domestic life or if children were to spend much more time with one parent than the other. It would be a future in which men and women participated in more or less equal numbers in every sphere of life, from infant care to different kinds of paid work to high-level politics. Thus it would no longer be the case that having no experience of raising children would be the practical prerequisite for attaining positions of the greatest social influence. Decisions about abortion and rape, about divorce settlements and sexual harassment, or about any other crucial social issues would not be made, as they often are now, by legislatures and benches of judges overwhelmingly populated by men whose power is in large part due to their advantaged position in the gender structure. If we are to be at all true to our democratic ideals, moving away from gender is essential. Obviously, the attainment of such a social world requires major changes in a multitude of institutions and social settings outside the home, as well as within it.

Such changes will not happen overnight. Moreover, any present solution to the vulnerability of women and children that is just and respects individual freedom must take into account that most people currently live in ways that are greatly affected by gender, and most still favor many aspects of current, gendered practices. Sociological studies confirm what most of us already infer from our own personal and professional acquaintances: there are no currently shared meanings in this country about the extent to which differences between the sexes are innate or environmental, about the appropriate roles of men and women, and about which family forms and divisions of labor are most beneficial for partners, parents, and children.[1] There are those, at one extreme, for whom the different roles of the two sexes, especially as parents, are deeply held tenets of religious belief. At the other end of the spectrum are those of us for whom the sooner all social differentiation between the sexes vanishes, the better it will be for all of us. And there are a thousand varieties of view in between. Public policies must respect people's views and choices. But they must do so only insofar as it can be ensured that these choices do not result, as they now do, in the vulnerability of women and children. Special protections must be built into our laws and public policies to ensure that, for those who choose it, the division of labor between the sexes does not result in injustice. In the face of these difficulties—balancing freedom and the effects of past choices against the needs of justice—I do not pretend to have arrived at any complete or fully satisfactory answers. But I shall attempt here to suggest some social reforms, including changes in public policies and reforms of family law, that may help us work toward a solution to the injustices of gender.

Marriage has become an increasingly peculiar contract, a complex and ambiguous combination of anachronism and present-day reality. There is no longer the kind of agreement that once prevailed about what is expected of the parties to a marriage. Clearly, at least in the United States, it is no longer reasonable to assume that marriage will last a lifetime, since only half of current marriages are expected to. And yet, in spite of the increasing legal equality of men and women and the highly publicized figures about married women's increased participation in the labor force, many couples continue to adhere to more or less traditional patterns of role differentiation. As a recent article put it, women are "out of the house but not out of the kitchen."[2] Consequently, often working part-time or taking time out from wage work to care for family members, especially children, most wives are in a very different position from their husbands in their ability to be economically self-supporting. This is reflected, as we have seen, in power differentials between the sexes within the family. It means also, in the increasingly common event of divorce, usually by mutual agreement, that it is the mother who in 90 percent of cases will have physical custody of the children. But whereas the greater need for money goes one way, the bulk of the earning power almost always goes the other. This is one of the most important causes of the feminization of poverty, which is affecting the life chances of ever larger numbers of children as well as their mothers. The division of labor within families has always adversely affected women, by making them economically dependent on men. Because of the increasing instability of marriage, its effects on children have now reached crisis proportions.

Some who are critical of the present structure and practices of marriage have suggested that men and women simply be made free to make their own agreements about family life, contracting with each other, much as business contracts are made.[3] But this takes insufficient account of the history of gender in our culture and our own psychologies, of the present substantive inequalities between the sexes, and, most important, of the well-being of the children who result from the relationship. As has long been recognized in the realm of labor relations, justice is by no means always enhanced by the maximization of freedom of contract, if the individuals involved are in unequal positions to start with. Some have even suggested that it is consistent with justice to leave spouses to work out their own divorce settlement.[4] By this time, however, the two people ending a marriage are likely to be far more unequal. Such a practice would be even more catastrophic for most women and children than is the present system. Wives in any but the rare cases in which they as individuals have remained their husbands' socioeconomic equals could hardly be expected to reach a just solution if left "free" to "bargain" the terms of financial support or child custody. What would they have to bargain *with*?

There are many directions that public policy can and should take in order to make relations between men and women more just. In discussing these, I shall look back to some of the contemporary ways of thinking about justice that I find most convincing. I draw particularly on Rawls's idea of the original position and Walzer's conception of the complex equality found in separate spheres of justice, between which I find no inconsistency. I also keep in mind critical legal theorists' critique of contract, and the related idea, suggested earlier, that rights to privacy that are to be valuable to all of us can be enjoyed only insofar as the sphere of life in which we enjoy them ensures the equality of its adult members and protects children. Let us begin by asking what kind of arrangements persons in a Rawlsian original position would agree to regarding marriage, parental and other domestic responsibilities, and divorce. What kinds of policies would they agree to for other aspects of social life, such as the workplace and schools, that affect men, women, and children and relations among them? And let us consider whether these arrangements would satisfy Walzer's separate spheres test—that inequalities in one sphere of life not be allowed to overflow into another. Will they foster equality within the sphere of family life? For the protection of the privacy of a domestic sphere in which inequality exists is the protection of the right of the strong to exploit and abuse the weak.

Let us first try to imagine ourselves, as far as possible, in the original position, knowing neither what our sex nor any other of our personal characteristics will be once the veil of ignorance is lifted.* Neither do we know our place in society or our particular conception of the good life. Par-

---

*I say so far as possible because of the difficulties already pointed out in chapter 5 of *Justice, Gender, and the Family*. Given the deep effects of gender on our psychologies, it is probably more difficult for us, having grown up in a gender-structured society, to imagine not knowing our sex than anything else about ourselves. Nevertheless, this should not prevent us from trying.

ticularly relevant in this context, of course, is our lack of knowledge of our beliefs about the characteristics of men and women and our related convictions about the appropriate division of labor between the sexes. Thus the positions we represent must include a wide variety of beliefs on these matters. We may, once the veil of ignorance is lifted, find ourselves feminist men or feminist women whose conception of the good life includes the minimization of social differentiation between the sexes. Or we may find ourselves traditionalist men or women whose conception of the good life, for religious or other reasons, is bound up in an adherence to the conventional division of labor between the sexes. The challenge is to arrive at and apply principles of justice having to do with the family and the division of labor between the sexes that can satisfy these vastly disparate points of view and the many that fall between.

There are some traditionalist positions so extreme that they ought not be admitted for consideration, since they violate such fundamentals as equal basic liberty and self-respect. We need not, and should not, that is to say, admit for consideration views based on the notion that women are inherently inferior beings whose function is to fulfill the needs of men. Such a view is no more admissible in the construction of just institutions for a modern pluralist society than is the view, however deeply held, that some are naturally slaves and others naturally and justifiably their masters. We need not, therefore, consider approaches to marriage that view it as an inherently and desirably hierarchical structure of dominance and subordination. Even if it were conceivable that a person who did not know whether he or she would turn out to be a man or a woman in the society being planned would subscribe to such views, they are not admissible. Even if there were no other reasons to refuse to admit such views, they must be excluded for the sake of children, for everyone in the original position has a high personal stake in the quality of childhood. Marriages of dominance and submission are bad for children as well as for their mothers, and the socioeconomic outcome of divorce after such a marriage is very likely to damage their lives and seriously restrict their opportunities.

With this proviso, what social structures and public policies regarding relations between the sexes, and the family in particular, could we agree on in the original position? I think we would arrive at a basic model that would absolutely minimize gender. I shall first give an account of some of what this would consist in. We would also, however, build in carefully protective institutions for those who wished to follow gender-structured modes of life. These too I shall try to spell out in some detail.

## Moving Away from Gender

First, public policies and laws should generally assume no social differentiation of the sexes. Shared parental responsibility for child care would be both assumed and facilitated. Few people outside of feminist circles seem willing to acknowledge that society does not have to choose between a system of female parenting that renders women and children seriously vulnerable and a system of total reliance on day care provided outside the home. While high quality day care, subsidized so as to be equally available to all children, certainly constitutes an important part of the response that society should make in order to provide justice for women and children, it is only one part.[5] If we start out with the reasonable assumption that women and men are equally parents of their children, and have equal responsibility for both the unpaid effort that goes into caring for them and their economic support, then we must rethink the demands of work life throughout the period in which a worker of either sex is a parent of a small child. We can no longer cling to the by now largely mythical assumption that every worker has "someone else" at home to raise "his" children.

The facilitation and encouragement of equally shared parenting would require substantial changes.[6] It would mean major changes in the workplace, all of which could be provided on an entirely (and not falsely) gender-neutral basis. Employers must be required by law not only completely to eradicate sex discrimination, including sexual harassment. They should also be required to make positive provision for the fact that most workers, for differing lengths of time in their working lives, are also parents, and are sometimes required to nurture other family members, such as their own aging parents. Because children are borne by women but can (and, I contend, should) be raised by both parents equally, policies relating to pregnancy and birth should be quite distinct from those relating to parenting. Pregnancy and childbirth, to whatever varying extent they require leave from work, should be regarded as temporarily disabling conditions like any others, and employers should be mandated to provide leave for all such conditions.[7] Of course, pregnancy and childbirth are far more than simply "disabling conditions," but they should be treated as such for leave purposes, in part because their disabling effects vary from one woman to another. It seems unfair to mandate, say, eight or more weeks of leave for a condition that disables many women for less time and some for much longer, while not mandating leave for illnesses or other disabling conditions. Surely a society as rich as ours can afford to do both.

Parental leave during the postbirth months must be available to mothers and fathers on the same terms, to facilitate shared parenting; they might take sequential leaves or each might take half-time leave. All workers should have the right, without prejudice to their jobs, seniority, benefits, and so on, to work less than full-time during the first year of a child's life, and to work flexible or somewhat reduced hours at least until the child reaches the age of seven. Correspondingly greater flexibility of hours must be provided for the parents of a child with any health problem or disabling condition. The professions whose greatest demands (such as tenure in academia or the partnership hurdle in law) coincide with the peak period of child rearing must restructure their demands or provide considerable flexibility for those of their workers who are also participating parents. Large-scale employers should also be required to provide high-quality on-site day care for children from infancy up to school age. And to ensure equal quality of day care for all young children, direct government subsidies (not tax credits, which benefit the better-off) should make up the difference between the cost of high-quality day care and what less well paid parents could reasonably be expected to pay.

There are a number of things that schools, too, must do to promote the minimization of gender. As Amy Gutmann has recently noted, in their present authority structures (84 percent of elementary school teachers are female, while 99 percent of school superintendents are male), "schools do not simply reflect, they perpetuate the social reality of gender preferences when they educate children in a system in which men rule women and women rule children." She argues that, since such sex stereotyping is "a formidable obstacle" to children's rational deliberation about the lives they wish to lead, sex should be regarded as a relevant qualification in the hiring of both teachers and administrators, until these proportions have become much more equal.[8]

An equally important role of our schools must be to ensure in the course of children's education that they become fully aware of the politics of gender. This does not only mean ensuring that women's experience and women's writing are included in the curriculum, although this in itself is undoubtedly important.[9] Its political significance has become obvious from the amount of protest that it has provoked. Children need also to be taught about the present inequalities, ambiguities, and uncertainties of marriage, the facts of workplace discrimination and segregation, and the likely consequences of making life choices based on assumptions about gender. They should be discouraged from thinking about their futures as *determined* by the sex to which they happen to belong. For many children, of course, personal experience has already "brought home" the devastating effects of the traditional division of labor between the sexes. But they do not necessarily come away from this experience with positive ideas about how to structure their own future family lives differently. As Anita Shreve has recently suggested, "the old home economics courses that used to teach girls how to cook and sew might give way to the new home economics: teaching girls *and boys* how to combine working and parenting."[10] Finally, schools should be required to provide high-quality after-school programs, where children can play safely, do their homework, or participate in creative activities.

The implementation of all these policies would significantly help parents to share the earning and the domestic responsibilities of their families, and children to grow up prepared for a future in which the significance of sex difference is greatly diminished. Men could participate equally in the nurturance of their children, from infancy and throughout childhood, with predictably great effects on themselves, their wives or partners, and their children. And women need not become vulnerable through economic dependence. In addition, such arrangements would alleviate the qualms many people have about the long hours that some children spend in day care. If one parent of a preschooler worked, for example, from eight to four o'clock and the other from ten to six o'clock, a preschool child would be at day care for only six hours (including nap time), and with each one or both of her or his parents the rest of the day. If each parent were able to work a six-hour day, or a four-day week, still less day care would be needed. Moreover, on-site provision of day care would enable mothers to continue to nurse, if they chose beyond the time of their parental leave.[11]

The situation of single parents and their children is more complicated, but it seems that it too, for a number of reasons, would be much improved in a society in which sex difference was accorded an absolute minimum of social significance. Let us begin by looking at the situation of never-married mothers and their children. First, the occurrence of pregnancy among single teenagers, which is almost entirely unintended, would presumably be reduced if girls grew up more assertive and self-protective, and with less tendency to perceive their futures primarily in terms of motherhood. It could also be significantly reduced by the wide availability of sex education and contraception.[12] Second, the added weight of responsibility given to fatherhood in a gender-free society would surely give young men more incentive than they now have not to incur the results of careless sexual behavior until they were ready to take on the responsibilities of being parents. David Ellwood has outlined a policy for establishing the paternity of all children of single mothers at the time of birth, and for enforcing the requirement that their fathers contribute to their support throughout childhood, with provision for governmental backup support in cases where the father is unable to pay. These proposals seem eminently fair and sensible, although the minimum levels of support suggested ($1,500 to $2,000 per year) are inadequate, especially since the mother is presumed to be either taking care of the child herself or paying for day care (which often costs far more than this) while she works.[13]

Third, never-married mothers would benefit greatly from a work structure that took parenthood seriously into account, as well as from the subsidization of high-quality day care. Women who grew up with the expectation that their work lives would be as important a part of their futures as the work lives of men would be less likely to enter dead-ended, low-skilled occupations, and would be better able to cope economically with parenthood without marriage.

Most single parenthood results, however, not from single mothers giving birth, but from marital separation and divorce. And this too would be significantly altered in a society not structured along the lines of gender. Even if rates of divorce were to remain unchanged (which is impossible to predict), it seems inconceivable that separated and divorced fathers who had shared equally in the nurturance of their children from the outset would be as likely to neglect them, by not seeing them or not contributing to their support, as many do today. It seems reasonable to expect that children after divorce would still have two actively involved parents, and two working adults economically responsible for them. Because these parents had shared equally the paid work and the family work, their incomes would be much more equal than those of most divorcing parents today. Even if they were quite equal, however, the parent without physical custody should be required to contribute to the child's support, *to the point where the standards of living of the two households were the same.* This would be very different from the situation of many children of divorced parents today, dependent for both their nurturance and their economic support solely on mothers whose wage work has been interrupted by primary parenting.

It is impossible to predict all the effects of moving toward a society without gender. Major current injustices to women and children would end. Men would experience both the joys and the responsibilities of far closer and more sustained contact with their children than many have today. Many immensely influential spheres of life—notably politics and the professional occupations—would for the first time be populated more or less equally by men and women, most of whom were also actively participating parents. This would be in great contrast to today, when most of those who rise to influential positions are either men who, if fathers, have minimal contact with their children, or women who have either forgone motherhood altogether or hired others as full-time caretakers for their children because of the demands of their careers. These are the people who make policy at the highest levels—policies not only *about* families and their welfare and about the education of children, but about the foreign policies, the wars and the weapons that will determine the future or the lack of future for all these families and children. Yet they are almost all people who gain the influence they do in part by never having had the day-to-day experience of nurturing a child. This is probably the most significant aspect of our gendered division of labor, though the least possible to grasp. The effects of changing it could be momentous.

## Protecting the Vulnerable

The pluralism of beliefs and modes of life is fundamental to our society, and the genderless society I have just outlined would certainly not be agreed upon by all as desirable. Thus when we think about constructing relations between the sexes that could be agreed upon in the original position, and are therefore just from all points of view, we must also design institutions and practices acceptable to those with more traditional beliefs about the characteristics of men and women, and the appropriate division of labor between them. It is essential, if men and women are to be allowed to so divide their labor, as they must be if we are to respect the current pluralism of beliefs, that society protect the vulnerable. Without such protection, the marriage contract seriously exacerbates the initial inequalities of those who entered into it and too many women and children live perilously close to economic disaster and serious social dislocation; too many also live with violence or the continual threat of it. It should be noted here that the rights and obligations that the law would need to promote and mandate in order to protect the vulnerable need not—and should not—be designated in accordance with sex, but in terms of different functions or roles performed. There are only a minute percentage of "househusbands" in this country, and a very small number of men whose work lives take second priority after their wives'. But they can quite readily be protected by the same institutional structures that can protect traditional and quasi-traditional wives, so long as these are designed without reference to sex.

Gender-structured marriage, then, needs to be regarded as a currently necessary institution (because still chosen by some) but one that is socially problematic. It should be subjected to a number of legal requirements, at least when there are children.[14]* Most important, there is no need for the division of labor between the sexes to involve the economic dependence, either complete or partial, of one partner on the other. Such dependence can be avoided if both partners have *equal legal entitlement* to all earnings coming into the household. The clearest and simplest way of doing this would be to have employers make out wage checks equally divided between the earner and the partner who provides all or most of his or her unpaid domestic services. In many cases, of course, this would not change the way couples actually manage their finances; it would simply codify what they already agree on—that the household income is rightly shared, because in a real sense jointly earned. Such couples recognize the fact that the wage-earning spouse is no more supporting the homemaking and child-rearing spouse than the latter is supporting the former; the form of support each offers the family is simply different. Such couples might well take both checks, deposit them in a joint account, and really share the income, just as they now do with the earnings that come into the household.

In the case of some couples, however, altering the entitlement of spouses to the earned income of the household as I have suggested *would* make a significant difference. It would make a difference in cases where the earning or higher-earning partner now directly exploits this power, by refusing to make significant spending decisions jointly, by failing to share the income, or by psychologically or physically abusing the non-earning or low-earning partner, reinforced by the notion that she (almost always the wife) has little option but to put up with such abuse or to take herself and her children into a state of destitution. It would make a difference, too, in cases where the higher-earning partner indirectly exploits this earning power in order to perpetuate the existing division of labor in the family. In such instances considerable changes in the balance of power would be likely to result from the legal and societal recognition that the partner who does most of the domestic work of the family contributes to its well-being just as much, and therefore rightly *earns* just as much, as the partner who does most of the workplace work.

What I am suggesting is *not* that the wage-working partner pay the homemaking partner for services rendered. I do not mean to introduce the cash nexus into a personal relationship where it is inappropriate. I have simply suggested that since both partners in a traditional or quasi-traditional

---

*I see no reason why what I propose here should be restricted to couples who are legally married. It should apply equally to "common law" relationships that produce children, and in which a division of labor is practiced.

marriage work, there is no reason why only one of them should get paid, or why one should be paid far more than the other. The equal splitting of wages would constitute public recognition of the fact that the currently unpaid labor of families is just as important as the paid labor. If we do *not* believe this, then we should insist on the complete and equal sharing of both paid and unpaid labor, as occurs in the genderless model of marriage and parenting described earlier. It is only if we *do* believe it that society can justly allow couples to distribute the two types of labor so unevenly. But in such cases, given the enormous significance our society attaches to money and earnings, we should insist that the earnings be recognized as equally earned by the two persons. To call on Walzer's language, we should do this in order to help prevent the inequality of family members in the sphere of wage work to invade their domestic sphere.

It is also important to point out that this proposal does not constitute unwarranted invasion of privacy or any more state intervention into the life of families than currently exists. It would involve only the same kind of invasion of privacy as is now required by such things as registration of marriages and births, and the filing of tax returns declaring numbers and names of dependents. And it *seems* like intervention in families only because it would alter the existing relations of power within them. If a person's capacity to fulfill the terms of his or her work is dependent on having a spouse at home who raises the children and in other ways sustains that worker's day-to-day life, then it is no more interventionist to pay both equally for their contributions than only to pay one.

The same fundamental principle should apply to separation and divorce to the extent that the division of labor has been practiced within a marriage. Under current divorce laws, as we have seen, the terms of exit from marriage are disadvantageous for almost all women in traditional or quasi-traditional marriages. Regardless of the consensus that existed about the division of the family labor, these women lose most of the income that has supported them *and* the social status that attached to them because of their husband's income and employment, often at the same time as suddenly becoming single parents, and prospective wage workers for the first time in many years. This combination of prospects would seem to be enough to put most traditional wives off the idea of divorcing even if they had good cause to do so. In addition, since divorce in the great majority of states no longer requires the consent of both spouses, it seems likely that wives for whom divorce would spell economic and social catastrophe would be inhibited in voicing their dissatisfactions or needs within marriage. The terms of exit are very likely to affect the use and the power of voice in the ongoing relationship. At worst, these women may be rendered virtually defenseless in the face of physical or psychological abuse. This is not a system of marriage and divorce that could possibly be agreed to by persons in an original position in which they did not know whether they were to be male or female, traditionalist or not. It is a fraudulent contract, presented as beneficial to all but in fact to the benefit only of the more powerful.

For all these reasons, it seems essential that the terms of divorce be redrawn so as to reflect the gendered or nongendered character of the marriage that is ending, to a far greater extent than they do now.[15] The legal system of a society that allows couples to divide the labor of families in a traditional or quasitraditional manner *must* take responsibility for the vulnerable position in which marital breakdown places the partner who has completely or partially lost the capacity to be economically self-supporting. When such a marriage ends, it seems wholly reasonable to expect a person whose career has been largely unencumbered by domestic responsibilities to support financially the partner who undertook these responsibilities. This support, in the form of combined alimony and child support, should be far more substantial than the token levels often ordered by the courts now. *Both postdivorce households should enjoy the same standard of living.* Alimony should not end after a few years, as the (patronizingly named) "rehabilitative alimony" of today does; it should continue for at least as long as the traditional division of labor in the marriage did and, in the case of short-term marriages that produced children, until the youngest child enters first grade and the custodial parent has a real chance of making his or her own living. After that point, child support should continue at a level that enables the children to enjoy a standard of living equal to that of the noncustodial parent. There can be no reason consistent with principles of justice that some should suffer economically vastly more than others from the breakup of a relationship whose asymmetric division of labor was mutually agreed on.

I have suggested two basic models of family rights and responsibilities, both of which are currently needed because this is a time of great transition for men and women and great disagreement about gender. Families in which roles and responsibilities are equally shared regardless of sex are far more in accord with principles of justice than are typical families today. So are families in which those who undertake more traditional domestic roles are protected from the risks they presently incur. In either case, justice as a whole will benefit from the changes. Of the two, however, I claim that the genderless family is more just, in the three important respects that I spelled out at the beginning of this book: it is more just to women; it is more conducive to equal opportunity both for women and for children of both sexes; and it creates a more favorable environment for the rearing of citizens of a just society. Thus, while protecting those whom gender now makes vulnerable, we must also put our best efforts into promoting the elimination of gender.

The increased justice to women that would result from moving away from gender is readily apparent. Standards for just social institutions could no longer take for granted and exclude from considerations of justice much of what women now do, since men would share in it equally. Such central components of justice as what counts as productive labor, and what count as needs and deserts, would be greatly affected by this change. Standards of justice would become humanist, as they have never been before. One of the most important effects of this would be to change radically the situation of women as citizens. With egalitarian families, and with institutions such as workplaces and schools designed to accommodate the needs of parents and children, rather than being based as they now are on the traditional assumption that "someone else" is at home, mothers would not be virtually excluded from positions of influence in politics and the workplace. They would be represented at every level in approximately equal numbers with men.

In a genderless society, children too would benefit. They would not suffer in the ways that they do now because of the injustices done to women. It is undeniable that the family in which each of us grows up has a deeply formative influence on us—on the kind of persons we want to be as well as the kind of persons we are.[16] This is one of the reasons why one cannot reasonably leave the family out of "the basic structure of society," to which the principles of justice are to apply. Equality of opportunity to become what we want to be would be enhanced in two important ways by the development of families without gender and by the public policies necessary to support their development. First, the growing gap between the economic well-being of children in single-parent and those in two-parent families would be reduced. Children in single-parent families would benefit significantly if fathers were held equally responsible for supporting their children, whether married to their mothers or not; if more mothers had sustained labor force attachment; if high-quality day care were subsidized; and if the workplace were designed to accommodate parenting. These children would be far less likely to spend their formative years in conditions of poverty, with one parent struggling to fulfill the functions of two. Their life chances would be significantly enhanced.

Second, children of both sexes in gender-free families would have (as some already have) much more opportunity for self-development free from sex role expectations and sex-typed personalities than most do now. Girls and boys who grow up in highly traditional families, in which sex difference is regarded as a determinant of everything from roles, responsibilities, and privileges to acceptable dress, speech, and modes of behavior, clearly have far less freedom to develop into whatever kind of person they want to be than do those who are raised without such constraints. It is too early for us to know a lot about the developmental outcomes and life choices of children who are equally parented by mothers and fathers, since the practice is still so recent and so rare. Persuasive theories such as Chodorow's, however, would lead us to expect much less differentiation between the sexes to result from truly shared parenting.[17] Even now, in most cases without men's equal fathering, both the daughters and the sons of wage-working mothers have been found to have a more positive view of women and less rigid views of sex roles; the daughters (like their mothers) tend to have greater self-esteem and a more positive view of themselves as workers, and the sons, to expect equality and shared roles in their own future marriages.[18] We might well expect that with mothers in the labor force and with fathers as equal parents, children's attitudes and psychologies will become even less correlated with their sex. In a very crucial sense, their opportunities to become the persons they want to be will be enlarged.

Finally, it seems undeniable that the enhancement of justice that accompanies the disappearance of gender will make the family a much better place for children to develop a sense of justice. We can no longer deny the importance of the fact that families are where we first learn, by example and by how we are treated, not only how people do relate to each other but also how they *should.* How would families not built on gender be better schools of moral development? First, the example of co-equal parents with shared roles, combining love with justice, would provide a far better example of human relations for children than the domination and dependence that often occur in traditional marriage. The fairness of the distribution of labor, the equal respect, and the interdependence of his or her parents would surely be a powerful first example to a child in a family with equally shared roles. Second, as I have argued, having a sense of justice requires that we be able to empathize, to abstract from our own situation and to think about moral and political issues from the points of view of others. We cannot come to either just principles or just specific decisions by thinking, as it were, as if we were nobody, or thinking from nowhere; we must, therefore, learn to think from the point of view of others, including others who are different from ourselves.

To the extent that gender is de-emphasized in our nurturing practices, this capacity would seem to be enhanced, for two reasons. First, if female primary parenting leads, as it seems to, to less distinct ego boundaries and greater capacity for empathy in female children, and to a greater tendency to self-definition and abstraction in males, then might we not expect to find the two capacities better combined in children of both sexes who are reared by parents of both sexes? Second, the experience of *being* nurturers, throughout a significant portion of our lives, also seems likely to result in an increase in empathy, and in the combination of personal moral capacities, fusing feelings with reason, that just citizens need.[19]

For those whose response to what I have argued here is the practical objection that it is unrealistic and will cost too much, I have some answers and some questions. Some of what I have suggested would not cost anything, in terms of public spending, though it would redistribute the costs and other responsibilities of rearing children more evenly between men and women. Some policies I have endorsed, such as adequate public support for children whose fathers cannot contribute, may cost more than present policies, but may not, depending on how well they work.[20] Some, such as subsidized high quality day care, would be expensive in themselves, but also might soon be offset by other savings, since they would enable those who would otherwise be full-time child carers to be at least part-time workers.

All in all, it seems highly unlikely that the *long-term* costs of such programs—even if we count only monetary costs, not costs in human terms—would outweigh the long-term benefits. In many cases, the cycle of poverty could be broken—and children enabled to escape from, or to avoid falling into, it—through a much better early start in life.[21] But even if my suggestions would cost, and cost a lot, we have to ask: How much do we care about the injustices of gender? How much do we care that women who have spent the better part of their lives nurturing others can be discarded like used goods? How ashamed are we that one-quarter of our children, in one of the richest countries in the world, live in poverty? How much do we care that those who raise children, *because* of this choice, have restricted opportunities to develop the rest of their potential, and very little influence on society's values and direction? How much do we care that the family, our most intimate social grouping, is often a school of day-to-day injustice? How much do we *want* the just families that will produce the kind of citizens we need if we are ever to achieve a just society?

## Endnotes

1. See *Justice, Gender, and the Family*, chap. 3, pp. 67–68.

2. "Women: Out of the House But Not Out of the Kitchen," *The New York Times*, February 24, 1988, pp. A1, C10.

3. See, for example, Marjorie Maguire Schultz, "Contractual Ordering of Marriage: A New Model for State Policy," *California Law Review* 70, no. 2 (1982); Lenore Weitzman, *The Marriage Contract: Spouses, Lovers, and the Law* (New York: The Free Press, 1981), parts 3–4.

4. See, for example, David L. Kirp, Mark G. Yudof, and Marlene Strong Franks, *Gender Justice* (Chicago: University of Chicago Press, 1986), pp. 183–185. Robert H. Mnookin takes an only slightly less laissez-faire approach, in "Divorce Bargaining: The Limits on Private Ordering," *University of Michigan Journal of Law Reform* 18, no. 4 (1985).

5. It seems reasonable to conclude that the effects of day care on children are probably just as variable as the effects of parenting—that is to say, very widely variable depending on the quality of the day care and of the parenting. There is no doubt that good out-of-home day care is expensive—approximately $100 per half-time week in 1987, even though child-care workers are now paid only about two-thirds as much per hour as other comparably educated women workers (Victor Fuchs, *Women's Quest for Economic Equality* [Cambridge: Harvard University Press, 1988], pp. 137–38). However, it is undoubtedly easier to control its quality than that of informal "family day care." In my view, based in part on my experience of the excellent day-care center that our children attended for a total of seven years, good-quality day care must have small-scale "home rooms" and a high staff-to-child ratio, and should pay staff better than most centers now do. For balanced studies of the effects of day care on a poor population, see Sally Provence, Audrey Naylor, and June Patterson, *The Challenge of*

*Day Care* (New Haven: Yale University Press, 1977); and, most recently, Lisbeth B. Schorr (with Daniel Schorr), *Within Our Reach—Breaking the Cycle of Disadvantage* (New York: Anchor Press, Doubleday, 1988), chap. 8.

6. Much of what I suggest here is not new; it has formed part of the feminist agenda for several decades, and I first made some of the suggestions I develop here in the concluding chapter of *Women in Western Political Thought* (Princeton: Princeton University Press, 1979). Three recent books that address some of the policies discussed here are Fuchs, *Women's Quest*, chap. 7; Philip Green, *Retrieving Democracy: In Search of Civic Equality* (Totowa, NJ: Rowman & Allanheld, 1985), pp. 96–108; and Anita Shreve, *Remaking Motherhood: How Working Mothers Are Shaping Our Children's Future* (New York: Fawcett Columbine, 1987), pp. 173–178. In Fuchs's chapter he carefully analyzes the potential economic and social effects of alternative policies to improve women's economic status, and concludes that "childcentered policies" such as parental leave and subsidized day care are likely to have more of a positive impact on women's economic position than "labor market policies" such as antidiscrimination, comparable pay for comparable worth, and affirmative action have had and are likely to have. Some potentially very effective policies, such as on-site day care and flexible and/or reduced working hours for parents of young or "special needs" children, seem to fall within both of his categories.

7. The dilemma faced by feminists in the recent California case *Guerra* v. *California Federal Savings and Loan Association*, 107 S. Ct. 683 (1987) was due to the fact that state law mandated leave for pregnancy and birth that it did *not* mandate for other disabling conditions. Thus to defend the law seemed to open up the dangers of discrimination that the earlier protection of women in the workplace had resulted in. (For a discussion of this general issue of equality versus difference, see, for example, Wendy W. Williams, "The Equality Crisis: Some Reflections on Culture, Courts, and Feminism," *Women's Rights Law Reporter* 7, no. 3 [1982].) The Supreme Court upheld the California law on the grounds that it treated workers equally in terms of their rights to become parents.

8. Amy Gutmann, *Democratic Education* (Princeton: Princeton University Press, 1987), pp. 112–115; quotation from pp. 113–114. See also Elisabeth Hansot and David Tyack, "Gender in American Public Schools: Thinking Institutionally," *Signs* 13, no. 4 (1988).

9. A classic text on this subject is Dale Spender, eds., *Men's Studies Modified: The Impact of Feminism on the Academic Disciplines* (Oxford: Pergamon Press, 1981).

10. Shreve, *Remaking Motherhood*, p. 237.

11. Although 51 percent of infants are breast-fed at birth, only 14 percent are entirely breast-fed at six weeks of age. Cited from P. Leach, *Babyhood* (New York: Alfred A. Knopf, 1983), by Sylvia Ann Hewlett, in *A Lesser Life: The Myth of Women's Liberation in America* (New York: Morrow, 1986), p. 409, note 34.

     Given this fact, it seems quite unjustified to argue that lactation *dictates* that mothers be the primary parents, even during infancy.

12. In Sweden, where the liberalization of abortion in the mid-1970s was accompanied by much expanded birth-control education and information and reduced-cost contraceptives, the rates of both teenage abortion and teenage birth decreased significantly. The Swedish teenage birth-rate was by 1982 less than half what it had been in the 1970s. Mary Ann

Glendon, *Abortion and Divorce in Western Law* (Cambridge: Harvard University Press, 1987), p. 23 and note 65. Chapter 3 of Schorr's *Within Our Reach* gives an excellent account of programs in the United States that have proven effective in reducing early and unplanned pregnancies. Noting the strong correlation between emotional and economic deprivation and early pregnancy, she emphasizes the importance, if teenagers are to have the incentive not to become pregnant, of their believing that they have a real stake in their own futures, and developing the aspirations and self-assertiveness that go along with this. As Victor Fuchs points out, approximately two-thirds of unmarried women who give birth are twenty or older (*Women's Quest*, p. 68). However, these women are somewhat more likely to have work skills and experience, and it seems likely that many live in informal "common law marriage" heterosexual or lesbian partnerships, rather than being *in fact* single parents.

13. David Ellwood, *Poor Support: Poverty in the American Family* (New York: Basic Books, 1988), pp. 163–174. He estimates that full-time day care for each child can be bought for $3,000 per year, and half-time for $1,000. He acknowledges that these estimated costs are "modest." I think they are unrealistic, unless the care is being provided by a relative or close friend. Ellwood reports that, as of 1985, only 18 percent of never-married fathers were ordered to pay child support, and only 11 percent actually paid any (p. 158).

14. Mary Ann Glendon has set out a "children first" approach to divorce (Glendon, *Abortion and Divorce*, pp. 94ff.); here I extend the same idea to ongoing marriage, where the arrival of a child is most often the point at which the wife becomes economically dependent.

15. My suggestions for protecting traditional and quasi-traditional wives in the event of divorce are similar to those of Lenore Weitzman in *The Divorce Revolution: The Unexpected Social and Economic Consequences for Women and Children in America* (New York: The Free Press, 1985), chap. 11, and Mary Ann Glendon in *Abortion and Divorce*, chap. 2. Although they would usually in practice protect traditional wives, the laws should be gender-neutral so that they would equally protect divorcing men who had undertaken the primary functions of parenting and homemaking.

16. Here I paraphrase Rawls's wording in explaining why the basic structure of society is basic. "The Basic Structure as Subject," *American Philosophical Quarterly* 14, no. 2 (1977), 160.

17. See chap. 6, note 58, in *Justice, Gender, and the Family*.

18. Shreve, *Remaking Motherhood*, chaps. 3–7.

19. See, for example, Sara Ruddick, "Maternal Thinking," *Feminist Studies* 6, no. 2 (1980); Diane Ehrensaft, "When Women and Men Mother," in *Mothering: Essays in Feminist Theory*, ed. Joyce Trebilcot (Totowa, NJ: Rowman & Allanheld, 1984); Judith Kegan Gardiner, "Self Psychology as Feminist Theory," *Signs* 12, no. 4 (1987), esp. 778–780.

20. David Ellwood estimates that "if most absent fathers contributed the given percentages, the program would actually save money" (*Poor Support*, p. 169).

21. Schorr's *Within Our Reach* documents the ways in which the cycle of disadvantage can be effectively broken, even for those in the poorest circumstances.

# Journal/Discussion Questions

✍ *In what ways did gender play a role in your own family as you were growing up? If you become a parent, what changes—if any—would you like to see in regard to the place of gender in your family?*

1. Okin argues that "A just future would be one without gender. In its social structures and practices, one's sex would have no more relevance than one's eye color or the length of one's toes." How does this compare to your vision of a just future? In what ways do you agree? Disagree? Explain.

2. In a gender neutral society, what changes does Okin foresee in the workplace? Do you think such changes would be a good thing? Why or why not?

3. How, according to Okin, would elementary school education change in a gender-neutral society? Do you think that elementary school education in today's society perpetuates sexism and roles based on gender? Ideally, how would you like to see children educated in regard to gender?

4. In discussing single parenthood and divorce, Okin suggests that "the parent without physical custody should be required to contribute to the child's support, *to the point where the standards of living of the two households were the same.*" Do you agree or disagree? Discuss your reasons.

# QUESTIONS FOR DISCUSSION AND REVIEW

## Where Do You Stand Now?

**Instructions:**

You have already answered the following questions in your moral problems self-quiz at the beginning of this book. Now that you have studied the material in this section, take a moment to answer the same questions again.

|  | Strongly Agree | Agree | Undecided | Disagree | Strongly Disagree | **Chapter 5: Gender** |
|---|---|---|---|---|---|---|
| 21. | ❑ | ❑ | ❑ | ❑ | ❑ | Women's moral voices are different from men's. |
| 22. | ❑ | ❑ | ❑ | ❑ | ❑ | Women are still discriminated against in the workplace. |
| 23. | ❑ | ❑ | ❑ | ❑ | ❑ | Sexual harassment should be illegal. |
| 24. | ❑ | ❑ | ❑ | ❑ | ❑ | Affirmative action helps women. |
| 25. | ❑ | ❑ | ❑ | ❑ | ❑ | Genuine equality for women demands a restructuring of the traditional family. |

Compare your answers to the present self-quiz with the answers to the initial self-quiz. How, if at all, have your answers changed? How have the *reasons* for your answers changed?

## Journal/Discussion Questions

✍ *Do you think the fact that you are a male or female has influenced your attitude toward any of the readings or ideas you encountered in this chapter? Discuss.*

1. What do you see as the ideal role of sex and gender in society? What do you think are the greatest liabilities associated with your view? The greatest assets? How does your view of this ideal relate to the views of the authors in this section?

2. Do you think that women are still discriminated against in today's society? Discuss the evidence for your position. If discrimination still exists, how should we as a society respond to it?

3. The issue of raising children is a central concern to many people, and is particularly troublesome to those who want to insure equality between the sexes. Discuss the potential conflict between child-raising and sex equality and explain how you think our society should deal with this issue. Relate your position to those presented in this chapter.

# FOR FURTHER READING:
# A BIBLIOGRAPHICAL GUIDE
# TO GENDER

## Journals

In addition to the standard journals in ethics discussed in the Appendix, there are several excellent journals devoted to issues of feminism. *Signs* is one of the oldest, and is a genuinely interdisciplinary journal devoted to issues relating to women; *Hypatia* is a philosophy journal created by members of the Society of Women in Philosophy; see also *Feminist Studies* and *Differences: A Journal of Feminist Cultural Studies.*

## Review Articles; Overviews

For an excellent overview of feminist ethics, see Alison M. Jaggar, "Feminist Ethics," *Encyclopedia of Ethics*, ed. Lawrence C. Becker and Charlotte B. Becker (New York: Garland, 1992), vol. I, pp. 361–370; Jane Grimshaw, "The Idea of a Female Ethic," *A Companion to Ethics*, ed. Peter Singer (Oxford: Blackwell, 1991), pp. 491–499. For an excellent overview of various positions, see Rosemarie Tong, *Feminine and Feminist Ethics* (Belmont, CA: Wadsworth, 1993) and *Feminist Frameworks*, ed. Alison M. Jaggar and Paula S. Rothenberg, 2nd ed. (New York: McGraw-Hill, 1984).

## Anthologies, Articles, and Books

There are a number of excellent anthologies on feminism and ethics, including Eva Feder Kittay and Diana Meyer's *Women and Moral Theory* (Savage, MD: Rowman & Littlefield, 1987); *Feminism and Political Theory,* ed. Cass R. Sunstein (Chicago: University of Chicago Press, 1990); Claudia Card's *Feminist Ethics* (Lawrence, KS: University of Kansas Press, 1991), which contains an excellent bibliography; *Explorations in Feminist Ethics*, ed. Eva Browning Cole and Susan Coultrap-McQuin (Bloomington: Indiana University Press, 1992), which also has an excellent bibliography; *Ethics: A Feminist Reader*, ed. Elizabeth Frazer, Jennifer Hornsby, and Sabina Lovibond (Oxford: Blackwell, 1992); *Women and Values: Readings in Recent Feminist Philosophy*, 2nd ed, ed. Marilyn Pearsall (Belmont, CA: Wadsworth, 1993). For a lively, representative selection of contemporary articles on feminism, see *Feminism: Opposing Viewpoints*, ed. Carol Wekesser (San Diego, CA: Greenhaven Press, 1995).

Rita C. Manning, *Speaking from the Heart: A Feminist Perspective on Ethics* (Lantham, MD: Rowman & Littlefield, 1992) is one of many excellent defenses of feminist perspectives in ethics. For a critical look at some elements in contemporary feminism, see Katie Roiphe, *The Morning After: Sex, Fear, and Feminism* (Boston: Little, Brown, 1993) and Christina Hoff Sommers, *Who Stole Feminism?* (New York: Simon & Schuster, 1994).

## Gender and Moral Voices

Carol Gilligan's *In a Different Voice* (Cambridge: Harvard University Press, 1982) has had a profound impact in a wide range of disciplines; her more recent work is to be found in a collection of essays that she co-edited with Janie Victoria Ward and Jill McLean Taylor, *Mapping the Moral Domain* (Cambridge: Center for the Study of Gender, Education and Human Development, 1988) and in *Meeting at the Crossroad*, by Lyn Mikel Brown and Carol Gilligan (Cambridge: Harvard University Press, 1992). Nel Noddings's *Caring* (Berkeley: University of California Press, 1984) and, more recently, her book *Women and Evil* (Berkeley: University of California Press, 1989) have also been influential in articulating a distinctive moral voice for women.

Several journal exchanges are also of particular relevance here, most of which have appeared in *Ethics*: the Kohlberg-Flanagan exchange on "Virtue, Sex, and Gender" *Ethics* 92, no. 3 (April 1982), 499–532; Lawrence Blum's "Gilligan and Kohlberg: Implications for Moral Theory" *Ethics* 98, no. 3 (April 1988), 472–491; and the symposium on "Feminism and Political Theory," *Ethics* 99, no. 2 (January 1989). Owen Flanagan's *Varieties of Moral Personality* (Cambridge: Harvard University Press, 1991) contains several excellent chapters (esp. chaps. 9–11) on this issue. Blum's essay, along with his previously unpublished "Gilligan's 'Two Voices' and the Moral Status of Group Identity," are both to be found in his *Moral Perception and Particularity* (New York: Cambridge University Press, 1994). Also see the essays in Part III of Claudia Card's anthology *Feminist Ethics*, cited above.

## Pornography and Hate Speech

For a survey of the ethical issues surrounding pornography, as well as an excellent bibliography, see Donald VanDeVeer, "Pornography," *Encyclopedia of Ethics*, ed. Lawrence C. Becker and Charlotte B. Becker (New York: Garland, 1992), vol. II, pp. 991–993. See the now classic pieces in *Take Back the Night*, ed. Laura Lederer (New York: William Morrow, 1980). For strong statements of opposition to pornography, see Andrea Dworkin, *Pornography: Men Possessing Women* (New York: Perigree Books, 1983), Catharine A. MacKinnon, *Only Words* (Cambridge: Harvard University Press, 1993). For a representative selection of philosophical positions on this issue, see *Pornography and Censorship*, ed. David Copp and Susan Wendell (Buffalo, NY: Prometheus Books, 1983).

The issue of banning hate speech has received a lot of attention in the past decade. Some of the most influential essays are gathered together in Mari J. Matsuda, et al., *Words That Wound: Critical Race Theory, Assaultive Speech, and the First Amendment* (Boulder, CO: Westview Press, 1993) and Henry Louis Gates, Jr., et al., *Speaking of Race, Speaking of Sex, Hate Speech, Civil Rights, and Civil Liberties*, with an introduction by Ira Glesser (New York: New York University Press, 1994); see also Gates's "Let Them Talk: Why Civil Liberties Pose No Threat to Civil Rights," *The New Republic* 209, no. 12–13 (September 20, 1993), 37 ff.; Andrew Altman, "Liberalism and Campus Hate Speech: A Philosophical Examination," *Ethics* 103, no. 2 (January 1993), 302–317. On the more general issue of sexist language, see *Sexist Language: A Modern Philosophical Analysis*, ed. Mary Vetterling-Braggin (n. p.: Littlefield, Adams, 1981).

## Sexual Harassment

See the review article "Sexual Abuse and Harassment" by Naomi Scheman in *Encyclopedia of Ethics*, ed. Lawrence C. Becker and Charlotte B. Becker (New York: Garland, 1992), vol. II, pp. 1139–1141. Also see Catharine MacKinnon, *Sexual Harassment of Working Women* (New Haven:

Yale University Press, 1979) for a view of sexual harassment as sex discrimination. See also the excellent anthology, *Sexual Harassment: Confrontations and Decisions*, ed. Edmund Wall (Buffalo, NY: Prometheus Books, 1992)

## Affirmative Action

For a general bibliography of affirmative action, see the references mentioned in the bibliography for the chapter on race and ethnicity. For a perceptive analysis of the ways in which certain practices result in sex discrimination, see Mary Anne Warren, "Secondary Sexism and Quota Hiring," *Philosophy and Public Affairs* 6 (1977), 240–261. In addition, see Susan D. Clayton and Faye J. Crosby, *Justice, Gender, and Affirmative Action* (Ann Arbor: University of Michigan Press, 1992).

# 6

# Sexual Orientation

**Videotape:**

*Topic:* Teaching about Families That Are Different
*Source:* *Nightline* (September 8, 1992)
*Anchors:* Ted Koppel; Dave Marash

# EXPERIENTIAL ACCOUNTS

André Dubus
"A Quiet Siege: The Death and Life of a Gay Naval Officer"

*André Dubus's most recent work is* Broken Vessels, *a collection of essays.*

*In this essay, Dubus recounts the story of the Commander of the Air Group aboard the carrier USS Ranger in the early 1960s. Dubus shows the way in which a naval investigation into the Commander's sexual orientation led to his suicide.*

〜

He was a Navy pilot in World War II and in Korea, and when I knew him in 1961 for a few months before he killed himself he was the Commander of the Air Group aboard the USS Ranger, an aircraft carrier, and we called him by the acronym CAG. He shot himself with his .38 revolver because two investigators from the Office of Naval Intelligence came aboard ship while we were anchored off Iwakuni in Japan and gave the ship's captain a written report of their investigation of CAG's erotic life. CAG was a much-decorated combat pilot, and his duty as a commander was one of great responsibility. The ship's executive officer, also a commander, summoned CAG to his office, where the two investigators were, and told him that his choices were to face a general court-martial or to resign from the Navy. Less than half an hour later CAG was dead in his stateroom. His body was flown to the United States; we were told that he did not have a family, and I do not know where he was buried. There was a memorial service aboard ship, but I do not remember it; I only remember a general sadness like mist in the passageways.

I did not really know him. I was a first lieutenant then, a career Marine; two years later I would resign and become a teacher. On the Ranger I was with the Marine detachment; we guarded the planes' nuclear weapons stored belowdecks, ran the brig, and manned one of the antiaircraft gun mounts. We were fifty or so enlisted men and two officers among a ship's crew of about 3,000 officers and men. The Air Group was not included in the ship's company. They came aboard with their planes for our seven-month deployment in the western Pacific. I do not remember the number of pilots and bombardier-navigators, mechanics and flight controllers, and men who worked on the flight deck, but there were plenty of all, and day and night you could hear planes catapulting off the front of the deck and landing on its rear.

The flight deck was 1,052 feet long, the ship weighed 81,000 tons fully loaded, and I rarely felt its motion. I came aboard in May for a year of duty, and in August we left our port in San Francisco Bay and headed for Japan. I had driven my wife and three young children home to Louisiana, where they would stay during the seven months I was at sea, and every day I longed for them. One night on the voyage across the Pacific I sat in the wardroom drinking coffee with a lieutenant commander at one of the long tables covered with white linen. The wardroom was open all night because men were always working. The lieutenant commander told me that Soviet submarines tracked us, they recorded the sound of our propellers and could not be fooled by the sound of a decoy ship's propellers, and that they even came into San Francisco Bay to do this; our submarines did the same with Soviet carriers. He said that every time we tried in training exercises to evade even our own submarines we could not do it, and our destroyers could not track and stop them. He said, "So if the whistle blows we'll get a nuclear fish up our ass in the first thirty minutes. Our job is to get the birds in the air before that. They're going to Moscow."

"Where will they land afterward?"

"They won't. They know that."

The voyage to Japan was five or six weeks long because we did not go directly to Japan; the pilots flew air operations. Combat units are always training for war, but these men who flew planes, and the men in orange suits and ear protectors who worked on the flight deck during landings and takeoffs, were engaging in something not at all as playful as Marine field exercises generally were. They were imperiled. One pilot told me that from his fighter-bomber in the sky the flight deck looked like an aspirin tablet. On the passage to Japan I became friendly with some pilots, drinking coffee in the wardroom, and I knew what CAG looked like because he was CAG. He had dark skin and alert eyes, and he walked proudly. Then in Japan I sometimes drank with young pilots. I was a robust twenty-five-year-old, one of two Marine officers aboard ship, and I did not want to be outdone at anything by anyone. But I could not stay with the pilots; I had to leave them in the bar, drinking and talking and laughing, and make my way back to the ship to sleep and wake with a hangover. Next day the pilots flew; if we did not go to sea, they flew from a base on land. Once I asked one of them how he did it.

"The pure oxygen. Soon as you put on the mask, your head clears."

It was not simply the oxygen, and I did not understand any of these wild, brave, and very efficient men until years later when I read Tom Wolfe's *The Right Stuff*.

It was on that same tour that I saw another pilot die. I worked belowdecks with the Marine detachment but that warm gray afternoon the entire ship was in a simulated condition of war, and my part was to stand four hours of watch in a small turret high above the ship. I could move the turret in a circular way by pressing a button, and I looked through binoculars for planes or ships in the 180-degree arc of our port side. On the flight deck planes were taking off; four could do this in quick sequence. Two catapults launched planes straight off the front of the ship, and quickly they rose and climbed. The third and fourth catapults were on the port side where the flight deck angled sharply out to the left, short of the bow. From my turret I looked down at the ship's bridge and the flight deck. A helicopter flew low near the ship, and planes were taking off. On the deck were men in orange suits and ear protectors; on both sides of the ship, just beneath the flight deck, were nets for these men to jump into, to save themselves from being killed by a landing plane that veered or skidded or crashed. One night I'd inspected a Marine guarding a plane on the flight deck; we had a sentry there because the plane carried a nuclear bomb. I stepped from a hatch into the absolute darkness of a night at sea and into a strong wind that lifted my body with each step. I was afraid it would lift me off the deck and hurl me into the sea, where I would tread water in that great expanse and depth while the ship went on its way; tomorrow they would learn that I was missing. I found the plane and the Marine; he stood with one arm around the cable that held the wing to the deck.

In the turret I was facing aft when it happened: men in orange were at the rear of the flight deck, then they sprinted forward, and I rotated my turret toward the bow and saw a plane in the gray sea and an orange-suited pilot lying facedown in the water, his parachute floating beyond his head, moving toward the rear of the ship. The plane had dropped off the port deck and now water covered its wing, then its cockpit, and it sank. The pilot was behind the ship; his limbs did not move, his face was in the sea, and his parachute was filling with water and starting to sink. The helicopter hovered low and a sailor on a rope descended from it; he wore orange, and I watched him coming down and the pilot floating and the parachute sinking beneath the waves. There was still some length of parachute line remaining when the sailor reached the pilot; he grabbed him; then the parachute lines tightened their pull and drew the pilot down. There was only the sea now beneath the sailor on the rope.

Then he ascended.

I shared a stateroom with a Navy lieutenant, an officer of medical administration, a very tall and strong man from Oklahoma. He had been an enlisted man, had once been a corpsman aboard a submarine operating off the coast of the Soviet Union, and one night their periscope was spotted, destroyers came after them, and they dived and sat at the bottom and listened by sonar to the destroyers' sonar trying to find them. He told me about the sailor who had tried to save the pilot. In the dispensary they gave him brandy, and the sailor wept and said he was trained to do that job, and this was his first time, and he had failed. Of course he had not failed. No man could lift another man attached to a parachute filled with water. Some people said the helicopter had not stayed close enough to the ship while the planes were taking off. Some said the pilot was probably already dead; his plane dropped from the ship, and he ejected himself high into the air, but not high enough for his parachute to ease his fall. This was all talk about the mathematics of violent death; the pilot was killed because he flew airplanes from a ship at sea.

He was a lieutenant commander, and I knew his face and name. As he was being catapulted, his landing gear on the left side broke off and his plane skidded into the sea. He was married; his widow had been married before, also to a pilot who was killed in a crash. I wondered if it were her bad luck to meet only men who flew; years later I believed that whatever in their spirits made these men fly also drew her to them.

I first spoke to CAG at the officers' club at the Navy base in Yokosuka. The officers of the Air Group hosted a party for the officers of the ship's company. We wore civilian suits and ties, and gathered at the club to drink. There were no women. The party was a matter of protocol, probably a tradition among pilots and the officers of carriers; for us young officers it meant getting happily drunk. I was doing this with pilots at the bar when one of them said, "Let's throw CAG into the pond."

He grinned at me, as I looked to my left at the small shallow pond with pretty fish in it; then I looked past the pond at CAG, sitting on a soft leather chair, a drink in his hand, talking quietly with two or three other commanders sitting in soft leather chairs. All the pilots with me were grinning and saying yes, and the image of us lifting CAG from his chair and dropping him into the water gave me joy, and I put my drink on the bar and said, "Let's go."

I ran across the room to CAG, grabbed the lapels of his coat, jerked him up from his chair, and saw his drink spill onto his suit; then I fell backward to the floor, still holding his lapels, and pulled him down on top of me. There was no one else with me. He was not angry yet, but I was a frightened fool. I released his lapels and turned my head and looked back at the laughing pilots. Out of my vision the party was loud, hundreds of drinking officers who had not seen this, and CAG sounded only puzzled when he said, "What's going on?"

He stood and brushed at the drink on his suit, watching me get up from the floor. I stood not quite at attention but not at ease either. I said, "Sir, I'm Marine Lieutenant Dubus. Your pilots fooled me." I nodded toward them at the bar, and CAG smiled. "They said, 'Let's throw CAG into the pond.' But, sir, the joke was on me."

He was still smiling.

"I'm very sorry, sir."

"That's all right, Lieutenant."

"Can I get the Commander another drink, sir?"

"Sure," he said, and told me what he was drinking, and I got it from the bar, where the pilots were red-faced and happy, and brought it to CAG, who was sitting in his chair again with the other commanders. He smiled and thanked me, and the commanders smiled; then I returned to the young pilots and we all laughed.

Until a few months later, on the day he killed himself, the only words I spoke to CAG after the party were greetings. One night I saw him sitting with a woman in the officers' club, and I wished him good evening. A few times I saw him in the ship's passageways; I recognized him seconds before the features of his face were clear: he had a graceful, athletic stride that dipped his shoulders. I saluted and said, "Good morning, sir" or "Good afternoon, sir." He smiled as he returned my salute and greeting, his eyes and voice mirthful, and I knew that he was seeing me again pulling him out of his chair and down to the floor, then standing to explain myself and apologize. I liked being a memory that gave him sudden and passing amusement.

On a warm sunlit day we were anchored off Iwakuni, and I planned to go with other crew members on a bus to Hiroshima. I put on civilian clothes and went down the ladder to the boat that would take us ashore. I was not happily going to Hiroshima; I was going because I was an American, and I felt that I should look at it and be in it. I found a seat on the rocking boat, then saw CAG in civilian clothes coming down the ladder. There were a few seats remaining, and he chose the one next to me. He asked me where I was going, then said he was going to Hiroshima, too. I was relieved and grateful; while CAG was flying planes in World War II, I was a boy buying savings stamps and bringing scrap metal to school. On the bus he would talk to me about war, and in Hiroshima I would walk with him and look with him, and his seasoned steps and eyes would steady mine. Then from the ship above us the officer of the deck called down, "CAG?"

CAG turned and looked up at him, a lieutenant junior grade in white cap and short-sleeved shirt and trousers.

"Sir, the executive officer would like to see you."

I do not remember what CAG said to me. I only remember my disappointment when he told the boat's officer to go ashore without him. All I saw in CAG's face was the look of a man called from rest back to his job. He climbed the ladder, and soon the boat pulled away.

Perhaps when I reached Hiroshima CAG was already dead; I do not remember the ruins at ground zero or what I saw in the museum. I walked and looked, and stood for a long time at a low arch with an open space at the ground, and in that space was a stone box that held the names of all who died on the day of the bombing and all who had died since because of the bomb. That night I ate dinner ashore, then rode the boat to the ship, went to my empty room, climbed to my upper bunk, and slept for only a while, till the quiet voice of my roommate woke me: "The body will be flown to Okinawa."

I looked at him standing at his desk and speaking into the telephone.

"Yes. A .38 in the temple. Yes."

I turned on my reading lamp and watched him put the phone down. He was sad, and he looked at me. I said, "Did someone commit suicide?"

"CAG."

"CAG?"

I sat up.

"The ONI investigated him."

Then I knew what I had not known I knew, and I said, "Was he a homosexual?"

"Yes."

My roommate told me the executive officer had summoned CAG to his office, shown him the report, and told him that he could either resign or face a general court-martial. Then CAG went to his room. Fifteen minutes later the executive officer phoned him; when he did not answer, the executive officer and the investigators ran to his room. He was on his bunk, shot in the right temple, his pilot's .38 revolver in his hand. His eyelids fluttered; he was unconscious but still alive, and he died from bleeding.

"They ran?" I said. "They ran to his room?"

Ten years later one of my shipmates came to visit me in Massachusetts; we had been civilians for a long time. In my kitchen we were drinking beer, and he said, "I couldn't tell you this aboard ship, because I worked in the legal office. They called CAG back from that boat you were on because he knew the ONI was aboard. His plane was on the ground at the base in Iwakuni. They were afraid he was going to fly it and crash into the sea and they'd lose the plane."

All 3,000 of the ship's crew did not mourn. Not every one of the hundreds of men in the Air Group mourned. But the shock was general and hundreds of men did mourn, and each morning we woke to it, and it was in our talk in the wardroom and in the passageways. In the closed air of the ship it touched us, and it lived above us on the flight deck and in the sky. One night at sea a young pilot came to my room; his face was sunburned and sad. We sat in desk chairs, and he said, "The morale is very bad now. The whole Group. It's just shot."

"Did y'all know about him?"

"We all knew. We didn't care. We would have followed him into hell." Yes, they would have followed him; they were ready every day and every night to fly with him from a doomed ship and follow him to Moscow, to perish in their brilliant passion.

## Journal/Discussion Questions

✍ *Do you know people who have had to conceal their sexual orientation? Discuss the moral issues that surround this situation.*

1. One of the interesting aspects of this essay is the way in which the CAG's sex-ual orientation is irrelevant to his position as Air Group Commander. In what ways is sexual orientation simply a personal matter? In what ways is it public?

2. Discuss the moral issues raised by this story.

# AN INTRODUCTION
# TO THE MORAL ISSUES

Let's begin by considering what type of discrimination occurs against gays and lesbians in contemporary American society. Then we shall turn to a discussion of the arguments advanced against homosexuality, the competing ideals of the place of sexual orientation in society, and the means for attaining those ideals.

## Discrimination against Gays and Lesbians

Discrimination against gays and lesbians differs in several ways from the previous two types of discrimination we have considered: racism and sexism. One of the principal reasons for this is that sexual orientation is generally much less apparent than either race or sex. Because they are less easily identifiable, gays and lesbians are less likely to be subject to certain kinds of discrimination. Homosexuals have not formally been denied voting rights as women and African Americans have been, apparently do not suffer from a lower level of income than their heterosexual counterparts, and have not usually encountered restrictions on their individual right to hold property. In these ways, they are not in need of the same kinds of affirmative action programs that have been defended for racial minorities and women.

*What types of discrimination do gays and lesbians experience in our society?*

Despite these differences that favor gays and lesbians, they are discriminated against in ways that would not be tolerated today if such discrimination were directed against racial minorities or women. They are not permitted to serve openly in the military; they are not permitted to marry one another, with both the emotional and financial costs that such prohibitions incur; they are often discriminated against in child-related matters such as child custody during divorces, adoption, foster parenting, Big Brothers, the Boy Scouts, and the like. Consider, for example, one the financial costs of not being permitted to marry. When a husband dies, his estate may pass to his wife without taxes; when a gay person's life-partner dies, transferred assets are heavily taxed.

Moreover, gays and lesbians—and their families—usually experience a very painful process when they begin to let their sexual orientation become public. Again, there is nothing comparable for racial minorities or for women. Announcements of one's race or gender rarely come as surprises to one's family and loved ones in the way that revealing one's sexual orientation often does.

Finally, it is important to realize that some gays and lesbians experience discrimination because of the radical character of their beliefs and "lifestyles." Here it is difficult to draw the line, but it would seem that at least part of the criticism and opposition they experience is directed primarily against their radicalness, not their gayness.

Let's now turn to a consideration of two specific areas of discrimination—gays and lesbians in the military, and homosexual marriage—and the more general issue raised by these particular problems, the issue of protection for gay rights.

## Gays and Lesbians in the Military

After he was elected in 1992, President Clinton attempted to lift the ban against homosexuals in the military and thereby ignited a heated debate about whether open homosexuals should be officially allowed to serve in the armed forces. Various arguments were advanced against lifting the ban, many of which centered around the effect on heterosexual military personnel "unit cohesion" and "combat effectiveness." Interestingly, some of the same arguments advanced against gays could also be advanced against women in the armed forces, and many of the arguments about the possibility of sexual harassment and unwanted sexual attention—if taken seriously—could certainly provide a welcome amount of protection for many women in the military.

## Homosexual Marriage

Presently in the United States, only heterosexual marriages are recognized by law. Some gay rights supporters have advocated the legalization of gay and lesbian marriages. Because they cannot be legally married, committed gay and lesbian couples are often denied the emotional and financial supports that a legally sanctioned marriage provides. Making a lifelong commitment is often difficult under any circumstances, and it becomes more so when one's commitment has no legal standing. This has particularly been a source of anguish for gays since the onset of AIDS, when gays have cared for dying partners but have not been given the recognition of one who has lost a spouse. Some of the obstacles they face include denial of hospital visitation rights, challenges to durable power of attorney by blood-related family, the denial of rights to pass property without taxation, and challenges to the wills of the deceased by blood families. Other gay rights advocates have argued that marriage does not provide the path to liberation that Andrew Sullivan and others have claimed.

## Gay and Lesbian Civil Rights

The more general issue raised by a number of supporters of gay rights is whether it ought to be legal to discriminate against people simply because of their sexual orientation. Should landlords be allowed to turn down potential tenants because of sexual orientation? Should schools and daycare centers be allowed to fire (or refuse to hire) individuals because they are gay or lesbian? Some advocates of gay and lesbian rights maintain that discrimination against individuals because of sexual orientation should be banned, just as we have banned such discrimination when based on race or gender.

# Arguments against Homosexuality

Opponents of homosexuality and of equal rights for homosexuals advance several different kinds of arguments in support of their position. These can be classified into three main types: (a) *religious arguments*, which usually proceed from some prohibitions against homosexuality in religious texts; (b) *intrinsic arguments*, that is, arguments asserting that there is something intrinsically immoral about homosexuality; and (c) *extrinsic arguments*, arguments that claim that homosexuality ought to be prohibited because of factors usually associated with, but not necessary to, homosexuality. Let's examine each of these three types of arguments.

## Religious Arguments

Religious arguments against homosexuality tend to be of two types, and those two types generally overlap. The first type of argument is narrowly *textual*—that is, it maintains that the tradition's religious text(s) condemn homosexuality, and therefore it is wrong. The second type is what we can call a *tradition* argument. It maintains that a given religious tradition and a certain worldview, taken together, are incompatible with homosexuality. Let's consider each of these.

*Is religion compatible with homosexuality?*

*Textual arguments.*   Religious arguments against homosexuality often appeal to some specific passage in the Bible, the Koran, or whatever religious text is central to that tradition, and then interpret that passage as a condemnation of homosexuality. The structure of such arguments is simple: $x$ (in this case, $x$ = homosexuality) is wrong because it is condemned by God, and we know that God condemns it because he says so in our religious text.

Two difficulties are often raised in regard to such arguments. First, is the passage actually being interpreted correctly? Here issues of translation and context are crucial, and such texts are often open to multiple interpretations. Second, do we—and ought we to—do everything espoused by that text. There are often many things our religious texts tell us to do that believers in fact reject. For example in the New Testament, verses in Mark 17–18 say that, as a sign, those that believe shall "pick up serpents," but few Christians do so or believe that they ought to do so. There is, in other words, a selectivity about textual arguments, at least taken in isolation, that makes them suspicious.

*Tradition arguments.*   The second, and often more thoughtful, kind of argument against homosexuality is one that asks "What are we, as a community and a tradition, all about?" Once having established the elements central to that tradition's identity, it then asks whether homosexuality is compatible with that tradition. This type of argument is much broader in scope and potentially much more subtle and textured. Instead of asking whether a specific kind of act is compatible with a selected religious text, this type of argument asks whether a particular religious tradition and way of life are compatible with a gay or lesbian life. Religious traditions show a wide range of variance on this issue, including the 1963 Quaker position that homosexual activity within a monogamous relationship is "natural" for some individuals and as much a gift of the Spirit as heterosexuality.

Notice that tradition arguments are not narrowly focused on the compatibility between a given religious tradition and the specific acts of gay or lesbian sex. Rather, they ask about the compatibility between their tradition and *a gay life*. This is a much broader question, made all the more complex by the fact that the term *a gay life* covers a wide range of different types of lives. We shall return to this issue below, in our discussion of the difference between intrinsic and extrinsic arguments.

*The act and the agent.*   Finally, it is important to note that some religiously based opposition to homosexuality distinguishes between (a) being a homosexual and (b) homosexual acts, and often reserves its condemnation—in the spirit of Augustine, who said to "Love the sinner, and hate the sin"—for homosexual acts while maintaining that *being* a homosexual does not exclude a person from the religious community in question. Within these traditions, celibate gays and lesbians are welcome into full membership in the community.

Many gays and lesbians reply to such a distinction by maintaining that their sexual orientation is so central to their identity as persons that to deny it through celibacy would be tantamount to denying a fundamental dimension of their identity as persons. It is, in other words, a distinction without a difference.

## Instrinsic Arguments

Those who argue that there is something intrinsically immoral about homosexuality usually say that it is "unnatural" or that it thwarts the "natural" purpose of sex, which is procreation. Let's consider each of these arguments.

*The argument from nature.*   Outside of a religious tradition, one of the arguments most frequently advanced against homosexuality is that it "goes against nature." This is an interesting argument, and much turns on the meaning of "nature." For the argument to work, two premises must be established: (1) that homosexuality is in fact "unnatural" in the required sense, and (2) that we ought not to do something that is "unnatural." Let's consider each of these claims in order.

First, in what sense, if any, is homosexuality "unnatural"? If we look just at the species of human beings, then we get two possible answers. Homosexuality is unnatural in the sense that it does not conform to the sexual orientation of the majority of human beings; however, homosexuality is natural in the sense that it is normal that a small percentage of human beings are (probably genetically, i.e., naturally) homosexual in their orientation. Edward Wilson, the sociobiologist, has argued in *On Human Nature*[1] that homosexuality in a certain percentage of the population is a normal condition that benefits humanity as a whole. Certainly, for homosexuals, their sexual orientation seems completely "natural" to them. Indeed, it would seem reasonable to argue that heterosexuality is natural for heterosexuals and homosexuality is natural for homosexuals. Furthermore, is homosexuality more "unnatural" than celibacy, a value and way of life highly esteemed by many religious and ethical traditions? If heterosexual sex is taken as the paradigm case of normalcy, the danger is that too little will count as normal in the end.

Yet there are a lot of things—such as war and death—that may be "natural," yet they would hardly qualify as good. This brings us to our second point: the words "natural" and "unnatural" must have some *normative* force if they are to generate a conclusion about the moral unacceptability of homosexuality. In other words, what is "unnatural" must be linked to what is bad or morally evil. Here the terrain becomes more difficult. On what basis can we say that the natural is good, especially if things like violence and death are natural? The only way is to say that not everything that is statistically normal—and "natural" in this sense—is natural in the sense of being morally good. Yet how do we make this judgment? In particular, how do we make it in a way that would show that homosexuality is unnatural in the moral sense? Traditionally, this has been done through an appeal to God's purpose in nature, but this again brings us back to religious arguments.

*Sex and procreation.*   The other way that the argument from nature establishes the moral sense of nature is through claiming that there are purposes in nature which provide the basis for the moral sense of the natural. In particular, one of our natural purposes is procreation, and advocates of this position maintain that homosexuality breaks an essential link between sex and procreation. This, they claim, is what makes homosexuality morally objectionable.

The difficulty with this argument is that, if it proves anything at all, it probably proves too much. If the argument were sound, it would seem to show that all sexual acts not aimed toward procreation (or at least in principle open to it) are immoral. In fact, this is the position that some—particularly Catholics—hold, but it seems to commit its adherents to condemning masturbators, people who practice birth control, and gays and lesbians equally.

## Extrinsic Arguments

Some opponents of homosexuality argue against homosexuality because of factors often (though perhaps erroneously) associated with it. For example, some might argue that gay relationships are not to be encouraged, since they tend not to be permanent in the way that heterosexual relationships (allegedly) are. Yet one has to be careful in assessing such arguments for at least two reasons. First, because homosexuality is often still condemned in our society, it is difficult to obtain reliable empirical data on such issues. Second, some of these alleged extrinsic factors might in fact be due to the very discrimination that gays and lesbians would like to see eliminated. For example, it is undoubtedly more difficult to maintain long-term committed relationships without the support of the law and one's family. To criticize gays and lesbians for (allegedly) not having committed relationships, and to then deny them the support of legally sanctioned relationships, is to beg the question.

An interesting extrinsic argument is often raised in the discussion of homosexuals in the military. If the presence of gays in the military makes heterosexual soldiers uncomfortable, is that an acceptable reason for banning gays? (Certainly we would not agree to this principle if we substituted race for sexual orientation.) Clearly, other people's reactions are something that is completely extrinsic to homosexuality.

*Drawing the line between intrinsic and extrinsic factors.* It is easy to find clear-cut cases of both extrinsic and intrinsic arguments. For example, some have advocated banning homosexuals from positions requiring a security clearance, since they may be more subject to blackmail than their heterosexual counterparts. But this is clearly an extrinsic argument, and it only has force in a society that discriminates against gays and lesbians. (Of course, it also further contributes to that discrimination.) Eliminate the discrimination, and the possibility for blackmail evaporates. Nothing intrinsic to homosexuality makes it susceptible to blackmail. On the other hand, being erotically attracted to someone of the same sex is intrinsic to being gay or lesbian, and arguments against such attraction would be applicable to all cases of homosexuality.

The line between intrinsic and extrinsic factors is less clear-cut. Some have advocated legally recognizing gay marriages, and Mr. Sullivan seems to mean "marriage" in the fairly traditional sense of a committed and monogamous relationship between two people. The principal difference, in Mr. Sullivan's case, is that he proposes allowing the two people to be of the same sex. Yet in his critique of Sullivan's position, Arkes raises the question of whether this would be sufficient in the eyes of many gay and lesbian rights activists. Aren't they advocating, Arkes asks, an endorsement—not just a silent tolerance—of the full range of sexual diversity? Aren't they, indeed, often opposed to fitting gays and lesbians into what they see as the straightjacket of traditional marriage? The question is whether this full range of sexual expression—which often includes multiple partners, anonymous sex, and the like—is intrinsic to homosexuality or not. This is a crucial issue for those who do not want to condemn homosexuality per se but do wish to affirm certain traditional values—such as intimacy, commitment, and monogamy—that are sometimes opposed by some representatives of gays and lesbians.

### Is Homosexuality a Matter of Choice?

Researchers remain uncertain about what the causes of homosexuality are. Some believe that the ultimate cause will turn out to be genetic, while others think it will center around early childhood experiences. Few believe that it is a matter of unimpeded adult choice, such as one might choose whether and how to part one's hair or what type of career to pursue. Most testimony indicates that sexual orientation is set, whatever the causes, by the time a person starts to be sexually aware. Sexual orientation, in other words, does not appear to be a *choice* in any significant sense.

This question is morally relevant for at least two reasons. First, we usually do not hold people responsible for things that they do not choose. It seems unjust to many people to condemn people for being homosexual if those people had no choice at all in their sexual orientation. Second, many people fear that interactions with gay persons may cause others to become gay. This is particularly an issue when gay adults are around children—as parents, foster parents, teachers, scout leaders, and the like. If sexual orientation is unaffected by such interactions, this issue may diminish in importance.

### Is Sexual Orientation Exclusively Either Heterosexual or Homosexual?

Finally, it is important to note that much of the contemporary discussion of these issues rests on the presumption that there is a sharp dividing line between, on the one hand heterosexuals and, on the other hand, gays and lesbians. The picture becomes more complex if, as some have suggested, sexual orientation may be bisexual. This has been argued in two quite distinct senses. First, some maintain that some individuals are naturally bisexual, just as some are naturally either heterosexual or homosexual. Second, a few theorists have argued that both sexual orientations are present in everyone to some degree, and that individuals are distinguished by the degree to which one orientation holds ascendancy over the other.

## Models of the Place of Sexual Orientation in Society

When we envision the ideal society as we would like to see it, what place does sexual orientation have in it? Is it a society composed solely of heterosexuals, or at least one in which homosexuals are not tolerated as members in good standing? Is it a society in which gays and lesbians are not discriminated against, but whose presence is also not stressed in any way? Or is it a society in which difference is celebrated and encouraged?

Our picture here is a complex one, because we actually have two separate—and sometimes conflicting—factors at work as individuals develop their own position on this issue. First, there is the issue of the morality of homosexuality, which is part of an individual's overall views on sexual morality. Second, there is the issue of societal rights and governmental protection of those rights.

Here the issue is the extent to which government ought to be involved in legislating matters of sexual morality.

Let's consider both of these factors intersect to form the major positions in this ongoing societal debate.

## The Traditional Model

Many conservatives espouse an ideal of society that has no room for gays and lesbians. In some versions, simply being homosexual is enough to eliminate a person from the community. In other versions, gays and lesbians would be allowed to have their sexual orientation, but not to engage in homosexual acts. They would, in other words, be sentenced to a life of involuntary chastity.

Defenders of conservative models offer two kinds of arguments. First, some maintain that homosexuality is intrinsically evil, and that therefore it should not be tolerated. Many defenders of this position cite religious sources as the foundation of their belief, while others appeal to some version of the "unnaturalness" argument discussed above. Second, some conservatives maintain that homosexuality contradicts important social and moral values—such as the value of family life—and should not be tolerated for that reason. Here the focus is not on homosexual *acts*, but on the *values* of homosexuals.

*What arguments support the traditional model of sexuality?*

Critics of the traditional model offer several replies. First, many defenders of homosexuality argue that it is not unnatural, a point we have already discussed above. Second, they point out that even if one believed something was unnatural and thus evil, it doesn't automatically follow that one is in favor of banning it. Many might think smoking cigarettes is bad, but that doesn't mean it should be completely banned. Third, they argue that it is consistent to support certain key social values, such as the value of family life, and yet not require that *everyone* live out that value in the same way. Many religious orders forbid their members from marrying, yet their presence is not seen in society as contradicting the value of family life. Fourth, many gays and lesbians support family life, and in some cases would even like to have the option of marriage open to them.

Perhaps the most telling reply to supporters of the traditional model is one that does not address their specific arguments, but rather the plight of individuals who are ostracized from society simply on the basis of who they are. If the traditional model were to prevail, gays and lesbians would be excluded from presenting themselves honestly in society simply because of their sexual orientation, not because of any specific, nonsexual actions or values. Where can these people go? They can either pretend they are straight, and thus gain some acceptance, or stand by their sexual orientation and be excluded from society. They must choose, in other words, between acceptance through denial of their own identity or exclusion as a result of affirming their sexual identity. A model of society that excludes a significant group in this way seems to be both a cruel and an unjust model.

## The Liberal Model

There is no single "liberal" position on the issue of gay and lesbian rights. However, there are two principal currents in the liberal tradition that discourage discrimination against homosexuals: the emphasis on individual autonomy and the importance of the right to privacy.

*Autonomy arguments.* Liberals characteristically believe that individual liberty is a very high priority, and consequently many hold that individuals should be free to have and express whatever sexual orientation they wish. In some versions of liberalism, this right is virtually absolute, limited only in those instances when its exercise infringes on someone else's autonomy, while other versions of liberalism believe that such rights may be restricted for other reasons as well.

*Privacy arguments.* Many liberals place a high value on the right to privacy, and see a person's sexual orientation as protected from public scrutiny by that right to privacy. A person's sexual orientation, they argue, is no one else's business, especially not the government's business. Privacy arguments are particularly important in regard to the issue of whether the state may forbid certain kinds of sexual acts between consenting adults in private.

*The difference between toleration, acceptance, and support.* Liberal positions differ in the degree to which they are supportive of gay and lesbian rights. We can distinguish three levels here.

- *Tolerance:* Gays and lesbians should not be discriminated against, but they also should not be encouraged. The "don't ask, don't tell" policy of the military may fall into this category, although many gays and lesbians see it as less than tolerant. Also in this category are people who believe homosexuality is bad but who also believe sexual morality shouldn't be legislated. Supporters of this position would be in favor of abolishing laws that forbid homosexual acts between consenting adults in private.

  *How strongly should society support gay rights?*

- *Acceptance:* Gays and lesbians should be allowed to express their sexual orientation openly to the same extent that heterosexuals are allowed to express their sexual orientation openly, and should not be discriminated against because of it. This would include support for legal protection against discrimination based on sexual orientation.

- *Endorsement:* Gay and lesbian sexual orientation and "lifestyles" should be presented as an option that is as valid and valuable as homosexual orientation and lifestyles. This may include presenting gay and lesbian families as models in public school curricula, legally sanctioning gay marriages, and so on.

Within the liberal tradition, there is a wide variation in the level of support for gay and lesbian rights.

## The Polymorphous Model

Finally, some in our society—and this includes some heterosexuals and some homosexuals—see sexuality as centered purely around pleasure, and they see no necessary link between sexuality and either procreation or intimacy. Whatever brings pleasure is good, and pleasure may come in many forms—that is, it may be polymorphous. Advocates of this view of sexuality hold that people should be allowed to engage in whatever kind of sexual activity they want and with whomever they want.

# Diversity and Consensus

Although there is relatively little common ground between the most extreme positions on this issue, there is the possibility of some reasonable consensus in the following way.

It seems reasonable that we, as a society, may want to encourage certain fundamental moral values in society. Although such encouragement need not take the form of legislating morality (in the sense of attempting to force people to hold particular moral values through legislative fiat), and although it need not deny individual freedom or the right to privacy (we can discourage something without outlawing it), we may indeed decide to encourage certain values (such as honesty, long-lasting commitment, monogamy, etc.) in our society as a whole, including both heterosexuals and homosexuals. We may further want to discourage certain values and their associated behaviors (such as treating people merely as sexual objects, anonymous sex, etc.), again for everyone, regardless of sexual orientation. The focus, in other words, for finding common ground is not on sexual orientation, but on values.

We can see how this could be applied to issues such as homosexuals in the military and to gay and lesbian marriages. Traditionally, the military has stood for certain values—patriotism, loyalty to one's unit, discipline, and so on—that could be affirmed for both homosexuals and heterosexuals. Indeed, this is in fact almost exactly the situation we have seen for decades (if not centuries). The gays and lesbians in the military have been committed first and foremost to military values, and have often served with great distinction, as the selection from André Dubus, "The Death and Life of a Gay Naval Officer," illustrates. The only difference would be to allow them to acknowledge their sexual orientation while still retaining their commitment to the values of the military.

A similar approach can be taken to the question of gay and lesbian marriages. It seems reasonable that society as a whole would want to encourage certain values such as commitment, individual caring, intimacy, and the like. Insofar as marriage is one of the institutions which helps to support these values, extending this to include gays and lesbians would seem reasonable, for it gives them the opportunity to participate in a highly important societal institution.

## Endnotes

1. Edward Wilson, *On Human Nature* (Cambridge, MA: Harvard University Press, 1978).

# THE ARGUMENTS

Barry Goldwater
"Job Protection for Gays"

*Barry Goldwater is the former senator from Arizona and the author of several books, including* The Conscience of a Conservative. *The present article appeared in 1994.*

*Former Senator Goldwater argues that equal job protection for gays is a necessary part of his conservative political philosophy. Conservatives, he argues, have long stood for a separation of church and state and for the principle that individuals ought to be able to live their lives as they wish, without government intrusion, as long as they do not hurt other people. Gays, he maintains, do not hurt others, and consequently there is no basis for discriminating against them.*

## As You Read, Consider This:

1. Goldwater argues for his position on the basis of *conservative* principles. Does his presentation of the conservative position seem accurate? How would members of the religious right challenge his vision of conservativism?

2. Why, according to Goldwater, is it in our national *economic* best interest to eliminate job discrimination against gays?

Last year, many who opposed lifting the ban on gays in the military gave lip service to the American ideal that employment opportunities should be based on skill and performance. It's just that the military is different, they said. In civilian life, they'd never condone discrimination.

Well, now's their chance to put up or shut up.

A bipartisan coalition in Congress has proposed legislation to protect gays against job discrimination. Congress is waking up to a reality already recognized by a host of Fortune 500 companies, including AT&T, Marriott and General Motors. These businesses have adopted policies prohibiting discrimination based on sexual orientation because they realize that their employees are their most important asset.

America is now engaged in a battle to reduce the deficit and to compete in a global economy. Job discrimination excludes qualified individuals, lowers work-force productivity and eventually hurts us all. Topping the new world order means attracting the best and creating a workplace environment where everyone can excel. Anything less makes us a second-rate nation. It's not just bad—it's bad business.

But job discrimination against gays and lesbians is real, and it happens every day. Cracker Barrel, a national restaurant chain, adopted a policy of blatant discrimination against employees suspected of being gay. Would anyone tolerate policies prohibiting the hiring of African Americans, Hispanics or women?

Today, in corporate suites and factory warehouses, qualified people live in fear of losing their livelihood for reasons that have nothing to do with ability. In urban and rural communities, hatred and fear force good people from productive employment to the public dole—wasting their talents and the taxpayers' money.

Gays and lesbians are a part of every American family. They should not be shortchanged in their efforts to better their lives and serve their communities. As President Clinton likes to say, "If you work hard and play by the rules, you'll be rewarded"—and not with a pink slip just for being gay.

It's time America realized that there was no gay exemption in the right to "life, liberty, and the pursuit of happiness" in the Declaration of Independence. Job discrimination against gays—or anybody else—is contrary to each of these founding principles.

Some will try to paint this as a liberal or religious issue. I am a conservative Republican, but I believe in democracy and the separation of church and state. The conservative movement is founded on the simple tenet that people have the right to live life as they please, as long as they don't hurt anyone else in the process. No one has ever shown me how being gay or lesbian harms anyone else. Even the 1992 Republican platform affirms the principle that "bigotry has no place in our society."

I am proud that the Republican Party has always stood for individual rights and liberties. The positive role of limited government has always been the defense of these fundamental principles. Our party has led the way in the fight for freedom and a free-market economy, a society where competition and the Constitution matter—and sexual orientation shouldn't.

Now some in our ranks want to extinguish this torch. The radical right has nearly ruined our party. Its members do not care enough about the Constitution, and they are the ones making all the noise. The party faithful must not let it happen. Anybody who cares about real moral values understands that this isn't about granting special rights—its about protecting basic rights.

It is for this reason that more than 100 mayors and governors, Republicans and Democrats, have signed laws and issued orders protecting gays and lesbians. In fact, nearly half the states have provided some form of protection to gays in employment. But of course many others have not, including my own state of Arizona.

It's not going to be easy getting Congress to provide job protection for gays. I know that firsthand. The right wing will rant and rave that the sky is falling. They've said that before—and we're still here. Constitutional conservatives know that doing the right thing takes guts and foresight, but that's why we're elected, to make tough decisions that stand the test of time.

My former colleagues have a chance to stand with civil rights leaders, the business community and the 74 percent of Americans who polls show favor protecting gays and lesbians from job discrimination. With their vote they can help strengthen the American work ethic and support the principles of the Constitution.

## Journal/Discussion Questions

✍ *Have you ever experienced—either first-hand or as a direct observer—discrimination against gays or lesbians in a work* *setting? Describe the incident and discuss what you perceive to be the motivations of the participants.*

1. Imagine that you have been asked by your senator to help to draft legislation to protect gays and lesbians from job discrimination. How would you word such legislation? What arguments would you outline in support of it? What objections would you expect to hear to it? How would you reply to such objections?

---

## Richard D. Mohr
## "Gay Rights"

*Richard D. Mohr is a professor of philosophy at the University of Illinois–Urbana. He specializes in Greek philosophy and social philosophy, and is the author of* The Platonic Cosmology; Gays/Justice: A Study of Ethics, Society, and Law; Gay Ideas: Outing and Other Controversies; *and* A More Perfect Union: Why Straight America Must Stand Up for Gay Rights.

*Mohr argues that gays are relevantly similar to classes already protected by the 1964 Civil Rights Act (either race or religion) and then shows that all attempts to mount good faith discriminations against gays fail the following principle: simply citing the current existence of prejudice, bigotry, or discrimination in a society against some group or citing the obvious consequences of such prejudice can never constitute good reason in trying to establish a good faith discrimination against that group.*

### As You Read, Consider This:

1. What does Mohr mean by a "good faith discrimination"? Give some examples of good faith discrimination that do not involve sexual orientation.

2. What does Mohr mean by the alfred dreyfus principle? What role does it play in Mohr's argument? Do you agree with the principle?

⌒

For Robert W. Switzer

In this paper I will suggest that there are no good moral reasons for exempting gays as a class from the protections which the 1964 Civil Rights Act affords racial, gender, ethnic and religious classes. These protections bar discrimination in private employment, housing, and public accommodations.[1]

I shall assume that it is a reasonable government function to eliminate arbitrariness regarding with whom we make contracts dealing with employment, housing, and public accommodations. The reasons for this are diverse,[2] and I shall not discuss them here. All but the most hardened of

Richard D. Mohr, "Gay Rights," *Social Theory and Practice* 8, no. 1 (Spring 1982). Reprinted by permission of the author.

libertarians would accept this, and even hardened libertarians are likely to hold that consistency demands that if some classes are afforded such protections, all relevantly similar classes should also be afforded such protections. And I take it that it is not in general the claim that one's sexual orientation is dissimilar in relevant respects to one's protected properties (race, religion) that forms the core of possible reasonable objections to the inclusion of gays within the protections of the Civil Rights Act. For on the one hand, if sexual orientation is something over which an individual has virtually no control, either for genetic or psychological reasons, then sexual orientation becomes relevantly similar to race, gender, and ethnicity. Discrimination on these grounds is deplorable because it holds a person accountable without regard for anything *he himself* has done. And to hold a person accountable for that over which he has no control is one form of prejudice. A similar argument from nonprejudicial consistency would seem persuasive for also including the physically and mentally challenged within the reach of the Civil Rights Act.

On the other hand, if one's sexual orientation is a matter of individual choice, it would seem relevantly similar to religion, which is a protected category. We would say that such a personal moral choice is not a reasonable ground for discrimination *even when* the private belief in and practice of it has very public manifestations, as when a religious person becomes involved in politics with a religious motive and a religious intent. And to claim that gay sex is in some sense immoral will not suffice to establish a relevant dissimilarity here. For the non-religious and the religious may consider each other immoral in this same sense and various religious sects will consider each other immoral, and yet all religious belief is protected.

Now a sufficient moral reason for the protection of private morality from discrimination in the public sphere is the following. In religious and sexual behavior as well as in other types of behavior, like excretory behavior, there is in our society a presumption of an *obligation* that they be carried out in private, even when there is virtually universal acceptance of the behavior, for example non-gay sex in missionary position for the sake of procreation; and this obligation in turn generates a *right* to privacy for these same practices. For society cannot consistently claim that these activities must be carried out in private (despite their manifest public consequences, like population growth) and yet retain a claim to investigate such activity and so make it *pro tanto* public behavior.[3] And by giving up the right to investigate such matters, *a fortiori* society gives up the right to discriminate based on them.

So I take it that there is a *prima facie* case for including sexual orientation within the ambit of the 1964 Civil Rights Act, since sexual orientation is relevantly similar to either race or religion. Now the Civil Rights Act reasonably enough has an exemption clause which allows for discrimination on the basis of a protected category when the discrimination against an otherwise protected category represents a "bona fide occupational qualification." This is a reasonable ground for exemption since it means that the discrimination ceases to be whimsical or arbitrary. Such discrimination would be discrimination in good faith. Two obvious examples of good faith discrimination are the following. It seems to me reasonable that a Chinese restaurant, for the sake of ambiance, should choose to hire only orientals. Further, it is good faith discrimination for the director of the movie "The Life of Martin Luther King, Jr." to consider only black actors for the title role.

Now I take it that the possibly reasonable attempt to argue that gays should not be afforded Civil Rights protections is that in the case of gays such exemptions swallow the rule, that is, that pretty much all discrimination against gays is discrimination in good faith, so that it would be disingenuous to include gays within the compass of protected classes. What I wish to argue in the rest of this paper is that virtually all attempts to justify discrimination against gays as discrimination in good faith fail, and therefore that there is nothing remotely approaching a general case to be made for exemptions of gays from Civil Rights protections. I shall take as my examples discriminations in the public sector, where, thanks to the Fourteenth Amendment's equal protection clause, there is already a general presumption against discrimination against gays and where such discrimination is permissible only if it is rationally related to a legitimate government concern.[4]

In trying to give an account of what constitutes good faith discrimination, we enter murky territory. In current practice there is no widely recognized and accepted taxonomy of what constitutes good faith discrimination, nor is there any obvious sufficient set of general principles governing what constitutes a good faith discrimination. Is it, for instance, a good faith discrimination for the new management of a bar that has gone gay to fire all the non-gay union employees of the former management, claiming that only gay waiters will make the bar's new clientele feel comfortable? This is an actual case that occurred recently in Toronto. The outcome of a legal challenge to the firings was that the same court which had ruled earlier that the new management of what was to become an Irish bar could fire all the previous non-Irish employees, ruled against the new gay management, claiming that "being gay is not as substantially different as being Irish." So stated, we seem to have bad grammar, dubious metaphysics, and liberal condescension all masking bigotry; but, I suggest that, for whatever bad reasons the court came up with this ruling, it was the correct ruling.

For I suggest that the following is a valid general principle governing the establishment of good faith discriminations. The principle is that simply citing the current existence of prejudice, bigotry or discrimination in a society against some group or citing the obvious consequences of such prejudice, bigotry, or discrimination can never constitute a good reason in trying to establish a good faith discrimination against that group.[5] Let us call this principle alfred dreyfus. Dreyfus tells us that stigmas which are entirely socially induced shall not play a part in our rational moral deliberations. I suggest, for instance, that a community could not legitimately claim that a by-law banning blacks from buying houses in the community was a good faith discrimination on the grounds that whenever blacks move into a heretofore white area, property values plummet. This is illegitimate, since it is only the current bigotry in the society that causes property values to drop, as the result of white flight and the subsequent reduction in size of the purchasing market.

In general, the fact that people discriminate can never be cited as a good reason for institutionalizing discrimination.[6] But even more clearly, the current existence of discrimination cannot ethically ground the continuance of the discrimination, when there are reasonable *prima facie* claims against discrimination.

If dreyfus is intuitively obvious (once attention is drawn to it) it has a direct bearing on almost every case where people try to justify discrimination against gays as discrimination in good faith. For one of its obvious ranges of application is cases where some joint project is a necessary part of a job. It is in this category of cases that good faith discriminations against gays are most often attempted.

Bans against gays in the armed forces and on police forces are classic cases of the attempt to establish such good faith discrimination against gays. The armed forces, after recently losing a series of court cases, have abandoned the strategy that gays make incompetent soldiers as the basis for their systematic discrimination against gays. In light of the Matlovich case, the Beller case, and others in which gay soldiers were shown to have sterling performance records, the armed forces no longer rest their policy on such contentions as the claims that all faggots have limp wrists; limp wrists cannot fire M16s; and therefore gays reduce combat readiness. Instead the Pentagon has placed renewed emphasis on the contention that gays cause a drop in morale and for this reason reduce combat readiness. As of January 16, 1981, the Pentagon has seven, official, articulated reasons for banning gays:

> The presence of such members adversely affects the ability of the armed forces 1) to maintain discipline, good order and morale, 2) to foster mutual trust and confidence among service members, 3) to insure the integrity of the system of rank and command, 4) to facilitate assignment and worldwide deployment of service members who frequently must live and work under close conditions affording minimal privacy, 5) to recruit and retain members of the armed forces, 6) to maintain the public acceptability of military service, and 7) to prevent breaches of security.[7]

Claims 1) through 6) form a group. I will discuss 7) in a separate context below. What all the first six claims have negatively in common is that none of them is based on the ability of gay soldiers to fulfill the duties of their stations. More generally, none of the claims is based on gays *doing* anything at all. So whatever else may be said for the policy, it lacks the virtue of being a moral stance, since it is a minimal requirement of a moral stance that people are judged and held culpable only for *actions* of their own doing. What the six reasons have positively in common is that their entire force relies exclusively on current widespread bigoted attitudes against gays. They appeal to the bigotry and consequent disruptiveness of non-gay soldiers (reasons 1, 2, 3, and 5) who apparently are made "up-tight" by the mere presence of gay soldiers and officers, and so claim that they cannot work effectively in necessary joint projects with gay soldiers. The reasons appeal to the anti-gay prejudices of our own society (reason 6), especially that segment of it which constitutes potential recruits (reason 5), and to the anti-gay prejudices of other societies (reason 4). No reasons other than currently existing widespread prejudice and bigotry of others are appealed to here in order to justify a discriminatory policy. So all six reasons violate dreyfus and are illegitimate.

Gay soldiers are being discriminated against on current Pentagon policy simply because currently existing bigotry and prejudice are counted as good reasons in trying to establish a good faith discrimination. To accept such a reasoning process as sound is to act like a right-wing terrorist who produces social disorder through indiscriminate bombings and then claims that what is needed is a police state. Clearly the social problem created by the bigoted soldiers and the terrorist is not solved by society acceding to their demands. It is soldiers who do not cease to be bigoted, not gay soldiers, who should be thrown out of the armed forces. Practically, of course, the solution to the problem is for the armed forces to re-educate its bigots and to expel those who are incorrigible. It should be remembered that until 1948 the U.S. armed forces were racially segregated on exactly the same grounds as those adduced now for barring gays, and especially on the ground that whites could not work with blacks. That year the forces were racially integrated and the skies did not fall. The West German armed forces have been gay/non-gay integrated in noncommissioned ranks and the skies have not fallen there either.

It is perhaps worthy of note that the current Pentagon policy on gays is simply a mirror image of the long-standing anti-gay policy of the International Association of Chiefs of Police, a policy which for the same reasons is equally illegitimate. That policy reads:

> Whereas, the life-style of homosexuals is abhorrent to most members of the society we serve, identification with this life-style destroys trust, confidence and esteem so necessary in both fellow workers and the general public for a police agency to operate efficiently and effectively; now, therefore, be it resolved, that the IACP . . . endorses a no hire policy for homosexuals in law enforcement.[8]

Despite the bogus appeal to "life-style," gays are here again being discriminated against not for anything they *do,* or on the basis of their ability to carry out police duties, but solely on the basis of the bigoted attitudes of others. If, as is quite possibly the case, the majority of society lacks trust and confidence in and finds abhorrent blacks, Latinos, women, and Jews *as* police officers, the argument would hold equally well against these groups, and yet the argument only singles out gays. So aside from being a bad argument, based entirely on violations of dreyfus, the policy fails to treat relevantly similar cases similarly.

I wish to give three other, I hope now obvious, examples of bad faith parading as good faith. The U.S. Civil Service has ceased as a matter of policy to discriminate against gays, but discrimination against gays is still systematic in the State Department, the CIA, the FBI, and the armed forces, on the alleged good faith discrimination that gays are security risks, since they are, it is claimed, subject to blackmail. That gays are subject to blackmail, though, is simply the result of currently existing prejudices and bigotries in the society, some of which are enshrined in law and government practice; so this argument violates dreyfus. Further, since it is the fact that one will be thrown out of the CIA (or any of the other organizations cited above) if exposed, that leads to the potential for blackmail, the argument also looks as though it is verging on being circular; for the government policy establishes the situation the government is trying to avoid, and then the government uses this situation as a reason for its policy. The practical solution is for the President to issue an executive order banning discrimination on the basis of sexual orientation in all branches of the government.[9]

Take as another example of bad faith discrimination the arguments used in lesbian child custody cases. Never has there been an area where socially endorsed stereotyping has been so flatfootedly appealed to in forming social policy as in child custody cases. In nearly all jurisdictions, there is a strong presumption in favor of giving custody to the mother, *unless* the mother is a lesbian, in which case the presumption of parental fitness shifts sharply in the direction of the father. Sometimes the argument for this sharp shift is merely a statement of bigotry. It runs: lesbians are evil; lesbians cause their children to be lesbians; and therefore, lesbians cause their children to be evil. When the shift is attempted to be justified as a good faith discrimination, the argument runs as follows: there is nothing inherently evil about mother or child being lesbian, but nevertheless, since, while the child is growing, there will be strong social recrimination from peers and other parents against the child as it becomes known in the community that the mother is a lesbian, only by discriminating against lesbian mothers are their children spared unnecessary suffering.[10] This argument, I take it, is an obvious violation of dreyfus. Currently existing bigotry and its consequences are cited as the only reason for perpetrating and institutionalizing discrimination. Note that if one does not think such discrimination is illegitimate *exactly because* it violates dreyfus, one would seem equally obliged to argue for the sterilization of inter-racial couples; for, only as such are their "progeny" spared the needless suffering created by the strong social recrimination which is directed against mixed-race children in current society.

Another bad faith argument is the widely held *Time* magazine (January 8, 1979) argument for discriminating against gay teachers.[11] It runs as follows: though openly gay teachers do not cause their students to become gay, nevertheless an openly gay teacher might (inadvertently or not) cause a closeted gay student to become openly gay; the life of an openly gay person is a life of misery and suffering; therefore, openly gay teachers must be fired, since they promote misery and suffering. It seems that the second premise, life of misery, if true in some way peculiar to gays, is so as the result of currently existing bigotry and discrimination in society of the very sort which the argument tries to enshrine into school board policy. So the argument violates dreyfus. But further, one cannot try to justify a social policy based on the consequences it is supposed to have, then attach negative sanctions or punishments to violations of the policy, and then say one was obviously correct in establishing the policy, citing as evidence that only behavior in conformity with the policy is producing good consequences. Stated more formally: it is illegitimate to give a rule-utilitarian rationale for a law, attach sanctions to the law and then show that one was correct in one's moral ground for the law by observing the consequence of implementing the sanctioned law. Sanctions make rule-utilitarian justifications self-fulfilling prophecies. If one passes sanctions against openly gay people, then obviously if one observes openly gay people beset by these sanctions one is going to claim one wouldn't want one's children to live that way. The solution, though, is to eliminate the sanctions which turn discriminations, based on alleged consequences of being openly gay, into self-fulfilling prophecies.

It should be noted that "purely moral" or religious claims to the effect that gays are wicked seem to bear no weight at all in establishing good faith discriminations. For what sort of job is being a non-sinner an essential job qualification? Nevertheless, most jurisdictions do require "good moral standing" for state and city licensing for a vast number of professional jobs ranging from doctors and lawyers to hairdressers and morticians. How these requirements are held to be reasonable or even desirable qualifications for these jobs is unclear. One wants as a lawyer someone who is shrewd, not someone who is pious. I suspect that eventually the courts will rule that these sorts of moral qualifications are so *vague* as to be incapable of fair application and so violate the due process clause of the Constitution. In the meanwhile, these requirements are abused in the most outrageous ways against gays. For in states which do not have consenting adult laws,[12] gays are selectively discriminated against as systematically violating the laws and so, allegedly, as necessarily lacking in good moral character.[13] Now I think this application of such qualifications against gays should also count as a violation of dreyfus. The claim that violating some law was the ground for a good faith discrimination would be legitimate, I suggest, only if the moral ground of the law turned out to be, independently of the enshrinement of the law, a good ground for a good faith discrimination. And on examination arguments against consenting adult laws turn out to be mere statements of prudery or merely religious or aesthetic claims.[14]

My hunch is that all anti-gay arguments that are cast as good faith discriminations violate dreyfus or are circular or are illegitimate self-fulfilling prophecies, but I do not presume to outguess human ingenuity in coming up with rationalizations for its hatreds and fears.

## Endnotes

1. A version of this paper was read to the Society for the Philosophy of Sex and Love at the meetings of the Eastern Division of the American Philosophical Association, December

1981. Many people have read and offered useful comments on earlier drafts of the paper. I would especially like to thank Professor Lee Rice of Marquette University and my colleague, Professor James Wallace, for their comments.

2. In unanimously finding the 1964 Civil Rights Act constitutional, the Supreme Court cited the Act's promotion of "personal dignity" as its most noteworthy justification for state action (*Heart of Atlanta Motel* v. *U.S.* 379 US 241 [1964]).

3. The legal correlate of this moral principle is that the mere presence of a police agent in an action that would otherwise be private or personal does not make the action a public action. This correlate has led the Massachusetts Supreme Court to rule on procedural due process grounds that the state's sodomy laws are unenforceable, without actually ruling the laws unconstitutional on substantive due process grounds (*Commonwealth* v. *Sefranka* Mass. 414 N. E. 2d 602 [Dec. 1980]).

4. This "rational relation" test was established for gays in the public sphere generally and the Civil Service specifically by *Norton* v. *Macy* 417 F.2d 1161 (D.C.Cir. 1969). The test for good faith discrimination in the Civil Rights Act is in fact a more stringent test. For "bona fide occupational qualification" is elaborated as that which is "reasonably necessary to the normal orientation" of a business. "Reasonably necessary" is a judicial oxymoron. For in equal protection cases, a rational relation or reasonable relation is simply a relation to a legitimate government concern, while a necessary relation is one which is *essential* to a *compelling* state interest. The tension of the phrase "reasonably necessary" notwithstanding, the courts have tended to interpret the Civil Rights Act as establishing a "business necessity test" (*Diaz* v. *Pan American Airways* 442 F.2d 385 [5th Cir. 1971]). If I can establish my claims operating with the weaker test, *a fortiori* my argument will hold for the more stringent test.

5. I take prejudice to be a species of bigotry. A bigot is an adult capable of reason who is willing to act on his moral opinions and who has no reason for his opinion, *or* who has a reason but it is prejudicial, is a rationalization, is merely a personal emotional response or is merely a parroting of someone *else's* reason, *or* who is unwilling to apply consistently the ethical principles which inform and give substance to his reason, once the relevant principles are pointed out to him, *or* whose principles themselves are so specialized as to be arbitrary.

6. See Ronald Dworkin, *Taking Rights Seriously* (Cambridge, MA: Harvard University Press, 1977), pp. 248–254.

7. San Francisco *Sentinel*, January 23, 1981. These regulations are published in the *Federal Register*, 46, no. 19 (Jan. 29, 1981), 9571–9578. They were largely constructed out of the holdings of the extremely anti-gay Beller case (*Beller* v. *Middendorf*, 632 F.2d 788 [9th Cir. 1980] denied US cert.). For a military case, though, which ended in a gay re-instatement see *benShalom* v. *Sec'y of Army* 22 F.E.P. 1396 (U.S. D.Ct E.D. Wis. 1980). This case is important, for in it the court recognized that the Army had violated the plaintiff's First Amendment rights and rights to substantive due process, in particular the right to privacy. In fact, the court recognized a constitutional right to sexual preference within the right to privacy.

8. San Francisco *Sentinel*, October 3, 1980.

9. In military cases and others where "security risk" is adduced as a reason for dismissal, the government has not once brought forth a case where a gay was blackmailed into disclosing secrets. This means that gays are being judged on the basis of stereotypes which have no factual basis. In sex discrimination cases, claims based on stereotypes and unsubstantiated fears

and apprehensions have been given no weight in attempts to establish bona fide occupational qualifications (*Weeks* v. *Southern Bell Telephone* 408 F.2d 228).

10. In fact it would seem that children in the custody of lesbian mothers do not suffer. On this subject allow me to recommend the movie on lesbian child custody cases *In the Best Interest of the Children* (Iris Films/Iris Feminist Collective, Berkeley, 1977). For a fairly recent discussion of gay parent custody cases see Donna Hitchens, "Social Attitudes, Legal Standards, and Personal Trauma in Child Custody Cases," in *Homosexuality and the Law*, ed. Donald Knutson (NY: Haworth Press, 1980) = *Journal of Homosexuality 5* (Fall 1979–Winter 1980), 89–95.

11. The current judicial status of discrimination against gay teachers is turbid. For an important and generally pro-gay case, see *Acanfora* v. *Bd. of Educ.* 491 F.2d 498 (4th Cir. 1974). For a recent anti-gay holding based on religious morality see *Gaylord v. Tacoma School Dist. #10* Wash. 559 P.2d 1340 (1981) denied US cert.

12. Approximately 65% of the U.S. population now lives in states with consenting adult laws. Twenty-two states have revoked their sodomy laws through legislative means: Alaska, California, Colorado, Connecticut, Delaware, Hawaii, Illinois, Indiana, Iowa, Maine, Nebraska, New Hampshire, New Jersey, New Mexico, North Dakota, Ohio, Oregon, South Dakota, Vermont, Washington, West Virginia, and Wyoming. In addition, the highest courts of Pennsylvania and New York have, on the basis of the right to privacy, declared unconstitutional their states' statutes prohibiting private, consensual sodomy between unmarried adults (*Commonwealth* v. *Bonadio* 490 Pa 91, 415 A.2d 47 [1980]; *People* v. *Onofre* 434 N.Y.S.2d 947, 51 NY2d 476, 415 N.E.2d 936 [1980] denied US cert.).

13. A recent landmark gay naturalization case will, it is to be hoped, clear up this area of administrative law: *Nemetz* v. *Immigration and Naturalization Service* 647 F.2d 432 (4th Cir. April 1981). This case ruled 1) that in cases of laws which are national in nature discriminations based on "moral turpitude" cannot be achieved merely by citing the violation of statutes which are peculiarly local, and even more importantly ruled 2) that determinations of good moral character or moral turpitude can only be made by appealing to public morality and that private sexual acts are not a matter of public morals: "The appropriate test in such cases is whether the act is harmful to the public or is offensive merely to a personal morality. Only those acts harmful to the public will be appropriate bars to a finding of good moral character" (at 436).

14. Anyone who doubts the truth of this claim might usefully read the floor debate surrounding H. Res. 208 (*Congressional Record–House* 673762, Oct. 1, 1981), by which the House by a nearly three-to-one margin quashed consenting adult laws which had been passed unanimously by the D.C. City Council.

## Journal/Discussion Questions

✍ *Mohr alludes to the question of whether sexual orientation is chosen or whether it is not a matter of choice. To what extent do you think a person's sexual orientation is a matter of choice? What moral relevance, if any, does this have?*

1. Mohr notes the way in which several of the arguments against allowing gays to serve in the military "appeal to the bigotry and consequent disruptiveness of non-gay soldiers." To what extent, if any, should such feelings be given weight in policy decisions? Are such feelings instances of "bigotry" in Mohr's sense?

2. To what extent should sexual orientation be considered a legitimate factor in court decisions involving child custody, surrogacy, and adoption?

---

## Jeffrey Jordan
## "Is It Wrong to Discriminate on the Basis of Homosexuality?"

*Jeffrey Jordan is an assistant professor in the department of philosophy, University of Delaware. He specializes in metaphysics and the philosophy of religion. He has both a theoretical and a practical interest in the protection of individual rights from the conventional orthodoxies of the day as well as from governmental intrusion.*

*Without passing judgment on the morality of homosexuality* per se, *Jordan argues that the public moral impasse about the rightness or wrongness of homosexuality provides a basis for discriminating on the basis of sexual orientation in certain public matters by, for example, not sanctioning same-sex marriages, since sanctioning such marriages would unnecessarily trample the moral rights of those who have religious objections to same-sex marriages.*

### As You Read, Consider This:

1. What does Jordan mean by the "parity thesis"? By the "difference thesis"? Which does he support?

2. Jordan distinguishes two ways of responding to public dilemmas. What are these ways? Under what conditions is each justified? Can you think of any other possible way?

◞

Much like the issue of abortion in the early 1970s, the issue of homosexuality has exploded to the forefront of social discussion. Is homosexual sex on a moral par with heterosexual sex? Or is homosexuality in some way morally inferior? Is it wrong to discriminate against homosexuals—to treat homosexuals in less favorable ways than one does heterosexuals? Or is some discrimination against homosexuals morally justified? These questions are the focus of this essay.

In what follows, I argue that there are situations in which it is morally permissible to discriminate against homosexuals because of their homosexuality. That is, there are some morally relevant differences between heterosexuality and homosexuality which, in some instances, permit a difference in treatment. The issue of marriage provides a good example. While it is clear that het-

Jeffrey Jordan, "Is It Wrong to Discriminate on the Basis of Homosexuality?" *Journal of Social Philosophy* 26, no. 1 (Spring 1995), 39–52. Copyright © 1995 *Journal of Social Philosophy*. Reprinted by permission of the *Journal of Social Philosophy*.

erosexual unions merit the state recognition known as marriage, along with all the attendant advantages—spousal insurance coverage, inheritance rights, ready eligibility of adoption—it is far from clear that homosexual couples ought to be accorded that state recognition.

The argument of this essay makes no claim about the moral status of homosexuality per se. Briefly put, it is the argument of this essay that the moral impasse generated by conflicting views concerning homosexuality, and the public policy ramifications of those conflicting views justify the claim that it is morally permissible, in certain circumstances, to discriminate against homosexuals.[1]

## 1. The Issue

The relevant issue is this: does homosexuality have the same moral status as heterosexuality? Put differently, since there are no occasions in which it is morally permissible to treat heterosexuals unfavorably, whether because they are heterosexual or because of heterosexual acts, are there occasions in which it is morally permissible to treat homosexuals unfavorably, whether because they are homosexuals or because of homosexual acts?

A negative answer to the above can be termed the "parity thesis." The parity thesis contends that homosexuality has the same moral status as heterosexuality. If the parity thesis is correct, then it would be immoral to discriminate against homosexuals because of their homosexuality. An affirmative answer can be termed the "difference thesis" and contends that there are morally relevant differences between heterosexuality and homosexuality which justify a difference in moral status and treatment between homosexuals and heterosexuals. The difference thesis entails that there are situations in which it is morally permissible to discriminate against homosexuals.

It is perhaps needless to point out that the difference thesis follows as long as there is at least one occasion in which it is morally permissible to discriminate against homosexuals. If the parity thesis were true, then on no occasion would a difference in treatment between heterosexuals and homosexuals ever be justified. The difference thesis does not, even if true, justify discriminatory actions on every occasion. Nonetheless, even though the scope of the difference thesis is relatively modest, it is, if true, a significant principle which has not only theoretical import but important practical consequences as well.[2]

A word should be said about the notion of discrimination. To discriminate against X means treating X in an unfavorable way. The word "discrimination" is not a synonym for "morally unjustifiable treatment." Some discrimination is morally unjustifiable; some is not. For example, we discriminate against convicted felons in that they are disenfranchised. This legal discrimination is morally permissible even though it involves treating one person unfavorably different from how other persons are treated. The difference thesis entails that there are circumstances in which it is morally permissible to discriminate against homosexuals.

## 2. An Argument for the Parity Thesis

One might suppose that an appeal to a moral right, the right to privacy, perhaps, or the right to liberty, would provide the strongest grounds for the parity thesis. Rights talk, though sometimes helpful, is not very helpful here. If there is reason to think that the right to privacy or the right to liberty encompasses sexuality (which seems plausible enough), it would do so only with regard to private acts and not public acts. Sexual acts performed in public (whether heterosexual or homosexual) are properly suppressible. It does not take too much imagination to see that the right to be free from offense would soon be offered as a counter consideration by those who find homosexuality morally problematic. Furthermore, how one adjudicates between the competing rights claims is far from clear. Hence, the bald appeal to a right will not, in this case anyway, take one very far.

Perhaps the strongest reason to hold that the parity thesis is true is something like the following:

1. Homosexual acts between consenting adults harm no one. And,

2. respecting persons' privacy and choices in harmless sexual matters maximizes individual freedom. And,

3. individual freedom should be maximized. But,

4. discrimination against homosexuals, because of their homosexuality, diminishes individual freedom since it ignores personal choice and privacy. So,

5. the toleration of homosexuality rather than discriminating against homosexuals is the preferable option since it would maximize individual freedom. Therefore,

6. the parity thesis is more plausible than the difference thesis.

Premise (2) is unimpeachable: if an act is harmless and if there are persons who want to do it and who choose to do it, then it seems clear that respecting the choices of those people would tend to maximize their freedom.[3] Step (3) is also beyond reproach: since freedom is arguably a great good and since there does not appear to be any ceiling on the amount of individual freedom—no "too much of a good thing"—(3) appears to be true.

At first glance, premise (1) seems true enough as long as we recognize that if there is any harm involved in the homosexual acts of consenting adults, it would be harm absorbed by the freely consenting participants. This is true, however, only if the acts in question are done in private. Public acts may involve more than just the willing participants. Persons who have no desire to participate, even if only as spectators, may have no choice if the acts are done in public. A real probability of there being unwilling participants is indicative of the public realm and not the private. However, where one draws the line between private acts and public acts is not always easy to discern; it is clear that different moral standards apply to public acts than to private acts.[4]

If premise (1) is understood to apply only to acts done in private, then it would appear to be true. The same goes for (4): discrimination against homosexuals for acts done in private would result in a diminishing of freedom. So (1)–(4) would lend support to (5) only if we understand (1)–(4) to refer to acts done in private. Hence, (5) must be understood as referring to private acts; and, as a consequence, (6) also must be read as referring only to acts done in private.

With regard to acts which involve only willing adult participants, there may be no morally relevant difference between homosexuality and heterosexuality. In other words, acts done in private. However, acts done in public add a new ingredient to the mix; an ingredient which has moral consequence. Consequently, the argument (1)–(6) fails in supporting the parity thesis. The argument (1)–(6) may show that there are some circumstances in which the moral status of homosexuality and heterosexuality are the same, but it gives us no reason for thinking that this result holds for all circumstances.[5]

# 3. Moral Impasses and Public Dilemmas

Suppose one person believes that X is morally wrong, while another believes that X is morally permissible. The two people, let's stipulate, are not involved in a semantical quibble; they hold genuinely conflicting beliefs regarding the moral status of X. If the first person is correct, then the second person is wrong; and, of course, if the second person is right, then the first must be wrong. This situation of conflicting claims is what we will call an "impasse." Impasses arise out of moral disputes. Since the conflicting parties in an impasse take contrary views, the conflicting views cannot all be true, nor can they all be false.[6] Moral impasses may concern matters only of a personal nature, but moral impasses can involve public policy. An impasse is likely to have public policy ramifications if large numbers of people hold the conflicting views, and the conflict involves matters which are fundamental to a person's moral identity (and, hence, from a practical point of view, are probably irresolvable) and it involves acts done in public. Since not every impasse has public policy ramifications, one can mark off "public dilemma" as a special case of moral impasses: those moral impasses that have public policy consequences. Public dilemmas, then, are impasses located in the public square. Since they have public policy ramifications and since they arise from impasses, one side or another of the dispute will have its views implemented as public policy. Because of the public policy ramifications, and also because social order is sometimes threatened by the volatile parties involved in the impasse, the state has a role to play in resolving a public dilemma.

A public dilemma can be actively resolved in two ways.[7] The first is when the government allies itself with one side of the impasse and, by state coercion and sanction, declares that side of the impasse the correct side. The American Civil War was an example of this: the federal government forcibly ended slavery by aligning itself with the Abolitionist side of the impasse.[8] Prohibition is another example. The Eighteenth Amendment and the Volstead Act allied the state with the Temperance side of the impasse. State mandated affirmative action programs provide a modern example of this. This kind of resolution of a public dilemma we can call a "resolution by declaration." The first of the examples cited above indicates that declarations can be morally proper, the right thing to do. The second example, however, indicates that declarations are not always morally proper. The state does not always take the side of the morally correct; nor is it always clear which side is the correct one

The second way of actively resolving a public dilemma is that of accommodation. An accommodation in this context means resolving the public dilemma in a way that gives as much as possible to all sides of the impasse. A resolution by accommodation involves staking out some middle ground in a dispute and placing public policy in that location. The middle ground location of a resolution via accommodation is a virtue since it entails that there are no absolute victors and no absolute losers. The middle ground is reached in order to resolve the public dilemma in a way which respects the relevant views of the conflicting parties and which maintains social order. The Federal Fair Housing Act and, perhaps, the current status of abortion (legal but with restrictions) provide examples of actual resolutions via accommodation.[9]

In general, governments should be, at least as far as possible, neutral with regard to the disputing parties in a public dilemma. Unless there is some overriding reason why the state should take sides in a public dilemma—the protection of innocent life, or abolishing slavery, for instance—the state should be neutral, because no matter which side of the public dilemma the state takes, the other side will be the recipient of unequal treatment by the state. A state which is partial and takes sides in moral disputes via declaration, when there is no overriding reason why it should, is tyrannical. Overriding reasons involve, typically, the protection of generally recognized rights.[10] In the case of slavery, the right to liberty; in the case of protecting innocent life, the right involved is the negative right to life. If a public dilemma must be actively resolved, the state should do so (in the absence of an overriding reason) via accommodation and not declaration since the latter entails that a sizable number of people would be forced to live under a government which "legitimizes" and does not just tolerate activities which they find immoral. Resolution via declaration is appropriate only if there is an overriding reason for the state to throw its weight behind one side in a public dilemma.

Is moral rightness an overriding reason for a resolution via declaration? What better reason might there be for a resolution by declaration than that it is the right thing to do? Unless one is prepared to endorse a view that is called "legal moralism"—that immorality alone is a sufficient reason for the state to curtail individual liberty—then one had best hold that moral rightness alone is not an overriding reason. Since some immoral acts neither harm nor offend nor violate another's rights, it seems clear enough that too much liberty would be lost if legal moralism were adopted as public policy.[11]

Though we do not have a definite rule for determining a priori which moral impasses genuinely constitute public dilemmas, we can proceed via a case by case method. For example, many people hold that cigarette smoking is harmful and, on that basis, is properly suppressible. Others disagree. Is this a public dilemma? Probably not. Whether someone engages in an imprudent action is, as long as it involves no unwilling participants, a private matter and does not, on that account, constitute a public dilemma.[12] What about abortion? Is abortion a public dilemma? Unlike cigarette smoking, abortion is a public dilemma. This is clear from the adamant and even violent contrary positions involved in the impasse. Abortion is an issue which forces itself into the public square. So, it is clear that, even though we lack a rule which filters through moral impasses designating some as public dilemmas, not every impasse constitutes a public dilemma.

## 4. Conflicting Claims on Homosexuality

The theistic tradition, Judaism and Christianity and Islam, has a clear and deeply entrenched position on homosexual acts: they are prohibited. Now it seems clear enough that if one is going to take seriously the authoritative texts of the respective religions, then one will have to adopt the views of those texts, unless one wishes to engage in a demythologizing of them with the result that one ends up being only a nominal adherent of that tradition.[13] As a consequence, many contemporary theistic adherents of the theistic tradition, in no small part because they can read, hold that homosexual behavior is sinful. Though God loves the homosexual, these folk say, God hates the sinful behavior. To say that act X is a sin entails that X is morally wrong, not necessarily because it is harmful or offensive, but because X violates God's will. So, the claim that homosexuality is sinful entails the claim that it is also morally wrong. And, it is clear, many people adopt the difference thesis just because of their religious views: because the Bible or the Koran holds that homosexuality is wrong, they too hold that view.

Well, what should we make of these observations? We do not, for one thing, have to base our moral conclusions on those views, if for no other reason than not every one is a theist. If one does not adopt the religion-based moral view, one must still respect those who do; they cannot just be dismissed out of hand.[14] And, significantly, this situation yields a reason for thinking that the difference thesis is probably true. Because many religious people sincerely believe homosexual acts to be morally wrong and many others believe that homosexual acts are not morally wrong, there results a public dilemma.[15]

The existence of this public dilemma gives us reason for thinking that the difference thesis is true. It is only via the difference thesis and not the parity thesis, that an accommodation can be reached. Here again, the private/public distinction will come into play.

To see this, take as an example the issue of homosexual marriages. A same-sex marriage would be a public matter. For the government to sanction same-sex marriage to grant the recognition and reciprocal benefits which attach to marriage would ally the government with one side of the public dilemma and against the adherents of religion-based moralities. This is especially true given that, historically, no government has sanctioned same-sex marriages. The status quo has been no same-sex marriages. If the state were to change its practice now, it would be clear that the state has taken sides in the impasse. Given the history, for a state to sanction a same-sex marriage now would not be a neutral act.

Of course, some would respond here that by not sanctioning same-sex marriages the state is, and historically has been, taking sides to the detriment of homosexuals. There is some truth in this claim. But one must be careful here. The respective resolutions of this issue whether the state should recognize and sanction same-sex marriages do not have symmetrical implications. The asymmetry of this issue is a function of the private/public distinction and the fact that marriage is a public matter. If the state sanctions same-sex marriages, then there is no accommodation available. In that event, the religion-based morality proponents are faced with a public, state-sanctioned matter which they find seriously immoral. This would be an example of a resolution via declaration. On the other hand, if the state does not sanction same-sex marriages, there is an accommodation available: in the public realm the state sides with the religion-based moral view, but the state can tolerate private homosexual acts. That is, since homosexual acts are not essentially public acts; they can be, and historically have been, performed in private. The state, by not sanctioning same-sex marriages is acting in the public realm, but it can leave the private realm to personal choice.[16]

## 5. The Argument from Conflicting Claims

It was suggested in the previous section that the public dilemma concerning homosexuality, and in particular whether states should sanction same-sex marriages, generates an argument in support of the difference thesis. The argument, again using same-sex marriages as the particular case, is as follows:

7. There are conflicting claims regarding whether the state should sanction same-sex marriages. And,

8. this controversy constitutes a public dilemma. And,

9. there is an accommodation possible if the state does not recognize same-sex marriages. And,

10. there is no accommodation possible if the state does sanction same-sex marriages. And,

11. there is no overriding reason for a resolution via declaration. Hence,

12. the state ought not sanction same-sex marriages. And,

13. the state ought to sanction heterosexual marriages. So,

14. there is at least one morally relevant case in which discrimination against homosexuals, because of their homosexuality, is morally permissible. Therefore,

15. the difference thesis is true.

Since proposition (14) is logically equivalent to the difference thesis, then, if (7)–(14) are sound, proposition (15) certainly follows.

Premises (7) and (8) are uncontroversial. Premises (9) and (10) are based on the asymmetry that results from the public nature of marriage. Proposition (11) is based on our earlier analysis of the argument (1)–(6). Since the strongest argument in support of the parity thesis fails, we have reason to think that there is no overriding reason why the state ought to resolve the public dilemma via declaration in favor of same-sex marriages. We have reason, in other words, to think that (11) is true.

Proposition (12) is based on the conjunction of (7)–(11) and the principle that, in the absence of an overriding reason for state intervention via declaration, resolution by accommodation is the preferable route. Proposition (13) is just trivially true. So, given the moral difference mentioned in (12) and (13), proposition (14) logically follows.

# 6. Two Objections Considered

The first objection to the argument from conflicting claims would contend that it is unsound because a similar sort of argument would permit discrimination against some practice which, though perhaps controversial at some earlier time, is now widely thought to be morally permissible. Take mixed-race marriages, for example. The opponent of the argument from conflicting claims could argue that a similar argument would warrant prohibition against mixed-race marriages. If it does, we would have good reason to reject (7)–(14) as unsound.

There are three responses to this objection. The first response denies that the issue of mixed-race marriages is in fact a public dilemma. It may have been so at one time, but it does not seem to generate much, if any, controversy today. Hence, the objection is based upon a faulty analogy.

The second response grants for the sake of the argument that the issue of mixed-race marriages generates a public dilemma. But the second response points out that there is a relevant difference between mixed-race marriages and same-sex marriages that allows for a resolution by declaration in the one case but not the other. As evident from the earlier analysis of the argument in support of (1)–(6), there is reason to think that there is no overriding reason for a resolution by declaration in support of the parity thesis. On the other hand, it is a settled matter that state protection from racial discrimination is a reason sufficient for a resolution via declaration. Hence, the two cases are only apparently similar, and, in reality, they are crucially different. They are quite different because, clearly enough, if mixed-race marriages do generate a public dilemma, the state should use resolution by declaration in support of such marriages. The same cannot be said for same-sex marriages.

One should note that the second response to the objection does not beg the question against the proponent of the parity thesis. Though the second response denies that race and sexuality are strict analogues, it does so for a defensible and independent reason: it is a settled matter that race is not a sufficient reason for disparate treatment; but, as we have seen from the analysis of (1)–(6), there is no overriding reason to think the same about sexuality.[17]

The third response to the first objection is that the grounds of objection differ in the respective cases: one concerns racial identity; the other concerns behavior thought to be morally problematic. A same-sex marriage would involve behavior which many people find morally objectionable; a mixed-race marriage is objectionable to some, not because of the participants' behavior, but because of the racial identity of the participants. It is the race of the marriage partners which some find of primary complaint concerning mixed-race marriages. With same-sex marriages, however, it is the behavior which is primarily objectionable. To see this latter point, one should note that, though promiscuously Puritan in tone, the kind of sexual acts that are likely involved in a same-sex marriage are objectionable to some, regardless of whether done by homosexuals or heterosexuals.[18] So again, there is reason to reject the analogy between same-sex marriages and mixed-race marriages. Racial identity is an immutable trait and a complaint about mixed-race marriages necessarily involves, then, a complaint about an immutable trait. Sexual behavior is not an immutable trait and it is possible to object to same-sex marriages based on the behavior which would be involved in such marriages. Put succinctly, the third response could be formulated as follows: objections to mixed-race marriages necessarily involve objections over status, while objections to same-sex marriages could involve objections over behavior. Therefore, the two cases are not strict analogues since there is a significant modal difference in the ground of the objection.

The second objection to the argument from conflicting claims can be stated so: if homosexuality is biologically based—if it is inborn[19]—then how can discrimination ever be justified? If it is not a matter of choice, homosexuality is an immutable trait which is, as a consequence, morally permissible. Just as it would be absurd to hold someone morally culpable for being of a certain race, likewise it would be absurd to hold someone morally culpable for being a homosexual. Consequently, according to this objection, the argument from conflicting claims "legitimizes" unjustifiable discrimination.

But this second objection is not cogent, primarily because it ignores an important distinction. No one could plausibly hold that homosexuals act by some sort of biological compulsion. If there is a biological component involved in sexual identity, it would incline but it would not compel. Just because one naturally (without any choice) has certain dispositions, is not in itself a morally cogent reason for acting upon that disposition. Most people are naturally selfish, but it clearly does not follow that selfishness is in any way permissible on that account. Even if it is true that one has a predisposition to do X as a matter of biology and not as a matter of choice, it does not follow that doing X is morally permissible. For example, suppose that pyromania is an inborn predisposition. Just because one has an inborn and, in that sense, natural desire to set fires, one still has to decide whether or not to act on that desire.[20] The reason that the appeal to biology is specious is that it ignores the important distinction between being a homosexual and homosexual acts. One is status; the other is behavior. Even if one has the status naturally, it does not follow that the behavior is morally permissible, nor that others have a duty to tolerate the behavior.[21]

But, while moral permissibility does not necessarily follow if homosexuality should turn out to be biologically based, what does follow is this: in the absence of a good reason to discriminate between homosexuals and heterosexuals, then, assuming that homosexuality is inborn, one ought not discriminate between them. If a certain phenomenon X is natural in the sense of being involuntary and nonpathological, and if there is no good reason to hold that X is morally problematic, then that is reason enough to think that X is morally permissible. In the absence of a good reason to repress X, one should tolerate it since, as per supposition, it is involuntary. The argument from conflicting claims, however, provides a good reason which overrides this presumption.

## 7. A Second Argument for the Difference Thesis

A second argument for the difference thesis, similar to the argument from conflicting claims, is what might be called the "no-exit argument." This argument is based on the principle that:

A.  no just government can coerce a citizen into violating a deeply held moral belief or religious belief.

Is (A) plausible? It seems to be since the prospect of a citizen being coerced by the state into a practice which she finds profoundly immoral appears to be a clear example of an injustice. Principle (A), conjoined with there being a public dilemma arising over the issue of same-sex marriages, leads to the observation that if the state were to sanction same-sex marriages, then persons who have profound religious or moral objections to such unions would be legally mandated to violate their beliefs since there does not appear to be any feasible "exit right" possible with regard to state sanctioned marriage. An exit right is an exemption from some legally mandated practice, granted to a person or group, the purpose of which is to protect the religious or moral integrity of that person or group. Prominent examples of exit rights include conscientious objection and military service, home-schooling of the young because of some religious concern, and property used for religious purposes being free from taxation.

It is important to note that marriage is a public matter in the sense that, for instance, if one is an employer who provides health care benefits to the spouses of employees, one must provide those benefits to any employee who is married. Since there is no exit right possible in this case, one would be coerced, by force of law, into subsidizing a practice one finds morally or religiously objectionable.[22]

In the absence of an exit right, and if (A) is plausible, then the state cannot morally force persons to violate deeply held beliefs that are moral or religious in nature. In particular, the state morally could not sanction same-sex marriages since this would result in coercing some into violating a deeply held religious conviction.

## 8. A Conclusion

It is important to note that neither the argument from conflicting claims nor the no-exit argument licenses wholesale discrimination against homosexuals. What they do show is that some discrimination against homosexuals, in this case the refusal to sanction same-sex marriages, is not only legally permissible but also morally permissible. The discrimination is a way of resolving a public policy dilemma that accommodates, to an extent, each side of the impasse and, further, protects the religious and moral integrity of a good number of people. In short, the arguments show us that there are occasions in which it is morally permissible to discriminate on the basis of homosexuality.[23]

## Endnotes

1. The terms "homosexuality" and "heterosexuality" are defined as follows. The former is defined as sexual feelings or behavior directed toward individuals of the same sex. The latter, naturally enough, is defined as sexual feelings or behavior directed toward individuals of the opposite sex.

   Sometimes the term "gay" is offered as an alternative to "homosexual." Ordinary use of "gay" has it as a synonym of a male homosexual (hence, the common expression, "gays and lesbians"). Given this ordinary usage, the substitution would lead to a confusing equivocation. Since there are female homosexuals, it is best to use "homosexual" to refer to both male and female homosexuals, and reserve "gay" to signify male homosexuals, and "lesbian" for female homosexuals in order to avoid the equivocation.

2. Perhaps we should distinguish the weak difference thesis (permissible discrimination on some occasions) from the strong difference thesis (given the relevant moral differences, discrimination on any occasion is permissible).

3. This would be true even if the act in question is immoral.

4. The standard answer is, of course, that the line between public and private is based on the notion of harm. Acts which carry a real probability of harming third parties are public acts.

5. For other arguments supporting the moral parity of homosexuality and heterosexuality, see Richard Mohr, *Gays/Justice: A Study of Ethics, Society and Law* (NY: Columbia, 1988); and see Michael Ruse, "The Morality of Homosexuality" in *Philosophy and Sex*, eds. R. Baker and F. Elliston (Buffalo, NY: Prometheus Books, 1984), pp. 370–390.

6. Perhaps it would be better to term the disputing positions "contradictory" views rather than "contrary" views.

7. Resolutions can also be passive in the sense of the state doing nothing. If the state does nothing to resolve the public dilemma, it stands pat with the status quo, and the public dilemma is resolved gradually by sociological changes (changes in mores and in beliefs).

8. Assuming, plausibly enough, that the disputes over the sovereignty of the Union and concerning states' rights were at bottom disputes about slavery.

9. The Federal Fair Housing Act prohibits discrimination in housing on the basis of race, religion, and sex. But it does not apply to the rental of rooms in single-family houses, or to a building of five units or less if the owner lives in one of the units. See 42 U.S.C. Section 3603.

10. Note that overriding reasons involve generally recognized rights. If a right is not widely recognized and the state nonetheless uses coercion to enforce it, there is a considerable risk that the state will be seen by many or even most people as tyrannical.

11. This claim is, perhaps, controversial. For a contrary view see Richard George, *Making Men Moral* (Oxford: Clarendon Press, 1993).

12. This claim holds only for smoking which does not affect other persons—smoking done in private. Smoking which affects others, second-hand smoke, is a different matter, of course, and may well constitute a public dilemma.

13. See, for example, Leviticus 18:22, 21:3; and Romans 1:22–32; and Koran IV:13

14. For an argument that religiously-based moral views should not be dismissed out of hand, see Stephen Carter, *The Culture of Disbelief: How American Law and Politics Trivialize Religious Devotion* (NY: Basic Books, 1993).

15. Two assumptions are these: that the prohibitions against homosexuality activity are part of the religious doctrine and not just an extraneous addition; second, that if X is part of one's religious belief or religious doctrine, then it is morally permissible to hold X. Though this latter principle is vague, it is, I think, clear enough for our purposes here (I ignore here any points concerning the rationality of religious belief in general, or in particular cases).

16. This point has implications for the moral legitimacy of sodomy laws. One implication would be this: the private acts of consenting adults should not be criminalized.

17. An *ad hominem* point: If this response begs the question against the proponent of the parity thesis, it does not beg the question any more than the original objection does by presupposing that sexuality is analogous with race.

18. Think of the sodomy laws found in some states which criminalize certain sexual acts, whether performed by heterosexuals or homosexuals.

19. There is some interesting recent research which, though still tentative, strongly suggests that homosexuality is, at least in part, biologically based. See Simon LeVay, *The Sexual Brain* (Cambridge, MA: MIT Press, 1993), pp. 120–122; and J. M. Bailey and R. C. Pillard, "A Genetic Study of Male Sexual Orientation," *Archives of General Psychiatry* 48 (1991), 1089–1096; and C. Burr, "Homosexuality and Biology," *The Atlantic* 271/3 (March 1993), 64; and D. Hamer, S. Hu, V. Magnuson, N. Hu, A. Pattatucci, "A Linkage Between DNA Markers on the X Chromosome and Male Sexual Orientation," *Science* 261 (16 July 1993), 321–327; and see the summary of this article by Robert Pool, "Evidence for Homosexuality Gene," *Science* 261 (16 July 1993), 291–292.

20. I do not mean to suggest that homosexuality is morally equivalent or even comparable to pyromania.

21. Even if one were biologically or innately impelled to do X, it clearly does not follow that one is thereby impelled to do X *in public*. Again, the public/private distinction is morally relevant.

22. Is the use of subsidy here inappropriate? It does not seem so since providing health care to spouses, in a society where this is not legally mandatory, seems to be more than part of a salary and is a case of providing supporting funds for a certain end.

23. I thank David Haslett, Kate Rogers, Louis Pojman, and Jim Fieser for helpful and critical comments.

## Journal/Discussion Questions

✍ *Talk with friends and acquaintances who are gay or lesbian. In what ways do they feel they have been discriminated against?* *What are their views on public policy issues such as homosexual marriage?*

1. The distinction between public and private acts is crucial to Jordan's argument. How does he draw that distinction? How does that affect his argument?

2. One possible objection to Jordan's position is that, if sound, it would also justify discriminating against things such as mixed race marriages. How does Jordan reply to this objection? Critically evaluate his replies.

3. What does Jordan mean by the "no exit" argument? Explain and critically evaluate that argument.

# QUESTIONS FOR DISCUSSION AND REVIEW

## Where Do You Stand Now?

**Instructions:**

You have already answered the following questions in your moral problems self-quiz at the beginning of this book. Now that you have studied the material in this section, take a moment to answer the same questions again.

| | Strongly Agree | Agree | Undecided | Disagree | Strongly Disagree | ***Chapter 6: Sexual Orientation*** |
|---|---|---|---|---|---|---|
| 26. | ❏ | ❏ | ❏ | ❏ | ❏ | Gays and lesbians should be allowed to serve openly in the military. |
| 27. | ❏ | ❏ | ❏ | ❏ | ❏ | Gays and lesbians should not be discriminated against in hiring or housing. |
| 28. | ❏ | ❏ | ❏ | ❏ | ❏ | Homosexuality is unnatural. |
| 29. | ❏ | ❏ | ❏ | ❏ | ❏ | Same-sex marriages should be legal. |
| 30. | ❏ | ❏ | ❏ | ❏ | ❏ | Homosexuality is a matter of personal choice. |

Compare your answers to the present self-quiz with the answers to the initial self-quiz. How, if at all, have your answers changed? How have the *reasons* for your answers changed?

## Journal/Discussion Questions

✍ *How well do you think the articles in this section have understood the experience of being gay? How well do you think they have understood the experience of being heterosexual? What do you think they have left out or misunderstood?*

1. Imagine that you have been hired by a congressional committee, which is charged with the responsibility of drafting new legislation to articulate the place of gays and lesbians in society. How would you advise the committee? What laws, if any, would you propose to add? To delete?

2. Should prominent gays and lesbians publicly reveal their sexual orientation? If they refuse to do so, are others—either gay or not—entitled to reveal it against their wishes?

3. Imagine a round-table discussion of the issue of whether openly gay individuals should be allowed to serve in the military. The participants include you, Senator Goldwater, and professors Mohr and Jordan. Recount the dialogue that would occur in which a discussion.

# FOR FURTHER READING:
# A BIBLIOGRAPHICAL GUIDE
# TO SEXUAL ORIENTATION

## Review Articles and Bibliographies

For a short overview of some of the philosophical issues about homosexuality, see Richard D. Mohr, "Homosexuality," *Encyclopedia of Ethics*, ed. Lawrence C. Becker and Charlotte B. Becker (New York: Garland, 1992), vol. I, pp. 552–554. For a bibliographical survey, see Robert B. Marks Ridinger, *The Homosexual and Society: An Annotated Bibliography* (New York: Greenwood Press, 1990).

## General Books, Anthologies, and Articles

Perhaps the best sympathetic philosophical approach to these issues is to be found in Richard D. Mohr's *Gays/Justice: A Study of Ethics, Society, and Law* (New York: Columbia University Press, 1988). For a much different perspective, see Roger Scruton, *Sexual Desire* (London: Weidenfeld and Nicolson, 1985). See also Michael Ruse, *Homosexuality: A Philosophical Inquiry* (New York: Basil Blackwell, 1968); *Homosexuality and Ethics*, ed. Edward Batchelor, Jr. (New York: Pilgrim Press, 1980); Roger J. Magnuson, *Are Gay Rights Right?: Making Sense of the Controversy*, rev. ed. (Portland, OR: Multnomah, 1990).

On the "social construction" of the concept of homosexuality, see Edward Stein, *Forms of Desire: Sexual Orientation and the Social Constructionist Controversy* (New York: Routledge & Kegan Paul, 1992); David Halperin's *One Hundred Years of Homosexuality* (London: Routledge & Kegan Paul, 1992); and John Thorp's "The Social Construction of Homosexuality," *Phoenix*, 46, no. 1 (Spring 1992), 54–61.

## Homosexual Marriage

On the issue of gay and lesbian marriages, see Susanne Sherman, *Lesbian and Gay Marriage* (Philadelphia: Temple University Press, 1992); John Stott, *Homosexual Partnerships?: Why Same-Sex Relationships Are Not a Christian Option* (Downers Grove, IL: InterVarsity Press, 1985); *Lesbian and Gay Marriage: Private Commitments, Public Ceremonies*, ed. Suzanne Sherman (Philadelphia: Temple University Press, 1992); *Fear of a Queer Planet: Queer Politics and Social Theory*, ed. Michael Warner (Minneapolis: University of Minnesota Press, 1993); *Is Gay Good? Ethics, Theology, and Homosexuality*, ed. W. Dwight Oberholtzer (Philadelphia, Westminster Press, 1971); John D'Emilio, *Making Trouble: Essays on Gay History, Politics and the University* (New York: Routledge & Kegan Paul, 1992); Henry Abelove, et. al., eds., *The Lesbian and Gay Studies Reader* (New York: Routledge & Kegan Paul, 1993); Michael Nava and Robert Dawidoff, *Created Equal: Why Gay Rights Matter to America* (New York: St. Martin's Press, 1994); and, most recently, Andrew Sullivan, *Virtually Normal* (New York: Knopf, 1995).

## Sexual Orientation and the Law

For an excellent introduction to some of the legal issues surrounding homosexuality, see *Harvard Law Review*, eds., *Sexual Orientation and the Law* (Cambridge: Harvard University Press, 1989) and William B. Rubenstein, ed., *Lesbians, Gay Men, and the Law* (New York: The New Press, 1993).

## Homosexuality and the Natural Law Tradition

For a discussion of *homosexuality and the natural law tradition*, see John M. Finnis, "Natural Law and Unnatural Acts," *Heythrop Journal*, 11 (1970), 365–387; and Harry V. Jaffa, *Homosexuality and the Natural Law* (Montclair, CA: Center for the Study of the Natural Law, Claremont Institute, 1990). On the positions of various churches on this issue, see G. Gordon Melton, *The Churches Speak On: Homosexuality* (Detroit: Gale Research, 1991). For an interesting exchange on the question of *whether homosexuality is unnatural* or not, see James A. Gould, "The 'Natural' and Homosexuality," *International Journal of Applied Philosophy* 4 (Fall 1988), 51–54 for a series of arguments about why homosexuality is not unnatural; the reply by Gerard J. Dalcourt, "Professor Gould and the 'Natural,'" *International Journal of Applied Philosophy* 5, no. 1 (Spring 1990), 75–77; a rejoinder to Dalcourt by Joseph J. Sartorelli, "Professor Dalcourt on the 'Natural'," *International Journal of Applied Philosophy* 8, no. 2 (Winter–Spring 1994), 49–52; Dalcourt's reply to Sartorelli, "Professor Sartorelli and the 'Natural'," *International Journal of Applied Philosophy* 8, no. 2 (Winter–Spring 1994), 53–56; and Gould's reply to everyone, "Is Homosexuality Natural?" *International Journal of Applied Philosophy* 8, no. 2 (Winter–Spring 1994), 57–58. On this issue, also see the exchange between Michael Level, "Why Homosexuality Is Abnormal," *The Monist* 67 (April 1984), 251–283 and the reply by Timothy F. Murphy, "Homosexuality and Nature: Happiness and the Law at Stake," *Journal of Applied Philosophy* 4 (October 1987), 195–204.

For a discussion of this issue within *Christianity*, see Charles E. Curran, "Homosexuality and Moral Theology: Methodological and Substantive Considerations," *The Thomist* 35 (July 1971), 447–481; Bruce A. Williams, "Homosexuality and Christianity: A Review Discussion," *The Thomist* 46 (October 1982), 609–625; Gerald D. Coleman, "The Vatican Statement on Homosexuality," *Theological Studies* 48 (1987), 727–734; and the reply by Anthony C. Daly, "Aquinas on Disordered Pleasures and Conditions," *The Thomist* 56, no. 4 (October 1992), 583–612. On a Buddhist perspective, see several of the essays in *Buddhism, Sexuality, and Gender*, ed. Jose I. Cabezon (Albany: SUNY Press, 1992).

## Gays and the Military

For a "novelistic" account of the United States military's treatment of gays and lesbians, see Randy Shilts, *Conduct Unbecoming* (New York: St. Martin's Press, 1993); also see the articles in R. D. Ray, *Gays: In or Out? The U.S. Military and Homosexuals—A Source Book* (McLean, VA: Brassey's (US), 1993).

# Poverty and Welfare

**Videotape:**

|  | | |
|---|---|---|
| | *Topic:* | Battle over Welfare Reform |
| | *Source:* | *Nightline* (January 10, 1995) |
| | *Anchor:* | Ted Koppel |

# EXPERIENTIAL ACCOUNTS

*Rosemary L. Bray is a former editor of* The New York Times Book Review. *She is at work on a book,* Unafraid of the Dark, *about African American attitudes and identity.*

*Ms. Bray describes her experiences growing up on welfare in Chicago and suggests ways in which the question of welfare is also one of race and women as well.*

⁓

Growing up on welfare was a story I had planned to tell a long time from now, when I had children of my own. My childhood on Aid to Families with Dependent Children (A.F.D.C.) was going to be one of those stories I would tell my kids about the bad old days, an urban legend equivalent to Abe Lincoln studying by firelight. But I know now I cannot wait, because in spite of a wealth of evidence about the true nature of welfare and poverty in America, the debate has turned ugly, vicious and racist. The "welfare question" has become the race question and the woman question in disguise, and so far the answers bode well for no one.

In both blunt and coded terms, comfortable Americans more and more often bemoan the waste of their tax money on lazy black women with a love of copulation, a horror of birth control and a lack of interest in marriage. Were it not for the experiences of half my life, were I not black and female and of a certain age, perhaps I would be like so many people who blindly accept the lies and distortions, half-truths and wrongheaded notions about welfare. But for better or worse, I do know better. I know more than I want to know about being poor. I know that the welfare system is designed to be inadequate, to leave its constituents on the edge of survival. I know because I've been there.

And finally, I know that perhaps even more dependent on welfare than its recipients are the large number of Americans who would rather accept this patchwork of economic horrors than fully address the real needs of real people.

My mother came to Chicago in 1947 with a fourth-grade education, cut short by working in the Mississippi fields. She pressed shirts in a laundry for a while and later waited tables in a restaurant, where she met my father. Mercurial and independent, with a sixth-grade education, my Arkansas-born father worked at whatever came to hand. He owned a lunch wagon for a time and prepared food for hours in our kitchen on the nights before he took the wagon out. Sometimes he hauled junk and sold it in the open-air markets of Maxwell Street on Sunday mornings. Eight years after they met—seven years after they married—I was born. My father made her quit her job; her work, he told her, was taking care of me. By the time I was 4, I had a sister, a brother and another brother on the way. My parents, like most other American couples of the 1950s, had their own American dream—a husband who worked, a wife who stayed home, a family of smiling children. But as was true for so many African-American couples, their American dream was an illusion.

The house on the corner of Berkeley Avenue and 45th Street is long gone. The other houses still stand, but today the neighborhood is an emptier, bleaker place. When we moved there, it was a street of old limestones with beveled glass windows, all falling into vague disrepair. Home was a four-room apartment on the first floor, in what must have been the public rooms of a formerly grand house. The rent was $110 a month. All of us kids slept in the big front room. Because I was the oldest, I had a bed of my own, near a big plate-glass window.

My mother and father had been married for several years before she realized he was a gambler who would never stay away from the track. By the time we moved to Berkeley Avenue, Daddy was spending more time gambling, and bringing home less and less money and more and more anger. Mama's simplest requests were met with rage. They fought once for hours when she asked for money to buy a tube of lipstick. It didn't help that I always seemed to need a doctor. I had allergies and bronchitis so severe that I nearly died one Sunday after church when I was about 3.

It was around this time that my mother decided to sign up for A.F.D.C. She explained to the caseworker that Daddy wasn't home much, and when he was he didn't have any money. Daddy was furious; Mama was adamant. "There were times when we hardly had a loaf of bread in here," she told me years later. "It was close. I wasn't going to let you all go hungry."

Going on welfare closed a door between my parents that never reopened. She joined the ranks of unskilled women who were forced to turn to the state for the security their men could not provide. In the sterile relationship between herself and the State of Illinois, Mama found an autonomy denied her by my father. It was she who could decide, at last, some part of her own fate and ours. A.F.D.C. relegated marginally productive men like my father to the ranks of failed patriarchs who no longer controlled the destiny of their families. Like so many of his peers, he could no longer afford the luxury of a woman who did as she was told because her economic life depended on it. Daddy became one of the shadow men who walked out back doors as caseworkers came in through the front. Why did he acquiesce? For all his anger, for all his frightening brutality, he loved us, so much that he swallowed his pride and periodically ceased to exist so that we might survive.

In 1960, the year my mother went on public aid, the poverty threshold for a family of five in the United States was $3,560 and the monthly payment to a family of five from the State of Illinois was $182.56, a total of $2,190.72 a year. Once the $110 rent was paid, Mama was left with $72.56 a month to take care of all the other expenses. By any standard, we were poor. All our lives were proscribed by the narrow line between not quite and just enough.

What did it take to live?

It took the kindness of friends as well as strangers, the charity of churches, low expectations, deprivation and patience. I can't begin to count the hours spent in long lines, long waits, long walks in pursuit of basic things. A visit to a local clinic (one housing doctors, a dentist and pharmacy in an incredibly crowded series of rooms) invariably took the better part of a day; I never saw the same doctor twice.

It took, as well, a turning of our collective backs on the letter of a law that required reporting even a small and important miracle like a present of $5.

All families have their secrets, but I remember the weight of an extra burden. In a world where caseworkers were empowered to probe into every nook and cranny of our lives, silence became defense. Even now, there are things I will not publicly discuss because I cannot shake the fear that we might be hounded by the state, eager to prosecute us for the crime of survival.

All my memories of our years on A.F.D.C. are seasoned with unease. It's painful to remember how much every penny counted, how even a gap of 25 cents could make a difference in any given week. Few people understand how precarious life is from welfare check to welfare check, how the word "extra" has no meaning. Late mail, a bureaucratic mix-up . . . and a carefully planned method of survival lies in tatters.

What made our lives work as well as they did was my mother's genius at making do—worn into her by a childhood of rural poverty—along with her vivid imagination. She worked at home endlessly, shopped ruthlessly, bargained, cajoled, charmed. Her food store of choice was the one that stocked pork and beans, creamed corn, sardines, Vienna sausages and potted meat all at 10 cents a can. Clothing was the stuff of rummage sales, trips to Goodwill and bargain basements, where thin cotton and polyester reigned supreme. Our shoes came from a discount store that sold two pairs for $5.

It was an uphill climb, but there was no time for reflection; we were too busy with our everyday lives. Yet I remember how much it pained me to know that Mama, who recruited a neighbor to help her teach me how to read when I was 3, found herself left behind by her eldest daughter, then by each of us in turn. Her biggest worry was that we would grow up uneducated, so Mama enrolled us in parochial school.

When one caseworker angrily questioned how she could afford to send four children to St. Ambrose School, my mother, who emphatically declared "My kids need an education," told her it was none of her business. (In fact, the school had a volume discount of sorts; the price of tuition dropped with each child you sent. I still don't know quite how she managed it.) She organized our lives around church and school, including Mass every morning at 7:45. My brother was an altar boy; I laid out the vestments each afternoon for the next day's Mass. She volunteered as a chaperone for every class trip, sat with us as we did homework she did not understand herself. She and my father reminded us again and again and again that every book, every test, every page of homework was in fact a ticket out and away from the life we lived

My life on welfare ended on June 4, 1976—a month after my 21st birthday, two weeks after I graduated from Yale. My father, eaten up with cancer and rage, lived just long enough to know the oldest two of us had graduated from college and were on our own. Before the decade ended, all of us had left the welfare rolls. The eldest of my brothers worked at the post office, assumed support of my mother (who also went to work, as a companion to an elderly woman) and earned his master's degree at night. My sister married and got a job at a bank. My baby brother parked cars and found a wife. Mama's biggest job was done at last; the investment made in our lives by the State of Illinois had come to fruition. Five people on welfare for 18 years had become five working, taxpaying adults. Three of us went to college, two of us finished; one of us has an advanced degree; all of us can take care of ourselves.

Ours was a best-case phenomenon, based on the synergy of church and state, the government and the private sector and the thousand points of light that we called friends and neighbors. But there was something more: What fueled our dreams and fired our belief that our lives could change for the better was the promise of the civil rights movement and the war on poverty—for millions of African-Americans the defining events of the 1960s. Caught up in the heady atmosphere of imminent change, our world was filled not only with issues and ideas but with amazing images of black people engaged in the struggle for long-denied rights and freedoms. We knew other people lived differently than we did, we knew we didn't have much, but we didn't mind, because we knew it wouldn't be long. My mother borrowed a phrase I had read to her once from Dick Gregory's auto-biography: Not poor, just broke. She would repeat it often, as often as she sang hymns in the kitchen. She loved to sing a spiritual Mahalia Jackson had made famous: "Move On Up a Little Higher." Like so many others, Mama was singing about earth as well as heaven.

These are the things I remember every time I read another article outlining America's welfare crisis. The rage I feel about the welfare debate comes from listening to a host of lies, distortions and exaggerations—and taking them personally.

I am no fool. I know of few women—on welfare or off—with my mother's grace and courage and stamina. I know not all women on welfare are cut from the same cloth. Some are lazy; some are ground down. Some are too young; many are without husbands. A few have made welfare fraud a lucrative career; a great many more have pushed the rules on outside income to their very limits.

I also know that none of these things justify our making welfare a test of character and worthiness, rather than an acknowledgment of need. Near-sainthood should not be a requirement for financial and medical assistance.

But all manner of sociologists and policy gurus continue to equate issues that simply aren't equivalent—welfare, race, rates of poverty, crime, marriage and childbirth—and to reach conclusions that serve to demonize the poor. More than one social arbiter would have us believe that we have all been mistaken for the last 30 years—that the efforts to relieve the most severe effects of poverty have not only failed but have served instead to increase and expand the ranks of the poor. In keeping women, children and men from starvation, we are told, we have also kept them from self-sufficiency. In our zeal to do good, we have undermined the work ethic, the family and thus, by association, the country itself.

So how did I get here?

Despite attempts to misconstrue and discredit the social programs and policies that changed—even saved—my life, certain facts remain. Poverty was reduced by 39 percent between 1960 and 1990, according to the Census Bureau, from 22.2 percent to 13.5 percent of the nation's population. That is far too many poor people, but the rate is considerably lower than it might have been if we had thrown up our hands and reminded ourselves that the poor will always be with us. Of black women considered "highly dependent," that is, on welfare for more than seven years, 81 percent of their daughters grow up to live productive lives off the welfare rolls, a 1992 Congressional report stated; the 19 percent who become second-generation welfare recipients can hardly be said to constitute an epidemic of welfare dependency. The vast majority of African-Americans are now working or middle class, an achievement that occurred in the past 30 years, most specifically between 1960 and 1973, the years of expansion in the very same social programs that it is so popular now to savage. Those were the same years in which I changed from girl to woman, learned to read and think, graduated from high school and college, came to be a working woman, a taxpayer, a citizen.

In spite of all the successes we know of, in spite of the reality that the typical welfare recipient is a white woman with young children, ideologues have continued to fashion from whole cloth the specter of the mythical black welfare mother, complete with a prodigious reproductive capacity and a galling laziness, accompanied by the uncaring and equally lazy black man in her life who will not work, will not marry her and will not support his family.

Why has this myth been promoted by some of the best (and the worst) people in government, academia, journalism and industry? One explanation may be that the constant presence of poverty frustrates even the best-intentioned among us. It may also be because the myth allows for denial about who the poor in America really are and for denial about the depth and intransigence of racism regardless of economic status. And because getting tough on welfare is for some a first-class career move; what better way to win a position in the next administration than to trash those people least able to respond? And, finally, because it serves to assure white Americans that lazy black people aren't getting away with anything.

Many of these prescriptions for saving America from the welfare plague not only reflect an insistent, if sometimes unconscious, racism but rest on the bedrock of patriarchy. They are rooted in the fantasy of a male presence as a path to social and economic salvation and in its corollary— the image of woman as passive chattel, constitutionally so afflicted by her condition that the only recourse is to transfer her care from the hands of the state to the hands of a man with a job. The largely ineffectual plans to create jobs for men in communities ravaged by disinvestment, the state-sponsored dragnets for men who cannot or will not support their children, the exhortations for women on welfare to find themselves a man and get married, all are the institutional expressions of the same worn cultural illusion—that women and children without a man are fundamentally damaged goods. Men are such a boon, the reasoning goes, because they make more money than women do.

Were we truly serious about an end to poverty among women and children, we would take the logical next step. We would figure out how to make sure women who did a dollar's worth of work got a dollar's worth of pay. We would make sure that women could go to work with their minds at ease, knowing their children were well cared for. What women on welfare need, in large measure, are the things key to the life of every adult woman: economic security and autonomy. Women need the skills and the legitimate opportunity to earn a living for ourselves as well as for people who may rely on us; we need the freedom to make choices to improve our own lives and the lives of those dear to us.

"The real problem is not welfare," says Kathryn Edin, a professor of sociology at Rutgers University and a scholar in residence at the Russell Sage Foundation. "The real problem is the nature of low-wage work and lack of support for these workers—most of whom happen to be women raising their children alone." Completing a five-year study of single mothers—some low-wage workers, some welfare recipients—Edin is quantifying what common sense and bitter experience have told millions of women who rotate off and on the welfare rolls: Women, particularly unskilled women with children, get the worst jobs available, with the least amount of health care, and are the most frequently laid off. "The workplace is not oriented toward people who have family responsibilities," she says. "Most jobs are set up assuming that someone else is minding the kids and doesn't need assistance."

But the writers and scholars and politicians who wax most rhapsodic about the need to replace welfare with work make their harsh judgments from the comfortable and supportive environs of offices and libraries and think tanks. If they need to go to the bathroom midsentence, there is no one timing their absence. If they take longer than a half-hour for lunch, there is no one waiting to dock their pay. If their babysitter gets sick, there is no risk of someone having taken their place at work by the next morning. Yet these are conditions that low-wage women routinely face, which inevitably lead to the cyclical nature of their welfare histories. These are the realities that many of the most vocal and widely quoted critics of welfare routinely ignore. In his book *The End of Equality*, for example, Mickey Kaus discusses social and economic inequity, referring to David

Ellwood's study on long-term welfare dependency without ever mentioning that it counts anyone who uses the services for at least one month as having been on welfare for the entire year.

In the heated atmosphere of the welfare debate, the larger society is encouraged to believe that women on welfare have so violated the social contract that they have forfeited all rights common to those of us lucky enough not to be poor. In no area is this attitude more clearly demonstrated than in issues of sexuality and childbearing. Consider the following: A *Philadelphia Inquirer* editorial of Dec. 12, 1990, urges the use of Norplant contraceptive inserts for welfare recipients—in spite of repeated warnings from women's health groups of its dangerous side effects—in the belief that the drug "could be invaluable in breaking the cycle of inner-city poverty." (The newspaper apologized for the editorial after it met widespread criticism, both within and outside the paper.) A California judge orders a woman on welfare, convicted of abusing two of her four children, to use Norplant; the judge's decision was appealed. The Washington state legislature considers approving cash payments of up to $10,000 for women on welfare who agree to be sterilized. These and other proposals, all centering on women's reproductive capacities, were advanced in spite of evidence that welfare recipients have fewer children than those not on welfare.

The punitive energy behind these and so many other Draconian actions and proposals goes beyond the desire to decrease welfare costs; it cuts to the heart of the nation's racial and sexual hysteria. Generated neither by law nor by fully informed public debate, these actions amount to social control over "those people on welfare"—a control many Americans feel they have bought and paid for every April 15. The question is obvious: If citizens were really aware of who receives welfare in America, however inadequate it is, if they acknowledged that white women and children were welfare's primary beneficiaries, would most of these things be happening?

Welfare has become a code word now. One that enables white Americans to mask their sometimes malignant, sometimes benign racism behind false concerns about the suffering ghetto poor and their negative impact on the rest of us. It has become the vehicle many so-called tough thinkers use to undermine compassionate policy and engineer the reduction of social programs.

So how did I get here?

I kept my drawers up and my dress down, to quote my mother. I didn't end up pregnant because I had better things to do. I knew I did because my uneducated, Southern-born parents told me so. Their faith, their focus on our futures are a far cry from the thesis of Nicholas Lemann, whose widely acclaimed book *The Promised Land* perpetuates the myth of black Southern sharecropping society as a primary source of black urban malaise. Most important, my family and I had every reason to believe that I had better things to do and that when I got older I would be able to do them. I had a mission, a calling, work to do that only I could do. And that is knowledge transmitted not just by parents, or school, or churches. It is a palpable thing, available by osmosis from the culture of the neighborhood and the world at large.

Add to this formula a whopping dose of dumb luck. It was my sixth-grade teacher, Sister Maria Sarto, who identified in me the first signs of a stifling boredom and told my mother that I needed a tougher, more challenging curriculum than her school could provide. It was she who then tracked down the private Francis W. Parker School, which agreed to give me a scholarship if I passed the admissions test.

Had I been born a few years earlier, or a decade later, I might now be living on welfare in the Robert Taylor Homes or working as a hospital nurse's aide for $6.67 an hour. People who think such things could never have happened to me haven't met enough poor people to know better. The avenue of escape can be very narrow indeed. The hope and energy of the 1960s—fueled not only by a growing economy but by all the passions of a great national quest—is long gone. The sense of possibility I knew has been replaced with the popular cultural currency that money and those who have it are everything and those without are nothing.

Much has been made of the culture of the underclass, the culture of poverty, as though they were the free-floating illnesses of the African-American poor, rendering them immune to other influences: the widespread American culture of greed, for example, or of cynicism. It is a thinly veiled continuation of the endless projection of "dis-ease" onto black life, a convenient way to sidestep a more painful debate about the loss of meaning in American life that has made our entire nation depressed and dispirited. The malaise that has overtaken our country is hardly confined to African-Americans or the poor, and if both groups should disappear tomorrow, our nation would still find itself in crisis. To talk of the black "underclass threat" to the public sphere, as Mickey Kaus does, to demonize the poor among us and thus by association all of us—ultimately this does more damage to the body politic than a dozen welfare queens.

When I walk down the streets of my Harlem neighborhood, I see women like my mother, hustling, struggling, walking their children to school and walking them back home. And I also see women who have lost both energy and faith, talking loud, hanging out. I see the shadow men of a new generation, floating by with a few dollars and a toy, then drifting away to the shelters they call home. And I see, a dozen times a day, the little girls my sister and I used to be, the little boys my brothers once were.

Even the grudging, inadequate public help I once had is fading fast for them. The time and patience they will need to re-create themselves is vanishing under pressure for the big, quick fix and the crushing load of blame being heaped upon them. In the big cities and the small towns of America, we have let theory, ideology and mythology about welfare and poverty overtake these children and their parents.

## Journal/Discussion Questions

✍ *Discuss your own experiences with welfare. Have you ever experienced it directly? Have you ever been close to anyone on welfare? Have you talked to them about the experience? In what ways was it helpful? In what ways was it either not helpful or perhaps even harmful to them?*

1. In light of Bray's article, what typically happens to *men* in families that receive A.F.D.C.? How can that issue be best addressed?

2. Currently, there is much talk about—and even legislative action toward—reducing or eliminating A.F.D.C. Discuss these proposals in light of Bray's description of her family's experience.

# AN INTRODUCTION TO THE MORAL ISSUES

## Introduction

We have only to walk down any major street in downtown New York—or any other major American city—to see the stark contrast between wealth and poverty in America. Gleaming limousines pull up next to homeless people seeking warmth from the heating grates of skyscrapers. Similarly, we have only to buy a cup of coffee to encounter the redistribution of some of that wealth in America—the tax on a cup of coffee, taken from the coffee drinker, is redistributed by the government. In these two experiences, we find the central questions about poverty and welfare in America today. *What*, first of all, *is the extent and nature of poverty in the United States*? Second, *what, if anything, should the government do about that poverty*?

## The Nature of Poverty in the United States

There is little doubt that poverty exists in the United States—it does not take a skilled economist to prove that, although the precise measurement of such poverty is a more difficult matter. Moreover, it is important to draw two initial distinctions as we approach the issue of poverty. First, we must realize that in most instances we are not talking as much about absolute poverty as we are about *relative impoverishment*. We are not concerned that the country as a whole is poor, but rather with the way in which some people in our country have less than others. Second, we must distinguish between *short-term poverty* and *long-term poverty*. Some people might be temporarily poor for a variety of reasons—they might just be beginning their careers, they might be temporarily between jobs, or the like. Yet our central concern is with those who experience long-term poverty—that is, are poor and have little prospect of changing their economic situation significantly.

*What are the nature and causes of poverty in the United States?*

The ways in which we explain the nature and causes of poverty have a profound influence on our moral understanding of poverty and the appropriate responses to it. Three competing models—none conclusively proven, but all psychologically powerful—dominate the contemporary popular discussion of poverty. Let's briefly consider each of these.

### The Discrimination Model of Poverty

Many people see poverty as the result of discrimination—primarily racism, but also sexism. Indeed, the correlation is easy to establish between low income and groups—most notably African Americans, Native Americans, and women—that have historically been objects of discrimination. Michael Harrington's *The Other America*[1] was one of the most influential early articulations of this view. *Causal* connections, of course, are more difficult to establish, but there is certainly an intuitive plausibility to the claim that the discrimination caused the poverty. However, other groups—Jews, many European ethnic groups including the Irish and the Italians, and Asians—

have been the objects of discrimination and yet have been more successful in overcoming poverty, and the discrimination model has difficulty in explaining these differences solely in terms of the forces of discrimination.

## The Random Market Forces Model of Poverty

Some see poverty in the United States as the result of forces that are essentially unconnected with either discrimination or individual merit; rather, the impersonal forces of the market rob some of jobs and reward others with an abundance of employment opportunities. Employment opportunities diminish in steel factories and increase in electronics plants, but steel workers cannot easily shift to another area of manufacturing—sometimes because it requires new skills, sometimes because the jobs are located in another city. Such changes create hapless victims and fortunate recipients.

## The Just Deserts Model of Poverty

Finally, some see poverty as the result of individual failings of character—that the poor are poor because on some level they have done something to deserve it. Advocates of this model see the poor as lazy, undisciplined, and wanting to be taken care of. In some versions of this position, the claim is made that a "culture of poverty"—to use the term coined by the sociologist Oscar Lewis—arises that undermines the motivation of the poor and encourages feelings of dependency, helplessness, and inferiority.

## The Case of the Children

One of the most troubling aspects of poverty is the plight of the children. We may argue about whether the parents deserve their fate, whether they should try harder to find employment, and the like, but there is little disagreement that children are the innocent victims in all this. Children don't decide where to be born, and there is no question of merit involved in their fate. A four-year-old child in a rich family is no more deserving of his or her fate than one in a poor family. If anything seems unfair, it is this.

*Does the fact that some of the poor are children affect our response to poverty?*

*Compassion.*    Two aspects about the issue of children stand out. First, our response to the fate of impoverished children is, first and foremost, an emotional one: *compassion.* We see their suffering, and on some fundamental level we identify with that suffering, realizing that it is just as valuable as ours. (In this respect, compassion is fundamentally different from pity. Whereas pity looks down on its object, compassion sees the one who is suffering as a moral equal. Although there may be moments when we appreciate the compassion of other people, none of us wants to be an object of pity, for pity always puts us down in relation to that pitier.) The strength of compassion as a motive for change is that it moves the whole person, not just the intellect.

*The cycle of poverty.*    There is a less visceral, but equally compelling, dimension to the problem of children and poverty. The danger that many people see is that a cycle of poverty arises in which poverty is passed on from one generation to another with little hope that individuals can break free from the cycle. Children who lack basic nutrition, children who do not receive regular medical care, children with little support for either their homes or their homework at home, children who are more afraid of being shot in school than receiving an "F"—these children can hardly be expected to fight against the odds and break out of the cycle of poverty they have known since birth. The focus of many welfare programs has been precisely here: to break the cycle of poverty by intervening with the children, giving them the skills and opportunities denied to their parents.

*How can we break the cycle of poverty?*

## Visions of the Ideal Role of Government in the Economy

The second major factor shaping our response to poverty is our vision of the ideal role of government in the operation of the economy. Some—conservative and libertarian thinkers occupy this camp—think that the economy will simply regulate itself; others—in the middle of the political spectrum—believe that some government intervention is necessary; and the remaining few—those on the far left of the political spectrum—believe that the government should actively and strongly intervene to guide the development of the economy.

### The Self-Regulating Model: Conservativism and Libertarianism

Ever since Adam Smith described the "invisible hand" of the market as guiding society's development, some theorists have maintained that the economy possesses a natural equilibrium which it finds without any external guidance. Indeed, those in this tradition generally feel that attempts to guide the economy will be more likely to produce greater problems than they solve.

Proponents of this model are divided about what kind of society this produces. Some see the invisible hand of the market as producing significant suffering and hardship, but maintain that this is simply and unavoidably the way things are. Others claim that, at least in the long run, such a society is in everybody's best interest. Certainly if such claims were true, many people's concern about the suffering of the poor would be greatly reduced.

### The Strong Interventionist Model: Communism and Socialism

At the other end of the political spectrum are those who maintain that a high degree of government intervention in the economy is justified, usually in order to produce a good society—one in which everyone is (roughly) economically equal, a society without rich or poor. This is the vision of society that inspired communism, and, to a large extent, socialism. In contrast to advocates of giving the market a free hand, egalitarians espouse a highly controlled market. Many maintain that the breakup of the Soviet Union marked the end of this kind of market.

### The Moderate Interventionist Model: Liberalism

Classical liberals have sought to stake out a middle ground between these two visions of the role of government in the economy, one that required the government to establish a minimum level—or floor—below which people would not be allowed to sink, but which imposed no maximum limits—or ceiling—on how high they could go. The intent of this model is to permit government intervention in the economy in order to eliminate extreme poverty but otherwise to restrict such intervention in order to preserve the incentives for individual initiative and hard work.

## Moral Frameworks for Responding to Poverty

Responses to poverty arise out of a combination of at least three factors: (1) one's views on the nature of poverty; (2) one's vision of the role of government in the economy, and (3) one's views on the moral framework—human rights, consequences, and compassion are the most important of these—that shape the way in which we move from the actual situation to the ideal. Let's now turn to a consideration of each of these three types of moral frameworks.

### Rights-Based Approaches to Poverty and Welfare

Those who see poverty in terms of the issue of rights fall along a predictable spectrum. At the one extreme—these are the *conservatives* and *libertarians*—are those who maintain (a) that poverty is a matter of individual desert and (b) that the government ought not to intervene in order to adjust the balance of wealth. At the other extreme—these are *socialists* and *communists*—are those who maintain (a) that poverty is not a matter of desert but a combination of bad luck and discrimination and (b) that the government ought to adjust the balance of wealth in such a way that all persons are approximately financially equal. In the middle are those—usually called *liberals*—who maintain that (a) at least some poverty is the result of factors beyond the impoverished individual's control and that (b) the government ought to intervene at least to ameliorate the more egregious effects of poverty, especially in those instances in which poverty is clearly not deserved. Notice that in each of these cases, the position is actually composed on two components, one dealing with the origins of poverty and the other dealing with the issue of government intervention.

*Negative and positive rights.* Philosophers typically distinguish between negative and positive rights. *Negative rights*, sometimes called *liberties*, are simply rights not to be interfered with in some particular way. *Positive rights*, sometimes called *welfare rights* or *entitlements*, go further, claiming that others are obligated to provide me with something so that I may successfully exercise my right. If I have a negative right to free speech, no one is allowed to prevent me from expressing my thoughts—they cannot confiscate my printing press, take away my microphone, or the like. If, however, I have a positive right to free speech, then I am entitled to more than just noninterference: others (society, the government) are obligated to provide me with the means for expressing my thoughts—they must give me access to printing press, microphone, and so on.

Of course, no right—despite the impression created by much of contemporary rhetoric—is absolute. At the very least, most advocates of negative rights draw the line at respecting a right when it infringes on someone else's similar right. I may have the right to free speech, but that does not mean I have the right to speak in such a way as to prevent others from speaking. Similarly, although this is seldom done, we must always recognize that rights are rarely absolute. Even something like the right to property presupposes a context, and it would seem odd to claim that individuals in a society that did not recognize private property would have a right to property.

The liberal approach to welfare rights during the last several decades in the United States has developed along an interesting path. The principal argument has not been in favor of adding new positive rights out of thin air, as it were. Rather, the argument has been that the effective exercise of certain already-recognized rights mandates certain welfare rights as necessary conditions for exercising other, more basic rights. Consider the right to equal treatment when applying to, say, medical school. Such equality of opportunity is of little practical benefit if it is not accompanied by a wider range of equal opportunities earlier in the student's life. If I did not have adequate nutrition to pay attention in elementary and secondary school, if I did not have access to educational benefits (such as computers) available to other students, if my teachers never believed in me because they thought no one of my race (or sex) was academically gifted, if I had to work full-time while going to school because my siblings and mother needed the income in order to just get by, then by the time I am twenty-two years old, it will make little difference to me that no one will arbitrarily bar me from medical school. In order to have genuine equality of opportunity at this stage, it would have been necessary to have equality of opportunity at many earlier stages—and such equality can only be insured through aggressive intervention by the government to insure positive rights.

## Consequentialist Approaches to Poverty

Some advocates of government intervention to reduce the problem of poverty sidestep the entire issue of whether individuals have a right to welfare and turn their attention instead to an examination of the (likely) consequences of either extending or withdrawing such support.

The main outline of consequentialist arguments on both sides of this issue is clear, even though there is significant disagreement about both facts and predictions. Consequentialist supporters of government intervention to reduce poverty maintain that, although money and services are ostensibly given only to the poor, in the long run everyone benefits from such actions. These benefits may be in the form of a more capable workforce, a physically healthier population (with less cost to the economy as a whole for sickness), less crime due to increased economic prosperity, and the like—all factors which would enhance the lives of everyone in society, not just the few who receive welfare benefits directly.

Consequentialist opponents of such intervention question the reliability of such claims in two ways. First, they ask whether present programs—perhaps, *any* programs—will produce the consequences that supporters claim. Will welfare programs, for example, produce a more capable workforce? Second, they ask whether such programs will not produce other, unwanted and undesirable consequences that their supporters ignore. For example, do such programs unintentionally foster dependency? Do programs such as Aid to Families with Dependent Children unintentionally undermine family structure? In "The Coming White Underclass," Charles Murray argues precisely this point, maintaining that A.F.D.C. is unintentionally producing an underclass, among both blacks and whites, by rewarding illegitimacy.

In response to such criticisms, defenders of consequentialist approaches to poverty are focusing more on programs that see welfare as a temporary measure intended to bring people into the workforce. The rise of interest in workfare has been symptomatic of this shift.

### Compassion-Based Approaches to Poverty

Finally, some approaches to the issue of poverty in our society appeal, first and foremost, to some central moral emotion—usually compassion—as the foundation of our response to poverty. Instead of seeing the reduction of poverty as an issue of rights or of consequences, advocates of this view see it simply as the humane and decent thing to do. We help the poor, they say, simply because we care about their suffering. To do anything less would be inhumane, and it would diminish our humanity as well as perpetuate the suffering of the poor.

*What role should compassion have in our response to poverty in America?*

Critics of this position are obviously in a difficult position, for they would seem to be forced into defending moral callousness, if not outright cruelty. Although some have been willing to bite the bullet, as it were, on this issue and simply accept the label of moral callousness, others have refused that characterization of their position. We must distinguish, conservatives such as Marvin Olasky—the author of *The Tragedy of American Compassion*—argue, between *feeling compassion* and *acting* on the basis of such feelings.[2] They endorse the feeling, but then argue that the proposed actions in fact fail (at least in the long run) to alleviate the suffering to which they are a response. Imagine someone snatching a crying baby from the hands of a physician who was performing a painful medical procedure intended to save the baby's life. Snatching the baby away might be well-motivated by compassion for the baby's suffering, but it may still be the wrong thing to do, ultimately probably causing more harm than good.

*Private charity.*   Whereas right-based approaches to poverty see basic subsistence as a right that the poor can claim, compassion-based approaches do not necessarily see the poor as having a *right* to welfare. Consequently, compassion-based approaches will be more likely to emphasize the importance of charity—and, especially, of private charity and individual acts of compassion.

## Diversity and Consensus

### Poverty and Welfare

Despite the deep divisions in our society over the issue of poverty and the ways in which we are to respond to it, there seems to be a reasonable prospect for achieving a common ground *if* certain empirical questions can be answered. The disagreements, at least between conservatives and liberals, seem to be more about empirical issues than value issues.

No one, for example, advocates creating dependency, just as no one—at least, neither conservatives nor liberals—is in favor of undermining the traditional family and its underlying values. The central issue, at least among both conservatives and liberals, is whether welfare works or not. This is primarily an empirical question, not a moral one.

Yet what happens if we find out that welfare does not work? We are still left with the problem of poverty in our society and with the task of finding other, more effective ways of responding to it.

## Endnotes

1. Michael Harrington, *The Other America* (New York: Penguin Books, 1992).
2. Marvin Olasky, *The Tragedy of American Compassion* (Wheaton, IL: Crossway Books, 1992).

# THE ARGUMENTS

James Sterba
"From Liberty to Welfare"

*James Sterba is professor of philosophy at the University of Notre Dame, and has published fourteen books—including* How to Make People Just—*and over 130 articles, most recently* Contemporary Social and Political Philosophy *and* Social and Political Philosophy: Classical Texts in Feminist and Multicultural Perspectives.

*Libertarians typically oppose welfare rights and the welfare state, in part because they represent an unwelcome intrusion of government into the private sphere. Sterba argues that such rights are justifiable even on libertarian grounds.*

## As You Read, Consider This:

1. What is the difference between Spencerian and Lockean libertarianism? How are the two conceptually related to one another? Why is this distinction important for Sterba's argument?

2. Throughout his article, Sterba presents his position and then considers a number of possible objections to his position and offers replies to those objections. As you read, make a note in the margin for each of these objections and for Sterba's replies.

⌒

Libertarians today are deeply divided over whether a night watchman state can be morally justified. Some, like Robert Nozick, hold that a night watchman state would tend to arise by an invisible-hand process if people generally respected each other's Lockean rights.[1] Others, like Murray Rothbard, hold that even the free and informed consent of all the members of a society would not justify such a state.[2] Despite this disagreement, libertarians are strongly united in opposition to welfare rights and the welfare state. According to Nozick, "the state may not use its coercive apparatus for the purpose of getting some citizens to aid others."[3] For Rothbard, "the libertarian position calls for the complete abolition of governmental welfare and reliance on private charitable aid."[4] Here I argue that this libertarian opposition to welfare rights and a welfare state is ill-founded. Welfare rights can be given a libertarian justification, and once this is recognized, a libertarian argument for a welfare state, unlike libertarian arguments for the night watchman state, is both straightforward and compelling. . . .

Libertarians have defended their view in basically two different ways. Some libertarians, following Herbert Spencer, have (1) defined liberty as the absence of constraints, (2) taken a right to liberty to be the ultimate political ideal, and (3) derived all other rights from this right to liberty. Other libertarians, following John Locke, have (1) taken a set of rights, including, typically, a right to life or self-ownership and a right to property, to be the ultimate political ideal, (2) defined liberty as the absence of constraints in the exercise of these fundamental rights, and (3) derived all other rights, including a right to liberty, from these fundamental rights.

Each of these approaches has its difficulties. The principal difficulty with the first approach is that unless one arbitrarily restricts what is to count as an interference, conflicting liberties will abound, particularly in all areas of social life.[5] The principal difficulty with the second approach is that as long as a person's rights have not been violated, her liberty would not have been restricted either, even if she were kept in prison for the rest of her days.[6] I don't propose to try to decide between these two approaches. What I do want to show, however, is that on either approach welfare rights and a welfare state are morally required.

## Spencerian Libertarianism

Thus suppose we were to adopt the view of those libertarians who take a right to liberty to be the ultimate political ideal. According to this view, liberty is usually defined as follows:

> *The Want Conception of Liberty:* Liberty is being unconstrained by other persons from doing what one wants.

This conception limits the scope of liberty in two ways. First, not all constraints whatever their source count as a restriction of liberty; the constraints must come from other persons. For example, people who are constrained by natural forces from getting to the top of Mount Everest do not lack liberty in this regard. Second, constraints that have their source in other persons, but that do not run counter to an individual's wants, constrain without restricting that individual's liberty. Thus, for people who do not want to hear Beethoven's Fifth Symphony, the fact that others have effectively proscribed its performance does not restrict their liberty, even though it does constrain what they are able to do.

Of course, libertarians may wish to argue that even such constraints can be seen to restrict a person's liberty once we take into account the fact that people normally want, or have a general desire, to be unconstrained by others. But other philosophers have thought that the possibility of such constraints points to a serious defect in this conception of liberty,[7] which can only be remedied by adopting the following broader conception of liberty:

> *The Ability Conception of Liberty:* Liberty is being unconstrained by other persons from doing what one is able to do.

Applying this conception to the above example, we find that people's liberty to hear Beethoven's Fifth Symphony would be restricted even if they did not want to hear it (and even if, perchance, they did not want to be unconstrained by others) since other people would still be constraining them from doing what they are able to do. . . .

Of course, there will be numerous liberties determined by the Ability Conception that are not liberties according to the Want Conception. For example, there will be highly talented students who do not want to pursue careers in philosophy, even though no one constrains them from doing so. Accordingly, the Ability Conception but not the Want Conception would view them as possessing a liberty. And even though such liberties are generally not as valuable as those liberties that are common to both conceptions, they still are of some value, even when the manipulation of people's wants is not at issue.

Yet even if we accept all the liberties specified by the Ability Conception, problems of interpretation still remain. The major problem in this regard concerns what is to count as a constraint. On the one hand, libertarians would like to limit constraints to positive acts (that is, acts of commission) that prevent people from doing what they are otherwise able to do. On the other hand, welfare liberals and socialists interpret constraints to include, in addition, negative acts (that is, of omission) that prevent people from doing what they are otherwise able to do. In fact, this is one way to understand the debate between defenders of "negative liberty" and defenders of "positive liberty." For defenders of negative liberty would seem to interpret constraints to include only positive acts of others that prevent people from doing what they otherwise are able to do, while defenders of positive liberty would seem to interpret constraints to include both positive and negative acts of others that prevent people from doing what they are otherwise able to do.[8]

Suppose we interpret constraints in the manner favored by libertarians to include only positive acts by others that prevent people from doing what they are otherwise able to do, and let us consider a typical conflict situation between the rich and the poor.

In this conflict situation, the rich, of course, have more than enough resources to satisfy their basic needs. By contrast, the poor lack the resources to meet their most basic nutritional needs even though they have tried all the means available to them that libertarians regard as legitimate for acquiring such resources. Under circumstances like these, libertarians usually maintain that the rich should have the liberty to use their resources to satisfy their luxury needs if they so wish. Libertarians recognize that this liberty might well be enjoyed at the expense of the satisfaction of the most basic nutritional needs of the poor. Libertarians just think that a right to liberty always has priority over other political ideals, and since they assume that the liberty of the poor is not at stake in such conflict situations, it is easy for them to conclude that the rich should not be required to sacrifice their liberty so that the basic nutritional needs of the poor may be met.

From a consideration of the liberties involved, libertarians claim to derive a number of more specific requirements, in particular, a right to life, a right to freedom of speech, press and assembly, and a right to property.

Here it is important to observe that the libertarian's right to life is not a right to receive from others the goods and resources necessary for preserving one's life; it is simply a right not to be killed unjustly. Correspondingly, the libertarian's right to property is not a right to receive from others the goods and resources necessary for one's welfare, but rather a right to acquire goods and resources either by initial acquisition or by voluntary agreement.

Rights such as these, libertarians claim, can at best support only a limited role for government. That role is simply to prevent and punish initial acts of coercion—the only wrongful actions for libertarians. And, as we noted before, libertarians are deeply divided over whether a government with even such a limited role, that is, a night watchman state, can be morally justified.

Of course, libertarians would allow that it would be nice of the rich to share their surplus resources with the poor. Nevertheless, according to libertarians, such acts of charity should not be coercively required, because the liberty of the poor is not thought to be at stake in such conflict situations.

In fact, however, the liberty of the poor is at stake in such conflict situations. What is at stake is the liberty of the poor to take from the surplus possessions of the rich what is necessary to satisfy their basic nutritional needs. When libertarians are brought to see that this is the case, they are often genuinely surprised, for they had not previously seen the conflict between the rich and the poor as a conflict of liberties.[9]

When the conflict between the rich and the poor is viewed as a conflict of liberties, we can either say that the rich should have the liberty to use their surplus resources for luxury purposes, or we can say that the poor should have the liberty to take from the rich what they require to meet their basic nutritional needs. If we choose one liberty, we must reject the other. What needs to be determined, therefore, is which liberty is morally preferable: the liberty of the rich or the liberty of the poor.

I submit that the liberty of the poor, which is the liberty to take from the surplus resources of others what is required to meet one's basic nutritional needs, is morally preferable to the liberty of the rich, which is the liberty to use one's surplus resources for luxury purposes. To see that this is the case we need only appeal to one of the most fundamental principles of morality, one that is common to all political perspectives, namely the "ought" implies "can" principle. According to this principle, people are not morally required to do what they lack the power to do or what would involve so great a sacrifice that it would be unreasonable to ask them to perform such an action.[10] For example, suppose I promised to attend a meeting on Friday, but on Thursday I am involved in a serious car accident which puts me into a coma. Surely it is no longer the case that I ought to attend the meeting now that I lack the power to do so. Or suppose instead that on Thursday I develop a severe case of pneumonia for which I am hospitalized. Surely I could legitimately claim that I no longer ought to attend the meeting on the grounds that the risk to my health involved in attending is a sacrifice that it would be unreasonable to ask me to bear.

Now applying the "ought" implies "can" principle to the case at hand, it seems clear that the poor have it within their power to willingly relinquish such an important liberty as the liberty to take from the rich what they require to meet their basic nutritional needs. Nevertheless, it would be unreasonable to require them to make so great a sacrifice. In the extreme case, it would involve requiring the poor to sit back and starve to death. Of course, the poor may have no real alternative to relinquishing this liberty. To do anything else may involve worse consequences for themselves and their loved ones and may invite a painful death. Accordingly, we may expect that the poor would acquiesce, albeit unwillingly, to a political system that denied them the welfare rights supported by such a liberty, at the same time that we recognize that such a system imposed an unreasonable sacrifice upon the poor—a sacrifice that we could not morally blame the poor for trying to evade.[11] Analogously, we might expect that a woman whose life was threatened would submit to a rapist's demands, at the same time that we recognize the utter unreasonableness of those demands.

By contrast, it would not be unreasonable to require the rich to sacrifice the liberty to meet some of their luxury needs so that the poor can have the liberty to meet their basic nutritional needs. Naturally, we might expect that the rich for reasons of self-interest and past contribution might be disinclined to make such a sacrifice. We might even suppose that the past contribution of the rich provides a good reason for not sacrificing their liberty to use their surplus for luxury purposes. Yet, unlike the poor, the rich could not claim that relinquishing such a liberty involved so great a sacrifice that it would be unreasonable to require them to make it; unlike the poor, the rich could be morally blameworthy for failing to make such a sacrifice.

Consequently, if we assume that however else we specify the requirements of morality, they cannot violate the "ought" implies "can" principle, it follows that, despite what libertarians claim, the right to liberty endorsed by libertarians actually favors the liberty of the poor over the liberty of the rich.

Yet, couldn't libertarians object to this conclusion, claiming that it would be unreasonable to require the rich to sacrifice the liberty to meet some of their luxury needs so that the poor could have the liberty to meet their basic nutritional needs? As I have pointed out, libertarians don't usually see the situation as a conflict of liberties, but suppose they did. How plausible would such an objection be? Not very plausible at all, I think.

Consider this: what are libertarians going to say about the poor? Isn't it clearly unreasonable to require the poor to sacrifice the liberty to meet their basic nutritional needs so that the rich can have the liberty to meet their luxury needs? Isn't it clearly unreasonable to require the poor to sit back and starve to death? If it is, then there is no resolution of this conflict that would be reasonable to require both the rich and the poor to accept. But that would mean that the libertarian ideal of liberty cannot be a moral ideal that resolves conflicts of interest in ways that it would be reasonable to require everyone affected to accept. Therefore, as long as libertarians think of themselves as putting forth such a moral ideal, they cannot allow that it would be unreasonable both to require the rich to sacrifice the liberty to meet some of their luxury needs in order to benefit the poor and to require the poor to sacrifice the liberty to meet their basic nutritional needs in order to benefit the rich. But I submit that if one of these requests is to be judged reasonable, then, by any neutral assessment, it must be the requirement that the rich sacrifice the liberty to meet some of their luxury needs so that the poor can have the liberty to meet their basic nutritional needs; there is no other plausible resolution, if libertarians intend to be putting forth a moral ideal that reasonably resolves conflicts of interest.

But might not libertarians hold that putting forth a moral ideal means no more than being willing to universalize one's fundamental commitments? Surely we have no difficulty imagining the rich willing to universalize their commitments to relatively strong property rights. Yet, at the same time, we have no difficulty imagining the poor and their advocates willing to universalize their commitments to relatively weak property rights. Consequently, if the libertarian's moral ideal is interpreted in this fashion, it would not be able to provide a basis for reasonably resolving conflicts of interest between the rich and the poor. But without such a basis for conflict resolution, how could societies flourish, as libertarians claim they would, under a minimal state or with no state at all?[12] Surely, in order for societies to flourish in this fashion, the libertarian ideal must resolve conflicts of interest in ways that it would be reasonable to require everyone affected to accept. But, as we have seen, that requirement can only be satisfied if the rich sacrifice the liberty to meet some of their luxury needs so that the poor can have the liberty to meet their basic nutritional needs.

It should also be noted that this case for restricting the liberty of the rich depends upon the willingness of the poor to take advantage of whatever opportunities are available to them for satisfying their basic needs by engaging in mutually beneficial work, so that failure of the poor to take advantage of such opportunities would normally either cancel or at least significantly reduce the obligation of the rich to restrict their own liberty for the benefit of the poor.[13] In addition, the poor would be required to return the equivalent of any surplus possessions they have taken from the rich once they are able to do so and still satisfy their basic needs. Nor would the poor be required to keep the liberty to which they are entitled. They could give up part of it, or all of it, or risk losing it on the chance of gaining a greater share of liberties or other social goods.[14] Consequently, the case for restricting the liberty of the rich for the benefit of the poor is neither unconditional nor inalienable.

Even so, libertarians would have to be disconcerted about what turns out to be the practical upshot of taking a right to liberty to be the ultimate political ideal. For libertarians contend that their political ideal would support welfare rights only when constraints are "illegitimately" interpreted to induce both positive and negative acts by others that prevent people from doing what they are otherwise able to do. By contrast, when constraints are interpreted to include only positive acts, libertarians contend, no such welfare rights can be justified.

Nevertheless, what the foregoing argument demonstrates is that this view is mistaken. For even when the interpretation of constraints favored by libertarians is employed, a moral assessment of the competing liberties still requires an allocation of liberties to the poor that will be generally sufficient to provide them with the goods and resources necessary for satisfying their basic nutritional needs.

One might think that once the rich realize that the poor should have the liberty not to be interfered with when taking from the surplus possessions of the rich what they require to satisfy their basic needs, it would be in the interest of the rich to stop producing any surplus whatsoever. Yet that would only be the case if first, the recognition of the rightful claims of the poor would exhaust the surplus of the rich and second, the poor would never be in a position to be obligated to repay what they appropriated from the rich. Fortunately for the poor both of these conditions are unlikely to obtain.

Of course, there will be cases where the poor fail to satisfy their basic nutritional needs, not because of any direct restriction of liberty on the part of the rich, but because the poor are in such dire need that they are unable even to attempt to take from the rich what they require to meet their basic nutritional needs. Accordingly, in such cases, the rich would not be performing any act of commission that prevents the poor from taking what they require. Yet, even in such cases, the rich would normally be performing acts of commission that prevent other persons from aiding the poor by taking from the surplus possessions of the rich. And when assessed from a moral point of view, restricting the liberty of these other persons would not be morally justified for the very same reason that restricting the liberty of the poor to meet their own basic nutritional needs would not be morally justified: it would not be reasonable to ask all of those affected to accept such a restriction of liberty. . . .

In brief, what this shows is that if a right to liberty is taken to be the ultimate political ideal, then, contrary to what libertarians claim, not only would a system of welfare rights be morally required, but also such a system would clearly benefit the poor.

## Lockean Libertarianism

Yet suppose we were to adopt the view of those libertarians who do not take a right to liberty to be the ultimate political ideal. According to this view, liberty is defined as follows:

> *The Rights Conception of Liberty:* Liberty is being unconstrained by other persons from doing what one has a right to do.

The most important ultimate rights in terms of which liberty is specified are, according to this view, a right to life understood as a right not to be killed unjustly and a right to property understood as a right to acquire goods and resources either by initial acquisition or voluntary agreement. In order to evaluate this view, we must determine what are the practical implications of these rights.

Presumably, a right to life understood as a right not to be killed unjustly would not be violated by defensive measures designed to protect one's person from life-threatening attacks. Yet would this right be violated when the rich prevent the poor from taking what they require to satisfy their basic nutritional needs? Obviously, as a consequence of such preventive actions poor people sometimes do starve to death. Have the rich, then, in contributing to this result, killed the poor, or simply let them die; and, if they have killed the poor, have they done so unjustly?

Sometimes the rich, in preventing the poor from taking what they require to meet their basic nutritional needs, would not in fact be killing the poor, but only causing them to be physically or mentally debilitated. Yet since such preventive acts involve resisting the life-preserving activities of the poor, when the poor do die as a consequence of such acts, it seems clear that the rich would be killing the poor, whether intentionally or unintentionally.

Of course, libertarians would want to argue that such killing is simply a consequence of the legitimate exercise of property rights, and hence, not unjust. But to understand why libertarians are mistaken in this regard, let us appeal again to that fundamental principle of morality, the "ought" implies "can" principle. In this context, the principle can be used to assess two opposing accounts of property rights. According to the first account, a right to property is not conditional upon whether other persons have sufficient opportunities and resources to satisfy their basic needs. This view holds that the initial acquisition and voluntary agreement of some can leave others, through no fault of their own, dependent upon charity for the satisfaction of their most basic needs. By contrast, according to the second account, initial acquisition and voluntary agreement can confer title of property on all goods and resources except those surplus goods and resources of the rich that are required to satisfy the basic needs of those poor who through no fault of their own lack opportunities and resources to satisfy their own basic needs.

Clearly, only the first of these two accounts of property rights would generally justify the killing of the poor as a legitimate exercise of the property rights of the rich. Yet it would be unreasonable to require the poor to accept anything other than some version of the second account of property rights. Moreover, according to the second account, it does not matter whether the poor would actually die or are only physically or mentally debilitated as a result of such acts of prevention. Either result would preclude property rights from arising. Of course, the poor may have no real alternative to acquiescing to a political system modeled after the first account of property rights, even though such a system imposes an unreasonable sacrifice upon them—a sacrifice that we could not blame them for trying to evade. At the same time, although the rich would be disinclined to do so, it would not be unreasonable to require them to accept a political system modeled after the second account of property rights—the account favored by the poor.

Consequently, if we assume that however else we specify the requirements of morality, they cannot violate the "ought" implies "can" principle, it follows that, despite what libertarians claim, the right to life and the right to property endorsed by libertarians actually support a system of welfare rights. . . .

Nevertheless, it might be objected that the welfare rights that have been established against the libertarian are not the same as the welfare rights endorsed by welfare liberals. We could mark this difference by referring to the welfare rights that have been established against the libertarian as "action welfare rights" and referring to the welfare rights endorsed by welfare liberals as both "action and recipient welfare rights." The significance of this difference is that a person's action welfare right can be violated only when other people through acts of commission interfere with a person's exercise of that right, whereas a person's action and recipient welfare right can be violated by such acts of commission and by acts of omission as well. However, this difference will have little practical import. For once libertarians come to recognize the legitimacy of action welfare rights, then in order not to be subject to the poor person's discretion in choosing when and how to exercise her action welfare right, libertarians will tend to favor two morally legitimate ways of preventing the exercise of such rights. First, libertarians can provide the poor with mutually beneficial job opportunities. Second, libertarians can institute adequate recipient welfare rights that would take precedence over the poor's action welfare rights. Accordingly, if libertarians adopt either or both of these ways of legitimately preventing the poor from exercising their action welfare rights, libertarians will end up endorsing the same sort of welfare institutions favored by welfare liberals.

Finally, once a system of welfare rights is seen to follow irrespective of whether one takes a right to liberty or rights to life and property as the ultimate political ideal, the justification for a welfare state becomes straightforward and compelling. For while it is at least conceivable that rights other than welfare rights could be adequately secured in a society without the enforcement agencies of a state, it is inconceivable that welfare rights themselves could be adequately secured without such enforcement agencies. Only a welfare state would be able to effectively solve the large-scale coordination problem necessitated by the provision of welfare. Consequently, once a system of welfare rights can be seen to have a libertarian justification, the argument for a welfare state hardly seems to need stating.[15]

## Endnotes

1. Robert Nozick, *Anarchy, State and Utopia* (New York: Basic Books, 1974), Part I.

2. Murray Rothbard, *The Ethics of Liberty* (Atlantic Highlands: Humanities Press, 1982), p. 230.

3. Nozick, *Anarchy, State and Utopia,* p. ix.

4. Murray Rothbard, *For a New Liberty* (New York: Collier Books, 1978), p. 148.

5. See, for example, James P. Sterba, "Neo-Libertarianism," *American Philosophical Quarterly* 15 (1978), 17–19; Ernest Loevinsohn, "Liberty and the Redistribution of Property," *Philosophy and Public Affairs* 6 (1977), 226–239; David Zimmerman, "Coercive Wage Offers," *Philosophy and Public Affairs* 10 (1981), 121–145. To limit what is to count as coercive, Zimmerman claims that in order for P's offer to be coercive:

   > (I)t must be the case that P does more than merely prevent Q *from taking from* P resources necessary for securing Q's strongly preferred preproposal situation; P must prevent Q *from acting on his own* (or with the help of others) *to produce or procure* the strongly preferred proposal situation.

   But this restriction seems arbitrary, and Zimmerman provides little justification for it. See David Zimmerman, "More on Coercive Wage Offers," *Philosophy and Public Affairs* 12 (1983), 67–68.

6. It might seem that this second approach could avoid this difficulty if a restriction of liberty is

understood as the curtailment of one's prima facie rights. But in order to avoid the problem of a multitude of conflicting liberties, which plagues the first approach, the specification of prima facie rights must be such that they only can be overridden when one or more of them is violated. And this may involve too much precision for our notion of prima facie rights.

7. Isaiah Berlin, *Four Essays on Liberty* (New York: Oxford University Press, 1969), pp. XXXVIII–XL.

8. On this point, see Maurice Cranston, *Freedom* (New York: Basic Books, 1953), pp. 52–53; C. B. Macpherson, *Democratic Theory* (Oxford: Oxford University Press, 1973), p. 95; Joel Feinberg, *Rights, Justice and the Bounds of Liberty* (Princeton, NJ.: Princeton University Press, 1980), chap. 1.

9. See John Hospers, *Libertarianism* (Los Angeles: Nash, 1971), chap. 7.

10. Alvin Goldman, *A Theory of Human Action* (Englewood Cliffs, NJ.: Prentice Hall, 1970), pp. 208–215; William Frankena, "Obligation and Ability," in *Philosophical Analysis,* ed. Max Black (Ithaca, NY: Cornell University Press, 1950), pp. 157–175.

    Judging from some recent discussions of moral dilemmas by Bernard Williams and Ruth Marcus, one might think that the "ought" implies "can" principle would only be useful for illustrating moral conflicts rather than resolving them.

    See Bernard Williams, *Problems of the Self* (Cambridge: Cambridge University Press, 1977), chaps. 11 and 12; Ruth Marcus, "Moral Dilemmas and Consistency," *The Journal of Philosophy* 80 (1980), 121–136. See also Terrance C . McConnell, "Moral Dilemmas and Consistency in Ethics," *Canadian Journal of Philosophy* 18 (1978), 269-287. But this is only true if one interprets the "can" in the principle to exclude only "what a person lacks the power to do." If one interprets the "can" to exclude in addition "what would involve so great a sacrifice that it would be unreasonable to ask the person to do it" then the principle can be used to resolve moral conflicts as well as state them. Nor would libertarians object to this broader interpretation of the "ought" implies "can" principle since they do not ground their claim to liberty on the existence of irresolvable moral conflicts.

11. See James P. Sterba, "Is There a Rationale for Punishment?" *The American Journal of Jurisprudence* 29 (1984), 29–44.

12. As further evidence, notice that those libertarians who justify a minimal state do so on the grounds that such a state would arise from reasonable disagreements concerning the application of libertarian rights. They do not justify the minimal state on the grounds that it would be needed to keep in submission large numbers of people who could not come to see the reasonableness of libertarian rights.

13. Obviously, the employment opportunities offered to the poor must be honorable and supportive of self-respect. To do otherwise would be to offer the poor the opportunity to meet some of their basic needs at the cost of denying some of their other basic needs.

14. The poor cannot, however, give up the liberty to which their children are entitled.

15. Of course, someone might still want to object to welfare states on the grounds that they "force workers to sell their labor" (see G. A. Cohen, "The Structure of Proletarian Unfreedom," *Philosophy and Public Affairs* 12 (1982), 3–33) and subject workers to "coercive wage offers." (See Zimmerman, "Coercive Wage Offers.") But, for a defense of at least one

form of welfare state against such an objection, see James P. Sterba, "A Marxist Dilemma for Social Contract Theory," *American Philosophical Quarterly* 21 (1981), 51–59.

## Journal/Discussion Questions

✍ *Imagine walking down the street and being approached for money by a homeless person. How would Sterba perceive that situation? Is this the same way that you would see it? Discuss.*

1. Sterba argues that "the liberty of the poor . . . is morally preferable to the liberty of the rich." Explain what he means by this. What conclusions does he draw from this? In what ways do you agree with him? Disagree?

2. Sterba sees the conflict between rich and poor in terms of a conflict of *liberties.* How does this affect his argument? In what other ways could that conflict be seen?

3. The rich, Sterba argues, would be morally blameworthy if they refused to sacrifice "their liberty to meet their luxury needs so that the poor can have the liberty to meet their basic nutritional needs." Do you agree with Sterba? Disagree? Discuss your reasons.

---

### Tibor Machan
### "The Nonexistence of Basic Welfare Rights"

*Born in Hungary at the beginning of World War II, Tibor Machan is a professor of philosophy at Auburn University and the author of numerous articles and books in social and moral philosophy, including* The Pseudo-Science of B. F. Skinner, Human Rights and Human Liberties, *and* Individuals and Their Rights, *from which the present selection is drawn.*

*Arguing specifically against James Sterba's "From Liberty to Welfare" and in general against liberalism, Machan here presents and defends a libertarian analysis of the issue of welfare rights.*

### As You Read, Consider This:

1. The word "liberty" may have several different meanings. Note the different senses of this term in the following essay.

2. What does Machan mean by "'ought' implies 'can'"? What role does this distinction play in his argument?

Reprinted from *Individuals and Their Rights* by Tibor Machan (LaSalle, Illinois: Open Court, 1989). Copyright © 1989, Open Court Publishing Company.

James Sterba and others maintain that we all have the right to "receive the goods and resources necessary for preserving" ourselves. This is not what I have argued human beings have a right to. They have the right, rather, not to be killed, attacked, and deprived of their property—by persons in or outside of government. As Abraham Lincoln put it, "no man is good enough to govern another man, without that other's consent."[1]

Sterba claims that various political outlooks would have to endorse these "rights." He sets out to show, in particular, that welfare rights follow from libertarian theory itself.[2] Sterba wishes to show that *if* Lockean libertarianism is correct, then we all have rights to welfare and equal (economic) opportunity. What I wish to show is that since Lockean libertarianism—as developed in this work—is true, and since the rights to welfare and equal opportunity require their violation, no one has these latter rights. The reason some people, including Sterba, believe otherwise is that they have found some very rare instances in which some citizens could find themselves in circumstances that would require disregarding rights altogether. This would be in situations that cannot be characterized to be "where peace is possible."[3] And every major libertarian thinker from Locke to the present has treated these kinds of cases.[4]

Let us be clear about what Sterba sets out to show. It is that libertarians are philosophically unable to escape the welfare-statist implication of their commitment to negative liberty. This means that despite their belief that they are only supporting the enforceable right of every person not to be coerced by other persons, libertarians must accept, by the logic of their own position, that individuals also possess basic enforceable rights to being provided with various services from others. He holds, then, that basic negative rights imply basic positive rights.

To Lockean libertarians the ideal of liberty means that we all, individually, have the right not to be constrained against our consent within our realm of authority—ourselves and our belongings. Sterba states that for such libertarians "Liberty is being unconstrained by persons from doing what one has a right to do."[5] Sterba adds, somewhat misleadingly, that for Lockean libertarians "a right to life [is] a right not to be killed unjustly and a right to property [is] a right to acquire goods and resources either by initial acquisition or voluntary agreement."[6] Sterba does realize that these rights do not entitle one to receive from others the goods and resources necessary for preserving one's life.

A problem with this foundation of the Lockean libertarian view is that political justice—not the justice of Plato, which is best designated in our time as "perfect virtue"—for natural-rights theorists presupposes individual rights. One cannot then explain rights in terms of justice but must explain justice in terms of rights.

For a Lockean libertarian, to possess any basic right to receive the goods and resources necessary for preserving one's life conflicts with possessing the right not to be killed, assaulted, or stolen from. The latter are rights Lockean libertarians consider to be held by all individual human beings. Regularly to protect and maintain—that is, enforce—the former right would often require the violation of the latter. A's right to the food she has is incompatible with B's right to take this same food. Both the rights could not be fundamental in an integrated legal system. The situation of one's having rights to welfare, and so forth, and another's having rights to life, liberty, and property is thus theoretically intolerable and practically unfeasible. The point of a system of rights is the securing of mutually peaceful and consistent moral conduct on the part of human beings. As Rand observes,

"Rights" are . . . the link between the moral code of a man and the legal code of a society, between ethics and politics. *Individual rights are the means of subordinating society to moral law.*[7]

Sterba asks us—in another discussion of his views—to consider what he calls "a *typical* conflict situation between the rich and the poor." He says that in his situation "the rich, of course, have more than enough resources to satisfy their basic needs. By contrast, the poor lack the resources to meet their most basic needs even though *they have tried all the means available to them that libertarians regard as legitimate for acquiring such resources*"[8] (my emphasis*).

The goal of a theory of rights would be defeated if rights were typically in conflict. Some bureaucratic group would have to keep applying its moral intuitions on numerous occasions when rights claims would *typically* conflict. A constitution is workable if it helps remove at least the largest proportion of such decisions from the realm of arbitrary (intuitive) choice and avail a society of men and women of objective guidelines that are reasonably integrated, not in relentless discord.

Most critics of libertarianism assume some doctrine of basic needs which they invoke to show that whenever basic needs are not satisfied for some people, while others have "resources" which are not basic needs for them, the former have just claims against the latter. (The language of resources of course loads the argument in the critic's favor since it suggests that these goods simply come into being and happen to be in the possession of some people, quite without rhyme or reason, arbitrarily [as John Rawls claims].)[9]

This doctrine is full of difficulties. It lacks any foundation for why the needs of some persons must be claims upon the lives of others. And why are there such needs anyway—to what end are they needs, and whose ends are these and why are not the persons whose needs they are held responsible for supplying the needs? (Needs, as I have already observed, lack any force in moral argument without the prior justification of the purposes they serve or the goals they help to fulfill. A thief has a basic need of skills and powers that are clearly not justified if theft is morally unjustified. If, however, the justification of basic needs, such as food and other resources, presupposes the value of human life, and if the value of human life justifies, as I have argued earlier, the principle of the natural rights to life, liberty and property, then the attainment or fulfillment of the basic need for food may not involve the violation of these rights.)

Sterba claims that without guaranteeing welfare and equal-opportunity rights, Lockean libertarianism violates the most basic tenets of any morality, namely, that "ought" implies "can." The thrust of "'ought' implies 'can'" is that one ought to do that which one is free to do, that one is morally responsible only for those acts that one had the power either to choose to engage in or to choose not to engage in. (There is debate on just how this point must be phrased—in terms of the will being free or the person being free to will something. For our purposes, however, all that counts is that the person must have [had] a genuine option to do X or not to do X before it can be true that he or she ought to do X or ought to have done X.) If an innocent person is forced by the actions of another to forgo significant moral choices, then that innocent person is not free to act morally and thus his or her human dignity is violated.

This is not so different from the commonsense legal precept that if one is not sound of mind one cannot be criminally culpable. Only free agents, capable of choosing between right and wrong, are open to moral evaluation. This indeed is the reason that many so-called moral theories fail to be anything more than value theories. They omit from consideration the issue of self-determination. If either hard or soft determinism is true, morality is impossible, although values need not disappear.[10]

If Sterba were correct about Lockean libertarianism typically contradicting "'ought' implies 'can,'" his argument would be decisive. (There are few arguments against this principle that I know of and they have not convinced me. They trade on rare circumstances when persons feel guilt for taking actions that had bad consequences even though they could not have avoided them.)[11] It is because Karl Marx's and Herbert Spencer's systems typically, normally, indeed in every case, violate this principle that they are not bona fide moral systems. And quite a few others may be open to a similar charge.[12]

Sterba offers his strongest argument when he observes that "'ought' implies 'can'" is violated "when the rich prevent the poor from taking what they require to satisfy their basic needs even though they have tried all the means available to them that libertarians regard as legitimate for acquiring such resources."[13]

Is Sterba right that such are—indeed, must be—typical conflict cases in a libertarian society? Are the rich and poor, even admitting that there is some simple division of people into such economic groups, in such hopeless conflict all the time? Even in the case of homeless people, many find help without having to resort to theft. The political factors contributing to the presence of helpless people in the United States and other Western liberal democracies are a hotly debated issue, even among utilitarians and welfare-state supporters. Sterba cannot make his argument for the typicality of such cases by reference to history alone. (Arguably, there are fewer helpless poor in near-libertarian, capitalist systems than anywhere else—why else would virtually everyone wish to live in these societies rather than those where welfare is guaranteed, indeed enforced? Not, at least originally, for their welfare-statist features. Arguably, too, the disturbing numbers of such people in these societies could be due, in part, to the lack of consistent protection of all the libertarian natural rights.)

Nonetheless, in a system that legally protects and preserves property rights there will be cases where a rich person prevents a poor person from taking what belongs to her (the rich person)—for example, a chicken that the poor person might use to feed herself. Since after such prevention the poor person might starve, Sterba asks the rhetorical question "Have the rich, then, in contributing to this result, killed the poor, or simply let them die; and if they have killed the poor, have they done so unjustly?"[14] His answer is that they have. Sterba holds that a system that accords with the Lockean libertarian's idea that the rich person's preventive action is just "imposes an unreasonable sacrifice upon" the poor, one "that we could not blame them for trying to evade." Not permitting the poor to act to satisfy their basic needs is to undermine the precept that "'ought' implies 'can'" since, as Sterba claims, that precept means, for the poor, that they ought to satisfy their basic needs. This they must have the option to do if they ought to do it. . . .

When people defend their property, what are they doing? They are protecting themselves against the intrusive acts of some other person, acts that would normally deprive them of something to which they have a right, and the other has no right. As such, these acts of protectiveness make it possible for men and women in society to retain their own sphere of jurisdiction intact, protect their own "moral space."[15] They refuse to have their human dignity violated. They want to be sovereigns and govern their own lives, including their own productive decisions and actions. Those who mount the attack, in turn, fail or refuse to refrain from encroaching upon the moral space of their victims. They are treating the victim's life and its productive results as though these were unowned resources for them to do with as they choose.

Now the argument that cuts against the above account is that on some occasions there can be people who, with no responsibility for their situation, are highly unlikely to survive without disregarding the rights of others and taking from them what they need. This is indeed possible. It is no less possible that there be cases in which someone is highly unlikely to survive without obtaining the services of a doctor who is at that moment spending time healing someone else, or in which there is a person who is highly unlikely to survive without obtaining one of the lungs of another person, who wants to keep both lungs so as to be able to run the New York City marathon effectively. And such cases could be multiplied indefinitely.

But are such cases typical? The argument that starts with this assumption about a society is already not comparable to the libertarianism that has emerged in the footsteps of Lockean natural-rights doctrine, including the version advanced in this book. That system is developed for a human community in which "peace is possible." Libertarian individual rights, which guide men and women in such an adequately hospitable environment to act without thwarting the flourishing of others, are thus suitable bases for the legal foundations for a human society. It is possible for people in the world to pursue their proper goals without thwarting a similar pursuit by others.

The underlying notion of society in such a theory rejects the description of human communities implicit in Sterba's picture. Sterba sees conflict as typically arising from some people producing and owning goods, while others having no alternative but to take these goods from the former in order to survive. But these are not the typical conflict situations even in what we today consider reasonably free human communities—most thieves and robbers are not destitute, nor are they incapable of doing something aside from taking other people's property in order to obtain their livelihood.

The typical conflict situation in society involves people who wish to take shortcuts to earning their living (and a lot more) by attacking others, not those who lack any other alternative to attacking others so as to reach that same goal. This may not be evident from all societies that team with human conflict—in the Middle East, or Central and South America, for example. But it must be remembered that these societies are far from being even near-libertarian. Even if the typical conflicts there involved the kind Sterba describes, that would not suffice to make his point. Only if it were true that in comparatively free countries the typical conflict involved the utterly destitute and helpless arrayed against the well-to-do, could his argument carry any conviction.

The Lockean libertarian has confidence in the willingness and capacity of virtually all persons to make headway in life in a free society. The very small minority of exceptional cases must be taken care of by voluntary social institutions, not by the government, which guards self-consistent individual rights.

The integrity of law would be seriously endangered if the government entered areas that required it to make very particular judgments and depart from serving the interest of the public as such. We have already noted that the idea of "satisfying basic needs" can involve the difficulty of distinguishing those whose actions are properly to be so characterized. Rich persons are indeed satisfying their basic needs as they protect and preserve their property rights. . . . Private property rights are necessary for a morally decent society.

The Lockean libertarian argues that private property rights are morally justified in part because they are the concrete requirement for delineating the sphere of jurisdiction of each person's moral authority, where her own judgment is decisive.[16] This is a crucial basis for the right to property. And so is the contention that we live in a metaphysically hospitable universe wherein people normally need not suffer innocent misery and deprivation—so that such a condition is usually the result of negligence or the violation of Lockean rights, a violation that has made self-development and commerce impossible. If exceptional emergencies set the agenda for the law, the law itself will disintegrate. (A just legal system makes provision for coping with emergencies that are brought to the attention of the authorities, for example, by way of judicial discretion, without allowing such cases to determine the direction of the system. If legislators and judges don't uphold the integrity of the system, disintegration ensues. This can itself encourage the emergence of strong leaders, demagogues, who promise to do what the law has not been permitted to do, namely, satisfy people's sense of justice. Experience with them bodes ill for such a prospect.)

Normally persons do not "lack the opportunities and resources to satisfy their own basic needs." Even if we grant that some helpless, crippled, retarded, or destitute persons could offer nothing to anyone that would merit wages enabling them to carry on with their lives and perhaps even flourish, there is still the other possibility for most actual, known hard cases, that is, seeking help. I am not speaking here of the cases we know: people who drop out of school, get an unskilled job, marry and have kids, only to find that their personal choice of inadequate preparation for life leaves them relatively poorly off. "'Ought' implies 'can'" must not be treated ahistorically—some people's lack of current options results from their failure to exercise previous options prudently. I refer here to the "truly needy," to use a shop-worn but still useful phrase—those who have never been able to help themselves and are not now helpless from their own neglect. Are such people being treated *unjustly*, rather than at most uncharitably, ungenerously, indecently, pitilessly, or in some other respect immorally—by those who, knowing of the plight of such persons, resist forcible efforts to take from them enough to provide the ill-fated with what they truly need? Actually, if we tried to pry the needed goods or money from the well-to-do, we would not even learn if they would act generously. Charity, generosity, kindness, and acts of compassion presuppose that those well enough off are not coerced to provide help. These virtues cannot flourish, nor can the corresponding vices, of course, without a clearly identified and well-protected right to private property for all.

If we consider the situation as we are more likely to find it, namely, that desperate cases not caused by previous injustices (in the libertarian sense) are rare, then, contrary to what Sterba suggests, there is much that unfortunate persons can and should do in those plausible, non-emergency situations that can be considered typical. They need not resort to violating the private-property rights of those who are better off. The destitute can appeal for assistance both from the rich and from the many voluntary social service agencies which emerge from the widespread compassion of people who know about the mishaps that can at times strike perfectly decent people.

Consider, as a prototype of this situation on which we might model what concerns Sterba, that if one's car breaks down on a remote road, it would be unreasonable to expect one not to seek a phone or some other way of escaping one's unfortunate situation. So one ought to at least try to obtain the use of a phone.

But should one break into the home of a perfect stranger living nearby? Or ought one instead to request the use of the phone as a favor? "'Ought' implies 'can'" is surely fully satisfied here. Actual practice makes this quite evident. When someone is suffering from misfortune and there are plenty of others who are not, and the unfortunate person has no other avenue for obtaining help than to obtain it from others, it would not be unreasonable to expect, morally, that the poor seek such help as surely might be forthcoming. We have no justification for assuming that the rich are all callous, though this caricature is regularly painted by communists and by folklore. Supporting and gaining advantage from the institution of private property by no means implies that one lacks the virtue of generosity. The rich are no more immune to virtue than the poor are to vice. The contrary view is probably a legacy of the idea that only those concerned with spiritual or intellectual matters can be trusted to know virtue—those concerned with seeking material prosperity are too base.

The destitute typically have options other than to violate the rights of the well-off. "'Ought' implies 'can'" is satisfiable by the moral imperative that the poor ought to seek help, not loot. There is then no injustice in the rich preventing the poor from seeking such loot by violating the right to private property. "'Ought' implies 'can'" is fully satisfied if the poor can take the kind of action that could gain them the satisfaction of their basic needs, and this action could well be asking for help.

All along here I have been considering only the helplessly poor, who through no fault of their own, nor again through any rights violation by others, are destitute. I am taking the hard cases seriously, where violation of "'ought' implies 'can'" would appear to be most probable. But such cases are by no means typical. They are extremely rare. And even rarer are those cases in which all avenues regarded as legitimate from the libertarian point of view have been exhausted, including appealing for help.

The bulk of poverty in the world is not the result of natural disaster or disease. Rather it is political oppression, whereby people throughout many of the world's countries are not legally permitted to look out for themselves in production and trade. The famines in Africa and India, the poverty in the same countries and in Central and Latin America, as well as in China, the Soviet Union, Poland, Rumania, and so forth, are not the result of lack of charity but of oppression. It is the kind that those who have the protection of even a seriously compromised document and system protecting individual negative human rights, such as the U.S. Constitution, do not experience. The first requirement for men and women to ameliorate their hardship is to be free of other people's oppression, not to be free to take other people's belongings.

Of course, it would be immoral if people failed to help out when this was clearly no sacrifice for them. But charity or generosity is not a categorical imperative, even for the rich. There are more basic moral principles that might require the rich to refuse to be charitable—for example, if they are using most of their wealth for the protection of freedom or a just society. Courage can be more important than charity or benevolence or compassion. But a discussion of the ranking of moral virtues would take us far afield. One reason that many critics of libertarianism find their own cases persuasive is that they think the libertarian can only subscribe to *political* principles or values. But this is mistaken.[17]

There can be emergency cases in which there is no alternative available to disregarding the rights of others. But these are extremely rare, and not at all the sort invoked by critics such as Sterba. I have in mind the desert-island case found in ethics books where instantaneous action, with only one violent alternative, faces persons—the sort we know from the law books in which the issue is one of immediate life and death. These are not cases, to repeat the phrase quoted from Locke by H. L. A. Hart, "where peace is possible." They are discussed in the libertarian literature and considerable progress has been made in integrating them with the concerns of law and politics.

Since we are here discussing law and politics, which are general systematic approaches to how we normally ought to live with one another in human communities, these emergency situations do not help us except as limiting cases. And not surprisingly many famous court cases illustrate just this point as they now and then confront these kinds of instances after they have come to light within the framework of civilized society. . . .

## Endnotes

1. Quoted in Harry V. Jaffa, *How to Think about the American Revolution* (Durham, NC: Carolina Academic Press, 1978), p. 41 (from *The Collected Works of Abraham Lincoln* [R. Basler (ed.), 1953], pp. 108–115).

2. See, in particular, James Sterba, "A Libertarian Justification for a Welfare State," *Social Theory and Practice*, vol. 11 (Fall 1985), 285–306 [reprinted above]. I will be referring to this essay as well as a more developed version, titled "The U.S. Constitution: A Fundamentally Flawed Document" in *Philosophical Reflections on the United States Constitution*, ed. Christopher Gray (1989).

3. H. L. A. Hart, "Are There Any Natural Rights?" *Philosophical Review* 64 (1955), 175.

4. See, for my own discussions, Tibor R. Machan, *Human Rights and Human Liberties* (Chicago: Nelson-Hall, 1975), pp. 213–222; "Prima Facie versus Natural (Human) Rights," *Journal of Value Inquiry* 10 (1976), 119–131; "Human Rights: Some Points of Clarification," *Journal of Critical Analysis* 5 (1973), 30–39.

5. Sterba, *op. cit.*, "A Libertarian Justification," 295.

6. Ibid.

7. Ayn Rand, "Value and Rights," in J. Hospers (ed.), *Readings in Introductory Philosophical Analysis* (Englewood Cliffs, NJ: Prentice Hall, 1968), p. 382.

8. Sterba, "The U.S. Constitution: A Fundamentally Flawed Document."

9. John Rawls, *A Theory of Justice* (Cambridge, MA: Harvard University Press, 1971), pp. 101–102. For a discussion of the complexities in the differential attainments of members of various ethnic groups—often invoked as evidence for the injustice of a capitalist system, see Thomas Sowell, *Ethnic America: A History* (New York: Basic Books, 1981). There is pervasive prejudice in welfare-state proponents' writings against crediting people with the ability to extricate themselves from poverty without special political assistance. The idea behind the right to negative liberty is to set people free from others so as to pursue their progressive goals. This is the ultimate teleological justification of Lockean libertarian natural rights. See Tibor R. Machan, *Human Rights and Human Liberties: A Radical Reconsideration of the American Political Tradition* (Chicago: Nelson-Hall, 1975). Consider also this thought from Herbert Spencer:

> The feeling which vents itself in "poor fellow!" on seeing one in agony, excludes the thought of "bad fellow," which might at another time arise. Naturally, then, if the wretched are unknown or but vaguely known, all the demerits they may have are ignored: and thus it happens that when the miseries of the poor are dilated upon, they are thought of as the miseries of the deserving poor, instead of being thought of as the miseries of undeserving poor, which in large measure they should be. Those whose hardships are set forth in pamphlets and proclaimed in sermons and speeches which echo throughout society, are assumed to be all worthy souls, grievously wronged; and none of them are thought of as bearing the penal-

ties of their own misdeeds. (*Man versus the State* [Caldwell, ID: Caxton Printers, 1940], p. 22)

10. Tibor R. Machan, "Ethics vs. Coercion: Morality of Just Values?" in L. H. Rockwell, Jr. et al., (ed.), *Man, Economy and Liberty: Essays in Honor of Murray N. Rothbard* (Auburn, AL: Ludwig von Mises Institute, 1988), pp. 236–246.

11. John Kekes, "'Ought' Implies 'Can' and Two Kinds of Morality," *The Philosophical Quarterly* 34 (1984), 459–467.

12. Tibor R. Machan, "Ethics vs. Coercion." In a vegetable garden or even in a forest, there can be good things and bad, but no morally good things and morally evil things (apart from people who might be there).

13. Sterba, "The U.S. Constitution: A Fundamentally Flawed Document."

14. Sterba, "A Libertarian Justification," pp. 295–296.

15. Robert Nozick, *Anarchy, State, and Utopia* (New York: Basic Books, 1974), p. 57. See, also, Tibor R. Machan, "Conditions for Rights, Sphere of Authority," *Journal of Human Relations* 19 (1971), 184–187, where I argue that "within the context of a legal system where the *sphere of authority* of individuals and groups of individuals cannot be delineated independently of the sphere of authority of the public as a whole, there is an inescapable conflict of rights specified by the same legal system." (186) See, also, Tibor R. Machan, "The Virtue of Freedom in Capitalism," *Journal of Applied Philosophy* 3 (1986), 49–58, and Douglas J. Den Uyl, "Freedom and Virtue," in Tibor R. Machan (ed.), *The Main Debate: Communism versus Capitalism* (New York: Random House, 1987), pp. 200–216. This last essay is especially pertinent to the understanding of the ethical or moral merits of coercion and coerced conduct. Thus it is argued here that "coercive charity" amounts to an oxymoron.

16. See, Machan, *op. cit.,* "The Virtue of Freedom in Capitalism" and "Private Property and the Decent Society," in J. K. Roth and R. C. Whittemore (eds.), *Ideology and American Experience* (Washington, DC: Washington Institute Press, 1986).

17. E.g., James Fishkin, *Tyranny and Legitimacy* (Baltimore, MD: Johns Hopkins University Press, 1979). Cf., Tibor R. Machan, "Fishkin on Nozick's Absolute Rights," *Journal of Libertarian Studies* 6 (1982), 317–320.

## Journal/Discussion Questions

✍ *Machan and Sterba differ on the question of whether "desperate cases" are usually caused by previous injustices or not. Discuss this issue in terms of your own experience.*

1. What is the difference between negative and positive liberty. Does negative liberty ultimately entail at least some positive liberties?

2. What role does a doctrine of basic human needs play for critics of libertarianism? For libertarians?

3. Why, according to Lockean libertarianism, are property rights fundamental? In what ways do you agree with this claim? Disagree?

Charles Murray
"The Coming White Underclass"

*Charles Murray, the author of* Losing Ground *and co-author of* The Bell Curve, *is the Bradley Fellow at the American Enterprise Institute.*

*In this article, which first appeared in* The Wall Street Journal *and was quickly and widely reprinted, Murray argues that the continuing rise in illegitimate birth constitutes a major problem for American society, both black and white. He advocates ending Aid to Families with Dependent Children because it encourages such illegitimacy.*

## As You Read, Consider This:

1. Murray draws a distinction between illegitimate children and their parents. What role does this distinction play in his argument?

❧

Every once in a while the sky really is falling, and this seems to be the case with the latest national figures on illegitimacy.

The unadorned statistic is that, in 1991, 1.2 million children were born to unmarried mothers, within a hair of 30 percent of all live births. How high is 30 percent? About four percentage points higher than the black illegitimacy rate in the early 1960s that motivated Daniel Patrick Moynihan to write his famous memorandum on the breakdown of the black family.

The 1991 story for blacks is that illegitimacy has now reached 68 percent of births to black women. In inner cities, the figure is typically in excess of 80 percent. But the black story, however dismaying, is old news. The new trend that threatens the United States is white illegitimacy.

In 1991, 707,502 babies were born to single white women, 22 percent of white births. A few months ago, a Census Bureau study showed that births to single women with college degrees doubled in the last decade to 6 percent from 3 percent. This is an interesting trend, but of minor social importance. The real news is that the proportion of single mothers with less than a high school education jumped to 48 percent from 35 percent in a single decade.

Women with college degrees contribute only 4 percent of white illegitimate babies, while women with high school educations or less contribute 82 percent. Women with family incomes of $75,000 or more contribute 1 percent of white illegitimate babies, while women with family incomes under $20,000 contribute 69 percent.

A Labor Department study that has tracked more than 10,000 youths since 1979 shows an even more dramatic picture. For white women below the poverty line in the year prior to giving birth, 44 percent of births have been illegitimate, compared with only 6 percent for women above the poverty line. White illegitimacy is overwhelmingly a lower-class phenomenon.

This brings us to the emergence of a white underclass. Now the overall white illegitimacy rate is 22 percent. The figure in low-income, working-class communities may be twice that. How much illegitimacy can a community tolerate? Nobody knows, but the historical fact is that the trend lines on black crime, dropout from the labor force and illegitimacy all shifted sharply upward as the overall black illegitimacy rate passed 25 percent.

I blame the revolution in social policy during that period, while others blame the sexual revolution, broad shifts in cultural norms, or structural changes in the economy. But the white illegitimacy rate is approaching that same problematic 25 percent region at a time when social policy is more comprehensively wrongheaded than it was in the mid-1960s, and the cultural and sexual norms are still more degraded.

The white underclass will begin to show its face in isolated ways. Look for certain schools in white neighborhoods to get a reputation as being unteachable, with large numbers of disruptive students and indifferent parents. Talk to the police; listen for stories about white neighborhoods where the incidence of domestic disputes and casual violence has been shooting up. Look for white neighborhoods with high concentrations of drug activity and large numbers of men who have dropped out of the labor force. As the spatial concentration of illegitimacy reaches critical mass, we should expect the deterioration to be as fast among low-income whites in the 1990s as it was among low-income blacks in the 1960s.

My proposition is that illegitimacy is the single most important social problem of our time—more important than crime, drugs, poverty, illiteracy, welfare or homelessness—because it drives everything else. Doing something about it is not just one more item on the American policy agenda, but should be at the top.

The constants are that boys like to sleep with girls and that girls think babies are endearing. Human societies have historically channeled these elemental forces of human behavior via thick walls of rewards and penalties that constrained the overwhelming majority of births to take place within marriage. The past 30 years have seen those walls cave in. It is time to rebuild them.

Bringing a child into the world when one is not emotionally or financially prepared to be a parent is wrong. The child deserves society's support. The parent does not.

To restore the rewards and penalties of marriage does not require social engineering. Rather, it requires that the state stop interfering with the natural forces that have done the job quite effectively for millennia.

I begin with the penalties, of which the most obvious are economic. Throughout human history, a single woman with a small child has not been a viable economic unit. Neither have the single woman and child been a legitimate social unit. In small numbers, they must be a net drain on the community's resources. In large numbers, they must destroy the community's capacity to sustain itself. Communities everywhere have augmented the economic penalties of single parenthood with severe social stigma.

Restoring economic penalties translates into the first and central policy prescription: to end all economic support for single mothers. The Aid to Families with Dependent Children payment goes to zero. Single mothers are not eligible for subsidized housing or for food stamps. An assortment of other subsidies and in-kind benefits disappear. Since universal medical coverage appears to be an idea whose time has come, I will stipulate that all children have medical coverage. But with that exception, the signal is loud and unmistakable: From society's perspective, to have a baby that you cannot care for yourself is profoundly irresponsible, and the government will no longer subsidize it.

How does a poor young mother survive without government support? The same way she has since time immemorial. If she wants to keep a child, she must enlist support from her parents, boyfriend, siblings, neighbors, church or philanthropies. She must get support from somewhere, anywhere, other than the government.

The objectives are threefold.

First, enlisting the support of others raises the probability that other mature adults are going to be involved with the upbringing of the child.

Second, the need to find support forces a self-selection process. One of the most shortsighted excuses made for current behavior is that an adolescent who is utterly unprepared to be a mother "needs someone to love." Childish yearning isn't a good enough selection device. We need to raise the probability that a young single woman who keeps her child is doing so volitionally and thoughtfully. Forcing her to find a way of supporting the child does this. It will lead many young women who shouldn't be mothers to place their babies for adoption. This is good. It will lead others, watching what happens to their sisters, to take steps not to get pregnant.

Third, stigma will regenerate. The pressure on relatives and communities to pay for the folly of their children will make an illegitimate birth the socially horrific act it used to be, and getting a girl pregnant something boys do at the risk of facing a shotgun. Stigma and shotgun marriages may or may not be good for those on the receiving end, but their deterrent effect on others is wonderful and indispensable. What about women who can find no support but keep the baby anyway? There are laws already on the books about the right of the state to take a child from a neglectful parent. Society's main response, however, should be to make it as easy as possible for those mothers to place their children for adoption at infancy.

The first step is to make adoption easy for any married couple who can show reasonable evidence of having the resources and stability to raise a child. Lift all restrictions on interracial adoption. Ease age limitations for adoptive parents.

The second step is to restore the traditional legal principle that placing a child for adoption means irrevocably relinquishing all legal rights to the child. The adoptive parents are parents without qualification. Records are sealed until the child reaches adulthood, at which time they may be unsealed only with the consent of biological child and parent.

Some small proportion of infants and larger proportion of older children will not be adopted. For them, the government should spend lavishly on orphanages. In 1993, we know a lot about how to provide a warm, nurturing environment for children, and getting rid of the welfare system frees up lots of money to do it. Those who prattle about the importance of keeping children with their biological mothers may wish to spend some time in a patrol car or with a social worker seeing what the reality of life with welfare-dependent biological mothers can be like.

One of the few concrete things that the government can do to increase the rewards of marriage is make the tax code favor marriage and children. Those of us who are nervous about using the tax code for social purposes can advocate making the tax code at least neutral.

A more abstract but ultimately crucial step in raising the rewards of marriage is to make marriage once again the sole legal institution through which parental rights and responsibilities are defined and exercised.

Little boys should grow up knowing from their earliest memories that if they want to have any rights whatsoever regarding a child that they sire; more vividly, if they want to grow up to be a daddy, they must marry. Little girls should grow up knowing from their earliest memories that if they want to have any legal claims whatsoever on the father of their children, they must marry. A marriage certificate should establish that a man and a woman have entered into a unique legal relationship. The changes in recent years that have blurred the distinctiveness of marriage are subtly but importantly destructive.

Together, these measures add up to a set of signals, some with immediate and tangible consequences, others with long-term consequences. They should be supplemented by others based on a re-examination of divorce law and its consequences.

That these policy changes seem drastic and unrealistic is a peculiarity of our age, not of the policies themselves. With embellishments, I have endorsed the policies that were the uncontroversial law of the land as recently as John Kennedy's presidency. Then, America's elites accepted as a matter of course that a free society such as America's can sustain itself only through virtue and temperance in the people.

Three decades after that consensus disappeared, we face an emerging crisis. The long, steep climb in black illegitimacy has been calamitous for black communities and painful for the nation.

The reforms I have described will work for blacks as for whites, and have been needed for years. But the brutal truth is that American society as a whole could survive when illegitimacy became epidemic within a comparatively small ethnic minority. It cannot survive the same epidemic among whites.

## Journal/Discussion Questions

✍ *In your own experience, is illegitimacy common in the United States? Do you think there is anything wrong with it?*

1. "Illegitimacy," Murray maintains, "is the single most important social problem of our time—more important than crime, drugs, poverty, illiteracy, welfare or homelessness—because it drives everything else." What support does he offer for this claim? Do you agree with him? Why or why not?

2. What role should the government have in regard to the issue of illegitimacy?

# QUESTIONS FOR DISCUSSION AND REVIEW

## Where Do You Stand Now?

### Instructions

You have already answered the following questions in your moral problems self-quiz at the beginning of this book. Now that you have studied the material in this section, take a moment to answer the same questions again.

| | | | | | |
|---|---|---|---|---|---|
| | *Strongly Agree* | *Agree* | *Undecided* | *Disagree* | *Strongly Disagree* |

*Chapter 7: Poverty and Welfare*

31. ❏ ❏ ❏ ❏ ❏    People are poor mainly because they do not have the proper ability, training, motivation, or interest in working hard.

32. ❏ ❏ ❏ ❏ ❏    Everyone has a right to a minimum income, whether they work or not.

33. ❏ ❏ ❏ ❏ ❏    Everyone has a right to a minimum income, if they want to work but cannot find a job.

34. ❏ ❏ ❏ ❏ ❏    Society ought to continue welfare support for women with illegitimate children.

35. ❏ ❏ ❏ ❏ ❏    Society ought to provide welfare support to elderly people who are no longer able to work.

Compare your answers to the present self-quiz with the answers to the initial self-quiz. How, if at all, have your answers changed? How have the *reasons* for your answers changed?

## Journal/Discussion Questions

✍ *Welfare reform remains a controversial issue in the United States today, one which elicits a tremendous amount of emotion. On the level of emotions, what responses do you feel to the welfare debate? What responses do you think other people experience?*

1. Imagine that you have just been hired by a new think-tank called BOBS, the Best of Both Sides. Knowing that you have read the selections in this chapter, they believe that you have an excellent grasp of the issues involved in welfare reform. They

want you to write a policy recommendation on the issue of welfare reform that incorporates the strengths of proposals by both advocates and critics of welfare without the accompanying liabilities—in other words, the best of both sides.

2. To what extent do you think the *government* should play a role in attempting to eliminate poverty? To what extent do *private individuals*, especially comparatively affluent ones, have an obligation to attempt to eliminate (or at least reduce) poverty?

# FOR FURTHER READING:
# A BIBLIOGRAPHICAL GUIDE
# TO POVERTY AND WELFARE

## The Nature of Poverty

William Julius Wilson, *The Truly Disadvantaged* (Chicago: University of Chicago Press, 1988); also see the symposium in *Ethics* 101, no. 3 (April 1991), 560–609, devoted to this work, with articles by Jennifer Hochschild, "The Politics of the Estranged Poor," and Bernard Boxill, "Wilson on the Truly Disadvantaged," and the response by Wilson.

## Poverty and Welfare

Among recent works on poverty and welfare in the United States, see Phoebe H. Cottingham and David T. Ellwood, eds., *Welfare Policy for the 1990s* (Cambridge, MA: Harvard University Press, 1989); William P. O'Hare, *Real Life Poverty in America: Where the American Public Would Set the Poverty Line* (Washington, DC: Center on Budget and Policy Priorities, 1990); Joel F. Handler and Yeheskel Hasenfield, *The Moral Construction of Poverty: Welfare Reform in America* (Newbury Park, CA: Sage, 1991); Christopher Jencks and Paul E. Peterson, *The Urban Underclass* (Washington: DC: Brookings Institution, 1991); Marvin Olasky, *The Tragedy of American Compassion* (Washington, DC: Regnery Gateway, 1992) and, for a conservative review of how the issue of single mothers with dependent children was handled in the nineteenth century, also see Olasky's "History's Solutions; Problems of Single Mother and Child Poverty," *National Review*, 46, no. 2 (February 7, 1994), 45 ff.; Jacqueline Jones, *The Dispossessed: America's Underclasses from the Civil War to the Present* (New York: Basic Books, 1992); for a more liberal view of these issues, see Mickey Kaus, *The End of Equality* (New York: Basic Books, 1992); Michael B. Katz, ed., *The "Underclass" Debate* (Princeton: Princeton University Press, 1993); R. Shep Melnick, *Between the Lines: Interpreting Welfare Rights* (Washington, DC: Brookings Institution, 1994). Theresa Funiciello's *Tyranny of Kindness: Dismantling the Welfare System to End Poverty in America* (New York: Atlantic Monthly Press, 1993) argues against the bureaucracy of the welfare system and in favor of a guaranteed minimal income. William J. Bennett and Peter Wehner, "Root Causes of Social Ills Lie in Welfare; Public Welfare Reform," *Insight on the News* 10, no. 9 (February 28, 1994), 32 ff.; Robert Rector, "Try the Difference Values Can Make; How Public Welfare Assistance Has Contributed to the Demise of Social, Moral, and Family Values," *Insight on the News* 9, no. 50 (December 13, 1993), 22 ff.; for a good overview of the various—primarily conservative—participants in the welfare discussion and their ideas, see Tom Bethell, "They Had a Dream; the Challenge of Welfare Reform," *National Review* 45; no. 16 (August 23, 1993), 31 ff.

## Narrative Accounts

For some extended narrative accounts of poverty, see Irene Glasser, *More Than Bread: Ethnography of a Soup Kitchen* (Tuscaloosa: University of Alabama Press, 1988); Elliot Liebow, *Tell Them Who I Am: The Lives of Homeless Women* (New York: Free Press, 1993); Valeria Polakow, *Lives on the Edge: Single Mothers and Their Children in the Other America* (Chicago: University of Chicago Press, 1993); Robert D. Bullard, ed., *Confronting Environmental Racism: Voices from the Grassroots* (Boston: South End Press, 1993). For some recent narrative accounts in newspapers, see Jeanie Russell Kasindorf, "Are They the Problem? Welfare Mothers; Interview," *New York Magazine* 28; no. 6 (February 6, 1995), 28 ff.; Barbara Vobejda, "Welfare an Afterthought, Teen Mothers Say," *The Washington Post,* February 14, 1995, A Section; pp. A1 ff.; Isabel Wilkerson, "An Intimate Look at Welfare: Women Who've Been There," *The New York Times,* February 17, 1995, Section A, pp. 1 ff.; and "Benefits and Doubts," *The Washington Post Magazine*, February 26, 1995, pp. 12 ff. For a good overview of some of the social issues and the available data, see David Whitman, Dorian Friedman, Mike Tharp, and Kate Griffin, "Welfare: The Myth of Reform," *U.S. News & World Report* 118, no. 2 (January 16, 1995), 30 ff., and the accompanying editorial, Mortimer B. Zuckerman, "Fixing the Welfare Mess, "*U.S. News & World Report* 118, no. 2 (January 16, 1995), 68 ff.

## Women and Poverty

The issue of poverty has a special impact on women. For some narrative accounts, see the Lievow and Polakow volumes cited above. Among the excellent recent studies of this issue are Paul E. Zoph, Jr., *American Women in Poverty* (Westport, CT: Greenwood Press, 1989); Lourdes Beneria and Shelley Feldman, eds., *Unequal Burden: Economic Crises, Persistent Poverty, and Women's Work* (Boulder, CO: Westview Press, 1992); Pamela D. Couture, *Blessed Are the Poor? Women's Poverty, Family Policy, and Practical Theology* (Nashville: Abingdon Press, 1991); Harrell R. Rodgers, Jr., *Poor Women, Poor Families: Single Mothers and Their Children in the Other America* (Chicago: University of Chicago Press, 1993).

## Race and Poverty

For contrasting views of *Latinos and poverty* in the United States, see Linda Chavez, *Out of the Barrio: Toward New Politics of Hispanic Assimilation* (New York: Basic Books, 1991) and Rebecca Morales and Frank Bonilla, eds., *Latinos in a Changing U.S. Economy: Comparative Perspectives on Growing Inequality* (Newbury Park, CA: Sage, 1993)

Among the works on *African Americans and poverty* (in addition to those already cited), see Maurence E. Lynn, Jr., and Michael G. H. McGeary, eds., *Inner-City Poverty in the United States* (Washington, DC: National Academy Press, 1990); Nicholas Lemann, *The Promised Land: The Great Black Migration and How It Changed America* (New York: Knopf, 1991); Gary Orfield and Carol Ashkinaze, *The Closing Door: Conservative Policy and Black Opportunity* (Chicago: University of Chicago Press, 1991); Christopher Jencks, *Rethinking Social Policy: Race, Poverty, and the Underclass* (Cambridge: Harvard University Press, 1992); Andrew Hacker, *Two Nations: Black and White, Separate, Hostile, Unequal* (New York: Scribner's, 1992); James Jennings, ed., *Race, Politics, and Economic Development: Community Perspectives* (New York: Verso, 1992); Douglas S. Massey and Nancy A. Denton, *American Apartheid: Segregation and the Making of the Underclass* (Cambridge: Harvard University Press, 1993).

## Distributive Justice

One of the central moral issues raised in this chapter has been the nature of distributive justice. Among the excellent anthologies in this area, see John Arthur and William Shaw, eds., *Justice and Economic Distribution* (Englewood Cliffs, NJ: Prentice Hall, 1978) and Virginia Held, ed., *Property, Profits, and Economic Justice* (Belmont, CA: Wadsworth, 1980). For a collection of libertarian pieces on this issue, see Tibor Machan, ed., *The Libertarian Alternative: Essays in Social and Political Philosophy* (Chicago: Nelson-Hall, 1977).

For a strong statement of the *liberal conception of justice*, see John Rawls, *A Theory of Justice* (Cambridge: Harvard, 1974) and, more recently, *Political Liberalism* (New York: Columbia, 1993); also see Brian Barry's *Theories of Justice* (Berkeley: University of California Press, 1989). For a strongly contrasting *libertarian conception of justice*, see: Robert Nozick's *Anarchy, State, and Utopia* (New York: Basic Books, 1974); the work of F. A. Hayek, especially *The Mirage of Social Justice*, which is volume 2 of his *Law, Legislation, and Liberty* (Chicago: University of Chicago Press, 1976); and Tibor Machan's *Individuals and Their Rights* (LaSalle, IL: Open Court, 1989). For an excellent attempt to *reconcile these and other widely divergent views of justice*, see James P. Sterba, *How to Make People Just: A Practical Reconciliation of Alternative Concepts of Justice* (Totowa, NJ: Rowman & Littlefield, 1988); for his most recent reply to Machan and others, see James P. Sterba, "From Liberty to Welfare," *Ethics* 105, 1 (October, 1994), 64–98. For an excellent short survey of distributive conceptions of justice, see Allen Buchanan, "Justice, Distributive," in *Encyclopedia of Ethics,* ed. Lawrence C. Becker and Charlotte B. Becker (New York: Garland, 1992), vol. I, pp. 655–661.

# World Hunger and Poverty

# EXPERIENTIAL ACCOUNTS

Lawrence B. Salander
"The Hunger"

*The author is president of Salander-O'Reilly Galleries in New York. He is also a painter with many solo and group exhibitions to his credit. He lives in New York.*

*In this article, Salander describes his experiences accompanying a CARE relief team to a famine-ridden town west of Mogadishu.*

Baidoa is a provincial town approximately 120 miles west of Mogadishu. The pre-famine population of this godforsaken place is anyone's guess. I've read figures that range from 40,000 to 60,000. There are more people than that here now. The place is teeming with refugees who have made their way here because they have heard that it is better. Better than what?

You don't see many young children in Baidoa, because most of them are dead. One report commissioned by the United Nations estimates that 71 percent of the children of Baidoa under 5 years old have died. The accuracy of the figure is debatable, but whatever the true number, it is clearly horrific. And it's not as though these kids are dying from anything exotic. The two biggest killers are diarrhea and the measles. The medicine and food they need sits in storage in Mogadishu.

Rancid, disease-carrying water. Life in a six-foot-square grass-covered hut, home to eight people. Mothers and fathers driven mad by the hopelessness of their situation, watching their children die. Many of them seem to refuse to believe it, and carry on as if everything were normal. Human feces are everywhere, and swarms of flies surround the children not yet sick enough to be out of pain, their hair turned orange by malnutrition before falling out in clumps. Many have silver-dollar-size oozing sores caused by a lice-like animal that bores through their skin to the bone. These children with their distended stomachs, half-naked and filthy. Each one coughing a death cough.

I traveled here under the auspices of CARE. With machine-gun fire as background music, one of the organization's employees, Mary Jane Hammond, who for the last several months has been a resident of Baidoa, began what seemed to be a daily exercise with these kids. Surrounded by thirty or forty of them, she started to count to ten, out loud in English. The children picked up the count. When they reached ten they all gave themselves a round of applause, and then all of them broke into the most wonderful smiles—made larger, it seemed, by their emaciated faces. The few optimistic moments in Baidoa clearly defined the almost unbearable misery. Death was not the worst of it.

I went to the "hospital" to visit the dying. As terrible as it was, it was almost a relief to see these kids out of pain. It's their parents who need our compassion. Two dark and damp ten-by-twenty-foot adjoining rooms serve as the "pediatric ward." Each room contains seven or eight beds—wooden platforms that two children often share. One mother pointed out her dying infant, who was too small to see at first. She searched my eyes for the hope I could not give her. A father took my arm and led me to the bed where his 5-year-old boy lay moments from death. He pulled back the cover to show me the boy's dissipated body, and then took my hand and placed it on what was left of his son's stomach.

We climbed back into our Jeep-like vehicle, with a crew of "security men" hired for the day by CARE. A 15-year-old manned the machine gun on the roof while two other riflemen rode shotgun. The driver was the boss, the oldest and the biggest. They were high from chewing khat all day. The next stop was the airstrip, and the man was in a hurry to get there. Moving targets must be harder to hit. The dust was flying as people scattered to avoid us. A young boy made a run for it, to join his friends across the street. The driver hit the brakes, and the kid froze. We missed him by inches.

This thug, the driver, got out of the car with a bamboo stick and chased the boy down. He hit him twice. I turned away in rage and disgust. But then I realized that this single, barbaric act was the most hopeful thing I'd seen all day. This guy was beating the child to teach him to be more careful. And that implies a belief in tomorrow, which in Baidoa is no small thing.

## Journal/Discussion Questions

✍ *Have you had any direct experience with relief efforts in countries with famines? If so, discuss those experiences in light of Salander's description of his own.*

1. Why did Salander describe the beating on the child as "hopeful"? Discuss your reactions to this description.

# AN INTRODUCTION TO THE MORAL ISSUES

## The Problem

We cannot help but be struck by the vast differences in standards of living between the United States (and other comparable industrialized nations) and developing countries. We have only to turn on the evening news to see clips of famine and starvation, natural disasters, and other political turmoil throughout the world. We may believe the political disagreements are best resolved among the disputants themselves. The natural disasters are transitory, but perhaps more evenly distributed among all the countries of the world. The hunger and starvation, however, are more disturbing, especially when we look around at our own affluence as a nation.

Should we help other nations, especially those in great poverty whose population is starving? Let's look more closely at these issues, beginning with the arguments in favor of helping other countries that are impoverished and whose population is starving.

## The Case for Helping Other Countries

There are a number of strong reasons for helping countries that are impoverished and starving. The first of these centers on our character, and in particular on the virtue of compassion. Others center on consequences, rights, and the duty to beneficence.

### The Argument from Virtue

*The moral force of suffering.* The mere sight of the deep suffering associated with poverty and starvation has a moral force all its own: it touches the deepest roots of human compassion to see such suffering. Anyone who possesses the virtue of compassion cannot help but respond to such suffering. To turn our backs in the face of such human misery would be cold-hearted indeed. Such a response would not only fail to relieve the suffering of others, but it would also diminish us, revealing a disturbing moral indifference. A virtuous person *must* respond to such suffering.

*How can we ignore the terrible suffering of starving nations?*

*The issue of luck.* Our moral disquiet about this poverty and hunger is intensified by the fact that we know we as individuals do not deserve this affluence any more or less than those in famine-ridden countries deserve their destitution and hunger. This is not to deny that we work hard. But if we had been born in Rwanda or Somalia, we could be working just as hard and starving to death. The overall affluence of our society is not something we have because of our merit; it is largely a matter of luck.

*The place of the children.* The children have a special place in all of this, but if there are any innocents left in the world, it is the children. Whatever we may say about the

*Are we under a greater obligation to the starving when they are children?*

408

political and economic leaders of a country, we cannot help but feel that the children deserve better. In a sea of suffering, their suffering stands out as having a special and undeniable moral force. It pulls us out of our moral complacency and demands a response from us.

*The statistics.* When we begin to look at the statistics, we realize that our impressionistic view of global inequalities and suffering is born out by the facts. The United States possesses a startling share of the world's wealth, consumes a highly disproportionate amount of its resources, and even produces an excessive percentage of its waste.

## The Issue of Complicity

We don't deserve to be born into an affluent society any more than we deserve to be born into an impoverished one. It is simply a matter of luck. But is it purely a matter of luck that some societies are rich and others are poor? Here the issue becomes more complex. The argument, put forth by many, is that the affluence of countries like the United States is built in part on the impoverishment of developing nations. The natural resources and labor of such nations are often exploited by major industrial nations in ways that are profoundly destructive to the social, economic, and political well-being of developing nations.

If this is the case, then the poverty and starvation of developing nations has an added moral force: we, the affluent, may be partly responsible for it. If this is the case, then we would seem to have some added duty to help relieve that suffering. We can understand the difference in terms of an analogy. Consider the different obligations in the following two situations. First, we see the victim of an automobile accident on the side of the road as we are driving by. Presumably we have some, although perhaps not always overriding, obligation to stop and try to help. Second, we cause an automobile accident that injures someone else. Presumably in this situation, we have a much greater obligation to render assistance, for we are responsible for the accident in the first place. The situation would seem to be similar with world poverty and starvation. If we are partly responsible for causing it, then we have a greater obligation to do something about it.

The complicity argument would seem to be most effective in creating obligations on the country-to-country level rather than the individual-to-individual level. For example, if the United States has systematically exploited Rouratania, then it seems that the United States has an obligation (all other things being equal) to Rouratania to make up for the harm that it has caused. It is less clear that individual citizens of the United States, some of whom might not have even agreed to the exploitive policies if they had been asked, would be obligated to the individual citizens of Rouratania. Moreover, even the country-to-country level has difficulties, since in many cases we are dealing with exploitation by corporations rather than by governments directly.

## The Group Egoist Argument

The compassionate response demands that we set aside self-interest and respond directly to relieve the suffering of others, even when we must make sacrifices to do so. This is a morally demanding response, and some have argued that we may not always be able or willing to respond so selflessly. Some in this tradition *Is it in our long-term interests to aid poor nations?* have argued that there are still good, self-centered moral reasons for trying to relieve the suffering of other countries.

The basic *moral premise* of this argument is what we may call group egoism, the belief that we ought to act in ways that further the interests of our group. In this case, we can take our group as being equivalent to the nation. The claim here is that it is in our best interests as a nation to help other, less affluent nations, even if there is a short-term cost to ourselves.

This moral premise must then be followed by an *empirical premise* that states that helping impoverished and starving countries contributes to our national welfare in the long run. Often such a premise is economic in character, and seems to be most plausible when discussing either a neighboring country or a country in a region where we have important economic interests. In both types of cases, our economic well-being is closely tied with the economic well-being of those other countries. If they fall upon hard times, we will also suffer. Thus, their prosperity is directly tied to ours.

Critics of this argument often attack the empirical premise in several ways. First, it is extremely difficult to prove such connections between countries conclusively, simply because of the complexity of the economic interactions and the fallibility of our predictive powers in this area. Second, some would argue that, far from benefiting from the well-being of other nations, we often benefit much more from their exploitability. Many actions intended to enhance another country's well-being might diminish its exploitability. Finally, critics point out that this argument, even if sound, really only obligates us to assist those countries in our direct economic sphere. We would seemingly be under no obligation to countries with which we have little economic contract.

## The Strict Utilitarian Argument

Utilitarianism, as we have said before, is a very demanding moral doctrine, for it asserts (1) that we should give our own happiness and pain no special weight, and (2) that we should always do what produces the *greatest* overall amount of utility. When we combine these principles, we begin to get a strong argument that morally requires rich nations to reduce the gap between themselves and poor nations until they are relatively equal. Once one accepts the strongly impartialist premise that anyone else's suffering counts just as much as your own in the moral calculus, then it is a comparatively short step to concluding that we should reduce everyone else's suffering to the same level as our own.

In order to take this short step to such a conclusion, however, one more premise is necessary, a premise about the moral difference between action and inaction. Critics of the argument outlined in the previous paragraph could maintain that, while we are obliged to *refrain* from actively doing anything to increase or perpetuate the suffering of those in impoverished countries, that alone does not entail that we are obliged to actively *do* something to reduce their suffering. In "Rich and Poor," Peter Singer supplies just such a premise, arguing that it is morally just as bad to let someone die (when you could save them without great cost to yourself) as to actively kill them.

Needless to say, this argument has many critics. Many simply reject utilitarianism as a whole, not just this particular application of it. Others try to retard the movement from a negative obligation to avoid harming others to a positive obligation to assist them. Some maintain that relief efforts do not in fact have the consequences that utilitarians intend them to have. Yet even if these objections could be met, there seems to be another, even more formidable problem about moral motivation. What would motivate the affluent to radically diminish their own lifestyles in order to help the poor and the hungry? Even more specifically, what would motivate the affluent to radically diminish the lifestyles of those they love in order to help complete strangers in distant lands? We shall return to this issue below in our discussion of moral particularity.

### The Basic Rights Argument

Some authors, including Henry Shue in *Basic Rights*, have argued that everyone has a right to minimal subsistence and that this is a positive right.[1] Recall the difference between a negative right and a positive one. If I have a negative right, that simply prohibits others from interfering with me in the exercise of that right. A negative right to free speech prevents others from silencing me, but it does not require them to give me a microphone, even if they have an extra one. A positive right, in contrast, obligates other people to assist me in the exercise of my right. If I

*Do all people have a right to basic subsistence?*

have a positive right to free speech, others (usually the state) must provide me with the opportunity and means for exercising that right. The right to subsistence, Shue argues, is a positive right that obligates others (particularly those with an overabundance of food) to assist me in continuing to subsist.

### The Kantian Imperfect Duty Argument

In his discussion of moral duties, Immanuel Kant distinguished between two types of duties. *Perfect duties* are those that require specific actions and put forth conditions that must be met at all times. The duty to tell the truth, for example, is a perfect duty. We must always tell the truth. *Imperfect duties*, in contrast, require that we perform some among a group of actions but do not mandate each and every action. The duty to benevolence is an imperfect duty. We are morally required, Kant says, to perform acts of benevolence toward those in need, but this does not mean that we are required to act benevolently toward each and every person in need and on each and every occasion of such need. We are morally obligated to act benevolently, but we have a considerable amount of moral freedom to decide about the particular occasions of such benevolence.

One of the strengths of Kant's position is that it allows us to find a middle ground between those who maintain that we have no duties to other countries and those who claim that we have seemingly overwhelming obligations to them. We have a duty to some benevolence, but we do not have a duty to reduce our standard of living to the point of equality with the poor of the world. In this respect, Kant's position seems to correspond with the moral intuitions of many people today.

## The Case against Helping Other Countries

Several different types of arguments have been advanced against claims that we should provide aid to impoverished and starving peoples.

### The Lifeboat Argument

In one of the most controversial articles ever written on this subject, Garrett Hardin in "Lifeboat Ethics" argues that we have a duty *not* to help the poor and starving of other countries. This is a strong and startling claim. Hardin is not simply saying that it was acceptable not to aid the poor—he is saying that it was *wrong* to help them.

*The lifeboat metaphor.*   Hardin suggests that rich nations are like lifeboats and that swimming around them are the poor of the world who are clambering to get into the lifeboat. If we let them into the lifeboat—that is, if we provide aid or permit immigration in significant degrees—then we will surely swamp the lifeboat and everyone, not just the poor already in the water, will be adrift. The answer—at least from the standpoint of those in the lifeboat—is not to take as many people in as possible until it is on the verge of sinking, but rather to preserve the integrity and long-term survivability of the boat itself. Hardin admits that it is purely a matter of luck that one is born in the lifeboat rather than the water, but he does not see this as changing his position. Those who really feel it is unfair can give up their places in the lifeboat to people in the water.

*Evaluating the metaphor.*   This has proved to be a powerful metaphor, but certainly not one without its misleading aspects. First, it presupposes that rich nations are like boats, and that the poor of the world are like individuals floundering in the water. This metaphor would seem to fit best when describing the relationship between a wealthy nation and a poor one whose government had collapsed. In most cases, however, the more accurate metaphor—if one wants to stay within this nautical range—would be numerous ships on the sea, some more seaworthy than others and some with a better store of provisions than others. (Other countries generally do not want to get into our boat; they simply do not want their own boat to sink.) Yet even this is misleading, since the notion of a "store of provisions" is a static one that fails to do justice to the dynamic ways in which food can be *produced* in countries. Second, this metaphor presupposes that the continuing existence and ultimate fate of those in the lifeboat is independent of the lives of those in the water. Yet this hardly seems to be the case. Countries are in constant and complex interactions with one another, interactions not captured by this metaphor. Certainly rich nations historically have exploited poor nations. Here the more adequate metaphor might be people swimming in the water after we have helped to sink their boat. Moreover, the continued existence of wealthy nations may well depend—in terms of politics and markets as well as labor and resources—on continuing interactions with poor nations. One philosopher, Onora O'Neill, has suggested that the more appropriate metaphor would be that *the earth* is a lifeboat.

*Immigration.*   Relief programs, Hardin points out, bring food to the starving; open immigration policies make it possible to bring people to the food. Hardin is equally opposed to open immigration policies, and for the same reason: such policies threaten to swamp the lifeboat.

## The Effectiveness Argument

Arguments that wealthy nations are obligated to aid poor nations contain not only a moral premise about obligation but also an implicit pragmatic premise that such aid can be effective. Some critics of aid have maintained that this issue can be settled on pragmatic grounds: aid, they argue, just doesn't *work*. And since it doesn't, we are under no moral obligation to do it. Here are some of the arguments they have advanced along these lines.

*Is economic aid to poor countries really effective in the long run?*

*Administration.*   Bureaucracies tend to perpetuate themselves, and often—in order to continue to exist—they need to perpetuate the problems they were originally created to eliminate. Overhead is tremendously high in many such relief efforts, both governmental and private. For these reasons, many have argued that relief efforts are inevitably about supporting relief agencies rather than eradicating hunger.

*Local economy.*   Some critics of relief projects to help the impoverished and the hungry in developing countries have argued that such assistance has significant negative consequences. A sudden influx of food from relief agencies into a local economy can, for example, depress the prices of existing crops, resulting in farmers' being unable to sell their crops at a profit. This, in turn, can mean that they will not have the money to buy seed for the next planting, and that will mean that they will soon be destitute and the country will find that the problem of starvation is even more severe next season.

*Dependency.*   It is easy to see, from the preceding paragraph, the way in which well-intentioned aid could inadvertently create dependency among the recipients. Critics of aid programs often espouse a kind of social Darwinism, claiming that we should avoid aid simply because it reduces people's ability to survive and promotes the survival of the weakest instead of the strongest.

*Futility.*   Moreover, some critics of aid advocate ceasing all aid right now because *eventually* it will prove futile. Aid, they argue, postpones problems but never ultimately solves them. Thus it might be possible, through massive relief efforts, to save the lives of 100,000 starving people this year, but that simply means that a decade from now we will be faced with the *impossible* task of saving 500,000 lives. Since that is impossible, what is the point—such critics ask—of saving some lives now? It only means that more will perish later. Given the ultimate futility of such relief efforts, these critics maintain that we should cease them now.

*Local corruption.*   Finally, some critics have pointed out that in some cases hunger is as much the result of political disagreements as of anything else. Indeed, in some cases starvation is used as a weapon for subjugating either opposing nations or internal groups within one's own nation. Similarly, food relief efforts are often hampered by local political opposition to the relief. In cases such as these, critics often conclude that those involved should be left to settle their own problems.

## The Libertarian Argument

Some claim that we have only negative rights and thus only negative duties. Libertarianism is the clearest political expression of this doctrine, and the work of Ayn Rand is the most popular literary expression of it. For a libertarian, the right to life is purely a negative one. No one is entitled to take my life away from me, but certainly no one is obligated to support my existence. Each person is solely responsible for his or her own existence, and society as a whole owes me nothing positive.

Furthermore, many in this tradition hold the right to property to be practically as strong as the right to life. This has important implications for any analysis of the unequal distribution of wealth. The libertarians maintain that the government has very few, if any, rights to deprive individuals of their property. (Many, for this reason, are strongly opposed to most taxes.) Thus libertarians see this issue as a conflict between an extremely weak or nonexistent claim (the right of the poor to aid) against a very strong claim (the right of individuals to acquire and retain their own property). For them, the choice is easy.

Critics of this position usually challenge the very foundations of ethical egoism. They maintain that it is simply moral callousness dressed up as moral theory. The moral life, they maintain, is not about selfishness, but about overcoming selfishness. Ethical egoism, they maintain, simply makes a virtue of what all other moral standpoints consider to be a vice.

## The Particularity Argument

*Special moral obligation to take care of our own.*   As we indicated above, there is something suspicious about a moral theory that requires us to care so much about strangers that we diminish the quality of life for those nearest and dearest to us. Consider this in relation to children. I love my daughter dearly, and I work hard to try to insure that she has the opportunities for a good life. If I am a utilitarian, am I obligated to give up money I would spend on my daughter in order to relieve the (admittedly, quite worse) suffering of complete strangers on the other side of the globe?

To raise this question is to call into doubt one of the most fundamental premises of most ethical theories: impartiality. Both Kantians and utilitarians would agree that the moral point of view is one of strict impartiality. I should not give more weight to the suffering of those I love than I do to the suffering of strangers. Yet in recent years this premise has come under increasing challenge, and some have argued that morality is not incompatible with particularity. In fact, some in this tradition would argue that there is something morally alienating about individuals who do not put the interests of those they love above the interests of strangers. This continues to be a point of great controversy among philosophers.

*The efficiency argument.*   Seeking a compromise between the impartialists and the particularists, some have argued that we can retain both. Impartiality, they agree, is the hallmark of the moral point of view. However, even while we admit that everyone's interests count equally in principle, it may be more *efficient* for us to allow individuals to protect the interests of those they care about. This moral division of labor would allow us to care for those we care about, and yet not completely surrender the notion that everyone's suffering has an equal moral weight. The difficulty with such an argument, of course, is that it presumes that everyone has people who care about them and who are able to do so effectively. Unfortunately, this is far from true.

*Epistemological considerations.*   There is a final dimension to the case for particularity. Some have argued that we know best what's good for our own citizens, other countries know best what's good for their own citizens. Here the claim is that we should "take care of our own" because we know best what they need and want in order to feel taken care of. Thus this is primarily an epistemological consideration, that is, a concern about what we can *know* about ourselves and other people.

The obvious reply to this argument is that, if people are starving to death, it is not difficult to know what they need. It is easy to see that people need water, food, medicine, and the like. Yet even here the matter proves to be more subtle, for that response is a very Western one, the response of a technocrat. To be sure, people may need these things, but those needs may be part of a larger, more complex set of physical, psychological, and spiritual needs that escape the notice of relief officials.

## The Liberal State Argument

The final argument that has been advanced against claims of obligations to impoverished and starving nations could be considered a political version of the particularity argument or a type of group egoism argument. The argument is a simple one. The liberal state can only function well—that is, provide the services to its citizens that it promises—if it rests on a solid economic foundation. If that foundation is threatened either through massive foreign aid or through massive immigration, then the state may no longer be able to provide any of its members with the traditional benefits of a liberal state. Education, defense, health care, construction and maintenance of infrastructure—all of these things would be drastically reduced if the liberal state were suddenly paying out huge sums for foreign aid or trying to meet the needs of a vast influx of immigrants.

Once again, this is an argument that contains both empirical and normative claims. On the empirical side is a claim that the minimal economic foundation of the liberal state will be eroded through massive aid or immigration. Social scientists and economists must determine whether this is true. The normative claim is less explicit, but it must be something to the effect that the continued existence of the liberal state is morally worth the suffering and death that could be averted in starving nations through massive aid. This is a much more difficult claim to support. Although it is presumably true that the continued existence of the liberal state is valuable to those who live in it, it is far from clear that it is of value to everyone, especially those who will die.

# Diversity and Consensus

## Short-Term Relief

Many of the issues surrounding relief, both short-term and long-term, are empirical issues concerning effectiveness. As we have already seen in our earlier discussion of efficiency, critics of even short-term relief often express their greatest doubts about the *efficacy* of such relief. One of the principal challenges to supporters of such aid is to show that such aid does more good than harm in the long run.

Despite these criticisms, the moral bottom line about short-term relief centers around the issue of compassion. How can we, in the face of such suffering and in the midst of our relative affluence, turn away in indifference? To fail to respond seems inhumane. The moral challenge is to discern how to respond wisely and effectively.

## Long-Term Assistance

Assistance programs are generally oriented toward helping recipient countries to become self-sustaining, rather than at establishing a long-term relationship of aid and dependency. How we can do this with skill and efficiency is an extremely complex question, but one that must be answered. In the process of answering it, we must also deal with questions about exploitation, population control, human rights, and respect for diverse cultural traditions. Moreover, we must figure out a way of determining how far we should go in offering assistance and support. The two extremes—Hardin, who advocates not helping at all, and Singer, who says we should help to the point of relative equality—leave a vast middle ground. Presumably the truth is somewhere in the middle here.

## A Common World

What kind of world do we envision for our future? Is it a world of vast inequities, the superfluously rich and the starving poor? Or, is it a world in which all human beings have the minimal conditions of a good life? And, if it is the latter type of world that we hope for, then we must ask ourselves how we shall achieve it.

## Endnotes

1. Henry Shue, *Basic Rights: Subsistence, Affluence, and U.S. Foreign Policy* (Princeton: Princeton University Press, 1980).

# THE ARGUMENTS

Garrett Hardin
"Lifeboat Ethics: The Case against Helping the Poor"

*Garrett Hardin is professor emeritus of biology at the University of California, Santa Barbara. A collection of his essays,* Naked Emperors, *appeared in 1983.*

*This is one of the most controversial articles published about the problem of world hunger, for in it Hardin argues that rich nations should not try to help poor, starving ones. Rich nations, Hardin suggests, are like lifeboats, sailing in a sea amidst drowning poor people who want to get into their boats. If the poor get in the boats, they will only sink them and everyone will perish.*

## As You Read, Consider This:

1. Much of what Hardin says depends on acceptance of the lifeboat metaphor. What are the strengths of this metaphor? In what ways is it misleading? In what ways is it different from the spaceship metaphor?

2. What does Hardin mean by "the tragedy of the commons"? What support is there for his claim that those who own property will care for it responsibly? What evidence is there against that claim?

Environmentalists use the metaphor of the earth as a "spaceship" in trying to persuade countries, industries and people to stop wasting and polluting our natural resources. Since we all share life on this planet, they argue, no single person or institution has the right to destroy, waste, or use more than a fair share of its resources.

But does everyone on earth have an equal right to an equal share of its resources? The spaceship metaphor can be dangerous when used by misguided idealists to justify suicidal policies for sharing our resources through uncontrolled immigration and foreign aid. In their enthusiastic but unrealistic generosity, they confuse the ethics of a spaceship with those of a lifeboat.

A true spaceship would have to be under the control of a captain, since no ship could possibly survive if its course were determined by committee. Spaceship Earth certainly has no captain; the United Nations is merely a toothless tiger, with little power to enforce any policy upon its bickering members.

If we divide the world crudely into rich nations and poor nations, two thirds of them are desperately poor, and only one third comparatively rich, with the United States the wealthiest of all. Metaphorically each rich nation can be seen as a lifeboat full of comparatively rich people. In the ocean outside each lifeboat swim the poor of the world, who would like to get in, or at least to share some of the wealth. What should the lifeboat passengers do?

First, we must recognize the limited capacity of any lifeboat. For example, a nation's land has a limited capacity to support a population and as the current energy crisis has shown us, in some ways we have already exceeded the carrying capacity of our land.

## Adrift in a Moral Sea

So here we sit, say fifty people in our lifeboat. To be generous, let us assume it has room for ten more, making a total capacity of sixty. Suppose the fifty of us in the lifeboat see 100 others swimming in the water outside, begging for admission to our boat or for handouts. We have several options: we may be tempted to try to live by the Christian ideal of being "our brother's keeper," or by the Marxist ideal of "to each according to his needs." Since the needs of all in the water are the same, and since they can all be seen as "our brothers," we could take them all into our boat, making a total of 150 in a boat designed for sixty. The boat swamps, everyone drowns. Complete justice, complete catastrophe.

Since the boat has an unused excess capacity of ten more passengers, we could admit just ten more to it. But which ten do we let in? How do we choose? Do we pick the best ten, the neediest ten, "first come, first served"? And what do we say to the ninety we exclude? If we do let an extra ten into our lifeboat, we will have lost our "safety factor," an engineering principle of critical importance. For example, if we don't leave room for excess capacity as a safety factor in our country's agriculture, a new plant disease or a bad change in the weather could have disastrous consequences.

Suppose we decide to preserve our small safety factor and admit no more to the lifeboat. Our survival is then possible, although we shall have to be constantly on guard against boarding parties.

While this last solution clearly offers the only means of our survival, it is morally abhorrent to many people. Some say they feel guilty about their good luck. My reply is simple: "Get out and yield your place to others." This may solve the problem of the guilt-ridden person's conscience, but it does not change the ethics of the lifeboat. The needy person to whom the guilt-ridden person yields his place will not himself feel guilty about his good luck. If he did, he would not climb aboard. The net result of conscience-stricken people giving up their unjustly held seats is the elimination of that sort of conscience from the lifeboat.

This is the basic metaphor within which we must work out our solutions. Let us now enrich the image, step by step, with substantive additions from the real world, a world that must solve real and pressing problems of overpopulation and hunger.

The harsh ethics of the lifeboat become even harsher when we consider the reproductive differences between the rich nations and the poor nations. The people inside the lifeboats are doubling in numbers every eighty-seven years; those swimming around outside are doubling, on the average, every thirty-five years, more than twice as fast as the rich. And since the world's resources are dwindling, the difference in prosperity between the rich and the poor can only increase.

As of 1973, the U.S. had a population of 210 million people, who were increasing by 0.8 percent per year. Outside our lifeboat, let us imagine another 210 million people (say the combined populations of Colombia, Ecuador, Venezuela, Morocco, Pakistan, Thailand and the Philippines), who are increasing at a rate of 3.3 percent per year. Put differently, the doubling time for this aggregate population is twenty-one years, compared to eighty-seven years for the U.S.

## Multiplying the Rich and the Poor

Now suppose the U.S. agreed to pool its resources with those seven countries, with everyone receiving an equal share. Initially the ratio of Americans to non-Americans in this model would be one-to-one. But consider what the ratio would be after eighty-seven years, by which time the Americans would have doubled to a population of 420 million. By then, doubling every twenty-one years, the other group would have swollen to 354 billion. Each American would have to share the available resources with more than eight people.

But, one could argue, this discussion assumes that current population trends will continue, and they may not. Quite so. Most likely the rate of population increase will decline much faster in the U.S. than it will in the other countries, and there does not seem to be much we can do about it. In sharing with "each according to his needs," we must recognize that needs are determined by population size, which is determined by the rate of reproduction, which at present is regarded as a sovereign right of every nation, poor or not. This being so, the philanthropic load created by the sharing ethic of the spaceship can only increase.

## The Tragedy of the Commons

The fundamental error of spaceship ethics, and the sharing it requires, is that it leads to what I call "the tragedy of the commons." Under a system of private property, the men who own property recognize their responsibility to care for it, for if they don't they will eventually suffer. A farmer, for instance, will allow no more cattle in a pasture than its carrying capacity justifies. If he overloads it, erosion sets in, weeds take over, and he loses the use of the pasture.

If a pasture becomes a commons open to all, the right of each to use it may not be matched by a corresponding responsibility to protect it. Asking everyone to use it with discretion will hardly do, for the considerate herdsman who refrains from overloading the commons suffers more than a selfish one who says his needs are greater. If everyone would restrain himself, all would be well; but it takes only one less than everyone to ruin a system of voluntary restraint. In a crowded world of less than perfect human beings, mutual ruin is inevitable if there are no controls. This is the tragedy of the commons.

One of the major tasks of education today should be the creation of such an acute awareness of the dangers of the commons that people will recognize its many varieties. For example, the air and water have become polluted because they are treated as commons. Further growth in the population or per-capita conversion of natural resources into pollutants will only make the problem worse. The same holds true for the fish of the oceans. Fishing fleets have nearly disappeared in many parts of the world, technological improvements in the art of fishing are hastening the day of complete ruin. Only the replacement of the system of the commons with a responsible system of control will save the land, air, water and oceanic fisheries.

In recent years there has been a push to create a new commons called a World Food Bank, an international depository of food reserves to which nations would contribute according to their abilities and from which they would draw according to their needs. This humanitarian proposal has received support from many liberal international groups, and from such prominent citizens as Margaret Mead, U.N. Secretary General Kurt Waldheim, and Senators Edward Kennedy and George McGovern.

A world food bank appeals powerfully to our humanitarian impulses. But before we rush ahead with such a plan, let us recognize where the greatest political push comes from, lest we be disillusioned later. Our experience with the "Food for Peace program," or Public Law 480, gives us the answer. This program moved billions of dollars worth of U.S. surplus grain to food-short, population-long countries during the past two decades. But when P.L. 480 first became law, a headline in the business magazine *Forbes* revealed the real power behind it: "Feeding the World's Hungry Millions: How It Will Mean Billions for U.S. Business."

And indeed it did. In the years 1960 to 1970, U.S. taxpayers spent a total of $7.9 billion on the Food for Peace program. Between 1948 and 1970, they also paid an additional $50 billion for other economic-aid programs, some of which went for food and food-producing machinery and technology. Though all U.S. taxpayers were forced to contribute to the cost of P.L. 480, certain special interest groups gained handsomely under the program. Farmers did not have to contribute the grain; the government, or rather the taxpayers, bought it from them at full market prices. The increased demand raised prices of farm products generally. The manufacturers of farm machinery, fertilizers and pesticides benefited by the farmers' extra efforts to grow more food. Grain elevators profited from storing the surplus until it could be shipped. Railroads made money hauling it to ports, and shipping lines profited from carrying it overseas. The implementation of P.L. 480 required the creation of a vast government bureaucracy, which then acquired its own vested interest in continuing the program regardless of its merits.

## Extracting Dollars

Those who proposed and defended the Food for Peace program in public rarely mentioned its importance to any of these special interests. The public emphasis was always on its humanitarian effects. The combination of silent selfish interests and highly vocal humanitarian apologists made a powerful and successful lobby for extracting money from taxpayers. We can expect the same lobby to push now for the creation of a World Food Bank.

However great the potential benefit to selfish interests, it should not be a decisive argument against a truly humanitarian program. We must ask if such a program would actually do more good than harm, not only momentarily but also in the long run. Those who propose the food bank usually refer to a current "emergency" or "crisis" in terms of world food supply. But what is an emergency? Although they may be infrequent and sudden, everyone knows that emergencies will occur from time to time. A well-run family, company, organization or country prepares for the likelihood of accidents and emergencies. It expects them, it budgets for them, it saves for them.

## Learning the Hard Way

What happens if some organizations or countries budget for accidents and others do not? If each country is solely responsible for its own well-being, poorly managed ones will suffer. But they can learn from experience. They may mend their ways, and learn to budget for infrequent but certain emergencies. For example, the weather varies from year to year, and periodic crop failures are certain. A wise and competent government saves out of the production of the good years in anticipation of bad years to come. Joseph taught this policy to Pharaoh in Egypt more than 2,000 years ago. Yet the great majority of the governments in the world today do not follow such a policy. They lack either the wisdom or the competence, or both. Should those nations that do manage to put something aside be forced to come to the rescue each time an emergency occurs among the poor nations?

"But it isn't their fault!" some kindhearted liberals argue. "How can we blame the poor people who are caught in an emergency? Why must they suffer for the sins of their governments?" The concept of blame is simply not relevant here. The real question is, what are the operational consequences of establishing a world food bank? If it is open to every country every time a need develops, slovenly rulers will not be motivated to take Joseph's advice. Someone will always come to their aid. Some countries will deposit food in the world food bank, and others will withdraw it. There will be almost no overlap. As a result of such solutions to food shortage emergencies, the poor countries will not learn to mend their ways, and will suffer progressively greater emergencies as their populations grow.

## Population Control the Crude Way

On the average, poor countries undergo a 2.5 percent increase in population each year; rich countries, about 0.8 percent. Only rich countries have anything in the way of food reserves set aside, and even they do not have as much as they should. Poor countries have none. If poor countries received no food from the outside, the rate of their population growth would be periodically checked by crop failures and famines. But if they can always draw on a world food bank in times of need, their population can continue to grow unchecked, and so will their "need" for aid. In the short run, a world food bank may diminish that need, but in the long run it actually increases the need without limit.

Without some system of worldwide food sharing, the proportion of people in the rich and poor nations might eventually stabilize. The overpopulated poor countries would decrease in numbers, while the rich countries that had room for more people would increase. But with a well-meaning system of sharing, such as a world food bank, the growth differential between the rich and the poor countries will not only persist, it will increase. Because of the higher rate of population growth in the poor countries of the world, 88 percent of today's children are born poor, and only 12 percent rich. Year by year the ratio becomes worse, as the fast-reproducing poor outnumber the slow-reproducing rich.

A world food bank is thus a commons in disguise. People will have more motivation to draw from it than to add to any common store. The less provident and less able will multiply at the expense of the abler and more provident, bringing eventual ruin upon all who share in the commons. Besides, any system of "sharing" that amounts to foreign aid from the rich nations to the poor nations will carry the taint of charity, which will contribute little to the world peace so devoutly desired by those who support the idea of a world food bank.

As past U.S. foreign-aid programs have amply and depressingly demonstrated, international charity frequently inspires mistrust and antagonism rather than gratitude on the part of the recipient nation.

## Chinese Fish and Miracle Rice

The modern approach to foreign aid stresses the export of technology and advice, rather than money and food. As an ancient Chinese proverb goes: "Give a man a fish and he will eat for a day; teach him how to fish and he will eat for the rest of his days." Acting on this advice, the Rockefeller and Ford Foundations have financed a number of programs for improving agriculture in the hungry nations. Known as the "Green Revolution," these programs have led to the development of "miracle rice" and "miracle wheat," new strains that offer bigger harvests and greater resistance to crop damage. Norman Borlaug, the Nobel Prize winning agronomist who, supported by the Rockefeller Foundation, developed miracle wheat, is one of the most prominent advocates of a world food bank.

Whether or not the Green Revolution can increase food production as much as its champions claim is a debatable but possibly irrelevant point. Those who support this well-intended humanitarian effort should first consider some of the fundamentals of human ecology. Ironically, one man who did was the late Alan Gregg, a vice president of the Rockefeller Foundation. Two decades ago he expressed strong doubts about the wisdom of such attempts to increase food production. He likened the growth and spread of humanity over the surface of the earth to the spread of cancer in the human body, remarking that "cancerous growths demand food; but, as far as I know, they have never been cured by getting it."

## Overloading the Environment

Every human born constitutes a draft on all aspects of the environment: food, air, water, forests, beaches, wildlife, scenery and solitude. Food can, perhaps, be significantly increased to meet a growing demand. But what about clean beaches, unspoiled forests, and solitude? If we satisfy a growing population's need for food, we necessarily decrease its per capita supply of the other resources needed by men.

India, for example, now has a population of 600 million, which increases by 15 million each year. This population already puts a huge load on a relatively impoverished environment. The country's forests are now only a small fraction of what they were three centuries ago, and floods and erosion continually destroy the insufficient farmland that remains. Every one of the 15 million new lives added to India's population puts an additional burden on the environment, and increases the economic and social costs of crowding. However humanitarian our intent, every Indian life saved through medical or nutritional assistance from abroad diminishes the quality of life for those who remain, and for subsequent generations. If rich countries make it possible, through foreign aid, for 600 million Indians to swell to 1.2 billion in a mere twenty-eight years, as their current growth rate threatens, will future generations of Indians thank us for hastening the destruction of their environment? Will our good intentions be sufficient excuse for the consequences of our actions?

My final example of a commons in action is one for which the public has the least desire for rational discussion—immigration. Anyone who publicly questions the wisdom of current U.S. immigration policy is promptly charged with bigotry, prejudice, ethnocentrism, chauvinism, isolationism or selfishness. Rather than encounter such accusations, one would rather talk about other matters, leaving immigration policy to wallow in the crosscurrents of special interests that take no account of the good of the whole, or the interests of posterity.

Perhaps we still feel guilty about things we said in the past. Two generations ago the popular press frequently referred to Dagos, Wops, Polacks, Chinks and Krauts, in articles about how America was being "overrun" by foreigners of supposedly inferior genetic stock. But because the implied inferiority of foreigners was used then as justification for keeping them out, people now assume that restrictive policies could only be based on such misguided notions. There are other grounds.

## A Nation of Immigrants

Just consider the numbers involved. Our government acknowledges a net inflow of 400,000 immigrants a year. While we have no hard data on the extent of illegal entries, educated guesses put the figure at about 600,000 a year. Since the natural increase (excess of births over deaths) of the resident population now runs about 1.7 million per year, the yearly gain from immigration amounts to at least 19 percent of the total annual increase, and may be as much as 37 percent if we include the estimate for illegal immigrants. Considering the growing use of birth-control devices, the potential effect of educational campaigns by such organizations as Planned Parenthood Federation of America and Zero Population Growth, and the influence of inflation and the housing shortage, the fertility rate of American women may decline so much that immigration could account for all the yearly increase in population. Should we not at least ask if that is what we want?

For the sake of those who worry about whether the "quality" of the average immigrant compares favorably with the quality of the average resident, let us assume that immigrants and native-born citizens are of exactly equal quality, however one defines that term. We will focus here only on quantity; and since our conclusions will depend on nothing else, all charges of bigotry and chauvinism become irrelevant.

## Immigration vs. Food Supply

World food banks *move food to the people*, hastening the exhaustion of the environment of the poor countries. Unrestricted immigration, on the other hand, *moves people to the food*, thus speeding up the destruction of the environment of the rich countries. We can easily understand why poor people should want to make this latter transfer, but why should rich hosts encourage it?

As in the case of foreign-aid programs, immigration receives support from selfish interests and humanitarian impulses. The primary selfish interest in unimpeded immigration is the desire of employers for cheap labor, particularly in industries and trades that offer degrading work. In the past, one wave of foreigners after another was brought into the U.S. to work at wretched jobs for wretched wages. In recent years the Cubans, Puerto Ricans and Mexicans have had this dubious honor. The interests of the employers of cheap labor mesh well with the guilty silence of the country's liberal intelligentsia. White Anglo-Saxon Protestants are particularly reluctant to call for a closing of the doors to immigration for fear of being called bigots.

But not all countries have such reluctant leadership. Most educated Hawaiians, for example, are keenly aware of the limits of their environment, particularly in terms of population growth. There is only so much room on the islands, and the islanders know it. To Hawaiians, immigrants from the other forty-nine states present as great a threat as those from other nations. At a recent meeting of Hawaiian government officials in Honolulu, I had the ironic delight of hearing a speaker, who like most of his audience was of Japanese ancestry, ask how the country might practically and constitutionally close its doors to further immigration. One member of the audience countered: "How can we shut the doors now? We have many friends and relatives in Japan that we'd like to bring here some day so that they can enjoy Hawaii too." The Japanese-American speaker smiled sympathetically and answered: "Yes, but we have children now, and someday we'll have grandchildren too. We can bring more people here from Japan only by giving away some of the land that we hope to pass on to our grandchildren some day. What right do we have to do that?"

At this point, I can hear U.S. liberals asking: "How can you justify slamming the door once you're inside? You say that immigrants should be kept out. But aren't we all immigrants, or the descendants of immigrants? If we insist on staying, must we not admit all others?" Our craving for intellectual order leads us to seek and prefer symmetrical rules and morals: a single rule for me and everybody else; the same rule yesterday, today, and tomorrow. Justice, we feel, should not change with time and place.

We Americans of non-Indian ancestry can look upon ourselves as the descendants of thieves who are guilty morally, if not legally, of stealing this land from its Indian owners. Should we then give back the land to the now living American descendants of those Indians? However morally or logically sound this proposal may be, I, for one, am unwilling to live by it and I know no one else who is. Besides, the logical consequence would be absurd. Suppose that, intoxicated with a sense of pure justice, we should decide to turn our land over to the Indians. Since all our wealth has also been derived from the land, wouldn't we be morally obliged to give that back to the Indians too?

## Pure Justice vs. Reality

Clearly, the concept of pure justice produces an infinite regression to absurdity. Centuries ago, wise men invented statutes of limitations to justify the rejection of such pure justice, in the interest of preventing continual disorder. The law zealously defends property rights, but only relatively recent property rights. Drawing a line after an arbitrary time has elapsed may be unjust, but the alternatives are worse.

We are all the descendants of thieves, and the world's resources are inequitably distributed. But we must begin the journey to tomorrow from the point where we are today. We cannot remake the past. We cannot safely divide the wealth equitably among all peoples so long as people reproduce at different rates. To do so would guarantee that our grandchildren, and everyone else's grandchildren, would have only a ruined world to inhabit.

To be generous with one's own possessions is quite different from being generous with those of posterity. We should call this point to the attention of those who, from a commendable love of justice and equality, would institute a system of the commons, either in the form of a world food bank, or of unrestricted immigration. We must convince them if we wish to save at least some parts of the world from environmental ruin.

Without a true world government to control reproduction and the use of available resources, the sharing ethic of the spaceship is impossible. For the foreseeable future, our survival demands that we govern our actions by the ethics of a lifeboat, harsh though they may be. Posterity will be satisfied with nothing less.

## Discussion Questions

✍ *Many people have a strong emotional reaction to Hardin's article. Describe your own emotional reaction to what he says. To what extent are your feelings supported by your arguments?*

1. Hardin argues that programs such as the world food bank appear humanitarian in motivation, but in fact are highly beneficial to many commercial interests. What is the force of this kind of objection? Does it undermine the value of such programs? Why? Why not?

2. Hardin cites Alan Gregg as saying that the spread of humanity is like a cancer. Discuss the strengths and weaknesses of this metaphor. What conclusions does acceptance of this metaphor lead to? Do you agree with those conclusions? Why or why not?

3. On what basis does Hardin object to current U.S. immigration policies? Criti-cally evaluate his position on this issue?

4. Hardin concludes that "the concept of pure justice produces an infinite regression to absurdity." Explain what he means by this conclusion. Discuss the reasons why you agree with him and why you disagree with him. Is his concept of "pure justice" a straw man?

Peter Singer
"Rich and Poor"

*Peter Singer, presently professor of philosophy and deputy director of the Center for Human Bioethics at Monash University (Melbourne), is the author of numerous works in ethics, especially in applied ethics. His books include* The Expanding Circle, Animal Lib-eration, Practical Ethics, *and, most recently,* Rethinking Life and Death *and* How Are We to Live? *He has also edited a number of books, including* A Companion to Ethics. *In his work, Singer sees himself as holding our conventional moral beliefs to a standard of con-sistency, coherence, and the avoidance of arbitrary distinctions. He finds that many of these traditional beliefs are remnants of earlier, religiously-inspired doctrines that he be-lieves many people no longer accept, while other beliefs survive only because they pro-mote some form of group selfishness.*

*Writing from a strict utilitarian standpoint, Singer argues that rich nations have an obligation to aid poor and starving ones up to the point of relative equality between rich and poor. Letting people starve to death when we could prevent it without giving up our own lives, Singer argues, is the moral equivalent of actively killing them—and since killing them is clearly wrong, so too is letting them starve to death under the present con-ditions. Singer considers various objections to his position, but finds none of them suffi-ciently strong to undermine his position.*

## As You Read, Consider This:

1. Singer maintains that "If we stopped feeding animals on grains and soybeans, the amount of food saved would—if distributed to those who need it—be more than enough to end hunger throughout the world." How do you think the issue of vegetarianism is related to world

Peter Singer, "Rich and Poor," from *Practical Ethics*, 2nd ed. (New York: Cambridge University Press, 1993). Copyright © 1993, Cambridge University Press. Reprinted by permission of the publisher and the author.

hunger? If people are asked to give up eating meat, are they being asked to give up something morally signficant, something to which they have a strong right?

2.  Singer maintains that if "allowing someone to die is not intrinsically different from killing someone, it would seem that we are all murderers." What is the moral difference between actively killing someone and passively letting someone die whom you could save? How does this issue play a role in the development of Singer's position? Do you agree with his principle, "if it is in our power to prevent something very bad from happening, without thereby sacrificing anything of comparable moral significance, we ought to do it"?

## Some Facts about Poverty

Consider these facts: by the most cautious estimates, 400 million people lack the calories, protein, vitamins and minerals needed to sustain their bodies and minds in a healthy state. Millions are constantly hungry; others suffer from deficiency diseases and from infections they would be able to resist on a better diet. Children are the worst affected. According to one study, 14 million children under five die every year from the combined effects of malnutrition and infection. In some districts half the children born can be expected to die before their fifth birthday.

Nor is lack of food the only hardship of the poor. To give a broader picture, Robert McNamara, when president of the World Bank, suggested the term "absolute poverty." The poverty we are familiar with in industrialized nations is relative poverty—meaning that some citizens are poor, relative to the wealth enjoyed by their neighbors. People living in relative poverty in Australia might be quite comfortably off by comparison with pensioners in Britain, and British pensioners are not poor in comparison with the poverty that exists in Mali or Ethiopia. Absolute poverty, on the other hand, is poverty by any standard. In McNamara's words:

> Poverty at the absolute level . . . is life at the very margin of existence. The absolute poor are severely deprived human beings struggling to survive in a set of squalid and degraded circumstances almost beyond the power of our sophisticated imaginations and privileged circumstances to conceive.
>
> Compared to those fortunate enough to live in developed countries, individuals in the poorest nations have:
>
> An infant mortality rate eight times higher
> A life expectancy one-third lower
> An adult literacy rate 60 per cent less
> A nutritional level, for one out of every two in the population, below acceptable standards;
> And for millions of infants, less protein than is sufficient to permit optimum development of the brain.

McNamara has summed up absolute poverty as "a condition of life so characterized by malnutrition, illiteracy, disease, squalid surroundings, high infant mortality and low life expectancy as to be beneath any reasonable definition of human decency."

Absolute poverty is, as McNamara has said, responsible for the loss of countless lives, especially among infants and young children. When absolute poverty does not cause death, it still causes misery of a kind not often seen in the affluent nations. Malnutrition in young children stunts both physical and mental development. According to the United Nations Development Programme, 180 million children under the age of five suffer from serious malnutrition. Millions of people on poor diets suffer from deficiency diseases, like goitre, or blindness caused by a lack of vitamin A. The food value of what the poor eat is further reduced by parasites such as hookworm and ringworm, which are endemic in conditions of poor sanitation and health education.

Death and disease apart, absolute poverty remains a miserable condition of life, with inadequate food, shelter, clothing, sanitation, health services and education. The Worldwatch Institute estimates that as many as 1.2 billion people—or 23 per cent of the world's population—live in absolute poverty. For the purposes of this estimate, absolute poverty is defined as "the lack of sufficient income in cash or kind to meet the most basic biological needs for food, clothing, and shelter." Absolute poverty is probably the principal cause of human misery today.

## Some Facts about Wealth

This is the background situation, the situation that prevails on our planet all the time. It does not make headlines. People died from malnutrition and related diseases yesterday, and more will die tomorrow. The occasional droughts, cyclones, earthquakes, and floods that take the lives of tens of thousands in one place and at one time are more newsworthy. They add greatly to the total amount of human suffering; but it is wrong to assume that when there are no major calamities reported, all is well.

The problem is not that the world cannot produce enough to feed and shelter its people. People in the poor countries consume, on average, 180 kilos of grain a year, while North Americans average around 900 kilos. The difference is caused by the fact that in the rich countries we feed most of our grain to animals, converting it into meat, milk, and eggs. Because this is a highly inefficient process, people in rich countries are responsible for the consumption of far more food than those in poor countries who eat few animal products. If we stopped feeding animals on grains and soybeans, the amount of food saved would—if distributed to those who need it—be more than enough to end hunger throughout the world.

These facts about animal food do not mean that we can easily solve the world food problem by cutting down on animal products, but they show that the problem is essentially one of distribution rather than production. The world does produce enough food. Moreover, the poorer nations themselves could produce far more if they made more use of improved agricultural techniques.

So why are people hungry? Poor people cannot afford to buy grain grown by farmers in the richer nations. Poor farmers cannot afford to buy improved seeds, or fertilizers, or the machinery needed for drilling wells and pumping water. Only by transferring some of the wealth of the rich nations to the poor can the situation be changed.

That this wealth exists is clear. Against the picture of absolute poverty that McNamara has painted, one might pose a picture of "absolute affluence." Those who are absolutely affluent are not necessarily affluent by comparison with their neighbors, but they are affluent by any reasonable definition of human needs. This means that they have more income than they need to provide themselves adequately with all the basic necessities of life. After buying (either directly or through their taxes) food, shelter, clothing, basic health services, and education, the absolutely affluent are still able to spend money on luxuries. The absolutely affluent choose their food for the pleasures of the palate, not to stop hunger; they buy new clothes to look good, not to keep warm; they move house to be in a better neighborhood or have a playroom for the children, not to keep out the rain; and after all this there is still money to spend on stereo systems, video-cameras, and overseas holidays.

At this stage I am making no ethical judgments about absolute affluence, merely pointing out that it exists. Its defining characteristic is a significant amount of income above the level necessary to provide for the basic human needs of oneself and one's dependents. By this standard, the majority of citizens of Western Europe, North America, Japan, Australia, New Zealand, and the oil-rich Middle Eastern states are all absolutely affluent. To quote McNamara once more:

> "The average citizen of a developed country enjoys wealth beyond the wildest dreams of the one billion Deonle in countries with per capita incomes under $200." These, therefore, are the countries—and individuals—who have wealth that they could, without threatening their own basic welfare, transfer to the absolutely poor.

At present, very little is being transferred. Only Sweden, the Netherlands, Norway, and some of the oil-exporting Arab states have reached the modest target, set by the United Nations, of 0.7 per cent of gross national product (GNP). Britain gives 0.31 per cent of its GNP in official development assistance and a small additional amount in unofficial aid from voluntary organizations. The total comes to about £2 per month per person, and compares with 5.5 per cent of GNP spent on alcohol, and 3 per cent on tobacco. Other, even wealthier nations, give little more: Germany gives 0.41 per cent and Japan 0.32 per cent. The United States gives a mere 0.15 per cent of its GNP.

## The Moral Equivalent of Murder?

If these are the facts, we cannot avoid concluding that by not giving more than we do, people in rich countries are allowing those in poor countries to suffer from absolute poverty, with consequent malnutrition, ill health, and death. This is not a conclusion that applies only to governments. It applies to each absolutely affluent individual, for each of us has the opportunity to do something about the situation; for instance, to give our time or money to voluntary organizations like Oxfam, Care, War on Want, Freedom from Hunger, Community Aid Abroad, and so on. If, then, allowing someone to die is not intrinsically different from killing someone, it would seem that we are all murderers.

Is this verdict too harsh? Many will reject it as self-evidently absurd. They would sooner take it as showing that allowing to die cannot be equivalent to killing than as showing that living in an affluent style without contributing to an overseas aid agency is ethically equivalent to going over to Ethiopia and shooting a few peasants. And no doubt, put as bluntly as that, the verdict is too harsh.

There are several significant differences between spending money on luxuries instead of using it to save lives, and deliberately shooting people.

First, the motivation will normally be different. Those who deliberately shoot others go out of their way to kill; they presumably want their victims dead, from malice, sadism, or some equally unpleasant motive. A person who buys a new stereo system presumably wants to enhance her enjoyment of music–not in itself a terrible thing. At worst, spending money on luxuries instead of giving it away indicates selfishness and indifference to the sufferings of others, characteristics that may be undesirable but are not comparable with actual malice or similar motives. Second, it is not difficult for most of us to act in accordance with a rule against killing people: it is, on the other hand, very difficult to obey a rule that commands us to save all the lives we can. To live a comfortable, or even luxurious life it is not necessary to kill anyone; but it is necessary to allow some to die whom we might have saved, for the money that we need to live comfortably could have been given away. Thus the duty to avoid killing is much easier to discharge completely than the duty to save. Saving every life we could would mean cutting our standard of living down to the bare essentials needed to keep us alive.[1] To discharge this duty completely would require a degree of moral heroism utterly different from that required by mere avoidance of killing.

A third difference is the greater certainty of the outcome of shooting when compared with not giving aid. If I point a loaded gun at someone at close range and pull the trigger, it is virtually certain that the person will be killed; whereas the money that I could give might be spent on a project that turns out to be unsuccessful and helps no one.

Fourth, when people are shot there are identifiable individuals who have been harmed. We can point to them and to their grieving families. When I buy my stereo system, I cannot know who my money would have saved if I had given it away. In a time of famine I may see dead bodies and grieving families on television reports, and I might not doubt that my money would have saved some of them; even then it is impossible to point to a body and say that had I not bought the stereo, that person would have survived.

Fifth, it might be said that the plight of the hungry is not my doing, and so I cannot be held responsible for it. The starving would have been starving if I had never existed. If I kill, however, I am responsible for my victims' deaths, for those people would not have died if I had not killed them.

These differences need not shake our previous conclusion that there is no intrinsic difference between killing and allowing to die. They are extrinsic differences, that is, differences normally but not necessarily associated with the distinction between killing and allowing to die. We can imagine cases in which someone allows another to die for malicious or sadistic reasons; we can imagine a world in which there are so few people needing assistance, and they are so easy to assist, that our duty not to allow people to die is as easily discharged as our duty not to kill; we can imagine situations in which the outcome of not helping is as sure as shooting; we can imagine cases in which we can identify the person we allow to die. We can even imagine a case of allowing to die in which, if I had not existed, the person would not have died—for instance, a case in which if I had not been in a position to help (though I don't help) someone else would have been in my position and would have helped.

Our previous discussion of euthanasia illustrates the extrinsic nature of these differences, for they do not provide a basis for distinguishing active from passive euthanasia. If a doctor decides, in consultation with the parents, not to operate on—and thus to allow to die—a Down's syndrome infant with an intestinal blockage, her motivation will be similar to that of a doctor who gives a lethal injection rather than allow the infant to die. No extraordinary sacrifice or moral heroism will be required in either case. Not operating will just as certainly end in death as administering the injection. Allowing to die does have an identifiable victim. Finally, it may well be that the doctor is personally responsible for the death of the infant she decides not to operate upon, since she may know that if she had not taken this case, other doctors in the hospital would have operated.

Nevertheless, euthanasia is a special case, and very different from allowing people to starve to death. (The major difference being that when euthanasia is justifiable, death is a good thing.) The extrinsic differences that *normally* mark off killing and allowing to die do explain why we *normally* regard killing as much worse than allowing to die.

To explain our conventional ethical attitudes is not to justify them. Do the five differences not only explain, but also justify, our attitudes? Let us consider them one by one:

1. Take the lack of an identifiable victim first. Suppose that I am a traveling salesperson, selling tinned food, and I learn that a batch of tins contains a contaminant, the known effect of which, when consumed, is to double the risk that the consumer will die from stomach cancer. Suppose I continue to sell the tins. My decision may have no identifiable victims. Some of those who eat the food will die from cancer. The proportion of consumers dying in this way will be twice that of the community at large, but who among the consumers died because they ate what I sold, and who would have contracted the disease anyway? It is impossible to tell; but surely this impossibility makes my decision no less reprehensible than it would have been had the contaminant had more readily detectable, though equally fatal, effects.

2. The lack of certainty that by giving money I could save a life does reduce the wrongness of not giving, by comparison with deliberate killing; but it is insufficient to show that not giving is acceptable conduct. The motorist who speeds through pedestrian crossings, heedless of anyone who might be on them, is not a murderer. She may never actually hit a pedestrian; yet what she does is very wrong indeed.

3. The notion of responsibility for acts rather than omissions is more puzzling. On the one hand, we feel ourselves to be under a greater obligation to help those whose misfortunes we have caused. (It is for this reason that advocates of overseas aid often argue that Western nations have created the poverty of third world nations, through forms of economic exploitation that go back to the colonial system.) On the other hand, any consequentialist would insist that we are responsible for all the consequences of our actions, and if a consequence of my spending money on a luxury item is that someone dies, I am responsible for that death. It is true that the person would have died even if I had never existed, but what is the relevance of that? The fact is that I do exist, and the consequentialist will say that our responsibilities derive from the world as it is, not as it might have been.

One way of making sense of the non-consequentialist view of responsibility is by basing it on a theory of rights of the kind proposed by John Locke or, more recently, Robert Nozick. If everyone has a right to life, and this right is a right *against* others who might threaten my life, but not a right to assistance from others when my life is in danger, then we can understand the feeling that we are responsible for acting to kill but not for omitting to save. The former violates the rights of others, the latter does not. Should we accept such a theory of rights? If we build up our theory of rights by imagining, as Locke and Nozick do, individuals living independently from each other in a "state of nature," it may seem natural to adopt a conception of rights in which as long as each leaves the other alone, no rights are violated. I might, on this view, quite properly have maintained my independent existence if I had wished to do so. So if I do not make you any worse off than you would have been if I had had nothing at all to do with you, how can I have violated your rights? But why start from such an unhistorical, abstract and ultimately inexplicable idea as an independent individual? Our ancestors were—like other primates—social beings long before they were human beings, and could not have developed the abilities and capacities of human beings if they had not been social beings first. In any case, we are not, now, isolated individuals. So why should we assume that rights must be restricted to rights against interference? We might, instead, adopt the view that taking rights to life seriously is incompatible with standing by and watching people die when one could easily save them.

4. What of the difference in motivation? That a person does not positively wish for the death of another lessens the severity of the blame she deserves; but not by as much as our present attitudes to giving aid suggest. The behavior of the speeding motorist is again comparable, for such motorists usually have no desire at all to kill anyone. They merely enjoy speeding and are indifferent to the consequences. Despite their lack of malice, those who kill with cars deserve not only blame but also severe punishment.

5. Finally, the fact that to avoid killing people is normally not difficult, whereas to save all one possibly could save is heroic, must make an important difference to our attitude to failure to do what the respective principles demand. Not to kill is a minimum standard of acceptable conduct we can require of everyone; to save all one possibly could is not something that can realistically be required, especially not in societies accustomed to giving as little as ours do. Given the generally accepted standards, people who give, say, $1,000 a year to an overseas aid organization are more aptly praised for above average generosity than blamed for giving less than they might. The appropriateness of praise and blame is, however, a separate issue from the rightness or wrongness of actions. The former evaluates the agent: the latter evaluates the action. Perhaps many people who give $1,000 really ought to give at least $5,000, but to blame them for not giving more could be counterproductive. It might make them feel that what is required is too demanding, and if one is going to be blamed anyway, one might as well not give anything at all.

(That an ethic that put saving all one possibly can on the same footing as not killing would be an ethic for saints or heroes should not lead us to assume that the alternative must be an ethic that makes it obligatory not to kill, but puts us under no obligation to save anyone. There are positions in between these extremes, as we shall soon see.)

Here is a summary of the five differences that normally exist between killing and allowing to die, in the context of absolute poverty and overseas aid. The lack of an identifiable victim is of no moral significance, though it may play an important role in explaining our attitudes. The idea that we are directly responsible for those we kill, but not for those we do not help, depends on a questionable notion of responsibility and may need to be based on a controversial theory of rights. Differences in certainty and motivation are ethically significant, and show that not aiding the poor is not to be condemned as murdering them; it could, however, be on a par with killing someone as a result of reckless driving, which is serious enough. Finally the difficulty of completely discharging the duty of saving all one possibly can makes it inappropriate to blame those who fall short of this target as we blame those who kill; but this does not show that the act itself is less serious. Nor does it indicate anything about those who, far from saving all they possibly can, make no effort to save anyone.

These conclusions suggest a new approach. Instead of attempting to deal with the contrast between affluence and poverty by comparing not saving with deliberate killing, let us consider afresh whether we have an obligation to assist those whose lives are in danger, and if so, how this obligation applies to the present world situation.

## The Obligation to Assist

### The Argument for an Obligation to Assist

The path from the library at my university to the humanities lecture theatre passes a shallow ornamental pond. Suppose that on my way to give a lecture I notice that a small child has fallen in and is in danger of drowning. Would anyone deny that I ought to wade in and pull the child out? This will mean getting my clothes muddy and either canceling my lecture or delaying it until I can find something dry to change into; but compared with the avoidable death of a child this is insignificant.

A plausible principle that would support the judgment that I ought to pull the child out is this: if it is in our power to prevent something very bad from happening, without thereby sacrificing anything of comparable moral significance, we ought to do it. This principle seems uncontroversial. It will obviously win the assent of consequentialists; but non-consequentialists should accept it too, because the injunction to prevent what is bad applies only when nothing comparably significant is at stake. Thus the principle cannot lead to the kinds of actions of which non-consequentialists strongly disapprove—serious violations of individual rights, injustice, broken promises, and so on. If non-consequentialists regard any of these as comparable in moral significance to the bad thing that is to be prevented, they will automatically regard the principle as not applying in those cases in which the bad thing can only be prevented by violating rights, doing injustice, breaking promises, or whatever else is at stake. Most non-consequentialists hold that we ought to prevent what is bad and promote what is good. Their dispute with consequentialists lies in their insistence that this is not the sole ultimate ethical principle: that it is an ethical principle is not denied by any plausible ethical theory.

Nevertheless the uncontroversial appearance of the principle that we ought to prevent what is bad when we can do so without sacrificing anything of comparable moral significance is deceptive. If it were taken seriously and acted upon, our lives and our world would be fundamentally changed. For the principle applies, not just to rare situations in which one can save a child from a pond, but to the everyday situation in which we can assist those living in absolute poverty. In saying this I assume that absolute poverty, with its hunger and malnutrition, lack of shelter, illiteracy, disease, high infant mortality, and low life expectancy, is a bad thing. And I assume that it is within the power of the affluent to reduce absolute poverty, without sacrificing anything of comparable moral significance. If these two assumptions and the principle we have been discussing are correct, we have an obligation to help those in absolute poverty that is no less strong than our obligation to rescue a drowning child from a pond. Not to help would be wrong, whether or not it is intrinsically equivalent to killing. Helping is not, as conventionally thought, a charitable act that it is praiseworthy to do, but not wrong to omit; it is something that everyone ought to do.

This is the argument for an obligation to assist. Set out more formally, it would look like this.

*First premise:* If we can prevent something bad without sacrificing anything of comparable significance, we ought to do it.

*Second premise:* Absolute poverty is bad.

*Third premise:* There is some absolute poverty we can prevent without sacrificing anything of comparable moral significance.

*Conclusion:* We ought to prevent some absolute poverty.

The first premise is the substantive moral premise on which the argument rests, and I have tried to show that it can be accepted by people who hold a variety of ethical positions.

The second premise is unlikely to be challenged. Absolute poverty is, as McNamara put it, "beneath any reasonable definition of human decency" and it would be hard to find a plausible ethical view that did not regard it as a bad thing.

The third premise is more controversial, even though it is cautiously framed. It claims only that some absolute poverty can be prevented without the sacrifice of anything of comparable moral significance. It thus avoids the objection that any aid I can give is just "drops in the ocean" for the point is not whether my personal contribution will make any noticeable impression on world poverty as a whole (of course it won't) but whether it will prevent some poverty. This is all the argument needs to sustain its conclusion, since the second premise says that any absolute poverty is bad, and not merely the total amount of absolute poverty. If without sacrificing anything of comparable moral significance we can provide just one family with the means to raise itself out of absolute poverty, the third premise is vindicated.

I have left the notion of moral significance unexamined in order to show that the argument does not depend on any specific values or ethical principles. I think the third premise is true for most people living in industrialized nations, on any defensible view of what is morally significant. Our affluence means that we have income we can dispose of without giving up the basic necessities of life, and we can use this income to reduce absolute poverty. Just how much we will think ourselves obliged to give up will depend on what we consider to be of comparable moral significance to the poverty we could prevent: stylish clothes, expensive dinners, a sophisticated stereo system, overseas holidays, a (second?) car, a larger house, private schools for our children, and so on. For a utilitarian, none of these is likely to be of comparable significance to the reduction of absolute poverty; and those who are not utilitarians surely must, if they subscribe to the principle of universalizability, accept that at least some of these things are of far less moral significance than the absolute poverty that could be prevented by the money they cost. So the third premise seems to be true on any plausible ethical view—although the precise amount of absolute poverty that can be prevented before anything of moral significance is sacrificed will vary according to the ethical view one accepts.

## Objections to the Argument

*Taking care of our own.* Anyone who has worked to increase overseas aid will have come across the argument that we should look after those near us, our families, and then the poor in our own country, before we think about poverty in distant places.

No doubt we do instinctively prefer to help those who are close to us. Few could stand by and watch a child drown; many can ignore a famine in Africa. But the question is not what we usually do, but what we ought to do, and it is difficult to see any sound moral justification for the view that distance, or community membership, makes a crucial difference to our obligations.

Consider, for instance, racial affinities. Should people of European origin help poor Europeans before helping poor Africans? Most of us would reject such a suggestion out of hand, and our discussion of the principle of equal consideration of interests in Chapter 2 [of *Practical Ethics*] has shown why we should reject it: people's need for food has nothing to do with their race, and if Africans need food more than Europeans, it would be a violation of the principle of equal consideration to give preference to Europeans.

The same point applies to citizenship or nationhood. Every affluent nation has some relatively poor citizens, but absolute poverty is limited largely to the poor nations. Those living on the streets of Calcutta, or in the drought-prone Sahel region of Africa, are experiencing poverty unknown in the West. Under these circumstances it would be wrong to decide that only those fortunate enough to be citizens of our own community will share our abundance. We feel obligations of kinship more strongly than those of citizenship. Which parents could give away their last bowl of rice if their own children were starving? To do so would seem unnatural, contrary to our nature as biologically evolved beings—although whether it would be wrong is another question altogether. In any case, we are not faced with that situation, but with one in which our own children are well-fed, well-clothed, well-educated, and would now like new bikes, a stereo set, or their own car. In these circumstances any special obligations we might have to our children have been fulfilled, and the needs of strangers make a stronger claim upon us.

The element of truth in the view that we should first take care of our own, lies in the advantage of a recognized system of responsibilities. When families and local communities look after their own poorer members, ties of affection and personal relationships achieve ends that would otherwise require a large, impersonal bureaucracy. Hence it would be absurd to propose that from now on we all regard ourselves as equally responsible for the welfare of everyone in the world; but the argument for an obligation to assist does not propose that. It applies only when some are in absolute poverty, and others can help without sacrificing anything of comparable moral significance. To allow one's own kin to sink into absolute poverty would be to sacrifice something of comparable significance; and before that point had been reached, the breakdown of the system of family and community responsibility would be a factor to weigh the balance in favor of a small degree of preference for family and community. This small degree of preference is, however, decisively outweighed by existing discrepancies in wealth and property.

*Property myths.*   Do people have a right to private property, a right that contradicts the view that they are under an obligation to give some of their wealth away to those in absolute poverty? According to some theories of rights (for instance, Robert Nozick's), provided one has acquired one's property without the use of unjust means like force and fraud, one may be entitled to enormous wealth while others starve. This individualistic conception of rights is in contrast to other views, like the early Christian doctrine to be found in the works of Thomas Aquinas, which holds that since property exists for the satisfaction of human needs, "whatever a man has in superabundance is owed, of natural right, to the poor for their sustenance." A socialist would also, of course, see wealth as belonging to the community rather than the individual, while utilitarians, whether social-ist or not, would be prepared to override property rights to prevent great evils.

Does the argument for an obligation to assist others therefore presuppose one of these other theories of property rights, and not an individualistic theory like Nozick's? Not necessarily. A the-ory of property rights can insist on our *right* to retain wealth without pronouncing on whether the rich *ought* to give to the poor. Nozick, for example, rejects the use of compulsory means like taxa-tion to redistribute income, but suggests that we can achieve the ends we deem morally desirable by voluntary means. So Nozick would reject the claim that rich people have an "obligation" to give to the poor, in so far as this implies that the poor have a right to our aid, but might accept that giv-ing is something we ought to do and failing to give, though within one's rights, is wrong—for there is more to an ethical life than respecting the rights of others.

The argument for an obligation to assist can survive, with only minor modifications, even if we accept an individualistic theory of property rights. In any case, however, I do not think we should accept such a theory. It leaves too much to chance to be an acceptable ethical view. For in-stance, those whose forefathers happened to inhabit some sandy wastes around the Persian Gulf are now fabulously wealthy, because oil lay under those sands; while those whose forefathers settled on better land south of the Sahara live in absolute poverty, because of drought and bad harvests. Can this distribution be acceptable from an impartial point of view? If we imagine ourselves about to begin life as a citizen of either Bahrain or Chad—but we do not know which—would we accept the principle that citizens of Bahrain are under no obligation to assist people living in Chad?

*Population and the ethics of triage.*    Perhaps the most serious objection to the argument that we have an obligation to assist is that since the major cause of absolute poverty is overpopulation, helping those now in poverty will only ensure that yet more people are born to live in poverty in the future.

In its most extreme form, this objection is taken to show that we should adopt a policy of "triage." The term comes from medical policies adopted in wartime. With too few doctors to cope with all the casualties, the wounded were divided into three categories: those who would probably survive without medical assistance, those who might survive if they received assistance, but other-wise probably would not, and those who even with medical assistance probably would not survive. Only those in the middle category were given medical assistance. The idea, of course, was to use limited medical resources as effectively as possible. For those in the first category, medical treat-ment was not strictly necessary; for those in the third category, it was likely to be useless. It has been suggested that we should apply the same policies to countries, according to their prospects of becoming self-sustaining. We would not aid countries that even without our help will soon be able to feed their populations. We would not aid countries that, even with our help, will not be able to limit their population to a level they can feed. We would aid those countries where our help might make the difference between success and failure in bringing food and population into balance. Ad-vocates of this theory are understandably reluctant to give a complete list of the countries they would place into the 'hopeless' category; Bangladesh has been cited as an example, and so have some of the countries of the Sahel region of Africa. Adopting the policy of triage would, then, mean cutting off assistance to these countries and allowing famine, disease, and natural disasters to reduce the population of those countries to the level at which they can provide adequately for all.

In support of this view Garrett Hardin has offered a metaphor: we in the rich nations are like the occupants of a crowded lifeboat adrift in a sea full of drowning people. If we try to save the drowning by bringing them aboard, our boat will be overloaded and we shall all drown. Since it is better that some survive than none, we should leave the others to drown. In the world today, according to Hardin, "lifeboat ethics" apply. The rich should leave the poor to starve, for otherwise the poor will drag the rich down with them.

Against this view, some writers have argued that overpopulation is a myth. The world produces ample food to feed its population, and could, according to some estimates, feed ten times as many. People are hungry not because there are too many but because of inequitable land distribution, the manipulation of third world economies by the developed nations, wastage of food in the West, and so on. Putting aside the controversial issue of the extent to which food production might one day be increased, it is true, as we have already seen, that the world now produces enough to feed its inhabitants—the amount lost by being fed to animals itself being enough to meet existing grain shortages. Nevertheless population growth cannot be ignored. Bangladesh could, with land reform and using better techniques, feed its present population of 115 million; but by the year 2000, according to United Nations Population Division estimates, its population will be 150 million. The enormous effort that will have to go into feeding an extra 35 million people, all added to the population within a decade, means that Bangladesh must develop at full speed to stay where it is. Other low-income countries are in similar situations. By the end of the century, Ethiopia's population is expected to rise from 49 to 66 million; Somalia's from 7 to 9 million, India's from 853 to 1041 million, Zaire's from 35 to 49 million.[2]

What will happen if the world population continues to grow? It cannot do so indefinitely. It will be checked by a decline in birth rates or a rise in death rates. Those who advocate triage are proposing that we allow the population growth of some countries to be checked by a rise in death rates—that is, by increased malnutrition, and related diseases; by widespread famines; by increased infant mortality; and by epidemics of infectious diseases.

The consequences of triage on this scale are so horrible that we are inclined to reject it without further argument. How could we sit by our television sets, watching millions starve while we do nothing? Would not that be the end of all notions of human equality and respect for human life? (Those who attack the proposals for legalizing euthanasia discussed in Chapter 7 [of *Practical Ethics*], saying that these proposals will weaken respect for human life, would surely do better to object to the idea that we should reduce or end our overseas aid programs, for that proposal, if implemented, would be responsible for a far greater loss of human life.) Don't people have a right to our assistance, irrespective of the consequences? Anyone whose initial reaction to triage was not one of repugnance would be an unpleasant sort of person. Yet initial reactions based on strong feelings are not always reliable guides. Advocates of triage are rightly concerned with the long-term consequences of our actions. They say that helping the poor and starving now merely ensures more poor and starving in the future. When our capacity to help is finally unable to cope—as one day it must be—the suffering will be greater than it would be if we stopped helping now. If this is correct, there is nothing we can do to prevent absolute starvation and poverty, in the long run, and so we have no obligation to assist. Nor does it seem reasonable to hold that under these circumstances people have a right to our assistance. If we do accept such a right, irrespective of the consequences, we are saying that, in Hardin's metaphor, we should continue to haul the drowning into our lifeboat until the boat sinks and we all drown. If triage is to be rejected it must be tackled on its own ground, within the framework of consequentialist ethics. Here it is vulnerable. Any consequentialist ethics must take probability of outcome into account. A course of action that will certainly produce some benefit is to be preferred to an alternative course that may lead to a slightly larger benefit, but is equally likely to result in no benefit at all. Only if the greater magnitude of the uncertain benefit outweighs its uncertainty should we choose it. Better one certain unit of benefit than a 10 percent chance of five units; but better a 50 per cent chance of three units than a single certain unit. The same principle applies when we are trying to avoid evils.

The policy of triage involves a certain, very great evil: population control by famine and disease. Tens of millions would die slowly. Hundreds of millions would continue to live in absolute poverty, at the very margin of existence. Against this prospect, advocates of the policy place a possible evil that is greater still: the same process of famine and disease, taking place in, say, fifty years' time, when the world's population may be three times its present level, and the number who will die from famine, or struggle on in absolute poverty, will be that much greater. The question is: how probable is this forecast that continued assistance now will lead to greater disasters in the future?

Forecasts of population growth are notoriously fallible, and theories about the factors that affect it remain speculative. One theory, at least as plausible as any other, is that countries pass through a "demographic transition" as their standard of living rises. When people are very poor and have no access to modern medicine their fertility is high, but population is kept in check by high death rates. The introduction of sanitation, modern medical techniques, and other improvements reduces the death rate, but initially has little effect on the birth rate. Then population grows rapidly. Some poor countries, especially in sub-Saharan Africa, are now in this phase. If standards of living continue to rise, however, couples begin to realize that to have the same number of children surviving to maturity as in the past, they do not need to give birth to as many children as their parents did. The need for children to provide economic support in old age diminishes. Improved education and the emancipation and employment of women also reduce the birth-rate, and so population growth begins to level off. Most rich nations have reached this stage, and their populations are growing only very slowly, if at all. If this theory is right, there is an alternative to the disasters accepted as inevitable by supporters of triage. We can assist poor countries to raise the living standards of the poorest members of their population. We can encourage the governments of these countries to enact land reform measures, improve education, and liberate women from a purely child-bearing role. We can also help other countries to make contraception and sterilization widely available. There is a fair chance that these measures will hasten the onset of the demographic transition and bring population growth down to a manageable level. According to United Nations estimates, in 1965 the average woman in the third world gave birth to six children, and only 8 per cent were using some form of contraception; by 1991 the average number of children had dropped to just below four, and more than half the women in the third world were taking contraceptive measures. Notable successes in encouraging the use of contraception had occurred in Thailand, Indonesia, Mexico, Colombia, Brazil, and Bangladesh. This achievement reflected a relatively low expenditure in developing countries—considering the size and significance of the problem—of $3 billion annually, with only 20 per cent of this sum coming from developed nations. So expenditure in this area seems likely to be highly cost-effective. Success cannot be guaranteed; but the evidence suggests that we can reduce population growth by improving economic security and education, and making contraceptives more widely available. This prospect makes triage ethically unacceptable. We cannot allow millions to die from starvation and disease when there is a reasonable probability that population can be brought under control without such horrors.

Population growth is therefore not a reason against giving overseas aid, although it should make us think about the kind of aid to give. Instead of food handouts, it may be better to give aid that leads to a slowing of population growth. This may mean agricultural assistance for the rural poor, or assistance with education, or the provision of contraceptive services. Whatever kind of aid proves most effective in specific circumstances, the obligation to assist is not reduced. One awkward question remains. What should we do about a poor and already overpopulated country that, for religious or nationalistic reasons, restricts the use of contraceptives and refuses to slow its population growth? Should we nevertheless offer development assistance? Or should we make our offer conditional on effective steps being taken to reduce the birth rate? To the latter course, some would object that putting conditions on aid is an attempt to impose our own ideas on independent sovereign nations. So it is—but is this imposition unjustifiable? If the argument for an obligation to assist is sound, we have an obligation to reduce absolute poverty; but we have no obligation to make sacrifices that, to the best of our knowledge, have no prospect of reducing poverty in the long run. Hence we have no obligation to assist countries whose governments have policies that will make our aid ineffective. This could be very harsh on poor citizens of these countries—for they may have no say in the government's policies—but we will help more people in the long run by using our resources where they are most effective. (The same principles may apply, incidentally, to countries that refuse to take other steps that could make assistance effective—like refusing to reform systems of land holding that impose intolerable burdens on poor tenant farmers.)

*Leaving it to the government.*   We often hear that overseas aid should be a government responsibility, not left to privately run charities. Giving privately, it is said, allows the government to escape its responsibilities. Since increasing government aid is the surest way of making a significant increase to the total amount of aid given, I would agree that the governments of affluent nations should give much more genuine, no-strings-attached, aid than they give now. Less than one-sixth of one per cent of GNP is a scandalously small amount for a nation as wealthy as the United States to give. Even the official UN target of 0.7 per cent seems much less than affluent nations can and should give—though it is a target few have reached. But is this a reason against each of us giving what we can privately, through voluntary agencies? To believe that it is seems to assume that the more people there are who give through voluntary agencies, the less likely it is that the government will do its part. Is this plausible? The opposite view—that if no one gives voluntarily the government will assume that its citizens are not in favor of overseas aid, and will cut its programme accordingly—is more reasonable. In any case, unless there is a definite probability that by refusing to give we would be helping to bring about an increase in government assistance, refusing to give privately is wrong for the same reason that triage is wrong: it is a refusal to prevent a definite evil for the sake of a very uncertain gain. The onus of showing how a refusal to give privately will make the government give more is on those who refuse to give.

This is not to say that giving privately is enough. Certainly we should campaign for entirely new standards for both public and private overseas aid. We should also work for fairer trading arrangements between rich and poor countries, and less domination of the economies of poor countries by multinational corporations more concerned about producing profits for shareholders back home than food for the local poor. Perhaps it is more important to be politically active in the interests of the poor than to give to them oneself—but why not do both? Unfortunately, many use the view that overseas aid is the government's responsibility as a reason against giving, but not as a reason for being politically active.

*Too high a standard?*   The final objection to the argument for an obligation to assist is that it sets a standard so high that none but a saint could attain it. This objection comes in at least three versions. The first maintains that, human nature being what it is, we cannot achieve so high a standard, and since it is absurd to say that we ought to do what we cannot do, we must reject the claim that we ought to give so much. The second version asserts that even if we could achieve so high a standard, to do so would be undesirable. The third version of the objection is that to set so high a standard is undesirable because it will be perceived as too difficult to reach, and will discourage many from even attempting to do so.

Those who put forward the first version of the objection are often influenced by the fact that we have evolved from a natural process in which those with a high degree of concern for their own interests, or the interests of their offspring and kin, can be expected to leave more descendants in future generations, and eventually to completely replace any who are entirely altruistic. Thus the biologist Garrett Hardin has argued, in support of his "lifeboat ethics," that altruism can only exist "on a small scale, over the short term, and within small, intimate groups"; while Richard Dawkins has written, in his provocative book *The Selfish Gene*: "Much as we might wish to believe otherwise, universal love and the welfare of the species as a whole are concepts which simply do not make evolutionary sense." I have already noted, in discussing the objection that we should first take care of our own, the very strong tendency for partiality in human beings. We naturally have a stronger desire to further our own interests, and those of our close kin, than we have to further the interests of strangers. What this means is that we would be foolish to expect widespread conformity to a standard that demands impartial concern, and for that reason it would scarcely be appropriate or feasible to condemn all those who fail to reach such a standard. Yet to act impartially, though it might be very difficult, is not impossible; The commonly quoted assertion that "ought" implies "can" is a reason for rejecting such moral judgments as "You ought to have saved all the people from the sinking ship," when in fact if you had taken one more person into the lifeboat, it would have sunk and you would not have saved any. In that situation, it is absurd to say that you ought to have done what you could not possibly do. When we have money to spend on luxuries and others are starving, however, it is clear that we can all give much more than we do give, and we can therefore all come closer to the impartial standard proposed in this chapter. Nor is there, as we approach closer to this standard, any barrier beyond which we cannot go. For that reason there is no basis for saying that the impartial standard is mistaken because "ought" implies "can" and we cannot be impartial.

The second version of the objection has been put by several philosophers during the past decade, among them Susan Wolf in a forceful article entitled "Moral Saints." Wolf argues that if we all took the kind of moral stance defended in this chapter, we would have to do without a great deal that makes life interesting: opera, gourmet cooking, elegant clothes, and professional sport, for a start. The kind of life we come to see as ethically required of us would be a single-minded pursuit of the overall good, lacking that broad diversity of interests and activities that, on a less demanding view, can be part of our ideal of a good life for a human being. To this, however, one can respond that while the rich and varied life that Wolf upholds as an ideal may be the most desirable form of life for a human being in a world of plenty, it is wrong to assume that it remains a good life in a world in which buying luxuries for oneself means accepting the continued avoidable suffering of others. A doctor faced with hundreds of injured victims of a train crash can scarcely think it defensible to treat fifty of them and then go to the opera, on the grounds that going to the opera is part of a well-rounded human life. The life-or-death needs of others must take priority. Perhaps we are like the doctor in that we live in a time when we all have an opportunity to help to mitigate a disaster. Associated with this second version of the objection is the claim that an impartial ethic of the kind advocated here makes it impossible to have serious personal relationships based on love and friendship; these relationships are, of their nature, partial. We put the interests of our loved ones, our family, and our friends ahead of those of strangers; if we did not do so, would these relationships survive? I have already indicated, in the response I gave when considering the objection that we should first take care of our own, that there is a place, within an impartially grounded moral framework, for recognizing some degree of partiality for kin, and the same can be said for other close personal relationships. Clearly, for most people, personal relationships are among the necessities of a flourishing life, and to give them up would be to sacrifice something of great moral significance. Hence no such sacrifice is required by the principle for which I am here arguing.

The third version of the objection asks: might it not be counterproductive to demand that people give up so much? Might not people say: "As I can't do what is morally required anyway, I won't bother to give at all." If, however, we were to set a more realistic standard, people might make a genuine effort to reach it. Thus setting a lower standard might actually result in more aid being given.

It is important to get the status of this third version of the objection clear. Its accuracy as a prediction of human behavior is quite compatible with the argument that we are obliged to give to the point at which by giving more we sacrifice something of comparable moral significance. What would follow from the objection is that public advocacy of this standard of giving is undesirable. It would mean that in order to do the maximum to reduce absolute poverty, we should advocate a standard lower than the amount we think people really ought to give. Of course we ourselves—those of us who accept the original argument, with its higher standard—would know that we ought to do more than we publicly propose people ought to do, and we might actually give more than we urge others to give. There is no inconsistency here, since in both our private and our public behavior we are trying to do what will most reduce absolute poverty.

For a consequentialist, this apparent conflict between public and private morality is always a possibility, and not in itself an indication that the underlying principle is wrong. The consequences of a principle are one thing, the consequences of publicly advocating it another. A variant of this idea is already acknowledged by the distinction between the intuitive and critical levels of morality, of which I have made use in previous chapters. If we think of principles that are suitable for the intuitive level of morality as those that should be generally advocated, these are the principles that, when advocated, will give rise to the best consequences. Where overseas aid is concerned, those will be the principles that lead to the largest amount being given by the affluent to the poor.

Is it true that the standard set by our argument is so high as to be counterproductive? There is not much evidence to go by, but discussions of the argument, with students and others have led me to think it might be. Yet, the conventionally accepted standard—a few coins in a collection tin when one is waved under your nose—is obviously far too low. What level should we advocate? Any figure will be arbitrary, but there may be something to be said for a round percentage of one's income like, say, 10 per cent—more than a token donation, yet not so high as to be beyond all but saints. (This figure has the additional advantage of being reminiscent of the ancient tithe, or tenth, that was traditionally given to the church, whose responsibilities included care of the poor in one's local community. Perhaps the idea can be revived and applied to the global community.) Some families, of course, will find 10 per cent a considerable strain on their finances. Others may be able to give more without difficulty. No figure should be advocated as a rigid minimum or maximum; but it seems safe to advocate that those earning average or above average incomes in affluent societies, unless they have an unusually large number of dependents or other special needs, ought to give a tenth of their income to reducing absolute poverty. By any reasonable ethical standards this is the minimum we ought to do, and we do wrong if we do less.

## Endnotes

1. Strictly, we would need to cut down to the minimum level compatible with earning the income which, after providing for our needs, left us most to give away. Thus if my present position earns me, say, $40,000 a year, but requires me to spend $5,000 a year on dressing respectably and maintaining a car, I cannot save more people by giving away the car and clothes if that will mean taking a job that, although it does not involve me in these expenses, earns me only $20,000.

2. Ominously, in the twelve years that have passed between editions of this book, the signs are that the situation is becoming even worse than was then predicted. In 1979 Bangladesh had a population of 80 million and it was predicted that by 2000 its population would reach 146 million; Ethiopia's was only 29 million, and was predicted to reach 54 million; and India's was 620 million and predicted to reach 958 million.

## Journal/Discussion Questions

✍ *In the concluding pages of his essay, Singer deals with the issue of whether his position is too demanding. On a personal level, do you feel that Singer's position places too high a set of expectations on you? Discuss this issue in light of his comments.*

1. Singer maintains that affluent *individuals* as well as affluent societies are obligated to help poor nations. What is the relationship between individual responsibility and collective responsibility? If we *as a nation* have an obligation to poorer nations, does it follow that each of us *as individuals* also has such an obligation? Discuss.

2. Singer considers five possible ways in which killing is morally different from letting die. What are these five possible differences? What reasons does Singer give for claiming that they do not undermine his claim that letting die is the moral equivalent of killing?

3. Singer maintains that "any consequentialist would insist that we are responsible for all the consequences of our actions." Do you think this is true? Can you imagine a situation in which you might not be responsible for all the consequences of your acts, even if those consequences are foreseeable?

4. How does Singer explain that "taking

care of our own" argument? Do you think his presentation of the argument puts that argument in its best light? What objections does Singer offer to this argument? Critically assess his objections.

5. What objections does Singer offer to the triage argument—and the related argument about population expansion—advanced by Hardin and others? Critically evaluate his objections.

## John Howie
## "World Hunger and a Moral Right to Subsistence"

*John Howie is a professor of philosophy at Southern Illinois University at Carbondale. He has published widely in the area of social and moral philospohy.*

*Subsistence, a basic and justified moral right, requires of others that they avoid depriving people of the* means *to subsistence,* protect *others from threats to it, and* aid *those unable to provide their own subsistence. The equivalent need condition, a limitation upon these three duties, indicates that a nation is not obligated to save another nation if that nation cannot act to rescue the sufferer without placing itself in a situation of equivalent need. None of the present-day affluent nations is under such limitations..*

### As You Read, Consider This:

1. What is the basis, according to Howie, for claims that human beings have basic rights, including a right to subsistence?
2. What does Howie mean by "the equivalent need condition"? What role does this concept play in his argument?

We live in a world in which one of every eleven persons does not get enough to eat. Each day more than ten thousand people die of starvation; thousands more, both adults and children, suffer brain damage and other functional abnormalities because of malnutrition. Often there is simply not enough drinking water or not enough food available. Some people must do without. A drought has come and some are allowed to die. Or, less food has been grown because less fertilizer was imported and hundreds or thousands die.

A deficiency in food, water, and shelter may underlie many of these deaths. It is by no means obvious that such deficiencies are not the result of human indulgence, extravagance, or simply unthinking neglect elsewhere on our globe. But, aside from indulgence, extravagance, and neglect, there are *other* causes of world hunger *directly* traceable to human agency and control. Consider a couple of examples. Call the first example a radical economic system change. A hypothetical case, it is typical none-the-less of what has often occurred in Latin American countries and is frequently present in situations of colonialism or empire-building by rich and affluent nations. Henry Shue, in

John Howie, "World Hunger and a Moral Right to Subsistence," *Journal of Social Philosophy* 18, no. 3 (Fall 1987), 27–31. Copyright © 1989 *Journal of Social Philosophy*. Reprinted by permission of the *Journal of Social Philosophy*.

his book, *Basic Rights*, has described clearly this type of case.[1] Imagine a country or area where there is barely enough food for the local population. Now, suppose there is a radical change in land-use from growing beans (a staple of the local diet) to raising flowers on the same land for export. The change, often undertaken by foreign investors, can diminish the quantity of food available and literally make it impossible for many of the local or regional inhabitants to get enough to eat. Some of these people as a consequence starve to death. Who is responsible for their deaths? Is this a violation of their right not to be killed? Is this a violation of their basic right to subsistence?

As another example take a "commodity pricing case" that Onora O'Neill discusses.[2] Suppose (as is often the case) that an underdeveloped country depends heavily on the price level of a few commodities. A sharp drop in the world price of coffee, or sugar, or cocoa may mean ruin and sharply lowered survival rates for whole regions. Sometimes such drops in price levels may be the result of factors beyond human control. On other occasions the drop in prices is a result of actions taken by investors, brokers, or governmental agencies. In taking these actions policies are chosen which will kill some people. Death in these situations is as likely as someone's pulling the trigger of a gun in a crowded room. The killing, of course, is not single-handed, often it is not instantaneous, nor are specific individuals selected to die. And, perhaps, in most cases, the people and agencies undertaking the action do not intend that anyone die. But, deaths occur, and those individuals or groups in collusion are the necessary condition of their occurrence. Who is to be blamed? Has a basic right to subsistence been violated?

O'Neill concludes appropriately for both sorts of cases:

> Only if we know that we were not part of any system of activities causing unjustifiable deaths could we have no duties to support policies which seek to avoid such deaths. Modern economic causal chains are so complex that it is likely that only those who are economically isolated and self-sufficient could know that they are part of no such systems of activities. Persons who believe that they are involved in some death-producing activities will have some of the same duties as those who think they have a duty to enforce others' rights not to be killed.[3]

What are these duties? What rights have been transgressed?

Both of these cases might be conceived as existing in an initial situation of plenty, or at least sufficiency. Then, action by some individuals or agencies and/or governments upsets the tenuous economic balance and people do starve.

It is hardly necessary to remark that in situations of scarcity or drought, or other natural disaster, the deaths may easily be multiplied. The tragedy of scarcity is that one person's gain is another person's loss. As Lappe and Collins have wisely emphasized:

> Drought is a natural phenomenon. Famine is a human phenomenon. Any link that does exist is precisely through the economic and political order of a society that can either minimize the human consequences or exacerbate them. While a people cannot change the weather, they can change the political and economic order.[4]

We cannot simply shrug our shoulders and murmur that famine is inevitable.

Famine is said correctly to be inevitable only *if* people do not curb their fertility, change their resource-wasting consumptive patterns, and avoid pollution and the resulting ecological catastrophes. But, all of these are policies we can choose or avoid. Our present choices produce, defer, or, perhaps at best, avoid famine. Present-day famines are the result, in large part, of yesterday's decisions. It is foolish and evasive to suppose that natural calamities and natural disasters cannot be, in some cases, avoided, and, in others, highly ameliorated. And it is clearly immoral not to avoid them when we can and to modify their devastating effects if they cannot be avoided.

If one is asked why are individuals and groups responsible for failure to curb fertility, resource-wasting consumption, pollution and attendant ecological disasters, the answer may be in part that whoever is responsible for these activities is also morally accountable for the effects or results of them. Even as a cause cannot be separated from its effects individuals or groups must be held morally accountable for whatever foreseeable repercussions follow as a result of their deeds. The activity or deed is always done in a specific context and to be willfully ignorant of consequences or repercussions is to be morally culpable.

Let us ask: What rights are being violated when famines occur? The rights that are being violated include (it seems) at least two "basic rights," the rights to *subsistence* and *physical security*. Borrowing the labels of Alan Gewirth, these rights are "basic" because they are "necessary conditions" for acting purposefully and with the likelihood of success.[5] Moreover, if one acts in accord with these rights, he/she will be acting in such a manner as to support the universally required conditions of any human agency. As Gewirth explains, "Basic rights have as their Objects the essential preconditions of action, such as life, physical integrity, [and] mental equilibrium."[6] These "basic" rights are to be distinguished from "nonsubtractive rights" (such as the right to a fair trial) and "additive" rights. They are "basic" because in their *absence* no other rights are even possible.

Of course, the protection of anyone's right to physical security requires positive actions, including providing for police forces, courts and orderly legal procedures (all of which openly insist upon the primacy of law over persons), and levying and collecting the taxes to support an enormous system for the prevention, detection and punishment of violations of personal security. These activities and institutions provide social guarantees for the individual's security.

The most fundamental of these two is the right to *subsistence*. In one respect it is what William Aiken calls "the right to be saved from preventable death due to deprivation."[7] What duties does this right require of us?

Henry Shue in his fascinating book gives an instructive three-fold answer: (1) we must *avoid depriving* other persons and other countries of their means of subsistence, (2) we must *protect* other persons and other countries when their means to subsistence is threatened and (3) we must *aid* those who are unable to provide for their own subsistence.[8] These are the moral duties that are entailed by the "basic" right to subsistence. The right to subsistence is a justified demand or claim that its enjoyment be socially guaranteed against usual threats. The duties placed on others on account of a right are explicitly to fulfill the right by securing it against the standard threats. The right to subsistence is reasonably secured when individuals avoid depriving others of the means to subsistence, protect others, in their employing such means to subsistence, and aid those who have been deprived of subsistence, whether by wrongful intent of others, indifference to their plight, or natural disaster.

This sketch of the right to subsistence with its corollary duties requires, however, that some limit to these duties be indicated. This limit has been wisely suggested by William Aiken. Using the limit in a somewhat different context he calls it "the equivalent need condition."[9] Briefly stated, the individual or nation, is not obligated to save another if the person or group cannot render the service or supply the goods without involving himself/herself or the group in a situation of equivalent or more extreme need than that of the sufferers.[10]

Let us note the full meaning of this limitation by considering it in relation to the tripartite duties that serve as guarantees for the right to subsistence. "Equivalent need" means as a limitation that we must avoid depriving other persons of their means of subsistence except in those rare circumstances where such avoidance would itself bring about an equivalent deprivation of the persons, or nation under duty to so act. Such a situation, it should be emphasized, is extremely unusual. It may be that such a situation would never empirically arise. Again, "equivalent need" circumscribes the duty to protect other persons when their means to subsistence is threatened. It is a duty to respond by providing such protection except when the provision of that protection requires an equivalent abandonment of such protection for one's own subsistence. Finally, the "equivalent need" limitation means that one is not obligated to aid those who are unable to provide for their own subsistence if such aid places the rescuer (rescuers) in a situation of equivalent or worse need.

The right to subsistence is a justifiable demand that those people and nations in crisis can make. No one of the three limitations suggested by "equivalent need" holds for the affluent nations such as the United States, the Soviet Union, England, France, to name only a few. To recognize ourselves as under obligations to fulfill this basic right would bring about radical and welcome changes in foreign and domestic policies.

## Endnotes

1. *Basic Rights, Subsistence, Affluence, and U.S. Foreign Policy* (Princeton: Princeton University Press, 1980), p. 46.

2. Onora O'Neill, "Lifeboat Earth," in *World Hunger and Moral Obligation*, ed. William Aiken and Hugh LaFollette (Englewood Cliffs, N.J.: Prentice-Hall, Inc., 1977), p. 158.

3. *Ibid.*, p. 159.

4. Frances Moore Lappe and Joseph Collins, *Food First, Beyond the Myth of Scarcity?* (New York: Ballantine Books, 1978), p. 95.

5. Ian Gewirth, *Human Rights: Essays on Justification and Applications* (Chicago: University of Chicago Press, 1982), p. 4.

6. *Ibid.*, pp. 18–19. Ronald Dworkin, in *Taking Rights Seriously* (Cambridge: Harvard University Press, 1978), calls these "background rights." For him they are rights that hold in an abstract way against decisions taken by society as a whole. Gewirth, by contrast, insists that individuals have these rights against other individuals as well as against the governments This is an important claim since it is the basis of individual responsibility in relation to rights.

7. William Aiken, in "The Right to Be Saved from Starvation," in *World Hunger and Moral Obligation*, p. 86.

8. *Basic Rights*, p. 53.

9. Aiken, *op. cit.*, p. 92.

10. *Ibid.*

# Journal/Discussion Questions

✐ *As a resident of one of the most affluent nations on earth, what do you think your own personal obligations are in regard to world hunger?*

1. In discussing cases of economic reversal such as a sharp drop in the world price of coffee, Howie asserts that "Death in these situations is as likely as someone's pulling the trigger of a gun in a crowded room." Critically evaluate this claim, paying special attention to the ways in which it resembles pulling the trigger of a gun in a crowed room and the ways in which it does not.

2. There has been considerable debate about the question of whether the "equivalent need" limitation is too strong. To what extent must we help others in dire need? How far are we morally obligated to go? How does Howie answer this question? What is your position on this issue?

# QUESTIONS FOR DISCUSSION AND REVIEW

## Where Do You Stand Now?

### Instructions

You have already answered the following questions in your moral problems self-quiz at the beginning of this book. Now that you have studied the material in this section, take a moment to answer the same questions again.

| | Strongly Agree | Agree | Undecided | Disagree | Strongly Disagree | |
|---|---|---|---|---|---|---|
| | | | | | | ***Chapter 8: World Hunger and Poverty*** |
| 36. | ❏ | ❏ | ❏ | ❏ | ❏ | Only the morally heartless would refuse to help the starving. |
| 37. | ❏ | ❏ | ❏ | ❏ | ❏ | We should help starving nations until we are as poor as they are. |
| 38. | ❏ | ❏ | ❏ | ❏ | ❏ | In the long run, relief aid to starving nations does not help them. |
| 39. | ❏ | ❏ | ❏ | ❏ | ❏ | Overpopulation is the main cause of world hunger and poverty. |
| 40. | ❏ | ❏ | ❏ | ❏ | ❏ | The world is gradually becoming a better place. |

Compare your answers to the present self-quiz with the answers to the initial self-quiz. How, if at all, have your answers changed? How have the *reasons* for your answers changed?

## Journal/Discussion Questions

✍ *Let's return to rock-bottom experiences. We are left with the fact that there are people throughout the world who are starving to death, slowly and painfully. We are—at least as a nation, and at least comparatively as individuals—affluent. How do you respond as a compassionate human being to the fact of such suffering?*

1. Imagine that you have been asked to address the annual convention of ethical egoists (ACEE) on the issue of world hunger. What could you say about world hunger to those who believe that their only moral duty is to promote their own welfare?

2. Imagine that you have been asked to address the annual convention of compassionate persons on the issue of world hunger and the *dangers* of compassion. What would you have to say to this audience of compassionate people about the dangers and pitfalls of compassionate responses to world hunger?

3. Imagine that you have been asked by the president of the United States to draft a policy statement on the question of how the United States should respond to world hunger. What main elements would it contain?

# FOR FURTHER READING:
# A BIBLIOGRAPHICAL GUIDE
# TO WORLD HUNGER AND POVERTY

## Journals

In addition to the standard ethics journals mentioned in the bibliographical essay at the end of Chapter 1, also see the journals *Ethics and International Affairs* and *World Development.*

## Review Articles

Nigel Dower's "World Poverty" in *A Companion to Ethics*, ed. Peter Singer (Cambridge: Blackwell, 1991) surveys the literature and argues "for a moderate but significant duty of caring in response to the evils of extreme poverty." Onora O'Neill, "International Justice: Distribution," *Encyclopedia of Ethics*, ed. Lawrence C. Becker and Charlotte B. Becker (New York: Garland, 1992), vol. I, pp. 624–628 provides an insightful and nuanced discussion of the issues of distributive justice, especially insofar as they relate to world hunger.

## Reports

Several reports on the state of the world have helped to share the international discussion of these issues. In the United States, the Presidential Commission on World Hunger, established by Jimmy Carter, issued *Overcoming World Hunger: The Challenge Ahead* (Washington, DC: Government Printing Office, 1980). For a more global perspective, see the *Brandt Report*, formally known as the Report of the Independent Commission on International Development Issues, *North-South: A Program for Survival* (Cambridge: M.I.T. Press, 1980). For replies to this, see Teresa Hayter, *The Creation of World Poverty: An Alternative View to the Brandt Report* (London: Pluto Press, 1981); Denis Goulet and Michael Hudson, *The Myth of Aid: The Hidden Agenda of the Development Reports* (New York: IDOC/Maryknoll Press, 1971); and Frances Moore Lappe, Joseph Collins, and David Kinley, *Aid as Obstacle: Twenty Questions about Our Foreign Aid and the Hungry* (San Francisco: Institute for Food and Development Policy, 1980/1981). Also see the *Brundtland Report*, formally known as the World Commission on Environment and Development, *Our Common Future* (New York: Oxford University Press, 1987). On the *Rio Report,* see *Agenda 21: The Earth Summit Strategy to Save Our Planet*, ed. Daniel Sitarz (Boulder: Earthpress, 1993). See also the excellent Worldwatch Institute Report on Progress toward a Sustainable Society, *State of the World 1994*, by Lester R. Brown et al., (New York: W. W. Norton, 1994).

Among the popular books that have been influential in this discussion, see Albert Gore, *Earth in the Balance: Ecology and the Human Spirit* (Boston: Houghton Mifflin, 1992). Frances Moore Lappe and Joseph Collins, *Food First: Beyond the Myth of Scarcity*, rev. ed. (New York: Ballantine Books, 1978) and also their *World Hunger: Twelve Myths* (San Francisco: Institute for Food and Development Policy, 1982). For a much more optimistic view, see Julian Simon, *The Ultimate Resource* (Princeton: Princeton University Press, 1981) and Julian Simon and Herman Kahn, *The Resourceful Earth* (Oxford: Blackwell, 1984).

## Anthologies

Several valuable anthologies are available. William Aiken and Hugh LaFollette's *World Hunger and Moral Obligation* (Englewood Cliffs, NJ: Prentice Hall, 1977) contains all the classic papers; see especially the pieces by Hardin, Singer, Arthur, Narveson, Slote, and O'Neill. *International Justice and the Third World*, ed. Robin Attfield and Barry Wilkins (New York: Routledge & Kegan Paul, 1992) contains eight papers discussing notions of global justice and its implications for the third world; the papers also relate third world development to sustainability, issues of gender, environmentalism, and third world debt. *Poverty, Justice, and the Law: New Essays on Needs, Rights, and Obligations*, ed. George R. Lucas (Lanham, MD: University Press of America, 1986) contains several excellent papers in this area. *Problems of International Justice*, ed. Stephen Luper-Foy (Boulder, CO: Westview Press, 1988) deals with more international issues than just world hunger, but the essays are uniformly excellent. Two volumes in the Opposing Viewpoints contain relevant material: *The Third World: Opposing Viewpoints*, ed. Janelle Rohr (San Diego: Greenhaven Press, 1989) and *Immigration: Opposing Viewpoints*, ed. William Dudley (San Diego: Greenhaven Press, 1990). Also see the essays in G. E. McCuen, ed., *World Hunger and Social Justice* (Ideas in Conflict Series, Wisconsin: G. E. McCuen, 1986).

These issues also arise within the context of environmental ethics. Among the excellent anthologies in this area, see Donald VanDeVeer and Christine Pierce, eds., *The Environmental Ethics and Policy Book* (Belmont, CA: Wadsworth, 1994) and Susan J. Armstrong and Richard G. Botzler, eds., *Environmental Ethics: Divergence and Convergence* (New York: McGraw Hill, 1993).

## Responses to Hardin

Garrett Hardin's "Lifeboat Ethics" (and relate versions of the same piece) stirred extensive discussion. A number of the articles in the Aiken and LaFollette, *World Hunger and Moral Obligation*, respond to Hardin; see especially Onora O'Neill's "Lifeboat Earth" in this collection. Also see some of the articles in *Problems of International Justice*, especially Onora O'Neill's "Hunger, Needs, and Rights" and William Aiken's "World Hunger, Benevolence, and Justice." Robert Coburn's "On Feeding the Hungry," *Journal of Social Philosophy* 7 (Spring 1976), 11–16, and Daniel Callahan's "Garrett Hardin's 'Lifeboat Ethic'," *Hastings Center Report* 4 (December 1974), 1–4, both strongly criticize Hardin's position. Jesse A. Mann, "Ethics and the Problem of World Hunger," *Listening* 16 (Winter 1982), 67–76, attempts to sketch out a middle ground between Singer and Hardin. Nick Eberstadt's "Myths of the Food Crisis," *New York Review of Books* (February 19, 1976), 32–37 challenges some of the assumptions that lead to Hardin's pessimism, while William W. Murdoch and Allan Oaten, "Population and Food: Metaphors and the Reality," *Bioscience*, September 9, 1975, pp. 561–567, offer a perceptive discussion of the underlying metaphors in Hardin's work. On the utilitarian dimensions of this issue, see Thomas L. Carson, "Utilitarianism and World Poverty," in *The Limits of Utilitarianism*, ed. Harlan B. Miller (Minneapolis: University Minnesota Press, 1982), pp. 242–251.

## General Defenses of the Duty to Aid Poor and Starving Nations

Henry Shue, *Basic Rights: Subsistence, Affluence, and U.S. Foreign Policy* (Princeton: Princeton University Press, 1980), offers a strong conceptual foundation for positive basic rights; see also his anthology (co-edited with Peter G. Brown), *Food Policy* (New York: The Free Press,

1977). Robert Goodin's *Protecting the Vulnerable* (Chicago: University of Chicago Press, 1986) is very carefully argued. Nicholas Dower, in *What Is Development? A Philosopher's Answer* (Glasgow University Centre for Development Studies: Occasional Paper Series no. 3, 1988) argues for significant but not overpowering obligation to aid poor nations. Onora O'Neill's *Faces of Hunger* (London: Allen & Unwin, 1986) derives the obligation to aid from people's right not to be killed. Amartya Sen, *Poverty and Famines: An Essay on Entitlement and Deprivation* (New York: Oxford University Press, 1981) stresses the way in which famines are rarely due to natural causes alone; also see Jean Drèze and Amartya Sen, *Hunger and Public Action* (Oxford: Clarendon Press, 1989). John Howie, in "World Hunger and a Moral Right to Subsistence," *Journal of Social Philosophy* 18 (Fall 1987), 27–31, argues in favor of a moral right to subsistence and the obligation of affluent nations to starving ones. Robert N. Van Wyk, "Perspectives on World Hunger and the Extent of Our Positive Duties," *Public Affairs Quarterly* 2 (April 1988), 75–90 seeks to find a middle way between Peter Singer's utilitarianism, which implies that we have a duty to do everything we can for the sake of the hungry, and Nozick's libertarianism, which says we have no positive duties at all. James P. Sterba's "The Welfare Rights of Distant Peoples and Future Generations: Moral Side-Constraints on Social Policy," *Social Theory and Practice* 7 (Spring 1981), 99–119 discusses the ways in which welfare rights of distant peoples "can be grounded on fundamental moral requirements to which many of us are already committed." Michael McKinsey's "Obligations to the Starving," *Nous* 15 (Spring 1981), 309–324, argues that the principles of benevolence that are most often appealed to as a source of individuals' obligations to the starving are all either false or do not in fact yield such obligations on the part of individuals, but there are obligations on the part of groups. In "Killing and Starving to Death," *Philosophy* 54 (April 1979), 159–171, James Rachels argues that it is morally just as bad to let someone starve as it is to kill them. Rodney G. Peffer argues for obligations of the rich nations to the poor in "World Justice, Population, and the Environment: A Programmatic and Philosophical Approach," *World Political Ecology*, ed. David Bell (York: York University Press, 1995). Chapter Four of Stanley Hoffmann's *Duties Beyond Borders: On the Limits and Possibilities of Ethical International Politics* (Syracuse, NY: Syracuse University Press, 1981) offers a nuanced account of the political dimensions of these issues.

## Arguments against the Duty to Aid

Jennifer Trusted, "The Problem of Absolute Poverty," in *The Environment in Question: Ethics and Global Issues*, ed. David E. Cooper (New York: Routledge & Kegan Paul, 1992), pp. 13–27, discusses the obligations of individuals in affluent countries to the third world, arguing that there can be no duty of general beneficence and that it is not wrong to favor those who are near and dear to us. James S. Fishkin, *The Limits of Obligation* (New Haven: Yale University Press, 1982), especially chap. 9: "The Famine Review Argument," on the limits of the obligations of rich nations to poor ones. Ruth Lucier, "Policies for Hunger Relief: Moral Considerations," in *Inquiries into Values*, ed. Sander H. Lee, (Lewiston, Mellen Press), pp. 477–493 suggests that food aid has moral ramifications stemming from present limitations on the aid available for distribution.

## Other Perspectives

Bhikkhu Sunanda Putuwar, "The Buddhist Outlook on Poverty and Human Rights," in *The Wisdom of Faith: Essays in Honor of Dr. Sebastian Alexander Matczak* (Lanham, MD: University Press of America, 1989).

# Living Together with Animals

**Videotape:**

| | | |
|---|---|---|
| | *Topic:* | Aspen's Fur Fight |
| | *Source:* | *Nightline* (February 1, 1990) |
| | *Anchor:* | Ted Koppel |

# EXPERIENTIAL ACCOUNTS

Peter Singer
"Down on the Factory Farm"

*Peter Singer, presently professor of philosophy and deputy director of the Center for Human Bioethics at Monash University (Melbourne), is the author of numerous works in ethics, especially in applied ethics. His books include* The Expanding Circle, Animal Liberation, Practical Ethics, *and, most recently,* Rethinking Life and Death *and* How Are We to Live? *He has also edited a number of books, including* A Companion to Ethics. *In his work, Singer sees himself as holding our conventional moral beliefs to a standard of consistency, coherence, and the avoidance of arbitrary distinctions. He finds that many of these traditional beliefs are remnants of earlier, religiously-inspired doctrines that he believes many people no longer accept, while other beliefs survive only because they promote some form of group selfishness.*

*One of the ways in which we avoid dealing with the issue of animal suffering is simply and literally by not seeing it. In this article, Peter Singer describes a number of the practices that are common in contemporary animal farming, concentrating on the treatment of chickens and veal calves.*

⌐

For most humans, especially those in modern urban and suburban communities, the most direct form of contact with non-human animals is at meal time: we eat them. This simple fact is the key to our attitudes to other animals, and also the key to what each one of us can do about changing these attitudes. The use and abuse of animals raised for food far exceeds, in sheer numbers of animals affected, any other kind of mistreatment. Hundreds of millions of cattle, pigs, and sheep are raised and slaughtered in the United States alone each year; and for poultry the figure is a staggering 3 billion. (That means that about 5,000 birds—mostly chickens—will have been slaughtered in the time it takes you to read this page.) It is here, on our dinner table and in our neighborhood supermarket or butcher's shop, that we are brought into direct touch with the most extensive exploitation of other species that has ever existed.

In general, we are ignorant of the abuse of living creatures that lies behind the food we eat. Consider the images conjured up by the word "farm": a house, a barn, a flock of hens, overseen by a strutting rooster, scratching around the farmyard, a herd of cows being brought in from the fields for milking, and perhaps a sow rooting around in the orchard with a litter of squealing piglets running excitedly behind her.

Very few farms were ever as idyllic as that traditional image would have us believe. Yet we still think of a farm as a pleasant place, far removed from our own industrial, profit-conscious city life. Of those few who think about the lives of animals on farms, not many know much of modern methods of animal raising. Some people wonder whether animals are slaughtered painlessly, and anyone who has followed a truckload of cattle must know that farm animals are transported in very crowded conditions; but few suspect that transportation and slaughter are anything more than the brief and inevitable conclusion of a life of ease and contentment, a life that contains the natural pleasures of animal existence without the hardships that wild animals must endure in the struggle for survival.

These comfortable assumptions bear little relation to the realities of modern farming. For a start, farming is no longer controlled by simple country folk. It is a business, and big business at that. In the last thirty years the entry of large corporations and assembly-line methods of production have turned farming into "agribusiness." . . .

The first animal to be removed from the relatively natural conditions of the traditional farms and subjected to the full stress of modern intensive farming was the chicken. Chickens have the misfortune of being useful to humans in two ways: for their flesh and for their eggs. There are now standard mass-production techniques for obtaining both these products.

Agribusiness enthusiasts consider the rise of the chicken industry to be one of the great success stories of farming. At the end of World War II chicken for the table was still relatively rare. It came mainly from small independent farmers or from the unwanted males produced by egg-laying flocks. Today "broilers"—as table chickens are now usually called—are produced literally by the million from the highly automated factory-like plants of the large corporations that own or control 98 percent of all broiler production in the United States.[1]

The essential step in turning the chicken from a farmyard bird into a manufactured item was confining them indoors. A broiler producer today gets a load of 10,000, 50,000, or even more day-old chicks from the hatcheries, and puts them straight into a long, windowless shed—usually on the floor, although some producers use tiers of cages in order to get more birds into the same size shed. Inside the shed, every aspect of the birds' environment is controlled to make them grow faster on less feed. Food and water are fed automatically from hoppers suspended from the roof. The lighting is adjusted according to advice from agricultural researchers: for instance, there may be bright light 24 hours a day for the first week or two, to encourage the chicks to gain quickly; then the lights may be dimmed slightly and made to go off and on every two hours, in the belief that the chickens are readier to eat after a period of sleep; finally there comes a point, around six weeks of age, when the birds have grown so much that they are becoming crowded, and the lights will then be made very dim at all times. The point of this dim lighting is to reduce the effects of crowding. Toward the end of the eight- or nine-week life of the chicken, there may be as little as half a square foot of space per chicken—or less than the area of a sheet of quarto paper for a 3½ lb. bird. Under these conditions with normal lighting the stress of crowding and the absence of natural outlets for the bird's energies lead to outbreaks of fighting, with birds pecking at each other's feathers and sometimes killing and eating one another. Very dim lighting has been found to reduce this and so the birds are likely to live out their last weeks in near-darkness.

Feather-pecking and cannibalism are, in the broiler producer's language, "vices." They are not natural vices, however—they are the result of the stress and crowding to which the modern broilerman subjects his birds. Chickens are highly social animals, and in the farmyard they develop a hierarchy, sometimes called a "pecking order." Every bird yields, at the food trough or elsewhere, to those above it in rank, and takes precedence over those below. There may be a few confrontations before the order is firmly established but more often than not a show of force, rather than actual physical contact, is enough to put a chicken in its place. As Konrad Lorenz, a renowned figure in the field of animal behavior, wrote in the days when flocks were still small:

> Do animals thus know each other among themselves? They certainly do. . . . Every poultry farmer knows that . . . there exists a very definite order, in which each bird is afraid of those that are above her in rank. After some few disputes, which need not necessarily come to blows, each bird knows which of the others she has to fear and which must show respect to her. Not only physical strength, but also personal courage, energy, and even the self-assurance of every individual bird are decisive in the maintenance of the pecking order.[2]

Other studies have shown that a flock of up to 90 chickens can maintain a stable social order, each bird knowing its place; but 10,000 birds crowded together in a single shed is obviously a different matter.[3] The birds cannot establish a social order, and as a result they fight frequently with each other. Quite apart from the inability of the individual bird to recognize so many other birds, the mere fact of extreme crowding probably contributes to irritability and excitability in chickens, as it does in humans and other animals. This is something farming magazines are aware of, and they frequently warn their readers:

> Feather-pecking and cannibalism have increased to a formidable extent of late years, due, no doubt, to the changes in technique and the swing towards completely intensive management of laying flocks and table poultry. . . . The most common faults in management which may lead to vice are boredom, overcrowding in badly ventilated houses . . . Lack of feeding space, unbalanced food or shortage of water, and heavy infestation with insect pests.[4]

Clearly the farmer must stop "vices," because they cost him money; but although he may know that overcrowding is the root cause, he cannot do anything about this, since in the competitive state of the industry, eliminating overcrowding could mean eliminating his profit margin at the same time. He would have fewer birds to sell, but would have had to pay the same outlay for his building, for the automatic feeding equipment, for the fuel used to heat and ventilate the building, and for labor. So the farmer limits his efforts to reducing the consequences of the stress that costs him money. The unnatural way in which he keeps his birds causes the vices; but to control them the poultryman must make the conditions still more unnatural. Very dim lighting is one way of doing this. A more drastic step, though one now almost universally used in the industry, is "debeaking." This involves inserting the chick's head in a guillotine-like device which cuts off part of its beak. Alternatively the operation may be done with a hot knife. Some poultrymen claim that this operation is painless, but an expert British Government committee under zoologist Professor F. W. Rogers Brambell appointed to look into aspects of intensive farming found otherwise:

> . . . between the horn and the bone is a thin layer of highly sensitive soft tissue, resembling the "quick" of the human nail. The hot knife used in de-beaking cuts through this complex of horn, bone and sensitive tissue, causing severe pain.[5]

De-beaking, which is routinely performed in anticipation of cannibalism by most poultrymen, does greatly reduce the amount of damage a chicken can do to other chickens. It also, in the words of the Brambell Committee, "deprives the bird of what is in effect its most versatile member" while it obviously does nothing to reduce the stress and overcrowding that lead to this unnatural cannibalism in the first place. . . .

"A hen," Samuel Butler once wrote, "is only an egg's way of making another egg." Butler, no doubt, was being humorous; but when Fred. C. Haley, president of a Georgia poultry firm that controls the lives of 225,000 laying hens, describes the hen as "an egg producing machine" his words have more serious implications. To emphasize his businesslike attitude Haley adds: "The object of producing eggs is to make money. When we forget this objective, we have forgotten what it is all about."[6]

Nor is this only an American attitude. A British farming magazine has told its readers:

> The modern layer is, after all, only a very efficient converting machine, changing the raw material—feedingstuffs—into the finished product—the egg—less, of course, maintenance requirements.[7]

Remarks of this kind can regularly be found in the egg industry trade journals throughout the United States and Europe, and they express an attitude that is common in the industry. As may be anticipated, their consequences for the laying hens are not good.

Laying hens go through many of the same procedures as broilers, but there are some differences. Like broilers, layers have to be de-beaked, to prevent the cannibalism that would otherwise occur in their crowded conditions; but because they live much longer than broilers, they often go through this operation twice. So we find a poultry specialist at the New Jersey College of Agriculture advising poultrymen to de-beak their chicks when they are between one and two weeks old because there is, he says, less stress on the chicks at this time than if the operation is done earlier, and in addition "there are fewer culls in the laying flock as a result of improper de-beaking." In either case, the article continues, the birds must be de-beaked again when they are ready to begin laying, at around twenty weeks of age.[8]

Laying hens get no more individual attention than broilers. Alan Hainsworth, owner of a poultry farm in upstate New York, told an inquiring local reporter that four hours a day is all he needs for the care of his 36,000 laying hens, while his wife looks after the 20,000 pullets (as the younger birds not yet ready to lay are called): "It takes her about 15 minutes a day. All she checks is their automatic feeders, water cups and any deaths during the night."

This kind of care does not make for a happy flock, as the reporter's description shows:

> Walk into the pullet house and the reaction is immediate—complete pandemonium. The squawking is loud and intense as some 20,000 birds shove to the farthest side of their cages in fear of the human intruders.[9]

Julius Goldman's Egg City, 50 miles northwest of Los Angeles, is one of the world's largest egg producing units, consisting of 2 million hens divided into block long buildings containing 90,000 hens each, five birds to a 16 by 18 inch cage. When the *National Geographic* magazine did an enthusiastic survey of new farming methods, Ben Shames, Egg City's executive vice-president, explained to its reporter the methods used to look after so many birds:

> We keep track of the food eaten and the eggs collected in 2 rows of cages among the 110 rows in each building. When production drops to the uneconomic point, all 90,000 birds are sold to

processors for potpies or chicken soup. It doesn't pay to keep track of every row in the house, let alone individual hens; with 2 million birds on hand you have to rely on statistical samplings.[10]

Nearly all the big egg producers now keep their laying hens in cages. Originally there was only one bird to a cage; and the idea was that the farmer could then tell which birds were not laying enough eggs to give an economic return on their food. Those birds were then killed. Then it was found that more birds could be housed and costs per bird reduced if two birds were put in each cage. That was only the first step, and as we have seen, there is no longer any question of keeping a tally of each bird's eggs. The advantages of cages for the egg producer now consist in the greater number of birds that can be housed, warmed, fed, and watered in one building, and in the greater use that can be made of labor-saving automatic equipment.

The cages are stacked in tiers, with food and water troughs running along the rows, filled automatically from a central supply. They have sloping wire floors. The slope—usually a gradient of 1 in 5—makes it more difficult for the birds to stand comfortably, but it causes the eggs to roll to the front of the cage where they can easily be collected by hand or, in the more modern plants, carried by conveyor belt to a packing plant.

When a reporter from the *New York Daily News* wanted to see a typical modern egg farm, he visited Frenchtown Poultry Farm, in New Jersey, where he found that

> Each 18 by 24 inch cage on the Frenchtown farm contains nine hens who seemed jammed into them by some unseen hand. They barely have enough room to turn around in the cages.
> "Really, you should have no more than eight birds in a cage that size," conceded Oscar Grossman, the farm's lessor. "But sometimes you have to do things to get the most out of your stock."[11]

Actually, if Mr. Grossman had put only eight birds in his cages they would still have been grossly overcrowded; at nine to a cage they have only 1/3 square foot per bird.

In 1968 the farm magazine *American Agriculturalist* advised its readers in an article headed "Bird Squeezing" that it had been found possible to stock at 1/3 square foot per bird by putting four birds in a 12 by 16 inch cage. This was apparently a novel step at the time; the steady increase in densities over the years is indicated by the fact that a 1974 issue of the same magazine describing the Lannsdale Poultry Farm, near Rochester, New York, mentions the same housing density without any suggestion that it is unusual.[12] In reading egg industry magazines I have found numerous reports of similar high densities, and scarcely any that are substantially lower. My own visits to poultry farms in the United States have shown the same pattern. The highest reported density that I have read about is at the Hainsworth farm in Mt. Morris, New York, where four hens are squeezed into cages 12 inches by 12 inches, or just one square foot—and the reporter adds: "Some hold five birds when Hainsworth has more birds than room."[13] This means 1/4, and sometimes 1/5, square foot per bird. At this stocking rate a *single sheet of quarto paper represents the living area of two to three hens.*

Under the conditions standard on modern egg farms in the United States and other "developed nations" every natural instinct the birds have is frustrated. They cannot walk around, scratch the ground, dustbathe, build a nest, or stretch their wings. They are not part of a flock. They cannot keep out of each other's way and weaker birds have no escape from the attacks of stronger ones, already maddened by the unnatural conditions. . . .

Intensive production of pigs and cattle is now also common; but of all the forms of intensive farming now practiced, the quality veal industry ranks as the most morally repugnant, comparable only with barbarities like the force-feeding of geese through a funnel that produces the deformed livers made into pate de foie gras. The essence of veal raising is the feeding of a high-protein food (that should be used to reduce malnutrition in poorer parts of the world) to confined, anemic calves in a manner that will produce a tender, pale-colored flesh that will be served to gourmets in expensive restaurants. Fortunately this industry does not compare in size with poultry, beef, or pig production; nevertheless it is worth our attention because it represents an extreme, both in the degree of exploitation to which it subjects its animals and in its absurd inefficiency as a method of providing people with nourishment.

Veal is the flesh of a young calf, and the term was originally reserved for calves killed before they had been weaned from their mothers. The flesh of these very young animals was paler and more tender than that of a calf that had begun to eat grass; but there was not much of it, since calves begin to eat grass when they are a few weeks old and still very small. So there was little money in veal, and the small amount available came from the unwanted male calves produced by the dairy industry. These males were a nuisance to the dairy farmers, since the dairy breeds do not make good beef cattle. Therefore they were sold as quickly as possible. A day or two after being born they were trucked to market where, hungry and frightened by the strange surroundings and the absence of their mothers, they were sold for immediate delivery to the slaughterhouse.

Once this was the main source of veal in the United States. Now, using methods first developed in Holland, farmers have found a way to keep the calf longer without the flesh becoming darker in color or less tender. This means that the veal calf, when sold, may weigh as much as 325 lbs., instead of the 90-odd lbs. that newborn calves weigh. Because veal fetches a premium price, this has made rearing veal calves a profitable occupation.

The trick depends on keeping the calf in highly unnatural conditions. If the calf were left to grow up outside, its playful nature would lead it to romp around the fields. Soon it would begin to develop muscles, which would make its flesh tough. At the same time it would eat grass and its flesh would lose the pale color that the flesh of newborn calves has. So the specialist veal producer takes his calves straight from the auction ring to a confinement unit. Here, in a converted barn or purpose-built shed, he will have rows of wooden stalls. Each stall will be 1 foot 10 inches wide and 4 feet 6 inches long. It will have a slatted wooden floor, raised above the concrete floor of the shed. The calves will be tethered by a chain around the neck to prevent them from turning around in their stalls. (The chain may be removed when the calves grow too big to turn around in such narrow stalls.) The stall will have no straw or other bedding, since the calf might eat it, spoiling the paleness of his flesh.

Here the calves will live for the next thirteen to fifteen weeks. They will leave their stalls only to be taken out to slaughter. They are fed a totally liquid diet, based on non-fat milk powder with added vitamins, minerals, and growth-promoting drugs. . . .

The narrow stalls and their slatted wooden floors are a serious source of discomfort for the calves. The inability to turn around is frustrating. When he lies down, the calf must lie hunched up, sitting almost on top of his legs rather than having them out to one side as he would do if he had more room. A stall too narrow to turn around in is also too narrow to groom comfortably in; and calves have an innate desire to twist their heads around and groom themselves with their tongues. A wooden floor without any bedding is hard and uncomfortable; it is rough on the calves' knees as they get up and lie down. In addition, animals with hooves are uncomfortable on slatted floors. A slatted floor is like a cattle grid, which cattle will always avoid, except that the slats are closer together. The spaces, however, must still be large enough to allow manure to fall or be washed through, and this means that they are large enough to make the calves uncomfortable.[14]

The special nature of the veal calf has other implications that show the industry's lack of genuine concern for the animals' welfare. Obviously the calves sorely miss their mothers. They also miss something to suck on. The urge to suck is strong in a baby calf, as it is in a baby human. These calves have no teat to suck on, nor do they have any substitute. From their first day in confinement—which may well be only the third or fourth day of their lives—they drink from a plastic bucket. Attempts have been made to feed calves through artificial teats, but the problems of keeping the teats clean and sterile are apparently too great for the farmer to try to overcome. It is common to see calves frantically trying to suck some part of their stalls, although there is usually nothing suitable; and if you offer a veal calf your finger he will immediately begin to suck on it, as a human baby sucks its thumb.

Later on the calf develops a desire to ruminate—that is, to take in roughage and chew the cud. But roughage is strictly forbidden and so, again, the calf may resort to vain attempts to chew the sides of its stall. Digestive disorders, including stomach ulcers, are common in veal calves, as are chronically loose bowel movements.

As if this were not enough, there is the fact that the calf is deliberately kept anemic. As one veal producers' journal has said,

> Color of veal is one of the primary factors involved in obtaining "topdollar" returns from the fancy veal market . . . "light color" veal is a premium item much in demand at better clubs, hotels and restaurants. "Light color" or pink veal is partly associated with the amount of iron in the muscle of the calves.[15]

So veal feeds are deliberately kept low in iron. A normal calf would obtain iron from grass or other forms of roughage, but since a veal calf is not allowed this he becomes anemic. Pale pink flesh is in fact anemic flesh. The demand for flesh of this color is a matter of snob appeal. The color does not affect the taste and it certainly does not make the flesh more nourishing—rather the opposite.

Calves kept in this manner are unhappy and unhealthy animals. Despite the fact that the veal producer selects only the strongest, healthiest calves to begin with, uses a medicated feed as a routine measure, and gives additional injections at the slightest sign of illness, digestive, respiratory and infectious diseases are widespread. It is common for a veal producer to find that one in ten of a batch of calves do not survive the fifteen weeks of confinement. Ten percent mortality over such a short period would be disastrous for anyone raising calves for beef, but the veal producer can tolerate this loss because of the high price restaurants are prepared to pay for his product. If the reader will recall that this whole laborious, wasteful, and painful process exists for the sole purpose of pandering to would-be gourmets who insist on pale, soft veal, no further comment should be needed.

### Endnotes

1. Harrison Wellford, *Sowing the Wind: The Politics of Food, Safety and Agribusiness* (New York: Grossman Press, 1971), p. 104.
2. K. Lorenz, *King Solomon's Ring* (London: Methuen, 1964), p. 147.

3. Ian Duncan, "Can the Psychologist Measure Stress?" *New Scientist*, October 18, 1973.

4. *The Smallholder*, January 6, 1962; quoted by Ruth Harrison, *Animal Machines* (London Vincent Stuart, 1964), p. 18.

5. *Report of the Technical Committee to Enquire into the Welfare of Animals Kept under Intensive Livestock Husbandry Systems* (London: Her Majesty's Stationery Office, 1965), para. 97.

6. *Poultry Tribune*, January 1974.

7. *Farmer and Stockbreeder*, January 30, 1962; quoted by Ruth Harrison, *Animal Machines*, p. 50.

8. *American Agriculturist*, July 1966.

9. *Upstate*, August 5, 1973, report by Mary Rita Kiereck.

10. *National Geographic*, February 1970.

11. *New York Daily News*, September 1, 1971.

12. *American Agriculturist*, August 1968, April 1974.

13. *Upstate*, August 5, 1973.

14. Ruth Harrison, *Animal Machines*, p. 72.

15. *The Wall Street Journal,* published by Provimi, Inc., Watertown, Wisconsin, November 1973.

## Journal/Discussion Questions

✍ *Do you have any direct experience with the raising and slaughtering of animals for food? (Did you grow up on a farm, or have you ever visited an animal farm or a slaughterhouse?) How have these experiences affected your views on animal rights? If you have not had any of these experiences, do you think this lack has affected your views? Discuss.*

1. If chickens are raised under the conditions that Singer describes, what implications—if any—does that have for eating eggs and meat from chickens under those conditions?

2. Singer stresses that modern animal agriculture is "big business," not the product of many small farmers. What moral implications, if any, does this have?

3. Why does Singer single out the "quality veal industry as the most morally repugnant" form of animal farming? Do you agree with his assessment? Discuss.

# AN INTRODUCTION TO THE MORAL ISSUES

## The Scope of the Moral Circle

In this chapter, we shall examine whether the circle of morality ought to be extended to include animals—and, if so, how this would transform our world. Certainly there are many areas of our daily lives which involve animals either directly or indirectly.

Many of us have pets, ride horses, visit zoos and places like Sea World, perhaps even go hunting or fishing. All of these involve animals directly. Many of us eat meat or fish, wear leather belts and shoes, use prescription medications, ride in cars with seat belts. Many of these involve animals indirectly as sources of food, as subjects of medical and safety research, and the like. Our relationship with animals pervades our daily lives in numerous, often unnoticed, ways.

*To what extent do animals have a moral standing in their own right?*

Many of these relationships with animals must be revised if we discover that animals are persons, or even that they have a moral status beyond the little that has traditionally been accorded to them. A variety of different types of concern—religious, rights, consequentialist, and character-based—have been offered as reasons for either modifying or retaining our present view of the moral status of animals. Let's consider each of these issues.

## Religious Concerns

Many advocates of animal rights and animal liberation maintain that religions, especially Christianity, have contributed strongly to the subjection and mistreatment of animals. Upon closer examination, however, we see that the picture is somewhat more complex than this, not only in Christianity, but in other religious traditions as well.

### Christianity

Many Western philosophers have criticized religion in general, and Christianity in particular, for fostering a morally insensitive attitude toward nonhuman animals. The critique is partly theological, partly political.

The theologically oriented critique is three-pronged, relating to the message of the book of Genesis in the Bible, to the incarnation, and to the notion of a human soul. *First*, in the opening chapters of Genesis, animals and the natural environment are depicted as existing solely for the sake of human beings and their salvation. Such a view gives animals only an instrumental value, denying that they may have any moral significance in themselves. *Second*, by seeing Jesus as the incarnation of God in a human being, critics maintain, Christianity sets human beings apart from all other beings. There is an ontological chasm between human beings and all other types of beings because God became a human being in order to save human beings. Animals simply did not figure into the picture. *Third*, and finally, Christian theology sees human beings as having an immortal soul, but animals do not have such a soul. This reinforces the ontological gap initiated by the incarnation, and further demotes animals when seen in relation to human beings. It is easy to see how C. S. Lewis, a Christian theologian, could conclude in "Pain and Animal Suffering," that "The beasts are to be understood only in their relation to man and, through man, to God. . . . Everything a man does to an animal is either a lawful exercise, or a sacrilegious abuse, of an authority by divine right."[1]

The politically oriented critique is more scathing, although it does not necessarily indicate anything as intrinsic to Christianity as its theological commitments. Here the structure of the critique is simply to point out that Christian churches, both implicitly and by default, have acted in ways that undermine the rights of animals. There is no shortage of examples, whether it be a nineteenth-century Pope forbidding the establishment of an anti-cruelty-to-animals office in Rome (allegedly because humans do not have duties to animals) or simply the long history of Christianity's endorsement of eating meat. As Tom Regan put it so succinctly in the title of one of his essays, "Christians Are What Christians Eat."[2]

Defenders of the Christian tradition often acknowledge its shortcomings, but reply to these criticisms by pointing out that there is another, albeit secondary, tradition in Christianity that does acknowledge the moral standing of animals. Genesis not only contains a model of domination, but also a model of stewardship which emphasizes the ways in which the entirety of creation is to be respected and taken care of. Some defenders of Christianity, such as Andrew Linzey,[3] even see Genesis as offering a religious foundation for vegetarianism: "I give you all plants that bear seed everywhere on earth, and every tree bearing fruit which yields seed: They shall be yours for food" (Genesis 1:29). Moreover, saints such as St. Francis of Assisi have kept this tradition alive with their devotion to animals.

## Buddhism

*Compassion and respect for life.*   The teachings of the Buddha explicitly urge respect for all life, not just human life, and this has had a profound impact on shaping the attitudes of Buddhists toward animals. The central moral stance of a Buddhist toward the world is one of compassion for suffering, and that compassion is directed as much toward animal suffering as human suffering.

*Reincarnation.*   Within the Buddhist tradition, as souls move through their journey of self-purification, they are reincarnated successively in different living beings, animals as well as human beings. Reincarnation in animals has a potentially profound impact on one's treatment of animals, since it opens up the possibility that the soul inhabiting an animal could—either in the past or the future—be the soul of a human being. This is in stark contrast with the Christian tradition, where the incarnation of God in Jesus separates human beings from all other animals.

## Native American Religious Traditions

*Harmony.*   Although Native American religions present a wide range of diverse beliefs and practices, it is certainly characteristic of most Native American religions that they emphasize the importance of a harmonious relationship with the natural world, that they see animals as often embodying both human and divine spirits, that the dividing line between human and animal is much less clearly marked than in Christian tradition, and that all animals are deserving of respect. Interestingly, this respect does not usually lead to absolute prohibitions on killing animals. Instead, it leads to prohibitions on unnecessary killing; moreover, it demands a respectful attitude toward even those animals that one kills. It is not inconsistent, in most Native American traditions, to kill an animal and to pray *to* (not just *for*) its spirit. Nor is it necessary to leave animals alone, as many strong supporters of animal rights seem to advocate. In the Native American tradition, human beings and animals interact with one another constantly, and harmony is to be achieved through rightly ordering those interactions.

*A proper space.*   One of the ways in which our relationships with animals can be rightly ordered is through proper spatial relationships. Many Native American traditions are highly spatial. Animals, human beings, and even the gods are seen as having particular places. (This, incidentally, is one reason why relocation was often so traumatic for Native Americans: their particular gods reside in a specific space, and to move to a new location was to move to a place where the gods would not know you.) Part of the harmonious relationship between humans and animals in the Native American tradition stemmed from a recognition of proper place, and often disastrous interactions between human beings and animals (for example, being bitten by a snake) are seen as an encroachment by human beings on the animal's space. Consequently, the way to avoid such problems is to be more respectful of the animal's space. This is in marked contrast with mainstream American attitudes, which are puzzled and outraged when, after building huge subdivisions that destroy the native habitat of wolves and other animals, wolves and other animals appear in residential areas. The Native American traditions emphasize a harmonious, respectful, and yet at the same time highly interactive view of the relationship between human beings and animals.

# Consequentialist Concerns

For many people, morality is primarily about consequences, about doing the thing that creates the most happiness and the least unhappiness. Yet the crucial question, at least in this context, is happiness *for whom*? Is it only happiness for human beings, or does the circle extend beyond this?

## Human-Centered Utilitarian Concerns

Utilitarianism initially was concerned only with the happiness or pleasure of human beings, and as such it would seem to consign animals to moral oblivion. However, even when we consider consequences solely for human beings, we notice that this by no means justifies all of our harmful treatment of animals in the past. Consider two examples: eating meat and cruelty to animals.

*First*, consider eating meat. Although vegetarianism is often espoused for the sake of animals, there may well be a strong, human-centered case for vegetarianism. What are the consequences of a diet rich in meat, especially red meat, for human beings? This is an empirical question, but it may well be the case that the overall effects of vegetarianism are significantly more healthful than the effects of a diet that contains meat. *Second*, consider cruelty to animals. Even if we leave aside for the moment the harmful effects on the animals themselves, it may well be the case that treating animals cruelly has harmful effects on human beings. Immanuel Kant, for example, argued that such cruelty makes us less morally sensitive beings and less likely to respond appropriately to the suffering of human beings. Cruelty to animals may well lead to cruelty to human beings, and is therefore to be avoided.

Thus, even when we assume a purely human-centered consequentialist approach to moral matters, we do not have to conclude that "anything goes" in regard to our treatment of animals. There may be important, human-centered constraints on our treatment of animals that have nothing to do with the moral status of the animals themselves.

## Speciesism

The fundamental moral question which was raised in the 1970s by Peter Singer in his book *Animal Liberation* was whether utilitarianism was being arbitrary when it considered the pleasure and pain of only human beings. If utilitarianism is fundamentally a doctrine about increasing pleasure and reducing pain and suffering, then shouldn't *all* pleasure and *all* pain and suffering count, not just the pleasure and pain of one species?

The argument for this position is simple and elegant. On what basis do we say that the suffering of one species counts and the suffering of another species doesn't? Presumably, for this line to be drawn justifiably, there must be some non-arbitrary criterion. It's not enough to say about some beings, "they're one of us," and about others, "they're not one of us." Yet what can this nonarbitrary criterion be? The only reasonable candidate, Singer and others argue, is the ability to suffer. Any other criterion, such as language or rationality, would in fact exclude some human beings, such as the severely mentally disabled or those in comas. The only acceptable nonarbitrary criterion is the ability to suffer.

The tendency to ignore the suffering of animals and the view that only human beings count is *speciesism.* Animal liberationists liken speciesism to racism and sexism, all of which draw arbitrary moral lines that undermine the moral standing of the other sex, of other races, or of other species. A truly consistent utilitarianism will recognize that the suffering of all living beings, not just human beings, counts from a moral point of view.

## Expanding the Circle of Utilitarianism: Animal Liberation

Once the suffering of animals has been acknowledged as having moral significance, the moral landscape changes dramatically. It is now populated by a myriad of different kinds of beings, not just human beings, and the moral calculation of consequences becomes much more complex. Moreover, they become more complex not just because more individual beings must be considered, but also because it is presumably more difficult to measure the extent to which animals are experiencing happiness, pleasure, pain, and suffering, since we cannot ask them directly in the same

*To what extent should the pain of animals count in weighing consequences?*

way that we can ask human beings. While some utilitarians—usually called *hedonistic* utilitarians—take pleasure and pain as the standard of utility, they are often criticized as having too base a standard. Other utilitarians—*eudaimonistic* utilitarians—take happiness and unhappiness as the standard. Although this seems to many to be a more appropriate standard, it is more difficult to quantify and apply, especially in the case of animals.

The utilitarian approach to the moral status of animals is subject to other difficulties as well, not the least of which is that it may not justify enough protection for animals. These are typical quandaries for utilitarians, irrespective of the issue of animals. Can one cow be killed if doing so will bring great pleasure to a dozen dogs? How do we treat the painless killing of animals? If a cow is killed instantaneously, painlessly, and without the cow's foreknowledge (so there is no anticipatory fear), does its death create any suffering to be considered in the utilitarian calculus?

Finally, if we grant that animals count in the moral world, *how much* do they count? Within the nonhuman animal world, is all animal suffering equal? Is the suffering of nonhuman animals of equal value to the suffering of humans? Is the suffering of a cow equal to the suffering of a worm? Of a human being?

## Considerations about Rights

Concerns about the strength of Singer's proposed utilitarian foundation for our attitude toward animals has led some philosophers, most notably Tom Regan, to shift the focus from the *liberation* of animals to animal *rights*. Nonhuman animals, Regan argues in our selection "The Case for Animal Rights" and in his book of the same name, have rights, just as human animals do. The crucial factor about rights is that they are, as Ronald Dworkin once suggested, like "trump cards." In other words, they take precedence over anything else, including considerations of utility. Thus, even if from a utilitarian point of view the killing of animals was sometimes justified, they still may be protected because they have a right to life.

### Who Has Rights?

Imagine that you were on a Star Trek mission to an unexplored planet, and that through a fluke accident you find yourself marooned on a planet that you know nothing about. Able to breathe the atmosphere, but lacking food and water, you are immediately faced with the question of what in your environment you may—both safely and morally—consume. Let's imagine that there is little plant matter, and the little that is available lacks nutritional content. You turn toward the living beings on the planet that are crawling, walking, hopping, running, and flying around the planet. Leaving aside the question of safety, how would you decide which creatures had a right to be respected and which creatures—if any—you were morally justified in eating?

As we tried to answer this question, presumably we would look for certain things—such as intelligence, language, culture, and the like—which would indicate that these beings are deserving of respect, are not to be used as a mere means to our nutritional goals. Similarly, when we look on earth at the nonhuman animal world around us, we must ask which animals have rights. The answer that animal rights advocates give is simple: the ability to feel pain (sentience) is what confers rights. What if the criterion is the ability to think and use language? Then certain kinds of animals—dolphins, chimps, and others—may qualify for rights, while other kinds of animals—slugs, worms, and so on—would not qualify, nor would certain human beings—most notably, those with severe mental disabilities and those in deep comas. The extent of animal rights depends directly on the criterion for conferring rights.

## How Do We Resolve Conflicts of Rights?

Authors such as Alasdair MacIntyre and Mary Ann Glendon have criticized the growing philosophical and political preoccupation with rights, and they have argued that the language of rights is only a fiction and that it leads to polarization and increased conflict. Certainly one of the difficulties is that rights are often presented as absolute, although the philosophically more defensible situation is to see virtually all rights as less than absolute. Otherwise we are left with the irresolvable situation of what to do when one absolute right conflicts with another absolute right. Obviously, we need some kind of hierarchy, some ordering of rights.

These considerations have a particular relevance in the area of animal rights. Advocates of animal rights have to answer three questions. *First*, what particular rights do all animals have? Do all animals have the right to life? The right not to suffer needlessly? The right to liberty? *Second*, do rights vary by species, or do all types of animals have equal rights? Does a worm have the same rights as a chimp and as a baby human being? *Third*, how do we resolve interspecies conflicts of rights? Is the right to life of a worm equal in moral standing to the right to life of a chimp and the right to life of a human infant? These are difficult questions, although not necessarily unanswerable. A strong defense of animal rights must, however, provide a plausible answer to these questions. In "The Case for Animal Rights," Tom Regan addresses each of these questions.

## Animal Rights and Abortion

There is an interesting corollary of one's position on animal rights. When a very broad right-conferring property such as the ability to feel pain is used as the principal basis for recognizing rights, then it would appear that fetuses have rights too. Often the arguments used against fetal rights—namely, that fetuses lack certain human characteristics such as self-consciousness or rationality—would not be sound if the broader, more inclusive definitions of right-conferring properties were in force.

# Concerns about Character

In addition to concerns about religion, consequences, and rights, defenders of animals have often pointed to the issue of *moral character* as providing a foundation for changing our attitudes toward animals. The argument has been that compassionate people will be more responsive to the suffering of animals, and that continuing mistreatment of animals in our society dulls our capacity for compassion in regard to all beings.

## Compassion

Almost everyone has had the experience of seeing an animal in pain, and for most of us our immediate response is to want to relieve the animal's suffering. We may nurse an injured bird back to health, wash the wounds of a dog that has been in a fight, even try to set the broken leg of a kitten. Sometimes, whether rightly or wrongly, we may conclude that the animal cannot recover and kill it in order to end its suffering. (Issues of animal rights prompt a reconsideration of euthanasia, not just abortion.)

Yet compassion initially seems to be a shaky foundation for our moral attitude toward animals. Sometimes, sympathy and compassion can turn into mere sentimentality—and some have criticized the animal rights movement for falling into the trap of sentimentality. In his article "Taking Sympathy Seriously," John A. Fisher develops and defends a sophisticated notion of sympathy as a foundation for our treatment of animals, one which he thinks is immune to the dangers of sentimentality.

## Proximity

Most people who eat meat in modern industrialized societies don't slaughter their own animals in order to do so, and this simple fact has important implications for the issue of character. If the cruelty of animal agriculture is kept from view, then sensitive and compassionate people may participate in such cruelty through ignorance. Of course, some would maintain that such ignorance is itself morally blameworthy, and some of the more visible protests by animal rights activists have been aimed at making cruelty to animals inescapably visible.

# Common Ground

The various moral concerns outlined in the preceding pages come directly into play when we seek a common ground on a number of pressing issues in regard to our moral attitude toward animals. Let's briefly consider several of these areas: medical experimentation on animals, commercial agriculture, the keeping of pets, and our interactions with wild animals.

### Medical Experimentation: Balancing Competing Concerns

One of the most difficult areas in which to assert animal rights is medical experimentation. When the choice is simply between preserving the lives of animals *versus* being able to save the lives of human beings, for most people the choice is easy: the human takes priority over the animal. Few would agree with Ingrid Newkirk, the national director of PETA (People for the Ethical Treatment of Animals), who claims that "Animal liberationists do not separate out the human animal, so there is no rational basis for saying that a human being has special rights. A rat is a pig is a dog is a boy. They're all mammals."[4]

*To what extent ought we to use animals in biomedical research?*

The difficulty is that we are rarely, if ever, presented with such a stark choice between the life of one human being and the life of one animal. The choices are more likely to be between the lives of hundreds of animals and the *possible* beneficial effects of some new drug for human beings. Often the issue of animal experimentation is about further confirmation of experimental results that are already available, or about determining what changes would occur if some small variable is altered. Sometimes the issue is simply training students and laboratory workers in experimental techniques.

Does animal suffering count at all? If we reject Newkirk's implied claim that animal suffering and human suffering are of equal value, then do we simply ignore animal suffering? Does it count at all? In "The Case for the Use of Animals in Biomedical Research," Carl Cohen argues that, once we reject the notion of speciesism, the suffering of animals is justified whenever it helps to reduce human suffering. Although he would be opposed to the *pointless* suffering of animals, he believes it is immoral to refuse to use animals in research when doing so would ultimately reduce human suffering and prolong human life. Cohen's article illustrates the way in which speciesism is tied closely—whether rightly or wrongly—with the wide-scale use of animals for human benefits. For him, animal suffering counts, but when measured against human suffering, it counts for very little indeed.

*The middle ground.    How much* should animal suffering count? If we are discontent with Cohen's wholesale endorsement of the use of animals in research, and if we have rejected Newkirk's claim that there is no morally significant difference between human suffering and animal suffering, then where do we stand? The middle ground here would seem to be that animal suffering should be reduced whenever possible. Questions should be raised about whether the research is really necessary, whether it absolutely has to include animals, whether it can involve fewer animals, whether the suffering of the animals can be reduced in any way.

## Commercial Animal Agriculture and Eating Meat

*The cruelty of animal farming.*   In his selection "Down on the Factory Farm," Peter Singer gives us a glimpse of what commercial animal agriculture is like, and it is a disturbing picture indeed. Animals are raised under extremely harsh and unnatural conditions that deprive them of many of the natural consolations of their lives, such as sucking, grooming, pecking, and the like. Even if we leave aside the fact that their lives eventually end in slaughter, many of us would find much to object to in the way in which such animals are treated.

*The vegetarian option.*   Many supporters of animal rights respond to this situation by espousing vegetarianism, since this is clearly the option that eliminates the need to raise and kill animals under these conditions. As we indicated earlier, vegetarianism has much to recommend it in addition to the issue of animal suffering. However, if vegetarianism for the entire world is not a realistic option at this time, it is important to ask whether there would be any conditions under which the raising of animals for food would be morally acceptable.

*Common ground.*   Two distinct issues arise in regard to raising animals for food: their deaths and their lives. Presumably it is morally better to kill animals painlessly (including a minimum of anticipatory fear as well as a minimum of physical pain) than painfully. If animals are slaughtered, it should be done in a way that minimizes their pain. Second, their lives should be (a) as free as possible from pain inflicted by human beings and (b) as natural as possible. The first requirement is clearly utilitarian in character, while the second relates to what we might call "quality of life." Part of respecting a being is that we recognize the natural rhythms and contours of that being's life, and we try to avoid unnecessarily disturbing them. For example, many animals groom themselves, and such grooming activity provides them with comfort on a variety of levels, psychological as well as physical. Whenever possible, we should raise animals in ways that allow them to follow their own natural inclinations.

## Pets

The issue of pets raises important questions about the moral status of animals, especially in regard to what we envision as the ideal relationship among the species. It's particularly interesting because we are not dealing with questions of cruelty and suffering— indeed, in many cases it is just the opposite. Pet owners love their pets, care for them deeply and attentively, and are often devastated when they die. Indeed, on the surface everyone—pets as well as people—seems to benefit from this relationship.

*How do you envision the ideal relationship between human beings and animals?*

Yet many supporters of animal rights/liberation argue strongly against the keeping of pets. For opponents of pets and domestication of animals in general, one of the mainstays of their position is the claim that, on the whole, pets are often mistreated. But even putting such mistreatment aside, they argue that the relationship between owner and pet is misconstrued. People see themselves as *owning* their pets as pieces of property, and the standard view of ownership is that people may do whatever they want to their property. Yet, if animals have rights, then they are not the proper objects of ownership anymore than people are proper objects of ownership.

What, then, is the ideal relationship between human beings and other species? Some advocates of animal liberation seem to envision a largely separatist future in which human beings live with only minimal interactions with other species. In contrast to this view, Vicki Hearne in "What's Wrong with Animal Rights," has presented an interesting and provocative view based in part on her experience as an animal trainer.[5] She sets aside the issue of animal rights and concentrates instead on the question of animal happiness. Animals, she maintains, often achieve their greatest happiness in relationships with human beings. It often seems, she implies, that animal rights advocates, although deeply concerned with reducing animal suffering, neither know animals intimately nor love them directly and immediately.

## Wild Animals: Zoos and Animal Preservation

How are we to interact with the wild animals of the world? Clearly we can't pretend that we don't interact with such animals and assume a "hands off" policy. Isolationism may have been a viable political option in the nineteenth century, but as we anticipate the coming of the twenty-first century, we can no longer reasonably expect to live in complete isolation from wild animals. Our paths increasingly cross, mainly because human beings intrude on their territory. Two issues relate immediately to this: zoos and hunting.

*Zoos.*   At one time, zoos were little more than a carnival side-show exhibiting the exotic and the bizarre. In recent years, in part because of pressure from animal liberation/rights groups, zoos are rethinking their goals and their place both in human society and in the course of natural evolution. Instead of seeing themselves as just providing people with an opportunity to see unusual animals, they see their mission to be educating the public about the importance of the animal world and the subtlety of its structures and interactions. They often are highly effective spokespersons for preserving the natural habitat of animals and protecting them from the encroachments of human civilization. Similarly, their role vis-à-vis the natural environment is changing. Whereas they previously existed in a largely parasitic relationship with the natural world, plucking out choice specimens at their pleasure, they now see themselves as supporting and preserving nature. Endangered species are protected and bred in zoos, and then returned whenever possible to the wild. The zoo then becomes part of the evolutionary chain.

Animal rights-based critics of zoos remain skeptical and dissatisfied. They feel that interventions in the natural chain of evolution are seldom successful since they are usually based on a weak gene pool. Moreover, zoos are still based on the assumption that human beings are entitled to capture other beings and put them on display for their own (i.e., the human beings') pleasure.

*Animal preservation.*   The larger issue raised by this critique of zoos is whether human beings should be involved at all in the project of animal preservation. The larger issue raised by this controversy is the ideal relationship between human beings and other species. At one extreme are those who see it in purely exploitative terms, the natural world being completely at the disposal of human beings. At the other extreme are those who see human beings as agents of harm and who thus maintain that human beings should simply assume a "hands off" policy toward the natural world as far as possible. In the middle are those who seek to develop a model of how human beings and animals can live together in ways that are mutually enhancing. The first challenge is to clearly articulate such a model; the second, even greater challenge, will be to realize it.

## Endnotes

1. Cited in Matthew Scully, "Creature Teachers," *National Review* 45, no. 9 (May 10, 1993), 56 ff.
2. Reprinted in Tom Regan, *The Thee Generation* (Philadelphia: Temple University Press, 1991), pp. 143–157.
3. See Andrew Linzey, *Animal Rights: A Christian Assessment* (London: SCM Press, 1976) and *Christianity and the Rights of Animals* (New York: Crossroad, 1988).
4. K. McCabe, "Who Will Live, Who Will Die?" *Washingtonian Magazine*, August 1986, 115.
5. Vicki Hearne, "What's Wrong with Animal Rights?" *Harper's Magazine*, September 1991, 59 ff.

# THE ARGUMENTS

Tom Regan
"The Case for Animal Rights"

*Tom Regan is one of the most articulate and powerful spokespersons for animal rights. He has published widely on a range of different topics, but his most influential work has been in the area of animal rights. His book,* Animal Rights, *is one of the foundational works in that area.*

*In this article, Regan argues that case for animal rights, maintaining that those who take animal rights seriously must be committed to abolishing the use of animals in science, animal agriculture, and commercial hunting and trapping. "The fundamental wrong," he writes, "is the system that allows us to view animals as our resources, here for us—to be eaten, or surgically manipulated, or exploited for sport or money." Regan considers and rejects several approaches to understanding our relationship to animals: indirect duty, contractarianism, and utilitarianism. Only a rights approach is able to recognize the inherent value of the individual, including the individual animal.*

## As You Read, Consider This:

1. Regan distinguishes between things that "make things worse" and the "fundmamental wrong." If we could eliminate the factors that "make things worse" for animals, do you think that would be enough? What of Regan's arguments supports the claim that there is a "fundamental wrong" here?

2. Regan sees the animal rights movement as "cut from the same cloth" as human rights movements that oppose racism and sexism. Are the kinds of arguments that Regan advances for animal rights the same kinds of arguments that were advanced for human rights?

I regard myself as an advocate of animal rights—as a part of the animal rights movement. That movement, as I conceive it, is committed to a number of goals, including:

- the total abolition of the use of animals in science;
- the total dissolution of commercial animal agriculture;
- the total elimination of commercial and sport hunting and trapping.

There are, I know, people who profess to believe in animal rights but do not avow these goals. Factory farming, they say, is wrong—it violates animals' rights—but traditional animal agriculture is all right. Toxicity tests of cosmetics on animals violates their rights, but important medical research—cancer research, for example—does not. The clubbing of baby seals is abhorrent, but not

Tom Regan, "The Case for Animal Rights." From *In Defence of Animals*, ed. Peter Singer (Oxford: Basil Blackwell, 1985). Reprinted by permission of the publisher.

the harvesting of adult seals. I used to think I understood this reasoning. Not any more. You don't change unjust institutions by tidying them up.

What's wrong—fundamentally wrong—with the way animals are treated isn't the details that vary from case to case. It's the whole system. The forlornness of the veal calf is pathetic, heart wrenching; the pulsing pain of the chimp with electrodes planted deep in her brain is repulsive; the slow, torturous death of the raccoon caught in the leg-hold trap is agonizing. But what is wrong isn't the pain, isn't the suffering, isn't the deprivation. These compound what's wrong. Sometimes—often—they make it much, much worse. But they are not the fundamental wrong.

The fundamental wrong is the system that allows us to view animals as our resources, here for us—to be eaten, or surgically manipulated, or exploited for sport or money. Once we accept this view of animals—as our resources—the rest is as predictable as it is regrettable. Why worry about their loneliness, their pain, their death? Since animals exist for us, to benefit us in one way or another, what harms them really doesn't matter—or matters only if it starts to bother us, makes us feel a trifle uneasy. . . .

In the case of animals in science, whether and how we abolish their use . . . are to a large extent political questions. People must change their beliefs before they change their habits. Enough people, especially those elected to public office, must believe in change—must want it—before we will have laws that protect the rights of animals. This process of change is very complicated, very demanding, very exhausting, calling for the efforts of many hands in education, publicity, political organization and activity, down to the licking of envelopes and stamps. As a trained and practicing philosopher, the sort of contribution I can make is limited but, I like to think, important. The currency of philosophy is ideas—their meaning and rational foundation—not the nuts and bolts of the legislative process, say, or the mechanics of community organization. That's what I have been exploring over the past ten years or so in my essays and talks and, most recently, in my book, *The Case for Animal Rights.* I believe the major conclusions I reach in the book are true because they are supported by the weight of the best arguments. I believe the idea of animal rights has reason, not just emotion, on its side.

In the space I have at my disposal here I can only sketch, in the barest outline, some of the main features of the book. Its main themes—and we should not be surprised by this—involve asking and answering deep, foundational moral questions about what morality is, how it should be understood and what is the best moral theory, all considered. I hope I can convey something of the shape I think this theory takes. The attempt to do this will be (to use a word a friendly critic once used to describe my work) cerebral, perhaps too cerebral. But this is misleading. My feelings about how animals are sometimes treated run just as deep and just as strong as those of my more volatile compatriots. Philosophers do—to use the jargon of the day—have a right side to their brains. If it's the left side we contribute (or mainly should), that's because what talents we have reside there.

How to proceed? We begin by asking how the moral status of animals has been understood by thinkers who deny that animals have rights. Then we test the mettle of their ideas by seeing how well they stand up under the heat of fair criticism. If we start our thinking in this way, we soon find that some people believe that we have no duties directly to animals, that we owe nothing to them, that we can do nothing that wrongs them. Rather, we can do wrong acts that involve animals, and so we have duties regarding them, though none to them. Such views may be called indirect duty views. By way of illustration: suppose your neighbor kicks your dog. Then your neighbor has done something wrong. But not to your dog. The wrong that has been done is a wrong to you. After all, it is wrong to upset people, and your neighbor's kicking your dog upsets you. So you are the one who is wronged, not your dog. Or again: by kicking your dog your neighbor damages your property. And since it is wrong to damage another person's property, your neighbor has done something wrong—to you, of course, not to your dog. Your neighbor no more wrongs your dog than your car would be wronged if the windshield were smashed. Your neighbor's duties involving your dog are indirect duties to you. More generally, all of our duties regarding animals are indirect duties to one another—to humanity.

How could someone try to justify such a view? Someone might say that your dog doesn't feel anything and so isn't hurt by your neighbor's kick, doesn't care about the pain since none is felt, is as unaware of anything as is your windshield. Someone might say this, but no rational person will, since, among other considerations, such a view will commit anyone who holds it to the position that no human being feels pain either—that human beings also don't care about what happens to them. A second possibility is that though both humans and your dog are hurt when kicked, it is only human pain that matters. But, again, no rational person can believe this. Pain is pain wherever it occurs. If your neighbor's causing you pain is wrong because of the pain that is caused, we cannot rationally ignore or dismiss the moral relevance of the pain that your dog feels.

Philosophers who hold indirect duty views—and many still do—have come to understand that they must avoid the two defects just noted: that is, both the view that animals don't feel anything as well as the idea that only human pain can be morally relevant. Among such thinkers the sort of view now favored is one or other form of what is called contractarianism.

Here, very crudely, is the root idea: morality consists of a set of rules that individuals voluntarily agree to abide by, as we do when we sign a contract (hence the name contractarianism). Those who understand and accept the terms of the contract are covered directly; they have rights created and recognized by, and protected in, the contract. And these contractors can also have protection spelled out for others who, though they lack the ability to understand morality and so cannot sign the contract themselves, are loved or cherished by those who can. Thus young children, for example, are unable to sign contracts and lack rights. But they are protected by the contract nonetheless because of the sentimental interests of others, most notably their parents. So we have, then, duties involving these children, duties regarding them, but no duties to them. Our duties in their case are indirect duties to other human beings, usually their parents.

As for animals, since they cannot understand contracts, they obviously cannot sign; and since they cannot sign, they have no rights. Like children, however, some animals are the objects of the sentimental interest of others. You, for example, love your dog or cat. So those animals that enough people care about (companion animals, whales, baby seals, the American bald eagle), though they lack rights themselves, will be protected because of the sentimental interests of people. I have, then, according to contractarianism, no duty directly to your dog or any other animal, not even the duty not to cause them pain or suffering; my duty not to hurt them is a duty I have to those people who care about what happens to them. As for other animals, where no or little sentimental interest is present—in the case of farm animals, for example, or laboratory rats—what duties we have grow weaker and weaker, perhaps to vanishing point. The pain and death they endure, though real, are not wrong if no one cares about them.

When it comes to the moral status of animals, contractarianism could be a hard view to refute if it were an adequate theoretical approach to the moral status of human beings. It is not adequate in this latter respect, however, which makes the question of its adequacy in the former case, regarding animals, utterly moot. For consider: morality, according to the (crude) contractarian position before us, consists of rules that people agree to abide by. What people? Well, enough to make a difference—enough, that is, collectively to have the power to enforce the rules that are drawn up in the contract. That is very well and good for the signatories but not so good for anyone who is not asked to sign. And there is nothing in contractarianism of the sort we are discussing that guarantees or requires that everyone will have a chance to participate equally in framing the rules of morality. The result is that this approach to ethics could sanction the most blatant forms of social, economic, moral and political injustice, ranging from a repressive caste system to systematic racial or sexual discrimination. Might, according to this theory, does make right. Let those who are the victims of injustice suffer as they will. It matters not so long as no one else—no contractor, or too few of them—cares about it. Such a theory takes one's moral breath away . . . as if, for example, there would be nothing wrong with apartheid in South Africa if few white South Africans were upset by it. A theory with so little to recommend it at the level of the ethics of our treatment of our fellow humans cannot have anything more to recommend it when it comes to the ethics of how we treat our fellow animals.

The version of contractarianism just examined is, as I have noted, a crude variety, and in fairness to those of a contractarian persuasion it must be noted that much more refined, subtle and ingenious varieties are possible. For example, John Rawls, in his *A Theory of Justice*, sets forth a version of contractarianism that forces contractors to ignore the accidental features of being a human being—for example, whether one is white or black, male or female, a genius or of modest intellect. Only by ignoring such features, Rawls believes, can we ensure that the principles of justice that contractors would agree upon are not based on bias or prejudice. Despite the improvement a view such as Rawls's represents over the cruder forms of contractarianism, it remains deficient: it systematically denies that we have direct duties to those human beings who do not have a sense of justice—young children, for instance, and many mentally retarded humans. And yet it seems reasonably certain that, were we to torture a young child or a retarded elder, we would be doing something that wronged him or her, not something that would be wrong if (and only if) other humans with a sense of justice were upset. And since this is true in the case of these humans, we cannot rationally deny the same in the case of animals.

Indirect duty views, then, including the best among them, fail to command our rational assent. Whatever ethical theory we should accept rationally, therefore, it must at least recognize that we have some duties directly to animals, just as we have some duties directly to each other. . . .

Some people think that the theory we are looking for is utilitarianism. A utilitarian accepts two moral principles. The first is that of equality: everyone's interests count, and similar interests must be counted as having similar weight or importance. White or black, American or Iranian, human or animal—everyone's pain or frustration matters, and matters just as much as the equivalent pain or frustration of anyone else. The second principle a utilitarian accepts is that of utility: do the act that will bring about the best balance between satisfaction and frustration for everyone affected by the outcome.

As a utilitarian, then, here is how I am to approach the task of deciding what I morally ought to do: I must ask who will be affected if I choose to do one thing rather than another, how much each individual will be affected, and where the best results are most likely to lie—which option, in other words, is most likely to bring about the best results, the best balance between satisfaction and frustration. That option, whatever it may be, is the one I ought to choose. That is where my moral duty lies.

The great appeal of utilitarianism rests with its uncompromising egalitarianism: everyone's interests count and count as much as the like interests of everyone else. The kind of odious discrimination that some forms of contractarianism can justify—discrimination based on race or sex, for example—seems disallowed in principle by utilitarianism, as is speciesism, systematic discrimination based on species membership.

The equality we find in utilitarianism, however, is not the sort an advocate of animal or human rights should have in mind. Utilitarianism has no room for the equal moral rights of different individuals because it has no room for their equal inherent value or worth. What has value for the utilitarian is the satisfaction of an individual's interests, not the individual whose interests they are. A universe in which you satisfy your desire for water, food and warmth is, other things being equal, better than a universe in which these desires are frustrated. And the same is true in the case of an animal with similar desires. But neither you nor the animal have any value in your own right. Only your feelings do.

Here is an analogy to help make the philosophical point clearer: a cup contains different liquids, sometimes sweet, sometimes bitter, sometimes a mix of the two. What has value are the liquids: the sweeter the better, the bitterer the worse. The cup, the container, has no value. It is what goes into it, not what they go into, that has value. For the utilitarian you and I are like the cup; we have no value as individuals and thus no equal value. What has value is what goes into us, what we serve as receptacles for; our feelings of satisfaction have positive value, our feelings of frustration negative value.

Serious problems arise for utilitarianism when we remind ourselves that it enjoins us to bring about the best consequences. What does this mean? It doesn't mean the best consequences for me alone, or for my family or friends, or any other person taken individually. No, what we must do is, roughly, as follows: we must add up (somehow!) the separate satisfactions and frustrations of everyone likely to be affected by our choice, the satisfactions in one column, the frustrations in the other. We must total each column for each of the options before us. That is what it means to say the theory is aggregative. And then we must choose that option which is most likely to bring about the best balance of totaled satisfactions over totaled frustrations. Whatever act would lead to this outcome is the one we ought morally to perform—it is where our moral duty lies. And that act quite clearly might not be the same one that would bring about the best results for me personally, or for my family or friends, or for a lab animal. The best aggregated consequences for everyone concerned are not necessarily the best for each individual.

That utilitarianism is an aggregative theory—different individuals' satisfactions or frustrations are added, or summed, or totaled—is the key objection to this theory. My Aunt Bea is old, inactive, a cranky, sour person, though not physically ill. She prefers to go on living. She is also rather rich. I could make a fortune if I could get my hands on her money, money she intends to give me in any event, after she dies, but which she refuses to give me now. In order to avoid a huge tax bite, I plan to donate a handsome sum of my profits to a local children's hospital. Many, many children will benefit from my generosity, and much joy will be brought to their parents, relatives and friends. If I don't get the money rather soon, all these ambitions will come to naught. The once-in-a-lifetime opportunity to make a real killing will be gone. Why, then, not kill my Aunt Bea? Oh, of course I might get caught. But I'm no fool and, besides, her doctor can be counted on to cooperate (he has an eye for the same investment and I happen to know a good deal about his shady past). The deed can be done . . . professionally, shall we say. There is very little chance of getting caught. And as for my conscience being guilt-ridden, I am a resourceful sort of fellow and will take more than sufficient comfort—as I lie on the beach at Acapulco—in contemplating the joy and health I have brought to so many others.

Suppose Aunt Bea is killed and the rest of the story comes out as told. Would I have done anything wrong? Anything immoral? One would have thought that I had. Not according to utilitarianism. Since what I have done has brought about the best balance between totaled satisfaction and frustration for all those affected by the outcome, my action is not wrong. Indeed, in killing Aunt Bea the physician and I did what duty required.

This same kind of argument can be repeated in all sorts of cases, illustrating, time after time, how the utilitarian's position leads to results that impartial people find morally callous. It is wrong to kill my Aunt Bea in the name of bringing about the best results for others. A good end does not justify an evil means. Any adequate moral theory will have to explain why this is so. Utilitarianism fails in this respect and so cannot be the theory we seek.

What to do? Where to begin anew? The place to begin, I think, is with the utilitarian's view of the value of the individual—or, rather, lack of value. In its place, suppose we consider that you and I, for example, do have value as individuals—what well call inherent value. To say we have such value is to say that we are something more than, something different from, mere receptacles. Moreover, to ensure that we do not pave the way for such injustices as slavery or sexual discrimination, we must believe that all who have inherent value have it equally, regardless of their sex, race, religion, birthplace and so on. Similarly to be discarded as irrelevant are one's talents or skills, intelligence and wealth, personality or pathology, whether one is loved and admired or despised and loathed. The genius and the retarded child, the prince and the pauper, the brain surgeon and the fruit vendor, Mother Teresa and the most unscrupulous used-car salesman—all have inherent value, all possess it equally, and all have an equal right to be treated with respect, to be treated in ways that do not reduce them to the status of things, as if they existed as resources for others. My value as an individual is independent of my usefulness to you. Yours is not dependent on your usefulness to me. For either of us to treat the other in ways that fail to show respect for the other's independent value is to act immorally, to violate the individual's rights.

Some of the rational virtues of this view—what I call the rights view—should be evident. Unlike (crude) contractarianism, for example, the rights view in principle denies the moral tolerability of any and all forms of racial, sexual or social discrimination; and unlike utilitarianism, this view in principle denies that we can justify good results by using evil means that violate an individual's rights—denies, for example, that it could be moral to kill my Aunt Bea to harvest beneficial consequences for others. That would be to sanction the disrespectful treatment of the individual in the name of the social good, something the rights view will not—categorically will not—ever allow.

The rights view, I believe, is rationally the most satisfactory moral theory. It surpasses all other theories in the degree to which it illuminates and explains the foundation of our duties to one another—the domain of human morality. On this score it has the best reasons, the best arguments, on its side. Of course, if it were possible to show that only human beings are included within its scope, then a person like myself, who believes in animal rights, would be obliged to look elsewhere.

But attempts to limit its scope to humans only can be shown to be rationally defective. Animals, it is true, lack many of the abilities humans possess. They can't read, do higher mathematics, build a bookcase or make baba ghanoush. Neither can many human beings, however, and yet we don't (and shouldn't) say that they (these humans) therefore have less inherent value, less of a right to be treated with respect, than do others. It is the similarities between those human beings who most clearly, most non-controversially have such value (the people reading this, for example), not our differences, that matter most. And the really crucial, the basic similarity is simply this: we are each of us the experiencing subject of a life, a conscious creature having an individual welfare that has importance to us whatever our usefulness to others. We want and prefer things, believe and feel things, recall and expect things. And all these dimensions of our life, including our pleasure and pain, our enjoyment and suffering, our satisfaction and frustration, our continued existence or our untimely death—all make a difference to the quality of our life as lived, as experienced, by us as individuals. As the same is true of those animals that concern us, . . . they too must be viewed as the experiencing subjects of a life, with inherent value of their own.

Some there are who resist the idea that animals have inherent value. "Only humans have such value," they profess. How might this narrow view be defended? Shall we say that only humans have the requisite intelligence, or autonomy, or reason? But there are many, many humans who fail to meet these standards and yet are reasonably viewed as having value above and beyond their usefulness to others. Shall we claim that only humans belong to the right species, the species Homo sapiens? But this is blatant speciesism. Will it be said, then, that all—and only—humans have immortal souls? Then our opponents have their work cut out for them. I am myself not ill-disposed to the proposition that there are immortal souls. Personally, I profoundly hope I have one. But I would not want to rest my position on a controversial ethical issue on the even more controversial question about who or what has an immortal soul. That is to dig one's hole deeper, not to climb out. Rationally, it is better to resolve moral issues without making more controversial assumptions than are needed. The question of who has inherent value is such a question, one that is resolved more rationally without the introduction of the idea of immortal souls than by its use.

Well, perhaps some will say that animals have some inherent value, only less than we have. Once again, however, attempts to defend this view can be shown to lack rational justification. What could be the basis of our having more inherent value than animals? Their lack of reason, or autonomy, or intellect? Only if we are willing to make the same judgment in the case of humans who are similarly deficient. But it is not true that such humans—the retarded child, for example, or the mentally deranged—have less inherent value than you or I. Neither, then, can we rationally sustain the view that animals, like them in being the experiencing subjects of a life, have less inherent value. All who have inherent value have it equally, whether they be human animals or not.

Inherent value, then, belongs equally to those who are the experiencing subjects of a life. Whether it belongs to others—to rocks and rivers, trees and glaciers, for example—we do not know and may never know. But neither do we need to know, if we are to make the case for animal rights. We do not need to know, for example, how many people are eligible to vote in the next presidential election before we can know whether I am. Similarly, we do not need to know how many individuals have inherent value before we can know that some do. When it comes to the case for animal rights, then, what we need to know is whether the animals that, in our culture, are routinely eaten, hunted and used in our laboratories, for example, are like us in being subjects of a life. And we do know this. We do know that many—literally, billions and billions—of these animals are the subjects of a life in the sense explained and so have inherent value if we do. And since, in order to arrive at the best theory of our duties to one another, we must recognize our equal inherent value as individuals, reason—not sentiment, not emotion—reason compels us to recognize the equal inherent value of these animals and, with this, their equal right to be treated with respect.

That, *very* roughly, is the shape and feel of the case for animal rights. Most of the details of the supporting argument are missing. They are to be found in the book to which I alluded earlier. Here, the details go begging, and I must, in closing, limit myself to four final points.

The first is how the theory that underlies the case for animal rights shows that the animal rights movement is a part of, not antagonistic to, the human rights movement. The theory that rationally grounds the rights of animals also grounds the rights of humans. Thus those involved in the animal rights movement are partners in the struggle to secure respect for human rights—the rights of women, for example, or minorities, or workers. The animal rights movement is cut from the same moral cloth as these.

Second, having set out the broad outlines of the rights view, I can now say why its implications for . . . science, among other fields, are both clear and uncompromising. In the case of the use of animals in science, the rights view is categorically abolitionist. Lab animals are not our tasters; we are not their kings. Because these animals are treated routinely, systematically as if their value were reducible to their usefulness to others, they are routinely, systematically treated with a lack of respect, and thus are their rights routinely, systematically violated. This is just as true when they are used in trivial, duplicative, unnecessary or unwise research as it is when they are used in studies that hold out real promise of human benefits. We can't justify harming or killing a human being (my Aunt Bea, for example) just for these sorts of reason. Neither can we do so even in the case of so lowly a creature as a laboratory rat. It is not just refinement or reduction that is called for, not just larger, cleaner cages, not just more generous use of anesthetic or the elimination of multiple surgery, not just tidying up the system. It is complete replacement. The best we can do when it comes to using animals in science is—not to use them. That is where our duty lies, according to the rights view. . . .

My last two points are about philosophy, my profession. It is, most obviously, no substitute for political action. The words I have written here and in other places by themselves don't change a thing. It is what we do with the thoughts that the words express—our acts, our deeds—that changes things. All that philosophy can do, and all I have attempted, is to offer a vision of what our deeds should aim at. And the why. But not the how.

Finally, I am reminded of my thoughtful critic, the one I mentioned earlier, who chastised me for being too cerebral. Well, cerebral I have been: indirect duty views, utilitarianism, contractarianism—hardly the stuff deep passions are made of. I am also reminded, however, of the image another friend once set before me—the image of the ballerina as expressive of disciplined passion. Long hours of sweat and toil, of loneliness and practice, of doubt and fatigue: those are the discipline of her craft. But the passion is there too, the fierce drive to excel, to speak through her body, to do it right, to pierce our minds. That is the image of philosophy I would leave with you, not "too cerebral" but disciplined passion. Of the discipline enough has been seen. As for the passion: there are times, and these not infrequent, when tears come to my eyes when I see, or read, or hear of the wretched plight of animals in the hands of humans. Their pain, their suffering, their loneliness, their innocence, their death. Anger. Rage. Pity. Sorrow. Disgust. The whole creation groans under the weight of the evil we humans visit upon these mute, powerless creatures. It is our hearts, not just our heads, that call for an end to it all, that demand of us that we overcome, for them, the habits and forces behind their systematic oppression. All great movements, it is written, go through three stages: ridicule, discussion, adoption. It is the realization of this third stage, adoption, that requires both our passion and our discipline, our hearts and our heads. The fate of animals is in our hands. God grant we are equal to the task.

## Journal/Discussion Questions

✍ *In your own life, what moral standing or importance do animals have? What difference does animal suffering make to you? How were you affected by Regan's article?*

1. What does Regan mean by "indirect duty views"? What criticisms does he offer of them? In what ways do you agree/disagree with his criticisms?

2. According to Regan, what is "contractari-anism"? What criticisms does he offer of the contractarian approach to morality?

3. Why, according to Regan, should we reject utilitarian approaches to the issue of our relationship to animals?

4. Why, according to Regan, is the rights view superior to all other approaches to the issue of our relationship to animals? Do you agree with Regan's assessment?

---

### Carl Cohen
### "The Case for the Use of Animals in Biomedical Research"

---

*Carl Cohen is a professor at the University of Michigan Medical School, Ann Arbor.*

*This article, which originally appeared in* The New England Journal of Medicine *in 1986, develops a strong critique of (1) the claim that animals have rights and (2) the claim that it is wrong to inflict avoidable suffering on sentient beings. Animals have no rights, Cohen argues, because they do not have any of the characteristics—free will, reason, self-consciousness, the ability to make free moral judgments, and the like—that are usually seen as the basis for attributing rights. Although we have duties to animals, the overall benefits to human beings of using animals in biomedical research clearly justifies their use. He further argues that we should continue testing on animals when other methods cannot provide us with equally reliable results and that we should, if anything, increase the number of animals used in testing in order to avoid the use of humans as test subjects whenever possible.*

### As You Read, Consider This:

1. Cohen considers a variety of possible standards for attributing rights to beings. What are these standards? Do animals have rights under these standards? Would severely mentally impaired human beings? Human beings in irreversible comas?
2. What, according to Cohen, is "speciesism"? Why does he defend it?

⌒

Using animals as research subjects in medical investigations is widely condemned on two grounds: first, because it wrongly violates the rights of animals,[1] and second, because it wrongly imposes on sentient creatures much avoidable suffering.[2] Neither of these arguments is sound. The first relies on a mistaken understanding of rights; the second relies on a mistaken calculation of consequences. Both deserve definitive dismissal.

## Why Animals Have No Rights

A right, properly understood, is a claim, or potential claim, that one party may exercise against another. The target against whom such a claim may be registered can be a single person, a group, a community, or (perhaps) all humankind. The content of rights claims also varies greatly: repayment of loans, nondiscrimination by employers, noninterference by the state, and so on. To comprehend any genuine right fully, therefore, we must know who holds the right, against whom it is held, and to what it is a right.

Alternative sources of rights add complexity. Some rights are grounded in constitution and law (e.g., the right of an accused to trial by jury); some rights are moral but give no legal claims (e.g., my right to your keeping the promise you gave me); and some rights (e.g., against theft or assault) are rooted both in morals and in law.

The differing targets, contents, and sources of rights, and their inevitable conflict, together weave a tangled web. Notwithstanding all such complications, this much is clear about rights in general: they are in every case claims, or potential claims, within a community of moral agents. Rights arise, and can be intelligibly defended, only among beings who actually do, or can, make moral claims against one another. Whatever else rights may be, therefore, they are necessarily human; their possessors are persons, human beings.

The attributes of human beings from which this moral capability arises have been described variously by philosophers, both ancient and modern: the inner consciousness of a free will (Saint Augustine)[3]; the grasp, by human reason, of the binding character of moral law (Saint Thomas)[4]; the self-conscious participation of human beings in an objective ethical order (Hegel)[5]; human membership in an organic moral community (Bradley)[6]; the development of the human self through the consciousness of other moral selves (Mead)[7]; and the underivative, intuitive cognition of the rightness of an action (Prichard).[8] Most influential has been Immanuel Kant's emphasis on the universal human possession of a uniquely moral will and the autonomy its use entails.[9] Humans confront choices that are purely moral; humans—but certainly not dogs or mice—lay down moral laws, for others and for themselves. Human beings are self-legislative, morally *auto-nomous*.

Animals (that is, nonhuman animals, the ordinary sense of that word) lack this capacity for free moral judgment. They are not beings of a kind capable of exercising or responding to moral claims. Animals therefore have no rights, and they can have none. This is the core of the argument about the alleged rights of animals. The holders of rights must have the capacity to comprehend rules of duty, governing all including themselves. In applying such rules, the holders of rights must recognize possible conflicts between what is in their own interest and what is just. Only in a community of beings capable of self-restricting moral judgments can the concept of a right be correctly invoked.

Humans have such moral capacities. They are in this sense self-legislative, are members of communities governed by moral rules, and do possess rights. Animals do not have such moral capacities. They are not morally self-legislative, cannot possibly be members of a truly moral community, and therefore cannot possess rights. In conducting research on animal subjects, therefore, we do not violate their rights, because they have none to violate.

To animate life, even in its simplest forms, we give a certain natural reverence. But the possession of rights presupposes a moral status not attained by the vast majority of living things. We must not infer, therefore, that a live being has, simply in being alive, a "right" to its life. The assertion that all animals, only because they are alive and have interests, also possess the "right to life"[10] is an abuse of that phrase, and wholly without warrant.

It does not follow from this, however, that we are morally free to do anything we please to animals. Certainly not. In our dealings with animals, as in our dealings with other human beings, we have obligations that do not arise from claims against us based on rights. Rights entail obligations, but many of the things one ought to do are in no way tied to another's entitlement. Rights and obligations are not reciprocals of one another, and it is a serious mistake to suppose that they are.

Illustrations are helpful. Obligations may arise from internal commitments made: physicians have obligations to their patients not grounded merely in their patients' rights. Teachers have such obligations to their students, shepherds to their dogs, and cowboys to their horses. Obligations may arise from differences of status: adults owe special care when playing with young children, and children owe special care when playing with young pets. Obligations may arise from special relationships: the payment of my son's college tuition is something to which he may have no right, although it may be my obligation to bear the burden if I reasonably can; my dog has no right to daily exercise and veterinary care, but I do have the obligation to provide these things for her. Obligations may arise from particular acts or circumstances: one may be obliged to another for a special kindness done, or obliged to put an animal out of its misery in view of its condition—although neither the human benefactor nor the dying animal may have had a claim of right.

Plainly, the grounds of our obligations to humans and to animals are manifold and cannot be formulated simply. Some hold that there is a general obligation to do no gratuitous harm to sentient creatures (the principle of nonmaleficence); some hold that there is a general obligation to do good to sentient creatures when that is reasonably within one's power (the principle of beneficence). In our dealings with animals, few will deny that we are at least obliged to act humanely—that is, to treat them with the decency and concern that we owe, as sensitive human beings, to other sentient creatures. To treat animals humanely, however, is not to treat them as humans or as the holders of rights.

A common objection, which deserves a response, may be paraphrased as follows:

> If having rights requires being able to make moral claims, to grasp and apply moral laws, then many humans—the brain-damaged, the comatose, the senile—who plainly lack those capacities must be without rights. But that is absurd. This proves [the critic concludes] that rights do not depend on the presence of moral capacities.[11]

This objection fails; it mistakenly treats an essential feature of humanity as though it were a screen for sorting humans. The capacity for moral judgment that distinguishes humans from animals is not a test to be administered to human beings one by one. Persons who are unable, because of some disability, to perform the full moral functions natural to human beings are certainly not for that reason ejected from the moral community. The issue is one of kind. Humans are of such a kind that they may be the subject of experiments only with their voluntary consent. The choices they make freely must be respected. Animals are of such a kind that it is impossible for them, in principle, to give or withhold voluntary consent or to make a moral choice. What humans retain when disabled, animals have never had.

A second objection, also often made, may be paraphrased as follows:

> Capacities will not succeed in distinguishing humans from the other animals. Animals also reason; animals also communicate with one another; animals also care passionately for their young; animals also exhibit desires and preferences.[12] Features of moral relevance—rationality, interdependence, and love—are not exhibited uniquely by human beings. Therefore [this critic concludes], there can be no solid moral distinction between humans and other animals.[13]

This criticism misses the central point. It is not the ability to communicate or to reason, or dependence on one another, or care for the young, or the exhibition of preference, or any such behavior that marks the critical divide. Analogies between human families and those of monkeys, or between human communities and those of wolves, and the like, are entirely beside the point. Patterns of conduct are not at issue. Animals do indeed exhibit remarkable behavior at times. Conditioning, fear, instinct, and intelligence all contribute to species survival. Membership in a community of moral agents nevertheless remains impossible for them. Actors subject to moral judgment must be capable of grasping the generality of an ethical premise in a practical syllogism. Humans act immorally often enough, but only they—never wolves or monkeys—can discern, by applying some moral rule to the facts of a case, that a given act ought or ought not to be performed. The moral restraints imposed by humans on themselves are thus highly abstract and are often in conflict with the self-interest of the agent. Communal behavior among animals, even when most intelligent and most endearing, does not approach autonomous morality in this fundamental sense.

Genuinely moral acts have an internal as well as an external dimension. Thus, in law, an act can be criminal only when the guilty deed, the actus reus, is done with a guilty mind, mens rea. No animal can ever commit a crime; bringing animals to criminal trial is the mark of primitive ignorance. The claims of moral right are similarly inapplicable to them. Does a lion have a right to eat a baby zebra? Does a baby zebra have a right not to be eaten? Such questions, mistakenly invoking the concept of right where it does not belong, do not make good sense. Those who condemn biomedical research because it violates "animal rights" commit the same blunder.

## In Defense of "Speciesism"

Abandoning reliance on animal rights, some critics resort instead to animal sentience—their feelings of pain and distress. We ought to desist from the imposition of pain insofar as we can. Since all or nearly all experimentation on animals does impose pain and could be readily forgone, say these critics, it should be stopped. The ends sought may be worthy, but those ends do not justify imposing agonies on humans, and by animals the agonies are felt no less. The laboratory use of animals (these critics conclude) must therefore be ended—or at least very sharply curtailed.

Argument of this variety is essentially utilitarian, often expressly so;[14] it is based on the calculation of the net product, in pains and pleasures, resulting from experiments on animals. Jeremy Bentham, comparing horses and dogs with other sentient creatures, is thus commonly quoted: "The question is not, Can they reason? nor Can they talk? but, Can they suffer?"[15]

Animals certainly can suffer and surely ought not to be made to suffer needlessly. But in inferring, from these uncontroversial premises, that biomedical research causing animal distress is largely (or wholly) wrong, the critic commits two serious errors.

The first error is the assumption, often explicitly defended, that all sentient animals have equal moral standing. Between a dog and a human being, according to this view, there is no moral difference; hence the pains suffered by dogs must be weighed no differently from the pains suffered by humans. To deny such equality, according to this critic, is to give unjust preference to one species over another; it is "speciesism." The most influential statement of this moral equality of species was made by Peter Singer:

> The racist violates the principle of equality by giving greater weight to the interests of members of his own race when there is a clash between their interests and the interests of those of another race. The sexist violates the principle of equality by favoring the interests of his own sex. Similarly the speciesist allows the interests of his own species to override the greater interests of members of other species. The pattern is identical in each case.[16]

This argument is worse than unsound; it is atrocious. It draws an offensive moral conclusion from a deliberately devised verbal parallelism that is utterly specious. Racism has no rational ground whatever. Differing degrees of respect or concern for humans for no other reason than that they are members of different races is an injustice totally without foundation in the nature of the races themselves. Racists, even if acting on the basis of mistaken factual beliefs, do grave moral wrong precisely because there is no morally relevant distinction among the races. The supposition of such differences has led to outright horror. The same is true of the sexes, neither sex being entitled by right to greater respect or concern than the other. No dispute here.

Between species of animate life, however—between (for example) humans on the one hand and cats or rats on the other—the morally relevant differences are enormous, and almost universally appreciated. Humans engage in moral reflection; humans are morally autonomous; humans are members of moral communities, recognizing just claims against their own interest. Human beings do have rights; theirs is a moral status very different from that of cats or rats.

I am a speciesist. Speciesism is not merely plausible; it is essential for right conduct, because those who will not make the morally relevant distinctions among species are almost certain, in consequence, to misapprehend their true obligations. The analogy between speciesism and racism is insidious. Every sensitive moral judgment requires that the differing natures of the beings to whom obligations are owed be considered. If all forms of animate life—or vertebrate animal life?—must be treated equally, and if therefore in evaluating a research program the pains of a rodent count equally with the pains of a human, we are forced to conclude (1) that neither humans nor rodents possess rights, or (2) that rodents possess all the rights that humans possess. Both alternatives are absurd. Yet one or the other must be swallowed if the moral equality of all species is to be defended.

Humans owe to other humans a degree of moral regard that cannot be owed to animals. Some humans take on the obligation to support and heal others, both humans and animals, as a principal duty in their lives; the fulfillment of that duty may require the sacrifice of many animals. If biomedical investigators abandon the effective pursuit of their professional objectives because they are convinced that they may not do to animals what the service of humans requires, they will fail, objectively, to do their duty. Refusing to recognize the moral differences among species is a sure path to calamity. (The largest animal rights group in the country is People for the Ethical Treatment of Animals; its co-director, Ingrid Newkirk, calls research using animal subjects "fascism" and "supremacism." "Animal liberationists do not separate out the human animal," she says, "so there is no rational basis for saying that a human being has special rights. A rat is a pig is a dog is a boy. They're all mammals.") [17]

Those who claim to base their objection to the use of animals in biomedical research on their reckoning of the net pleasures and pains produced make a second error, equally grave. Even if it were true—as it is surely not—that the pains of all animate beings must be counted equally, a cogent utilitarian calculation requires that we weigh all the consequences of the use, and of the nonuse, of animals in laboratory research. Critics relying (however mistakenly) on animal rights may claim to ignore the beneficial results of such research, rights being trump cards to which interest and advantage must give way. But an argument that is explicitly framed in terms of interest and benefit for all over the long run must attend also to the disadvantageous consequences of not using animals in research, and to all the achievements attained and attainable only through their use. The sum of the benefits of their use is utterly beyond quantification. The elimination of horrible disease, the increase of longevity, the avoidance of great pain, the saving of lives, and the improvement of the quality of lives (for humans and for animals) achieved through research using animals is so incalculably great that the argument of these critics, systematically pursued, establishes not their conclusion but its reverse: to refrain from using animals in biomedical research is, on utilitarian grounds, morally wrong.

When balancing the pleasures and pains resulting from the use of animals in research, we must not fail to place on the scales the terrible pains that would have resulted, would be suffered now, and would long continue had animals not been used. Every disease eliminated, every vaccine developed, every method of pain relief devised, every surgical procedure invented, every prosthetic device implanted—indeed, virtually every modern medical therapy—is due, in part or in whole, to experimentation using animals. Nor may we ignore, in the balancing process, the predictable gains in human (and animal) well-being that are probably achievable in the future but that will not be achieved if the decision is made now to desist from such research or to curtail it.

Medical investigators are seldom insensitive to the distress their work may cause animal subjects. Opponents of research using animals are frequently insensitive to the cruelty of the results of the restrictions they would impose.[18] Untold numbers of human beings—real persons, although not now identifiable—would suffer grievously as the consequence of this well-meaning but shortsighted tenderness. If the morally relevant differences between humans and animals are borne in mind, and if all relevant considerations are weighed, the calculation of long-term consequences must give overwhelming support for biomedical research using animals.

# Concluding Remarks

## Substitution

The humane treatment of animals requires that we desist from experimenting on them if we can accomplish the same result using alternative methods—*in vitro* experimentation, computer simulation, or others. Critics of some experiments using animals rightly make this point.

It would be a serious error to suppose, however, that alternative techniques could soon be used in most research now using live animal subjects. No other methods now on the horizon or perhaps ever to be available—can fully replace the testing of a drug, a procedure, or a vaccine, in live organisms. The flood of new medical possibilities being opened by the successes of recombinant DNA technology will turn to a trickle if testing on live animals is forbidden. When initial trials entail great risks, there may be no forward movement whatever without the use of live animal subjects. In seeking knowledge that may prove critical in later clinical applications, the unavailability of animals for inquiry may spell complete stymie. In the United States, federal regulations require the testing of new drugs and other products on animals, for efficacy and safety, before human beings are exposed to them.[19] We would not want it otherwise.

Every advance in medicine—every new drug, new operation, new therapy of any kind—must sooner or later be tried on a living being for the first time. That trial, controlled or uncontrolled, will be an experiment. The subject of that experiment, if it is not an animal, will be a human being. Prohibiting the use of live animals in biomedical research, therefore, or sharply restricting it, must result either in the blockage of much valuable research or in the replacement of animal subjects with human subjects. These are the consequences—unacceptable to most reasonable persons—of not using animals in research.

## Reduction

Should we not at least reduce the use of animals in biomedical research? No, we should increase it, to avoid when feasible the use of humans as experimental subjects. Medical investigations putting human subjects at some risk are numerous and greatly varied. The risks run in such experiments are usually unavoidable, and (thanks to earlier experiments on animals) most such risks are minimal or moderate. But some experimental risks are substantial.

When an experimental protocol that entails substantial risk to humans comes before an institutional review board, what response is appropriate? The investigation, we may suppose, is promising and deserves support, so long as its human subjects are protected against unnecessary dangers. May not the investigators be fairly asked, Have you done all that you can to eliminate risk to humans by the extensive testing of that drug, that procedure, or that device on animals? To achieve maximal safety for humans we are right to require thorough experimentation on animal subjects before humans are involved.

Opportunities to increase human safety in this way are commonly missed; trials in which risks may be shifted from humans to animals are often not devised, sometimes not even considered. Why? For the investigator, the use of animals as subjects is often more expensive, in money and time, than the use of human subjects. Access to suitable human subjects is often quick and convenient, whereas access to appropriate animal subjects may be awkward, costly, and burdened with red tape. Physician-investigators have often had more experience working with human beings and know precisely where the needed pool of subjects is to be found and how they may be enlisted. Animals, and the procedures for their use, are often less familiar to these investigators. Moreover, the use of animals in place of humans is now more likely to be the target of zealous protests from without. The upshot is that humans are sometimes subjected to risks that animals could have borne, and should have borne, in their place. To maximize the protection of human subjects, I conclude, the wide and imaginative use of live animal subjects should be encouraged rather than discouraged. This enlargement in the use of animals is our obligation.

## Consistency

Finally, inconsistency between the profession and the practice of many who oppose research using animals deserves comment. This frankly *ad hominem* observation aims chiefly to show that a coherent position rejecting the use of animals in medical research imposes costs so high as to be intolerable even to the critics themselves.

One cannot coherently object to the killing of animals in biomedical investigations while continuing to eat them. Anesthetics and thoughtful animal husbandry render the level of actual animal distress in the laboratory generally lower than that in the abattoir. So long as death and discomfort do not substantially differ in the two contexts, the consistent objector must not only refrain from all eating of animals but also protest as vehemently against others eating them as against others experimenting on them. No less vigorously must the critic object to the wearing of animal hides in coats and shoes, to employment in any industrial enterprise that uses animal parts, and to any commercial development that will cause death or distress to animals.

Killing animals to meet human needs for food, clothing, and shelter is judged entirely reasonable by most persons. The ubiquity of these uses and the virtual universality of moral support for them confront the opponent of research using animals with an inescapable difficulty. How can the many common uses of animals be judged morally worthy, while their use in scientific investigation is judged unworthy?

The number of animals used in research is but the tiniest fraction of the total used to satisfy assorted human appetites. That these appetites, often base and satisfiable in other ways, morally justify the far larger consumption of animals, whereas the quest for improved human health and understanding cannot justify the far smaller, is wholly implausible. Aside from the numbers of animals involved, the distinction in terms of worthiness of use, drawn with regard to any single animal, is not defensible. A given sheep is surely not more justifiably used to put lamb chops on the supermarket counter than to serve in testing a new contraceptive or a new prosthetic device. The needless killing of animals is wrong; if the common killing of them for our food or convenience is right, the less common but more humane uses of animals in the service of medical science are certainly not less right.

Scrupulous vegetarianism, in matters of food, clothing, shelter, commerce, and recreation, and in all other spheres, is the only fully coherent position the critic may adopt. At great human cost, the lives of fish and crustaceans must also be protected, with equal vigor, if speciesism has been forsworn. A very few consistent critics adopt this position. It is the reductio ad absurdum of the rejection of moral distinctions between animals and human beings.

Opposition to the use of animals in research is based on arguments of two different kinds— those relying on the alleged rights of animals and those relying on the consequences for animals. I have argued that arguments of both kinds must fail. We surely do have obligations to animals, but they have, and can have, no rights against us on which research can infringe. In calculating the consequences of animal research, we must weigh all the long-term benefits of the results achieved—to animals and to humans—and in that calculation we must not assume the moral equality of all animate species.

## Endnotes

1. T. Regan, *The Case for Animal Rights* (Berkeley, CA: University of California Press, 1983).

2. P. Singer, *Animal Liberation* (New York: Avon Books, 1977).

3. Augustine (A.D. 397), *Confessions* (New York: Pocketbooks, 1957), bk. 7, pp. 104–126.

4. Aquinas (A.D. 1273), *Summa Theologica* (Philosophic Texts) (New York: Oxford University Press, 1960), pp. 353–366.

5. G. W. F. Hegel (1821), *Philosophy of Right* (London: Oxford University Press, 1952), pp. 105–110.

6. F. H. Bradley, "Why Should I Be Moral?" in *Ethical Theories*, ed. A. I. Melden (New York: Prentice Hall, 1950), pp. 345–359.

7. G. H. Mead (1925), "The Genesis of the Self and Social Control" in *Selected Writings* ed. A. J. Reck (Indianapolis: Bobbs-Merrill, 1964), pp. 264–293.

8. H. A. Prichard (1912), "Does Moral Philosophy Rest on a Mistake?" in *Readings in Ethical Theory*, ed. W. Sellars and J. Hospers (New York: Appleton-Century-Crofts, 1952), pp. 149–163.

9. I. Kant (1785), *Fundamental Principles of the Metaphysic of Morals* (New York: Liberal Arts Press, 1949).

10. B. E. Rollin, *Animal Rights and Human Morality* (Buffalo, NY: Prometheus Books, 1981).

11. [See note 1 and] C. Hoff, "Immoral and Moral Uses of Animals," *New England Journal of Medicine* 302 (1980), 115–118.

12. [See note 11 and] D. Jamieson, "Killing Persons and Other Beings," in *Ethics and Animals*, ed. H. B. Miller and W. H. Williams (Clifton, NJ: Humana Press, 1983), pp. 135–146.

13. B. E. Rollin, *Animal Rights and Human Morality*.

14. P. Singer, "Ten Years of Animal Liberation," *New York Review of Books* 31 (1985), 46–52.

15. J. Bentham, *Introduction to the Principles of Morals and Legislation* (London: Athlone Press, 1970).

16. P. Singer, *Animal Liberation*.

17. K. McCabe, "Who Will Live, Who Will Die?" *Washingtonian*, August 1986, p. 115.

18. P. Singer, *Animal Liberation*.

19. U.S. Code of Federal Regulations, Title 21, Sect. 505(i). Food, Drug, and Cosmetic Regulations. U.S. Code of Federal Regulations, Title 16, Sect. 1500.40–2. Consumer Product Regulations.

# Journal/Discussion Questions

✍ *Have you ever been involved with animal experimentation? Do you know anyone who has been? What moral responses did you (or they) have to such experiments? Would you still be involved in them?*

1. What criteria does Cohen offer for determining whether a being has rights or not? Discuss the extent to which you agree or disagree with Cohen's list of criteria.

2. Why does Cohen believe that "Speciesism . . . is essential for right conduct, because those who will not make the morally relevant distinctions among species are almost certain, in consequence, to misapprehend their true obligations." In what ways will they misapprehend their true obligations? Do you agree here with Cohen's claim?

3. Cohen claims that "Scrupulous vegetarianism, in matters of food, clothing, shelter, commerce, and recreation, and in all other spheres, is the only fully coherent position the critic [of using animals in biomedical research] may adopt." Do you agree with Cohen? Do you think most critics of the use of animals in research would agree?

---

### Gary E. Varner
### "The Prospects for Consensus and Convergence in the Animal Rights Debate"

*Gary E. Varner is an assistant professor in the department of philosophy at Texas A&M University, College Station. He has published widely in the areas of environmental ethics and animal rights.*

*Despite political posturing, both sides in the animal rights debate—the "animal welfarists" and the "animal rightists"—in Varner's eyes have a surprising potential for agreeing at least at the level of policy (convergence), and sometimes even at the level of moral theory (consensus). Peter Singer's utilitarianism is less absolutist than often realized, and allows that animal experimentation may in some (rare and largely hypothetical) cases be justified. Often disagreements turn on empirical rather than moral matters—how much pain animals actually suffer and what benefits actually flow from a particular research project. Even Tom Regan's defense of animal rights recognizes that in some cases human interests clearly take precedence over animal interests. Varner concludes with a cautionary note about extremist statements on both sides of this debate.*

Gary E. Varner, "Prospects for Consensus and Convergence in the Animal Rights Debate," *Hastings Center Report* 24, no. 1 (January 1994). Copyright © 1994, The Hastings Center. Reprinted by permission of the publisher and the author.

## As You Read, Consider This:

1. How are animals welfarists distinguished—both philosophically and politically—from animal rightists?
2. Varner distinguishes between the approaches of Peter Singer and Tom Regan. What is the most important philosophical basis for distinguishing their positions?

Controversies over the use of nonhuman animals (henceforth animals) for science, nutrition, and recreation are often presented as clear-cut standoffs, with little or no common ground between opposing factions and, consequently, with little or no possibility for consensus-formation. As a philosopher studying these controversies, my sense is that the apparent intransigence of opposing parties is more a function of political posturing than theoretical necessity, and that continuing to paint the situation as a clear-cut standoff serves the interests of neither side. A critical look at the philosophical bases of the animal rights movement reveals surprising potential for convergence (agreement at the level of policy despite disagreement at the level of moral theory) and, in some cases, consensus (agreement at both levels).[1] Recognizing this should make defenders of animal research take animal rights views more seriously and could refocus the animal rights debate in a constructive way.

In response to the growth of the animal rights movement, animal researchers have begun to distinguish between animal rights views and animal welfare views, but they have not drawn the distinction the way a philosopher would. Researchers typically stress two differences between animal welfarists and animal rightists. First, welfarists argue for reforms in research involving animals, whereas rightists argue for the total abolition of such research. Second, welfarists work within the system, whereas rightists advocate using theft, sabotage, or even violence to achieve their ends. A more philosophical account of the animal rights/animal welfare distinction cuts the pie very differently, revealing that many researchers agree with some animal rights advocates at the level of moral theory, and that, even where they differ dramatically at the level of moral theory, there is some potential for convergence at the level of policy.

## Animal Welfare: The Prospects for Consensus

Peter Singer's *Animal Liberation* is the acknowledged Bible of the animal rights movement. Literally millions of people have been moved to vegetarianism or animal activism as a result of reading this book. PETA (People for the Ethical Treatment of Animals) distributed the first edition of the book as a membership premium, and the number of copies in print has been cited as a measure of growth in the animal rights movement. However, Singer wrote *Animal Liberation* for popular consumption, and in it he intentionally avoided discussion of complex philosophical issues.[2] In particular, he avoided analyzing the concepts of "rights" and "harm," and these concepts are crucial to drawing the animal rights/animal welfare distinction in philosophical terms.

In *Animal Liberation*, Singer spoke loosely of animals having moral "rights," but all that he intended by this was that animals (at least some of them) have some basic moral standing and that there are right and wrong ways of treating them. In later, more philosophically rigorous work—summarized in his *Practical Ethics*, a second edition of which has just been issued[3]—he explicitly eschews the term rights, noting that, as a thoroughgoing utilitarian, he must deny not only that animals have moral rights, but also that human beings do.

When moral philosophers speak of an individual "having moral rights," they mean something much more specific than that the individual has some basic moral standing and that there are right and wrong ways of treating him or her. Although there is much controversy as to the specifics, there is general agreement on this: to attribute moral rights to an individual is to assert that the individual has some kind of special moral dignity, the cash value of which is that certain things cannot justifiably be done to him or her (or it) for the sake of benefit to others. For this reason, moral rights have been characterized as "trump cards" against utilitarian arguments. Utilitarian arguments are based on aggregate benefits and aggregate harms. Specifically, utilitarianism is the view that right actions maximize aggregate happiness. In principle, nothing is inherently or intrinsically wrong, according to a utilitarian; any action could be justified under some possible circumstances. One way of characterizing rights views in ethics, by contrast, is that there are some things which, regardless of the consequences, it is simply wrong to do to individuals, and that moral rights single out these things.

Although a technical and stipulative definition of rights, this philosophical usage reflects a familiar concept. In day-to-day discussions, appeals to individuals' rights are used to assert, in effect, that there is a limit to what individuals can be forced to do, or to the harm that may be inflicted upon them, for the benefit of others. So the philosophical usage of rights talk reflects the common-sense view that there are limits to what we can justifiably do to an individual for the benefit of society.

To defend the moral rights of animals would be to claim that certain ways of treating animals cannot be justified on utilitarian grounds. But in *Practical Ethics* Peter Singer explicitly adopts a utilitarian stance for dealing with our treatment of nonhuman animals. So the author of "the Bible of the animal rights movement" is not an animal rights theorist at all, and the self-proclaimed advocates of animal welfare are appealing to precisely the same tradition in ethics as is Singer. Both believe that it is permissible to sacrifice (even involuntarily) the life of one individual for the benefit of others, where the aggregated benefits to others clearly outweigh the costs to that individual. (At least they agree on this as far as animals are concerned. Singer is a thoroughgoing utilitarian, whereas my sense is that most animal researchers are utilitarians when it comes to animals, but rights theorists when it comes to humans.)

Many researchers also conceive of harm to animals very similarly to Singer, at least where nonmammalian animals are concerned. In *Animal Liberation*, Singer employs a strongly hedonistic conception of harm. He admits that the morality of killing is more complicated than that of inflicting pain (p. 17) and that although pain is pain wherever it occurs, this "does not imply that all lives are of equal worth" (p. 20). This should be stressed, because researchers commonly say that according to animal rights philosophies, of which Singer's is their paradigm, all animals' lives are of equal value. No fair reading of Singer's *Animal Liberation* would yield this conclusion, let alone any fair reading of *Practical Ethics*, where he devotes four chapters to the question of killing.

The morality of killing is complicated by competing conceptions of harm. In *Animal Liberation*, Singer leaves the question of killing in the background and uses a strongly hedonistic conception of animal welfare. He argues that the conclusions reached in the book, including the duty to refrain from eating animals, "flow from the principle of minimizing suffering alone" (p. 21). To conceive of harm hedonistically is to say that harm consists in felt pain or lost opportunities for pleasure. For a utilitarian employing a hedonistic conception of harm, individuals are replaceable in the following sense. If an individual lives a pleasant life, dies a painless death, and is replaced by an individual leading a similarly pleasant life, there is no loss of value in the world. Agriculturalists appear to be thinking like hedonistic utilitarians when they defend humane slaughter in similar terms. Researchers employ a similarly hedonistic conception of harm when they argue that if all pain is eliminated from an experimental protocol then, ethically speaking, there is nothing left to be concerned about.

Singer conceives of harm to "lower" animals in hedonistic terms and thus agrees with these researchers and agriculturalists. He even acknowledges that the replaceability thesis could be used to defend some forms of animal agriculture, although not intensive poultry systems, where the birds hardly live happy lives or die painless deaths. However, Singer argues that it is implausible to conceive of harm in hedonistic terms when it comes to "self-conscious individuals, leading their own lives and wanting to go on living" (p. 125), and he argues that all mammals are self-conscious in this sense.

Singer equates being self-conscious with having forward-looking desires, especially the desire to go on living. He argues that such self-conscious individuals are not replaceable, because when an individual with forward-looking desires dies, those desires go unsatisfied even if another individual is born and has similar desires satisfied. With regard to self-conscious individuals, Singer is still a utilitarian, but he is a preference utilitarian rather than a hedonistic utilitarian. Singer cites evidence to demonstrate that the great apes are self-conscious in his sense (pp. 11–16) and states, without saying what specific research leads him to this conclusion, that neither fish nor chickens are (pp. 95, 133), but that "a case can be made, though with varying degrees of confidence," that all mammals are self-conscious (p. 132).

It is easy to disagree with Singer about the range of self-consciousness, as he conceives of it, in the animal kingdom.[4] Probably most mammals have forward-looking desires, but the future to which they look is doubtless a very near one. Cats probably think about what to do in the next moment to achieve a desired result, but I doubt that they have projects (long-term, complicated desires) of the kind suggested by saying that they are "leading their own lives and wanting to go on living."

However, even if we grant Singer the claim that all mammals have projects, so long as we remain utilitarians this just means that research on mammals carries a higher burden of justification than does research on "lower" animals like reptiles or insects, a point many researchers would readily grant. A preference utilitarian is still a utilitarian, and in at least some cases, a utilitarian must agree that experimentation is justified.

In the following passage from *Practical Ethics*, Singer stresses just this point:

> In the past, argument about animal experimentation has often . . . been put in absolutist terms: would the opponent of experimentation be prepared to let thousands die from a terrible disease that could be cured by experimenting on one animal? This is a purely hypothetical question, since experiments do not have such dramatic results, but as long as its hypothetical nature is clear, I think the question should be answered affirmatively—in other words, if one, or even a dozen animals had to suffer experiments in order to save thousands, I would think it right and in accordance with equal consideration of interests that they should do so. This, at any rate, is the answer a utilitarian must give. (p. 67)

Singer doubts that most experiments are justified, not because he believes experimentation is wrong simpliciter, but because he doubts that the benefits to humans significantly outweigh the costs to the animals. In the pages preceding the passage just quoted, Singer cites examples of experiments he thinks cannot plausibly be said "to serve vital medical purposes": testing of new shampoos and food colorings, armed forces experiments on the effects of radiation on combat performance, and H. E Harlow's maternal deprivation experiments. "In these cases, and many others like them," he says, "the benefits to humans are either nonexistent or uncertain, while the losses to members of other species are certain and real" (p. 66).

So the disagreement between Singer and the research establishment is largely empirical, about how likely various kinds of research are to lead to important human benefits. Researchers often argue that we cannot be expected to know ahead of time which lines of research will yield dramatic benefits. Critics respond that these same scientists serve on grant review boards, whose function is to permit funding agencies to make such decisions all the time. Here I want only to emphasize that this is an empirical dispute that cannot be settled a priori or as a matter of moral theory. One of the limitations of utilitarianism is that its application requires very detailed knowledge about the effects of various actions or policies. When it comes to utilitarian justifications for animal research, the probability—and Singer is correct that it is never a certainty—that various lines of research will save or significantly improve human lives must be known or estimated before anything meaningful can be said. Singer is convinced that most research will not meet this burden of proof; most researchers are convinced of just the opposite.

## Animal Rights: The Prospects for Convergence

Most animal researchers agree to a surprising extent with the Moses of the animal rights movement. Their basic ethical principles are the same (at least where nonhuman animals are concerned), and they apply to all animals the same conception of harm which Singer applies to all animals except mammals. Where they disagree with Singer is at the level of policy; they see the same ethical theory implying different things in practice. Dramatic disagreement at the level of moral theory emerges only when we turn to the views of Tom Regan, whose ethical principles and conception of harm are dramatically different from Singer's and the researchers'.

Regan's *The Case for Animal Rights*[5] is a lengthy and rigorous defense of a true animal rights position. It is impossible to do justice to the argument of a 400-page book in a few paragraphs, so here I will simply state the basic destination Regan reaches, in order to examine its implications for animal research.

For Regan, there is basically one moral right: the right not to be harmed on the grounds that doing so benefits others, and all individuals who can be harmed in the relevant way have this basic right. Regan conceives of harm as a diminution in the capacity to form and satisfy desires, and he argues that all animals who are capable of having desires have this basic moral right not to be harmed. On Regan's construal, losing an arm is more of a harm than stubbing one's toe (because it frustrates more of one's desires), but death is always the worst harm an individual can suffer because it completely destroys one's capacity to form and satisfy desires. As to which animals have desires, Regan explicitly defends only the claim that all mentally normal mammals of a year or more have desires, but he says that he does this to avoid the controversy over "line drawing," that is, saying precisely how far down the phylogenetic scale one must go to find animals that are incapable of having desires. Regan is confident that at least all mammals and birds have desires, but acknowledges that the analogical evidence for possession of desires becomes progressively weaker as we turn to herpetofauna (reptiles and amphibians), fish, and then invertebrates.[6]

Regan defends two principles to use in deciding whom to harm where it is impossible not to harm someone who has moral rights: the miniride and worse-off principles. The worse-off principle applies where noncomparable harms are involved, and it requires us to avoid harming the worse-off individual. Regan's discussion of this principle makes it clear that for him, harm is measured in absolute, rather than relative terms. If harm were measured relative to the individual's original capacity to form and satisfy desires, rather than in absolute terms, then death would be uniformly catastrophic wherever it occurs. But Regan reasons that although death is always the greatest harm which any individual can suffer (because it forecloses all of that individual's opportunities for desire formation and satisfaction), death to a normal human being is noncomparably worse than death to any nonhuman animal, because a normal human being's capacity to form and satisfy desires is so much greater. To illustrate the use of the worse-off principle, Regan imagines that five individuals, four humans, and a dog are in a lifeboat that can support only four of them. Since death to any of the human beings would be noncomparably worse than death to the dog, the worse-off principle applies, and it requires us to avoid harming the human beings, who stand to lose the most.

The miniride principle applies to cases where comparable harms are involved, and it requires us to harm the few rather than the many. Regan admits that, where it applies, this principle yields the same conclusions as the principle of utility, but he emphasizes that the reasoning is nonutilitarian. The focus, he says, is on individuals rather than the aggregate. What the miniride principle instructs us to do is minimize the overriding of individuals' rights, rather than to maximize aggregate happiness. To illustrate the miniride principle's application, Regan imagines that a runaway mine train must be sent down one of two shafts, and that fifty miners would be killed by sending it down the first shaft but only one by sending it down the second. Since the harms that the various individuals in the example would suffer are comparable (only humans are involved, and all are faced with death), the miniride principle applies, and we are obligated to send the runaway train down the second shaft.

Regan argues that the rights view (as he labels his position) calls for the total abolition of animal research. In terms of the basic contrast drawn above between rights views and utilitarianism, it is easy to see why one would think this. The fundamental tenet of rights views is opposition to utilitarian justifications for harming individuals, and as we saw above, researchers' justification for animal research is utilitarian. They argue that by causing a relatively small number of individuals to suffer and die, a relatively large number of individuals can live or have their lives significantly improved.

However, Regan's worse-off principle, coupled with his conception of harm, would seem to imply that at least some research is not only permissible but required, even on a true animal rights view. For as we just saw, Regan believes that death for a normal human is noncomparably worse than death for any nonhuman animal. So if we knew that by performing fatal research on a given number of nonhuman animals we could save even one human life, the worse-off principle would apply, and it would require us to perform the research. In the lifeboat case referred to above, Regan emphasizes that where the worse-off principle applies, the numbers do not matter. He says:

Let the number of dogs be as large as one likes; suppose they number a million; and suppose the lifeboat will support only four survivors. Then the rights view still implies that, special considerations apart, the million dogs should be thrown overboard and the four humans saved. To attempt to reach a contrary judgment will inevitably involve one in aggregative i.e., utilitarian considerations. (p. 325)

The same reasoning, in a hypothetical case like that described by Singer (where we know, with absolute certainty, that one experiment will save human lives) would imply that the experiment should be performed.

One complication is that the empirical dispute over the likelihood of significant human benefits emerging from various lines of research, which makes utilitarian justifications of experimentation so complex, will reappear here. Having admitted that some research is justified, animal rights advocates would doubtless continue to disagree with researchers over which research this is. Nevertheless, the foregoing discussion illustrates how the implications of a true animal rights view can converge with those of researchers animal welfare philosophy. Even someone who attributes moral rights in the philosophical sense to animals, and whose ethical theory thus differs dramatically from most animal researchers', could think that some medical research is justified. This warrants stressing, because researchers commonly say things like, "According to animal rightists, a rat is a pig is a dog is a boy," and, "Animal rightists want to do away with all uses of animals, including life-saving medical research." However, no fair reading of either Singer or Regan would yield the conclusion that they believe that a rat's or a pig's life is equal to a normal human's. And, consequently, it is possible for someone thinking with Singer's or Regan's principles to accept research that actually saves human lives.

It is possible, but Regan himself continues to oppose all animal research to benefit humans. His basis is not the worse-off principle, but that the principle applies, "special considerations apart." One of those considerations is that "risks are not morally transferrable to those who do not voluntarily choose to take them," and this, he claims, blocks application of the worse-off principle to the case of medical experimentation (p. 377). For example, subjects used to screen a new vaccine run higher risks of contracting the disease when researchers intentionally expose them to it. Humans can voluntarily accept these risks, but animals cannot. Consequently, the only kind of research on "higher" animals (roughly, vertebrates) that Regan will accept is that which tests a potential cure for a currently incurable disease on animals that have already acquired the disease of their own accord.

However, most people believe that in at least some cases, we can justifiably transfer risks without first securing the agreement of those to whom the risks are transferred. For instance, modifying price supports can redistribute the financial risks involved in farming, and changing draft board policies in time of war can redistribute the risk of being killed in defense of one's country. Yet most people believe such transfers are justifiable even if involuntary. In these cases, however, the individuals among whom risks are redistributed are all members of a polis through which, arguably, they give implicit consent to the policies in question. Still, in some cases there cannot plausibly be said to be even implicit consent. When we go to war, for instance, we impose dramatic risks on thousands or even millions of people who have no political influence in our country. But if the war is justified, so too, presumably, are the involuntarily imposed risks.

# The Prospects for Conversation

It has not been my purpose in this paper to decide which particular forms of experimentation are morally justifiable, so I will not further pursue a response to Regan's abolitionist argument. My goal has been to refocus the animal rights debate by emphasizing its philosophical complexity. The question is far more complicated than is suggested by simplistic portrayals by many researchers and in the popular media.

According to the common stereotype, an animal rights advocate wants to eliminate all animal research and is a vegetarian who even avoids wearing leather. But the first "serious attempt . . . to assess the accuracy of" this stereotype, a survey of about 600 animal activists attending the June 1990 "March for Animal Rights" in Washington, D.C., found that nearly half of all activists believe the animal rights movement should not focus on animal research as its top priority; over a third eat red meat, poultry, or seafood; and 40 percent wear leather.[7] I have often heard agriculturalists and scientists say that it is hypocritical for an animal rights advocate to eat any kind of meat, wear leather, or use medicines that have been developed using animal models. But it would only be hypocritical if there were a single, monolithic animal rights philosophy that unambiguously ruled them all out.

In this essay, I have stressed the philosophical diversity underlying the animal rights movement. The "animal rights philosophies" of which many researchers are so contemptuous run the philosophical gamut from a utilitarianism very similar to their own to a true animal rights view that is quite different from their own. On some of these views, certain kinds of animal agriculture are permissible, but even on a true animal rights view like Regan's, it is possible to endorse some uses of animals, including experimentation that is meaningfully tied to saving human lives.

Continuing to paint all advocates of animal rights as unreasoning, antiscience lunatics will not make that movement go away, any more than painting all scientists who use animal models as Nazis bent on torturing the innocent will make animal research go away. Animal protection movements have surfaced and then disappeared in the past, but today's animal rights movement is squarely grounded in two major traditions in moral philosophy and, amid the stable affluence of a modern, industrialized nation like the United States, cannot be expected to go away. By the same token, twentieth-century medical research has dramatically proven its capacity to save lives and to improve the quality of human life, and it cannot be expected to go away either. So the reality is going to involve some level of some uses of animals, including some kinds of medical research.

A more philosophical understanding of the animal welfare/animal rights distinction can help replace the current politics of confrontation with a genuine conversation. Researchers who understand the philosophical bases of the animal rights movement will recognize similarities with their own views and can rest assured that genuinely important research will not be opposed by most advocates of animal rights. In the last analysis, what animal rights views do is increase the burden of proof the defenders of research must meet, and this is as it should be. Too often, pain and suffering have been understood to be "necessary" whenever a desired benefit could not be achieved without them, without regard to how important the benefit in question was.[8]

When it comes to research on animals, "academic freedom" cannot mean freedom to pursue any line of research one pleases, even in the arena of medical research. In most areas of research, someone who spends her career doing trivial work wastes only the taxpayers' money. But a scientist who spends his career doing trivial experiments on animals can waste the lives of hundreds or even thousands of sentient creatures. There will be increasing public oversight of laboratory research on animals, because major traditions in Western ethical theory support at least basic moral consideration for all sentient creatures. Researchers who react by adopting a siege mentality, refusing to disclose information on research and refusing to talk to advocates of animal rights, only reinforce the impression that they have something to hide.

### Endnotes

1. I owe this account of the consensus/convergence distinction to Bryan G. Norton, *Toward Unity among Environmentalists* (New York: Oxford University Press, 1991), pp. 237–243.

2. Peter Singer, *Animal Liberation*, 2nd ed. (Avon Books: 1990), pp. x–xi.

3. Peter Singer, *Practical Ethics*, 2nd ed. (New York: Cambridge University Press, 1993).

4. In any case, as Raymond Frey has pointed out, it is not clear that having forward-looking desires is a necessary condition for being self-conscious. R. G. Frey, *Rights, Killing, and Suffering: Moral Vegetarianism and Applied Ethics* (Oxford: Basil Blackwell, 1983), p. 163.

5. Tom Regan, *The Case for Animal Rights* (Berkeley and Los Angeles: University of California Press, 1983).

6. This evidence is reviewed in my *In Nature's Interests? Interests, Animal Rights, and Environmental Ethics*, in manuscript.

7. S. Plous, "An Attitude Survey of Animal Rights Activists," *Psychological Science* 2 (May 1991), 194–196.

8. Susan Finsen, "On Moderation," in *Interpretation and Explanation in the Study of Animal Behavior*, ed. Marc Bekoff and Dale Jamieson, vol. 2 (Boulder: Westview Press, 1990), pp. 394–419.

## Journal/Discussion Questions

✍ *In your own life, do you find yourself looking for some middle ground between the animal rights position and those that Varner describes as "animal welfarists"? Discuss.*

1. Animal rights activists are sometimes portrayed as fanatics, yet Varner suggests that they are a much more diverse group than many outsiders recognize. What basis does he offer for this assertion? Do you think that animal rights activists are—as Carl Cohen asserted in a previous selection—inconsistent if they are not strict vegetarians?

2. According to Varner, is there a morally relevant difference between experimentation on mammals versus experimentation on nonmammals? Where do Singer and Regan stand on this issue? In what ways do you agree or disagree with them? Discuss your reasons.

3. Explain the *miniride* and the *worse-off principles*. Under what circumstances is each applicable? How do these affect Regan's views on animal experimentation?

# QUESTIONS FOR DISCUSSION AND REVIEW

## Where Do You Stand Now?

### Instructions

You have already answered the following questions in your moral problems self-quiz at the beginning of this book. Now that you have studied the material in this section, take a moment to answer the same questions again.

| | *Strongly Agree* | *Agree* | *Undecided* | *Disagree* | *Strongly Disagree* | |
|---|---|---|---|---|---|---|
| | | | | | | ***Chapter 9: Living Together with Animals*** |
| 41. | ❑ | ❑ | ❑ | ❑ | ❑ | There's nothing morally wrong with eating veal. |
| 42. | ❑ | ❑ | ❑ | ❑ | ❑ | It's morally permissible to cause animals pain in order to do medical research that benefits human beings. |
| 43. | ❑ | ❑ | ❑ | ❑ | ❑ | All animals have the same moral standing. |
| 44. | ❑ | ❑ | ❑ | ❑ | ❑ | Zoos are a morally good thing. |
| 45. | ❑ | ❑ | ❑ | ❑ | ❑ | There is nothing morally wrong with hunting. |

Compare your answers to the present self-quiz with the answers to the initial self-quiz. How, if at all, have your answers changed? How have the *reasons* for your answers changed?

## Journal/Discussion Questions

✍ *In light of the material in this chapter, how have your views changed on the ethical treatment of animals in regard to such issues as keeping pets, eating meat, wearing fur and animal products (such as leather shoes), using animals for testing shampoos, and using animals for medical research?*

1. In light of all the readings in this chapter, what changes (if any) do you think we should make in the ways in which animals are treated in our society? Why should people be motivated to make these changes if they involve some degree of sacrifice on their part?

2. If we grant animals rights, then we are accepting the general principle that nonhumans can have rights. One of the issues in the abortion debate has been the claim that the fetus is not (yet) a human being and thus does not have rights. If animals have rights, does this have moral implications for the rights of fetuses?

3. Drawing on the readings in this and the previous chapter, discuss the relationship between animals rights, vegetarianism,

and world hunger. To what extent could problems of world hunger be solved by vegetarianism, an option that would at the same time reduce animal suffering? How would a utilitarian answer this question? How do you answer it?

# FOR FURTHER READING:
# A BIBLIOGRAPHICAL GUIDE
# TO LIVING WITH ANIMALS

## Bibliographies

See Charles Magel, *A Bibliography of Animal Rights and Related Matters* (Washington, DC: University Press of America, 1981); and his *Keyguide to Information Sources on Animal Rights* (Jefferson, NC: McFarland, 1989).

## Journals

In addition to the standard journals in ethics discussed in the bibliographical guide at the end of Chapter 1, there are two journals devoted solely to issues related to animals: *Ethics and Animals* and *Between the Species.*

## Survey Articles

Tom Regan's "Treatment of Animals," in *Encyclopedia of Ethics*, ed. Lawrence Becker (New York: Garland, 1992), vol. I, pp. 42–46 provides an excellent, short survey of the principal ethical issues surrounding the treatment of animals; it includes a bibliography. Lori Gruen's "Animals," in *A Companion to Ethics*, ed. Peter Singer (Oxford: Blackwell, 1991), pp. 343–353 also provides a good summary of these issues along with a bibliography. For a broader social history of the animal rights movement, see "Man's Mirror; History of Animal Rights," *The Economist* 321, no. 7733 (November 16, 1991), pp. 21 ff.

## Anthologies

There are a number of excellent anthologies dealing with issues of the moral status of animals. *Animal Rights: Opposing Viewpoints*, ed. Janelle Rohr (San Diego: Greenhaven Press, 1989) contains an excellent collection of short articles; it also includes a list of organizations involved in the animal rights issue and how to contact them. *Animal Rights and Welfare*, ed. Jeanne Williams (New York: H. W. Wilson Company, 1991), in the series The Reference Shelf, vol. 63, no. 4, is a well-edited, short (168 pages) collection of short and often popular articles on the issues of animal rights, animals in research, and changes in the animal rights movement. *Ethics and Animals*, ed. Harlan B. Miller and William H. Williams (Clifton, NJ: Humana Press, 1983) is an excellent anthology of philosophical articles by well-known philosophers (including Tom Regan, Jan Narveson, Annette Baier, Bernard Rollin, Dale Jamieson, Lawrence Becker, James Rachels, R. G. Frey, and many others) and includes a very good bibliography. *On the Fifth Day: Animal Rights and Human Ethics*, ed. Richard Knowles Morriw and Michael W. Fox (Washington, DC: Acropolis Books, 1978) is volume sponsored by the Humane Society of the United States and contains twelve essays on the moral status of animals and a statement of the Principles of the Humane Society. *The Animal Rights/Environmental Ethics Debate*, ed. Eugene C. Hargrove (Albany: State University of New York Press, 1992) contains eleven very good articles dealing specifically with the question of the relationship between animal rights issues and issues about environmental ethics. *Animal Experimentation: The Moral Issues*, ed. Robert M. Baird and Stuart E. Rosenbaum (Buffalo, NY: Prometheus Books, 1991) contains fifteen articles on animal rights and experimentation and a short bibliography. Also see R. G. Frey, *Rights, Killing, and Suffering: Moral Vegetarianism and Applied Ethics* (Oxford: Basil Blackwell, 1983); *Animal Sacrifices: Religious Perspectives on the Use of Animals in Science*, ed. Tom Regan (Philadelphia: Temple University Press, 1986); *In Defence of Animals*, ed. Peter Singer (New York: Blackwell, 1985); and *Animals' Rights: A Symposium*, ed. David Paterson and Richard Ryder (Fontwell, Sussex: Centaur, 1979). Tom Regan and Peter Singer co-edited *Animal Rights and Human Obligations* (Englewood Cliffs, NJ: Prentice Hall, 1976). Peter Singer's *Ethics* (New York: Oxford, 1994) is not an anthology about animal rights, but rather a very interesting anthology about ethics *from the standpoint of* a strong advocate of animal rights.

## Single-Author Works

Although there are certainly some early works that defended the rights of animals, such as Lewis Gompertz's *Moral Inquiries on the Situation of Man and of Brutes* (1824) and Henry S. Salt, *Animals' Rights* (1892), it was not until the last three decades that strong defenses of animal rights gained significant ground. Peter Singer's *Animal Liberation*, now in its second edition (New York: Avon Books, 1990), first appeared in 1976. Also see his *Practical Ethics*, 2nd ed. (New York: Cambridge University Press, 1993). Equally influential has been the work of Tom Regan, whose *The Case for Animal Rights* (Berkeley, Calif.: University of California Press, 1983) and *The Thee Generation: Reflections on the Coming Revolution* (Philadelphia: Temple University Press, 1991), a collection of his recent essays, including "Christians Are What Christians Eat," have both had a wide impact. Mary Midgley, *Animals and Why They Matter* (Athens, GA: University of Georgia Press, 1983) is admirably argued, as is James Rachels, *Created from Animals: The Moral Implications of Darwinism* (New York: Oxford, 1991). Bernard E. Rollin, *The Unheeded Cry: Animal Consciousness, Animal Pain, and Science*, with a foreword by Jane Goodall (Oxford: Oxford University Press, 1989) surveys changing attitudes toward animal consciousness and deals specifically with the issue of how we can know and measure animal pain, and his *Animal Rights and Human Morality*, rev. ed. (Buffalo, NY: Prometheus Books, 1992) is a well-written, articulate defense of animal rights. In *The Animals Issue* (Cambridge: Cambridge University Press, 1992), Peter Carruthers defends a contractualist account of ethics and argues that animals do not have direct moral significance. Michael P. T. Leahy's *Against Liberation: Putting Animals in Perspective* (London and New York: Routledge & Kegan Paul, 1991) offers a Wittgensteinian critique of contemporary defenses of animal rights. In *Interests and Rights: The Case Against Animals* (Oxford: Clarendon Press, 1980), R. G. Frey argues that animals are part of the moral community, but that their lives are not of equal value to adult human lives. For a nuanced discussion of these issues by a philosopher whose primary concern is with the concept of rights rather than animals, see Chapter 6 of A. I. Melden, *Rights in Moral Lives* (Berkeley: University of California Press, 1988). Also see Steven F. Sapontzis, *Morals, Reason, and Animals* (Philadelphia: Temple University Press, 1987); Richard Ryder, *Victims of Science* (London: David-Poynter, 1975); Marian Stamp Dawkins, *Animal Suffering: The Science of Animal Welfare* (London and New York: Chapman and

Hall, 1980). In *The Case for Animal Experimentation* (Berkeley: University of California Press, 1986), Michael A. Fox argues that animals lack the critical self-awareness necessary for membership in the moral community; however, he renounced this view almost immediately after publication of the book. See Michael A. Fox, "Animal Experimentation: A Philosopher's Changing Views," *Between the Species*, vol. 3 (1987), 55–60.

Andrew Linzey, in *Animal Rights: A Christian Assessment* (London: SCM Press, 1976) and *Christianity and the Rights of Animals* (New York: Crossroad, 1988), develops a critique of Christianity's neglect of animals and offers a theological foundation for a more positive Christian attitude toward the rights of animals.

## Articles

In addition to the articles contained in the anthologies mentioned above, see Peter Singer's "Ten Years of Animal Liberation," *New York Review of Books* 31 (1985), 46–52; Dale Jamieson, "Utilitarianism and the Morality of Killing," *Philosophical Studies* 45, (1984), 209–221; R. G. Frey, "Moral Standing, the Value of Lives, and Speciesism," *Between the Species* 4, no. 3 (Summer 1988), 191–201; and M. Kheel, "The Liberation of Nature: A Circular Affair," *Environmental Ethics* 7, no. 2 (Summer 1985), 135–149.

# 10

# Environmental Ethics

**Videotape:**

     *Topic:*   Environment Movement Rival

     *Source:*  *Nightline* (February 4, 1992)

     *Anchor:*  Ted Koppel

# EXPERIENTIAL ACCOUNTS

N. Scott Momaday
"Native American Attitudes toward the Environment"

*Mr. Momaday is the author of numerous works, including* House Made of Dawn *(New York: New American Library, 1968) and* The Way to Rainy Mountain *(New York: Ballantine Books, 1969).*

*In an informal context, Mr. Momaday discusses the ways in which Native Americans understand their relationship to the natural environment. He focuses on several key ideas: the ways in which the relationship between human beings and the environment is one of mutual appropriation, the ways in which Native Americans understand what an "appropriate" relationship is between a person and the environment, and the important role played by imagination in understanding these issues.*

## As You Read, Consider This:

1. How does Mr. Momaday use stories to develop his ideas? Would you draw the same conclusions from his stories that Mr. Momaday does?
2. What does Mr. Momaday mean by "appropriateness"?

The first thing to say about the native American perspective on environmental ethics is that there is a great deal to be said. I don't think that anyone has clearly understood yet how the Indian conceives of himself in relation to the landscape. We have formulated certain generalities about that relationship, and the generalities have served a purpose, but they have been rather too general. For example, take the idea that the Indian reveres the earth, thinks of it as the place of his origin and thinks of the sky also in a personal way. These statements are true. But they can also be misleading because they don't indicate anything about the nature of the relationship which is, I think, an intricate thing in itself.

I have done much thinking about the "Indian worldview," as it is sometimes called. And I have had some personal experience of Indian religion and Indian societies within the framework of a worldview. Sometime ago I wrote an essay entitled "An American Land Ethic" in which I tried to talk in certain ways about this idea of a native American attitude toward the landscape. And in that essay I made certain observations. I tried to express the notion first that the native American ethic with respect to the physical world is a matter of reciprocal appropriation: appropriations in which man invests himself in the landscape, and at the same time incorporates the landscape into his own most fundamental experience. That suggests a dichotomy, or a paradox, and I think it is a paradox. It is difficult to understand a relationship which is defined in these terms, and yet I don't know how better to define it.

Secondly, this appropriation is primarily a matter of the imagination. The appropriation is realized through an act of the imagination which is moral and kind. I mean to say that we are all, I suppose, at the most fundamental level that we imagine ourselves to be. And this is certainly true of the American Indian. If you want a definition, you would not go, I hope, to the stereotype which has burdened the American Indian for many years. He is not that befeathered spectacle who is always chasing John Wayne across the silver screen. Rather, he is someone who thinks of himself in a particular way and his idea comprehends his relationship to the physical world, among other things. He imagines himself in terms of that relationship and others. And it is that act of the imagination, that moral act of the imagination, which I think constitutes his understanding of the physical world.

Thirdly, this imagining, this understanding of the relationship between man and the landscape, or man and the physical world, man and nature, proceeds from a racial or cultural experience. I think his attitude toward the landscape has been formulated over a long period of time, and the length of time itself suggests an evolutionary process perhaps instead of a purely rational and decisive experience. Now I am not sure that you can understand me on this point; perhaps I should elaborate. I mean that the Indian has determined himself in his imagination over a period of untold generations. His racial memory is an essential part of his understanding. He understands himself more clearly than perhaps other people, given his situation in time and space. His heritage has always been rather closely focused, centered upon the landscape as a particular reality. Beyond this, the native American has a particular investment in vision and in the idea of vision. You are familiar with the term "vision quest" for example. This is another essential idea to the Indian worldview, particularly that view as it is expressed among the cultures of the Plains Indians. This is significant. I think we should not lose the force of the idea of seeing something or envisioning something in a particular way. I happen to think that there are two visions in particular with reference to man and his relationship to the natural world. One is physical and the other is imaginative. And we all deal in one way or another with these visions simultaneously. If I can try to find an analogy, it's rather like looking through the viewfinder of a camera, the viewfinder which is based upon the principle of the split image. And it is a matter of trying to align the two planes of that particular view. This can be used as an example of how we look at the world around us. We see it with the physical eye. We see it as it appears to us, in one dimension of reality. But we also see it with the eye of the mind. It seems to me that the Indian has achieved a particularly effective alignment of those two planes of vision. He perceives the landscape in both ways. He realizes a whole image from the possibilities within his reach. The moral implications of this are very far-reaching. Here is where we get into the consideration of religion and religious ideas and ideals.

There is another way in which I think one can very profitably and accurately think of the Indian in relation to the landscape and in terms of his idea of that relationship. This is to center on such a word as *appropriate*. The idea of "appropriateness" is central to the Indian experience of the natural world. It is a fundamental idea within his philosophy. I recall the story told to me some years ago by a friend, who is not himself a Navajo, but was married for a time to a Navajo girl and lived with her family in Southern Utah. And he said that he had been told this story and was passing it on to me. There was a man living in a remote place on the Navajo reservation who had lost his job and was having a difficult time making ends meet. He had a wife and several children. As a matter of fact, his wife was expecting another child. One day a friend came to visit him and perceived that his situation was bad. The friend said to him "Look, I see that you're in tight straits, I see you have many mouths to feed, that you have no wood and that there is very little food in your larder. But one thing puzzles me. I know you're a hunter, and I know, too, there are deer in the mountains very close at hand. Tell me, why don't you kill a deer so that you and your family might have fresh meat to eat?" And after a time the man replied, "No, it is inappropriate that I should take life just now when I am expecting the gift of life."

The implications of that idea, and the way in which the concept of appropriateness lies at the center of that little parable is a central consideration within the Indian world. You cannot understand how the Indian thinks of himself in relation to the world around him unless you understand his conception of what is appropriate; particularly what is morally appropriate within the context of that relationship.

**QUESTION:**    Could you probe a little deeper into what lies behind the idea of appropriate or inappropriate behavior regarding the natural world. Is it a religious element? Is it biological or a matter of survival? How would you characterize what makes an action appropriate or inappropriate?

**MOMADAY:**    It is certainly a fair question but I'm not sure that I have the answer to it. I suspect that whatever it is that makes for the idea of appropriateness is a very complex thing in itself. Many things constitute the idea of appropriateness. Basically, I think it is a moral idea as opposed to a religious one. It is a basic understanding of right within the framework of relationships, and, within the framework of that relationship I was talking about a moment ago, between man and the physical world. That which is appropriate within this context is that which is *natural*. This another key word. My father used to tell me of an old man who has lived a whole life. I have often thought of this image. The old man used to come to my grandfather's house periodically to pay visits, and my father has very vivid recollections of this man whom I never knew. But his name was Chaney. Father says that Chaney would come to the house and he would make himself perfectly at home. He would be passing by going from one place to another, exercising his ethnic prerogative for nomadism. But he would make my grandfather's house a kind of resting place. He stayed there on many occasions. My father says that every morning when Chaney was there as a guest he would get up in the first light, paint his face, go outside, face the east, and bring the sun out of the horizon. Then he would pray. He would pray aloud to the rising sun. He did that because it was appropriate that he should do that. He understood. Or perhaps I should say that in terms of his own understanding, the sun was the origin of his strength. He understood the sun, within a more formal religious context, similar to the way someone else understands the presence of a deity. And in the face of that recognition, he acted naturally or appropriately. Through the medium of prayer, he returned some of his strength to the sun. He did this everyday. It was a part of his daily life. It was as natural and appropriate to him as anything could be. There is in the Indian worldview this kind of understanding of what is and what is not appropriate. It isn't a matter of intellection. It is respect for the understanding of one's heritage. It is a kind of racial memory and it has its origin beyond any sort of historical experience. It reaches back to the dawn of time.

**QUESTION:**    When talking about vision, you said that the Indians saw things physically and also with the eye of the mind, I think this is the way you put it. You also said that this was a whole image, and that it had certain moral implications. Would you elaborate further?

MOMADAY: I think there are different ways of seeing things. I myself am particularly interested in literature, and in the traditions of various peoples, the Indians in particular. I understand something of how this works within the context of literature. For example, in the nineteenth century in America, there were poets who were trying very hard to see nature and to write about it. This is one kind of vision. They succeeded in different ways, some succeeding more than others. They succeeded in seeing what was really there on the vision plain of the natural world and they translated that vision, or that perception of the natural world, into poetry. Many of them had a kind of scientific training. Their observations were trained through the study of botany, astronomy, or zoology, etc. This refers, of course, to one kind of vision.

But, obviously, this is not the sort of view of the landscape which characterizes the Indian world. His view rather is of a different and more imaginative kind. It is a more comprehensive view. When the native American looks at nature, it isn't with the idea of training a glass upon it, or pushing it away so that he can focus upon it from a distance. In his mind, nature is not something apart from him. He conceives of it, rather, as an element in which he exists. He has existence within that element, much in the same way we think of having existence within the element of air. It would be unimaginable for him to think of it in the way the nineteenth century "nature poets" thought of looking at nature and writing about it. They employed a kind of "esthetic distance," as it is sometimes called. This idea would be alien to the Indian. This is what I meant by trying to make the distinction between two sides of a split image.

QUESTION: So then, presumably in moral terms, the Indian would say that a person should not harm nature because it's something in which one participates oneself.

MOMADAY: This is one aspect of it. There is this moral aspect, and it refers to perfect alignment. The appropriation of both images into the one reality is what the Indian is concerned to do: to see what is really there, but also to see what is *really* there. This reminds me of another story. It is very brief. It was told to me by the same fellow who told me about the man who did not kill the deer. (To take a certain liberty with the title of a novel that I know well.) He told me that while he himself was living in southern Utah with his wife's family, he became very ill. He contracted pneumonia. There was no doctor, no physician nearby. But there was a medicine man close at hand. The family called in a diagnostician (the traditional thing to do), who came and said that my friend was suffering from a particular malady whose cure would be the red-ant ceremony. So a man who is very well versed in that ceremony, a seer, a kind of specialist in the red-ant ceremony, came in and administered it to my friend. Soon after that my friend recovered completely. Not long after this he was talking to his father-in-law, and he was very curious about what had taken place. He said, "I wonder about the red-ant ceremony. Why is it that the diagnostician prescribed that particular ceremony for me?" His father-in-law looked at him and said, "Well, it was obvious to him that there were red ants in your system, and so we had to call in a seer to take the red ants out of your system." At this point, my friend became very incredulous, and said, "Yes, but surely you don't mean that there were red ants inside of me." His father-in-law looked at him for a moment, then said, "Not ants, but ants." Unless you understand this distinction, you might have difficulty understanding something about the Indian view of the natural world.

## Note

This paper was adapted from transcriptions of oral remarks Professor Momaday made on this subject, informally, during a discussion with faculty and students.

## Journal/Discussion Questions

✍ *Mr. Momaday suggests that "appropriateness" is a central concept in terms of which Native Americans understand their relationship to the natural world. In your own life, what role—if any—does this notion play in your understanding of your own relationship to the natural world. Does this concept shed light on any parts of your experience that you hadn't reflected on before?*

1. Explain what Mr. Momaday means by "appropriateness." How could this idea be used to develop environmental policies?

2. Think about the way in which Mr. Momaday responds to questions. He usually tells a story. What does this suggest about the way in which Native Americans maintain and transmit moral wisdom? How does this relate to the role of imagination?

# AN INTRODUCTION TO THE MORAL ISSUES

## Introduction

Perhaps more than any of the other issues that we have considered in this book, questions about our relationships with animals and the environment take us to the heart of a fundamental clash of worldviews. It is, moreover, not like the familiar clashes between liberal and conservative, theist and atheist, or the like; it is, rather, a clash between a *scientific and techno-logical worldview*—which encompasses liberal and conservative, theist and atheist, and other divisions familiar to us—and a diverse set of *natural worldviews*—many of them echoing the cultures of indigenous peoples—which emphasize the continuity and interdependence of human beings and the natural world.

*Should we view the world in scientific or natural terms?*

One of the by-products of this clash of worldviews is that much of environmental ethics calls into question the foundations of traditional (i.e., western European) ethics. This has been both an asset and a liability for the development of environmental ethics. On the plus side, it has resulted in a number of interesting discussions that illuminate aspects of the foundations of Western ethics that might not otherwise be brought as sharply into focus. In particular, it has called attention to the ways in which Western ethics conceptualizes the natural world and understands the place of human beings in it. On the negative side, however, the concern with such foundational questions has detracted, at least in the eyes of some, from environmental ethic's principal task as *applied* ethics. Rather than concentrating on specific moral issues facing those concerned with the environment (as well as those who are not concerned with it!), environmental ethics has concentrated on issues that exist on such a high level of abstraction that they are not immediately fruitful for making decisions about the specific environmental issues.

## The Central Questions

As we turn toward a consideration of environmental ethics, three questions present themselves:

(1) *Who,* or what, *has moral weight* (i.e., is deserving of direct moral consideration)?
(2) *How much* moral weight does each (type of) entity have?
(3) How do we make *decisions* when there are *conflicts* among different types of beings, each of which have moral weight?

An adequate environmental ethic must eventually provide answers to all three of these questions. In recent work by environmentalists, considerable attention has been paid to the first of these questions. Here the debate has centered around the question of whether individual animals, species, plants, rivers, etc. have moral weight; that is, whether we should give moral consideration to the question of their well-being or continued flourishing. Sometimes this question is posed in relation to individuals (e.g., this specific plant) and sometimes it is posed in relation to species (e.g., the spotted owl). In the next section of this introduction, we shall examine a number of specific answers to these questions.

The second question—how much moral standing something has—is both crucial and usually neglected. It is crucial because ethics must eventually provide guidance for our actions, and if we have no way of ranking how much moral consideration a given entity merits, we are left without assistance in resolving conflicts among morally considerable beings. The answer to the third question obviously presupposes an answer to the first two questions. We shall consider each of these three questions here, but first sketch out an overview of the main schools of thought in environmental ethics.

# An Overview

Since this is relatively uncharted territory for many of us, it may be helpful to see an overview of the conceptual terrain and the various positions that have been marked out on it by the current participants in the discussion of environmental ethics. We may initially divide these approaches into two categories. *Human-centered approaches* to the environment take human beings as their moral point of reference and consider questions of the environment solely from that perspective. They ask, in other words, environmental questions from the standpoint of the effects of the answers to such questions on human beings in one way or another. In contrast to these approaches, we find in recent years that a number of *expanded-circle approaches* (to borrow a term from the title of Peter Singer's *The Expanding Circle*) that draw the circle of morally considerable beings—that is, entities deserving of moral respect in some way—with an increasingly wide radius. Let's examine each of these in somewhat more detail.[1]

## Human-centered Approaches

Human-centered approaches to the environment do not necessarily neglect the environment, but typically they recognize as valid moral reasons only those reasons acceptable to traditional moral theories. These theories are of the various types we discussed in the Introduction to this book.

*Ethical egoists* recognize only reasons of self-interest as an adequate moral justification for treating the environment in a particular way. For example, ethical egoists could well imagine people wanting a particular landscape preserved because it provided them personally with an aesthetically-pleasing view, but it would also see those who wanted to strip mine that particular landscape as morally justified if it maximized their own self-interest.

*Group egoists* are also concerned with self-interest, but the net of self-interest is more broadly cast to include not only one's personal interests, but the interests of the group with which one most strongly affiliates. The boundaries of the group may be comparatively narrow (one's family), intermediate (one's neighborhood, one's corporation, one's church group), or quite broad (one's nation, all those who share one's religious beliefs). What is characteristic of these approaches is that only the interests of one's group are to be given moral weight in making decisions. Similarly, there are approaches in *virtue ethics* which concentrate on developing those character traits that contribute to the welfare of the group: loyalty, a spirit of self-sacrifice, obedience to authority, and so on. Aristotle, for example, sought to determine those character traits that would make a person a good member of the *polis*, the Greek city-state. Much more recently, William Bennett and others have sought to determine the virtues we should foster in order to have a better civic and communal life in the United States. One of the principal differences between group egoist and virtue ethics is that egoism focuses on the question of what actions we should perform, while virtue ethics looks at the kind of person we should be.

*Utilitarianians*, like egoists, are consequentialists, that is, they determine whether particular actions are right or wrong by looking at their consequences. However, whereas the ethical egoist looks at consequences only insofar as they affect the egoist personally, the utilitarian looks at consequences insofar as they affect all human beings. Often courses of action that would be justified from the standpoint of ethical egoism are not morally justified from a utilitarian standpoint, since they may benefit the egoist but not provide sufficient benefit to humanity as a whole (when judged in relation to competing courses of action).

Preserving the natural environment may be an important value to utilitarians if doing so provides the maximal benefit to humanity. There are a variety of ways in which this could be so. For example, preservation—or at least careful management—of the natural environment may provide long-term resources for all of humanity. Thus we may want to preserve the rain forests because, even though destroying them might bring short-term profit to a small group of people, preserving them provides irreplaceable benefits to humanity in terms of air quality, natural resources, etc. Notice that there is no claim here that the rain forest is valuable in itself; its value derives from the ways in which it contributes to human well-being. If in the long run human well-being would best be served by destroying the rain forests, then utilitarianism would not only permit this, it would require it.

## Expanded-Circle Approaches

*Expanded utilitarianism.* Traditionally, utilitarianism has been concerned with the effects of various actions on the well-being of human beings. The underlying rationale has been that the whole point of ethics is to increase pleasure or happiness and to decrease pain, suffering, or unhappiness. As we saw in the previous chapter, a number of philosophers, most notably Peter Singer, have taken the next step and asked why only *human* suffering counts in the utilitarian calculus. If we are concerned with reducing suffering, should we be concerned with reducing the suffering of *all* sentient beings. Thus this version of utilitarianism has expanded the circle of morally considerable beings to include nonhuman animals. Although this is far from a full-fledged environmental ethic, it is an important step beyond a purely anthropocentric ethic.

*Biocentrism* represents the first step toward a genuinely environmental ethic, for it maintains that all living beings—this includes plants, fauna, etc., as well as human and nonhuman animals—are deserving of moral consideration in their own right. Biocentric approaches focus on individual entities, and the premise here seems to be primarily a teleological one. All living beings have some *telos* or final goal, and this is usually understood in terms of flourishing or growing in some sense. They are thus entitled to moral consideration from us—that is, we should not act in ways that thwart their movement toward their natural goal.

*Ecocentrism,* which is often called deep ecology by its supporters, expands the circle to its maximal terrestrial limits by taking the entirety of what exists on the earth as morally considerable, inanimate as well as animate. It comes in two versions, the latter of which is much more plausible than the former. *Individualistic ecocentrism* gives moral weight to each and every entity within the ecosystem. The difficulty with this approach flows from the fact that individualistic ecocentrism has been unable to provide a criterion for assigning different weights to different individuals—and if everything has an equal moral weight, then it is virtually impossible to arrive at a decision procedure in particular cases in which precedence must be given to one individual over another.

The more plausible variant of ecocentrism is to be found in *holistic ecocentrism,* which gives moral weight to each species, type, etc. in the ecosystem. Thus holistic ecocentrism is concerned with the preservation of species, and concern about individuals is only a means to the end of species-preservation. Similarly, ecocentric environmentalists may be concerned about the preservation of particular types of environments—wetlands, sand dunes, rainforests—both in their own right and insofar as they are parts of larger ecosystems. The ultimate ecosystem is the earth as a whole. The following diagram illustrates the various ways of expanding the circle of morality that philosophers have proposed.

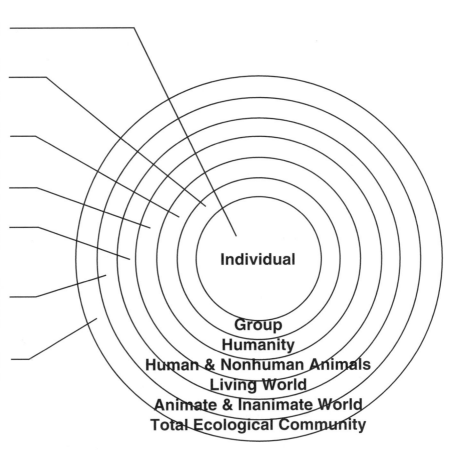

**Individual Ethical Egoism:**
*Concerned Only with One's Self*

**Group Ethical Egoism, Aristotelian Virtue Theory:**
*Concerned Only with One's Group (Community, City-State, Nation, etc.)*

**Traditional Utilitarianism, Deontology:**
*Directly Concerned Only with Human Beings*

**Expanded Utilitarianism:**
*Directly Concerned with the Welfare of All Sentient Beings*

**Biocentrism:**
*Directly Concerned with All Individual Entities in the Living World*

**Individualistic Ecocentrism:**
*Directly Concerned with All Individual Entities in the World*

**Holistic Ecocentrism:**
*Directly Concerned with All Species and Groups*

**Individual**

**Group**
**Humanity**
**Human & Nonhuman Animals**
**Living World**
**Animate & Inanimate World**
**Total Ecological Community**

As we have already seen in Chapter 9, many philosophers argued that the moral circle ought to be expanded to include nonhuman animals. As we shall see in this chapter, some philosophers want to expand this circle even further to include all of the natural environment.

# Criteria of Moral Considerability

Clearly, those who want to "expand the circle" are claiming that entities that previously had not been recognized as having moral weight should now be given moral consideration. On what basis should they be accorded this moral respect? In nonanthropocentric approaches, it must be on the basis of some property that they possess, rather than on the basis of their impact on human beings. In the previous chapter, we examined several proposed criteria for expanding the circle of moral considerability to include nonhuman animals, but most of those criteria were limited to the world of humans and animals. When the circle is extended even further, criteria such as the ability to use language or manipulate tools are of little help. Several proposals have been advanced for criteria of moral considerability that extend the moral domain beyond humans and animals.

## Intrinsic Value

To say that something has intrinsic value is to say that it can't be used merely as a means. Most people admit that human beings have intrinsic value—that is, that we can't morally use people merely as a means to our own ends. On the other hand, we would all agree that something like a hammer has no intrinsic value—we can use it for whatever purposes we want, whether to pound nails or as a doorstop, without worrying about being disrespectful to the hammer. Indeed, we can even destroy it without feeling like we are violating the hammer in some morally significant way. It has no intrinsic value, and thus in itself merits no moral respect.

Yet what quality or characteristic accords intrinsic value to human beings and not to hammers—and what other types of beings share this characteristic? Claims about intrinsic value turn out to be mere resting places along the path of a longer argument, for advocates of intrinsic value must then specify the characteristics that form the basis of intrinsic value. Some philosophers, like Immanuel Kant, have maintained that *rationality* is the foundation of intrinsic value; thus any being possessing rationality would merit moral respect. More recently, Kenneth Goodpaster and others have argued that being alive should be our criterion of moral considerability and that all *living* beings have intrinsic value.[2] At least one philosopher has maintained that the only nonarbitrary criterion of moral considerability and intrinsic value is "*being in existence.*"[3] On this view, everything that exists would have intrinsic value.

It is clear that the appeal to intrinsic value in itself sheds little light on the issue of moral considerability, since such an appeal must quickly be filled in with a specification of the basis for attributing intrinsic value—and at this point we are back to the broader issue of criteria of moral considerability. However, this discussion indirectly illuminates an interesting and sometimes neglected background issue. In modern industrialized countries like the United States, the assumption is often that things have *only* instrumental value unless there is evidence to the contrary. This is in sharp contrast to other cultures that make the opposite assumption: they assume that everything is deserving of respect, and that we ought not to use things as mere means unless there is a good justification for doing so. The burden of proof is then on the other side.

## Teleology

A second way of approaching this problem has been to argue that, at least in the living world, there is a natural teleology: plants move toward flowering, animals toward reproduction, and so on. Certainly this is true, and one simply has to walk through a lush forest to understand what natural flourishing is like. Similarly, one only has to walk through a forest that has been clear-cut to understand what devastation induced by human beings is like. So there is something intuitively plausible about appeals to teleology.

Yet the teleological argument does not take us far enough, or at least does not yield the conclusions that some environmentalists would like to see. First, we get different and conflicting views of flourishing, depending on whether we consider the flourishing of the individual, the species, or the ecosystem. What promotes the flourishing of one might not promote the flourishing of the others. The flourishing of individual animals often depends on killing other animals. The flourishing of a species may well depend on preventing overpopulation of the species, and that may in turn depend on the early deaths of a certain percentage of the species. Similarly, the flourishing of the ecosystem may depend on diminishing or destroying certain species. Flourishing in an ecosystem is a complex phenomenon, and it includes things such as animals killing one another and forest fires and floods and droughts.

Second, the flourishing of one individual or species is often bought at the price of the flourishing of another. Yet environmentalists often seem to advocate some form of noninterference with the environment, which seems at odds with the way in which species often seem to conflict with, and prey upon, one another. Teleology doesn't seem to provide much support for an ethic of noninterference with the environment.

Third, how do we think about the natural teleology of human beings? It seems reasonable to maintain that human beings need many things to flourish that may be harmful to the environment. Again, it would seem that teleology might well justify much that many environmentalists oppose.

## Aesthetic Value

Certainly one of the most powerful motivating forces in the work of many environmentalists has been their appreciation of the beauty of nature. If you have experienced the beauty of nature, then you understand how compelling this motivation can be. If you have not experienced it, it is unlikely that any description will convince you of the power of the experience.

Yet there are difficulties associated with allowing the moral weight of nature to depend on its aesthetic value. We have already alluded to one of those difficulties in the previous paragraph: beauty, while not perhaps solely in the eye of the beholder, is not universally and objectively accessible. The Florida Everglades are a good example—beautiful to some, a bug-infested swamp to others. Moreover, even if there were relatively widespread agreement about beauty, is *all* of nature beautiful? It seem improbable that some of it wouldn't be ugly—and if so, does it deserve less moral consideration than the beautiful parts?

*To what extent should we respect nature because of its beauty?*

Finally, even granting the beauty of the natural world, are we willing to commit ourselves to a principle that aesthetic value outweighs other types of value? It seems unlikely that we would be willing to do so outside of environmental ethics, so allowing the moral value of nature to rest on its aesthetic value seems to be a risky proposition.

## Sacredness

Religious traditions have played a major role in shaping people's attitudes toward the environment, although we often find within a single religious tradition different and at times conflicting ways of understanding and appreciating the environment. Consider the Christian, the Native American, and the Taoist traditions.

*The Christian traditions: Dominion and stewardship.*   Throughout its history, there have been two distinct traditions in Christianity about the relationship between human beings and the environment. The dominant tradition has been one of *dominion,* and its origins are in found in the first chapter of Genesis, where human beings are given control over the world to use it to their own ends. The other tradition, perhaps never dominant but often more powerful than it has been in the twentieth century, is one of *stewardship,* in which human beings are seen as being charged by God with the task of preserving the natural environment. Environmentalists typically criticize the former tradition in Christianity, while they tend—if they acknowledge its existence—to laud the latter.

*Native American traditions: Reciprocity and respect.*   Although there is a considerable degree of diversity within Native American religious traditions, in general Native American traditions emphasize the sacredness of nature—the natural world is much more imbued with spirits than it is for, say, the traditional Christian—and the ways in which it therefore merits respect. However, in contrast to many contemporary environmentalists who espouse noninterference by humans in the natural world, Native Americans see the relationship between human beings and the natural world as one of reciprocal interaction. Hunting, for example, is an important activity in many Native American traditions; although unnecessary killing of animals is prohibited, hunting in order to meet one's own basic needs (and the needs of one's family) is not only permitted, but on occasion even celebrated. Interestingly, killing an animal is not seen as necessarily incompatible with respecting it.

# Future Generations, Predictibility, and the Environment

Concern for the environment is all the more complex because often the principal issue is not the immediate effects of one particular action, but rather the long-range effects of a policy carried out for decades, perhaps even centuries. Two aspects of this issue are especially troublesome: the moral status of future generations, and the limits of our predictive powers.

## Future Generations: Their Rights, Our Responsibilities

Part of this complexity centers around the issue of future generations. Often we are concerned, not just about the short-term effects on the environment at present, but even more about the long-term effects of policies on the environment and the impact of the resulting changes on the lives of our descendants. Nuclear waste, for example, might be a significant problem now, but it could well be a mammoth, unmanageable problem in another century if present trends continue.

*What do we owe future generations in terms of the environment we leave them?*

A number of philosophical perplexities surround the issue of future generations. Perhaps the most pressing of these concerns the issue of the kind of rights that future generations can have. Since future generations do not exist yet (by definition), then how is it possible for non-existent beings to have rights? Indeed, if we pursue certain environmentally destructive courses of action, they may well never exist. In what sense, if any, can counter-factual individuals—persons who would have existed if we had acted differently—exert a moral claim on us? This is slippery conceptual terrain, and it is not clear that we can traverse it without stumbling.

The more promising way of dealing with this issue is to leave aside the issue of the rights of future generations and concentrate on the maxims that guide our own situation. Some moral guideline—for example, that we should leave the earth in no worse a condition than we received it—might provide a basis for considering the interests of future generations. Or we might make metaphorical use of the concept of parenthood as a foundation for our concern for the well-being of future generations. We are all children of parents; some of us may also be (or become) parents ourselves; all of us can pass on parental concern, whether biologically grounded or not, by acting in ways which promote the welfare of future generations. These lines of argumentation seem more plausible than a concern with the narrowly-defined issue of the rights of future generations.

## Predictability

The other way in which this whole issue is complex centers around the issue of predictability. As we deal with increasingly complex systems, it becomes more and more difficult to know reliably in advance precisely what will occur. Our predictions are often accompanied by a restriction: "all other things being equal." Yet in complex systems, other things are rarely if ever equal.

*To what extent can we predict the long-term environmental consequences of our actions?*

In recent years, an entire branch of mathematics—called "chaos theory"—has been devoted solely to this issue. Chaos theory grew in part out of the difficulties in forecasting the weather, and chaos theorists now maintain that it is impossible *in principle,* not just in practice, to predict the weather with absolute accuracy, even with an infinite number of weather sensors covering the entire globe. Infinitesimal variations—a butterfly fluttering its wings in South America—produce unanticipated results—a thunderstorm in New York two months later.

Coupled with this is the fact that we cannot easily foretell what additional developments, particularly technological ones, will have an impact on our predictions. A century ago, for example, dire predictions warned that New York City would eventually be overcome by horse manure, given the steadily increasing amount of horse traffic on the city streets. The advent of the automobile eliminated this problem while substituting other types of problems in its place. So, too, we are unsure of the ways in which future inventions may reshape our environmental problems.

What are we to conclude from this? Clearly, we cannot simply give up on prediction. In fact, our predictions are often accurate. However, we must be especially aware of our own fallibility, our own ability to make mistakes, as we make predictions on a global scale about long-term future events and trends. However, such an awareness should not be seen as a justification of complacency based in a feeling of futility about prediction.

## Endnotes

1. This typology draws on several sources, most notably Carolyn Merchant's "Environmental Ethics and Political Conflict," reprinted below, and J. Baird Callicott's "Environmental Ethics," *Encyclopedia of Ethics,* ed. Lawrence and Charlotte Becker (New York: Garland, 1992), vol. I, pp. 311–315.

2. Kenneth E. Goodpaster, "On Being Morally Considerable," *Journal of Philosophy* LXXV, 6 (June, 1978), 308–324.

3. W. Murray Hunt, "Are Mere Things Morally Considerable?" *Environmental Ethics* 2 (Spring 1980), 59–65.

# THE ARGUMENTS

Carolyn Merchant
"Environmental Ethics and Political Conflict: A View from California"

*Carolyn Merchant is professor of environmental history, philosophy, and ethics at the University of California, Berkeley. She is the author of* The Death of Nature: Women, Ecology, and the Scientific Revolution; Radical Ecology: The Search for a Livable World, *and, most recently,* Earthcare: Women and the Environment.

*Merchant examines three approaches to environmental ethics and illustrates them with examples from California. An* egocentric ethic *is grounded in the self and based on the assumption that what is good for the individual is good for society. A* homocentric ethic *is grounded in society and is based on the assumption that policies should reflect the greatest good for the greatest number of people and that, as stewards of the natural world, humans should conserve and protect nature for human benefit. An* ecocentric ethic *is grounded in the cosmos, or whole environment, and is based on the assignment of intrinsic value to nonhuman nature. This threefold taxonomy may be useful in identifying underlying ethical assumptions in cases where ethical dilemmas and conflicts of interest develop among entrepreneurs, government agencies, and environmentalists.*

## As You Read, Consider This:

1. Note Merchant's objections to each of these approaches. Do you think that there are any advantages to egocentric or homocentric ethics that she neglects or underestimates? Do you think that there any any liabilities to ecocentric approaches that she doesn't appreciate?

2. Merchant discusses the ways in which different worldviews underlie different approaches to environmental ethics. As you read, note some of these connections. Also observe the connections between these ethics and religious traditions.

## Introduction

In his *Nichomachean Ethics,* Aristotle noted that "all knowledge and every pursuit aims at some good."[1] But whether this is an individual, social, or environmental good lies at the basis of many real world ethical dilemmas. Here I offer a taxonomy of ethical approaches—egocentric, homocentric, and ecocentric—that often underlie the political positions of various interest groups engaged in struggles over land and natural resource uses. Conflicts of interest among private individuals and corporations, government agencies, and environmentalists often reflect these ethical approaches. Because they are the culmination of sets of associated political, religious, and ethical

Carolyn Merchant, "Environmental Ethics and Political Conflict: A View from California," *Environmental Ethics* 12, no. 1 (Spring 1990). Copyright 1990, Environmental Ethics, Inc. Reprinted by permission of the publisher and the author.

trends developing in Western culture since the seventeenth century, they may be illustrated through examples from the history of environmental and natural resource problems in California

## Egocentric Ethics

An egocentric ethic is grounded in the self. It is based on an individual ought focused on individual good. In its applied form, it involves the claim that what is good for the individual will benefit society. The individual good is thus prior to the social good which follows from it as a necessary consequence. An egocentric ethic's orientation does not derive from selfishness or narcissism, but rather is based on a philosophy that treats individuals (or private corporations) as separate, but equal social atoms. Historically, the egocentric ethic rose to dominance in Western culture during the seventeenth century. As the classic ethic of liberalism and laissez faire capitalism, in the United States it has been the guiding ethic of private entrepreneurs and corporations whose primary goal is the maximization of profit from the development of natural resources. Only the "silken bands of mild government," as Hector St. John de Crevecoeur put it in 1782, inhibit individual actions. Industry is "unfettered and unrestrained, because each person works for himself."[2]

Environmentally, an egocentric ethic permits individuals (or corporations) to extract and use natural resources to enhance their own lives and those of other members of society, limited only by the effects on their neighbors. Traditionally, the use of fire, common water sources, and rivers were regulated by laws. Under common law during the American colonial period, for example, one could not obstruct a river with a dam because it would interfere with its natural course and reduce the privileges of others living along it. By the late eighteenth century, however, individual privileges increasingly prevailed when profits were at stake. Entrepreneurs could erect dams on the grounds that "the public whose advantage is always to be regarded, would be deprived of the benefit which always attends competition and rivalry."[3]

Egocentric ethics often reflects the Protestant ethic. An individual is responsible for his or her own salvation through good actions. During the seventeenth century, American Christianity moved away from the doctrine of the early Puritans that only the elect would be saved toward the Arminian doctrine that any individual could assure his or her own salvation by leading an ethical life.[4] In the seventeenth century, the Protestant ethic dovetailed with the Judeo-Christian mandate of Genesis 1:28: "Be fruitful and multiply, and replenish the earth and subdue it." From an environmental perspective, as University of California historian Lynn White, Jr., argues, the Judeo-Christian ethic legitimated the domination of nature.[5] Early economic development in America was reinforced by this biblical framework. As the Arabella, bearing the first Puritan settlers of the Massachusetts Bay colony, left England for the New World in 1629, John Winthrop quoted the Genesis 1 passage.[6] In justifying American expansion into Oregon in 1846, John Quincy Adams asserted that the objectives of the U.S. were to "make the wilderness blossom as the rose; to establish laws, to increase, multiply, and subdue the earth, which we are commanded to do by the first behest of the God Almighty."[7] Likewise, Thomas Hart Benton that same year, in his famous address to the Twenty-ninth Congress, insisted that the white race had "alone received the divine command to subdue and replenish the earth: for it is the only race that . . . hunts out new and distant lands, and even a New World, to subdue and replenish. . . ."[8] Similar biblical passages reinforced God's command to transform nature from a wilderness into a civilization. Reverend Dr.

Dwinell's sermon, commemorating the joining of the Central Pacific and Union Pacific railroads in 1869, quoted the Bible as a sanction for human alteration of the natural landscape. "Prepare ye the way of the Lord, make straight in the desert a highway before our God. Every valley shall be exalted, and every mountain and hill shall be made low and the crooked shall be made straight and the rough places plain. . . ."[9]

Egocentric ethics as a basis for environmental policy is rooted in the philosophy of seventeenth-century political philosopher Thomas Hobbes. In turn, Hobbes' approach forms the foundation for the environmental ethic of University of California ecologist Garrett Hardin, whose "Tragedy of the Commons" influenced environmental policy in the 1970s.[10] For Hobbes, humans are basically competitive. In *Leviathan* Hobbes asserts that people are by nature unfriendly, hostile, and violent. In the state of nature, everyone has an equal right to everything, for "Nature has given all to all." But for Hobbes, nature is not a garden of Eden or a utopia in which everyone shares its fruits as earlier communal theories of society held. Instead, everyone is competing for the same natural resources. In *De Cive* he wrote, "For although any man might say of every thing, this is mine, yet he could not enjoy it, by reason of his neighbor, who having equal right and equal power, would pretend the same thing to be his."[11] Thus, because of competitive self-interest, the commons could not be shared, but must be fought over.

By Hobbes' time, the English commons were losing their traditional role as shared sources of life-giving grass, water, and wood to be used by all peasants as had been the case in feudal Europe. Instead they could be owned and enclosed by individual landlords who could use them to graze sheep for the expanding wool market. In fact, if lords did not compete, they could lose their lands and fortunes and be ridiculed by their peers. "For he that should be modest and tractable and perform all he promises," wrote Hobbes, " . . . should but make himself a prey to others and procure his own certain ruin."[12]

The commons was thus like a marketplace or a battleground in need of law and order. The solution to the disorder that prevailed in the state of nature was the social contract. By common consent, people gave up their freedom to fight and kill and out of fear accepted governance by a sovereign. Through the rational acceptance by each citizen of a set of rules for individual ethical conduct, social order, peace, and control could be maintained. The state was thus an artificial ordering of individual parts, a Leviathan, "to which we owe . . . our peace and defense."[13] Hobbes' egocentric ethic therefore was based on the assumption that human beings, as rational agents, could overcome their "natural" instincts to fight over property.

Hardin's "Tragedy of the Commons" and his "lifeboat ethics" are both grounded in this egocentric ethic. Like Hobbes, Hardin's (unstated) underlying assumptions are that people are naturally competitive, that capitalism is the "natural" form of economic life, and that the commons is like a marketplace. In his "Tragedy of the Commons," Hardin argues that individuals tended to graze more and more sheep on the commons because the economic gain was +1 for each sheep. On the other hand, the cost of overgrazing (environmental deterioration) was much less than −1 because the costs were shared equally by all. Thus there was no incentive to reduce herds. In the modern analogy, the seas and air are a global commons. Resource depletion and environmental pollution of the commons are shared by all; hence there is no incentive for individuals or nations to control their own exploitation. The costs of acid rain and chloroflourocarbons in the air, oil spills and plastics in the oceans, and the depletion of fish, whales, and seals are shared equally by all who fish, breathe, and live. The solution, for Hardin as for Hobbes, is mutual coercion, mutually agreed upon. People, corporations, and nation states voluntarily consent to rational regulation of resources.[14]

Similarly Hardin's "Living on a Lifeboat" is an egocentric ethic.[15] When an overloaded boat capsizes, there will be insufficient lifeboats to save all. Those individuals who are saved are those who are strong enough to help themselves. When a population outstrips its food resources, some individual nations will institute population control policies and some will not. These nations can at best be selectively helped through a policy of triage such as that developed for wartime injury victims.[16] Under triage, limited wartime medical resources are used first to help those with severe injuries who can survive only with aid and second to those with moderate injuries who would survive anyway. Those with massive fatal injuries who would die despite medical aid are not helped beyond pain reduction. Analogously, developed nations with food surpluses should help developing nations which voluntarily agree to control population growth. Those who cannot or will not agree to population control policies should not receive assistance. The lifeboat ethic is thus an egocentric ethic of individual choice based on human reason. Nations, like individual atoms, are rational decision makers who can decide whether or not to save themselves. Having arrived at that choice through reason, they either voluntarily submit to coercion, i.e., population control, in order to save their countries or accept catastrophe.

Egocentric ethics is rooted in the mechanistic science of the seventeenth century.[17] Mechanism is based on several underlying assumptions that are consistent with liberal social theory. First, mechanistic science is based on the assumption that matter is made up of individual parts. Atoms are the real components of nature, just as individual humans are the real components of society. Second, the whole is equal to the sum of the individual parts. The law of identity in logic, or a = a, is the basis for the mathematical description of nature. Likewise, society is the sum of individual rational agents, as in Hobbes' depiction of the body of the sword-carrying sovereign as made up of the sum of the individual humans who have submitted themselves to his rule. Third, mechanism involves the assumption that external causes act on inert parts. In accordance with Newton's first law of mechanics, a body remains at rest or in motion in a straight line unless acted on by an external force. Similarly, in society, rules and laws handed down by a sovereign or representative governing body are obeyed by a passive populace. Fourth, change occurs by the rearrangement of parts. In the billiard-ball universe of mechanistic scientists, the initial amount of motion (or energy) introduced into the universe by God at its creation is conserved and simply redistributed among the parts as they come together or separate to form the bodies of the phenomenal world. In much the same way, individuals in society associate and dissociate in corporate bodies or business ventures. Fifth, mechanistic science is often dualistic. Philosophers such as René Descartes and scientists such as Robert Boyle and Isaac Newton posited a world of spirit separate from that of matter. Nature, the human body, and animals could all be described, repaired, and controlled, as could the parts of a machine, by a separate human mind acting according to rational laws. Similarly, in the rhetoric of the founders of the American Constitution, democratic society is a balance of powers as in a pendulum clock, and government operates as do the well-oiled wheels and gears of a machine controlled by human reason. Mind is separate from and superior to body; human society and culture are separate from and superior to nonhuman nature. Just as mechanistic science gives primacy to the individual parts that make up a corporeal body, so egocentric ethics gives primacy to the individual humans that make up the social whole.

How has egocentric ethics been actuated with respect to the California environment? In *The Fisherman's Problem,* environmental historian Arthur McEvoy describes the management of the California fisheries in terms of the problem of the depletion of the commons. After the settlement of California by Euro-Americans in the eighteenth and nineteenth centuries, exploitation of river and ocean fish by individuals superseded the communal management of fishing by native American groups. Fish, like gold nuggets, were commodities to be extracted from the state of nature and turned into profits. As in the tragedy of the commons, "American authorities recognized . . . that pollution and overharvesting could degrade inland fisheries. But the problem was that those forces were so diffused over society, every individual contributing a negligible share, as to be legally uncontrollable." By the late nineteenth century, depletion of the rivers made it essential that fishing be regulated through laws and managed by government agencies—the "mutual coercion mutually agreed upon" of Hobbes and Hardin. The law as a form of rational human cognition regulated exploitation. Conflict of interest cases resulted in the curtailing of fishing by minority groups such as the Chinese. The newly created federal fishing agency and the state board of fish commissioners studied the problem scientifically and restocked the rivers with exotic fish.[18]

A more recent example of the environmental effects of the egocentric ethic in California is the Santa Barbara oil spill. Union Oil Company of California, part of a consortium that had leased the rights from the federal government to drill for oil in a tract off the Santa Barbara coast, experienced a blowout of one of its deep water wells on 28 January 1969. Union's development reflected an egocentric ethic of self-interest. A corporation founded in the Santa Barbara area having assets of $2.4 billion, its directors sought to maximize profits and to elevate it from the eleventh largest oil company in the United States to a place among the Big Ten. Its oil drilling, petrochemical, tanker, and manufacturing operations made it an industrial giant. The blowout caused a large oil slick which spread toward Santa Barbara invading the commons of water, air, and public beaches. Ecological effects included the damaging of barnacles, surf grass, California sea lions, and thousands of birds including grebes, loons, murres, cormorants, brown pelicans, and sea gulls, as well as introducing aromatic hydrocarbons into the food chain. Hardin's analysis applies to this "tragedy of the commons." First, the advantage to Union Oil in using the ocean commons to drill for oil was +1, while the environmental consequences to them of polluting the commons were much less than −1 because the costs were shared by other oil companies and the public. Second, the oil spill resulted in stricter controls and fines on environmental pollution, the development of a growing body of environmental law—Hardin's "mutual coercion, mutually agreed upon,"—and a "Declaration of Environmental Rights" that includes the statement, "We must extend ethics beyond social relations to govern man's contact with all life forms and with the environment itself."[19]

An egocentric ethic underlies the actions of private developers in current environmental disputes in which the goals of entrepreneurs dedicated to promoting their individual good conflict with those of government agencies charged with preserving the public good, and with those of environmentalists defending the good of nonhuman nature. For example, discharges of toxic chemicals by computer chip manufacturers in "Silicon Valley" on the San Francisco peninsula conflict with the regulatory mandates of water quality control agencies protecting ground water quality. Likewise, the efforts of Dow Chemical Corporation to locate a chemical processing plant in the Suisuin Marsh area of the San Francisco Bay conflict with the public interest ethics of air and water quality control boards and with the ethics of environmentalists who wish to preserve the marsh as habitat for the endangered salt marsh harvest mouse.

From an environmental point of view, the egocentric ethic that legitimates laissez faire capitalism has a number of limitations. Because egocentric ethics is based on the assumption that the individual good is the highest good, the collective behavior of human groups or business corporations is not a legitimate subject of investigation. Second, because it includes the assumption that humans are "by nature" competitive and capitalism is the "natural" form of economics, ecological effects are external to human economics and cannot be adjudicated. In the nineteenth century, however, the first of these problems was dealt with through a new form of environmental ethics—the homocentric or utilitarian ethic. In the twentieth century, the problem of internalizing ecological externalities was addressed through the development of ecocentric ethics.

## Homocentric Ethics

A homocentric (or anthropocentric) ethic is grounded in society. A homocentric ethic underlies the social interest model of politics and the approach of environmental regulatory agencies that protect human health. According to the utilitarian ethics of Jeremy Bentham and John Stuart Mill, for example, a society ought to act in such a way as to insure the greatest good for the greatest number of people. The social good should be maximized, social evil minimized. For both Bentham and Mill, the utilitarian ethic has its origins in human sentience. Feelings of pleasure are good; those of pain are evil and are to be avoided. Because people have the capacity for suffering, society has an obligation to reduce suffering through policies that maximize social justice for all.[20]

Utility, according to Bentham, "is that property in any object whereby it tends to produce benefit, advantage, good, or happiness . . . or to prevent the happening of mischief, pain, evil, or unhappiness." For Bentham, the interest of the community is the "sum of the interests" of the individuals that compose it and actions are good in conformity with their tendency to "augment the happiness of the community." While Bentham spoke of the community and the sum of the individual interests that make up this "ficticious body," Mill cast his arguments in terms of the "general interests of society," "the interest of the whole," and "the good of the whole."[21] Each individual, he assumed, is endowed with feelings that promote the general good. "Utilitarian morality recognizes in humans the power of sacrificing their own greatest good for the good of others." Each person should associate his or her happiness with "the good of the whole." People therefore have primary duties and obligations to other humans, not just to themselves.[22] "Actions," he said, "are right in proportion as they tend to promote happiness; wrong as they tend to produce the reverse of happiness."[23]

In developing an ultimate sanction for the principle of utility, Mill went beyond the simple prohibitions against killing and robbery in the Mosaic decalogue and the Hobbesian idea that it is "natural" for individuals freely to kill each other unless they give up that right and receive protection from a sovereign. "I feel I am bound not to rob or murder, betray or deceive; but why am I bound to promote the general happiness?" he asked. The answer lies in education. The more "education and general cultivation," the more powerful is the enforcement. Moral feelings overcome selfish motives and create deeply rooted feelings of unity with other humans. These feelings are not innate, but acquired. Mill claimed that a sequence of ethical standards develops as "civilization" advances and mankind is "further removed from a state of savage independence." The spirit of the utilitarian ethic is expressed in the Golden Rule. "'To do as you would be done by,' and 'To love your neighbor as yourself,'" Mill wrote, "constitute the ideal perfection of utilitarian morality." This sequence from an individually based egocentric to a socially based utilitarian or homocentric ethic was further extended by Wisconsin ecologist Aldo Leopold in the 1930s in his formulation of a land ethic enhanced through education.[24]

In the United States, the conservation movement of the late nineteenth and early twentieth centuries was sanctioned by a homocentric ethic that extended utilitarianism to the natural environment. Gifford Pinchot's conservation ethic is based on the principle that natural resources should be used wisely to create "the greatest good for the greatest number [of people] for the longest time." Progressive era conservation policy centralized the management of forests, rivers, grazing lands, and minerals in government agencies. The ground for decision making in these agencies is that society should be benefited through extending the lives of renewable natural resources and conserving nonrenewable resources. Leopold contrasts Pinchot's formulation of the utilitarian ethic as a conservation ethic with an ecological ethic in his discussion of the A-B cleavage—the land as commodity production versus the land as biota.[25]

As in egocentric ethics, the homocentric *ought* reflects a religious formulation. Humans are stewards and caretakers of the natural world. Scholars such as ecologist René Dubos and philosophers John Passmore and Robin Attfield have pointed out that the Bible contains numerous passages that countervene the stark domination ethic of Genesis 1.[26] In Genesis 2, thought to be derived from a different historical tradition than Genesis 1, the animals are helpmeets for humans. God, according to Dubos, "placed man in the Garden of Eden not as a master but rather in a spirit of stewardship."[27] Like egocentric ethics, stewardship ethics were enunciated by seventeenth-century scientists and theologians concerned about the atheistic implications of mechanism as formulated by Hobbes. John Ray and William Derham developed a theology of stewardship consistent with Newtonian science, human progress, and the management of nature for human benefit. They quote such New Testament passages as Matthew 25:14: "That these things are the gifts of God, they are so many talents entrusted with us by the infinite Lord of the world, a stewardship, a trust reposed in us; for which we must give an account at the day when our Lord shall call." Additionally, in Luke 16:2, God said to the unfaithful steward, "Give an account of thy stewardship, for thou mayest no longer be steward." In stewardship ethics, God as the wise conservator and superintendent of the natural world made humans caretakers and stewards in his image. Stewardship ethics, however, is fundamentally a homocentric ethic. Humans must manage nature for the benefit of the human species, not for the intrinsic benefit of other species.[28]

Like egocentric ethics, homocentric ethics are consistent with the assumptions of mechanistic science, especially as extended by nineteenth-century scientists to include the fields of thermodynamics, hydrology, and electricity and magnetism. Scientific experts could use these laws for the efficient management of natural resources. Yet certain assumptions that characterize later ecocentric ethics are melded with the homocentric. Both nature (as in Darwinian evolution) and society are described in terms of organic metaphors. As Supreme Court Justice Oliver Wendell Holmes, Jr., put it in 1903, "In modern societies, every part is so organically related to every other part that what affects any portion must be felt more or less by all the rest."[29]

How have homocentric ethics been actuated in California? A particularly salient example is the building of dams for water and hydraulic power for cities and states. The controversy in the early twentieth century over whether to dam Hetch Hetchy Valley in Yosemite National Park as a source for water and power for the city of San Francisco is a case in point. Pinchot, arguing for San

Francisco, pointed out that a water supply for the city was a greater good for a greater number of people than leaving the valley in the state of nature for a few hikers and nature lovers. John Muir, on the other hand, viewed the valley as one of God's cathedrals and the proponents of the dam as temple destroyers, an ethic based on the valley's intrinsic right to remain as created. Today water control agencies such as the San Francisco Water Department or the Metropolitan Water District of Los Angeles are quite explicit in their claim that they must consider the greatest good for the greatest number of people in distributing water to their customers in time of shortages.[30]

The controversy over the damming of the Stanislaus River in the 1970s is another example. Federal officials wanted to provide flood control and water delivery for farmers, whereas environmentalists asserted that the river had a right to continue in its own state of nature as a wild river. The New Melones dam was proposed as part of the Bureau of Reclamation's Central Valley Project in the 1930s to control flooding and to recharge ground-water sources, and in 1962 the plans were expanded to include hydropower, irrigation, and recreation. Congressman John McFall, who fought for authorization to build the dam, adopted a utilitarian stance, arguing that a "larger project will bring more benefits for my people." After lengthy planning, review, and litigation involving public agencies such as the federal Bureau of Reclamation, the Army Corps of Engineers, and the State Water Resources Control Board and environmental groups such as the Environmental Defense Fund, the Friends of the River, and the Sierra Club, the dam was finally authorized and built, with high waters reaching and covering the white waters of the Stanislaus in the spring of 1983.

In his protest over the dam in 1979, environmentalist Mark Dubois chained himself to a rock to prevent the river, endangered wildlife, and the rocks from losing their rights to remain free. "All the life of this canyon, its wealth of archaeological and historical roots to our past, and its unique geological grandeur are enough reasons to protect this canyon just for itself," he wrote to the Army Corps of Engineers. "But in addition, all the spiritual values with which this canyon has filled tens of thousands of folks should prohibit us from committing the unconscionable act of wiping this place off the face of the earth." The controversy may be viewed as a conflict among interest groups with different underlying ethics. Here farmers and corporate agribusiness ventures, whose egocentric ethics promoted the individual's good, along with federal water control agencies, whose homocentric ethics saw water development as the greatest good for the greatest number, conflicted with the ecocentric ethics of those environmentalists who supported the river's intrinsic right to remain wild.[31]

This conflict points up one of the main problems of both egocentric and homocentric ethics—their failure to internalize ecological externalities. Ecological changes and their long-term effects are outside the human/society framework of these ethics. The effects of ecological changes such as salinity buildup in farming soils that use the dam's water or the loss of indigenous species when a valley is flooded are not part of the human-centered calculus of decision making. One approach offered by ethicists is to extend homocentric ethics to include other sentient species. Animal liberationists Peter Singer and Tom Regan, for example, extend the pleasure-pain principle of Bentham and Mill to animals, arguing that conditions for the well-being of animals should be maximized while conditions that lead to pain, such as overcrowded conditions, liquid diets, and cruel experimentation, should be minimized.[32] A similar extension of stewardship ethics to include nonhuman species and future human beings is made by Robin Attfield.[33] The alternative rejected by Attfield and the animal liberationists is to formulate a radically different form of environmental ethics—ecocentric ethics.

## Ecocentric Ethics

An ecocentric ethic is grounded in the cosmos. The whole environment, including inanimate elements, rocks, and minerals along with animate plants and animals, is assigned intrinsic value. The eco-scientific form of this ethic draws its ought from the science of ecology. Recognizing that science can no longer be considered value free, as the logical positivists of the early twentieth century had insisted, proponents of ecocentric ethics look to ecology for guidelines on how to resolve ethical dilemmas. Maintenance of the balance of nature and retention of the unity, stability, diversity, and harmony of the ecosystem are its overarching goals. Of primary importance is the survival of all living and nonliving things as components of healthy ecosystems. All things in the cosmos as well as humans have moral considerability

Modern ecocentric ethics were first formulated by Leopold during the 1930s and 1940s and published as "The Land Ethic," the final chapter of his posthumous *A Sand County Almanac.* Some of Leopold's inspiration for the land ethic seems to have derived from Mill's *Utilitarianism.* Like Mill, who wrote about the "influences of advancing civilization," the "removal from the state of savage independence," and the utilitarian Golden Rule as superseding the basic prohibitions against robbing and murdering, Leopold thought ethics developed in sequence: "The first ethics," he wrote, "dealt with the relation between individuals; the Mosaic Decalogue is an example. Later accretions dealt with the relation between the individual and society. The Golden Rule tries to integrate the individual to society." The land ethic, he argued, extends the sequence a step further. It enlarges the bounds of the community to include "soils, waters, plants, and animals, or collectively, the land." It "changes the role of *Homo sapiens* from conqueror of the land-community to plain member and citizen of it. It implies respect for his fellow members and also respect for the community itself."[34] In putting the land ethic into practice, Leopold urged that each question be judged according to what is both ethically and aesthetically right. Perhaps influenced by Mill's phraseology that "actions are right in proportion as they tend to promote happiness; wrong as they tend to produce the reverse of happiness," Leopold wrote: "A thing is right when it tends to preserve the integrity, beauty, and stability of the biotic community. It is wrong when it tends otherwise." Like Mill who argued for the importance of education in creating obligations toward other people, Leopold argued that in order to overcome economic self-interest, ethical obligations toward the land must be taught through conservation education.[35]

J. Baird Callicott has pointed out that Leopold's conception of community is derived from the community ecology of Frederic Clements and Charles Elton.[36] Clements conceptualized plant succession as the process through which a plant community changes from a young to a mature organism, just as a child grows into a mature adult. Elton included animals as well as plants in his community model of ecology. In an unpublished manuscript, written in the 1920s, Leopold discusses the concept espoused by the Russian philosopher Ouspensky that land is a living organism whose parts—soil, mountains, rivers, atmosphere, etc.—are like the organs of a coordinated whole. This whole has all the characteristics of a living thing, but because of its enormous size and the slowness of its life processes, people do not recognize it as such. "We cannot destroy the earth with moral impunity," Leopold admonished, " . . . the 'dead' earth is an organism possessing a certain kind and degree of life, which we intuitively respect as such."[37] In 1935, Arthur Tansley replaced Clements' and Elton's anthropomorphic language of the collective organism with the term *ecosystem.* By the time that Leopold completed *A Sand County Almanac,* his earlier earth ethic had become a land ethic and he had replaced the term *biology* with *ecology*. The organismic metaphor lingered, however, in what he called the A-B cleavage—his distinction between the utilitarian view of land as "slave and servant" versus the ecological concept of land as "collective organism."[38]

At the University of California, Santa Barbara, environmental historian Roderick Nash has elaborated Leopold's land ethic in an article "Do Rocks Have Rights?" Rocks are part of the pyramid of animate and inanimate things governed by the laws of ecology. Even though rocks are not sentient like animals, rocks as well as plants can be assigned interests that can be represented and adjudicated. Yet such a concept might still be used to protect rocks in the interest of humans. Pushing it further, Nash argues, we can "suppose that rocks, just like people, do have rights in and of themselves. It follows that it is the rock's interest, not the human interested in the rock, that is being protected." Other cultures such as Native Americans, Zen Buddhists, and Shintos, he points out, assume that rocks are alive—a mystical religious belief not usually held by Western philosophers and scientists.[39]

Ecocentric ethics are rooted in a holistic, rather than a mechanistic, metaphysics.[40] There are five basic assumptions implicit in this holistic perspective. (1) *Everything is connected to everything else.* The whole qualifies each part, conversely, a change in one of the parts changes the other parts and the whole. Ecologically, this has been illustrated by the idea that no part of an ecosystem can be removed without altering the dynamics of the cycle. If too many changes occur, an ecosystem collapses. Alternatively, to remove the parts from the environment for study in the laboratory may result in a distorted understanding of the ecological system as a whole.[41]

(2) *The whole is greater than the sum of the parts.* Unlike the concept of identity, in which the whole equals the sum of the parts, ecological systems experience synergy: the combined action of separate parts produce an effect greater than the sum of the individual effects. This can be exemplified by the dumping of organic sewage and industrial pollutants into lakes and rivers. The bacterial increases may cause those drinking or swimming in the water to become ill. But if the bottom of the lake is covered with metallic mercury, the overall hazard is more than doubled because the bacteria may also transform the metallic mercury into toxic methyl mercury which becomes concentrated in the food chain.[42]

(3) *Meaning is context dependent.* As opposed to the context independence assumption of mechanism, in holism each part at any instant takes its meaning from the whole. For example, in a hologram, produced by directing laser light through a half-silvered mirror, each part of the three-dimensional image contains information about the whole object. There are many-to-one and one-to-many relationships, rather than the point-to-point correspondences between object and image found in classical optics. Similarly, in perception, objects are integrated patterns. The whole is perceived first with an awareness of hidden aspects, background, and recognition of patterns, as when one views a tree or a house.[43]

(4) *Process has primacy over parts.* As opposed to the closed isolated equilibrium and near equilibrium systems studied in classical physics (such as the steam engine), biological and social systems are open. These are steady-state systems in which matter and energy are constantly being exchanged with the surroundings. Living things are dissipative structures, resulting from a continual flow of energy, just as a vortex in a stream is a structure arising from the continually changing water molecules swirling through it. Ilya Prigogene describes an open, far-from-equilibrium thermodynamics in which new order and organization can arise spontaneously. Nonlinear relationships occur in which small inputs can spontaneously produce large effects.[44] Continual change and

process are not only significant in ecology, but also are fundamental to the new physics. Physicist David Bohm in his book *Wholeness and the Implicate Order* describes process as originating from an undivided multidimensional wholeness called a holomovement. Within the holomovement is an implicate order that unfolds to become the explicate order of stable, recurring elements observed in the everyday world. The holomovement is life-implicit, the ground of both inanimate matter and of life.[45]

(5) *Humans and nonhuman nature are one.* In holism there is no nature/culture dualism: humans and nature are part of the same organic cosmological system. While theoretical ecologists often focus their research on natural areas removed from human impact, human (or political) ecologists study the mutual interactions between society and nonhuman nature.

In California, the philosophical change from the dominant mechanistic worldview to an ecological worldview, or *deep ecology* (a term coined by Norwegian philosopher Arne Naess), is a subject investigated by sociologist Bill Devall of Humboldt State University in Arcata and philosopher George Sessions of Sierra College. Devall and Sessions put forward eight basic principles of deep ecology including the idea that "the well-being and flourishing of human and nonhuman Life on Earth have value in themselves (synonyms: intrinsic value, inherent value). These values are independent of the usefulness of the nonhuman world for human purposes." They argue that policies should be implemented that maintain the richness and diversity of life, while also allowing for the fulfillment of basic human needs.[46]

The shift from a mechanistic, atomistic paradigm to an ecological, holistic paradigm is the focus of investigations by the Elmwood Institute in Berkeley, founded by physicist Fritjof Capra. The institute engages in a continent-wide education program and reaches out to the international community in its efforts to connect the ecological paradigm with a new ecological ethic. A second organization devoted to the promotion of a new world view is the Center for the Study of the Postmodern World in Santa Barbara, directed by founder David Griffin. Together with the Center for Process Studies, affiliated with the School of Theology at Claremont, the Center for the Study of a Postmodern World sponsors lecture series, conferences, and a book series on constructive postmodern thought. A third organization devoted to the emergence of a new consciousness that broadens the boundaries of science is the Institute of Noetic Sciences in Sausalito, directed by Willis Harman, an engineer and University of California regent.[47]

Just as mechanism dovetailed with certain political assumptions, so holism has been seen to imply particular kinds of politics. Holism found favor among philosophers and ecologists during the 1920s. In the 1930s, however, its emphasis on the whole over and above the parts was viewed as being consistent with fascism. This contributed to the replacement of holistic and organismic assumptions in biology by mechanistic modes of description. In the 1960s and 1970s holistic ideas returned with the blossoming of small-scale back-to-the-land communes and households in which decision making was vested in the consensus of the whole group. Drawing on holistic assumptions, the bioregional movement in California emphasizes living within the resources of the local watershed and developing them to sustain the human and nonhuman community as an ecological whole. Recently the emergence of green politics has given rise to a California political movement dedicated to the establishment of an ecologically viable society. [48]

Three examples illustrate the application of the ecocentric ethic in California: (1) restoration ecology, (2) the biological control of insect pests, and (3) sustainable agriculture. Restoration is the process of restoring human-disturbed ecosystems to earlier pristine forms. Leopold initiated the current movement when he began to replant an abandoned farm outside the University of Wisconsin at Madison with the original prairie plants that had grown there prior to white settlement. The project was continued after his death and is now the Curtis prairie in the university's arboretum. Using ecological guidelines, species are planted according to their original distributions in close proximity to each other. Over time a process occurs in which synergistic relationships are reestablished among soils, plants, insect pollinators, and animals to recreate the prairie ecosystem. Like a doctor healing a patient or a helmsperson steering a boat, restoration is a process of synthesis in which humans put nonhuman nature back together again. It contrasts with the mechanistic model in which nature is like a clock that can be taken apart through analysis and repaired through external intervention. An ecocentric ethic thus guides the restoration of forests, marshes, prairies, and rivers.[49]

An example of restoration in California is the replanting of the redwoods in Big Basin Redwoods State Park in the Santa Cruz mountains. The land where the park is today was set aside in 1902 after it had been scarred by heavy use, soil compaction, and erosion caused by lumber operations. As the old trees died new ones did not regenerate. In 1968, the Santa Cruz Lumber Company, which had held off cutting a stand of old-growth redwoods in what is now the park's interior core, went out of business and threatened to cut the timber if the state did not immediately exercise its option to purchase the land. Successful efforts to purchase and protect the threatened areas were followed by restoration. Guided by an implicit ecocentric ethic of management, restorers planted young trees, ferns, huckleberries, and ground cover, enriched the soil with redwood chips and removed old parking lots and remnants of lumber operations. Restoring the native plant species helped to establish the ecological conditions under which insect, mammal, and bird communities could also regenerate themselves. A new whole was created, helping to recreate the major elements of the presettlement ecosystem.[50]

Biological control is a second example of an ecocentric ethic of management. Using ecological guidelines, natural insect enemies are introduced into the ecosystem to control population levels of pests. The technique was pioneered by the Divisions of Biological Control of the University of California at Berkeley and at Riverside. One of the first successful uses of biological control in California occurred in 1888. The cottony-cushion scale introduced from Australia was destroying citrus groves in southern California. Acting on the inspiration of entomologist C. V. Riley, Albert Koebele traveled to Australia and brought back the vedalia, a lady beetle that fed on the scale. One thousand beetles soon cleared acres of orange groves, saving the industry. This ecological strategy was vindicated in the 1940s when DDT killed so many of the vedalia that a resurgence of the scale occurred.[51]

The assumptions that underlie biological control and its related strategy, integrated pest management (IPM), are ecologically grounded. According to Carl Huffaker of the University of California at Berkeley, the basis of IPM is that "biological control, together with plant resistance, forms nature's principal means of keeping phytophagous insects within bounds in environments otherwise favorable to them. They are the core around which pest control in crops and forests should be built."[52] Likewise, Ray Smith, also of the University of California at Berkeley, has noted that ecology provides the model for insect control strategies: "We cannot afford any longer to disregard the considerable capabilities of pest organisms for countering control efforts. . . . It is for this prudent reason that we must understand Nature's methods of regulating populations and maximize their application."[53] Biological control and IPM assume that humans are only one part of an interrelated ecological complex and that insects and humans must coexist. This management strategy is based on the recognition that insect populations will not be totally obliterated, but their numbers can be controlled so that humans may harvest crops. Reservoirs of insect pests, however, will continue to exist. This ecological interdependence implies that all organic and inorganic parts of the ecosystem have intrinsic value. Biological control is based therefore on an ecocentric rather than an egocentric or homocentric ethic.

According to environmental historian John Perkins, the ecocentric assumptions underlying biological control and IPM contrast with the human-centered stewardship ethics of the chemical-control paradigm that relies on broad spectrum chemicals to manage insects. This latter paradigm assumes that humans are above nature and can legitimately use chemicals to obliterate populations of insects for human benefit. Humans are "stewards of the natural world and both [can] and should do what [is] needed to protect their interests."[54] Chemical control is thus based on a homocentric or utilitarian ethic in which humans are the most important parts of the complex social and natural world and their high status legitimates their manipulation of the world for the good of human society.

A third example of an ecocentric ethic is sustainable agriculture, an ecologically based form of farm management. This strategy has been developed as an alternative to the industrial approach to agriculture based on optimizing purchased inputs to produce outputs at the least cost. The "evolution from labor intensive to energy and capital intensive farming," writes Miguel Altieri of the University of California at Berkeley, "was not influenced by rational decisions based on ecological considerations, but mainly by the low cost of energy inputs." In contrast to this egocentric approach, aimed primarily at maximizing a farmer's profits, the ecological approach is based on principles that conserve the renewable resource base and reduce the need for external technological inputs. According to Gordon Douglass of Pomona College in southern California, its principles include "1) the optimization of farm output over a much longer time period than is usual in industrial farming activities; 2) the promotion and maintenance of diversified agroecosystems whose living components perform complementary functions; 3) the building up of soil fertility with organic matter and the protection of nutrients from leaching; 4) the promotion of continuous cover and the extensive use of legume-based rotations, cover crops, and green manures; and 5) the limiting of imported fertilizer applications and pesticide uses."[55]

Sustainable agriculture can be further extended to integrate the human community with the agroecosystem. "This holistic approach to farming communities," Douglass points out, "draws attention to interactions not only within Landl among farming families and other human member[s] of rural communities, but also between nonhuman components such as crops with crops, crops with animals, soil conditions and fertility with insects, and disease in crops and livestock." Sustainable agriculture is thus based on an ecocentric ethic of management in which the land is considered as a whole, its human components being only one element. Policy decisions must be based on considerations of what is best for the soil, vegetation, and animals (including humans) on the farm as well as outside sources of water, air, and energy. As a result, humans and the land are sustained together.[56]

Like egocentric and homocentric ethics, ecocentric ethics have a religious formulation. Whereas the eco-scientific form of the ethic is rooted in the science of ecology, the eco-religious form is based on the faith that all living and nonliving things have value. In California, one such formulation is the process theology developed by John Cobb, Jr., David Ray Griffin, and others of the Center for Process Studies at Claremont Graduate School in southern California. Process theology owes its origins to British philosopher Alfred North Whitehead who taught at Harvard University and to philosopher Charles Hartshorne, a teacher of Cobb at the University of Chicago. According to Cobb and Griffin, process philosophy asserts that "process is fundamental. It does not assert that everything is in process . . . but to be *actual is* to be a process." It substitutes a theory of internal relations, according to which entities are qualitatively changed in interactions, for the nineteenth-century billiard ball model of unilinear causation in which entities are independent and left unchanged, affecting each other only through external relations. According to its theology of nature, God created the world out of chaos (rather than *ex nihilo*) and each stage in the evolutionary process represents an increase in divine goodness. Each *individual* thing, whether a living organism or an atom, has intrinsic value and there is a continuity between human and nonhuman experience. One's attitude toward a dog, which is a compound individual, differs from that toward a plant, which is also a compound individual, but has no center of enjoyment, and toward a rock, which, as a mere aggregate, has no intrinsic value. All three, however, have instrumental value in supporting each other in the ecosystem.[57]

Process thought is consistent with an ecological attitude in two senses: (1) its proponents recognize the "interconnections among things, specifically between organisms and their total environments," and (2) it implies "respect or even reverence for, and perhaps a feeling of kinship with, the other creatures." Cobb and Griffin argue that process philosophy implies an ecological ethic and a policy of social justice and ecological sustainability. "The whole of nature participates in us and we in it. We are diminished not only by the misery of the Indian peasant but also by the slaughter of whales and porpoises, and even by the 'harvesting' of the giant redwoods. We are diminished still more when the imposition of temperate-zone technology onto tropical agriculture turns grasslands into desert that will support neither human nor animal life."[58]

Cobb's student Jay McDaniel argues that intrinsic value includes the entire physical world. Atoms as individual things have intrinsic value. Rocks express the energy inherent within their atoms. They too have intensity and intrinsic value, albeit less than that of living organisms. Outer form is an expression of inner energy. The assumption that rocks have intrinsic value, however, does not mean that rocks and sentient beings would necessarily have equal ethical value, but rather that they would all be treated with reverence. This could result in a new attitude by Christians toward the natural world, one that involves both objectivity and empathy.[59]

Susan Armstrong-Buck of Humboldt State University in Arcata also sees Whitehead's philosophy as providing an adequate foundation for an environmental ethic. She argues that the assignment of intrinsic value to nonhuman nature is an integral component of Whitehead's metaphysics. Process is the continuity of occasions or events that are internally related—each present occasion is an integration of all past occasions. Occasions, Whitehead wrote, are "drops of experience complex, and interdependent." The world is itself a process of fluent energy; actual entities are self-organizing wholes. Differences exist in the actual occasions that constitute each entity. Intrinsic value, according to Armstrong-Buck, is based not on an extension of self-interest to the rest of nature, but on the significance to the entity itself of each occasion and its entire interdependent past history. The basis for assigning preferences to biosystems will be based on the degree of diversity, stability freedom of adaptation, and integration of actual occasions inherent in each system.[60]

Despite the efforts of Leopold and others, ecocentric ethics, like egocentric and homocentric ethics, has a number of philosophical difficulties. Finding a philosophically adequate justification for the intrinsic value of nonhuman beings has been called by some environmental philosophers the central axiological problem of environmental ethics. In mainstream Western culture, only human beings have traditionally had inherent worth, while the rest of nature has been assigned instrumental value as a resource for humans. Thus within an egocentric or homocentric ethic, it is not *morally* wrong to kill or use the last of a species of animal, plant, or mineral when human survival is at stake. Within an ecological ethic, however, such a decision could depend on finding an adequate justification for the intrinsic value of the nonhuman species, as well as on the particular circumstances. At bottom, ecocentric ethics may have a homocentric justification.[61]

A second problem stems from the distinction between facts and values. The separation of observable facts from humanly assigned values, or is from *ought*, has been a mainstay of Western science since the work of David Hume in the eighteenth century. Can a property such as the goodness or richness of animals, rocks, or the biosphere be inferred through the senses as an objective, intrinsic characteristic of the entities in question? Can there properly be such a thing as an ecological ethic, when ecology is an objective science and ethics is a subjective value system? Environmental philosophers have proposed a number of answers to the question, but they remain "wicked" problems for them, i.e., ones that demand transdisciplinary analysis. One approach is to question the possibility that facts can be separated from values in science and philosophy. Another is to recognize that descriptions of what is can include intrinsic value, while questions of what one ought to do belong to a different category.[62]

A third difficulty with Leopold and Nash's formulation of ecocentric ethics lies in the validity of their supposition that ethics develops sequentially. The advancement of civilization does not necessarily imply the evolution of more sophisticated ethics. The assumption that the earliest ethics dealt with the relations between individuals imposes the assumptions of Hobbes' hypothetical "state of nature" and the individualism of laissez faire capitalism onto the earliest peoples. Critics argue that in fact the sequence may be exactly reversed. American Indian and other indigenous cultures seem to have developed an ecocentric ethic that treats animals, plants, and rocks as if they were animate, sensitive persons. Conversely, the narcissism of twentieth-century Americans is a reflection of an extreme form of individualism focusing primarily on the self.[63]

Despite these underlying difficulties, egocentric, homocentric, and ecocentric environmental ethics have all received attention and have been further developed since the environmental movement of the 1970s and 1980s. When conflicts of interest over environmental and quality of life issues are at stake, the above taxonomy may be useful in analyzing the implicit ethical positions assumed by interested parties. Such an understanding could in turn lead to the improved environmental policies that are needed if both people and nonhuman nature are successfully to thrive together in the next century.

## Acknowledgments

The research for this paper was supported by Agricultural Experiment Station, project no. CA-B*-CRS-4720-H. The author thanks Miguel Altieri, J. Baird Callicott, David Griffin, Michael Heiman, Alan Miller, Pamela Muick, and Charles Sellers for helpful suggestions and criticisms.

## Endnotes

1. Aristotle, *Nichomachean Ethics,* in Richard McKeon, ed., *The Basic Works of Aristotle* (New York: Random House, 1941), 1095al3-l5, p. 937.

2. J. Hector St. John de Crevecoeur, "What Is an American?" in *Letters from an American Farmer* (New York: E. P. Dutton, 1957), p. 36.

3. *Palmer* v. *Mulligan,* 1805, quoted in Morton J. Horwitz, *The Transformation of American Law: 1780–1860* (Cambridge: Harvard University Press, 1981), p. 3.

4. Edmund S. Morgan, *The Puritan Dilemma: The Story of John Winthrop* (Boston: Little, Brown, 1958), pp. 7–8, 28.

5. Lynn White, Jr., "The Historical Roots of Our Ecologic Ethic," *Science* 155 (1967), 1203–1207.

6. John Winthrop, "Winthrop's Conclusions for the Plantation in New England," in *Old South Leaflets* (Boston, 1629), no. 50, pp. 4–5.

7. John Quincy Adams, in U.S. Congress, House, *Congressional Globe* 29th Cong., 1st Sess., I (9 February 1846), pp. 339–342. Adams omits the biblical phrase "replenish the earth."

8. Thomas Hart Benton, in U.S. Congress, Senate, *Congressional Globe* 29th Cong. 1st Sess., I (6 June 1846), pp. 917–918. Note that Benton reverses the biblical word ordering from "replenish the earth and subdue it" to "subdue and replenish the earth."

9. Reverend Dwinell, quoted in John Todd, *The Sunset Land or the Great Pacific Slope* (Boston: Lee and Shepard, 1870), p. 252.

10. Garrett Hardin, "The Tragedy of the Commons," *Science* 162 (1968), 1243–1248; Garrett Hardin and John Baden, eds., *Managing the Commons* (San Francisco: W. H. Freeman 1977).

11. Thomas Hobbes, "The Philosophical Rudiments Concerning Government and Society," in William Molesworth, ed., *English Works, 11 vols.* (Aalen, Germany: Scientia, 1966), vols. 2, 11.

12. Hobbes, *Leviathan,* in *English Works,* 3, p. 145. On the transformation of the use of the commons, see Carolyn Merchant, *The Death of Nature: Women, Ecology, and the Scientific Revolution* (San Francisco: Harper & Row, 1980), pp. 42–68, 209–213. Also Susan Jane Buck Cox, "No Tragedy on the Commons," *Environmental Ethics 7* (1985), 49–61.

13. Hobbes, *Leviathan,* p. 158.

14. Hardin, "Tragedy of the Commons," in *Managing the Commons,* pp. 20–21, 26–28. Hardin argues against the principle of Adam Smith that "decisions reached individually will, in fact, be the best decisions for an entire society," since it would imply laissez faire population control methods. He does not, however, question Smith's fundamental assumption that under capitalism an individual who "intends only his own gain," is "led by an invisible hand to promote . . . the public interest" (p. 19).

15. Hardin, "Living on a Lifeboat," in *Managing the Commons,* pp. 261–279.

16. Garrett Hardin, *Promethean Ethics: Living with Death, Competition, and Triage* (Seattle:

University of Washington Press, 1980). On the concept of triage, see also David H. Bennett, "Triage as a Species Preservation Strategy," *Environmental Ethics* 8 (1986), 47–58.

17. On the assumptions of mechanistic science and philosophy, see Merchant, *Death of Nature,* pp. 227–235.

18. Arthur McEvoy, *The Fisherman's Problem: Ecology and Law in the California Fisheries: 1850–1980* (New York: Cambridge University Press, 1980); idem., "Toward an Interactive Theory of Nature and Culture: Ecology, Production, and Cognition in the California Fishing Industry," *Environmental Review* 11 (1987), 293.

19. Robert Easton, *Black Tide: The Santa Barbara Oil Spill and Its Consequences* (New York: Delacorte, 1972), pp. ix, 5–6, 17–30, 250–264; Roderick Nash, "The Santa Barbara Oil Spill," in Roderick Nash, ed., *The American Environment: Readings in the History of Conservation* (Reading, MA: Addison-Wesley, 1976), p. 299. The Declaration of Environmental Rights is an extension of the natural rights doctrine of liberal economic theory to include the environment.

20. Jeremy Bentham, *An Introduction to the Principles of Morals and Legislation* (London: W. Pickering, 1823), 1:2. John Stuart Mill, *Utilitarianism* (Indianapolis: Bobbs Merrill, 1957), p. 10.

21. Bentham, *Principles of Morals and Legislation,* pp. 2–3. "An action . . . may be said to be conformable to the principle of utility, or for shortness sake, to utility (meaning with respect to the community at large), when the tendency it has to augment the happiness of the community is greater than any it has to diminish it" (p. 3). See also Mill, *Utilitarianism,* pp. 22–23.

22. Mill, *Utilitarianism,* p. 22. See also the following statements by Mill on the primacy of the good of the whole over that of the individual: "The happiness which forms the utilitarian standard of what is right in conduct is not the agent's own happiness but that of all concerned. As between his own happiness and that of others, utilitarianism requires him to be as strictly impartial as a disinterested and benevolent spectator" (p. 22). "Utility would enjoin first, that laws and social arrangements would place the happiness or the interest of every individual as nearly as possible in harmony with the interest of the whole" (p. 22). " . . . a direct impulse to promote the general good may be in every individual one of the habitual motives of action, and the sentiments connected therewith may fill a large and prominent place in every human being's sentient existence" (p. 23).

23. Ibid., p. 10.

24. Ibid., pp. 34, 36, 40, 22. Compare Aldo Leopold, *A Sand County Almanac* (London: Oxford University Press, 1949). *DD.,* pp. 202–203.

25. Gifford Pinchot, *Breaking New Ground* (New York: Harcourt Brace Jovanovich, 1947), p. 505: "Conservation is the foresighted utilization, preservation, and/or renewal of forests, waters, lands, and minerals, for the greatest good of the greatest number for the longest time." For a discussion of Pinchot's policies, see Samuel P. Hays, *Conservation and the Gospel of Efficiency: The Progressive Conservation Movement, 1890–1920* (New York: Atheneum, 1975). Leopold, *A Sand County Almanac,* pp. 221–223.

26. René Dubos, "Conservation, Stewardship, and the Human Heart," *Audubon Magazine,* Sep-

tember 1972, pp. 21–28; John Passmore, *Man's Responsibility for Nature* (New York: Scribner's, 1974), chap. 2, "Stewardship and Cooperation with Nature"; Robin Attfield, *The Ethics of Environmental Concern* (New York: Columbia University Press, 1983).

27. Dubos, "Conservation," p. 27.

28. Merchant, *Death of Nature,* pp. 246–252.

29. Oliver Wendell Holmes in *Diamond Glue Co.* v. *United States Glue Co.,* 1903, quoted in McEvoy, "Toward an Interactive Theory," p. 294.

30. Roderick Nash, "Hetch Hetchy," in *Wilderness and the American Mind* (New Haven: Yale University Press, 1977), chap. 10, pp. 161–181; Carolyn Merchant, "Women of the Progressive Conservation Movement, 1900–1916," *Environmental Review* 8 (1984), 76–80. On current water issues, see Carl Nolte, "Bay Area May Buy Water from Southern California," *San Francisco Chronicle,* 24 February 1989, p. A1.

31. Tim Palmer, *Stanislaus: The Struggle for a River* (Berkeley: University of California Press, 1982), pp. 53, 163; Palmer, *Endangered Rivers and the Conservation Movement* (Berkeley: University of California Press, 1986), pp. 125–128.

32. Peter Singer, *Animal Liberation: A New Ethics for Our Treatment of Animals* (New York: Avon Books, 1975); Tom Regan, *All That Dwell Therein—Essays on Animals Rights and Environmental Issues* (Berkeley: University of California Press, 1982). In *Utilitarianism,* Mill wrote, "The standard of morality . . . may accordingly be defined [as] 'the rules and precepts for human conduct' by the observance of which an existence such as has been described might be, to the greatest extent possible, secured to all mankind; and not to them only, but, so far as the nature of things admits, to the whole sentient creation" (p 16).

33. Attfield, *Ethics of Environmental Concern.*

34. Mill, *Utilitarianism,* pp. 40, 34, 22; see discussion above. Leopold, *A Sand County Almanac,* pp. 224–225.

35. Mill, *Utilitarianism,* p. 10; on education, see p. 35. Leopold, *A Sand County Almanac,* pp. 224–225; on education, see pp. 207–214.

36. J. Baird Callicott, ed., *Companion to A Sand County Almanac: Interpretative and Critical Essays* (Madison: University of Wisconsin Press, 1987), pp. 198ff.

37. Aldo Leopold, "Some Fundamentals of Conservation in the Southwest," *Environmental Ethics* I (1979), 131–141. For a discussion see Susan Flader, "Leopold's 'Some Fundamentals of Conservation': A Commentary," *Environmental Ethics* I (1979), 143–148 and Callicott, *Companion,* pp. 201–202.

38. Leopold, *A Sand County Almanac,* p. 223, as discussed in Callicott, *Companion,* pp. 201–202.

39. Roderick Nash, "Do Rocks Have Rights?" *The Center Magazine,* November/December 1977, p. 10.

40. On holism see J. C. Smuts, *Holism and Evolution* (New York: Macmillan, 1926). For a critique of holistic thinking, see D. C. Phillips, *Holistic Thought in Social Science* (Stanford: Stanford University Press, 1976).

41. Barry Commoner, *The Closing Circle: Nature, Man, and Technology* (New York: Bantam,

1972), pp. 29–35, 188. For a critique of Commoner's holism, see Don Howard, "Commoner on Reductionism," *Environmental Ethics* 1 (1979), 159–176.

42. Commoner, *Closing Circle,* pp. 221–223.

43. John P. Briggs and F. David Peat, *Looking Glass Universe: The Emergence of Wholeness* (New York: Simon & Schuster, 1984), pp. 249–252.

44. llya Pngogine and Isabelle Stengers, *Order out of Chaos: Man's New Dialogue with Nature* (New York: Bantam, 1984).

45. David Bohm, *Wholeness and the Implicate Order* (Boston: Routledge & Kegan Paul, 1980), pp. 1–26, 172–213.

46. Bill Devall and George Sessions, *Deep Ecology* (Salt Lake City: Peregrine Smith Books, 1985). See also Michael Tobias, ed., *Deep Ecology* (San Diego: Avant Books, 1985).

47. Fritjof Capra, *The Tao of Physics: An Exploration of the Parallels between Modern Physics and Eastern Mysticism* (Berkeley: Shambhala, 1975); idem., *The Turning Point: Science, Society and the Rising Culture* (New York: Simon & Schuster, 1982). David Griffin, ed., *The Reenchantment of Science: Postmodern Proposals* (Albany: State University of New York Press, 1988); idem., *Spirituality and Society: Postmodern Visions* (Albany: State University of New York Press, 1988); Willis Harman, *An Incomplete Guide to the Future* (New York: Norton, 1979). Other California authors whose books have addressed the shift to an ecological paradigm include John B. Cobb, Jr. (see n. 57); Theodore Roszak, *Where the Wasteland Ends: Politics and Transcendence in Postindustrial Society* (Garden City, NY: Doubleday, 1972); Ernest Callenbach, *Ecotopia* (Berkeley: Banyan Tree Books, 1977); Joseph W. Meeker, *Minding the Earth: Thinly Disguised Essays on Human Ecology* (Alameda, CA: Latham Foundation, 1988); Gary Snyder, *Turtle Island* (New York: New Directions, 1974); Gregory Bateson, *Steps to an Ecology of Mind* (New York: Chandler, 1972); Bateson, *Mind and Nature: A Necessary Unity* (New York: E. P. Dutton, 1979).

48. Donald Worster, *Nature's Economy: The Roots of Ecology* (San Francisco: Sierra Club Books, 1977), pp. 329–330, 339–348. Peter Berg, *Figures of Regulation: Guides for Re-Balancing Society with the Biosphere* (San Francisco: Planet Drum Foundation, n.d.); idem., ed., *Reinhabiting a Separate Country: A Bioregional Anthology of Northern California* (San Francisco: Planet Drum Foundation, 1978); Raymond Dasmann and Peter Berg, "Reinhabiting California," *The Ecologist* 7 (1980), 399–401; Raymond Dasmann, "Future Primitive: Ecosystem People versus Biosphere People," *Coevolution Quarterly* (Fall 1976), 26–31; idem., "Biogeographical Provinces," *Coevolution Quarterly* (Fall 1976), 32–37; Fritjof Capra and Charlene Spretnak, *Green Politics: The Global Promise* (New York: E. P. Dutton, 1984).

49. On the philosophy of restoration, see William R. Jordan, "Thoughts on Looking Back," *Restoration and Management Notes* 1, no. 3 (Winter 1983), 2; William R. Jordan "On Ecosystem Doctoring," *Restoration and Management Notes* 1, no. 4 (Fall 1983), 2; Carolyn Merchant "Restoration and Reunion with Nature," *Restoration and Management Notes* 4, no. 2 (Winter 1986), 68–70. On Leopold and restoration, see "Looking Back: A Pioneering Restoration Project Turns Fifty," *Restoration and Management Notes* 1, no. 3 (Winter 1983), 4–10. On the techniques of restoration, see John Cairns, Jr., "Restoration, Reclamation, and

Regeneration of Degraded or Destroyed Ecosystems," in Michael Soulé, ed., *Conservation Biology: The Science of Scarcity and Diversity* (Sunderland, MA: Sinauer, 1986), pp. 465–484. Restoration is not only used to reestablish natural areas such as parks and nature reserves, but also as mitigation in development. Thus, an airport may expand by filling in a marsh to construct an airstrip. As mitigation for the construction, the developer must artistically reconstruct another marsh in the vicinity. Here the ethical goals and guidelines are more consistent with homocentrism than ecocentrism.

50. John J. Berger, *Restoring the Earth* (New York: Knopf, 1985), pp. 69–78; see also pp. 155–171 on the restoration of falcons in California. For other examples of restoration projects see articles in *Restoration and Management Notes.*

51. Richard L. Doutt, "Vice, Virtue, and the Vedalia," *Bulletin of the Entomological Society of America* 4 (1958), 119–123; K. S. Hagen and J. M. Franz, "A History of Biological Control," *History of Entomology* (Palo Alto, CA: Annual Reviews, 1973), pp. 433–476, see pp. 433–435, 441–444; Richard L. Doutt, "A Tribute to Parasite Hunters," in Cynthia Westcott, ed., *Handbook on Biological Control of Insect Pests* (New York: Brooklyn Botanic Garden Record, Plants and Gardens, 1960), p. 51; Paul Debach, *Biological Control by Natural Enemies* (London: Cambridge University Press, 1974), pp. 92–100.

52. F. Wilson and C. B. Huffaker, "The Philosophy, Scope and Importance of Biological Control," in C. B. Huffaker and P. S. Messenger, eds., *Theory and Practice of Biological Control* (New York: Academic Press, 1976), p. 4.

53. R. F. Smith, J. L. Apple, and D. G. Bottrell, "The Origin of Integrated Pest Management Concepts for Agricultural Crops," in J. L. Apple and R. F. Smith, eds., *Integrated Pest Management* (New York: Plenum Press, 1976), p. 12.

54. Perkins, *Insects, Experts, and the Insecticide Crisis: The Quest for New Pest Management Strategies* (New York: Plenum Press, 1982), p. 184. For a critique of chemical controls by an advocate of biological control, see Robert van den Bosh, *The Pesticide Conspiracy* (New York: Doubleday Anchor, 1980).

55. Miguel Altieri, "Ecological Diversity and the Sustainability of California Agriculture," in *Sustainability of California Agriculture: A Symposium* (Davis: University of California Sustainability of California Agriculture Research and Education Program, 1985), p. 106; Gordon K. Douglass, "Sustainability of What? For Whom?" in *Sustainability of California Agriculture: A Symposium* (Davis: University of California Sustainability of California Agriculture Research and Education Program, 1985), p. 38. See the remainder of these proceedings for additional examples of sustainable agriculture in California; also Miguel Altieri, James Davis, and Kate Burroughs, "Some Agroecological and Socioeconomic Features of Organic Farming in California: A Preliminary Study," *Biological Agriculture and Horticulture* I (1983), 97–107. Sustainable agriculture could also be conceptualized as a homocentric ethic of stewardship oriented primarily to the good of human communities. See George E. Brown, Jr., "Stewardship in Agriculture," in Gordon K. Douglass, ed., *Agricultural Sustainability in a Changing World Order* (Boulder, CO: Westview Press, 1984), pp. 147–158.

56. Douglass, "Sustainability of What?" p. 40.

57. John B. Cobb, Jr., and David Ray Griffin, *Process Theology* (Philadelphia: Westminister

Press 1976), p. 14; see also 23, 65–67, 76, 79, 152–153; John B. Cobb, Jr., "Process Theology and an Ecological Model," in Philip N. Joranson and Ken Butigan, eds., *Cry of the Environment: Rebuilding the Christian Creation Tradition* (Santa Fe: Bear & Company, 1984), pp. 329–336; John B. Cobb Jr., "Ecology, Ethics, and Theology," in *Herman E. Daly,* ed., *Economics, Ecology, Ethics: Essays Toward a Steady-State Economy* (San Francisco: W. H. Freeman, 1973), pp. 162–176; Charles Birch and John Cobb, Jr., *The Liberation of Life: From the Cell to the Community* (Cambridge: Cambridge University Press, 1981); Alfred North Whitehead, *Process and Reality,* ed. David Ray Griffin and Donald W. Sherburne (New York: Free Press, 1978). The Center for Ethics and Social Policy in Berkeley, California has also addressed the question of an ecological approach to Christian religion. See Joranson and Butigan, *Cry of the Environment.* Conrad Bonifazi of Humboldt State University in Arcata is the author of *The Soul of the World: An Account of the Inwardness of Things* (Lanham, MD: University Press of America, 1978).

58. Cobb and Griffin, *Process Theology,* pp. 76, 79, 155.

59. Jay McDaniel, "Physical Matter as Creative and Sentient," *Environmental Ethics* 5 (1983), 291–317; McDaniel, "Christian Spirituality as Openness to Fellow Creatures," *Environmental Ethics* 8 (1986), 33–46.

60. Susan Armstrong-Buck, "Whitehead's Metaphysical System as a Foundation for Environmental Ethics," *Environmental Ethics* 8 (1986), 243, 246.

61. On the problem of intrinsic value, see J. Baird Callicott, "Intrinsic Value, Quantum Theory, and Environmental Ethics," *Environmental Ethics* 7 (1985), 257–275.

62. On ecology and values, see Holmes Ralston III, "Is There an Ecological Ethic?" *Ethics* 85 (1975), 93–104. Wicked problems are a class of complex value-laden problems to which there are no solutions that are disciplinary in nature. Their resolution depends on new transdisciplinary methods of conceptualization.

63. Donald Worster, "Conservation and Environmentalist Movements in the U.S.: Comment on Nash and Hays," in Kendall E. Bailes, ed., *Environmental History: Critical Issues in Comparative Perspective* (Lanham, MD: University Press of America, 1985), p. 262. On ancient ideas of an animate earth and its ethical implications, see J. Donald Hughes, "Gaia: Environmental Problems in Chthonic Perspective," ibid., pp. 64–82 and Merchant, *Death of Nature,* p. 141. On the way in which the animate view of nature held by American Indian tribes regulated hunting and gathering, see Calvin Martin, *Keepers of the Game: Indian-Animal Relationships and the Fur Trade* (Berkeley: University of California Press, 1978) and G. Reichel-Dolmatoff, "Cosmology as Ecological Analysis: A View from the Rain Forest," *The Ecologist* 7, no. 1 (1977), 4–11.

## Journal/Discussion Questions

✍ *Merchant recounts the story of Mark Dubois and his 1979 protest against a dam project. Discuss your reactions to Dubois' protest. Do you think he was right to do what he did?*

1. According to Merchant, what are the lim-

itations of the egocentric approach to environmental issues? To the homeocentric approach? To the ecocentric approach? What limitations do *you* see in the ecocentric approach? Which approach most closely resembles your own?

2. Merchant discusses Roderick Nash's article, "Do Rocks Have Rights?" How would you answer Nash's question? Do you agree with Merchant's position on this issue?

3. What, according to Merchant, are the basic assumptions of holism? What is the opposite of holism?

---

### Lynn Scarlett
### "Clear Thinking about the Earth"

*Lynn Scarlett is vice-president of research at the Reason Foundation in Los Angeles. The primary focus of her research is on environmental policy, including solid waste, recycling, and air emissions issues.*

*In this article, Scarlett explores the ways in which people's basic presuppositions— their worldviews—shape the ways in which they see the world and, more specifically, the ways in which they understand both the causes of environmental problems and their solutions. She argues that the basic presupposition underlying Vice President Al Gore's worldview is a deeply pessimistic and surprisingly static one; she contrasts this with a more optimistic, dynamic view of our relationship to the environment.*

### As You Read, Consider This:

1. How, according to Scarlett, does the static nature of Gore's worldview affect his views on natural resources? How does the dynamic nature of her own worldview affect Scarlett's views?

~

"Rashamon," a celebrated Japanese film, presents four witnesses observing a single crime. Each witness perceives the situation so differently that the audience experiences what appear to be four distinct events.

Current discourse on the environment raises a "Rashamon-like" specter of competing perceptions. The world presents us with a single reality; but expositors on the environment view that world and its workings through multiple and radically different lenses. Among this medley of lenses, two perspectives predominate.

On the one hand, we have what I will call the pessimists. They see a world in trouble. They focus on the moment, see despoliation, and predict doom. They believe we can evade doom, but

Lynn Scarlett, "Clear Thinking about the Earth," reprinted with the Permission of the Pacific Research Institute for Public Policy from *Environmental Gore*, ed. John A. Baden (San Francisco: Pacific Research Institute for Public Policy, 1994). Copyright 1994, Pacific Research Institute for Public Policy.

only through sweeping changes wrought through single-minded pursuit of an environmental imperative.

On the other hand are the optimists. They view today as one moment on a long and largely progressive landscape of human achievement, a landscape in which human action propels us forward in a never-ending problem-solving quest.

Vice President Albert Gore fits squarely among the pessimistic visionaries. In *Earth in the Balance,*[1] he tells us that "our children will inherent a wasteland," unless we "dramatically change our civilization and our way of thinking about the relationship between humankind and the earth" (p. 163).

## Gore's Worldview

This is Gore's overarching vision. What are the elements of that vision?

Gore's vision is of a (relatively) static world. He purports to look far into the future, but his view of the present is static—like a snapshot of a moment. He sees current patterns of resource use, projects those patterns into the future, and labels them "unsustainable."

This snapshot view also gives rise to a basic pessimism about technology and human action. Understandably, in a snapshot world view, technologies look like the problem rather than an evolving sequence of solutions. In Gore's snapshot focus, past ills are forgotten, leaving us to dwell only on present woes, which, in turn, are easy to blame on present technologies. His snapshot view compels us to forget that those technologies were the answer to some earlier challenge. Indeed, for Gore, change and adaptation are themselves suspect: "our willingness to adapt," he says, "is an important part of the underlying problem. . . . believing that we can adapt to just about anything is ultimately a kind of laziness" (p. 240).

Gore's freeze-frame world view has three chief consequences. First, it underplays the omnipresence of trade-offs in human action. Gore tends to focus on a single problem (or set of problems) at a single point in time, which then prompts him to propose "solutions" to these problems outside of any historical context. This results in an ignoring of past problems whose redress may have given rise to present problems. It leads him to ignore (or at least greatly underplay) how his proposed "solutions" themselves may mitigate one problem, while giving rise to others. It results in what American Enterprise Institute economist Robert Hahn calls Gore's "kitchen sink" approach to problem-solving—throw every tool at the problem with no thought given to costs and adverse (including environmental) impacts.[2]

Second, with technologies identified as the culprit for current problems, this leads Gore easily to the conclusion that the only remedies to the problems before us lie in fundamental changes in our thinking. Our effort, he writes in *Earth in the Balance,* "has to involve more than a search for mechanical solutions" (p. 161). He then adds that we need to "find a way to dramatically change our civilization and our way of thinking about the relationship between humankind and the earth" (p. 163).

Third, since technology springs primarily out of the world of industry, this view makes industry a leading offender standing in the way of a cleaner environment.

Resilience and adaptation are natural components of a dynamic world—a world in which human action is a constant process of confronting problems, adjusting, and readjusting. By contrast, in a freeze-frame world, problems take on a more cataclysmic cast. Problems are "out there," the product of accumulated human actions. And "solutions" take the form of some imagined "new" picture of the world, some set of endpoints like "clean air," "clean water," protected wetlands and forests, some future Eden.

With a set of endpoints in mind, reaching that future becomes, then, a process of prescribing new "managed" technologies, new products, new lifestyles, new mandates for action. A freeze-frame view thus often gives rise to an emphasis on prescriptive regulations and pre-defined solutions.

This freeze-frame view also nourishes a sense that "we are running out of resources." At any point in time, the mix of resources that are "out there" appears to be finite and fixed. If we are running out of resources, then recycling and reduced consumption become compelling requirements for sustainable development.

This is a tough theme to refute. Intuitively, it would seem self-evident that most of the earth's resources are finite. There are, of course, exceptions. These include resources that reproduce—like plant matter. Or those that are recreated in never-ending cycles—like water. And they include resources that we take advantage of but do not deplete in the process—like the sun.

However, rocks and minerals, and plant matter like old-growth forests that took eons to come to their present majesty, and fragile environments that house critters in a delicate balance, all these resources surely are finite in some real sense.

In fact, this emphasis on scarcity highlights an important constraint on human activity. Economics is all about the decisions by which we marshal scarce resources to satisfy virtually infinite desires and needs. But this scarcity in an economic sense does not imply that we are "running out of resources" in the sense set forth by so many who share Gore's apocalyptic world view.

## Another Worldview

How could this be? Looking at the environment through a different lens gives us a different interpretation of the world around us. A longer time horizon that stretches into the past and projects into the future helps nourish a more optimistic view of our resource base for several reasons.

For example, this longer time frame allows us to focus on the processes of change—how we moved from a Stone Age to a Bronze Age to an Iron Age and eventually on into the present Information Age. This focus invites two observations.

First, this perspective underscores that it is the attributes of particular raw materials that we seek, not each stone, chemical, or organic product per se. We seek fuel, not necessarily oil; material that can be woven, not just cotton, wool, or nylon; materials that are malleable, strong, or conductive, not copper or iron or silica per se. This opens up vast possibilities for invention, exploration, substitution, and expansion of our resource base. It is human action that turns a sow's ear into silk—or, more realistically, sewage sludge into energy, oil into usable fuel, or old plastic scrap into tennis ball fuzz.

This is not mere speculation. In the 1970s, authors of a best-selling book, *Limits to Growth*, predicted that gold, silver, mercury, zinc, and lead would have been thoroughly depleted by the year 2000. Instead, as Harvard economist Robert Stavins points out in a 1993 article, "reserves have increased; demand has changed; substitution has occurred; and recycling has been stimulated."[3]

One dramatic example helps us to understand how, even in the face of population growth and increasing incomes, we do not appear to be "running out of resources." Consider our telecommunications system—the linchpin of the modern age. In the 1950s some doomsayers, eyeing the increasing consumption of copper to provide communications wire, presaged severe copper shortages and impending interruptions of our worldwide communications network.

What, instead, has come to pass? Today, copper wire is increasingly being replaced by fiber optic cable. We are moving away from the relatively high-value copper to abundant sand as our basic input into communications networks. The impact on resources is stunning. We consume 25 kilograms of sand to produce a cable that can carry 1,000 times the messages over its length as a cable made from one ton of copper.

This example does not settle the issue. Not all efforts at substitution yield such compelling results. Examples such as these, however, should at least cause us to ask under what conditions this evolution occurs, whether it applies to all resources, and what the implications are for general concern about resource conservation. The historical world view prompts questions about process and change that the freeze-frame view unwittingly neglects.

There is another point that a longer time horizon and a focus on dynamic processes makes apparent. Changing circumstances give rise to changing priorities. When requirements for basic food and shelter absorbed the attention of most of humankind, it is not surprising that certain environmental values were neglected. As those more fundamental needs have been met, we naturally have developed a revised hierarchy of values, one in which environmental amenities, conservation, and long-term health concerns become top priorities. This is, however, an evolutionary, not a revolutionary process.

It is likewise not surprising that technological innovations of earlier decades and centuries turned more toward efforts to efficiently produce food, clothing, shelter, and other tangible consumption items than toward redressing environmental problems. As our hierarchy of values has changed, however, so, too, do our innovations evolve to satisfy new goals and overcome new problems.

The apocalyptic worldview, with its shorter time frame, neither perceives nor appreciates this evolutionary and iterative process. Hence, again, problems appear cataclysmic, with their resolution depending on revolutionary alterations in human action.

None of the adjustment process described by optimists occurs by magic. This prompts us to ask under what conditions these evolutionary changes take place. One economic structure seems especially pivotal to this process of change, conservation, and resource stewardship: prices.

Free-market prices emerge through the dynamic transactions of buyers and sellers. They fluctuate, depending on supply and demand, giving us information about the relative scarcities of different resources, labor, and capital. They tell us—in a relative sense—which resources are becoming scarcer. They thus help us to conserve where it matters most at any point in time. And they provide a common denominator—a yardstick—with which we can compare and prioritize our multiple preferences, values, and needs. They tell us how much (in monetary terms) of a set of resources (including raw materials, energy, labor, capital, and, increasingly, environmental "goods") are required to satisfy our different needs.

This picture is imperfect. Not all "costs" associated with certain activities are incorporated into pricing systems. In fact, imperfect pricing is at the heart of many current resource problems—we don't "pay" for the air we use, or we don't pay the full costs for the water we drink, for example. Thus, the adjustment process only imperfectly encompasses our quest for enhancing environmental values.

There is another side issue here worth mentioning. Our "environment" is more than simply a set of "resources" ready and waiting for transformation into items useful for human consumption. For many, the concern about the environment goes beyond ensuring a steady supply of resources to meet tangible human needs. For example, historian Lynn White has repudiated what he calls the "axiom that nature has no reason for existence save to serve man."[4] White called for the "spiritual autonomy of all parts of nature," a theme that Gore has repeated. Gore writes in *Earth in the Balance* that people have lost sight of the "intrinsic" value of nature. He states, "so many people now view the natural world merely as a collection of resources; indeed to some people nature is like a giant data bank that they can manipulate at will" (p. 203).

While it makes no philosophical sense to talk about flora or fauna or geological formations having "intrinsic" value, it is plausible to imagine that some of us value the earth and its living components for the aesthetic or spiritual nourishment they arouse.

"Intrinsic value" implies value outside the "valuer"—value beyond the presence of any moral consciousness. Spiritual values, however, do exist: they emerge from the moral choices and preferences of individuals. For these kinds of values, the economic dynamics of substitution offer little solace. As the oft-repeated poem puts it, "a rose is a rose is a rose." If that rose—or the gray whale or an Alpine lake—disappears, those who derive spiritual contentment from that rose will not find consolation in the prospect that other natural wonders still exist or that substitution processes will prevent our "running out" of those instrumental resources that we use for human consumption of tangible goods.

This leads us to the second important economic structure important to the dynamic processes of change, conservation, and resource stewardship: property rights. In a pathbreaking 1968 article, Garret Hardin warned us of the perils of the "tragedy of the commons." Unfettered access to commonly owned resources, Hardin argued, leads us to despoliation of the environment. In a book Hardin edited in 1977 he wrote, "Individuals locked into the logic of the commons are free only to bring on universal ruin."[5]

Hardin identified a fundamental environmental problem, but many later commentators on his work did not draw the obvious conclusion from Hardin's observations about the commons. Instead of seeing the advantages of introducing property rights where they do not exist and sustaining them where they do, they saw regulations or more common ownership as the remedy.

Yet property rights, for all the negative emotional baggage and ambiguous issues they raise, establish conditions of responsibility. Property rights sustain responsibility because they directly link "actors" to the outcomes of their actions. It is (though with many caveats) the property owner that suffers from the consequences of poor stewardship. Hence, property rights promote stewardship. As Rob Stavins has pointed out, "the reason why some resources—water, forests, fisheries, and some species of wildlife—are threatened while others—principally minerals and fossil fuels—are not is that the scarcity of the latter group (the nonrenewable resources) is well reflected in market prices, while this is much less the case for the former group, which, in fact, are characterized by being *open access* or *common property* resources."[6]

Property rights also establish boundaries for individual human action, by restricting the spheres within which one can act autonomously. Beyond those spheres, where individuals bump shoulders with one another, autonomous actions are circumscribed at a minimum by a "do no harm to others" principle. But within those spheres, individuals can pursue self-defined values. This means instrumental values—for example, using land for grazing. And it means spiritual values—the "nature as cathedral" values that Gore worries about.

Without property institutions, the alternative remains the give-and-take of the political process, which means the processes of coerced compromise. Or one can, like Gore, press for a religious transformation, a sort of consciousness-raising whereby we all adopt a shared appreciation of "nature as cathedral" and environmental goals as the single organizing principle for our actions. One wonders where Gore can point to for a successful model of "consciousness raising" of the scope he proposes. The most far-reaching attempts (revolutionary socialism) to create a "new human being" have been accompanied with massive coercive efforts. The legacy of such efforts has thus mostly been loss of freedom and only dubious accomplishments toward a better world.

## The Limits of World Visions

Competing world visions make dialogue about appropriate actions difficult, since different visions produce different interpretations even of what "the problem" is. And, by definition, different world visions produce different understandings of how the world works.

Sorting out the components of competing visions can help us explore where opportunities for better communications might lie. Yet this exploration will not dissolve differences. Gore blurs two very different aspects of human thought and sentiment. World visions are all about how we think the world works; they are not about what we "value." To some extent, world visions can be altered by honing our powers of observation and understanding—by taking a bird's eye view where we had previously looked only with feet planted on the ground.

Values, however, spring from a complex interplay of reasoned thought and human sentiment. Thus, at least part of the environmental policy debate is a tug-of-war between those who value, for example, "freedom of human action" not for any utilitarian results it might have, but because it "feels good" to be free. The same can be said for those who embrace the "nature as cathedral" notion. They value nature because it "feels good" to walk in its beauty.

This is why so much talk of "market mechanisms" to address environmental problems misses the central questions. If markets are *only* about finding lower-cost ways to achieve predefined goals, these mechanisms simply push aside values questions. And the embrace of these market mechanisms in terms of "problem-solving" puts these tools on a level with proposed new technologies or new regulations. All three are merely instruments to solve problems.

On the other hand, there is another way of looking at markets—a way that views markets as a set of decentralized institutions and decision processes through which individuals "reveal" their preferences and through which they undertake mutually agreeable transactions. This is another way of saying that, through their choices among competing options, individuals translate their values into sets of actions. And they do so through what amounts to a give-and-take process of negotiation. Markets, thus, are about individual freedom.[7]

A historical lens, with an emphasis on evolution and adjustment, permits us to see a dynamic world and to focus on process rather than particular "freeze-frame" outcomes. The focus on process moves us away from the "markets-as-tools" notion toward an appreciation of markets as a means by which individuals pursue their individual hierarchies of values. It is the feedback loops of decentralized market decision-making institutions that will allow individuals to pursue those values into the future. And it is those same feedback loops that will make environmental values rise higher and higher on the hierarchy as our other needs are met and as these tangible environmental and spiritual values loom larger.

## Endnotes

1. Al Gore, *Earth in the Balance* (Boston: Houghton Mifflin, 1992).

2. See Chapter 2 of *Environmental Gore*, edited by John A. Baden (San Francisco: Pacific Research Institute for Public Policy, 1992).

3. Robert Stavins, "Comments on 'Lethal Model 2: The Limits to Growth Revisited,' by William Nordhaus," in *Brookings Papers on Economic Activity*, 1993.

4. Lynn White, cited in Robert James Bidinotto, "The Green Machine," *IOS Journal*, May 1993.

5. Garret Hardin, ed., "The Tragedy of the Commons," *Managing the Commons* (New York, W. H. Freeman, 1977), p. 29.

6. Stavins, *op. cit.*

7. This is a notion of freedom strongly at odds with that put forth by Gore. Gore claims that "freedom is a necessary condition for an effective stewardship of the environment" (p. 179). Yet he means by freedom the political empowerment to demand remedies to problems.

## Journal/Discussion Questions

✍ *Scarlett stresses the importance of worldviews in shaping our basic perception of the world. In what ways does your own worldview affect the ways in which you perceive environmental issues? Be as specific as possible.*

1. Scarlett describes Gore's position as an "apocalyptic worldview." What does she mean by this term? Do you agree with her? To what extent do you think an apocalyptic attitude is a major part of contemporary environmental philosophy?

2. What, according to Scarlett, are the environmental advantages of an increasing emphasis on property rights? Do you agree with her? Discuss your reasons.

## Thomas E. Hill, Jr.
## "Ideals of Human Excellence and Preserving the Natural Environment"

*Thomas Hill, a professor of philosophy at the University of North Carolina at Chapel Hill, specializes in Kant's moral philosophy. He is the author of numerous articles as well as two recent books,* Autonomy and Self-Respect *(1991) and* Dignity and Practical Reason in Kant's Moral Theory *(1992).*

*In this article, Hill is concerned with exploring the kind of moral character that may be associated with particular attitudes toward the environment. For the sake of argument, Hill asks us to imagine that the case for environmentalism cannot be established either through a weighing of consequences or an appeal to rights. There is still something morally important to consider: how does indifference to nonsentient nature fit in with human excellences (virtues) that we want to encourage? Hill argues that such indifference may be a sign of ignorance, of self-importance, of a lack of self-respect, of a lack of an aesthetic sense, or a lack of gratitude.*

### As You Read, Consider This:

1. In the first two sections of his article, Hill considers and rejects a number of possible foundations for environmental ethics. As you read, number each position and note Hill's reasons for setting each one aside.

2. What human excellences does Hill find to be incompatible with an insensitivity to the environment? What arguments does he offer in support of his claim?

~

# I

A wealthy eccentric bought a house in a neighborhood I know.[1] The house was surrounded by a beautiful display of grass, plants, and flowers, and it was shaded by a huge old avocado tree. But the grass required cutting, the flowers needed tending, and the man wanted more sun. So he cut the whole lot down and covered the yard with asphalt. After all it was his property and he was not fond of plants.

It was a small operation, but it reminded me of the strip mining of large sections of the Appalachians. In both cases, of course, there were reasons for the destruction, and property rights could be cited as justification. But I could not help but wonder, "What sort of person would do a thing like that?"

Many Californians had a similar reaction when a recent governor defended the leveling of ancient redwood groves, reportedly saying, "If you have seen one redwood, you have seen them all."

Incidents like these arouse the indignation of ardent environmentalists and leave even apolitical observers with some degree of moral discomfort. The reasons for these reactions are mostly

Thomas E. Hill, Jr., "Ideals of Human Excellence and Preserving the Natural Environment," *Environmental Ethics* 5 (1983). Copyright 1983, Environmental Ethics, Inc. Reprinted by permission of the publisher and the author.

obvious. Uprooting the natural environment robs both present and future generations of much potential use and enjoyment. Animals too depend on the environment; and even if one does not value animals for their own sakes, their potential utility for us is incalculable. Plants are needed, of course, to replenish the atmosphere quite aside from their aesthetic value. These reasons for hesitating to destroy forests and gardens are not only the most obvious ones, but also the most persuasive for practical purposes. But, one wonders, is there nothing more behind our discomfort? Are we concerned solely about the potential use and enjoyment of the forests, etc., for ourselves, later generations, and perhaps animals? Is there not something else which disturbs us when we witness the destruction or even listen to those who would defend it in terms of cost/benefit analysis?

Imagine that in each of our examples those who would destroy the environment argue elaborately that, even considering future generations of human beings and animals, there are benefits in "replacing" the natural environment which outweigh the negative utilities which environmentalists cite.[2] No doubt we could press the argument on the facts, trying to show that the destruction is shortsighted and that its defenders have underestimated its potential harm or ignored some pertinent rights or interests. But is this all we could say? Suppose we grant, for a moment, that the utility of destroying the redwoods, forests, and gardens is equal to their potential for use and enjoyment by nature lovers and animals. Suppose, further, that we even grant that the pertinent human rights and animal rights, if any, are evenly divided for and against destruction. Imagine that we also concede, for argument's sake, that the forests contain no potentially useful endangered species of animals and plants. Must we then conclude that there is no further cause for moral concern? Should we then feel morally indifferent when we see the natural environment uprooted? . . .

# III

What sort of person, then, would cover his garden with asphalt, strip mine a wooded mountain, or level an irreplaceable redwood grove? Two sorts of answers, though initially appealing, must be ruled out. The first is that persons who would destroy the environment in these ways are either shortsighted, underestimating the harm they do, or else are too little concerned for the well-being of other people. Perhaps too they have insufficient regard for animal life. But these considerations have been set aside in order to refine the controversy. Another tempting response might be that we count it a moral virtue, or at least a human ideal, to love nature. Those who value the environment only for its utility must not really love nature and so in this way fall short of an ideal. But such an answer is hardly satisfying in the present context, for what is at issue is *why* we feel moral discomfort at the activities of those who admittedly value nature only for its utility. That it is ideal to care for nonsentient nature beyond its possible use is really just another way of expressing the general point which is under controversy.

What is needed is some way of showing that this ideal is connected with other virtues, or human excellences, not in question. To do so is difficult and my suggestions, accordingly, will be tentative and subject to qualification. The main idea is that, though indifference to nonsentient nature does not *necessarily* reflect the absence of virtues, it often signals the absence of certain traits which we want to encourage because they are, in most cases, a natural basis for the development of certain virtues. It is often thought, for example, that those who would destroy the natural environment must lack a proper appreciation of their place in the natural order, and so must either be ignorant or have too little humility. Though I would argue that this is not necessarily so, I suggest that, given certain plausible empirical assumptions, their attitude may well be rooted in ignorance, a narrow perspective, inability to see things as important apart from themselves and the limited groups they associate with, or reluctance to accept themselves as natural beings. Overcoming these deficiencies will not guarantee a proper moral humility, but for most of us it is probably an important psychological preliminary. Later I suggest, more briefly, that indifference to nonsentient nature typically reveals absence of either aesthetic sensibility or a disposition to cherish what has enriched one's life and that these, though not themselves moral virtues, are a natural basis for appreciation of the good in others and gratitude.[3]

Consider first the suggestion that destroyers of the environment lack an appreciation of their place in the universe.[4] Their attention, it seems, must be focused on parochial matters, on what is, relatively speaking, close in space and time. They seem not to understand that we are a speck on the cosmic scene, a brief stage in the evolutionary process, only one among millions of species on Earth, and an episode in the course of human history. Of course, they know that there are stars, fossils, insects, and ancient ruins; but do they have any idea of the complexity of the processes that led to the natural world as we find it? Are they aware how much the forces at work within their own bodies are like those which govern all living things and even how much they have in common with inanimate bodies? Admittedly scientific knowledge is limited and no one can master it all; but could one who had a broad and deep understanding of his place in nature really be indifferent to the destruction of the natural environment?

This first suggestion, however, may well provoke a protest from a sophisticated anti-environmentalist.[5] "Perhaps *some* may be indifferent to nature from ignorance," the critic may object, "but I have studied astronomy, geology, biology, and biochemistry, and I still unashamedly regard the nonsentient environment as simply a resource for our use. It should not be wasted, of course, but what should be preserved is decidable by weighing long-term costs and benefits." "Besides," our critic may continue, "as philosophers you should know the old Humean formula, 'You cannot derive an *ought* from an *is.*' All the facts of biology, biochemistry, etc., do not entail that I ought to love nature or want to preserve it. What one understands is one thing; what one values is something else. Just as nature lovers are not necessarily scientists, those indifferent to nature are not necessarily ignorant."

Although the environmentalist may concede the critic's logical point, he may well argue that, as a matter of fact, increased understanding of nature tends to heighten people's concern for its preservation. If so, despite the objection, the suspicion that the destroyers of the environment lack deep understanding of nature is not, in most cases, unwarranted, but the argument need not rest here.

The environmentalist might amplify his original idea as follows: "When I said that the destroyers of nature do not appreciate their place in the universe, I was not speaking of intellectual understanding alone, for, after all, a person can *know* a catalog of facts without ever putting them together and seeing vividly the whole picture which they form. To see oneself as just one part of nature is to look at oneself and the world from a certain perspective which is quite different from being able to recite detailed information from the natural sciences. What the destroyers of nature lack is this perspective, not particular information."

Again our critic may object, though only after making some concessions: "All right," he may say, "*some* who are indifferent to nature may lack the cosmic perspective of which you speak, but again there is no *necessary* connection between this failing, if it is one, and any particular evaluative attitude toward nature. In fact, different people respond quite differently when they move to a wider perspective. When I try to picture myself vividly as a brief, transitory episode in the course of nature, I simply get depressed. Far from inspiring me with a love of nature, the exercise makes me sad and hostile. You romantics think only of poets like Wordsworth and artists like Turner, but you should consider how differently Omar Khayyam responded when he took your wider perspective. His reaction, when looking at his life from a cosmic viewpoint, was 'Drink up, for tomorrow we die.' Others respond in an almost opposite manner with a joyless Stoic resignation, exemplified by the poet who pictures the wise man, at the height of personal triumph, being served a magnificent banquet, and then consummating his marriage to his beloved, all the while reminding himself, 'Even this shall pass away.'"[6] In sum, the critic may object, "Even if one should try to see oneself as one small transitory part of nature, doing so does not dictate any particular normative attitude. Some may come to love nature, but others are moved to live for the moment; some sink into sad resignation; others get depressed or angry. So indifference to nature is not necessarily a sign that a person fails to look at himself from the larger perspective."

The environmentalist might respond to this objection in several ways. He might, for example, argue that even though some people who see themselves as part of the natural order remain indifferent to nonsentient nature, this is not a common reaction. Typically, it may be argued, as we become more and more aware that we are parts of the larger whole we come to value the whole independently of its effect on ourselves. Thus, despite the possibilities the critic raises, indifference to nonsentient nature is still in most cases a sign that a person fails to see himself as part of the natural order.

If someone challenges the empirical assumption here, the environmentalist might develop the argument along a quite different line. The initial idea, he may remind us, was that those who would destroy the natural environment fail to *appreciate* their place in the natural order. "Appreciating one's place" is not simply an intellectual appreciation. It is also an attitude, reflecting what one values as well as what one knows. When we say, for example, that both the servile and the arrogant person fail to *appreciate* their place in a society of equals, we do not mean simply that they are ignorant of certain empirical facts, but rather that they have certain objectionable attitudes about their importance relative to other people. Similarly, to fail to appreciate one's place in nature is not merely to lack knowledge or breadth of perspective, but to take a certain attitude about what matters. A person who *understands* his place in nature but still views nonsentient nature merely as a resource takes the attitude that nothing is *important* but human beings and animals. Despite first appearances, he is not so much like the pre-Copernican astronomers who made the intellectual error of treating the Earth as the "center of the universe" when they made their calculations. He is more like the racist who, though well aware of other races, treats all races but his own as insignificant.

So construed, the argument appeals to the common idea that awareness of nature typically has, and should have, a humbling effect. The Alps, a storm at sea, the Grand Canyon, towering redwoods, and "the starry heavens above" move many a person to remark on the comparative insignificance of our daily concerns and even of our species, and this is generally taken to be a quite fitting response.[7] What seems to be missing, then, in those who understand nature but remain unmoved is a proper humility.[8] Absence of proper humility is not the same as selfishness or egoism, for one can be devoted to self-interest while still viewing one's own pleasures and projects as trivial and unimportant.[9] And one can have an exaggerated view of one's own importance while grandly sacrificing for those one views as inferior. Nor is the lack of humility identical with belief that one has power and influence, for a person can be quite puffed up about himself while believing that the foolish world will never acknowledge him. The humility we miss seems not so much a belief about one's relative effectiveness and recognition as an attitude which measures the importance of things independently of their relation to oneself or to some narrow group with which one identifies. A paradigm of a person who lacks humility is the self-important emperor who grants status to his family because it is *his*, to his subordinates because *he* appointed them, and to his country because *he* chooses to glorify it. Less extreme but still lacking proper humility is the elitist who counts events significant solely in proportion to how they affect his class. The suspicion about those who would destroy the environment, then, is that what they count important is too narrowly confined insofar as it encompasses only what affects beings who, like us, are capable of feeling.

This idea that proper humility requires recognition of the importance of nonsentient nature is similar to the thought of those who charge meat eaters with "species-ism." In both cases it is felt that people too narrowly confine their concerns to the sorts of beings that are most like them. But, however intuitively appealing, the idea will surely arouse objections from our anti-environmentalist critic. "Why," he will ask, "do you suppose that the sort of humility I *should* have requires me to acknowledge the importance of nonsentient nature aside from its utility? You cannot, by your own admission, argue that nonsentient nature is important, appealing to religious or intuitionist grounds. And simply to assert, without further argument, that an ideal humility requires us to view nonsentient nature as important for its own sake begs the question at issue. If proper humility is acknowledging the relative importance of things as one should, then to show that I must lack this you must first establish that one *should* acknowledge the importance of nonsentient nature."

Though some may wish to accept this challenge, there are other ways to pursue the connection between humility and response to nonsentient nature. For example, suppose we grant that proper humility requires only acknowledging a due status to sentient beings. We must admit, then, that it is logically possible for a person to be properly humble even though he viewed all nonsentient nature simply as a resource. But this logical possibility may be a psychological rarity. It may be that, given the sort of beings we are, we would never learn humility before persons without developing the general capacity to cherish, and regard important, many things for their own sakes. The major obstacle to humility before persons is self-importance, a tendency to measure the significance of everything by its relation to oneself and those with whom one identifies. The processes by which we overcome self-importance are doubtless many and complex, but it seems unlikely that they are exclusively concerned with how we relate to other people and animals. Learning humility requires learning to feel that something matters besides what will affect oneself and one's circle of associates. What leads a child to care about what happens to a lost hamster or a stray dog he will not see again is likely also to generate concern for a lost toy or a favorite tree where he used to live.[10] Learning to value things for their own sake, and to count what affects them important aside from their utility, is not the same as judging them to have some intuited objective property, but it is necessary to the development of humility and it seems likely to take place in experiences with nonsentient nature as well as with people and animals. If a person views all nonsentient nature merely as a resource, then it seems unlikely that he has developed the capacity needed to overcome self-importance.

# IV

This last argument, unfortunately, has its limits. It presupposes an empirical connection between experiencing nature and overcoming self-importance, and this may be challenged. Even if experiencing nature promotes humility before others, there may be other ways people can develop such humility in a world of concrete, glass, and plastic. If not, perhaps all that is needed is limited experience of nature in one's early, developing years; mature adults, having overcome youthful self-importance, may live well enough in artificial surroundings. More importantly, the argument does not fully capture the spirit of the intuition that an ideal person stands humbly before nature. That idea is not simply that experiencing nature tends to foster proper humility before other people; it is, in part, that natural surroundings encourage and are appropriate to an ideal sense of oneself as part of the natural world. Standing alone in the forest, after months in the city, is not merely good as a means of curbing one's arrogance before others; it reinforces and fittingly expresses one's acceptance of oneself as a natural being.

Previously we considered only one aspect of proper humility, namely, a sense of one's relative importance with respect to other human beings. Another aspect, I think, is a kind of *self-acceptance*. This involves acknowledging, in more than a merely intellectual way, that we are the sort of creatures that we are. Whether one is self-accepting is not so much a matter of how one attributes *importance* comparatively to oneself, other people, animals, plants, and other things as it is a matter of understanding, facing squarely, and responding appropriately to who and what one is, e.g., one's powers and limits, one's affinities with other beings and differences from them, one's unalterable nature and one's freedom to change. Self-acceptance is not merely intellectual awareness, for one can be intellectually aware that one is growing old and will eventually die while nevertheless behaving in a thousand foolish ways that reflect a refusal to acknowledge these facts. On the other hand, self-acceptance is not passive resignation, for refusal to pursue what one truly wants within one's limits is a failure to accept the freedom and power one has. Particular behaviors, like dying one's gray hair and dressing like those twenty years younger, do not *necessarily* imply lack of self-acceptance, for there could be reasons for acting in these ways other than the wish to hide from oneself what one really is. One fails to accept oneself when the patterns of behavior and emotion are rooted in a desire to disown and deny features of oneself, to pretend to oneself that they are not there. This is not to say that a self-accepting person makes no value judgments about himself, that he likes all facts about himself, wants equally to develop and display them; he can, and should feel remorse for his past misdeeds and strive to change his current vices. The point is that he does not disown them, pretend that they do not exist or are facts about something other than himself. Such pretense is incompatible with proper humility because it is seeing oneself as better than one is.

Self-acceptance of this sort has long been considered a human excellence, under various names, but what has it to do with preserving nature? There is, I think, the following connection. As human beings we are part of nature, living, growing, declining, and dying by natural laws similar to those governing other living beings; despite our awesomely distinctive human powers, we share many of the needs, limits, and liabilities of animals and plants. These facts are neither good nor bad in themselves, aside from personal preference and varying conventional values. To say this is to utter a truism which few will deny, but to accept these facts, as facts about oneself, is not so easy—or so common. Much of what naturalists deplore about our increasingly artificial world reflects, and encourages, a denial of these facts, an unwillingness to avow them with equanimity.

Like the Victorian lady who refuses to look at her own nude body, some would like to create a world of less transitory stuff, reminding us only of our intellectual and social nature, never calling to mind our affinities with "lower" living creatures. The "denial of death," to which psychiatrists call attention, reveals an attitude incompatible with the sort of self-acceptance which philosophers, from the ancients to Spinoza and on, have admired as a human excellence.[11] My suggestion is not merely that experiencing nature causally promotes such self-acceptance, but also that those who fully accept themselves as part of the natural world lack the common drive to disassociate themselves from nature by replacing natural environments with artificial ones. A storm in the wilds helps us to appreciate our animal vulnerability, but, equally important, the reluctance to experience it may *reflect* an unwillingness to accept this aspect of ourselves. The person who is too ready to destroy the ancient redwoods may lack humility, not so much in the sense that he exaggerates his importance relative to others, but rather in the sense that he tries to avoid seeing himself as one among many natural creatures.

## V

My suggestion so far has been that, though indifference to nonsentient nature is not itself a moral vice, it is likely to reflect either ignorance, a self-importance, or a lack of self-acceptance which we must overcome to have proper humility. A similar idea might be developed connecting attitudes toward nonsentient nature with other human excellences. For example, one might argue that indifference to nature reveals a lack of either an aesthetic sense or some of the natural roots of gratitude.

When we see a hillside that has been gutted by strip miners or the garden replaced by asphalt, our first reaction is probably, "How ugly!" The scenes assault our aesthetic sensibilities. We suspect that no one with a keen sense of beauty could have left such a sight. Admittedly not everything in nature strikes us as beautiful, or even aesthetically interesting, and sometimes a natural scene is replaced with a more impressive architectural masterpiece. But this is not usually the situation in the problem cases which environmentalists are most concerned about. More often beauty is replaced with ugliness.

At this point our critic may well object that, even if he does lack a sense of beauty, this is no moral vice. His cost/benefit calculations take into account the pleasure others may derive from seeing the forests, etc., and so why should he be faulted?

Some might reply that, despite contrary philosophical traditions, aesthetics and morality are not so distinct as commonly supposed. Appreciation of beauty, they may argue, is a human excellence which morally ideal persons should try to develop. But, setting aside this controversial position, there still may be cause for moral concern about those who have no aesthetic response to nature. Even if aesthetic sensibility is not itself a moral virtue, many of the capacities of mind and heart which it presupposes may be ones which are also needed for an appreciation of other people. Consider, for example, curiosity, a mind open to novelty, the ability to look at things from unfamiliar perspectives, empathetic imagination, interest in details, variety, and order, and emotional freedom from the immediate and the practical. All these, and more, seem necessary to aesthetic sensibility, but they are also traits which a person needs to be fully sensitive to people of all sorts. The point is not that a moral person must be able to distinguish beautiful from ugly people; the point is rather that unresponsiveness to what is beautiful, awesome, dainty, dumpy, and otherwise aesthetically interesting in nature probably reflects a lack of the openness of mind and spirit necessary to appreciate the best in human beings.

The anti-environmentalist, however, may refuse to accept the charge that he lacks aesthetic sensibility. If he claims to appreciate seventeenth-century miniature portraits, but to abhor natural wildernesses, he will hardly be convincing. Tastes vary, but aesthetic sense is not *that* selective. He may, instead, insist that he *does* appreciate natural beauty. He spends his vacations, let us suppose, hiking in the Sierras, photographing wildflowers, and so on. He might press his argument as follows: "I enjoy natural beauty as much as anyone, but I fail to see what this has to do with preserving the environment independently of human enjoyment and use. Nonsentient nature is a resource, but one of its best uses is to give us pleasure. I take this into account when I calculate the costs and benefits of preserving a park, planting a garden, and so on. But the problem you raised explicitly set aside the desire to preserve nature as a means to enjoyment. I say, let us enjoy nature fully while we can, but if all sentient beings were to die tomorrow, we might as well blow up all plant life as well. A redwood grove that no one can use or enjoy is utterly worthless."

The attitude expressed here, I suspect, is not a common one, but it represents a philosophical challenge. The beginnings of a reply may be found in the following. When a person takes joy in something, it is a common (and perhaps natural) response to come to cherish it. To cherish something is not simply to be happy with it at the moment, but to care for it for its own sake. This is not to say that one necessarily sees it as having feelings and so wants it to feel good; nor does it imply that one judges the thing to have Moore's intrinsic value. One simply wants the thing to survive and (when appropriate) to thrive, and not simply for its utility. We see this attitude repeatedly regarding mementos. They are not simply valued as a means to remind us of happy occasions; they come to be valued for their own sake. Thus, if someone really took joy in the natural environment, but was prepared to blow it up as soon as sentient life ended, he would lack this common human tendency to cherish what enriches our lives. While this response is not itself a moral virtue, its may be a natural basis of the virtue we call "gratitude." People who have no tendency to cherish things that give them pleasure may be poorly disposed to respond gratefully to persons who are good to them. Again the connection is not one of logical necessity, but it may nevertheless be important. A non-religious person unable to "thank" anyone for the beauties of nature may nevertheless feel "grateful" in a sense; and I suspect that the person who feels no such "gratitude" toward nature is unlikely to show proper gratitude toward people.

Suppose these conjectures prove to be true. One may wonder what is the point of considering them. Is it to disparage all those who view nature merely as a resource? To do so, it seems, would be unfair, for, even if this attitude typically stems from deficiencies which affect one's attitudes toward sentient beings, there may be exceptions and we have not shown that their view of nonsentient nature is itself blameworthy. But when we set aside questions of blame and inquire what sorts of human traits we want to encourage, our reflections become relevant in a more positive way. The point is not to insinuate that all anti-environmentalists are defective, but to see that those who value such traits as humility, gratitude, and sensitivity to others have reason to promote the love of nature.

## Endnotes

1. The author thanks Gregory Kavka, Catherine Harlow, the participants at a colloquium at the University of Utah, and the referees for *Environmental Ethics,* Dale Jamieson and Donald Scherer for helpful comments on earlier drafts of this paper.

2. When I use the expression "the natural environment," I have in mind the sort of examples with which I began. For some purposes it is important to distinguish cultivated gardens from forests, virgin forests from replenished ones, irreplaceable natural phenomena from the replaceable, and so on; but these distinctions, I think, do not affect my main points here. There is also a broad sense, as Hume and Mill noted, in which all that occurs, miracles aside, is "natural." In this sense, of course, strip mining is as natural as a beaver cutting trees for his dam, and, as parts of nature, we cannot destroy the "natural" environment but only alter it. As will be evident, I shall use *natural* in a narrower, more familiar sense.

3. The issues I raise here, though perhaps not the details of my remarks, are in line with Aristotle's view of moral philosophy, a view revitalized recently by Philippa Foot's *Virtue and Vice* (Berkeley: University of California Press, 1979), Alasdair MacIntyre's *After Virtue* (Notre Dame: Notre Dame Press, 1981), and James Wallace's *Virtues and Vices* (Ithaca and London: Cornell University Press, 1978), and other works. For other reflections on relationships between character and natural environments, see John Rodman, "The Liberation of Nature," *Inquiry* (1976), 83–131 and L. Reinhardt, "Some Gaps in Moral Space: Reflections on Forests and Feelings," in Mannison, McRobbie, and Routley, eds., *Environmental Philosophy* (Canberra: Australian National University Research School of Social Sciences, 1980).

4. Though for simplicity I focus upon those who do strip mining, etc., the argument is also applicable to those whose utilitarian calculations lead them to preserve the redwoods, mountains, etc., but who care for only sentient nature for its own sake. Similarly the phrase "indifferent to nature" is meant to encompass those who are indifferent *except* when considering its benefits to people and animals.

5. For convenience I use the labels *environmentalist* and *anti-environmentalist* (or *critic*) for the opposing sides in the rather special controversy I have raised. Thus, for example, my "environmentalist" not only favors conserving the forests, etc., but finds something objectionable in wanting to destroy them even aside from the costs to human beings and animals. My "anti-environmentalist" is not simply one who wants to destroy the environment: he is a person who has no qualms about doing so independent of the adverse effects on human beings and animals.

6. "Even this shall pass away," by Theodore Tildon, in *The Best Loved Poems of the American People,* ed. Hazel Felleman (Garden City, NY: Doubleday, 1936).

7. An exception, apparently, was Kant, who thought "the starry heavens" sublime and compared them with "the moral law within," but did not for all that see our species as comparatively insignificant.

8. By "*proper* humility" I mean that sort and degree of humility that is a morally admirable character trait. How precisely to define this is, of course, a controversial matter; but the point for present purposes is just to set aside obsequiousness, false modesty, underestimation of one's abilities, and the like.

9. I take this point from some of Philippa Foot's remarks.

10. The causal history of this concern may well depend upon the object (tree, toy) having given the child pleasure, but this does not mean that the object is then valued only for further pleasure it may bring.

11. See, for example, Ernest Becker, *The Denial of Death* (New York: Free Press, 1973).

## Journal/Discussion Questions

✍ *To what extent do you think that humility is a virtue? In your own life, has humility played an important role? How, if at all, has it affected your attitude toward the environment?*

1. Hill considers and rejects three possible nonutilitarian justifications of our discomfort at the destruction of parts of the natural environment. What are these proposed justifications? What are Hill's objections? Do you agree with him?

2. In Part III of his article, Hill develops a dialogue between the environmentalist and the person who is indifferent to the environment. Critically assess this dialogue. Are there more plausible or more powerful objections or replies on either side that Hill has overlooked? Could either side's position be strengthened? How?

3. Hill talks about "proper humility." What, precisely, is proper humility? How do we draw a line between proper humility and improper humility? How does this tie in with the idea of valuing things for their own sake?

4. Can you sketch out a portrait of an antienvironmentalist who is not open to the kinds of criticisms that Hill levels against those insensitive to nonsentient nature?

# QUESTIONS FOR DISCUSSION AND REVIEW

## Instructions

You have already answered the following questions in your moral problems self-quiz at the beginning of this book. Now that you have studied the material in this section, take a moment to answer the same questions again.

| | Strongly Agree | Agree | Undecided | Disagree | Strongly Disagree | |
|---|---|---|---|---|---|---|
| | | | | | | **Chapter 10: Environmental Ethics** |
| 46. | ❑ | ❑ | ❑ | ❑ | ❑ | Nature is just a source of resources for us. |
| 47. | ❑ | ❑ | ❑ | ❑ | ❑ | The government should strictly regulate toxic waste. |
| 48. | ❑ | ❑ | ❑ | ❑ | ❑ | We should make every effort possible to avoid infringing on the natural environment any more than we already have. |
| 49. | ❑ | ❑ | ❑ | ❑ | ❑ | We owe future generations a clean and safe environment. |
| 50. | ❑ | ❑ | ❑ | ❑ | ❑ | We should not impose our environmental concerns on developing nations. |

Compare your answers to the present self-quiz with the answers to the initial self-quiz. How, if at all, have your answers changed? How have the *reasons* for your answers changed?

# FOR FURTHER READING:
# A BIBLIOGRAPHICAL GUIDE
# TO ENVIRONMENTAL ETHICS

## Journal

In addition to the standard journals in ethics discussed in the bibliographical essay in Chapter 1, see especially *Environmental Ethics*, which has been a rich source of scholarship and theory on issues of environmental ethics; also see the journal *Environmental Values*, edited by Alan Holland at Lancaster University, UK.

## Review Articles

See the review articles by J. Baird Callicott, "Environmental Ethics," *Encyclopedia of Ethics*, ed. Lawrence C. Becker and Charlotte B. Becker (New York: Garland, 1992), vol. I, pp. 311–314, and Robert Elliot, "Environmental Ethics," *A Companion to Ethics*, ed. Peter Singer (Oxford: Blackwell, 1991), pp. 284–293. Also see the articles in *Environmental Philosophy: From Animal Rights to Radical Ecology*, discussed below.

## Anthologies

*The Environmental Crisis: Opposing Viewpoints*, ed. Neal Bernards (San Diego: Greenhaven Press, 1991) contains chapters on pesticides, garbage, toxic waste, air and water pollution, and environmental protection. *Taking Sides: Clashing Views on Controversial Environmental Issues*, 5th ed., edited, selected, and with introductions by Theodore D. Goldfarb (Guilford, CT: Dushkin Group, 1993) also covers a wide range of issues with a balanced selection of readings as does Donald VanDerVeer and Christine Pierce, eds., *People, Penguins, and Plastic Trees* (Belmont: Wadsworth, 1986). *The Environment in Question: Ethics and Global Issues*, ed. David E. Cooper and Joy A. Palmer (London: Routledge, 1992) contains a good balance of theoretical and applied issues. *Earthbound: New Introductory Essays in Environmental Ethics*, ed. Tom Regan (New York: Random House, 1984) in a very interesting collection of original essays on such topics as pollution, energy, economics, ocean resources, agriculture, rare species, future generations, and moral theory. See also Donald Scherer and Thomas Attig, eds., *Ethics and the Environment* (Englewood Cliffs, NJ: Prentice Hall, 1983). *Environmental Philosophy: From Animal Rights to Radical Ecology*, ed. Michael E. Zimmerman et al. (Englewood Cliffs, NJ: Prentice Hall, 1993) is a superb collection of essays, with introductions for individual sections done by representatives of each tradition, including ecofeminism, deep ecology, and social ecology.

*Responsibilities to Future Generations*, ed. Ernest Partridge (Buffalo: Prometheus Books, 1980), *Obligations to Future Generations*, ed. R. I. Sikora and Brian Barry (Philadelphia: Temple University Press, 1978), and *Obligations to Future Generations*, ed. E. Partridge (Buffalo: Prometheus Books, 1981) all contain articles about the issue of our responsibility to future generations for not destroying the natural environment.

## Articles

Richard Routley's "Is There a Need for a New, an Environmental Ethic?" in *Proceedings of the 15th World Congress of Philosophy*, ed. Bulgarian Organizing Committee (Sophia, Bulgaria: Sophia-Press, 1973), vol. 1, pp. 205–210, was one of the first statements of a need for a new environmental ethic.

Kenneth E. Goodpaster, "On Being Morally Considerable," *Journal of Philosophy* 22 (1978), 308–325, argues that it is the capacity to live (not mere sentience) that gives an entity moral considerability; also see his "From Egoism to Environmentalism," in *Ethics and Problems of the 21st Century*, ed. K. E. Goodpaster and K. M. Sayre (Notre Dame: University of Notre Dame Press, 1979).

On the issue of the relationship between human beings and nature, see Bryan G. Norton, "Environmental Ethics and Weak Anthropocentrism," *Environmental Ethics* 6 (1984), 131–148; Tom Regan, "The Nature and Possibility of an Environmental Ethic," *Environmental Ethics* 3 (1981), 19–34; Peter Singer, "Not for Humans Only: The Place of Non-humans in Environmental Issues," in *Ethics and Problems of the 21st Century*, ed. Kenneth E. Goodpaster (Notre Dame, Ind.: University of Notre Dame Press, 1979); and Donald VanDeVeer, "Interspecies Justice," *Inquiry* 22 (1979), 55–70.

J. Ronald Engel, "Ecology and Social Justice: The Search for a Public Environmental Ethic," in *Issues of Justice: Social Sources and Religious Meanings*, ed. Warren Copeland and Roger Hatch (Macon, GA: Mercer Press, 1988), pp. 243–266. On the relationship between feminism and environmental issues, see Karen Warren, "Feminism and Ecology: Making Connections," *Environmental Ethics* 9 (1987), 3–20.

## Books

Aldo Leopold's *A Sand County Almanac: With Essays on Conservation from Round River* (New York: Ballantine Books, 1970) is a classic of the environmental movement; J. Baird Callicott's *In Defense of the Land Ethic: Essays in Environmental Philosophy* (Albany: State University of New York Press, 1988) is a development of, and defense of, Leopold's land ethic. In this same tradition is Rolston Holmes, III, *Environmental Ethics: Duties to and Values in the Natural World* (Philadelphia: Temple University Press, 1988) and *Philosophy Gone Wild: Essays in Environmental Ethics* (New York: Prometheus Books, 1986).

Among the more important works in this area, see Robin Attfield, *The Ethics of Environmental Concern* (New York: Columbia University Press, 1983); Eugene C. Hargrove, *Foundations of Environmental Ethics* (Englewood Cliffs, NJ: Prentice Hall, 1989); John Passmore, *Man's Responsibility for Nature: Ecological Problems and Western Traditions* (New York: Scribner's, 1974); W. F. Baxter, *People or Penguins: The Case for Optimal Pollution* (New York: Columbia University Press, 1974); and Christopher Manes, *Radical Environmentalism and the Unmaking of Civilization* (Boston: Little, Brown, 1990); Mark Sagoff, *The Economy of the Earth: Philosophy, Law, and the Environment* (Cambridge: Cambridge University Press, 1988). See also Paul W. Taylor, *Respect for Nature: A Theory of Environmental Ethics* (Princeton: Princeton University Press, 1986) defends a biocentric account of ethics; Lawrence E. Johnson, *A Morally Deep World: An Essay on Moral Significance and Environmental Ethics* (Cambridge: Cambridge University Press, 1991); and Richard Sylvan, *A Critique of Deep Ecology* (Canberra: Research School of Social Sciences, Australian National University, 1985).

# Appendix

## Reading, Analyzing, and Constructing Philosophical Arguments

I remember what it was like when I first began reading philosophy. All too often, the language seemed stilted, the examples contrived and improbable, and the reasoning tortuous. I fought my way through difficult texts, and in the process learned how to read such texts more efficiently—that is, I learned how to get more out of them, and to do so faster. But I picked it up on my own; no one taught me. Certainly no one ever offered me a set of tips or guidelines on how to do it.

I hope the following remarks help you acquire some of these skills more quickly and easily. Very little of what follows is absolute, for reading and writing well are much more of an art than a science. I hope the following suggestions help you in acquiring that art.

### Philosophy as Conversation

Philosophy is often a dialogue. Plato used the dialogue format explicitly, but it is implicit in much of contemporary philosophical writing, especially in articles. Essentially, articles are snippets out of a conversation. One philosopher (it's rare for philosophical articles to be co-authored) is explicating, commenting on, criticizing, or fine-tuning the work of other philosophers. We often see the thread of a conversation running through a group of articles, each of which comments on and attempts to improve upon its predecessors, thereby giving rise to yet further contributions to the conversation. Part of the greatness of key philosophical works—such as Plato's dialogues, Aristotle's *Metaphysics*, Augustine's *Confessions*, Aquinas's *Summa Theologica*, Descartes's *Meditations*, Hume's *Treatise*, Kant's three *Critiques*, Hegel's *Phenomenology*, or Heidegger's *Being and Time*—lies precisely in their ability to initiate a wealth of such conversations, sometimes continuing for centuries.

The conversational character of philosophical discourse has some important implications for how you can best read philosophical texts. Keep the following points in mind:

- If philosophy is a conversation, then you are walking into the middle of a conversation when you pick up a journal article. A lot has been said before you arrived, and one of the challenges to you as a reader will be to figure out what you missed.

- Some authors help you to understand the conversation by telling you what one (or more) of the previous participants said about the issue at hand. As a result, philosophical works may contain a summary of previous positions, and often these positions are not the author's own. *Be careful not to attribute to authors positions that they are only recounting in order to subsequently refute them.*

Philosophical writing is often quite different from textbook writing. Once you are aware of the difference, it may be easier to follow.

Just as the philosophy you are reading is part of a conversation, so, too, your reading may become conversational. Ideally, reading is not a passive process of mere assimilation, but an active—indeed, interactive—process quite similar to a conversation between you and the author. The text talks to you, you listen and respond with questions, and often the text yields up further answers to your questions. It is precisely this back-and-forth movement that is at the heart of philosophical understanding.

## Active Reading

Reading in the way just indicated is one way of reading *actively*. In *Reading Critically, Writing Well*, Rise B. Axelrod and Charles R. Cooper outline six strategies for critical reading. Five of these are particularly helpful for us in this context.

### Previewing

Before you begin to read the body of an article or book, try to figure out what to expect. If the author (or someone else) has provided an abstract, read that carefully. Pay attention to the title. Read the introduction and conclusion. All of this helps you to begin your reading with a cognitive map of what to expect, and this makes it much easier to process the information. You may have to revise details of that map, but it is a lot easier to navigate with it than with none at all.

### Annotating

Read with a pencil or pen in your hand, and don't hesitate—unless it's a library book—to mark up the book. Put question marks by things that are unclear—and if later they become clear, erase the question mark. Put numbers in the margin whenever points are enumerated. If you find a phrase like "My second argument is . . . ," make sure you know what the *first* one was. Circle key terms. Put a star by references in the footnotes that you want to look up.

Many of us use highlighters for underlining a text. These are visually helpful, but much less sophisticated than a pencil. If you find that you're highlighting everything, something's wrong—the whole idea of highlighting is to make the main points stand out more clearly.

### Outlining

When you annotate, you are already beginning to outline. See if the article is divided into sections. Use any title the author gives for sections or subsections. If only numbers are given, supply your own titles. Look for the overall structure of the piece. Many philosophical pieces will be divided into arguments, objections, and replies.

## Summarizing

It is often helpful to try to put someone else's argument into your own words. Summaries don't seem creative, but doing a summary can often teach us a lot. We have to understand what the author is saying in order to reformulate it in our own words. Moreover, the process of summarizing something forces us to focus on what is important in the piece, and that focus is very valuable. Finally, you will often find that you discover a lot about the holes in an author's arguments by summarizing an article or book. By summarizing in your own words, you have to ask yourself continually exactly what did the author mean by a particular claim. This process often reveals hidden ambiguities and shortcomings in an argument.

## Analyzing

The process of summarizing is usually a first step toward analysis. When we analyze a piece, we are usually asking two questions. First, does the author provide adequate support for the claims that are advanced? Here we use the standards of logic to evaluate how well the author has succeeded in justifying his or her conclusions.

Second, do you agree or disagree with the points an author is making? It is important to try to figure out where you stand on these issues. Sometimes this is a slow and difficult process. Sometimes we come to understand our own position initially only in bits and pieces.

# Writing a Moral Problems Paper

Imagine that you want to—or, perhaps, must—write a term paper in a moral problems course. Let's look at the steps you will go through, taking as our example a paper on euthanasia.

## Choosing a Topic

Look for a topic that interests you, first and foremost. It will be easier to do and more worthwhile for you. Narrow it down to the point that you can cover the topic in the time and space you have available for it.

Let's assume that you know you want to write a paper on the morality of euthanasia. Initially, your topic simply reads:

*The morality of euthanasia.*

That's a vast topic, and the first thing you need to do is to *narrow it down*. Are you interested in discussing euthanasia in regard to newborns with severe birth defects? Adults in the final stages of a terminal disease? Those with extremely painful disorders who are not necessarily on the brink of death? It makes a difference which group you discuss, since somewhat different moral issues arise in each case. In the case of newborns, there is no possibility of obtaining consent from them, since they are incapable of consent by virtue of their age. With adults in the final stages of a terminal disease, it is possible to ask them what their preferences are, and they may already have indicated those preferences in a living will. In any case, their death is imminent; one is hastening a process which is already near its end. In the case of those with chronic, painful, but nonfatal disorders, the situation is different. One is not hastening the inevitable, or at least not the imminently inevitable. Let's say that you decide to do a paper on the third group. Your topic is now:

*The morality of euthanasia for people with chronic, painful disorders.*

As you work on your paper, you may find that you are refining you topic further and further. You realize that "painful" is a little vague, and that you really want to consider the extreme cases of great pain. Thus you make the topic a little more precise:

*The morality of euthanasia for people with chronic, extreme pain.*

You realize that you will need to have one section of your paper that details exactly what you mean by "chronic, extreme pain."

Presumably you are concerned with those cases in which people make a choice to die, not those cases in which others simply kill them. Thus your topic is a bit more precise:

*The morality of voluntary euthanasia for people with chronic, extreme pain.*

However, you make a note to yourself that "voluntary" is a tricky concept here, because sometimes people can want one thing while they are in pain, and later be glad they are alive.

Confining yourself to euthanasia for people with chronic, painful disorders, you have to consider whether you want to look at (a) passive euthanasia, which is just withholding life-saving treatment, or (b) active euthanasia, which involves taking some active measures to terminate the person's life. After thinking a moment, you realize that passive euthanasia doesn't help many of the people with chronic pain, since they will continue to live (but in great pain) even if treatment is withheld. So, you decide to consider active euthanasia, and you realize that somewhere in your paper you will have to explain why this distinction is important for the group of people you want to consider. Your topic is now:

*The morality of voluntary, active euthanasia for people with chronic, extreme pain.*

But even this may not be specific enough, because you realize that one of the central issues is whether doctors should perform euthanasia or not. Now your topic is:

*The morality of voluntary, physician-assisted, active euthanasia for people with chronic, extreme pain.*

This raises a number of issues specifically about physicians' responsibilities, and you realize that one section of your paper will be devoted to this. Perhaps the most difficult thing is that physicians are committed to preserving life, and doing something that actively brings about its termination would seem to violate their professional code. You make a mental note to yourself to consult those professional codes of ethics to see what they have to say about this issue.

In all likelihood, these refinements won't all happen at once. The refinements will occur over a process of time as you work on the paper. That's fine.

## Constructing an Outline of Issues

Some people write from outlines, some don't. Most of us, however, at least make a list of the things we want to discuss in a paper, even if it isn't a full outline. From the process of refining your topic, you already have several issues for your outline:

- Describing the condition of those with "chronic, extreme pain."
- Detailing what counts as "voluntary" for people in such conditions.
- Discussing why passive euthanasia is not enough for people in this situation.
- Outlining the responsibilities of physicians in regard to euthanasia requests.

Now you have the start of a structure for your paper. You will revise this structure continually as you work on your paper. Again, that's fine.

Also, don't hesitate to make notes to yourself along the way. For example, next to "the responsibilities of physicians . . . ," you might make a note, "Check AMA guidelines." Don't forget to go back later and check over these notes and reminders.

## Developing Your Thesis

It's one thing to choose a topic, but quite another to develop a thesis about that topic. Your *topic* indicates the area you want to work on; the *thesis statement* indicates what you want to prove about that area. The crucial first step here is to begin to think through exactly what you believe. You may be uncertain, and that's all right. Then at least try to jot down the things you think are wrong. Gradually you will be developing your central thesis, the main claim that you want to defend in your paper.

In our euthanasia paper example, your initial thesis statement might be:

*Doctors should not perform euthanasia.*

As we saw before with your topic, you will probably refine your thesis statement as you work on your paper. For example, the word "should" is ambiguous here. Does it mean that physician-assisted euthanasia should be *illegal*, or does it mean that it is *morally wrong*, or does it mean *both*? Let's imagine that you mean that it is morally wrong. Then your revised thesis statement is:

*It is immoral for physicians to assist in euthanasia.*

Notice that we've already begun to incorporate some of the revisions from our statement of topic. Let's incorporate the rest of them now:

*It is immoral for physicians to assist in voluntary euthanasia for people with chronic, extreme pain.*

Notice that there is now a very specific focus for your topic: it is on the morality of the *physician's* actions.

Once again, it is important to realize that developing your thesis may take time. This is part of the normal give-and-take of writing a paper.

## Getting Sources

Now that you have a sense of your topic, it's time to get some sources to use in developing your paper. This is rarely a one step process. Expect to make several trips to the library, for each batch of reading—in footnotes, bibliographies, and so on—will suggest additional sources that you may want to consult.

*Card catalogs.* The first thing to consult at your library is the card catalog. These are now often computerized, and this may allow you to search by subject and also to look for any key words in the title. Pay particular attention to anthologies and books with extensive bibliographies. If you see anthologies with something like "the basic issues" in the title or subtitle, make sure you look at it—it will probably be a valuable asset in getting an overview of the issues involved.

*Databases.* Computerized databases make it incredibly easy to search for books and articles on a specific topic. (In fact, the problem is usually getting too much information, rather than too little.) Some databases, like *InfoTrack*, survey popular sources as well as some scholarly ones. In philosophy, the most valuable resource is *The Philosopher's Index*, which is available in many libraries on CD-ROM. (Otherwise, it is probably available in hard cover.)

Here are a few hints about searching databases. First, you may have to search under several different words to cover your topic. A search on "euthanasia" may have to be supplemented with one on "mercy killing." Some databases contain a thesaurus with lists of alternative words to consult, etc.

Second, many of these programs support sophisticated search logic, and this can help you eliminate unwanted references as well as uncover all the relevant ones. Since your interest is in physician-assisted euthanasia, you may well want to do a search on physicians and either euthanasia or mercy killing. If you are only interested in things done in the last five years, you may add a further restriction to eliminate anything before 1990. Consult the guide for the particular program you are using to determine how it handles search logic.

Third, databases often contain abstracts of articles and books. These can be invaluable. Once you know what a particular article discusses and tries to prove, you can more easily decide whether you want to track it down and read the whole thing or not. Make sure you select the proper option on your search to insure that you get the abstracts if they are available.

Fourth, you can often download your search results onto a floppy disk and then transfer this to your own computer, if you have one. This makes it much easier to organize and work with your bibliography.

*Anthologies, bibliographies, and encyclopedia and review articles.* It's difficult and time-consuming to survey a new area without help. Review articles, encyclopedia articles, and annotated bibliographies can save you a tremendous amount of work in this area. Look for these in your bibliographical searches.

If you were looking for sources on euthanasia, look at the many anthologies—such as this one—available on contemporary moral problems. They have often done much of your work for you, and if you find certain articles being mentioned or reprinted in several of them, that's a good indication that it is an important piece to read. Also, there are specialized anthologies—some in philosophy, some more general—that may contain a wide range of articles. Prometheus Books has a series called "Contemporary Issues," which is very well done; there is one on euthanasia entitled *Euthanasia: The Moral Issues* (ed. Robert M. Baird and Stuart E. Rosenbaum). The Dushkin Publishing Group publishes a long series of anthologies in its series "Taking Sides." Greenhaven Press has a very nice "Opposing Viewpoint" series, including one on *Euthanasia: Opposing Viewpoints.* Both the Dushkin and Greenhaven series contain both selections from the popular press and more specialized sources, and both contain bibliographical guides; the Greenhaven series also typically includes a list of relevant organizations and information about how to contact them.

In some areas, you will find entire books that are devoted just to a bibliographical guide in a particular area. Although they may appear overwhelming, these are almost always divided into subtopics. If you use them cautiously and selectively, they can be valuable without being overwhelming.

Encyclopedias often publish helpful articles, and it is worth consulting them. There are both general encyclopedias—like the *Encyclopedia Britannica*, which still has the highest standards of scholarship—and special-interest encyclopedias. In philosophy in general, *The Encyclopedia of Philosophy* (1967, ed. Paul Edwards) is now fairly dated, but it still has some excellent pieces. In ethics, the two-volume *Encyclopedia of Ethics* (New York: Garland, 1992, ed. Lawrence and Charlotte Becker) is a superb collection of articles on a wide range of issues in ethics; *A Companion to Ethics* (Oxford: Blackwell, 1991, ed. Peter Singer) contains fewer articles, but they tend to be longer than those in *The Encyclopedia of Ethics*. Both also contain excellent bibliographical suggestions, and both are quite recent. Also, journals occasionally publish review articles that survey the literature on a given problem. *American Philosophical Quarterly* often has such articles (e.g., "Recent Work on Punishment"), and they provide an excellent way of understanding what the recent issues are in a given area.

*Journals.* There are a number of philosophy journals that specialize in ethics. These include *Ethics, Philosophy and Public Affairs, The Journal of Value Inquiry, Social Philosophy & Policy, The Journal of Social Philosophy, Public Affairs Quarterly*, and *The Journal of Applied Philosophy*. These are often worth just browsing through, even when you do not have a specific reference, for they contain a wealth of articles and book reviews that may have some bearing on your topic.

There are numerous other, more specialized journals that you should also be aware of. For example, the *Hastings Center Report* contains excellent articles and reviews in biomedical ethics and related fields. Some of the more specialized journals are listed in the bibliographical guides in each chapter of this book.

*The Internet.* The resources on the Internet are increasing every day. For an up-to-date listing of ethics-related resources on the Internet, visit my home page mentioned in the Preface of this book. It contains listings of current articles, discussion groups, and links to all the other ethics sites that I know about.

*Books.* Single-author books in ethics often offer a sustained and detailed articulation of a single point of view on a particular moral question. They are invaluable, for it is only in this context that authors are able to develop their position both broadly and in depth. For readers, they also require a significant investment of time compared with articles. Try to discover the author's thesis early in your reading of the book and learn to read them efficiently.

## Reading Your Sources

One of the best pieces of advice I ever got in high school was to always read with a pencil in my hand. Read actively, outlining and making marginal notes (unless it's a library book, then put your notes on a separate piece of paper). When you're reading in preparation for writing a paper, you should continually be asking yourself two questions. First, what is the author's position and what support is offered for it? The focus here is on understanding the article or book on its own terms. Second, how does the author's position relate to my own? Here the focus is on developing your own position. As you read, note particular arguments that may provide support for your own position as well as possible objections to your position. These will be invaluable when you turn to writing your paper.

## The First Draft

*A sense of the problem.* Why should I care about what you are going to say in your paper? It's often helpful at the beginning of your paper to give the readers a sense of (a) why your topic is an important one and (b) why your thesis is significant. In your euthanasia paper, you could show that the *topic* is important by pointing to ballot initiatives to legalize it in parts of the United States, by legalization efforts in other countries, and so on. To show that your thesis is significant, you can point to a number of physicians publicly involved in euthanasia. (Articles from two of them are included in this anthology.)

*A preview of where you're going.* Once you've generated a sense of why readers should care about what you're going to say, then you should give them some indication of where you're going in the paper. Usually, you would begin by developing your position first and then turning to the arguments on the other side. In this case, however, since physician-assisted euthanasia is currently illegal, you will probably want to consider first the arguments in favor of physician-assisted euthanasia. This heightens the readers' sense that there is a real issue here, a genuine moral question to be answered, and that there is real controversy over the correct answer.

*An outline of the paper.* Develop an outline of the paper that allows the development to flow well. The simplest outline for the euthanasia paper might be something like this:

I. Introduction
II. Arguments in Favor of Legalizing Physician-Assisted Euthanasia
III. Arguments against Legalizing Physician-Assisted Euthanasia
IV. Replies to Arguments against Legalizing Physician-Assisted Euthanasia
V. Conclusion

This is a simple, almost simplistic, structure, but it gets the job done. Each of the three major parts will then have a number of subdivisions dealing with specific issues such as the Hippocratic oath, the danger of a slippery slope, the rights of physicians to refuse, the pressure from insurance companies, and so on.

An alternative outline might well take each of the individual topics separately and consider the pros and cons of each topic. Then the initial outline might look more like this:

I. Introduction
II. The Physician's Duty to Do No Harm: The Hippocratic Oath
III. The Physician's Right to Refuse Euthanasia Requests

The arguments for and against your position in regard to each of these issues would then be contained in a single section. The second outline provides more continuity than the previous outline on specific issues, whereas the previous outline gives a clear picture of the coherence of the overall position.

## Constructing Arguments

Once you have a rough outline, begin to sketch the arguments. Consult your reading notes, for these should contain virtually everything that you want to discuss in your paper. Jot down the various arguments you want to consider under each issue.

*Example: The slippery slope argument.* Consider the issue of the possible abuses that could occur if physician-assisted euthanasia were legalized. These are often called "slippery slope" arguments because as a group they usually claim that, if we take the first step down this slope (legalizing euthanasia), then we will slide the rest of the way down. You might have one argument about how the eugenics program in Nazi Germany included euthanasia and the way in which that led to hundreds of thousands of deaths. The initial general structure of an argument like this is:

*Premise 1:* Legalizing euthanasia in Nazi Germany led to massive abuses of the system;

*Conclusion:* Legalizing euthanasia in the United States will lead to massive abuses.

Of course, as soon as we see the argument stated in this way, we realize that we need an additional premise to establish the relevant similarities between the United States and Nazi Germany. Clearly we can't say "Whatever happened in Nazi Germany will happen in the United States." Instead, we might try something like this:

*Premise 2:* The situation in the United States is like the situation in Nazi Germany.

But now that we have spelled out this premise, we realize that it is far from strong. Presumably there are lots of ways in which Nazi Germany was different from the United States, including its myth of Aryan racial superiority.

Are there any other cases in which euthanasia has been tried in circumstances more similar to those in the United States? The example of Holland comes immediately to mind, for they have legalized (at least to some extent) physician-assisted euthanasia and they are a society that is at least more similar to ours than Nazi Germany.

*Premise 1:* Legalizing euthanasia in Holland has led to abuses of the system;

*Premise 2:* The situation in the United States is like the situation in Holland;

*Conclusion:* Legalizing euthanasia in the United States will lead to massive abuses.

The second premise here seems much less controversial than in the preceding example. Now, however, the difficulty is with Premise 1. Whatever abuses may occur in Holland, they are nowhere near those of Nazi Germany. The way to strengthen this argument is to provide additional support for Premise 1.

Even if we can support the conclusion of this argument, we need to go further. We need to provide additional support in order to conclude that we should not legalize euthanasia. The argument might begin with the conclusion of the preceding argument.

*Premise 1:* Legalizing euthanasia in the United States will lead to massive abuses.

*Premise 2:* We should avoid doing anything that will lead to massive abuses.

*Conclusion:* We should avoid legalizing euthanasia.

Once again, we have to provide support for our premises, and here the troublesome one will be the second premise.

*Counterexamples.* How might we attack the second premise? Well, we could point to things that lead to massive abuses but which we nonetheless have legalized. Drinking alcohol comes immediately to mind. It leads to massive abuses and extremely high personal as well as social costs. When we begin to argue in this fashion, we are examining a counterexample. Philosophers often use counterexamples to criticize the positions of their opponents, and they are a powerful argumentative technique.

Of course, someone might try to object that euthanasia is a matter of life and death and thus that it is dissimilar to drinking. This type of reply attempts to show a dissimilarity between the original case and the counterexample in order to weaken the relevance of the counterexample. However, the defender of the argument could reply that drinking often leads to death either from alcohol-related illnesses or from accidents caused by intoxication. Such a reply strengthens the counterexample by reinforcing the similarities between it and the original case.

*Types of premises.* The premises of an argument may be of several different types. Some premises are *conceptual*, dealing primarily with the meaning of our words. Others are *normative*, making claims about what we ought to do. Finally, some are *empirical*, giving us relevant facts about the world. Consider the following argument.

*Empirical Premise:* Dr. Kevorkian is practicing euthanasia.

*Conceptual Premise:* Euthanasia involves the intentional taking of another person's life.

*Normative Premise:* It is always morally wrong to intentionally take another person's life.

*Conclusion:* What Dr. Kevorkian is doing is morally wrong.

It is important to distinguish among these three types of premises, since each is evaluated and supported in different ways. *Empirical premises* are in principle the easiest to test, since they usually make claims about empirically verifiable matters of fact. In this case, we might substitute the name of a different doctor—Dr. Koop, for example, the former Surgeon General of the United States—and we would find that it was clearly false. *Conceptual premises* are largely a matter of definition. Sometimes there is no absolute right or wrong in these matters, but it is always important to be certain that everyone is using key terms in the same way. In this case, the conceptual premise could be refined considerably. For example, there is no mention of the distinction between voluntary and involuntary euthanasia, nor is there any reference to the distinction between active and passive euthanasia. *Normative premises* are sometimes the most difficult to prove, and they often demand great refinement. The normative premise given in this argument—"It is always morally wrong to intentionally take another person's life"—is one that only absolute pacifists would accept. Most people think it is morally permissible to intentionally kill another human being in self-defense and in warfare.

## The Second Draft

Many of us find that we have to go through several drafts before a paper is satisfactory. After you finish your first draft, here are some things you may consider to develop the paper further.

*Outlining.* Near the end of the process, try doing an outline of what you've written, even if you didn't have a detailed one at the beginning. Outline what's there, and then you can do two things. First, you can check to see if you've stayed on track in your paper. You can compare what you've written in a given paragraph with your outline in order to make sure that everything in that paragraph actually contributes to your topic. If it doesn't, you may want either to delete it or to move it to another paragraph or section. If you work on a word processor, it is particularly easy to move paragraphs around, and sometimes we accidentally have some of our ideas out of place.

Second, look over your outline and make sure that you haven't left anything out. Sometimes we miss the forest for the trees, and sometimes in our own arguments we miss glaring holes because we are concerned with tiny details. Outlining helps us to see the general structure and the large gaps.

Third, if there are important topics that you have not considered, make sure that you indicate (probably in your introduction) that you are aware of them and have consciously chosen to set them aside. In a euthanasia paper, for example, you may realize that there are important difficulties about the meaning of "voluntary." Does it refer to a choice made in great pain, or only to one made in a pain-free reflective state, or only to a choice reaffirmed over a long period of time? If you are not going to consider certain issues such as this in your paper, tell the reader.

*Avoid common mistakes.* Read over your draft, and check for various kinds of common mistakes. Try to eliminate rhetorical questions by changing them into straightforward assertions. Get rid of gender-specific language wherever possible. (I prefer to use plural constructions to do this.) Don't use words whose meaning isn't completely clear to you. Proofread carefully, even if you use a computerized spell-check program. A spell check will not indicate anything is wrong with a sentence like, "I red the book." It takes a human being to realize that it should say, "I read the book."

*Quotations.* Generally, make sure that you have kept direct quotations to a minimum. Unless there is a special reason to do so, summarize the ideas in your own words. It will preserve the flow of the paper and show the reader that you have mastered these ideas. Give a direct quote, however, if the author's specific wording is important.

## Academic Integrity

It goes without saying that you shouldn't cheat on a term paper—and cheating on an ethics paper seems particularly outrageous! However, even when people don't intend to cheat, they sometimes do so through a combination of carelessness and ignorance.

Plagiarism is the unacknowledged use of another person's words or ideas as your own. If you are using someone else's exact words, they must be enclosed in quotation marks and a reference must be given to the source. If you are using someone else's idea (reformulated in your own words), then a reference should be given to the source.

Be careful not to plagiarize accidentally. If you make notes on your reading, and if you have direct quotations in your notes, then make sure that you have them enclosed in quotation marks in your notes. Otherwise, you might put them into your paper as your own words, not realizing that they were originally a quotation.

## One Final Comment

Remember, finally, that your paper is a chance for you to develop your thinking on a topic that is important to you. Take the opportunity to do so.